A Galic and English dictionary. Containing all the words in the Scotch and Irish dialects of the Celtic, ... By the Rev. William Shaw, ... Volume 1 of 2

William Shaw

PRINT EDITIONS

A Galic and English dictionary. Containing all the words in the Scotch and Irish dialects of the Celtic, ... By the Rev. William Shaw, ... Volume 1 of 2

Shaw, William
ESTCID: T147710
Reproduction from British Library
Vol. 2 is entitled: 'An English and Galic dictionary'.
London : printed for the author, by W. and A. Strahan; and sold by J. Murray; P. Elmsly; C. Elliot, J. Balfour, and R. Jamieson, Edinburgh; D. Prince, Oxford; Messrs. Merril, Cambridge; Wilson, Dublin; and Pissot, Paris, 1780.
2v. ; 4°

Eighteenth Century
Collections Online
Print Editions

Gale ECCO Print Editions

Relive history with *Eighteenth Century Collections Online*, now available in print for the independent historian and collector. This series includes the most significant English-language and foreign-language works printed in Great Britain during the eighteenth century, and is organized in seven different subject areas including literature and language; medicine, science, and technology; and religion and philosophy. The collection also includes thousands of important works from the Americas.

The eighteenth century has been called "The Age of Enlightenment." It was a period of rapid advance in print culture and publishing, in world exploration, and in the rapid growth of science and technology – all of which had a profound impact on the political and cultural landscape. At the end of the century the American Revolution, French Revolution and Industrial Revolution, perhaps three of the most significant events in modern history, set in motion developments that eventually dominated world political, economic, and social life.

In a groundbreaking effort, Gale initiated a revolution of its own: digitization of epic proportions to preserve these invaluable works in the largest online archive of its kind. Contributions from major world libraries constitute over 175,000 original printed works. Scanned images of the actual pages, rather than transcriptions, recreate the works *as they first appeared.*

Now for the first time, these high-quality digital scans of original works are available via print-on-demand, making them readily accessible to libraries, students, independent scholars, and readers of all ages.

For our initial release we have created seven robust collections to form one the world's most comprehensive catalogs of 18th century works.

Initial Gale ECCO Print Editions collections include:

History and Geography
Rich in titles on English life and social history, this collection spans the world as it was known to eighteenth-century historians and explorers. Titles include a wealth of travel accounts and diaries, histories of nations from throughout the world, and maps and charts of a world that was still being discovered. Students of the War of American Independence will find fascinating accounts from the British side of conflict.

Social Science

Delve into what it was like to live during the eighteenth century by reading the first-hand accounts of everyday people, including city dwellers and farmers, businessmen and bankers, artisans and merchants, artists and their patrons, politicians and their constituents. Original texts make the American, French, and Industrial revolutions vividly contemporary.

Medicine, Science and Technology

Medical theory and practice of the 1700s developed rapidly, as is evidenced by the extensive collection, which includes descriptions of diseases, their conditions, and treatments. Books on science and technology, agriculture, military technology, natural philosophy, even cookbooks, are all contained here.

Literature and Language

Western literary study flows out of eighteenth-century works by Alexander Pope, Daniel Defoe, Henry Fielding, Frances Burney, Denis Diderot, Johann Gottfried Herder, Johann Wolfgang von Goethe, and others. Experience the birth of the modern novel, or compare the development of language using dictionaries and grammar discourses.

Religion and Philosophy

The Age of Enlightenment profoundly enriched religious and philosophical understanding and continues to influence present-day thinking. Works collected here include masterpieces by David Hume, Immanuel Kant, and Jean-Jacques Rousseau, as well as religious sermons and moral debates on the issues of the day, such as the slave trade. The Age of Reason saw conflict between Protestantism and Catholicism transformed into one between faith and logic -- a debate that continues in the twenty-first century.

Law and Reference

This collection reveals the history of English common law and Empire law in a vastly changing world of British expansion. Dominating the legal field is the *Commentaries of the Law of England* by Sir William Blackstone, which first appeared in 1765. Reference works such as almanacs and catalogues continue to educate us by revealing the day-to-day workings of society.

Fine Arts

The eighteenth-century fascination with Greek and Roman antiquity followed the systematic excavation of the ruins at Pompeii and Herculaneum in southern Italy; and after 1750 a neoclassical style dominated all artistic fields. The titles here trace developments in mostly English-language works on painting, sculpture, architecture, music, theater, and other disciplines. Instructional works on musical instruments, catalogs of art objects, comic operas, and more are also included.

The BiblioLife Network

This project was made possible in part by the BiblioLife Network (BLN), a project aimed at addressing some of the huge challenges facing book preservationists around the world. The BLN includes libraries, library networks, archives, subject matter experts, online communities and library service providers. We believe every book ever published should be available as a high-quality print reproduction; printed on-demand anywhere in the world. This insures the ongoing accessibility of the content and helps generate sustainable revenue for the libraries and organizations that work to preserve these important materials.

The following book is in the "public domain" and represents an authentic reproduction of the text as printed by the original publisher. While we have attempted to accurately maintain the integrity of the original work, there are sometimes problems with the original work or the micro-film from which the books were digitized. This can result in minor errors in reproduction. Possible imperfections include missing and blurred pages, poor pictures, markings and other reproduction issues beyond our control. Because this work is culturally important, we have made it available as part of our commitment to protecting, preserving, and promoting the world's literature.

GUIDE TO FOLD-OUTS MAPS and OVERSIZED IMAGES

The book you are reading was digitized from microfilm captured over the past thirty to forty years. Years after the creation of the original microfilm, the book was converted to digital files and made available in an online database.

In an online database, page images do not need to conform to the size restrictions found in a printed book. When converting these images back into a printed bound book, the page sizes are standardized in ways that maintain the detail of the original. For large images, such as fold-out maps, the original page image is split into two or more pages

Guidelines used to determine how to split the page image follows:

• Some images are split vertically; large images require vertical and horizontal splits.
• For horizontal splits, the content is split left to right.
• For vertical splits, the content is split from top to bottom.
• For both vertical and horizontal splits, the image is processed from top left to bottom right.

~~379. g.~~

~~2118. 4. g~~

~~382. g~~

~~12978 k 8.~~

1502 | 410

GALIC AND ENGLISH

DICTIONARY.

CONTAINING

All the Words in the SCOTCH and IRISH Dialects of the CELTIC,
that could be collected from the Voice, and Old Books and MSS.

By the Rev. WILLIAM SHAW, A. M.

VOLUME I.

———————

LONDON:

Printed for the AUTHOR, by W. and A. STRAHAN;
And sold by J. MURRAY, Fleet-street; P. ELMSLY, Strand; C. ELLIOT, J. BALFOUR,
and R. JAMIESON, Edinburgh; D. PRINCE, Oxford; Messrs. MERRIL, Cambridge;
WILSON, Dublin; and PISSOT, at Paris.
MDCCLXXX.

TO

HIS GRACE.

ALEXANDER,

DUKE OF GORDON, MARQUIS AND EARL OF HUNTLY,
LORD BADENOCH, BARON ENZIE, &c. &c. &c.
ONE OF THE SIXTEEN PEERS OF SCOTLAND, AND
KNIGHT OF THE MOST ANTIENT ORDER OF THE THISTLE.

MY LORD,

IN writing a Dedication to YOUR GRACE, an extenſive field for Panegyric is opened to my view.—It would be no flattery to YOUR GRACE, were I to mention the Greatneſs and Antiquity of the Houſe of GORDON, and enumerate the heroic Deeds and generous Actions of a long train of Anceſtors, who have made a truly conſpicuous figure in the Annals of Caledonia. Their Virtues, MY LORD, have deſcended to our Days.—Every one who has the Honour of being known to YOUR GRACE, may, with delight, ſurvey the private virtues of Domeſtic Life, united with true Patriotiſm and Generoſity, to ſtand forth in defence of your Country, when Danger threatens our happy Conſtitution in Church and State.

The

DEDICATION.

The early Encouragement YOUR GRACE was pleaſed to give this Undertaking, has inclined me to put the Reſult of my Labours under your Protection, as the Friend of Letters. It is a Depoſit of the dying Language of YOUR GRACE's Anceſtors, which was once famous in the Weſtern World, and is ſtill the ſpeech of many of his Majeſty's faithful and loyal Subjects, who have ever been the firm Friends of Regal Government, and over whom YOUR GRACE is ſo conſiderable a Chieftain.

I am happy in having this opportunity of ſhewing my attachment to YOUR GRACE; and have the honour to be, with the moſt profound reſpect,

MY LORD,

YOUR GRACE's

Much obliged, and

Moſt obedient humble Servant,

LONDON,
May 26, 1780.

W. SHAW.

PREFACE.

THE human mind, from an innate curiofity, and the pleafure received from the contemplation of melancholy images, is more delighted by a retrofpective view of the paft, than any conjectures fhe can form of the future. How much foever difconnected by fituation, birth, or other circumftances, the patriotifm, virtue, learning, and bravery of individuals; the wealth, power, cuftoms, and manners, national character, and extent of territory, with the gradual decay and difmemberment of a people, fhe confiders with an attention highly interefted, and gently perplexed.

And although, by the contingencies of human affairs, and the ufual fate of empires, a nation be reduced from its antient fplendour to an inconfiderable ftate amongft neighbouring powers, yet the underftanding of the philofophical enquirer, fet at liberty from the low and narrow dictates of a felfifh fpirit, being acceffible to truth, and friendly to mankind, and having foregone the little diftinctions of party, with liberal capacioufnefs of mind, indulgeth intellectual appetites from every opening fource of gratification. Whoever affords entertainment for mental defires, or information to the fpeculative, renders an acceptable fervice to the friends of literature.

Senfible of this, his inclination would have led the Compiler to embrace the prefent opportunity of enquiring into the different migrations of the Celtic nations over the various kingdoms of Europe, and of giving an account of their empire and power, attended with numerous viciffitudes, fince they parted with their progenitors Japhet and Gomer, in Afia, until their prefent gradual decline and eve of exiftence as a feparate people in the Britifh Ifles, and prefent the reader with every gratification fuch an inveftigation might afford; but as this would lead into a tedious difcuffion of what hath been lately written for and againft Scoto and Ibero-Celtic antiquities, and exceed the compafs of a Preface, I fhall referve that for a feparate difquifition, and confine myfelf to an account of the prefent undertaking.

The general encouragement the prefent age hath fo generoufly given to every work that can afford either pleafure or inftruction, hath induced many to become candidates for fame in the republic of letters. Every fcience and art is improved;

every

PREFACE.

every subject hath been impartially discussed. Whatever can tend to information, to promote knowledge and the improvement of life, hath, on whatever subject and from whatever source offered, been cheerfully received. Not insensible to the impulse of ambition, nor indifferent in the pursuit of honest fame, originally prompted by patriotism, and instigated by some learned men, I have been ambitious to cast my mite into the stores of Literature, gleaned from the remains of the venerable Celtic.

The approbation which the curious have been pleased to signify of the Analysis of the Scotch Dialect of the Galic, published at London in 1778, encouraged me to turn my thoughts towards the present work. But the difficulties attending such a laborious undertaking seemed so numerous and insurmountable, that my expectations, however sanguine in theory, appeared irreducible to practice. Some learned friends observed, that such a work could only be effected under the immediate auspices of the Scotch and Irish nations by a public subscription; as a tour through these countries, to complete a Dictionary, must be performed. Being however inwardly persuaded, that whatever is the business of many is the business of nobody, I was discouraged from any application of that nature. As the Public hath often been imposed upon, proposals were made for printing by subscription a Galic Dictionary; and that my countrymen might be more convinced of my zeal and real intention of publishing, payment only on delivery of the book was the condition.

Observing with regret the indolence and inactive zeal of my compatriots in the cause of their expiring language, with the most ardent enthusiasm I was impelled to attempt snatching from oblivion, and in her last struggles for existence preserve in a Dictionary, as much as possible of the greatest monument of antiquity perhaps now in the world : for the Galic is the language of Japhet, spoken before the Deluge, and probably the speech of Paradise.

Encouraged by the good wishes of my friends, excited by a partiality for the subject, and a hope of realizing what had hitherto been little thought of or neglected by my countrymen, in the spring of 1778 I undertook a journey from London to the Highlands of Scotland. Having made a progress into almost every corner of the Highland part of the continent, and visited the most considerable of the Hebrides, exposed to much fatigue and many inconveniencies, I passed over to Ireland, there also to pursue the Galic ; and returned to London in February 1779, after a perambulation of about three thousand miles, with a collection of near thirty thousand articles for a Dictionary.

In the Highlands, there being few books, and still fewer MSS. in the Scotch dialect, the language in the living voice was the only source from which I could glean vocables. In the island of Mull, however, Mr. Macarthur, one of the ministers there, who understands the language well, laid before me about two hundred words, part of which I transcribed, uncertain whether I had seen them before.

The

PREFACE.

The better clafs of the people every where with alacrity afforded every poffible information, and for that purpofe feldom fpoke to me but in the antient tongue, turning the converfation to various fubjects, to give an opportunity of catching new words. But the common people, who are generally poffeffed of whatever narration remains in the country, muft all be bought. They told me, I had been well paid by his Majefty for what I undertook, otherwife I fhould not have been at fo much pains, and therefore they feldom opened their mouths before they were paid.

Sir James Foulis, although of the Low Country of Scotland, and confequently once a ftranger to the Galic, by ftudy is now better acquainted with it than many of the natives. This gentleman, in the fequeftered vale of life, hath employed his leifure hours in gleaning and depofiting in his library whatever remains of Celtic antiquities he could reach at; and perceiving that my defign was not to boaft of what learning the Galic contained, whilft I concealed it from public view, but at once prefent the world with the language itfelf, unlike to others, hid not the refult of his inveftigations and long labours under a bufhel, but generoufly allowed me the ufe of his manufcript collection His knowledge of a tongue, believed impoffible to learn, is a living inftance of what application, and a tafte for antient learning, can do, fome Bard, therefore, will write his epitaph, and every patriot Gaedheal add a ftone to his carn.

In Ireland I have been chiefly obliged to Lieut. Col Vallancy, who, by indefatigable induftry, has acquired a thorough acquaintance with the Galic, and deferves much of all the friends of the antiquities of that nation. There are many valuable MSS. in his poffeffion, the ufe of which he generoufly granted me. Trinity College Library contains many books and MSS. in the old letter, and on a variety of fubjects, to which I had free accefs by means of Dr. Cleghorn, and the indulgence of Dr. Leland. Thefe volumes, elegantly tranfcribed, but fealed books to moft of the prefent age, whilft I furveyed and examined them, and looked back to the ancient ftate of this once bleffed and lettered ifland, produced emotions eafier conceived than defcribed.

Having, thus, collected my materials at a confiderable expence and wafte of time, I fat down to arrange the whole, probably facrificing more ufeful purfuits to a defire of recording what in a few years no labour or induftry could recover. The fmall number of fubfcribers, and the expence I had already been at in procuring materials, made me apprehenfive I fhould never be able to publifh; and I was about to depofit my MSS. in fome public library, when fome Gentlemen in London, with true patriotifm in the republic of letters, encouraged the work on the plan of fubfcription. Amongft thefe I hold myfelf particularly indebted to Lieut. General Melvill, who, adding to military fcience a tafte for ancient as well as modern learning, fhewed himfelf a zealous promoter of this undertaking in favour

of

of the Galic language. By thefe means I have been enabled to fend this work to the prefs, although on a more contracted plan than I at firft propofed. It however contains nearly every word in both the Scotch and Irifh dialects, with an Englifh tranflation oppofite, in the Firft Volume; and the moft neceffary articles in the Englifh, with their oppofite Galic terms, in the Second. The Galic reader will find no innovations in orthography; for I have confidered it my bufinefs rather to record words as they have been written in the ancient Irifh MSS. than attempt to write a Dictionary, by altering the fpelling from the received method, to what I might conceive it ought to be, according to the powers of the letters, and the philofophy of language.

A fpeech fo fingular in its inflections, fo ancient in its ftructure, and fo copious in words as the Galic, although much written, cannot be fo fixed in its orthography as thofe tongues which enjoy the benefit of Printing. With the Irifh, however, (whofe dialect has always been the written and ftudied language) the difference was very inconfiderable. One vowel or diphthong is fometimes fubftituted for a fimilar one, and the commutable confonants and combinations are interchanged. This has been the cafe with the Greek and Latin languages, as well as with the Galic.— The perfection to which the laft arrived in Ireland in fuch remote ages is aftonifhing, and of which the perufal of this Dictionary is an indubitable proof. I have, however, fometimes written the abftract termination Orachd, for Mhorachd, Al, for Amhuil, and Lachd, for Amhuilachd.—Oppofite every Englifh word there are as many different Galic words as I could collect. The moft common are firft, and the more ancient or obfolete laft, which the curious Orientalift may compare with fimilar words in the Eaftern tongues.

As a Dictionary becomes perfect only by different editions, and the induftry and abilities of the different editors, I do not intrude the prefent work upon the Public as a book to which nothing can be added. It will anfwer the purpofes of a Galic and Englifh, and Englifh and Galic Dictionary; and by it, and the affiftance of the Analyfis or Grammar, one may acquire a confiderable degree of knowledge in the language, and be more able to form a juft idea of Celtic learning. If my labour affords the defired affiftance to thofe at home who may wifh to improve the knowledge of their mother tongue, or fatisfaction to the curious abroad, that may be inclined to compare words in it with other dialects of the Celtic, or the Oriental languages; and if, in thefe books, I have preferved in an intelligible and rational ftate, a tongue more copious, nervous, and fofter than is commonly allowed, I have obtained my wifh—for whatever adds to the ftores of Literature, I reckon gain.

A

LIST of SUBSCRIBERS.

A.

HIS Grace the Duke of Argyle.
His Grace the Duke of Athol.
The Right Hon. the Earl of Aberdeen.
The Right Hon. the Earl of Aylesford.
Robert Adam, Esq;
Mr. David Andrew, Throgmorton-street.

B.

His Excellency the Earl of Buckinghamshire,
    Lord Lieutenant of Ireland.
Right Hon. the Earl of Berkeley.
Right Hon. Lord Binning.
The Hon. Daines Barrington.
Sir Patrick Blake, Bart.
Christopher Blake, Esq;
Joseph Banks, Esq; F. R. S. &c.
Rev. R. Beadon, Archdeacon of London.
James Brodie, of Brodie, Esq;
Edmund Burke, Esq;
Michael Burke, Esq.
Doctor Beattie.
Gustavus Brander, Esq;
James Boswell, Esq; Advocate.
James Bryant, Esq.
Isaac Hawkins Browne, Esq; Shropshire.

C.

His Grace the Archbishop of Canterbury.
The Right Hon. Lord Cadogan.
The Right Hon. Lord Frederic Campbell.
    3 Copies.
Sir David Carnegie, Bart.
Sir George Colquhoun, Bart.
Sir James Campbell, of Ardkinlass, Bart.
John Campbell, of Calder, Esq;
Col. Charles Campbell, of Barbreck.
Niel Campbell, of Duntroon, Esq;
John Campbell, of Airds, Esq;
Alexander Campbell, of Glenure, Esq;
Alexander Campbell, Esq; London.
Alexander Campbell, Esq, Chamberlain of
    Kyntire.
Mr. Archibald Campbell, Minister of Inve-
    rary.
Mr. William Campbell, Minister of Lochow.
Robert Campbell, of Asknish, Esq, Sheriff
    of Argyle.
James Campbell, Esq; of St. John's.
Colin Campbell, of Scamadale, Esq;
James Campbell, Esq; Provost of Inve-
    rary.
Alexander Chisholm, of Chisholm, Esq;
W. Cunningham, of Entricken, Esq;

W. Calderwood, Efq; Captain of the Firft Troop of Horfe Guards.

Mr. John Clerk, Land Surveyor, Edinburgh.

Captain Robert Cook.

Mr. James Campbell, Covent Garden, 4 Copies.

Mr. Colvil, Burleigh-ftreet, London.

Mr. D. Campbell, Merchant, Campbeltown.

D.

The Right Hon. the Earl of Dunmore.

The Right Hon. Vifcount Dudley.

Henry Dundafs, Efq; Lord Advocate.

G. Dempfter, Efq, M. P.

The Hon. John Drummond.

Col. Debbeigh.

Henry Dagge, Efq,

James Dundafs, of Dundafs, Efq;

Thomas Dundafs, Efq;

W. Dalrymple, Efq,

D. Davidfon, of Cantray, Efq;

Mr. H. Davidfon, London. 2 Copies.

Harry Davidfon, Efq,

G. Drummond, Efq; Lincoln's Inn Fields.

E.

The Right Hon. Earl of Eglintoune.

The Countefs of Elgin.

Bifhop of Ely.

Lord Elliock.

Mr. James Elphinfton.

Edinburgh, Univerfity of.

Mr. Charles Elliot, Bookfeller, Edinburgh. 3 Copies.

F.

The Right Hon. Earl of Fife.

General Frafer, of Lovat.

Archibald Frafer, Efq;

Sir James Foulis, of Colington, Bart.

Sir James Forbes, Bart.

James Fordyce, of Ayton, Efq;

G. Fordyce, M. D.

Alexander Frafer, of Struy, Efq;

Alexander Frafer, of Culduthil, Efq;

H. Frafer, of Efkadale, Efq.

James Frafer, of Belladruim, Efq;

Simon Frafer, of Daltullich, Efq;

Donald Frafer, of Ballone, Efq;

John Frafer, of Garthmore, Efq;

Mr. W. Frafer, Writer, at Invernefs.

Mr. Arch. Fletcher, Writer, Edinburgh.

Hugh Frafer, Efq; Lieutenant in the Navy.

Mr. Paul Frafer, Minifter of Craignifh.

G.

His Grace the Duke of Gordon. 5 Copies.

The Right Hon. the Earl of Gower.

Lord Adam Gordon.

Baron Gordon.

James Grant, of Shuglie, Efq;

Alexander Grant, of Corimonie, Efq;

Alexander Grant, Efq, Lieutenant in the 71ft Regiment.

Patrick Grant, of Glenmorifton, Efq;

—— Gordon, of Whitely, Efq; Advocate.

Lieut. Col. Harry Gordon.

Glafgow, Univerfity of.

W. Grey, Efq; of Jamaica.

Mr. John Geddes, Valladolid.

Mr. Alexander Geddes, Fochabers.

Mr. Alexander Gordon, Paris.

H.

Lord Haddo.

Sir George Home, Bart.

W. Hunter, M. D. Phyfician to the Queen.

The Rev. W. T. Harvey, A. M. Rector of Quadrington and Normanton, Lincolnfhire.

William Hall, Efq;

Archibald Hamilton, Efq;

LIST OF SUBSCRIBERS.

I.

Alexander Johnfon, M. D. London.
Samuel Johnfon, L. L. D.
Edward Jones, Efq,
Invernefs, Library of.

K.

The Right Hon. Earl of Kelly.
Michael Keene, Efq, Counfellor at Law,
   St. Vincents.
The Rev. Doctor Kippis.
The Rev. Mr. John Kelly.

L.

The Right Hon. Marquis of Lothian.
J. Lamont of Lamont, Efq,
John Lloyd, Efq, of Denbighfhire.
Martin Lindfay, Efq, Lothbury, London.

M.

The Right Hon. Lord Mountftuart.
Sir Allan Maclean, Bart.
The Hon. Major General Mackay.
Major Montgomery.
Normand Macleod, of Macleod, Efq;
Donald Maclachlan, of Clanlachlan, Efq;
Lieutenant General Melvill.
Angus Macalafter, of Loup, Efq;
D. Macdonnel, of Glengary, Efq;
Alexander Maclean, of Coll, Efq,
Lachlane Maclean, of Torlifk, Efq;
James Mackintofh, of Faon, Efq,
W. Mackintofh, of Holm, Efq;
Andrew Macpherfon, of Benachar, Efq;
Lachlan Macpherfon, Efq; of Ralia.
John Macpherfon, of Uvie, Efq;
Captain John Macpherfon (of Colonel
   Maclean's Regiment).
John Macpherfon, Efq; M. P.
Donald Mackintofh, of Dalmageree, Efq;

James Macpherfon, Efq; London.
Ranald Macdonnel, of Scothoufe, Efq;
John Macleod, of Raafay, Efq;
Captain Mackintofh, of Balinefpick.
David Melvill, Efq, Dublin.
Mr. Robert Macfarlane, Walthamftow.
John Mackenzie, Efq; Inner Temple.
Archibald Maclean, of Lochbuy, Efq;
Charles Mackintofh, Efq, late of Gibral-
   tar.
G. G. Munro, of Breamore, Efq;
Colonel Archibald Macnab.
Dugald Malcolm, Efq, London.
James Morifon, Efq, London, 2 Copies.
Colin Mackenzie, Efq, London.
Donald Maclean, Efq, junior, of Kinger-
   loch.
John Macniel, of Ugdale, Efq,
Niel Mac Neale, Efq, of Tirfargus.
Patrick Macdougal, of Galanach, Efq;
Charles Maclean, of Kenlochallin, Efq;
Mr. Kenneth Maclenan, Watchmaker, Lon-
   don.
Mr. Maclaurin, Edinburgh.
Mr. Duncan Mackay, Probationer.
Mr. John Macdonald, Arran.
Mr. Edmund Macqueen, Minifter of Barra.
Mr. Allan Macqueen, Minifter of North-
   Uift.
Mr. John Mackinnon, Argyle-ftreet.
John Mackintofh, Efq, Lieutenant of Ma-
   rines.
Mr. Donald Macleod, Minifter of Glenelg.

N.

His Grace the Duke of Northumberland.

O.

Right Hon. Lord Onflow.
The Hon. Sir Adolphus Oughton.
Richard Ofwald, Efq.

P.

The Right Hon. the Earl of Pembroke.
Dr. Percy, Dean of Carlifle.
Sir John Pringle, Bart.
John Preftwich, Efq; London.
Mr. William Purfe, Strand.

Q.

His Grace the Duke of Queenfberry.

R.

Right Hon. the Marquis of Rockingham.
Right Hon. Lord Ravenfworth.
Col. W. Roy.
David Rae, Efq; Advocate.
Allan Ramfay, Efq;

S.

The Right Hon. Earl of Sandwich.
Right Hon. Lord Sandys.
Sir George Shuckburgh, Bart.
G. Lewis Scot, Efq;
Robert Shuttleworth, Efq; Lancafhire.

Rev. G. Strahan, A.M. Rector of Iflington.
G. Stewaft, Efq; Devonfhire-ftreet, Cavendifh-fquare.
John Stewart, of Balachaolifh, Efq;
Major John Small.
John Hamilton Smythe, Efq;
Mr. Alexander Shaw, London.
Mr. John Shaw, Arran.
St. Andrews (Univerfity of).

T.

Governor Trapaud, Fort Auguftus.
W. Tod, Efq; London.
John Townfon, Efq; Grey's Inn.

V.

The Right Hon. Earl Verney.
Lieut. Col. Vallancy.

W.

Lady Mary Walker.
John White, of Benochy, Efq;
John Henley Wall, Efq;
Mr. W. Wright, Leith.

A

GALIC AND ENGLISH

DICTIONARY.

A

A, In Galic called Ailm, is the firſt letter of the Alphabet, is pronounced broad, as in the Italian and French languages, or a in the Engliſh fall, tall. It has too many different ſignifications in the old MSS. and printed books, the principal of which are as follow. Vide Galic Analyſis.

A. His, her, it's.

A. An aſcent, hill, or promontory.

A. Improperly a ſign of the preſent and future tenſe.

A. Improperly a ſign of the vocative.

A. Thus marked a' is the article an, as a' bhean for an bhean.

A. For ag, ſign of the participle preſent, ought always to be written at length ag.

A. No ſign properly of the vocative; it ſhould be written o, as a Dhia, o Dhia.

A. No ſign of the infinitive.

A. Is often improperly written for *as*, out of.

A B A

A. The relative *that.*

A. A wain, carr, or chariot. Vide Gloſſary of Collum Cille.

Ab A lord, father, abbot. Vide Hebrew Abh, Chaldaic Abba, and the Greek and Latin Abbas.

Aba. Cauſe, matter, buſineſs.

Aba. Father.

Ab, or ap. An ape, in the antient Gaulic any little animal: hence the Welſh ap a ſon, and Greek nepos.

Ab. Negative, not, un.

Abac. Vide Abhac.

Abach. The entrails of a beaſt, a proclamation.

Abaidh. A bud. Vide Abbuidh.

Abaidachd. Abbacy.

Abail, & abailt. Death.

Abair. Say thou.

Abairam, or abram. To ſay, ſpeak.

Abairt. Speech, articulation; alſo education, politeneſs, breeding.

• Abaiſe,

Abaife. Cuftom, manner.

Abact. Ironical joking. Vide Gloffary of C. Cille.

Abadh. A fatire, a lampoon.

Abhac. A terrier, a ferret, inde abhaftrach.

Abhach. A dwarf, or fprite.

Abacho. Gain, great doings.

Abhadh. A camp, a fmall net in form of a fack, to catch fifh.

Abhacoide. An advocate, not Galic.

Abhal. An apple-tree, an apple. Vide Ubhal.

Abhalghort. An orchard.

Abhain. Vide Amhuin.

Abar. A marfh, a boggy piece of land.

Abhantur. The good luck or fuccefs of an undertaking.

Abhaftrach. The barking of a dog.

Abhar, or adbhar. Caufe, motive.

Abhdhac. Lordly courage.

Abheil. Vide Aidhbheil.

Abhcaid. A jeft.

Abhlan. A wafer.

Abhlan coifrigte. The Euchariſt.

Abhlan. Whatever is eat with bread in way of condiment or fauce, vulgarly called kitchen.

Abhlabhra. Mute, dumb. Vide Amhlabhra.

Abhaiſt. Cuftom, habit, fafhion.

Abharach. A youth under age, but who acts as a man.

Abhmbathair. Mother abbefs.

Abhra, abhraid. Eyelid. Vide Fabhradha.

Ablach. A carcafe.

Abra. A fpeech, faying, a poem.

Abhra. Dark.

Abrad. Far removed, exalted, from brad in the Gaulic a fummit, fovereign. *It made many braide.* Chaucer. Fab. of Dido. Vide Braid.

Abhran. A fong. Vide Amhran.

Abraim. Vide Abaraim.

Abran, abraon. The month of April.

Abrann. Luftful, lecherous; alfo bad news.

Abhras. A ready anfwer.

Abhras. Spinning; flax and wool.

Abhus. A wild beaft of any fort, a ſtall for cattle.

Abſdal. An apoftle.

Abſdalachd. Apoftlefhip.

Abhſan. A furrow or hollow place.

Abſdoltachadh. Effectual.

Abu ! The war cry of the antient Irifh, a common interjection.

Abuigh. Ripe, ready, expert, alert.

Abuigham. To ripen.

Abughadh. Ripening.

Abulta. Able, ftrong, capable.

Abultachd. Ability.

Ac. A refufal, denial.

Ac. Speech, tongue.

Ac. A fon.

Aca-damh. Academy. Vide Damh.

Acain vel acfuin. Tackle, furniture, tools.

Acaideadh. An inhabitant, a tenant.

Acalla. A converfation.

Acartha. Profit, the loan or ufe of a thing.

Acca, accafa. With them, their.

Accarachd. Gentlenefs, moderation, refpect.

Accartha. Gentle, moderate, refpectful, obliging.

Accain, ag accain. Complaining, fighing.

Accaire. An anchor, an acre of land.

Accarfaid. A port, harbour.

Accaſtair. An axle.

Accuin. Vide Acfuin.

Accuil. Backwards.

Acfuin. Tools, tackle.

Acfuinach. Having tools or tackling, able, fufficient.

Ach, achd. But, except.

Ach,

Ach. A fkirmifh.

Acha. A mound or bank.

Achaidh. An abode.

Achadh. A field.

Achamair. Soon, timely, abridged.

Achamaireachd. Abridging, abbreviation.

Achd. Cafe, ftate, condition.

Achiar, acar. Sharp, tart, four.

Achdra. An expedition at fea.

Achdran, achdranach. An adventurer, a foreigner.

Achar. A diftance.

Acaran. Lumber.

Acais. Poifon.

Achran. Intricacy.

Achranach. Intricate.

Achd cheana. However.

Acharradh. A diminutive being, a fprite.

Achdam. To chafe.

Achlais. Arm, arm-pit.

Achmhufan. A rebuke, cenfure, reprehenfion.

Achmhufanaicham. To rebuke, cenfure.

Achfal. An angel.

Acht. A body.

Acladh, aclaidh. A fifhery.

Aclaidhe. Smooth, fine, foft.

Acmac. A circuit, compafs.

Acht. Danger, peril.

Acht. A ftatute, decree, deed.

Achtam. To pafs an act of parliament, to ordain, order, command.

Acht. A nail, or claw.

Achlaid. Chafing, purfuing.

Acmhaing, acmhaingeach. Puiffant, copious, rich.

Ach beg. Almoft.

Acomialam. To heap together, increafe.

Acomal. An affembly, or heaping together.

Acon. A refufal, denial.

Acor, acobhair. Covetoufnefs, avarice, penury.

Acras. Hunger. Vide Ocras.

Acrafach. }
Acrach. } Hungry.

Acram. I come, agree.

Acrann. A knot.

Acrannach. Entangled.

Achrannam. To entangle.

Acuil. An eagle.

A d'. For a do, to thee, only a verb intervenes, a d' mharbadh, come to kill thee.

A' d'. For ann do.

Adag A fhock of corn, a haddock.

Ad. Water.

Ada. Victory.

Adamhain. }
Adamhair. } Play, diverfion, fport.

Adamhairam. To play, fport.

Adamhra. Admiration.

Adair. An adder ; I believe not Irifh.

Adbatham. To die.

Adbath. Slaughter, deftruction.

Adfed. Chafte.

Adfia. It is yours, your property; an imperfonal verb.

Adh. A law.

Adh. Fit to do any thing.

Adh, agh. Felicity, good luck.

Adhmhor. Fortunate, lucky.

Adharc. A horn, trumpet.

Adharcach. Having horns.

Adhaircain. A lapwing, touchet.

Agh feidh. A hind.

Adhart, adhartan. A pillow, bolfter.

Adhairt. Front, van.

Adhartar. A dream.

Adantachd. A blufh.

Adhailg. Defire, will.

Adhailgne. The toll of a mill, military law, poverty,

Adhaghabhail. A lawful taking.

Adhamhrach. Bleffedly.

Adhamh. Adam.

Adhamhradham. To blefs.

Adhainnam,

Adhainnam. To lighten.

Adhal. A flesh hook.

Adhall. Dull, deaf.

Adhall. Sin, corruption.

Adhaltan. A dull stupid fellow.

Adhaltranach. An adulterer.

Adhaltranas Adultery.

Adhann. A pan or cauldron; the herb Coltsfoot.

Adbanta. Kindled, exasperated.

Adhna. Kindling of the fire, fervour, heat.

Adharadh. Adoration.

Adharam. To adore, worship.

Adhradair. ⎫
Adharach. ⎬ Worshipper, adorer.

Adhaftair. An halter.

Adhmoilaim. To neglect.

Admhulich. Warrant, surety.

Adhmhud. Timber.

Adharadh. To join, to stick close to.

Adhas. Good.

Adhbbha, Adhbhadhan. Instrument.

Adhbhadh. A house, room, habitation, garrison, fortress, palace.

Adhbhachd. A harmless joke.

Adhbhachdach. Jocose; gross, fat, corpulent.

Adhbharfeach. A comber of wool or flax.

Adhbhal. Nimble, quick, thrifty.

Adhbhal. Vide Aidhbheil.

Adhbhan trireach. A sort of musick.

Adhbhar. A cause, reason, matter, business.

Adhbharas. Carded wool.

Adhbhe. Hail! may you live!

Adhbo. A shout, war cry, of which every Irish prince had one.

Adhbhchlos. Great fame, vanity.

Adhbhclas. Pleasure, joy.

Adhbhchlofach. Vainglorious.

Adhbhuidh. Joy, merriment; a foundation.

Adheitchidhe. Ugly.

Adhflath. Rightful, sovereign.

Adhuathmhorra. Odious, detestable.

Adhuathmharachd. Abomination.

Adhghair. Lawful.

Adhlacam. To bury, inter.

Adhlacadh. ⎫
Adhlachan. ⎬ A burial.

Adhlacanach. Burier of the dead, an undertaker.

Adhlacte. Buried, interred.

Adhlaic. A longing desire after what is good.

Adhlan. A champion.

Adhm. Knowledge.

Adhma. Knowing.

Adhmhollam. To extol, praise.

Adhmholladh. Praise.

Adhnacal. ⎫
Admachd. ⎬ A burial, interment.

Adhnaclach. A sexton.

Adhnadh. A kindling of fire.

Adhnairc. Shamefacedness.

Adhnaidhe. Old, antient.

Adhram. To adore, worship.

Adhradh. ⎫
Adhras. ⎬ Adoration.

Adhrac. A refusal.

Admhall. Wandering, desultory, wanton.

Adonathad. Sovereignty, old laws.

Adudh. A circle, fire.

Aduath. Horror, detestation.

Aduathmhorra. Terrible, horrid, dreadful.

Aduathmhorrachd. Horror, abomination.

Aduain. A stranger, foreigner.

Ae, aodh. The liver.

Ae. One.

Aedh. The eye.

Aeghe. The liver.

Aeidh. A trade, craft.

Aerdha. Vide Athargha.

Aerdhaite. Sky-coloured.

Aedhar, *rather* Athar. The air, sky.

Aesfhear. God.

Aetharag.

Aetharag. A walking spirit.

Afost. Gold.

Afraighe. Arising to battle.

Afrionn. Mass or Eucharist offering.

Ag. Sign of the present participle.

Aga. A space, the bottom of any depth; why? wherefore?

Agad. For *Ag do*, with thee, thine.

Agall. A speech.

Agalladh. A dialogue.

Agallam. To speak.

Agamh. A doubt, suspicion.

Agamhal. Doubtful.

Agam, ag mi. With or at me, in my possession.

Againn, againne. With us, our.

Agaibh, agaibhse. With you, your.

Agaram, agartam. To plead, pursue, dispute, plea.

Agart. Pleading, pursuing.

Agartas. A suit, plea.

Agartach. Litigious.

Agamus. The action of striking.

Agan. Precious, dear.

Agag. An habitation or settlement.

Agarach. A pretender, claimer.

Agart. Pursuing, revenge.

Agarthach. Vindictive, litigious.

Agh. Good fortune. Vide Adh.

Agh. An ox, bull, or cow.

Agh. Fear, astonishment, awe.

Agh. A conflict, battle.

Aghaim. To be afraid or astonished.

Aghach. Warlike, brave.

Aghaidh. Be merry.

Aghaisach. Easy.

Aghai, aghaidh. The face, countenance.

Aghais. Ease.

Aghaisaicham. To ease.

Aghmhor. Vide Adhmhor.

Aghnas. Pleading, argumentation.

Aghnaidhasam. To plead.

Aghanidhe. An advocate, pleader.

Agharam. To expostulate, challenge.

Aghgha. Contentious.

Aghthar. A hot skirmish.

Aghet. Old wine.

Agna, eagnai. Wisdom, prudence.

Agsal. Generous, noble.

Agurad. Mild, coaxing, deceitful.

Agus. And.

Ai. A cause or controversy.

Ai. A swan.

Ai, aoi. An herd; also a sheep or cow.

Ai, aoi. A region, tract or territory.

Ai. Learned.

Ai, aoi. Inheritance of land, possession.

Aibh, aoibh. Similitude.

Aibheis. The sea; great boasting, a gulf, emptiness.

Aibghitir. ⎫
Aiblitir. ⎬ Alphabet.

Aibhseach. Wonderful, enormous, arrogant.

Aibhseoir. ⎫ Adversary, the devil, a gasconader.
Aibhasdair. ⎬

Aibhseoirachd. Cursing, imprecating, rodomontade.

Aibhreann. A castrated buck-goat.

Aibrean. April.

Aibhsioch. Great; gay, joyous.

Aibhche. A scholar.

Aibhe. All hail!

Aibhidach. Huge, great.

Aibhse. A diminutive contemptible creature, a sprite.

Aibhsuigham. To be astonished, frightened.

Aibid. A habit.

Aibhle. A spark.

Aibhleach. Singed.

Aibhleog. A red coal, a sparkle, a flake of snow.

Aibhleoga. Sparkling.

Aic. A tribe or family; nourishing, desire.

Aice. A prop.

      Aice.

Aice. At or with her, hers.

Aice, aiceachd. Leading.

Aiceam. To lead.

Aice. Near, clofe.

Aicfeacht. Power.

Aicear. Angry, cruel, fevere.

Aicid. Difeafe, ficknefs.

Aicideach. Sick perfon, difeafed.

Aicide. Accident.

Aiccidach. Unfortunate, that meets with accidents.

Aicim. To pray, befeech, entreat.

Aicle. }
Aicde. } A veil.

Aicde A bodkin, a ring.

Aicde. A building, foundation.

Aice. Led.

Aicme. A fort or kind, tribe.

Aicme, Beauty.

Aichear. Sharp, keen.

Aicidhad. A ftich, pain, ficknefs.

Aicidheach. Full of pains.

Aichill. Great lamentation.

Aichill. Able, potent.

Aichillidh. Dexterous, handy.

Aicillidhachd. Dexterity.

Aicir. Vide Athair.

Aicne. Nature.

Aicre. }
Aicfi. } Inheritance, patrimony.

Aidhbean Evil; long.

Aid. A piece, portion.

Aid. Cold.

Aidhbhean. Remote.

Aidhbhean. A ftranger, foreigner.

Aidhbhean. An inn.

Aidhbhrugh. Bewitching, eye-biting.

Aidhbham. To fafcinate.

Aidhbheil. Huge, vaft, enormous.

Aidhbheil. A wonder, a boafting.

Aidhbhfi. An old fort of Irifh cronan or fong.

Aidhbhfin. A phantom or fprite.

Aidhchleadh. }
Aidhceall. } Mifchief, eye-biting.

Aidheach. A milch-cow.

Aidheitige. Ugly, deformed.

Aidhidhe. Bafhful, faithful, true.

Aidhilgneach. A dairy-maid.

Aidhfidheach. Demonftration.

Aidhle. A cooper's adz.

Aidide. Humble, refpectful.

Aidhme. Apparel, raiment, goods, chattels.

Aidhmhe. An inftrument.

Aidhme. A military drefs.

Aidhme. Coarfe or rough land.

Aidhne. Age.

Aidhmhillam. To confume, deftroy, pervert.

Aidhmhos. Vide Aighnas. Pleading.

Aidhneas. Pleading.

Aidhnaidhe. An advocate, pleader.

Aidhnaireachd. Pleading.

Aidhneafoir. An opponent.

Aidmhuigham. }
Aidmhailam. } To confefs, declare, to own.
Aidmham. }

Aidmhal. A confeffion, profeffion, declaration.

Aidmhalach. A profeffor.

Aidhmhean. Refuge.

Aidmhighte Confeffed.

Aifir. Blame, fault.

Aifrionn. Holy mafs.

Aig. At.

Aige. At or with him, it, his.

Aighe. A beam, prop

Aighe. A hind, a hill.

Aighe. Stout, valiant.

Aigh. Generous, valiant.

Aighar. Gladnefs, joy.

Aigharach. Glad, joyful.

Aigein. The deep, the ocean.

Aigefin. Thereat.

Aigeam. To go on.

Aigeach.

Aigeach. The founder of a deep.

Aighean. Vide Adhann.

Aigionta. Intentions.

Aigine. Vide Aigne. Mind, intention.

Aighreile. A judge.

Aighreiram. To judge.

Aigantach. Chearful, high-minded, festive.

Aigantachd. }
Aigantas. } Jollity, chearfulness.

Aighneachd. Liberality, generosity.

Aightha. Faces.

Aigbheile. Terror.

Aigcorachd. Arguing.

Aigeoram. To argue.

Aigal. Puffed up, elate.

Aigailam. To grieve, vex.

Aigalain. Ear-ring, taffel, chain, tag.

Aigilne. Truth.

Aigal. Bottom of a valley.

Aighne. Nature.

Aighneach. Liberal.

Ail. A stone.

Ail. Shamefaced, noble, beautiful.

Ail. A sting, or prickle.

Aill. Will, pleasure.

Ail. Arms, weapons.

Ail. A rebuke.

Ail. Mouth.

Ail. A petition, request.

Ail. Time, while.

Ail. A blot in an escutcheon.

Ailbhin. A small flock.

Ailc. A stone.

Ailcne. Paving stones.

Ailce. Manners, behaviour.

Ailbhech. Stones.

Ailcith. A strand stone.

Ailcar. A porch.

Ailcneachan. A paver.

Ailcneachachd. Paving.

Ailec, aileach. A stone-horse

Ailfes. A bridle-bit.

Ailgean. Noble offspring.

Ailghean. Powerful, strong; soft, smooth.

Ailghean. Want.

Ailgeas. A desire, longing.

Ailgine. Softness, smoothness.

Ailgeadh. Forgiveness.

Ailag. Hickup.

Aile. Smell.

Aillagan. A gew-gaw, any thing pretty.

Ailbhag cluaise. An ear-ring.

Ailen. Orts.

Aille. }
Aillad. } Handsomeness.

Ailne. Beauty.

Ailim. To entreat, pray.

Ailam. To foster, nourish.

Aill. A journey.

Aill. A steep bank washed by the water.

Aill. A bridle.

Aill. Noble.

Aill. Praise.

Aill. Course, place, stead, turn.

Aillam. To go, come.

Aillbhil. A bridle-bit.

Aillbhruachach. Having steep or rocky banks.

Aillim. Alum.

Ailleann. Elecampane.

Aille. Praise.

Ailleachd. Handsomeness.

Aillean. A causeway.

Aillean. A pet, a beau, a minion.

Ailleanam. To make fine.

Aillgean. Smooth, soft.

Aillgeasachd. Ardency.

Aillgeasdha. Ardent.

Ailliadh, ailliath. Roaring.

Aillis. Vide Aillse. A canker

Aillinbhus. A great salmon.

Aillse. A fairy, diminutive creature, a canker; delay.

Ailm. An elm; the name of the letter a.

Ailmeadh. A prayer.

Ailmeog. The elm.

Ailionta.

Ailionta. Airy. Of the air.

Ailidh. White.

Ailligham. To beautify, make handsome.

Aillionnoir. A caterer.

Ailmh. A flint stone.

Aillin. Another.

Ailmse. Mistake.

Ailp. Any gross lump.

Ailt. Stately, noble, grand.

Ailt. Rather *Rult*, joints.

Ailt. A house.

Ailtire An architect, a carpenter.

Aimhdheoin. ⟩ Unwilling, against consent,
Aindeoin. ⟨ in spite of.

Aimheogan. Vide Aigain.

Aimhean. Pleasant, agreeable.

Aimhe. Growing.

Aimid. A foolish woman.

Aimirtne. Voracity, greediness.

Aimhleas. Hurt, detriment, ruin.

Aiminn. Smooth, pleasant.

Aimbeart. Evil device, mischief.

Aimbeartach. Mischievous, poor.

Aimhleisg. Drowsiness, laziness.

Aimhleasach. Foolish, imprudent.

Aimhleathan. ⟩ Narrow, strait.
Aimhlionn. ⟨

Aimhnach. Full of rivers.

Aimhneart. Force, violence.

Aimhreidh. Disquieted, disturbed.

Aimhreidham. To disagree.

Aimhreit. Disturbance, quarrel.

Aimhreis. Difficult.

Aimhreitach. Quarrelsome, litigious.

Aimsir. Weather, season, time.

Aimsiral. ⟩ Temporal.
Aimsirtha. ⟨

Aimhreidhe. Defiles, straights, fastnesses.

Aimhriar. Mismanagement.

Aimhrioch. Disguise.

Aimrid. Barren, steril.

Aimsiugham. To tempt.

Aimhgh eur. Edgeless.

Ain. Honourable, praise-worthy, respectful.

Ain. Not, un.

Aine. Delight, joy, pleasure.

Aine. Agility, expedition, music, harmony, experience.

Aine. A platter.

Aineas. Joy.

Ainbeachlach. Rough, rugged.

Ainbheach. Manifold; great rain.

Ainbheach. A drone.

Ainbheil. Impudence, shame.

Ainbhfhios. Ignorance, rudeness.

Ainbhfhiosach. Rude, ignorant, headstrong, resentful.

Ainbhfeile. Impudence, stinginess.

Ainbhfeithach. Rude, ignorant.

Ainbhfine. A foreign tribe.

Ainbhigh. Rainy weather.

Ainble. Naughtiness, badness, malice.

Ainbhreagh.

Ainbhith. A savage or ferocious animal.

Ainbhfoil. Brave, valiant, intrepid.

Aincheardach. A buffoon, an ingenious fallacious fellow.

Aincheas. ⟩ A doubt, dilemma, danger.
Aincheist. ⟨

Ainching. A champion.

Aincheantais. A toy or trifle.

Ainchial, ainchialtachd. Peevishness, frowardness.

Ainchialtha. Testy, peevish.

Ainchliu. A peevish person.

Aindeas. Awkward.

Aindeise. Affliction, calamity.

Aindear. A young woman fit for marriage.

Aindhiarrigh. Angry.

Aindligheadh. Trespass.

Aindligheach. Transgressor, lawless.

Aineach. Horsemanship.

Aindiuid. Obstinacy in sin.

Aineamh. A blemish, stain, blot.

Aineamhach.

Aineamhach. Blemiſhed, maimed.

Ainneart. Vide Aimhneart. Violence.

Aineolas. Ignorance.

Aineolach. Ignorånt.

Ainfheadh. Plenteous, abundant.

Aingeis. A curſe, malediction.

Ainbhthinne. A ſtorm.

Ainbhtheann. A ſpring tide, a flood.

Ainblem. A battle.

Ainchead. To bury.

Ainceoil. Evil upon them.

Aincinneach. Skilled.

Aincidh. A doubt.

Aincredhnis. Very thrifty.

Ainchrionailt. Acuteneſs.

Ainchrionnadh. Acute.

Ainciſeachd. Rejecting.

Aindreanngha. Peeviſh.

Aineadargnaidh. Renowned, famous.

Aineaſach. Brave, hardy.

Aineaſgair. Unpoliſhed, rude.

Aincis. A ſkin or hide.

Ainfreagaraighte. Accountable.

Ainer. Great, powerful, noble.

Ainbhfheoil. Proud fleſh.

Ainghean. Exceſſive love.

Aingeal. An angel or meſſenger, fire, light, funſhine.

Ainglidh. Angelical.

Aingen. The holy ones.

Aingidh. Wicked, malicious.

Aingidheachd. Wickedneſs, malice.

Ainghiorradh. A ſhort cut.

Ainicam. To ſhun, avoid.

Ainiarmharthach. Too powerful, too many.

Ainm. Name, noun.

Ainmal.
Ainmneamhuil. } Famous, noted.

Ainmunach. Nominative.

Ainmunaiche. Denominator.

Ainimhneach. A blemiſh.

Ainadh. A gnaſh, gaping at.

Ainan. Liver.

Ainmlite.
Ainmchlar. } A catalogue.

Ainleog. A ſwallow; a ſting, a ſnare.

Ainleog-mhara. A black martin.

Ainleogam. To entrap, enſnare.

Ainmhidh. Animal, brute.

Ainbhfhiach. A debt.

Ainfhuail. Chamber-pot.

Aindioſlachd. Infidelity.

Ainnamhag. A phœnix.

Ainnir. A maid, virgin.

Ainnis. Needy.

Ainniſachd. Low condition.

Ainghniomh. Wicked; an evil deed.

Ainghniomhach. Facinorous.

Ainmnuigham. To name, denominate.

Ainmnighte. Denominated.

Aininne. Anger, ill will.

Ainin. The herb Coltsfoot.

Ainnimh. A wilderneſs.

Ainiocht. Oppreſſion, cruelty.

Ainiochdmhor. Oppreſſive, tyrannical.

Ainghlimam.
Ainghlearam. } To perſecute.

Ainiomh. A ſpot, blemiſh in reputation.

Ainiomad. Too much.

Ainius. A ſoothſayer.

Ainle. A wild cat.

Ainle. Fair, well featured.

Ainleachd. Fairneſs, beauty.

Ainleanmhuinam. To perſecute.

Ainleanmhuin. Perſecution.

Ainleas. Diſſervice, miſchief, theft.

Ainleathrom. Oppreſſion, injuſtice.

Ainmne. Patience.

Ainmheid. A wonder.

Ainmheaſartha. Huge, immoderate, intemperate.

Ainmeaſarthachd. Intemperance.

Ainmheas. Recompence.

Ainmhidhachd. Brutality.

Ainmhinte. A brute.

Ainmidighthe. Like a brute.

Ainmhiann. Defire, luft, paffion.

Ainmhiannach. Luftful, paffionate.

Ainn. A circle, ring.

Ainne. A ring.

Ainneadh. Patience.

Ainnighte. Made patient or tame.

Ainram. I underftand.

Ainriochd. A pitiful condition.

Ainfearc. Hatred; vehement love.

Ainfgian. Fury.

Ainfgianach. Furious.

Ainfgianta. Broken down, raging.

Ainfpiamach. A cruel perfon.

Ainfrianta. Obftinate, debauched, unbridled.

Ainfriantas. Libertinifm.

Ainfriantach. A Libertine.

Ainteach. A faft from flefh.

Ainteann. Very ftout, bold, ftiff.

Ainteas. Exceffive heat, inflamation.

Ainteafuighachd. Feverifhnefs.

Aintigharna. A tyrant, oppreffor.

Aintigharnas. Tyranny, oppreffion.

Ainteift. Falfe witnefs.

Aintreun. Ungovernable, very powerful.

Ainteach. Boaftful.

Aipol. Apollo.

Air. Upon.

Air. Slaughter.

Air. Arife.

Air, airfan. On him, it.

Air. Number thou.

Air. Deftroyed.

Airbhe. Ribs.

Airbhe. A ftory.

Airbhthe. Ribbed, furrowed.

Air ais. Back, backwards.

Airbheadha. Divifions.

Airbheadham. To divide.

Airbire. An armful.

Airbhre. A multitude, legion, hoft, army.

Airbheart. Meaning.

Airbheartach. Sagacious.

Airbheartam. To lead, to move about.

Airbheartbhith. Life.

Airc. A cheft, or large granary.

Airc. Difficulty, ftraight.

Aircifeach. Difficult, ftraight, hungry.

Airc. A lizard.

Airc-luachrach. An emmet.

Airceachd. Herefy.

Airchealladh. Theft.

Airchealtrach. A hind of the third year, a cow.

Airchean. The end, border of a country.

Airc. A fow.

Airceadal. Prophecy.

Airchealladh. Sacrilege.

Airceann. Certain, pofitive.

Airceas. Maturity.

Airceas. Straightnefs, difficulty.

Aircheana. From thence forward.

Aircheafd. Waiting, meeting.

Airceaftair. Genuine mirth.

Aircillam. To lie in wait.

Aircineach. Taking one with the other.

Aircinneach. Chief of a clan.

Airchionn. A fide.

Airciofach. Greedy, gluttonous.

Airchis. A complaint.

Airchifam. To expoftulate.

Airchis. A pledge.

Airchifde. Lamentation for the dead.

Airceach. Ingenious.

Airceach. A plunderer.

Airchill. Keeping.

Airc. Cork-tree.

Aircain. A ftopper for a bottle.

Airceadh. An earneft penny.

Aird. A coaft, quarter, cardinal point.

Aird. State, order, improvement.

Aird. Happinefs.

Airdbheandham. To cut.

Airdcheannas Superiority.

Airdcheann. A fuperior.

Airde. Height, eminence, highnefs.

Aireach.

Aireach. A shepherd, herd.

Airachas. Feeding of cattle, the office of a shepherd, pastoral life.

Airidh. Shielding, keeping of cattle in the mountains.

Airamhain. Complaining, missing the absence of any thing.

Airdceim. Dignity, eminence.

Airdceimam. To dignify, step majestically.

Airdceimneachd. Dignity.

Airdheanna. Position of a thing.

Airdchur. Power.

Airdhe, airdheal. A sign.

Airdhi. A wave.

Airdgheoin. Great noise, tempest, hurricane.

Airdhiobhadh. Execution, death, destruction.

Airdinntin. Haughtiness, arrogance, high spirit.

Airdfhogharach. Altisonant.

Airdinntinach. High-minded.

Airdeannaibh. Constellations.

Airdreachd. A synod.

Airdreim. High stile, magnificence, flight in poetry, rant.

Airdleog. A sudden jerk, a pull.

Airdriogh. A monarch.

Airdriaghlaigham. To rule supreme.

Airdsgeimhleoir. A curious inquisitive person.

Airdthigarna. ⎱
Airdthriath. ⎰ Supreme lord, sovereign.

Aire. Notice, attention.

Aire. A fishing weir.

Aire A name to the different ranks of nobility

Aire. A judge.

Aire. A servant.

Aireach. Noble, a noble person.

There were six degrees of aireachs or nobles distinguished by the antient Irish, in gradation, between the common people and the king, as expressed in the following Brehon law, which was enacted soon after the reception of Christianity. Cai caite techta cach adnacal o thuaich do gach grad iar na miad do Eclais? What are the lawful fees of burial, from the rustic upwards, according to the rule of the church? Imna ocairach tri seoit no a logh Imna bo-aireach u seoit no a logh. Imna aireach deasa X seoit no a logh. Imna aireach-ard u seoit X no a logh. Imna aireach treisiu, XX seoit no a logh. Imna aireach-foirgill XXX seoit no a logh. Imna un cumala no a logh. i. e. Hymns for an ocaireach, three cows, or an equivalent. Hymns for a bo-aireach, five cows, or an equivalent. Hymns for an aireach-desa, ten cows, or an equivalent. Hymns for an aireach-ard, fifteen cows, or an equivalent. Hymns for an aireach-tresiu, twenty cows, or an equivalent. Hymns for an aireach-foirgill, thirty cows, or an equivalent. Hymns for a king, seven cumala of cows (forty-two), or an equivalent. Hence we may range them in the following order.

1. The king.
2. Aireach-foirgill.
3. Aireach-treisiu, who has ennobled himself in war.
4. Aireach-ard.
5 Aireach-desa, from his lands.
6. Bo-aireach, from his cattle.
7. Oc-aireach, from his eloquence and learning.

Aireach. Vigilant, attentive, subtle.

Aireach. Violent, hostile.

Aireac. Ingenuity.

Aireadha. Excellent, famous.

Aireamh. A number, numbering, numeration.

Aireamham. To number.

Aireamhach. A numerator, accomptant.

Aireamhachd. Numbering, numeration.

       Aireannach.

Aireannach. A beginning.

Airear. A bay or harbour.

Airear. Satisfaction, choice.

Airear. Food, pleasant.

Aireasg. The apple of the eye, sight.

Aireardha. Pleasant.

Airel. A bed.

Airghe. A herd.

Airghean. A bridle rein, symptoms, air-gheanna a bhais, symptoms of death.

Airelam. To lay in bed.

Aireleach. A sleepy person.

Airfidach. Harmonious.

Airfideadh. Harmony.

Airg. A prince.

Airgeadh. Regard.

Airgeadham. To regard.

Airgad. Silver, money.

Airghir. A cow-calf.

Airgim. To ask, seek, demand.

Airgad-beo. Quickfilver.

Airgadeach. That hath money.

Airgadgha. Silver, of silver.

Airgad-toit. Hearth-money.

Airgim. To plunder, spoil, drive away.

Airgne. }
Airgnadh. } Robbery.

Airgtheach. }
Airgthoir. } A spoiler, plunderer.

Airidhe. Spectres, visions.

Airid. Certain, particular, especial.

Airigh. Chief, sovereign.

Airigh. Deserving.

Airigheachd. Sovereignty.

Airilleach. A law.

Airde-tuath. The North.

Airde-deas. The South.

Airde-near. The East.

Airde-niar. The West.

Airillean. A fashion.

Airiocht. Factions, parties.

Airiochtas. Tumultuous meetings.

Airiocht. A cantred.

Airiomh. Plowing.

Airis. Knowledge.

Airse, and airisin. Rehearsal.

Airisin. An appointment, order.

Airleacam. To lend, borrow.

Airleacadh. Lending, borrowing.

Airleacthach. Ready, willing, he that lends.

Airguinam. To plunder.

Airle. Counsel, loan.

Airleog. A fling, jostle, toss.

Airis. History.

Airis. Charcoal, a firebrand.

Airiseach. A rehearser.

Airisam. Vide Aithrisam, to rehearse, re-cite, repeat.

Airisne. Hereafter.

Airleach. Skirmish.

Airliochtoir. Ufurer.

Airm. Arms.

Airm. A place.

Airmchrios. A belt.

Airmeart. An order or custom.

Airmghein. Well-born.

Airmheadh. A measure.

Airmheacht. Distinction.

Airmheadham. To weigh.

Airmid. Honour, worship, reverence.

Airmidineach. Venerable, respectful.

Airmhidh. An interdict, a vow, promise.

Airmide. A custom.

Airmid. A swan.

Airmham. To number, reckon.

Airne. Sloe, plumb.

Airne. Kidney.

Airne. A watching, fiting up.

Airneag. A little floe.

Airsneal. Fatigue, wearinefs.

Airneadha. The feed of fhrub trees.

Airneadhach. Shrubby.

Airneamh, airtneamh. A grinding-ftone, hone.

Airm-theine. Fire-arms.

Airmfhilgte. Miffive weapons.

Airneis. Cattle, chattels, moveables, furniture.

Airmlann. Armoury.

id. A plum.

Airri. A tyrant.

Air neo. Elfe, otherwife.

Airrfce. The hinder part of the neck.

Airrfe. A vault.

Airrfidh. An arcade, arch.

Airteagal. Article.

Airtin. A pebble.

Airtine. A flint ftone.

Airteamh. An inch.

Airfneal. Fatigue, wearinefs.

Airfge. Contemplation.

Ais. Back.

Ais. Hill, covert, ftrong-hold.

Ais. Dependence.

Ais. A loan.

Ais. Carr, wain, cart.

Ais. Bafhful.

Ais. Shingles to cover houfes.

Aifag. ⎫
Aifioc. ⎬ Reftoration, a ferry, a vomit.

Aifc. A requeft, petition.

Aifc. Damage, trefpafs, a reproach, chaftifement.

Aifg. A fpot or blemifh.

Aifg. A gift.

Aifgidh. Gratis, freely.

Aifcam. To requeft, crave, fearch for.

Aifceir. A ridge of high mountains.

Aifde. ⎫
Aifdeadh. ⎬ A poem, ingenuity.

Aifdeach. A gay, diverting fellow, gamefome.

Aifde. Out of her, it.

Aifdeachan. ⎫
Aifdigheachd. ⎬ Sports, diverfions, jefts.

Aifdighoir. Jefter, player.

Aifcheimnigham. To retire, withdraw.

Aifdar. Vide Aftar.

Aifdrein. An exchange.

Aifdridh. A tranflation, digreffion.

Aifdrigham. To tranflate.

Aifdruighadh. Viciffitude, revolution

Aifeirgham. To rife again.

Aifeal. Jollity.

Aifeirghidh. Refurrection, fome part of a mill.

Aifeilg. Behind.

Aifne. A rib.

Aifghairmam. ⎫
Aifghleodham. ⎬ To call back.

Aificeach. Crafty.

Aifghinalaigham. To degenerate.

Aifigam. To ferry over, reftore, to vomit.

Aifeilgam. To ftay behind.

Aifreimnuigham To reciprocate.

Aifreimnughadh. Reciprocation.

Aifreimnuighach. Reciprocal.

Aisfealbha. Reftitution.

Aisfeidhmeachd. Difbanding.

Aisfeidmam. To difband.

Aifgeadh. A defire.

Airgire. A petitioner.

Aifiocam. Vide Aifagam.

Aifion. A crown, diadem, a relick.

Aifios. Inclination to vomit.

Aifling. A dream.

Aiflear. A fpring tide.

Aifleine. A fhrowd.

Aiflingam. Dream.

Aiflingeach. A dreamer.

Aifphillam. To retort, return.

Aifneidham. To name or tell.

Aifneis. Naming, telling.

Aifneifam. To make manifeft.

Aifteidh. The hatches of a fhip.

Aiftior. Vide Aftar.

Aiftiorach. A traveller.

Aiftigheadh. Compofition, invention.

Aiftigham. To feign, invent.

Aiftighthoir. A merry Andrew, Jack Pudding.

Aiftrioch. Inconftant.

Aifbrioghadh.

Aiſtrioghadh. A progreſs, journey.

Aiſtruigham. To travel.

Ait, aite. A place, ſtead.

Ait. Glad, joyful.

Aitas. Gladneſs, joy.

Aiteamh. A proof, convincing argument.

Aitchim. To pray, beg.

Aitcheas. The concubine of a warrior.

Aiteann. Furz.

Aitigham. To inhabit; to prove.

Aitaghas. Inhabiting, dwelling, a colony.

Aitchimeach. A petitioner.

Aiteach. Anxious, careful.

Aith. Quick, ſharp.

Aithche. A kiln, kilns.

Aith. Vide Ath, again, an iterative particle.

Aithamh. A fathom.

Aith. An hill, an eminence.

Aith. A ſkirmiſh.

Aithadh. Elfſhot.

Aitham. To deny.

Aithnigham. To know, perceive.

Aithchreidamh. Apoſtacy.

Aithbhe. The ebb of the tide.

Aithbhioradham. To blame, reprove.

Aithbhioradh. Reproach, blame.

Aithcheaſam. To illumine, to play the whore.

Aithcheas. A whore.

Aithcham. To deny.

Aithchimam. To border, welt, embroider.

Aithchumar. Brief, compendious.

Aithcheodham. To diſapprove, condemn.

Aithe. Revenge.

Aithe. Keen.

Aitheach. A ſon, a giant, clown.

Aitheach. Gigantick.

Aithne. Commandment, precept.

Aithnam. To command, enjoin.

Aithne. ⎱
Aitheantas. ⎰ Knowledge, acquaintance.

Aithnighte. Known.

Aithnuighadh. Knowing, knowledge.

Aitheantam. To know, comment.

Aitheirgam. To riſe again.

Aitheas. A blemiſh, an upbraiding.

Aitheaſc. Admonition.

Aitheiſdacht. An appeal.

Aithfene. Redemption.

Aithghear. Brief, inſtantaneous.

Aithghinam. To regenerate.

Aithgheinte. Regenerate.

Aithghein. ⎱
Aithgheimamhin. ⎰ Regeneration.

Aithghein. Like.

Aithid. A ſerpent, aſp.

Aithidin. A little venomous creature, a little beaſt.

Aithiobhar. Baniſhment, expulſion.

Aithigh. Giants.

Aithine. A fire-brand.

Aithine. Charcoal.

Aithir-lus. Ground-ivy.

Aithiorach. A myſtery; trade, art, ſcience.

Aithis. A check, affront, abuſe.

Aithin. Liver.

Aithiſam. ⎱
Aithiſuigham. ⎰ To abuſe, affront.

Aithiſeach. An abuſive perſon.

Aithiſughadh. Defamation.

Aithle. An old rag.

Aithle. After.

Aithlinughadh. Delineation.

Aithlionadh. Reinforcement, recruiting.

Aithleoireachd. Amuſing.

Aithmheal. Compunction, repentance.

Aithmheas. The ebbing of the ſea.

Aithn an la. Height of day.

Aithne. Store.

Aithneach. Treaſured, hoarded up.

Aithre. An ox, bull, cow.

Aithreach. Penitent, ſorry.

Aithreachas. Repentance, regret.

Aithreas. Healing, curing.

Aithridhe. Tears, grief, ſadneſs, repentance.

Aithridach.

Aithridhach. Sorrowful.

Aithrin. A sharp point, a scold.

Aithrine. A calf.

Aithriogham. To dethrone.

Aithrigham. To awake.

Aithris. Imitation, recital, rehearsal, report, narration.

Aithrisam. To recite, repeat, rehearse.

Aithriseadh. Tautology.

Aithriseach. }
Aithristeach. } An imitator, a tale-bearer.

Aithsgriobham. To transcribe.

Aithsgriobhadair. A transcriber, copyist.

Aithsgriobhadh. A transcript copy.

Aitide. Submission.

Aitreabh. }
Aitne. } Dwelling, houses, offices.

Aitreabhach. An inhabitant.

Aitreach. A farmer.

Aitreabham. To inhabit.

Aitreabhach Habitable.

Aitrisam. To bid, order, command.

Aiti. Moist.

Aitiol. Juniper.

Al. A rock, stone.

Al. Nurture, food.

Al. Fear.

Al, alach. Brood of any young.

Al. A horse.

Alach. A brood, crew, tribe, generation; the nails in a boat.

Alach ramh. A set or bank of oars.

Aladh. Wisdom, skill, craft.

Alach. Activity, alacrity, a request.

Ala. Nursing.

Ala. A trout.

Ala. A wound.

Aladhnach. Comical, crafty.

Ala. Speckled.

Alacht. Big with young.

Aladh. Malice, a lye.

Alaim. To salute, hail, to nurse.

Alaim. To sing praise.

6

Al-eile. One by another.

Alain. White, bright, clear.

Alaineacht. Beauty.

Alaim. To seize upon.

Alba. }
Albin. } Scotland.

Albanach. Scotchman, Scotch.

Alb. Vide Ailp. Height

Albard. Halberd.

Alfat. Cause, reason.

Alfalach. Thoroughly hid.

Alga. }
Algac. } Noble, great.

Algachd. Nobility.

All. Great, prodigious.

All. A bridle.

All. Another.

All. A nobleman's hall.

All. Foreign.

All. A rock, cliff.

All. A generation, race.

Alla. Wild, the Most High.

Allabhair. Echo.

Allabhair. A great army.

Allabhar. Strange, wild, savage.

Allaidh. Savage, wild.

Alloil. Noble.

Alladh. To go, to meet.

Alladh. Excellency, fame.

Allan. }
Allod. } In former times.

Allbuadhach. A prince's hall.

Allbuadhach. Victorious.

Allchur. Transposition.

Allgloir. Jargon, gibberish.

Allglois. Mischief.

Allghort. An orchard.

Allmharach. A stranger, foreigner.

Allmhargha. Exotic.

Allmharghachd. Barbarity.

Allmuirceadh. The encrease of days.

Allmo. A drove, herd of cattle.

Allod. Formerly, antrently.

Alliaon.

Allraon. A foreign expedition or journey.

Allrion. Yonder road or way.

Allfmhain. Knotty, full of knots.

Allfmuainn. A great float or buoy.

Alltadh. Wild, favage.

Alltachd. Savagenefs.

Alltarach. Oppofite, reverfe.

Alluigh. Wild.

Allun. A hind.

Alluin. Fair, handfome.

Almchadha. Charitable.

Almoine. Almonds.

Alpa. Mountains. See Ailp.

Alon. A ftone.

Alt. Nurfing.

Alt. A high place.

Alt. A brook, a valley.

Alt. An action, deed, or fact.

Alt. A condition, ftate, order.

Alt. A leap, foon.

Alt. A part, fection of a book, time.

Alt. A joint.

Alt. Exaltation.

Altuigham. To give thanks, to falute.

Altoir. An altar.

Altughadh. Giving thanks, faluting, thankfgiving, grace at meat.

Altra.
Altranas. } Foftering.

Altramam. To fofter, nurfe.

Altram. Nurfing.

Altrach. One that fofters.

Altcheangal. Articulation, inofculation, anafatamofis.

Altamhuil. Arthritick.

Altan. A fmall brook.

Aluda. Wounds in battle.

Alughain. Potters clay.

Aluin. Handfome. Vide Alluin.

Am. Time, feafon, convenience.

Amamhuil. Timely.

Am. A prepofitive negative particle in place of an before words beginning with f, b, p.

Am. Soft, moift.

Ama The collar of a cart-horfe.

Amach. A vulture or ravenous bird.

Amach. Out.

Amad.
Amadan. } A fool.

Amadan-montich. A dotterill.

Amadanach.
Amadanta. } Foolifh.

Amidachd.
Amadanachd. } Folly.

Amail. Broken, loft; evil, mifchief.

Amall. A vifit.

Amain fheithide. Amphibious beafts.

Amain. Occupation.

Amail.
Amhuil. } Like, as.

Aman. A river.

Amarcam. To be fond of, kind to.

Amas. Hitting, marking.

Amaifam. To hit.

Amaraich. Scurvy-grafs.

Amafgidh. Profane, helter fkelter.

Amafgidhachd. Profanenefs.

Ambeath. Quick, nimble, active.

Ameafg. Among.

Amghar. Affliction, tribulation.

Amh. Raw, unfodden, crude, bad, naughty.

Amh. Even, alfo.

Amh. Ocean.

Amh. A fool, fimpleton.

Amh. Denial.

Amha. A man, perfon.

Amhach. A dwarf. Vide Abhach.

Amhain.
Amhuin. } River.

Amhain. Only, alone.

Amhaon. Twins, plurality.

Amhar. Mufick.

Amharc.

Amhar. A veſſel to hold malt in.

Amharc. The ſight, look.

Amharag. Muſtard.

Amharcam. To look.

Amharc. A fault.

Amhairg. Woe.

Amhantas. } Good luck, royal privi-
Amhantur. } lege.

Amharcoll. } The letter X.
Amhancoll. }

Amharas. Doubt, ſuſpicion.

Amhraſach. Doubtful, ſuſpicious.

Amhraſachadh. Doubting.

Amharaſaigham. To miſtruſt.

Amhas. A wild ungovernable man, madman.

Amhaſach. Dull, ſtupid.

Amhaſan. A ſentry, freſh man.

Amhaſag. Silly woman.

Amhra. A dream, poem.

Amhran. A ſong.

Amhluadh. Confuſion, diſtreſs.

Amhra. Noble, great, good; dark.

Amhra. Hilt of a ſword.

Amharchull. Aphthongs.

Amhdhadh. Permitting, ſuffering.

Amhradh. Mourning, lamentation.

Amhghar. Affliction, tribulation.

Amhgharach. Afflicted ſorely, troubled.

Amhlabhair. Mute, dumb.

Amhlaiſg. Bad beer.

Amhlaiſgach. A brewer of taplaſh.

Amhlair. A fool, oaf.

Amhnas. Impudent.

Amhnian. Folly.

Amhne. Himſelf.

Amhnur. Shameleſs.

Amhus. Reſtleſs.

Amhuilam. To ſpoil.

Amid. A fooliſh woman.

Amlagach. } Curling.
Amlach. }

Amm. Miſchievous, bad.

Amm. To refuſe.

Ammar. A trough.

Ammar-baiſdaidh. A font.

Ammar-fuail. Chamber-pot.

Amni. Generous.

Amri. A cupboard.

Amuidh. A fool.

Amuigh. Without, out.

Amus. An ambuſh, ſurprize, violent onſet.

Amus. Leiſure.

Amuſach. One that keeps his appointment.

An. The article the.

An. Interrogative particle, *an gabh thu?* will you take?

An. Privative, evil, not, un.

An. A kind of veſſel, water.

An. Still, quiet.

An. True, pleaſant, noble, ſwift.

An. A lie.

An. Pure.

Ana. Riches.

Ana. Continuance of fair weather.

Ana. A ſilver cup.

Ana. Truly.

Anabbuidh. Unripe.

Anach. A cleaning, waſhing.

Anach. A path.

Anacail. Quietneſs.

Anacal. A quiet perſon.

Anaclam. To preſerve, watch over.

Anacail. Preſervation.

Anachain. Danger, misfortune.

Anachaim. To avoid, ſhun, preſerve.

Anac. A wound.

Anachan. One that keeps in the way.

Anacht. Quietneſs, tranquillity.

Anachrach. Full of pity.

Anachradh. A wretch, an object of pity.

Anachras. Pity, compaſſion.

Anaclachd. Reſtleſſneſs.

Anacair. Affliction. Reſtleſſneſs.

Anainbreadh. Unſatiable.

Anart. Linen.

Anart-buird. Table-cloth.

Ann aird. Aloft.

Anart-canaich. Fuſtian.

Anairth. Gentle, mild, humane.

Anais. Backward, reverfed.

Anaifgam. To crave, beg.

Anaithne. A private man.

Anaithnam. I know not.

Anaithnighte. Unknown.

Anal. Breath.

Anal. } Not Irifh. Annals, chroni-
Analaih. } cle.

Analam. To breathe.

Annall. } From beyond.
Anallod. }

Anam. Soul, life.

Anamoch. Late.

Anamhac. An animal.

Anamhach. Lively.

Anamchara. A bofom friend.

Annamh. Rare.

Anamchoidh. Brave.

Anamhain. A panegyrift.

Anaoibhin. Woe.

Anafcaim. To mix.

Anafcacht. Mixture.

Anaois. Nonage.

Anat. Plain, manifeft.

Anafgar. Reftlefs, irkfome.

Anabas. Offscourings.

Anabarrach. Exceffive.

Anabar. Excefs, too much.

Anaculach. Lean.

Anabhirach. Very pointed, fharp.

Anaceift. Difficulty.

Anacneafda. Cruel, difhoneft, unfafe.

Anacreidmhach. Infidel.

Anacreideamh. Infidelity.

Anacleachda. Inexperience.

Anachuram. Care, anxiety.

Anacomhthrom. } Injuftice.
Anaceartas. }

Anabeachdalachd. Haughtinefs.

Anachintach. Uncertain.

Anamhras. Sufpicion, diftruft.

Anaghlais. Hog-wafh.

Anafda. Stormy.

Anaghoirafach. Inconvenient.

Anacaithach. Squanderer.

Anachaoinam. To deplore.

Anachruas. Avarice.

Anacoimfeach. Vaft, infinite.

Anamhfheoil. Proud flefh.

Anbhaine. Extafy.

Anbhal. Prodigious.

Anbhaine. Weaknefs.

Anbhail. Shamelefs, haughty.

Anbhann. } Weak.
Anmhann. }

Anbhor. A great fwelling.

Anbhas. A fudden death.

Anbhfoil. Courageous.

Anbrith. Large, prodigious.

Anbhrod. A tyrant.

Anbhrodaim. To tyrannize.

Anbhochd. Very poor.

Anbhuineachd. Weaknefs, faintnefs.

Anbhathadh. Deluge.

Anchaint. Ill language, faucinefs.

Anchaitham. To fquander.

Anceadna. Exceffive.

Andan. Foolhardy.

Andanadas. Prefumption.

Andiugh. To-day.

Ande. Yefterday.

Andeirach. Mournful, of many tears.

Andeiftin. Squeamifhnefs.

Andach. Anger.

Andach. Evil.

Andadh. Juft.

Andeas. South.

Andon. Although.

Andolas. Sadnefs.

Andochafach. Sanguine, prefumptuous.

Andualarafc. Catechrefis.

Androbhlafach. A great fquanderer.

Andras. A fury, infernal divinity.

Anduine. A wicked man.

Andul. Avidity.

Andlighach. A tranfgreffor, illegal.

Andoigh. Bad eftate, condition.

Andrafd & aris. Ever and anon.
Anebhachdach. Ineffectual.
Anebhachd. Inefficacy.
Aneaibam. To diftruft.
Anearbfa. Diftruft.
Anc ande. Yefterday.
Aneagal. Aftonifhment.
Aneadargnaidh. A ftranger.
Aneis. A fkin, hide.
Anfobhrachd. A fkeleton.
Anfhairfuing. Vaft.
Anfhuras. Impatience.
Anfadh. A ftorm.
Anfadhach. Stormy.
Anfam. To ftay.
Anfhlath. A tyrant.
Anfas. Fear, dread.
Anfhocain. Peril, danger.
Anfhoralamh. Conftraint, danger.
Anfhorlan. Puiffance, oppreffion, plundering.
Anfhoth. Very watchful.
Ang. Renown, great.
Ang. A ftring, twift.
Ang. Rank.
Angach. Vide Ingnach. Full of nails.
Angadh. The guffet of a fhirt.
Angangach A fnare.
Angathlonnach. Glittering.
Angclu. A champion.
Angar. A ftall for cattle.
Angbhaidh. Valiant, ftout; hard, unjuft.
Angcoire. An anchorite.
Anglonn. Adverfity, danger.
Anglonn. Very ftrong.
Anghlaodh. A loud fhout.
Angna. Refpite, delay.
Angnatha. Relations.
Angnathach. Unufual.
Angradh. Doating love.
Angradhaeh. Loving.
Angrais. An engine.
Angraibh. A ruler, chief.
Anios. Up.

Aniochd. Cruelty.
Aniochdmhor. Cruel.
Aniuid. Error, depravity.
Aniudadh. Depraved.
Anius. A foothfayer.
Anluchduigham. To furcharge.
Anmhaoin. Strife, great riches.
Anmeinidhe. Evil doing.
Anmhiann. Concupifcence.
Anmhodh. Difrefpect.
Anmhor. Very great.
Anmhugean. Oftentation.
Anmhunam. To ftay, tarry.
Annan. A name of Ireland.
Anndeigh. After.
Anniugh. To day.
Ann. In there, in him, it.
Ann a' dheigh fin. After that, afterwards.
Annac. Evil.
Annac. Anger.
Annach. Clean.
Annaicte. Cleanfed.
Annactam. To cleanfe, purify.
Annadh. Delay.
Annamh. Seldom, rare, a wildernefs.
Ann ceann a cheile. Together.
Annas. Rarity.
Anncein. Afar, far off.
Ann-cois. Nigh to, by, along.
Ann-cais. Prefently.
Ann car. Near to.
Ann crochadh. Depending, impending.
Ann-coinamh. Oppofite.
Annradh. Diftrefs, ftorm at fea, tempeft.
Annranach. Stormy.
Annam. In me.
Annad. In thee.
Anninne. In us.
Annta. In them.
Annfa. Dear, beloved; in the.
Annfachd. Affection, the beloved.
Annofach. Strange, unufual.
Annoid. A church.

Annunn.

Annunn. Over to the other fide.

Annroir. Laft night.

Annracht. The higheft degree of poetry next the ollamh; a fit of crying.

Annfin. } In that place, there, then.
Annfud. }

Anois. Now.

Anochd. To night.

Anpaccair cear. A fole, flounder.

Anradh. A poet in the next degree of honour to an ollamh, a boon, a petition.

Anraim. To feek a boon.

Anradham. To grieve, afflict.

Anro. Abundance.

Anrod. Tribulation.

Anrodhach. Afflicted.

Anfhocair. Reftleffnefs, difquietude.

Anfhocrach. Reftlefs.

Anfhogh. Adverfity.

Anfgaineadh. A chafm.

Anfcairt. A great clamour, a great thicket of brambles.

Anfcairtach. Shouting loudly.

Anfcairtam. To fhout, bawl.

Anflogh. A great hoft.

Anfhran. A ladle.

Anfamhlachd. Incomparability.

Anfamhluighte. Incomparable.

Anfant. Covetoufnefs, avarice.

Anfantach. Covetous, a greedy gut, gormandizer.

Antrath. Wrong feafon.

Antrathach. Abortive.

Antoil. Luft.

Antoilal. Wilful, obftinate.

Antoilalachd. Wilfulnefs, obftinacy.

Antlachd. Difpleafure, diflike.

Antlas. A great fair of cattle, a merry trick.

Antlafach. A facetious merry fellow.

Antlafam. To play pranks.

Antoirdhear. The eaft.

Antrom. Grievous.

Antromuigham. To aggravate.

Antromughadh. Aggravating.

Antruas. Great pity, fympathy.

Antruacanta. Pitiful, compaffionate.

Antomhaill. Gluttony.

Antogradh. Evil defire.

Antomhailtoir. A glutton.

Anuinn. The eaves of a houfe.

Anualach. A burden, over weight.

Anualigham. To buiden.

Anuair. A ftorm.

An uair. When.

Anuafal. Mean, ignoble.

Anuas. Down.

Anuabhair. Exceffive pride.

Anuaibhrach. Proud.

Anuais. Fierce.

Aobhach. } Chearful.
Aobhin. }

Aobrunn. Uncle.

Aobh. Similitude.

Aobhdha. Beautiful.

Aobhdhachd. Beauty.

Aodann. The face, forehead.

Aodannach-freine. Front ftall of a bridle.

Aodh. Fire, the liver.

Aodach. Cloth.

Aodhar. A fiery defolation.

Aodarman. A bladder.

Aodh. A fheep.

Aodhaire. A fhepherd, paftor.

Aodhnaire. An owner.

Aodhaireachd. Tending fheep.

Aodochas. Defpair.

Aodochafach. Full of defpair.

Aogafg. Likenefs, image.

Aogh. Hugh.

Aoi. A ftranger, gueft.

Aoi. A fwan, confederacy, compact.

Aoi. Inftruction, knowledge.

Aoi. Honour, refpect.

Aoi. An ifland, a trade, a hill, poffeffion.

Aoibh. A courteous, civil look.

Aoibh. A patrimony.

Aoibh. Pleafant, comely.

Aoibheal. Rejoicing, merriment.

Aoibheal. Fire.

Aoibheamhuil. Grateful, fatisfied.

Aoibhnach. Glad, joyful.

Aoibhnas. Gladnefs, joyfulnefs.

Aoibhioll. Giddy.

Aoibhillam. To be giddy, hairbrained.

Aoibhinn. Joyful, pleafant, fair.

Aoibhle. A fign, token, omen.

Aoibhligham. To mark, explain an omen.

Aoide. A web.

Aoide. A youth.

Aoideanach. Well behaved.

Aoideach. Youthful.

Aoideag. A hair lace, fillet.

Aoidain. A leak.

Aoideogaim. To bind the hair.

Aoidaineach. Leaky.

Aoidhe. A fkilful perfon.

Aoidheach. } A ftranger, gueft.
Aoidhidhe. }

Aoidheachd. Hofpitality, lodging, enter-tainment.

Aoidheachdam. To entertain, lodge.

Aoig. A fkeleton.

Aoigh. A hero.

Aoil. The mouth.

Aoil. Pleafant, fair.

Aoilbbhreo. Limekiln.

Aoileach. A gazing-ftock.

Aoileach. Dung.

Aoilean. Fine, excellent, charming.

Aoileanta. Beautiful.

Aoileannacht. Beauty.

Aoilbhinn. A fmall herd, flock.

Aoilfeog. A caterpillar.

Aoilleadh. To chew.

Aoin. A rufh, honour, a faft.

Aoinchineamhuin. One event.

Aoine. Skill.

Aoinneann. Pleafant.

Aoine. Friday.

Aineach. Fafting.

Aoinam. To faft.

Aoir. A curfe, a fatire, railing.

Aoire. A fatirift.

Aoirain A ploughman.

Aoireagradh. A reftipulation.

Aoireadh. Sheet or corner of a fail, a field.

Aoirfuigham. To enhance the value of.

Aoireachdin. Exclaiming againft, blaming.

Aois. Age.

Aoll. Lime.

Aolain. Learning.

Aolainaiche, oileamhnach. A ftudent.

Aolainaigham. To educate.

Aolam. To inftruct.

Aollam. To lime.

Aolladoir. Plafterer.

Aol-tigh. A fchool, college.

Aoll-phlafda. A parget, or plafter.

Aolte. Inftructed.

Aollphlafduiche. A plafterer.

Aolamh. Vide Ollamh.

Aolthoir. Fofterer.

Aon. Excellent, noble.

Aomam. To incline, bend.

Aon. One, a country.

Aomadh. Bending, inclination.

Aonach. A hill, fir.

Aonagraicham. To wallow.

Aonar. Alone, folitary.

Aonarachd. Singularity.

Aonaran. A folitary perfon.

Aonghnethach. Homogeneous.

Aonranach. } Solitary.
Aonardha. }

Aondeug. Eleven.

Aoncathairach. Of the fame city.

Aonda. Particular.

Aongam. To move, ftir.

Aonachd. Unity.

Aonghuthach. Confonous.

Aonbhith. Co-effentiality.

Aoninntin. One mind, unanimous.

Aondathach.

Aondathach. Of one colour.

Aonadharcach. Unicorn.

Aonracan. A folitary perfon, widower.

Aono. The one, firft.

Aonracanach. Alone.

Aono-deug. Eleventh.

Aonracanachd. Solitude.

Aonflaith. Monarch.

Aonflaithachd. Monarchy.

Aonfuirt. Wallowing. 2 Sam. ix.

Aonta. A leafe, licence, confent.

Aontach. Acceffary.

Aonta. A man unmarried, celibacy.

Aontuigham. To confent

Aonriogh. Monarch.

Aontachd. Acquiefcence.

Aontigheas. } Cohabiting.
Antigheachd. }

Aos. A community, fet of people.

Aofda. } Old, aged.
Aofmhor. }

Aofmhureachd. } Age, antiquity.
Aofdachd. }

Aofdan. A foothfayer.

Aontromas. Madnefs, levity. Vide Eat-
romas.

Aoth. A bell, a crown.

Aothadh. Clean, pure.

Aothachd. Ringing of bells.

Aothaim. To ring bells.

Ap. } Ripe.
Apaidh. }

Apa, apag. An ape.

Aprainn. Mercy.

Apran. Apron.

Apthach. Mortal.

Ar. Our.

Ar. Slaughter.

Ar. Ploughing, hufbandry.

Ar. A bond, tye.

Ar. Guiding, conduct.

Ara. A conference.

Ara. The loin.

Ara. A bier.

Arac. A conflict.

Arach. A ploughfhare.

Arach. Strength, power, authority, re-
ftraint.

Arach. A tye, bond, or collar on a beaft,
fifhing ware.

Arachas. Infurance.

Aracoir. Infurer.

Arachair. Rowing.

Aracul. A cell or grotto, hut.

Arad. Strong, brave.

Arada. A fevere punifhment.

Arad. } A ladder.
Aradh. }

Aradh. The reins, loins.

Aradhain. Abufe.

Aradain. A defk, pulpit.

Araigh. The reins of a bridle.

Araim. To plough.

Aramhuil. Officious.

Aran. Bread.

Aran cruinneachd. Wheaten bread.

Aran donn. Brown bread.

Aran milis. Gingerbread.

Aran. The Kidneys.

Aran. Familiar converfation; aran bodaigh
air bothar, a clown's converfation on the
highway.

Aranailt. A pannier, bread bafket.

Arancha. A pantry.

Aranoir. A baker.

Araoid. A cover, table-cloth.

Araon. Both.

Aras. Vide Aros. A houfe, village, fettlement.

Arafach. Habitable.

Arafach. An inhabitant.

Aarafaim. To dwell, inhabit.

Arba. Yet, neverthelefs.

Arbhadh. Deftruction.

Arbhar. Corn, grain; an hoft, army.

Arbaim. To deftroy.

Arbharach.

Arbharach. Fertile, full of corn.

Arbharachd. Embattling an army.

Arbharain. To array.

Arbhra. Vide Arbhar.

Arbhraigneach. Scarce of corn.

Arbhraigneach. A fnare.

Arbhraignam. To enfnare.

Arc. Vide Airc. A cheft, ark.

Arc. A body.

Arc. A dwarf.

Arc, arcain. A little pig.

Arc. A bee, a wafp.

Arc. A lizard.

Arc. Impoft, tribute.

Arcan. A cork, ftopper.

Arc luachrach. An adder, lizard.

Archu. A chained dog.

Archon. A fierce dog.

Archuifg. An experiment.

Archur. Sucking.

Arcis. A hide.

Ard. High, lofty, eminent, excellent.

Ardan. A height, eminence, pride.

Ardanach. High, proud, elate.

Ardaigham. To elevate, extol.

Ardruich. A houfe.

Ardaghadh. Honour, elevation, preferment.

Ardarc. A blazon, coat of arms.

Ardaingal. Archangel.

Ardchnoc-faire. A great or chief beacon, guide.

Ardeafbuig. Archbifhop.

Ard-dhuic. Archduke.

Ardorus. Lintel of a door.

Ardbheandiuc. An archduchefs.

Ardchantoir. Archchanter.

Ardbhreithamh. Chief juftice.

Ardcheimnigham. To ftalk.

Ardghuth. A great fhout, cry.

Ardfhogharach. Altifonant.

Ardghlorach, a. Loud fpeaking.

Ardghloir. Altiloquence, bombaft.

Ardmharaich. An admiral.

Ardollamh. Hiftoriographer royal.

Ardchathair. Metropolis.

Ardriogh. Sovereign, monarch.

Ardfhuidhidhoir. Prefident.

Ardfgol. College.

Ardfhagart. High-prieft.

Ardinmhe. High rank, eminence.

Ardinmhach. Eminent.

Ardfgeimhleoir. A curious perfon.

Ardchumhachd. } Supreme power.
Ardchomas.

Ardcheannas. Supreme dominion.

Ardfeadhmanach. High-fteward.

Ardghaois. A liberal art.

Ardghaoifire. A mafter of arts.

Ardghul. Loud lamentations.

Ardhachdach. Great, grand.

Ardhamh. A plough ox.

Ardharch. A blazon, coat of arms.

Ardhafach. High, ftately.

Ardreachtas. A convention, affembly.

Ardog. Vide Ordog. A thumb.

Argdha. Military, warlike.

Arg. A champion.

Argnach. } A robber, plunderer.
Argnoir.

Argnadh. Robbery, plundering.

Aig. A corn fkep.

Argnaim. To rob, plunder.

Argairim. To keep, herd.

Arguin. An argument.

Argthoir. A deftroyer.

Arigh. Chiefs.

Arinn. Friendfhip.

Aris. Again.

Arleog. A high flight, a project.

Arleogach. Full of projects.

Arling. A corps de referve.

Arlogh. Some part of the fide.

Arlodh. Bringing home the harveft, feifd an arloigh, harveft home feaft.

Arm. The army, armour.

Armal. ⎫
Armach. ⎭ Armed, warlike.

Armailte. An army.

Aimailteach. Having armies.

Armachd. Feats of arms.

Armam. To arm.

Armann. A chief, a prince.

Armara. A rebuke, check.

Armaire. A cupboard, closet.

Armhaigh. A buzzard.

Armcha. ⎫
Armthaisg. ⎭ An armoury, magazine.

Armhindam. To reverence, respect.

Armtha, armte. Armed.

Armuinte. Blessed.

Armuintam. To bless.

Arn. A judge.

Arnaidh. A band, surety.

Arnath. Swollen, puffed up.

Aroch. Straight.

Aroch. A hamlet, a little shielding.

Aroich. Field of battle.

Arne. A sloe, reins, kidneys. Vide Airne.

Aros. A house, habitation.

Aroll. Great slaughter, great deal, many.

Arol. Other.

Arr. A stag, a hind.

Arra. Treachery.

Arra. A pledge.

Arrachar. Steering, rowing.

Arrach. ⎫ A pigmy, dwarf, a spectre, appa-
Arracht. ⎭ rition, centaur.

Arrachtach. Manly, effectual, puissant.

Arrachtas. Power.

Arradh. An ornament.

Arraghaidach. Negligent.

Arradh. Vide Earradha.

Arraidh. Evil actions.

Arraing. A stitch, convulsions.

Arraisam. To arrive or reach at.

Arrchoghaidh. The hound that first winds or comes up with the deer.

Arroid. Vice.

Arridh. Generous.

Arroidam. To corrupt.

Arronnach. Becoming, fit.

Arronaidham. To fit.

Arrsantach. Old, ancient.

Arruisach. Obvious.

Arsa eisan. Said he.

Arsachd. Age, being old.

Arsuighoir. An antiquary.

Arsuighachd. Antiquity.

Arson. For, in room of.

Arsneall. Sadness, sorrow.

Arsnalach. Sad, sorrowful.

Art. A bear.

Art. A stone, a tent, tabernacle, house.

Art. A limb.

Art. God.

Art. Flesh.

Artach. Stoney, a quarry.

Artarach. A ship boat.

Artchailair. A quarry, stone pit.

Artene. Pebbles, sand.

Arteine. A flint.

Arthrach. A ship, wherry, boat.

Arther. Easterly.

Arthraigham. To navigate, to enlarge.

Artragam. To do or make.

Artuirdhis. Augmentation.

Arusc. A lord.

Arusg. The neck.

As. Out, out of, out of him or it.

Asam. Out of me.

Asad. Out of thee.

Asinn, asinne. From, out of us.

Asibh Out of, from you.

Asda. Out of, from them.

As. Milk, ale, beer.

Asach. A shoemaker.

Asach. Milky, watery.

Asaighte. Shod.

Asadh. Anchoring, resting, settling.

Asam. To kindle a fire.

Asafirmam. To remove.

Asaidh.

Afaidh. A refting, repofing, ftanza.

Afaire. A fhoemaker.

Afaidham. To rebel, revolt.

Afaitigham. To abandon, evacuate.

Afal. An afs.

Afam. To do, make.

Afanta. Sedition.

Afarlaighachd. Magic, divination, intoxication.

Afaid. Debate.

Afardoir. A litigious perfon.

Afcaim. To afk, beg.

Afcairt. A budding, fprouting; hards, tow.

Afgan. A grig.

Afgidh. Gratis, free.

Afguil. The bofom, armpit.

Afcal. A conference; onfet; flowing of the tide.

Afcaoin. Curfe, excommunication.

Afcaointam. To curfe, excommunication.

Afcar. A gueft.

Afcath. A foldier, champion.

Afchu. A water-dog.

Afcnaim. To enter.

Afcnamh. Afcenfion.

Afdar. A journey, way.

Afdaraigham. To travel.

Afdairaiche. A traveller.

Afdaroir. A porter.

Afal. An afs.

Afinnleachd. Devices.

Afnag. A fan to winnow corn with.

Afgach. A winnower.

Afgaim. To winnow, cleanfe.

Afion. A crown.

Afleach. A requeft, temptation.

Aflaigham. To beg, requeft.

Aflonnadh. A difcovery, telling.

Afurlaigham. To fupport.

Affain. Plates.

Afcuch. An efcape.

Afcuchaim. To efcape.

Aftas. A fpear, javelin.

Afteach. In, into.

Aftigh. In, within.

Aftharruing. Abftract.

Aftranach. A gueft, ftranger, traveller.

At. A fwelling.

Atmhor. Swelling.

Ata. Is, am.

Ata. A hat, cap.

Atan. A cap, garland.

Atach. A requeft.

Atach. Fermentation.

Atachanam. To prate.

Atail. Deaf.

Atamhneachd. Redemption.

Atais. Woe.

Atchuifle. Aneurifm.

Ath. Again, equal to re in Latin, proximate.

Ath. A ford.

Ath, or aith. A kiln.

Athair. A father.

Athar. The air, fky.

Athair-ceile.   } Father-in-law.
Athair-ann-dlighe. }

Athairamhuil. Fatherly.

Atha. A blaft of wind.

Athach. A giant.

Athach. Waves.

Athach gaoith. A blaft.

Athach. A fpace.

Athaile. Inattention.

Athainne. A firebrand.

Athair-baifdaich. A godfather.

Athair-faoifaidin. A father confeffor.

Athair-lufa. Groundivy.

Athairamhlachd. Fatherlinefs.

Athairaighachd. A patrimony.

Athaireog. An aunt by the father

Athais. A rebuke.

Athaifam. To rebuke.

Athaifeach. Reviling.

Athal. Deaf.

Athal. A flesh hook.

Athairdham. To adopt.

Athairdhadh. Adoption.

Athargadh. A sharp engagement.

Athairgaibh. Importunity, solicitation.

Atharmactadh. Parricide.

Atharaigham. To change, flit, alter.

Atharaghadh. Alteration, change.

Athathad. Reunion.

Athbhach. Strength.

Athbhath. Second death.

Athbheoghaicham. To re-kindle, re-animate.

Athcaoid. Sickness, ailments

Athcaoideach. Sickly.

Athcaoin. Complaint.

Athchagnam. To chew the cud, ruminate.

Athchagnadh. Chewing the cud.

Athcairt. Renewal of a lease.

Athcasam. To return, to attack, to twist again.

Athchasachdich. A repeated cough.

Athchasta. Strongly twisted.

Athchomair. Brief, short.

Athbhualam. To re-act.

Atha na suil. Corner of the eye.

Athghairrid. Short, brief, a short way.

Athbhrodam. To resuscitate.

Athbhar. Aftercrop.

Atharamharc. Aeoroscopy.

Athareolas. Aeoromancy.

Athar-iul. Aerology.

Atharmheigh. A barometer.

Athailte. A scar.

Athchasaidam. To re-charge.

Athchoimhearan. A register.

Athchoimhire. An abridgement.

Athchomhaircam. To shout out again.

Athchraim. To restore.

Athcharam. To mend, repair.

Athchuimhnigham. To recollect.

Athchuimirc. Rehearsal of a cause.

Athchuimhne. Recollection.

Athchuinge. A request.

Athchruinnigham. To rally.

Athchuingam. To request.

Athcheimnigham. To recapitulate.

Athchuiram. To surrender; to banish.

Athcheasnigham. To re-examine.

Athchuir. Banishment.

Athchuimain. To deform, transform.

Athbharram. To call again, to repeat, to echo.

Athlamh. Expert, ready.

Athamhal. A looking after, perceiving.

Athchostas. Aftercost.

Aththinnas clainne. Afterpains.

Athlagham. To procrastinate.

Athlaghadh. Procrastination.

Athghabham. } To take back, retake, resume.
Athghlacam. }

Athghearram. To shorten, abbreviate.

Athghlanam. To refine, furbish.

Athnuadhaicham. To renew.

Athnuadhachadh. Renovation.

Athsmuintuigham. To reflect, think, consider.

Athsgalam. To resound.

Athsmuintughadh. Reflection.

Athsmuintidh. Second thought.

Athdhiolam. To refund.

Ath-la. Next day.

Athlan-mara. Reflux of the sea, next tide.

Athghloram. To resound.

Athmhalairtam. To make a second exchange.

Athmhalairt. Another or second exchange.

Athnacham. To give up, deliver.

Athneartuigham. To reinforce.

Athnamh. Great store, spoil.

Athleimam. To resound.

Athrach. A boat, wherry.

Athuamhortha. Terrible, horrid, detestable.

Athuamhorthachd. Abomination.

Ath-uair. Second time.

Aththogam.

Aththogam. To rebuild.
Aththoifaigham. To recommence.
Athrainnam. To fubdivide.
Athrochin Recovering.
Athreoruigham. ⟩ To reconduct, to re-
Athfdiuram. ⟨ trieve.
Athgheinmhin. Regeneration.
Athgheinam. To regenerate.

Athleafluigham. To reform.
Athleaffughadh. Reformation.
Athfgriobham. To tranfcribe.
Athfhealladh. Retrofpect.
Athfhealbhachadh. Reverfion.
Athchuinginam. To retrieve.
Attin. Furze.
Audhallam. To be deaf.

B.

B Is the fecond letter of the Irifh alphabet, and is called beth, i. e. birch
It is a labial letter, and the article an is
changed to am before it, as an bolg, the
belly, is am bolg in nouns of the mafculine gender. For further information I
refer the reader to the Galic Analyfis.

Ba. *Was, were, have been.* It ought to be
written b'e, for bu e.
Ba. Cows. Plural of bo.
Ba. Good.
Ba. Under.
Ba. Death.
Baan. The matrix of a cow.
Bab, baban. A babe, baby.
Baban. Short pieces of yarn or thread, a
taffel.
Babanach. Having taffels.
Babhachd. Innocence, fweetnefs.
Babhoidin. Taffels.
Babhuin. A bulwark, an inclofure for cat-
tle, a milking place for cows.
Bac, bacal, bacadh. A let, ftop, hindrance,
a prop, crook, fulcrum.
Bac. ⟩ A hook, hinge of a door.
Bacan. ⟨
Bacach. Lame, halt.

Bacag. A trip or fall.
Bacam, bacaigham. To ftop, hinder, to
make lame or halt.
Bacal. An obftacle, hindrance.
Bacaifach. Hindering.
Bacuidhe. Lamenefs.
Bachul. A ftaff, crofier, crook.
Bachlag. A lifp or ftop in the fpeech; a
little curl.
Bachlagach. ⟩ Full of curls.
Bachlach. ⟨
Bacudhas. Oven.
Bacala. A bakehoufe.
Bacalta. Baked.
Bacan. Hinge of a door, any little hook.
Bacal. A flave, prifoner.
Bach. Loving.
Bach. A breach, violent attack or fur-
prize.
Bachanta. Prating.
Bachantachd. Garrulity.
Bach. Drunkennefs.
Bachaire. A drunkard.
Bachairiughadh. Drinking, fotting.
Bachaim. To make drunk.
Bachallam. To clip round, to trim.
Bachla. A cup, chalice.

Bachar.

Bachar. A beech maſt, an acorn, the herb Lady's Glove.

Bachla. An armful.

Bachlobhra. Pimples in the face from drinking.

Bachthorman. The noiſe of drunkards.

Bachoide. The boſs of a ſhield.

Bachtna. Strife, contention.

Bad. A bunch, buſh, cluſter, tuft.

Bad-mulaich. The top cluſter, the hair on the top of the head.

Bad. A boat.

Bad-aiſaig. A ferry-boat.

Bad-fada. A long-boat.

Badan. A tuft of trees or hair.

Badanach. Tufted.

Badach. Having boats, boat like.

Badachd. Boating.

Badh. Love, friendſhip.

Badhach. Loving, friendly.

Badhbh. A vulture, Royſton crow, any ravenous bird.

Badhbh. A fairy woman, a ſcold; the North.

Badhghaire. A ſot, a fool, a coquet.

Badhbha. Evident, manifeſt.

Badhbhachd. Croaking like a raven, hawk, or vulture.

Badhon. A little haven, road, rampart, bulwark, a bay of the ſea.

Baganta. }
Bagach. } Warlike, corpulent, tight.

Bagach. Fighting.

Bagar. A threat.

Bagaram. To threaten.

Bagart. Threatening.

Bagh, badh. Kindneſs; an eſtuary.

Bagh. A promiſe, tie, bond.

Bagh-thinnas. A ſurfeit.

Bagham. To give or pledge one's word.

Baghach, badhach. Kind, friendly, loving.

Baghadh. Fighting, quarrelling.

Baidal. A tower.

Baghlach. Dangerous.

Baghthroidam. To wrangle.

Baidalach. Towering.

Baigh. Love, kindneſs, friendſhip.

Baichbheurla. A ſoleciſm.

Baic. A twiſt, turn.

Baicham. To touch, ſtrike.

Baidh. A wave.

Baidhe. Predicting, prophecying.

Baidheal. A cow-ſtall.

Baidheach. A co-adjutor, comrade.

Baidheach. }
Baighal. } Friendly, fair, noble.

Baidheachd. Friendſhip.

Baidheamhlachd. Prophecying.

Baidheachas. Grace, favour.

Baidhte. Waſhed, drowned.

Baidham. To endear, to give one's word, to prophecy.

Baidin. A yawl, a little boat.

Baiſphiaſt. A toad.

Baigham. To ſpeak to.

Baighin. A waggon.

Baighle. A fawn.

Bail. A place, reſidence.

Bail. Proſperity, good luck.

Bail. The allowance of a mill to the poor.

Bailc. Bold, ſtrong, alſo a ſtraight, or ligature.

Bailceach. A ſtrong ſtraight man.

Baile. A town, village; plur. Bailte.

Baile mor. A large town.

Baile. A clan, tribe.

Baile margaidh. A market town.

Baile-geamhraidh. Ground always plowed.

Baile puirt. A ſea port.

Baillam. To drink.

Bailli. A bailiff.

Baillein. A boſs, ſtud, any round thing.

Baillen. A drink.

Baillcog.

Bailleog. A twig, fprout, or fucker.

Bailleagach. Full of twigs or fuckers.

Bailm. Balm, balfam.

Bailigheachd. A bailiwick, province, diftrict.

Bailteach. Full of towns.

Bailgfhionn. Having a white or fpeckled belly.

Bailtachas. Planting towns, colonizing.

Baine. Milk.

Baine. A drop

Bainbh A little pig.

Bainbhidheachd Pigging, farrowing.

Bainbhin A fucking pig.

Baincheadach. Authorized.

Bainceadam To authorize.

Baine-milis. New milk.

Baine-goirt. Butter-milk.

Baine-binntighte. Thickened milk.

Baine-nuis. Bieftings.

Baine ramhar. Curdled milk.

Baine-gamhnach. Honey-fuckle.

Baineach. Milky.

Baine bo Cow's milk.

Baine caorach. Sheep milk.

Bainne. Whither.

Bainalach. A dropping of rain.

Baineafag. A ferret.

Bainfirinfce. The epicene gender.

Bainnfhreagaradh. A bond, ftipulation.

Baing. On a fudden.

Bainghearrachd. A goddefs.

Bainni. Madnefs, fury, rage.

Bainnionn. Female.

Bainnionnas. Muliebrity

Bainnfe. Of tne wedding. Vide Banis.

Bainfeach. A plain or field, fheepwalk, a folitary place.

Bainfeachd. Feafting.

Bainfeaghadh. Deftroying, defolating.

Bainfgeal. A ftar.

Bainfpireag. A fparrow-hawk.

Bainteoladh. A woman thief.

Baintigharna. A lady, a gentlewoman.

Baintreabhach. A widow.

Bairche. Strong, brave.

Bairche. A battle.

Bair A game, battle, a game at hurling.

Bairchne. A fight by women.

Baiidheis. The end or point.

Bairdheifam. To point.

Bairead. A bonnet, cap.

Baireatrom. Light-headed, quick, nimble.

Bairefc The froth of water.

Baircin. A ferret.

Baircin. Crofs fticks or fide timbers for a houfe.

Bairgeanta. Swift.

Baiighean. A cake.

Bairghean. A floor, plot of ground.

Bairghin. A begotten fon.

Bairghintach. A bringer forth of fons.

Baiiin. A cake of bread.

Bairile. A helmet, a barrel.

Bairinn. A firebrand.

Bairneach. Filial.

Bairneach. Perverfe, fretful.

Bairnigham. To fret.

Bairneachd. Judging.

Bairnam. To judge.

Bairribhuaghbhail. A founding horn.

Bairricin. A ferret.

Bairfeach. A fcold, fhrew.

Bairfgeoig. Top of the windpipe.

Bairfeachd. Scolding, a fatire.

Bairfeog. A young fcold.

Bairfigham. To fcold.

Bais. Water.

Baifc. Round.

Baifchaile. Ruddle.

Baifceall. A wild perfon.

Baifcne. A tree.

Baifeach. Flat.

Baifeachd. Palmiftry.

Baifde.

Baifde, baifdeoir. Baptift ; a fornicator.

Baifdadh. Baptifm, rain.

Baifdeam. To baptize ; to dip.

Baife. Of the palm of the hand. See Bas.

Baifeal. Pride.

Baifealach. Proud.

Baifin. A bafon.

Baifleach. An ox, a handful of water, or any thing.

Baite. Drowned.

Baifter, baiter. Water.

Baiftidhe. Drops from a houfe.

Baitheann. Inevitable, prefent death.

Baithis. The forehead, brow.

Baiteach. Vide Bodach.

Baitin. A little ftick.

Baitineachd. Beating with a ftick.

Ball. A fpot, mark , a place, a ball, globe; a weapon, member, a cable.

Ballach. Spotted.

Balach. A giant, a fturdy fellow, a fellow.

Baladh. Fighting.

Balaighe. Profit, advantage.

Balbh. Dumb, mute.

Balbhachd. Dumbnefs.

Balbhan. A dumb perfon.

Balbhanam. To ftrike dumb.

Balc. A hardnefs or cruftnefs in the earth occafioned by the weather.

Balc. Strong, ftout.

Balcmhar. Great, corpulent.

Balg. A man of erudition.

Balgan-feidaidh. Fuz-ball.

Balla. A wall, rampart.

Ball-deife. An inftrument, tool, ufeful weapon.

Ball-fampuill. An example, fpecimen.

Ball-oibre. A tool to work.

Ball-toirmaifg. An obftacle.

Ballan. A teat, udder ; a fhell, covering ; broom, a churn.

8

Ballan-lofguin. A mufhroom.

Ball-feirc. Beauty fpot.

Ball-dobhrain. A mole.

Ballan-tinntachaidh. A cheefe vat.

Ball-faobhrach. An edged tool.

Ball-feargha. Membrum virile.

Ballardadh. Proclamation.

Ballaidham. To proclaim.

Ballghalar. Plague.

Ballnafg A joint.

Ballog. The fkull.

Ballog. A blot.

Balt. A belt.

Ballfgoid. A blifter.

Ballfgoidam. To blifter.

Balt. A welt, border.

Ballach. Striped.

Baltaidhe. Fetters.

Baltin. Health, fafety.

Ballchrith. Trembling.

Ban. Pale, white, true ; copper, copper mine.

Banag. Any thing white, a fhilling.

Bannach. A bannock, cake.

Bann. A bond, bill ; a chain, a girth, belt ; a proclamation, a ball.

Bannal. A number, many, croud, women.

Bannlamh. A cubit, handcuffs.

Bani. Madnefs, frenzy.

Ban-talamh. Lay ground.

Bann-taifbeunaidh. A bond of appearance.

Ban. A woman, light. Vide Bean.

Bana. Death.

Banab. Abbefs.

Banaigham. To lay wafte, to bleach, whiten, grow pale.

Banaghadh. Laying wafte, whitening.

Banais. A wedding.

Banaiteach. Serious.

Banbh. A pig.

Banchonganta. A midwife.

Banchoigle.

Banchoigle. A cup companion, a female goffip.

Banfhlufga. Fluxus muliebris.

Banda. Female.

Bang. A nut, the touch, hindrance.

Bangadh. A promife.

Banmhac. A fon-in-law.

Ban-mhathair. A mother-in-law.

Bann. Marching, journeying.

Bann duirne. A wriftband.

Banna. A band, troop.

Bannach. Active.

Bannach. A fox.

Bannachd. Subtlety.

Bannamh. A female faint.

Bannleanaim. To act the midwife.

Bannaoin. A goddefs.

Bannfach. An arrow.

Bannfhaor. Free by law.

Bannfhaorfachd. Freedom by law, licence, patent.

Bannfhaorfaigham. To licence.

Bannfhorn. A kind of gridle or bake-ftone.

Bannfhompla. An example.

Banoglach. A fervant maid.

Banrach. A fold, a fmock.

Banracham. To pent up.

Banfgal. A woman; effeminate.

Banfglabha. A bondmaid.

Banfcoth. A fon-in-law.

Banfear. A filly.

Banta. A niece.

Bantrach. Fingal's feraglio.

Baodh. Wild, foolifh.

Baodhan. A calf.

Baodrod. Vide Bairfeachd.

Baoghal. Danger.

Baoghalach. Dangerous, perilous.

Baoibh. A foolifh mad woman.

Baoil. Water; madnefs, a fit of mad-nefs.

Baothan. A jack fprat, nidget.

Baothleimnach. Wild-leaping.

Baois. Luft, concupifcence, levity, mad-nefs.

Baoifgal. Shining, glittering

Baoifeach. Lafcivious.

Baoifgam. To peep, look in.

Baoifleach. A brothel.

Baoith. Youthful, light.

Baoithchreidmhach. Credulous

Baos. Capricious.

Baofrach. Frenzy.

Baoth. Weak, foft, fimple.

Baothan. A blockhead.

Baothchaifigh. Riotous.

Bar. Bread.

Bar. A fon, a learned man

Bar. A dart.

Barr. A top, a crop, the hair of the head, overplus.

Bar a bhrigein. Silver-weed.

Bar braonan nan con. Tormentil.

Bara. Going, marching, anger.

Bara. A barrow.

Bara-roth. A wheelbarrow.

Baramhuil. An opinion, fuppofition, con-jecture.

Baramhlaigham. To fuppofe, conjecture.

Baramhlaghadh. Suppofing.

Baramhlach. Cenforious.

Barantas. A warrant, pledge, pawn.

Baranta. Warrantee, furety.

Baran A baron.

Baranachd. A barony.

Barantaicham. To warrant.

Barantamhuil. Warrantable.

Barath. Lying in wait.

Barbrog. The barberry bufh.

Barran. The tops of mountains

Barran. A hedge of thorns by a wall, ed-der.

Barrachaol. A pyramid.

Barrach.

Barrach. Tow, hards.

Barrachd. Overplus.

Barriall. A thong, latchet.

Bar-baile. } Battlements, bartizans.
Barmor.

Barc. A bark, fmall fhip.

Barc. A book.

Barclann. A library.

Barcachd. An embarkation.

Barcaim. To embark

Bard. A poet.

Bard. Corporation.

Bardachd. Poetry, corporation town.

Bardal. A drake.

Bardamhuil. Like a poet, fatirift.

Bardas. A lampoon, fatire.

Barg. Red hot.

Barn. A nobleman, a judge, a battle.

Barra. A barr, fpike.

Barr. Helmet, fon, head, top, end, fcum, heap.

Barrachad. A cottage, hut.

Barradh. A hindrance.

Barraghlach. Tops or branches of trees.

Barraighain. A mitre, turband.

Barraift. Borage, green cale.

Barramhuil. Gay, genteel, fprightly, generous.

Barrabhailc. Entablature.

Barrachas. Curled hair.

Barrchfaighte. Trimmed, clipped.

Barrbhuidhe. Yellow-head.

Barrdog. A box, pannier, hamper.

Barrog. A young girl.

Barrag A ftitch, oppreffion in ficknefs; grappling, wreftling.

Barrfhionn. White-topped.

Barrog. A knit, rod, fwitch.

Barrogam. To grapple, to embrace.

Barlin. A rolling fea.

Barneach. A limpet, a cunner.

Bard-coimhioc. } A dramatift.
Bard-dealbhchluith.

Barddidhas. }
Bardachd.   } Satire.
Barfeas.   }

Barrag. Weeds that float in water.

Barradhriopair. A butler.

Barramhais. A cornice.

Barrthonn. } Pericranium.
Barrchuft. }

Bas, bos. The palm of the hand.

Bas. Death.

Bafmhor. Mortal.

Bafmhorachd. Mortality.

Bafuigham. To die, ftarve.

Bafgluaidhe. Vermilion, red lead.

Bafal. Judgment.

Bafafcanas. The bafs in mufic.

Bafbaire. A fencer.

Bafbruidheach. Lecherous.

Bafbruidheachd. Lechery.

Bafc. Red.

Bafc. Round.

Bafcach. A catchpole, a bailiff.

Bafcam. To apprehend.

Bafcairm. A circle.

Bafcaid. A bafket.

Bafcall. A wild man in the woods.

Bafcarnach. Lamentation.

Bafcart. Cinnamon.

Bafc-charnte. Globular.

Bafc-chriadh Ruddle.

Bafdard. A baftard.

Bafgam. To ftop, ftay.

Bafgaire. A mournful clapping of hands.

Baflog. A place of execution.

Baflach. The palmful.

Bafmun. I fuppofe fomething medicinal.

Baffoile. Vaffal.

Baffa. Fate, fortune.

Bata. A ftick, ftaff, baton.

Batail. A fkirmifh, fight.

Batair. A cudgeller.

Bataireachd. Cudgelling.

Bath.

Bath. The fea.

Bath. Slaughter, death, murder.

Bath. Thirſt.

Bath. }
Bathadh. } Drowning.

Batham. To drown, die, periſh, to faint.

Bhthainte. A booty of cattle.

Bathais. Forehead.

Bathghorm. A light blue.

Bathlach, balach. A clown.

Bathlan. The flux of the fea, a calm.

Bathlaodh. A helmet.

Bathroid. A token.

Bathſhruth. A calm ſtream.

Batros. Roſemary.

Bathar. Wares.

B'e, for bu e. It was.

Be. Night.

Be. A woman.

Be. Life.

Beabh. A tomb, grave.

Beabham. To die.

Beacan. A muſhroom.

Beac. }
Beachan. } A bee.

Beachan chapul. A waſp.

Beacarna. A common proſtitute.

Beacht. A multitude, a ring.

Beacht. Perfect.

Beacht. A covenant, furety.

Beacht. Perception, feeling, idea.

Beachta. Carriage, behaviour.

Beachtam. To compaſs, embrace, to criticize.

Beachligham. To certify, aſſure.

Beachdam. To meditate, confider, perceive.

Beachtaire. A critic.

Beachtamhuil. Circular, roundiſh.

Beachdidh Sure, certain.

Beachlann. A bee houſe.

Beachran. Wandering, ſtraying.

Beachrainnam. To grieve, to put aſtray.

Bead. Mournful, forrowful news.

Bead. Flattery, a trick, pity.

Beadidheacht. Sweet mouthed, forwardneſs.

Beadidh. Forward, impudent.

Beadighan. A ſcoffer, paraſite.

Beadidham. To be forward, to act the paraſite.

Beadighe. A flatterer.

Beadag. Lying woman, a goſſip.

Beaddarach. Frolickſome, ſportive, fond.

Beadan. Calumny.

Beadradh. Fondling, toying.

Beadanachd. Calumniating.

Beadfhoraobhadh. A regiſter, commentary.

Beag. Little, fmall; is beag orm, I value not, I hate.

Beag nach. Almoſt.

Beagan. A little, a few.

Beaganam. To make little.

Beagchionta. A foible.

Beagdhata. A ſtingy fellow.

Beageaglach. Void of fear.

Beagluach. Of little value.

Beal. Vide Beul.

Beal, or Beul. An orifice, hole.

Beal. The god Belus.

Beala. A veil.

Beala. To die.

Beali. Broom.

Bealach. A gap, a highway or road.

Bealadh. Anointing.

Bealbhach. A bit for the mouth.

Bealbhan-ruadh. A fort of hawk.

Bealcainteach. Talkative.

Bealchrabhadh. Hypocriſy.

Bealchrabhach. A hypocrite.

Bealdruidam. To ſilence.

Bealfhothargain. A gargariſm.

Bealgach. Prattling, babbling.

Bealgradh. Diſſimulation, flattery.

Bealradh. A phraſe, ſpeech.

Bealraidhteach. Famous, talkative.

Bealtaine. A compact, agreement.

[K]   Bealteine.

Bealteine. The firſt of May. Teine Beil, or fire of the god Belus, i. e. Mayday in Iriſh, ſo called from the fires which the Druids lighted on the ſummits of the higheſt hills, into which they drove the four-footed beaſts, uſing at the ſame time certain ceremonies to expiate for the ſins of the people. This Pagan ceremony of lighting thoſe fires in honour of the Aſiatic God Belus, gave its name to the entire month of May, which to this day is called Mios na Bealteine, in the Iriſh language. Dr. Keating ſays, the deſign of it was to keep off contagious diſorders from them for that year, and that all the inhabitants of Ireland quenched their fires on that day, and kindled them again out of ſome part of that fire.

Bean. A woman.

Beann. A degree, ſtep; a horn; a ſkirt, a drinking cup.

Beann. A mountain; plur. Beannta.

Bean. A goat.

Bean. Quick, nimble.

Bean. For Buin, touch thou.

Beanadh. Dulneſs, bluntneſs.

Bean-bainnſe. ⎫
Bean-nuadhphoſda. ⎬ A bride.

Bean-laoch. ⎫
Bean-ghaiſgaiche. ⎬ A heroine.

Bean-tighe. A landlady, goodwife.

Beanachas tighe. Houſewifery.

Bean-tuath. A country wench.

Beanaltra. A nurſe.

Bean-choimhaidachd. A waiting maid, a bride maid.

Bean-chioch. A wet nurſe.

Beancharaid. A female friend.

Beanchinnaidh. A female nameſake.

Beanoglach. A maid ſervant.

Bean-ghluin. A midwife.

Beantigharna. A lady, gentlewoman.

Bean-leoghain. A lioneſs.

Bean-nighaidh. A waſherwoman.

Beanriogh. A queen.

Bean-ſdiubhard. A houſekeeper.

Bean-ſdiubhardachd. Houſekeeping

Bean-ſhiubhladh. A woman in childbed.

Beanphriunnſa. A princeſs.

Beaniarla. Counteſs.

Beanuaſal. A lady or gentlewoman

Beanbhochd. A beggar woman.

Beandiuc. Dutcheſs.

Beanleigh. A female phyſician.

Beandalta. A foſter daughter.

Bean-oſd. An hoſteſs.

Beanridir. A knight's lady.

Beanabharain. A baroneſs.

Beanbaile. The lady of the place or Ilk.

Beanmhaiſdair A miſtreſs.

Beanarach. A ſhepherdeſs or milkmaid.

Beandia. Goddeſs.

Beanogha. A grand-daughter.

Beanchliamhuin. A daughter-in-law, or ſiſter-in-law.

Beanbhuachaile. A ſhepherdeſs.

Beanchruitire. A female harper.

Beanchuiſlainach. A female piper.

Beancheile. A ſpouſe.

Beanſhniomh. A ſpinſter.

Beanamhuil. Modeſt, like a woman.

Beantrach. A houſe of women, ſeraglio.

Beanntach. Full of mountains.

Beannachd. A bleſſing, farewell.

Beannuicham To bleſs.

Beandraoith. Enchantreſs, ſorcereſs.

Beanadhaltranach. Adultreſs.

Beannachadh. A bleſſing, benediction, grace to meat.

Beannuighte. Bleſſed.

Beannan. A little hill.

Beanam. To reap, mow, cut down.

Beandachd. Effeminacy.

Beangan. A branch, bough.

Beanchomharba. A dowager.

Beanchobar. A horn.

Beanann.

Beanann. Furniture, goods.
Beannach. Horned, skirted, chequered.
Beannaim. To steal, thieve, cornute.
Beannog. A coif, linen cap.
Beanoighre. Heiress.
Bear. A spit. Vide Bior.
Bear. A bear.
Beara. A judge.
Bearacht. Judgment.
Bearaim. To take away, to give. Vide Beiram
Bearan. A young man, a pin.
Bearbhadh. Seethed, boiled.
Bearbhaim. To melt, dissolve.
Bearbhoir. A refiner of metals.
Bearg. Anger, a champion.
Beargachd. Diligence.
Beargna. The vernacular language of a place.
Bearla. Vide Beurla.
Bearla Fene. Lawyer's Irish.
Bearla tebidh. Mixed dialect.
Bearna. A gap, breach.
Bearnan-bride. Dandelion.
Bearnach. Full of gaps.
Bearr. Short, brief.
Bearra. A spear.
Bearra. Short hair.
Bearrasgian. A razor.
Bearradan. Scissars, snuffers.
Bearram. To clip, shear.
Bearra. A cut, shred, slice, segment.
Bearradh. Tripping along, light.
Bearradh. The tops or cliffs of mountains and rocks.
Bearrg. Angry, outrageous.
Bearrthoir. ⎤
Bearradair. ⎬ A barber, shearer.
Bearrthach. ⎦
Bearna-mhiol. The hare lip.
Beart. An engine, machine, frame, mode of doing any thing, a bundle, truss.
Beart treabhaidh. A plow.

Beart-fhighaidh. A weaver's loom.
Beart-uchd. A poitrel.
Beartach. Rich.
Beartas. Riches.
Beartaigham. To yoke, begin, to brandish, flourish, play, meditate.
Bearrthog. A razor.
Beart. Judgment, clothes.
Beart. Carried. Vide Beiram.
Beart. A game at tables.
Beart. A covenant, agreement.
Beart. Threatening.
Beartaire. A brandisher.
Beartam. To threaten, point.
Bearrtha. Shaved, cropped.
Beartrach. A pair of tables, chess-board.
Beartha. Clean, fine, genteel.
Beas. Behaviour, manners, custom.
Beas. Certain, correct.
Beascnadh. Peace ; a speech, dialect.
Beasach. Well behaved.
Beascnaidh. Accommodation, agreement.
Beascnaigham. To accommodate, agree.
Beascon. A syllogism.
Beasg. A harlot.
Beastan. A grievance.
Beath. Birch tree.
Beatha. Life.
Beathach. A beast, animal.
Beathaigham. To feed, nourish.
Beathaghadh. Food, nourishment, education, benefice, bread, or place.
Beathmhan. A bee.
Beathodach. A beaver.
Beathog. A bee, beech-tree.
Beathoguighte. Stung by a bee.
Beathra. Water.
Bec. A point, bill of a bird.
Bechnel. Gavelkind.
Bechdalachd. Ambition.
Bed. A deed or action, injury, pity.
Bed. Mournful, dismal.
Bed. Fruit.

Bedfoiriobhadh. A commentary.

Beg. Vide Beag. Little.

Beic. An outcry, roar.

Beicam. To roar.

Beicaire. Bawler, prating fellow.

Beicighil. Outcry, roaring.

Beidadh. Patching.

Beichare. A beehive.

Beidhaidh. A lamprey.

Beicleimnach. Dancing, skipping.

Beile. A meal of meat.

Beille. A kettle, caldron.

Beillean. Blame, reproach.

Beilbhag. Corn poppy

Beilt. Of a belt, or cingle.

Beim A stroke, blow, cut.

Beim. A tribe, stock, generation.

Beim. Help, a beam, piece of timber.

Beimcheip. A whipping-stock.

Beimnach. Vehement, cutting, reproachful.

Beinnid. Cheese-rennet.

Beinc. A bin.

Beinc. A separation, disjunction.

Beine. A champion ; the evening.

Beinin. A little woman.

Beinn. A mountain, hill, the summit.

Beirbhis. Anniversary feast, vigil.

Beiram. To take, give, bring forth, bear,
to carry. Vide Bearaim.

Beiram fanear. To observe.

Beirt. Two persons.

Beirt. Help, assistance.

Beirt. A burden.

Beirthe. Birth, born, brought forth.

Beirtin. A little burden.

Beistin. A little beast.

Beisgne. Peace, quiet.

Beit. Twain, both.

Beith. A birch tree.

Beitha. Of birch, birchen.

Beitin. The scorched or frost-bitten grafs
of the hills.

Beithniur. St. John's wort.

Beithir. A bear.

Beitir. Clean, neat.

Belra. A parish, an ecclesiastical division
of land.

Beltine. Month of May.

Ben. Vide Bean. A woman.

Beneigin. A rape.

Beo. Living, alive.

Beo. Cattle, any living creature.

Beochomhan. A warren.

Beodhacht. Courage, vigour.

Beodhaim. To quicken, enliven.

Beochan. A small fire.

Beochanta. Vigorous.

Beo-eachdairachd. Biography.

Beo-luath. Hot embers.

Beoghaineamh. Quicksand.

Beoill. Fatness.

Beoil. Verbal.

Beol. A robber.

Beolaoch. A lively lad.

Beolach. Talkative.

Beolidhachd. } Oral tradition.
Beoloidas. }

Beo-radharc. Quick sight.

Beoshlainte. Life rent.

Beothachal. Lively.

Beothach. A beast.

Beoir. Beer.

Beoir-laidir. Strong beer.

Beoir-chaol. Small beer.

Beothal. Waving.

Beosach. Bright, glittering, brisk, dapper,
spruce.

Beosaigham. To beautify, deck out.

Beosgaradh. A divorce.

Beo-thorrach. Ready to lie in.

Beo-thuismighthach. Viviparous.

Bes. And.

Bes. The belly ; art, trade.

Bes. Manner, custom.

Bes. Exact, careful.

Bes.

Bes. Vide Baos.

Befcna. Peace, country.

Bet. A chariot.

Betheacht. Effeminate.

Bethcignachadh. Forcing a woman.

Beterlach. The old law.

Bethluifnion. The alphabet.

Beth. Birch, the letter B.

Beul. The mouth. Vide Beal.

Beuloidas. Tradition.

Beul. The god Belus.

Beulmhach. ⎱ The bit of a bridle.
Beulanach. ⎰

Beuldhraoithachd Incantation.

Beulbochd. Pleading of poverty.

Beulphurgaid. Gargarifm.

Beulach. Fair fpoken.

Beulais. Prating, babbling.

Beul bi. A pretty little mouth.

Beul-maothain. Scrobiculum cordis.

Beum. A cut, gap, reproach.

Beumnach. Full of cuts, gaps.

Beud. A deed, an evil deed. Vide Bed.

Beudag. A little, idle, goffiping woman.

Beus Moral virtue, quality.

Beufach. Moral, civil, courteous.

Beurtha. Genteel, well-fpoken.

Beurla. Speech, a word, phrafe; the Englifh language.

Bha. Imperfect tenfe of atam, was.

Bhar. Your.

Bhi. Vide Bha.

Bhos. On this fide.

Bi. Killing, murdering.

B'i. For bu i, it was fhe. Vide Analyfis, Ata.

Bi. Small, little, fine.

Bi. Living.

Biach. Membrum virile.

Biachachd. A priapifm.

Biadh. Meat, food.

Biadh ur eunan. Wood forrel.

Biadhta. Fatted.

Biadhchluan. A kitchen.

Biadhtach. An hofpitable man; a certain order of tenants in Ireland who procured provifions for the nobles.

Biadhor. Efculent.

Biail. An hatchet, an ax.

Bial. Water.

Bian. A pelt, fkin, hide.

Bian-leaffaiche. A currier.

Bias, biafd A beaft.

Biafd donn (or) dubh. An otter.

Biata, biatach. Vide Biadhtach.

Biatach. A raven.

Biatas. Betony.

Bibhfi. Deprivation.

Bicheaib, bichim. Mercury, quickfilver.

Biceir. A cup.

Bicheardcha. A tavern, victualling-houfe.

Bidain. A little bit.

Bidag. A dirk, ftilletto.

Bid. A hedge.

Bidgh, bidhgadh. A fudden ftart.

Bidhis. A fciew.

Big. Little.

Bigeun. A coif, cap, hair-lace.

Bigh. Glue, birdlime.

Bil. Good.

Bil. A beard, the mouth, a bird's bill.

Bil. A bloffom.

Bile. A tree, clufter of trees.

Bile. A border, welt.

Bili. Lips.

Bille. A bill.

Bille. Poor, mean, weak.

Bille. A rag.

Bill. A leper, a fool.

Billeachd. Poverty.

Billeog. Leaf of tree.

Billeog-bhaite. Water Lily.

Bileogan nan eun A fort of acid plant.

Billeoga an fpon. Tuffilago or Coltsfoot.

Bilich. Tuft.

Bilich chuige. Marigold.

Bim. Vide Bitham.

Binn. True, sweet, melodious, harmonious.

Binn. Vide Beinn. A hill, the hopper of a mill.

Binn. Accusation, sentence.

Binn. A voice.

Binnain. A pinnacle or top.

Binndain. Rennet.

Binnteach. Coagulative.

Binndealan. Biadiol. } A forehead-cloth.

Binne. More melodious.

Binne. Binnas. } Harmony, melody.

Binnalach. Melodious chirping.

Binneach. Hilly, having horns.

Binnealta. Binnealtach. } Pretty, neat, fine, melodious.

Binneaduin. Hill of Howth.

Binnean. A bell

Binntigham. To coagulate.

Binnear. A hill.

Binnear. A hair pin, a bodkin for the hair.

Binse. A bench.

Biochionnta. Common, general.

Biodh. The world.

Biochiontas. State of being common.

Biodh. For Bithadh. Vide Ata, Analysis.

Biochuram. Anxiety.

Biodanach. A tatler.

Biodhbha. An enemy.

Biodhbhanas. Discord.

Biodhg. A start.

Biodhgam. To start up.

Biodhgamhuil Active, lively.

Biol. A musical instrument.

Biolar. Cresses.

Biolasgadh. Talking, prattling.

Biolasgach. Talkative.

Biolgada. Rowing.

Bion. Readily, usually.

Bior. A spit, pin, bodkin.

Biorfhiacul. A toothpick.

Bioi. Water, a well or fountain.

Bior nam buide. Dandelion.

Biorach. A two year old heifer.

Biorach. Sharp-pointed, piercing, mucronated.

Biorshuilach. Sharp-sighted

Bioran A little stake, pin, needle.

Biorchoil. An instrument for beheading.

Bioian. Strife.

Bioranach. A contentious person, a pincushion.

Bioranachan. A pinmaker.

Bioranaighte. Vexed.

Biorar. Watercresses.

Bioriasg. A fishing bait.

Biorbhogha. A rainbow.

Biorbhuafan. A water serpent.

Biorchomhladh. A water sluice.

Biordhach. Watery.

Biorgon. A floodgate, a dam.

Biorphota. Urn.

Bioror. The brink of any water.

Biorra an t iasgair. Biorra. Biorra cruidin. } The bird called Kingfisher.

Biorrach. A boat, skiff.

Biorrac. A marshy field.

Biorraidh. A bullock.

Biorraid. Strife, an osier twig, a cap or helmet.

Biorranam. To hamper, perplex, distract.

Biorran. Anguish of mind

Biorranach. Distracted.

Biorranaire. A fomentor of strife.

Biorros. Water Lily.

Biorrfraobh. The old bed of a river.

Biosar. Silk,

Bioth—

Bioth-eoin. Birdlime, glue.

Bioth, bigh. } Gum of trees, pith of
Bioth-craoibh. } wood.

Biothanach. A thief.

Bioth, bith. Life, exiftence, a being.

Bioth. The world.

Biolar. Dainty, fine, fpruce.

Biothbhuan. Everlafting, perpetual, eternal.

Biothbhuantachd. Eternity, everlafting.

Biothghrabhachd. Cofmography.

Bir, bior. Water.

Bir. A fpit. Vide Bior.

Bir. Short.

Birag. The foretooth in brutes.

Birag lodain. A bandftickle.

Biread. A cap, bonnet.

Biraidach. High-headed.

Birfheadan. A water-pipe.

Birfhion. Metheglin.

Birid A breeding cow.

Birmhein. Oozinefs, moifture.

Birin. A little pin.

Birrae. Standing water.

Birt. Loads, bundle. Vide Beirt.

Birt. Hilt, haft, handle.

Bis. A buffet, box.

Bis eagha. Icicles hanging from the eaves of houfes.

Bifeach. Profperity, encreafe.

Bith. A wound.

Bith. The world, a being, exiftence, being, life.

Bith. Cuftom, habit.

Bithbheo. Everlafting.

Bitheamhnach. A thief.

Bithbhrigh. Effence.

Bithe. Female, belonging to the female fex.

Bithre Life-time.

Bitheamhanta. Thievifh.

Bithfhior. Everlafting.

Bitiorra. Chearful, blithe.

Bitis. Beets.

Bieci A ftrong man.

Bla. A town, village.

Bla. Piety, devotion.

Bla. The fea, a green field.

Bla. Healthy, fafe, well.

Bla. Yellow.

Bla. A cry, fhout.

Bla. Fruit of the womb.

Bla. Praife, renown.

Bla. In the Brehon laws, *be it enacted.* Vide Cairbre Liffeachar's code.

Blachd. A word.

Bladh. Renown, fame.

Bladh. Smooth.

Bladh. A flower, a garland of flowers.

Bladh, blaidh. A part, fragment, portion.

Bladh. Encreafe of fame.

Bladh. Flattery.

Blaidham, bladham. To break.

Bladaire. A flatterer, foother.

Blad. A dirty mouth.

Bladairam. To flatter.

Bladhach. Buttermilk.

Bladhachd. Breaking or crumbling to pieces.

Bladhm. A flirt, a brag, boaft.

Blaghair. A blaft.

Blaghaire. A boafter.

Blaghaiream. To boaft.

Blaghantas. Boafting.

Blaghmanach. A boafting fellow.

Blai. The womb.

Blanag. Fat, tallow.

Blanigach. Fat.

Blaifam. To tafte.

Blaith. Plain, fmooth.

Blaithe. Smoother.

Blaith. A bloffom.

Blaitheafch. Smooth, polifhed.

Blaithfleafg. A garland of flowers.

Blaitham. To fmooth, polifh.

Blaithliog.

Blaithliog. A polished stone.

Blaithin. A small blossom.

Blame. Sound, healthy.

Blandar. Flattery.

Blanc. A farthing.

Blaoc. A whale.

Blaodh-cun. A bird-call.

Blaodh. A shout or calling, breath.

Blaodhag. A noisy girl or woman.

Blaodhrach. Clamorous.

Blaor. A cry.

Blaoram. To cry.

Blar. A field, green, a spot, a battle.

Blaran. A little field, green, spot.

Blaosc. A husk or shell.

Blaoscin. The skull.

Blas. Taste, flavour.

Blasaim. To taste.

Blasachd. Tasting.

Blasda. Savoury.

Blasdachd. Sweetness.

Blaspog. A sweet kiss.

Blath. A form or manner.

Blath. ⎫ A flower, blossom, fruit, ef-
Blathan. ⎬ fects.

Blath. Praise.

Blath. White, clean, warm.

Blathliag. A pumice-stone.

Blathach. Butter-milk.

Blathaigham. To flower; to polish, smooth.

Blathaille. Mark of a stroke.

Blathoibriughadh. Embroidery.

Blatuigham. To warm.

Bleachd. Kine, milk.

Blathas. Warmth.

Bleachdaire. A soothing, undermining fellow.

Blathor. Having warmth.

Bleagham. ⎫ To milk.
Bleaghanam. ⎬

Bleasghanach. Emulgent.

Bleathach. That grindeth.

Bleatham. To grind.

Bleathmhor. Fruitful.

Bleathghlunach. In-kneed.

Bleid. A cajole, or wheedling.

Bleidh. A cup, goblet.

Bleidh-mhiol. A whale.

Blein. A harbour for boats.

Bleun. The flank, groin.

Bliaghain, blianadh. A year.

Bliaghanamhuil. Yearly.

Bliaghainchain. An annuity.

Blidham. To milk.

Blimh, blinn. Spittle, froth of a dead body.

Blincain. A torch, link.

Bliocht. Profit of a milk cow.

Bliochdmhaire. Full of milk.

Blionach. A slow handless person.

Blioch. A whole.

Bliochan. Yellow marsh anthericum.

Bliosan. An artichoke.

Blipfeachd. War.

Blith. Grinding

Bloach. A whale.

Blob. Thick-lipped.

Blobaran. A stutterer.

Bloc. Orbicular, round.

Blocan. A little block.

Blochbharram. To turn in a lathe.

Blodh. A fragment, piece.

Blodhach. Broken in pieces.

Blodham. To break in pieces.

Blodhaire. A battery, a place from which an attack is made.

Blodhuideog. A fragment.

Bloinigain-garaidh. Spinnage.

Blomas. Ostentation.

Blor. A voice.

Blorach. Noisy.

Bloracan. A noisy fellow.

Blos. Open, plain, manifest.

Blosam. To make manifest.

Blosc. A congregation, light.

Bloscach. A robust clown.

Bloscaire. A collector.

Bloscam.

Blofcam.　To found a horn or trumpet, to explode.

Blofgadh.　A found, report.

Blofcmhaor.　A cryer to a court.

Blot.　A cave or den.

Blotach.　One that dwells in a cave.

Blotlach　A cave, den.

Bluch.　Fatnefs.

Bluiiid.　Pinched.

Bluirc.　Crumbs, a fragment.

Blufar.　A noife, outcry.

Bo.　A cow.

Bo.　A fawn.

Bo allaidh.　A buffalo.

Boag.　A fea lark.

Lobhaith.　A cow flaughter.

Bo-bhainnadh.　A milch-cow.

Bobhadh.　A bow.

Boban.　Papa.

Bobeloth.　An antient name of the alphabet.

Bobas.　I would not.

Bobgurnac.　A blaft, fart.

Bobo ! O ! ftrange !

Boc.　Deceit, fraud, a blow, ftroke, box.

Boc.　A he-goat, a buck.

Bocadh.　A difcuffing or fifting of a matter.

Bocaide.　The knobs in a fhield, a bofs.

Bocam.　To fwell; to fkip as a deer.

Bocan.　A hobgoblin, fprite.

Bocan.　A covering, cottage.

Bocan bearach.　A mufhroom.

Bocan.　A hook or crook.

Bocanach.　Hooked, bent.

Bocanam.　To bend, make crooked.

Bocar.　Cow-dung.

Bochan.　A cottage.

Boch.　Heyday.

Bochd.　Poor, needy.

Bochna.　The fea, a narrow fea, mouth of a river.

Bocht.　A breach ; fire.

Bocht.　Reaping, cutting down.

Bochdam.　To impoverifh.

Bochdaine.　Poverty.

Bochthonn.　A fwelling furge.

Bofca.　A coffer, box.

Bocoide.　Studds, boffes

Bocum　A covering.

Bod.　A tail, a man's yard.

Bodach.　A ruftic, old man, an Englifh pint.

Bodach-ruadh.　A cod-fifh.

Bodachamhuil.　Surly, ruftic, boorifh.

Bodar. } Deaf.
Bodhar. }

Bodhar.　Vide Bothar.

Bodh-ar.　Murrain of cattle.

Bodharfach.　A deftroyer of cows.

Bodog.　Rage, anger, fury; a yearling calf.

Bodogachd.　Fury, rage.

Bodagachd.　An heifer that wants the bull.

Boel.　Pith of any ftalk.

Boghtain.　A building, roof, a vault.

Boghtainam.　To build, roof, vault.

Bog.　Soft, penetrable.

Bogach. } A marfh, moor, bog, fwamp.
Boglach. }

Bogadach.　Gefture.

Bogadh.　Tendernefs.

Bogaleo.　A bumpkin.

Bogam.　To move, put in motion, to wag, wave.

Bogaicham.　To foften, to mellow.

Bogan.　An egg in embryo.

Boganach.　A foft fellow.

Bog-ghiogan.　Sow-thiftle.

Bogghluafachd.　Floating, moving.

Bogha.　A bow.

Boghadair.　An archer.

Bogha-frais.　A rainbow.

Bogham.　To bend like a bow.

Boghar.　Vide Bodhar.

Boglus, buglofs.　Ox tongue.

Bogbhuine. } A bulrufh.
Bogluachair. }

Bogun. Bacon.

Bogur. Threatening.

Boguram. To threaten.

Boicinach. A boy fourteen years old.

Boichde. Poverty.

Boichde. Poorer.

Boid. A vow.

Boidam. To vow.

Boideach. Tolerable well.

Boideachan. A bodkin.

Boideis. Drunkenness.

Boidh. Neat, trim, spruce.

Boidhe. Vide Buidhe. Yellow.

Boidhean. Yellow-hammer.

Boidheach. Pretty.

Boidhad. Beauty.

Boidheasach. Yellow-jaundice.

Boidheog. A goldfinch.

Boidham. To thank.

Boidhlia. Puddle.

Boidhliath. Pale yellow.

Boidhmhios. The month July.

Boidrealt. A comet.

Boigbheulach. Open-mouthed.

Boigh. A teat.

Boige. Softness.

Boigiun. A bulrush.

Boigrean. Flummery.

Boigshibhin. A bulrush.

Boil. Issue, success, use.

Boile. Rage.

Boileach. Altogether.

Boilg, builg. A bubble.

Boilgphiast. A belly-worm, maw-worm.

Boilg. Husks of seeds.

Boilgain, bolgan. A quiver.

Boilgain beic. The spongy mushroom.

Boill. A knob, or boss.

Boillrinn. A ring.

Boillsgeanachd. Bulging out.

Boillsgeanaibh. Hills, mountains.

Boillsgeanam. To make round and bulging.

Boiltnigham. } To smell.
Boillteanasam. }

Boin. A cow.

Boinnaid. A bonnet.

Boinnaid an losgain. Brown boletus.

Boineadh. Budding, sprouting.

Boinne. A drop.

Boinean. A bud, sprout.

Boinneach. Sprouting.

Boinnanta. Stout, well-built.

Boineadh. A running sore.

Boinneog. A cake, bannock.

Boir. An elephant.

Boirb. The brow of a ridge.

Boirbe. Fiercer.

Boirbeachd. Fierceness.

Boirb bhriathrach. Vain-glorious, fierce-speaking.

Boirche. An elk, buffalo.

Boirchriadh. A kind of fat clay.

Boisag. A box on the ear.

Boisceall. A hind, a savage man or woman.

Boisgadh. A flash.

Boisgam. To flash.

Boisaid. A belt.

Boitain. A bundle of hay or straw.

Boiteall. Haughtiness, arrogance.

Boiteallgha. Arrogant, presumptuous.

Bol. A poet, art, skill.

Bol. A cow.

Bolachd. Poetry.

Bolann. An ox-stall.

Boladh. Smell.

Bolb. A sort of caterpillar.

Bolg. A bag, budget, belly.

Bolg-saighaid. A quiver.

Bolg. A pair of bellows.

Bolgan beicach. A fuzball.

Bolg. A pimple.

Bolg an t sollair. A magazine.

Bolgach. The small-pox.

Bolgach Fhrancach. The French-pox.

Bolgam.

Bolgam.   To blow, swell, or blister.

Bolgam.   A sip, gulp, a mouthful, dram.

Bolgan.   A small budget, or quiver.

Boll.   Boss of a bridle, a gorget.

Bolla.   A bowl or goblet.

Bolla.   Eighteen pecks.

Bolla.   A sort of bladder upon nets.

Bollog.   A shell, a skull, top of the head.

Bollog.   A bullock.

Bollsaire.   An antiquary, herald, master of ceremonies, cryer of a court.

Bollsgaire buird.   A meat carver at a prince's table amongst the Irish.

Bollsgairam   To proclaim.

Bollsgaire.   A bawler, boaster.

Bolltadh.   A bolt, bar.

Boltanas.   A smell.

Boltnigham.   To smell.

Boluigh.   Scented.

Bolunta.   Fine, exquisite.

Bomanam.   To boast, vaunt.

Bomanachd.   Boasting, vaunting.

Bomannachd.   Spotted, chequered.

Bomlachd.   The cow and profit.

Bonn.   A base, sole, bottom, foundation, pedestal.

Bonn.   A piece of money, a coin.

Bonn-sia.   A halfpenny.

Bonn.   Good.

Bonnaine.   A lacquey, footman.

Bonnamh.   A tribe or family.

Bonnan.   A bittern.

Bonna.   A sudden blast.

Bonnog.   A leap or jump.

Bonnseach.   A dart, javelin.

Bonnsachd.   Leaping, jumping.

Bonnsaigham·   To dart.

Bor.   A swelling, pride.

Borb.   Fierce, cruel, savage, barbarous, haughty, luxuriant, rank, ignorant.

Borb.   A tyrant.

Borbam.   To swell.

Borba.   Haughtiness, fierceness, barbarity.

Borbara.   Barbarous.

Bord.   A table, a board.

Bord-beula.   Starboard.

Bord luinge.   The deck of a ship.

Bord-cula.   Larboard.

Bord.   Border, boast, brink.

Bord-mor.   Table of the green cloth.

Borg.   A village.

Boroimhe.   A tribute of cows and other cattle.

Borr.   A knob.

Borr.   Great, noble, grand, splendid.

Borrach.   A haughty man.

Borrachas.   Hectoring.

Borra.   A swelling.

Borrocha.   A bladder.

Borradh.   A file of soldiers.

Borradh.   A swelling.

Borral.   Proud.

Borradh.   Parched.

Borradhach.   Valiant.

Borraidh.   Borrage.

Borram.   To swell, grow big and proud, to parch.

Borras.   Sodder.

Borbham.   To bail.

Boruaim.   Noise.

Borrshuileach.   Full-eyed.

Borrthoradh.   Greatness, majesty.

Borrun.   The haunch, or buttock.

Bos.   A palm, hand.

Bossag.   A slap on the face.

Bos.   Certain, abject, mean, low.

Bosan.   A purse.

Bosarguin.   Destruction.

Bosd.   Boasting.

Bosbhualadh.   Clapping of hands.

Bosdal.   Boasting.

Bosgaire.   Applause.

Bosgairdam.   To applaud.

Bosluath.   Applause, also nimble-handed, brisk.

Bosuaillam.   To extol.

Bot.

Bot. Fire, a cluster, a bunch.

Botach. A reedy bog.

Botigar. A fork.

Both. ⎱ A cottage, hut, tent, bower,
Bothag. ⎰ shade.

Bothach. Full of tents.

Bothach, A fen, a bog.

Bothigh. An ox-stall, cow-house.

Bothar. A lane, road, street.

Botin, botis. A boot.

Boudach. A pimp.

Botinicham. To put on boots.

Boudag. A bawd.

Bra. Brow.

Brac. An arm.

Braca. A breaker, harrow.

Bracam. To break, harrow.

Bracadh. Cabin, hut.

Bracaim. To embrace.

Bracan. Broth.

Braccaille. A sleeve, bracelet

Braich. Barley, malt.

Brachadh. Fermentation, malting.

Bracham. To malt, ferment.

Brachan. Any thing fermented, leaven.

Brachadair. A maltman.

Brachd. Hatred.

Brachd. A drop, increase of wealth, reaping, mowing.

Brachd. Sap, juice.

Brachdach. Substantial.

Brachag. A pimple, sore eyes.

Brachshuileach. Blear-eyed.

Bradag. A sly roguish girl.

Bradan A salmon.

Bradach. Thievish.

Bradhadair. fuel.

Braduighe. A thief.

Bradham. To oppress.

Bradhrudh. Ambush.

Bradogam. To flatter, charm.

Brac. A market, shop.

Brafal. Deceit.

Braghad. The neck, the top of the neck.

Braghadgha. Jugular.

Braghairt. A truss.

Bragharuighibh. A gibbet.

Braiche. ⎱ A stag, buffalo.
Braicheamh. ⎰

Braicam. A pack-saddle.

Braicne. A cat.

Braicht. A mouth.

Braid. Upper part.

Braigh. The throat, neck, upper part of any thing, tops of mountains.

Braigh. ⎱ An hostage.
Braighdean thairis. ⎰

Braighaidain. A collar.

Braighe. A monosyllable.

Braigheachd. Imprisonment, constraint.

Braighaidanas. Slavery, bondage.

Braighid. The neck.

Braighislaid. A collar.

Braidhadh. A clap of noise, or thunder.

Braighire. A bag or budget.

Braile. Heavy rain.

Brailam. To feel; reject, slight.

Brain. A chieftain, also large, extensive.

Brain. Beginning, front.

Braine. ⎱ Captain of a ship.
Braineach. ⎰

Brainn. The womb.

Brain. A quern.

Brais. Fabulous, fertile in invention; paroxysm.

Braisad. Rapidity.

Braisgeul. A fable, romance.

Braiseagnach. ⎱ A false accusation.
Braisionlach. ⎰

Braithcheim. A stag, wild ox.

Braitheoir. An overseer, spectator.

Braitham. To inspect, oversee, observe.

Braithlis. Wort.

Bramach. A colt.

Bramaire. ⎱ A noisy fellow.
Bramanach. ⎰

Braman. A crupper.

Bramanta. Unpolished, boorish, sulky.

Bran. Poor, black.

Bran. A raven, rook.

Branar. Fallow ground.

Brancas. A halter.

Brandubhan. A spider.

Branghaire. A corpse left in the open air.

Brann A burning coal or ember.

Brann. A woman.

Brannra. The collar bones.

Brannradh. A trivet.

Brannumh. Chesmen.

Brannumh. A coat of mail.

Brannrach. A pen, fold.

Braoch. The border of a country.

Braoi. Eyebrows.

Araoighille. A crack, flaw.

Braoighille. A heavy shower of rain.

Braonan. An earth nut.

Braoighillam. To crack, crumble.

Braollaid. Raving, dreaming.

Braoilladh. A rattling noise.

Braoilag. A whortle-berry.

Braon. A drop.

Braoilag-nan-con. Bear-berries.

Braonach. Dropping.

Braonam. To drop.

Braos. ⎫
Braoisg. ⎬ A gape, yawn.

Braosach. ⎫
Braoisgeach. ⎬ Gaping.

Bras. Brisk, active, lively, sudden.

Brasailte. A panegyrick.

Brasaire-buird. A sycophant.

Brasargnaidhe. A sophister.

Braschomhrac. Justs, tilts, tournaments.

Braschomnadh. Counterfeiting.

Brasgalladh. A declamation.

Brasgan. Vide Prasgan. The mob.

Brasluidhe. Perjury.

Brasgeul. A romance.

Brat. A cloke, mantle, veil, or covering.

Biathlon. A sheet.

Brat. Judgment.

Brat-urlair. A carpet.

Bratag. A worm, caterpillar, a rag.

Brat-broin. Mortcloth.

Bratham. To betray.

Brath. Treachery, destruction, design, a mafs, a lump.

Biath, pronounced Brach. For ever.

Brathadair. A betrayer.

Brathair. A brother.

Brathair ceile. Brother-in-law.

Braithairal. Brotherly.

Brathairalachd. Brotherliness.

Brathair-bochd. A frier.

Brathcadh. Corruption.

Brathaireog. An aunt by the father.

Breab. A kick.

Breabam. To kick, spurn.

Breaban. A patch.

Bre. A hill, headland.

Breabadair. A weaver, kicker.

Breac. Speckled, spotted, parti-coloured; the small-pox.

Breac-feunain. A freckle.

Breac. A trout, a salmon, a wolf.

Breac-bedi. A loach.

Breacam. To chequer, embroider, to pick a millstone, to carve, to mix.

Breac an t siol. ⎫
Bricein baintigharna. ⎬ A wagtail.

Breachoi. Indifference.

Breacan. A Scotch plaid.

Breacfhoilfigham. To glimmer.

Breacfhollus. Twilight.

Breacag. A little cake.

Breachd. Doubt.

Breachtaire. A graving tool, a graver.

Breachdan. Wheat, a custard, fresh butter.

Breaclion. A drag-net.

Breachdnuighte. Made party-coloured, mixed.

Breacmhuch. A magpye.

[N]   Bread.

Bread. A breach.

Breadh. Fine. Vide Breagh.

Breadhachd. Finery.

Breag. A lie.

Breagach. Falfe.

Breagaire. A liar, diffembler.

Breagnuigham. To belie.

Breagarfidh. Imagination.

Breagh. Fine, dreffed

Breagchrabhadh. Hypocrify.

Breaghaicham. To adorn.

Breaghaidh. An enthufiaft.

Breaghachd. Ornaments.

Breagfaidhachd. Enthufiafm.

Breaghaflach. A dream.

Breagluigham. To forfwear.

Breaghaflaicham. To dream.

Breaghna. The river Boyne.

Breagradh. Chearful.

Breall. A phymofis.

Breallach. That hath a phymofis.

Brean Filthy, ftinking.

Breanan. A dunghill.

Breananam. To ftink.

Breancrann. A certain tree.

Breantas. Filth, ftink, putrefaction.

Breantadh. The fifh Bream.

Breantag. A ftinking flut.

Breas. A prince, potentate.

Breas. A voice, great noife.

Breafam. To reign.

Breafaontaidh. The royal affent

Breafchathair. A throne.

Breas-cholbh. A fceptre.

Breafda. Principal, active, lively.

Breasfnora. A throne.

Breaflang. Deceit.

Breaflann. A palace, a court of juftice.

Breafnion. A royal mandate.

Breafoirchifde. A prince's treafure.

Breafrod. A king's road.

Breath. Judgment, cenfure, confidence.

Breath. Clean, pure.

Breathach. Judicial, critical.

Breathamh. A judge.

Breathas. Folly.

Breathamhnas. Judgment.

Breathnach. A Welfhman

Breathnas. A clafp, bodkin, fkewer, tongue of a buckle.

Breathnuigham. To perceive, judge.

Brec. A wolf, brock, badger.

Breicin. A fprat, fmall trout.

Breichneoras. Sculpture.

Breid. A kerchief, or head attire for women.

Breid-uchd. A ftomacher.

Breidin. A coif or little rag, a web of frize.

Breifne. A man's nail, a hole.

Breifneach. Full of holes.

Breig. A ruftic, boor.

Breignigh. A fiction.

Breig. Falfe, counterfeit.

Breigriochlam To difguife.

Breigfhios. Enthufiafm.

Breim. Breaking wind backwards.

Brein. A ftink.

Breinan-brothach. Great daify.

Breine. More ftinking.

Breis. A tear, a diftilling.

Breifg. Quick, active, brifk.

Breifgthe. Moved, provoked.

Breifam. To break, crack, tear.

Breifim. A war cry.

Brefnion. A writ, mandamus.

Breith. Taking, carrying, bearing, bringing forth.

Breith. Judgment, penance.

Breitheamh. A judge.

Breitheamhnas. Judgment, fentence.

Breithantach. Judicious.

Breithiontoir. A tiller.

Breithir. A word.

Breithireach. Full of words.

Breitireachd. Interpretation.

Breo. Fine.

Breoch. A brim, brink.

Breochloch.

Breochloch. A flint.

Breochual. A bonfire, a funeral pile.

Breochoire. A warming-pan.

Breodhraoithachd. Pyromancy.

Breog. A leveret.

Breogam. To pound, bruise.

Breog. }
Breoghte. } Weak, feeble.

Breogach. A baker.

Breogam. To bake.

Breoillean. Darnel.

Breoghteachd. Illness, sickliness.

Breon. A blur or spot.

Breonam. To blur or spot.

Breothadh. Consumption.

Breothan Wheat.

Breug. A lie.

Breuntas. Vide Breantas.

Breugach. Lying. Vide Breagach.

Breugnaicham. To gainsay.

Breugnaichoir. A gainsayer.

Breugriochd. Disguise.

Breun. Stinking. Vide Brean.

Bri. Anger, wrath; a word, a hill, rising ground.

Bri. Near to, an effort, essence.

Briagh. A mortal wound.

Brian. A word, composition.

Briana. A warrant, an author, composition.

Brianach. Full of fair speeches.

Briar. A prickle, thorn, pin.

Briathar. A word, a verb; victory, conquest.

Briathrachas. Elocution, phraseology.

Briathram. } To affirm, to dictate, to
Briathraigham. } swear to.

Brib A bribe, a small sum of money.

Bribheadaghan. One that affects difficult words.

Brice. A brick.

Brichath Greyish.

Bridne. A freckle.

Bridag. Part of the jaw.

Brideach. A virgin, bride, a dwarf.

Brigh. A hill, price, value; virtue, force, a tomb, a miracle.

Brighide. A hostage.

Brillin. Clitoris.

Brin. A dream, reverie.

Brindealan. A frontlet.

Brindealbhadh. Painting, sculpture, pourtraying.

Brindealbhoir. A painter, carver.

Brinneach. A hag, old woman, mother of children.

Brinnighte. Hagridden.

Briocht. Sorcery, witchcraft; colour, complexion.

Briocht. A wound, art, trade, a beauty.

Briochtaic. An amulet

Briogh. An effort, capacity, essence, elixir.

Brioghach, briogmhor. Efficacious, substantial.

Brioghach. Hilly.

Briollan. A piss-pot, a urinal, a foolish ignorant fellow.

Briollaire. A whoremonger.

Briollog. An illusion.

Briollsgaire. A bully, busybody.

Brion. A fiction, a lie; a drop.

Brionach. A liar.

Brionnach. Flattering, fair.

Briondatham. To counterfeit.

Briongarsacht. } A dream.
Briongloid. }

Briot. Speckled. Chitter-chatter.

Brisgam. To start up.

Brisargnaidhe. Sophister.

Brisgarnach. Crackling.

Brionnal. Flattery.

Brisam. To break.

Brigis. Breeches.

Bristhroisgam. To breakfast.

Brisglorach. That hath small talk.

Brisadh. Breaking, assimilation.

Brisg. Brittle.

Brisgaid.

Brifgaid. Bifcuit.

Briflean. White tanfy.

Brifleach. The derout of an army.

Britheaghlaidh. Kind, gentle.

Brium. An helmet.

Bro. Old, antient.

Bro. A champion, a grindftone.

Broas. Old age.

Brochan. Pottage.

Broc. A badger, grey.

Brod. A goad, prickle, fting, a fpot, blemifh.

Brocach. Speckled in the face.

Brcd. Chaftifement, pride.

Broclach. A warren.

Brodamhuil. Proud.

Brodam. To fpur, ftir up.

Brodghaınamh. Gravel.

Brodh. A ftraw, a ftem.

Brodiafg. Needle-fifh.

Brog }
Brogbhreid. } A fandal, fhoe.

Brogach. Shod.

Broga-na cumhaig. Butterwort.

Brogh. Filthinefs.

Broghach. Filthy.

Brog. Sorrow; a houfe.

Broghadh. Encreafe, profit.

Broghaidhil. Filth, dirt.

Broghaın. Excefs, abufe.

Broghdha. Exceffive, fuperfluous.

Broghdha. Forcibly.

Broghdha. A footman.

Broice, broicne. A mole or freckle.

Broicneach. Freckled.

Broidineall. A rich garb.

Broidinealta. Embroidered.

Broigheal. A cormorant, fea-raven.

Broimeis. Anger, boldnefs.

Broinn. Belly.

Broinnag. A little rag, tatter.

Broin. A height, large company.

Broinndeargan. Robin-Redbreaft.

I

Bronnthach. A girth.

Bronnag. A gudgeon.

Broifgam. To excite, provoke.

Broifnin. A fmall faggot.

Broith. Carnation colour.

Brolofgadh. Talkative.

Brollach. The breaft, bofom.

Brollach. A prologue.

Brollachan. A ragged, naked perfon.

Brollaigh. Boldnefs

Brom. Breaking of wind.

Bromach. A colt.

Bromam. To break wind.

Broman. A boor, ruftick.

Bromanach. Ruftic, rude.

Bromurrudhufach. Bold, confident.

Bron. Mourning, forrow, fafting.

Bron-muilinn. A millftone.

Bron. Perpetual.

Bronach. Sad, forrowful.

Bronadh. Deftruction.

Bronnghabhal. Conception.

Bronnghabham. To conceive.

Bronn. The belly, womb.

Bronn. }
Bronntas. } A gift, favour, track.

Bronnam. To give, beftow.

Bronnfgaole. A flux.

Bronnta. Beftowed.

Brofdughadh. An incentive.

Brofduigham. To excite.

Brofgaladh. Exciting.

Brofgadh. An exhortation.

Brofgalach. Prompt.

Brofna. A faggot.

Brot. Broth.

Broth. A mole, ditch.

Broth. A ftraw, flefh, fire.

Broth-luachra. A rufh.

Brothaire. A cauldron.

Brothairne. Down, fur.

Brothaireargadh. }
Brothigh. } Shambles, butchery.

Brothas. Farrago, brewis.
Brothag. Bosom.
Brothlach. A place to dress meat.
Brothladh. Intent on mischief.
Bru. The womb; a hind.
Bru. A country, a bank.
Bruach. A border, brink, edge.
Bruachan. A little brink, a fawn.
Bruachairachd. Hovering about.
Bruachbhaile. Suburbs.
Bruachda. Magnificent.
Bruachdha. A footman.
Bruaidh. A peasant.
Bruadar. A dream.
Bruadaram. To dream.
Bruchag. A chink, cranny, eyelet.
Bruchd. A belch, ejaculation.
Brucach. Speckled in the face.
Bruchdam. To pour forth, belch.
Bruchdadh. } Pouring forth, going for-
Bruchdal. } ward.
Bruchlas. The fluttering of birds going to rest.
Brudan. A salmon, simmering.
Brudham. To bruise, squeeze.
Brudhadh. A squeezing, pounding.
Brughadhoir. A pestle.
Brudeag. A soliciting.
Brudhaiteach. A threadbare coat.
Brug, brugh. A large house, a village, borough, a little hillock, the residence of fairies.
Brugh. An heap, monument; the belly, a fast.
Brughan. Faggots.
Brudan. A simmering noise.
Brughach. The face of a hill.
Brughte. Bruised.
Bruidhann. Noise of men, strife.
Bruid. Captivity; pointed.
Bruidam. To torture.
Bruidhann. Noise.
Bruidhnach. Noisy.
Brughaidhe. A farmer, burgher.

Bruí. The belly.
Bruide. A brute.
Bruidamhuil. Beastly, brutish.
Bruidamhlachd Brutality.
Bruidhachd. A colony.
Bruidhlionta. Cloyed.
Bruighin. A fairy hill.
Bruighe. A farmer, a farm.
Bruighean. A palace
Brughseach. A womb with young.
Bruimfheur. Switch-grass.
Bruin. A cauldron, belly.
Bruinneach. A nurse, mother.
Bruinneadach. An apron.
Bruinneach. A glutton.
Bruinnin. Knap of cloth.
Bruindeargan. A Robin-Redbreast.
Bruinteach. Great with child.
Bruis. Shivers.
Bruit. Curtains.
Bruite. Vide Brughte.
Bruith. Seethed, boiled.
Bruitham. To boil.
Bruithne. A refiner.
Bruitin. The measles.
Bruithneach. Glowing hot.
Brullsgeantach. Impetuous.
Brum. A broom.
Brun. A firebrand.
Brumaire. A pedant.
Brus. Browse.
Brusam. To browse.
Bruscar. Baggage, broken ware.
Bruth. Hair of the head.
Bruth. Heat in the skin.
Bruth. Any thing red hot.
Bruthchan. Broth, soup.
Bruthneach. Sultry.
Bruthmhaireachd. Fainting through heat.
Bu. Was. Vide Anal. Ata.
Buabhal. Apron, unicorn.
Buachar. Cow-dung.
Buadhbhall. Conquering.

Buadh-

Buadhbhalachan. A trumpeter.
Buac. Buck-yarn, cloth, bleaching.
Buac. Brow of a hill, crown of a vault, a cap.
Buachach. Fine, beauish.
Buacachan. A bleecher.
Buachail. A cow-herd, shepherd.
Buachailleach. Pastoral.
Buacais. Wick of a candle.
Buadh. Food.
Buaidh. } Victory, virtue, attri-
Buaidh-laraich. } bute.
Buadhach. Victorious, having virtues.
Buadhal. Triumphant.
Buadharg. A victorious champion.
Buadhach. Tribute.
Buadhghallan. Ragweed.
Buadhaire. A conqueror.
Buadhartha. Grieved, vexed.
Buadhghuth. Clamorous, shouting
Buadhas. Victory, triumph.
Buadhmhor. Sway, victorious.
Buac. Settlement.
Buaibhthe. Threatening.
Buaf. A toad.
Buafadh. Poisoned, menacing.
Buafach. Virulent.
Buafare. A viper.
Buafathair. An adder.
Buag. A spigot, plug.
Buagaire. A faucet.
Buagairam. To tap.
Buaice. A wave.
Buaiceach. Giddy.
Buaicin. A veil, lappet.
Buaicinam. To blindfold.
Buaicis. A small wick.
Buaidham. To conquer, overcome.
Buaidhirt. Tumult.
Buairthe. A conqueror.
Buaidhradh. Temptation, disturbance.
Buaidhram. To vex, disturb, tempt.
Buaidhradair. Disturber, tempter.
Buaifeach. Angry, fretting

Buaific. An antidote.
Buail. A step, degree.
Buaileach. An oxstall.
Buailidh. Dairy-house.
Buailam. To strike, afflict.
Buailtair. A thresher.
Buailteach. That striketh, liable.
Buailtain. A flail.
Buaillite. Water-lily.
Buailt. A locker, a niche.
Buailteachan. A flying camp.
Buailte Beaten, threshed.
Buainam. To cut, reap.
Buain. Cutting, reaping.
Buain. Equality.
Buain. Deprivation.
Buaine. More durable.
Buaine. Perpetuity.
Buaintoir. A reaper, mower.
Bual. Physick; water.
Bualadh. Remedy, cure.
Bualadh. Threshing, beating.
Bual a chrag. Balm-cricket.
Bualainle. A sea-lark.
Bualchrannach. A float, raft.
Bualchomhla. A sluice.
Buallghas. A millpond.
Buallachd. A drove of cows.
Bualtrach. Cow-dung.
Buan. Lasting, durable.
Buan. Good, harmonious.
Buan. A nurse.
Buana. } A hewer, reaper.
Buanidh. }
Buan-mharthanach. Everlasting.
Buanna. A billetted soldier.
Buannachd. Quartering of soldiers.
Buanas. Perpetuity.
Buanigham. To last.
Bunchuimhne. Chronicle.
Buannachd. Profit, gain.
Buansheasam. To persevere.
Buar. Oxen.

Buarach.

Buarach. A fetter for cows in time of milking.

Buas. The belly.

Buasarea. The diaphragm.

Buas. A breach, rout.

Buas. A trade, art.

Buban. A coxcomb.

Buc. Cover of a book, bulk.

Bucamhuil. Bulky.

Bucla. A buckle.

Buclaigham. To buckle.

Budh. The world.

Budh A breach, rout

Bugha. Fear; a leek.

Bugan. An unlaid egg.

Bugsa. Box-tree, a box.

Buich. A breach.

Buic. Stags, goats.

Buicead. A mouthful.

Buicaid. A bucket, knob.

Buicain. A pimple.

Buichiu. A young buck.

Buidal. A bottle, anchor.

Buidh. Thanks.

Buidin. A prickle.

Buidhe. Yellow.

Buidhe nan ningean. Spurge.

Buidheach. Thankful.

Buidhach. The jaundice.

Buidhachas. Thanks.

Buidhead. Yellowness.

Buidhag-bhuachaire. A yellow-hammer.

Buidheann. A troop, company.

Buidheacan. Yolk of an egg.

Buig-bhuinne. ⎫
Buigneach. ⎬ Bullrushes.

Buige. Softer.

Buil. Fruits, effects.

Buile. Vide Baoil.

Builigham. To improve.

Buille. A blow.

Builleach. That giveth blows.

Builin. A loaf.

Builinach. A baker.

Builg. Bellows.

Builgain. A bubble, blister, pimple, vesicle.

Builg. A distemper amongst cattle.

Builg. Seeds of herbs.

Builginach. Full of husks, blisters.

Builgam. To swell, blister.

Builgas. A blister.

Builgeasach. Spotted.

Buillsgein. Center, middle.

Buime. A nurse, mother.

Buinne. A tap, spout, ulcer.

Buinne. ⎫
Buinneog. ⎬ A twig, sprout, hem.

Buinneach. A flux, lax.

Buinnean-leana. A bittern.

Buinneamh. Effusion.

Buinean. Feminine.

Buinnire. A footman.

Buinteach. One troubled with a flux.

Buinam. To touch, meddle, to belong, to take.

Buintin. Touching, belonging.

Buirbain. A cancer.

Buirbe. Fierceness, more fierce.

Buireadh. Roaring, bellowing.

Buireadh. Gore, pus.

Buiream. To roar, bellow.

Buireadhach. Warlike.

Bnirfeach. An outcry, bellowing.

Buirgeisach. A burgess.

Buirling. A sort or boat.

Buiscin. A thigh, haunch, thigh armour.

Buiste. A pouch, scrip.

Buite. A firebrand.

Buitealach. Great fire.

Buitse. An icicle.

Buitealadh. Fierce.

Buitfach. A witch.

Buitsachas. Witchcraft.

Bul. Manner, fashion.

Bulistair. A bullace, sloe.

I

Bulla. A bowl, ball.

Bulos. A prune.

Bullach. The fish called Connor.

Bunbhean. A woman of discreet years.

Bun. Keeping, taking care of.

Bun. Stump, root, bottom, stock.

Bunabhas. An element.

Bunach. Tare of flax.

Bunadh. Origin, stock.

Bunadhas. ⎫ Foundation, radix, authority,
Bunachar. ⎬ etymology.

Bunudhasach. Authentic.

Bunailte, bunailtach. Steady, fixed, authentic.

Bunait. A foundation.

Bunaitam. To possess, inherit.

Buntata. Potatoes.

Buncios. Chief rent.

Bunchiall. A moral.

Bundunach. Ungainly.

Bunchiosaiche. A pensioner.

Bundun. The fundament, blunder.

Bunaithigham. To found, establish.

Bunn. Work.

Bunfhath. Absolute cause.

Bunnluchd. Aborigines.

Bunmhais. Buttock.

Bunnos. An old custom.

Bunnseacha. Rods, osiers.

Buntop. Sudden, hasty.

Bunntais. Perquisites.

Bunnan. A bittern.

Bhur. Vide Bhar. Your.

Bur. ⎫
buridh. ⎬ A clown, boor, chuff.

Bur. A swelling, anger.

Burach. Exploits, a file of soldiers.

Buralach. Sulky, crying.

Burach. A swelling, fore.

Buraim. To fret, make fore.

Buramaid. Wormwood.

Burdan. A gibe, a sing-song.

Burris. Caterpillar.

Burg. A village.

Buirdaisach. ⎫
Burgaire. ⎬ A burgess, citizen.

Buricaidach. A big fellow.

Burr. Great.

Burne. Water.

Bus. Mouth, snout, a kiss.

Busach. Sulky, having a snout.

Busgam. To dress; to stop, hinder.

Bus-dubh. Name of a dog.

Busgadh. Coiffure, head-dress.

Busiall. Muzzle.

Butis. A boot.

Buth. A shop, tent.

Buta. A short ridge, a tun, boot.

Buthal. A pot-hook.

Buthal raimh. Fulcrum of an oar.

C.

THE third letter of the alphabet, called Coll, i. e. Hazel; for the Irish named their letters after natural objects and trees, when the names began with suitable initials. The letters are called Feadha, i. e. Wood. The C is pronounced hard, as K in English. Vide Analysis.

Ca.

Ca. A houfe.

Ca'as. Whence?

Caab. Concord in finging.

Cab. The mouth, a head, a gap.

Caba. Cap, covering of the head.

Cabach. Toothlefs, full of gaps.

Cabach. Babbling, talkative; a hoftage.

Cabag. A cheefe.

Cabag. A toothlefs woman.

Cabaga. A drab, a ftrumpet.

Cabaile. A fleet, navy.

Cabaire. A babbler.

Cabaifachd. } Prating, babbling.
Cabaireachd. }

Caban. A capon; tent, booth.

Cabadh. Breaking of land.

Cabam. To indent, break land, to catch.

Cabhag. A great hurry, a jack-daw.

Cabhagach. Sudden, hafty.

Cachanach. Day-break.

Cabhlach. A fleet.

Caban. A cottager.

Cabar. A joint, confederacy.

Cabar. A lath, a deer's horn, antler.

Cabrach. Branching.

Cabartha. United.

Cabhair. Help, aid.

Cabhar. Any old bird.

Cabhairam. To help, affift, relieve.

Cabharthach. Helpful, affifting.

Cabafdah. A fort of curb.

Cabhan. A field, plain.

Cabhanfhail. Prop or beam of a houfe.

Cabhara. Vide Cathbhar.

Cabhfair. A caufeway, pavement.

Cabfanta. Dry, fnug.

Cabhfairaiche. A paver.

Cabal. A cable.

Cabluighe. Ship tackle.

Cablacan. A mariner.

Cablachda. Naval.

Cabog. A prater.

Cabig. A pillory.

Cabhra. Auxiliary.

Cabhrach. An auxiliary.

Cabraim. To join, unite, couple.

Cac. Human excrement.

Cacam. To go to ftool.

Cacach. Dirty, filthy.

Caca. A cake.

Cach. The reft.

Cacadh. A yawl.

Cacaim. To idle.

Cachain. They fung.

Cachan. Profit, ufe.

Cachla. A gate.

Cachnam. To effect, finifh.

Cacradh. Cacophony.

Cacht. A maid fervant, the world.

Cacht. Confinement; generally.

Cacht. A faft, fafting.

Cacht. A fhout.

Cachta. Hunger.

Cachtamhuil. Servile.

Cad. Vide Coid.

Cad. High

Cad. A friend, holy.

Cadach. Friendfhip.

Cadachas. Atonement.

Cadad. An eclipfe.

Cadaim. To fall, to chance.

Cadal. Delay, fleep.

Cadalam. To fleep, delay.

Cadall. A battle.

Cadaltach. Sleepy.

Cadam. The fork of the hair.

Cadam. Ruin.

Cadamach. Ruinous.

Cadan, cadas. Cotton, a pledget.

Cadarus. Contention.

Cadarafaim. To argue.

Cadarus. Whither? which way?

Cadhal. A bafon; hide, fkin.

Cadhal. Fair, beautiful.

Cadhal. Colewort, rail.

Cadhan. A wild goofe, barnacle.

Cadhas. }
Cadas. } Friendship, honour.

Cadhafach. Refpectful, honourable.

Cadhla. A goat.

Cadhla. Fat of the guts.

Cadhlachal. A goat-herd.

Cadhlaidh. A joker.

Cad-luibh. Cudwort.

Cadhmus. Haughtinefs.

Cadhnamha. Equal, alike.

Cado. A blanket.

Cadnaice. Poffeffion.

Cadnaicam. To poffefs.

Cadranta. Stubborn, obftinate.

Cadran. Contention.

Cae. A feaft, banquet.

Cae. A hedge.

Caec. Blind.

Caemh. A feaft.

Caemh. Fine, handfome, pleafant.

Cag. Vide Cabhag.

Cafradh. Vide Cathbrith.

Caghaidh. Lawful, juft.

Cagaidh. Strangenefs.

Cagailt. Frugality.

Cagal. The herb cockle.

Cagalam. To fpare.

Cagallach. Frugal.

Cagar, cagairt. A whifper, whifpering.

Cagaram. To whifper.

Cagladh. Sparing, frugal.

Cagnam. To chew.

Cai. A way, road.

Cai. A houfe.

Cai. The cuckow's bird.

Caibhais. Giggling, laughing.

Caibhdean. A multitude, a harlot.

Caibhne. Friendfhip.

Caibal. A chapel, burying-place.

Caibidil. A chapter.

Caibne. The mouth.

Caibinnachd. Prating.

Caicmhe. A neck-ornament.

Caid. A rock, fummit.

Caid. A part, fhare.

Caidhce. Fine, calm.

Caideal. A pump.

Caideacha. A fpot, a ftain.

Caidh. Chafte.

Caidh. Order, manner.

Caidh. Vide Cath.

Caidhe. Dirt, a blemifh.

Caidheach. Polluted.

Caidheachd. Chaftity.

Caidheamhuil. Decent.

Caidhean. Alone, folitary.

Caidhean. A turtle-dove.

Caidhean. The leader of a flock of goats.

Caidhidhe. Covered with a hide.

Caidhidhe. The cover of a houfe.

Caidhni. A virgin.

Caidiol. A fun-dial.

Caidhle. Finifhing.

Caidhlighte. Finifhed.

Caidhliche. Thick fur.

Caidreadh. Friendfhip, cherifhing; commerce.

Caidreach. }
Caidreamhach. } Converfant, fond.

Caidreadh. Difcourfe, converfation.

Caidram. To converfe, to fondle.

Caigalam. To lay up, to cover the fire.

Caigne, caignean. A fan to winnow.

Caigionnam. To link.

Cail. Condition, conftitution, voice.

Cail. A fpear, fhield.

Cail. A ward, defire, longing.

Cail. An appearance, or look.

Cail. An affembly, commendation.

Cail. Difpofition; behind.

Cailbhe. A mouth, orifice.

Cailbheach. Wide-mouthed.

Cailbheacht. Yawning.

Cailbhearb. A cow-herd.

Cailc. Shield, buckler.

Cailc. Chalk, lime.

Cailceata.

Cailceata. Hard.

Cailcamhuil. Chalky.

Cailcin. A little shield.

Cailcin. A disorder of the eyes.

Caile. A young girl, a quean.

Caile-bhalaich. A cot-quean.

Caile. A strumpet, harlot.

Caileonta. ⎞
Caileamhuil. ⎠ Girlish.

Caileachdar. Passion of the mind.

Caileach. Vide Caolach.

Caileachd. Nature.

Caileas. Lethargy.

Cailegin. Something.

Cailaing. A seed, husk.

Cailainag. Seedy, husky.

Cailg. A sting, resentment.

Cailgeamhuil. Pungent.

Cailgam. To stick, to prick.

Cailicin. An old woman.

Cailidhir. Snot, phlegm.

Cailidheachd. Qualification, quality, genius.

Cailigheach. A humourist.

Cailis. A chalice.

Cailindha. Calends.

Cailin. A little girl.

Caill. A loss, a trick.

Caill. To name.

Caillam. To lose.

Caillchula. Old wives tales.

Caille. A veil or cowl.

Cailleach. An old woman, a nun.

Cailleachag-cheanndubh. A titmouse.

Cailleach. A coward.

Cailleach-chosach. A milliped.

Cailleachas. Dotage.

Cailleach-oiche. An owl.

Cailleadh. Emasculation.

Cailleasg. A horse or mare.

Cailleamhain. Loss, damage.

Cailleamhnach. Defective.

Cailleam. To castrate.

Cailliog. A loss.

Cailtean, cailteanach. An eunuch.

Cailtearnach. A shrubby place.

Cailmhion. A light helmet.

Cailpig. A mug, or jug.

Caillte. Lost.

Cailtin. Hazle.

Caime. ⎞
Caimad. ⎠ Crookedness.

Caim. A fault.

Caimeacan. Humpbacked.

Caimein. A mote.

Caimean. Reproved, blemished.

Caimhdean. A multitude.

Caimheach. A protector.

Caimis. A shirt.

Caimse. A shift.

Caimleir. A bent stick used by butchers.

Caimneach. Chaste.

Caimpear. A champion.

Caimsiog. Falsehood.

Cain. Chaste; beloved.

Cain. Rent, tribute, a fine.

Caineach. A satire, dispraise.

Cainam. To satirise, dispraise.

Caindeal. A candle.

Caindigheacht. A quantity.

Caineog. A mote; a farthing.

Caineog. Barley and oats.

Caineog. Female privity.

Cainficam. To fine, amerce.

Caingeal. A hurdle, a reason.

Caingean. A rule, cause.

Caingean. A supplication, petition.

Caingean. A compact, covenant.

Caingnam. To argue, plead.

Cainam. To dispraise.

Cainneal. A channel, cinnamon.

Cainneabhar. Dirt, filth.

Cainseadh. Lavishment.

Cainseoir. A scolder.

Cainseoiracht. Scolding.

Cainsi. The face, countenance.

Caint. Speech

Cainteach.

Cainteach. Talkative, malicious.

Cainteachd. Pronunciation.

Cainteal. A prefs, a lump.

Cainteoir. A babbler.

Caintic. A canticle, fong.

Cair.　　　⎫
Cairain.　⎬ The gum, a grin.
　　　　　⎭

Cair. An image.

Cairb. A plank; a chariot.

Cairban. A fail-fifh.

Cairb. A fufee; a fhip.

Cairbh. A carcafe.

Cairbhecan. A fhip-boy.

Cairbham. To man a fleet; to fhake, to quiver.

Cairbhin. A little fhip.

Cairam. To mend; fend away, lay up.

Cairbhin. The gums.

Cairbineach. A toothlefs perfon.

Cairbne. A charioteer.

Cairc. Hair, furr.

Cairche. Mufick.

Cairceach. Hairy; eager.

Caircheas. A twift.

Caircheas. A little veffel.

Caircheafam. To twift.

Cairde. A bofom friend.

Cairde. Friendfhip; delay, refpite.

Cairde-gaoil. Kinsfolk.

Cairdeas. Friendfhip, a fponfor.

Cairdeamhuil.　⎫
Cairdeach.　　 ⎬ Friendly.
　　　　　　　⎭

Cairdamhlachd. Friendlinefs.

Cairdhearg. A blufh.

Caireachan. A big-mouthed perfon.

Caireamhan. A fhoemaker.

Caireog. A prating wench.

Cairrfhiadh. A hart, ftag.

Cairghios. Lent.

Cairgham. To abftain.

Cairgain. An herb.

Cairam. To endear.

Cairin. A darling.

Cairin. Lean meat.

Cairine. Legs.

Cairle. Tumbled, toffed.

Cairleam.　　　　 ⎫
Cairleacanam.　　⎬ To beat, tofs about.
　　　　　　　　⎭

Cairmeal. Wild peafe.

Cairneach. A prieft; an ofprey; ftoney.

Cairpe. Accurfed.

Cairigham. To mend.

Cairreal. Noife.

Carraic. A rock.

Carbthoir. A charioteer.

Cairrfe. A club.

Cairreir. A carrier.

Cairt. Bark, rind, a cart, card, chart.

Cairt. A rock, ftone.

Cairtcheap. A cart-wheel.

Cairteog. A tumbril.

Cairteal. Quarters, lodging, a challenge.

Carteoir. A carter, waggoner.

Cairthe. A chariot.

Cairtlan. A cartulary.

Caife. Cheefe.

Cais. Regard, love, efteem.

Cais. Vide Cuis.

Cais. An eye; rent, hafte.

Cais. Spruce, trim.

Caifan. Hoarfenefs, phlegm.

Caifchiabh. A curl.

Caifchiabhach. Curled.

Caffe. A ftream, a cake, quicknefs.

Caife. A wrinkle, fold, paffion.

Caife. A mufhroom.

Caife. Difcord.

Caifan. Hoarfenefs.

Caifeach. Wrinkled.

Cais-fhion. White-footed, name of a cow.

Caifeal. A bulwark, wall.

Caifad. Steepnefs, fuddenefs.

Caifeog. The ftem of a weed.

Caifeamhan. A fhoemaker.

Caifearbhan. Dandelion.

Caifg. Eafter.

Caifgam.

Caisgam. To stop.
Caisiol. A stone building.
Caisleach-spuinc. Touchwood.
Caislleachta. Polished, smoothed.
Caislithe. Wrinkled, folded.
Caislean. A castle, garrison.
Caisleoir. A projector.
Caisli. Polished.
Caismeachd. Alarm, march tune.
Caismeart. Heat of battle, armour, a band
  of men for fight.
Caissiolachd. Battlements.
Caismiortach. An armed man.
Caisreag. A wrinkle.
Caisreabhachd. Legerdemain.
Caisdeal. A castle.
Cait. A sort or kind.
Caisriminidhe. A wrinkle.
C'ait. Where? for cia ait.
C'ait as. Whence?
Caiteach, caiteog. A basket.
Caiteach. Chaff.
Caiteach. Expensive, prodigal.
Caiteach. A ship's main-sheet.
Caiteachas. Prodigality.
Caiteog. A butter-pot, butter.
Caith. Chaff, a blemish.
Caith. Chaste, mild.
Caitheach. } A spendthrift.
Caithmhach. }
Caitheadh. Spending.
Caithte. Spent, old.
Caithfeach. Nigh to.
Caitham. To winnow.
Caithmham. To consume, shoot, wear.
Caithbheartach. A sorner.
Caithfidh. It behoves, becomes.
Caithear. } Oportet.
Caithfighear. }
Caithlioch. Chaff, husks.
Caithamh. Consuming.
Caithmhileadh. A soldier.
Caithleam. We must.
Caithreim. Triumph, famous.

Caithreamadh. Information.
Caithriodhnach. A cave.
Caithris. Watching.
Caitin. Shagg, nap of cloth.
Caitin. Blossom of osier.
Caitin. A little cat.
Caitineach. Curled.
Caitineach. A cloth dresser.
Caitit. A pin, bodkin.
Caitsloan. Chaff.
Caitte. How?
Caitte. Necessary.
Caittiughadh. Invalid.
Cal. Colewort, kail; a joke.
Cal-colag. Cauliflower.
Cal. Sleep, slumber.
Cal-cearslach. Cabbage.
Cal. To keep safe.
Cala. Hard; frugal, thrifty.
Cala. } A port, harbour, ferry.
Caladh. }
Calam. To enter port.
Calain. A Couch.
Calaire. A cryer.
Calaireachd. Burying, interring.
Calaim. To sleep.
Calaois. A cheat.
Calaoiseach. A juggler.
Calb. The head.
Calbh. Hardiness.
Calbh. Bald.
Calbhachd. Baldness.
Calcare. To drive, caulk.
Calchearcain. Shuttlecock.
Calpa. Calf of the leg.
Calbhthas. A buskin.
Calbhualadh. A hot battle.
Calc. Chalk.
Calcam. To drive with a hammer, to caulk.
Calcam. } To harden.
Calcaigham. }
Calcaighte. Hardened.
Calcughadh. Obduracy.

Caldach. Mifchief; fharp, pointed.

Calg. A fword, a prickle, fting, hair.

Calgach. Sharp, prickly.

Calghaois. A cheat.

Calgaire. A wheedler.

Calgbhruid. Falfe imprifonment.

Calis. chalice.

Calgbhruidhan. Butcher's broom.

Call. A church, veil, hood.

Call. Lofs.

Callach. A bat, a boar.

Calldachd. Loffes.

Callaidhe. A partner.

Callaid. A cap.

Callaidh. Active, nimble.

Calla. Tame.

Callaind. Kalends.

Callaicham. To tame.

Callaire. A crier.

Callaireachd. Crying.

Callan. Noife, fhouting.

Callanach. Clamorous.

Callois. Buffoonery.

Callagam. To flatter.

Calloid. A funeral cry, elegy.

Caltag. Black guillemot.

Calltarnach. A trufs of weeds.

Calma. Strong.

Calman. A pigeon.

Calmachd. }
Calmadas. } Courage, ftrength.

Cam. A quarrel, duel.

Cam. Crooked.

Cam. Deceit.

Cama. Brave.

Camam. To bend, to make wry.

Camaillte. Rubbed.

Camalta. Demure.

Camchofach. Bow-legged.

Camceachdta. The north pole.

C'a mead. How much?

Camglas. A redfhank.

Camach. Power.

Camal. A camel.

Caman. A hurling-club.

Camanachd. Game of hurling.

Camhaoir. Break of day.

Camdhan. Iambick.

Camaran. An ideot.

Camlurgin. Club-foot.

Camluirginach. Club-footed.

Camhnaidh. Reft, dwelling, building.

Camhnaidhachd. Settlement.

Cam-mhuigarlach. Club-footed.

Cam-mhuinal. The bird wryneck.

Camog. A fmall bay, a clafp.

Camog. A curl, the temples.

Camogach. Crooked, curled.

Camoigin. A curled-headed child.

Campa. A camp.

Campuigham. To encamp.

Campthuaim. Entrenchment.

Campur. Champion.

Campar. Anger, grief.

Camparach. Vexing, grievous.

Camrath. A gutter, fewer, jakes.

Camfhuileach. Squint-eyed.

Cramfhronach. Crook-nofed.

Camus. A bay, regio perineum.

Can. Whilft, when.

Can, can as. From whence?

Can. A lake.

Cana. A whelp, pup, a moth.

Canach. Standing water, cotton, cat's tail, mofs-crops, deceit.

Canach. A tribute; bombaft, a porpoife.

Canachd. Taxing.

Canaen. The collector of a tax.

Canaigh. Dirt.

Canam. To fing.

Cangaruicham. To fret, vex, canker.

Cantin. Speaking, finging.

Canaighte. Sung.

Canaib. Hemp.

Canal. A canal, conduit.

Canamhuin. A language.

Canbhas.

Canbhas. Canvas, failcloth.

Canmhuin. Pronunciation, accent.

Cann. A refervoir.

Cannoin. Muttering.

Cann. A veffel, full moon.

Canna. Moths.

Cannran. Contention, grumbling.

Canna. A cann.

Cannach. Sweet-willow, myrtle.

Canoin. A rule, canon.

Canaranam. To grumble.

Cannta. A lake, puddle.

Cantach. Dirty.

Canntic. A fong, canticle.

Cantaighoir. Singer.

Cantail. Voting for, finging, auction.

Cantaireachd. Singing by note.

Cantalam. To fell by auction.

Cantach. Dirty, muddy.

Cantaoir. A prefs.

Cante. The quince-tree.

Cantlamh. } Strife.
Cantol.

Cantol. Grief.

Canuichte. Mulcted.

Canur. Cotton.

Caob. A clod.

Caobhan. A prifon.

Caobh. A bough, a branch.

Caoch. Blind.

Caoch nan cearc. Henbane.

Caochag. A nut without a kernel.

Caocham. To blind.

Caocidis. A fortnight.

Caochan. The fundament, a mole.

Gaochan. An eddy of air, or a ftream or rill; whifgy in the firft procefs of diftillation.

Caochog. Mufhroom, puff-ball.

Caochag. A turned fhell.

Caochag. Blindman's-buff.

Caochlan. A fwift rill.

Caochlaigham. To change.

Caochladh. A change.

Caochlaidach. Changeable, variable.

Caod Colum-cille, caod. St. John's wort.

Caodam. To come.

Caoda. How?

Caodh. A tear.

Caodh. Good order, condition.

Caoidham. To weep.

Caodhamhlachd. Competency.

Caoidh. Lamentation, a tear.

Caodhan. A perfon in good condition.

Caogam. To wink.

Caogadh. Winking.

Caogad. Fifty.

Caogado. Fiftieth.

Caoi. A cuckow, ways and means.

Caoiche, caoichad. Blindnefs.

Caoil. The waift.

Caoile. Smallnefs.

Caoille. Land.

Caoimh. } Gentle, mild, beloved.
Caoimhal.

Caoimheach. A bedfellow.

Caoimheachas. Society.

Caoimheachan. An entertainer.

Caoimhnal. Kindly.

Caomhfgiath. A buckler, fhield.

Caoimhnalachd. Kindnefs.

Caoimhtheacht. Protection, a county.

Caoimhnas. Kindnefs.

Caoimin. The herb eye-bright.

Caoimin. The murrain.

Caoiminach. A common for cattle.

Caoin. Delightful, pleafing.

Caoin. Right fide.

Caoin. Mild-tempered, dry.

Caoineadh. Irifh lamentation.

Caoineachas. Peace.

Caoineach. Stubbles, mofs.

Caoinuigham. To dry.

Caoineachan. A polifher of ftone.

Caoinam. To lament, cry.

Caoinfhuarach. Indifferent.

Caoinafgar. A garrifon.

Caointeach.

Caointeach. Sad, forrowful.
Caoirbheirthach. Bearing berries.
Caoirin. A little berry, a little sheep.
Caoirin-leana. Great wild valerian.
Caoile. A club.
Caoirleachd. Tossing with clubs.
Caoirlam. To beat with clubs.
Caois. A furrow, a young pig.
Caoileachan. A swine-herd.
Caol. Slender, small.
Caol. A calling an assembly.
Caol an duirne. The wrift.
Caolach. The herb fairy-flax.
Caolach. A cock.
Caolach-dubh. The black cock.
Caolach-fraoich. Heathcock.
Caolach-gaoith. A weather-cock.
Caolach-fraincach   Turkey-cock.
Caolach-uifge. A water-wheel, a bird called waterin.
Caolach-aifrionn. Bell to prayers.
Caolach-mios. Purging-flax.
Caolam. To leffen.
Caolan. Small gut.
Caolfail. Nettles, the herb heiriff.
Caolfhairge. A ftrait.
Caolghlorach. Shrill.
Caolas. A ftrait, frith.
Caolmhaor. An apparitor.
Caolmhiofachan. Purging-flax.
Caomh   Gentle, mild, little
Caomh. A feaft, running together.
Caomhadh. Refemblance.
Caomha. Skill, knowledge, nobility.
Caomhalach. Kindly.
Caomhaigh. A man expert at arms.
Caomham. To protect, fpare.
Caomhan. A noble perfon.
Caomhantadh. Protected.
Caomharrach. Private, fecret.
Caomhchlodh. Exchange of lands.
Caomhchladhach. One changing abode often.

Caomhdha. Poetry, verfification.
Caomhloife. A pleafant blaze of the fire.
Caomhnadh. Protection, a friend.
Caomhna. Nourifhment.
Caomhnach. A friend, feeder.
Caomhnadh. Frugality.
Caomhnam. To fpare, fave, referve.
Caomhnaidhe. A bofom friend.
Caomhnafgar. Defence.
Caomhantach. Saving, frugal.
Caomhfhrath. A pleafant village.
Caomhfaidhoir. A rehearfer.
Caomhtha. Society.
Caomthach. An affociate, chum.
Caomhtheachd. Company.
Caon. A refemblance.
Caonam. To refemble, to hide.
Caonar. Cotton.
Caonaran. A folitary perfon.
Caonnag. A neft of wild bees, a fkirmifh.
Caonnagach. Riotous.
Caonbhuidhe. Gratitude.
Caondualach. A carver.
Caondubhrachd. Devotion.
Caonach. Mofs.
Caonta. Private.
Caor. A berry, a candle.
Caor. A firebrand, a thunderbolt.
Caora. Bunches of berries.
Caora-bad-minn. Stone-bramble.
Caoradh. A fheep.
Caorachd. Sheep.
Caorbhearthach. Bacciferous.
Caoran. A dry clod.
Caorgheal. Red hot.
Caorlann. A fheepfold.
Caor-talmhain. Earth nuts.
Caor-teintidh. A thunderbolt.
Caor-dromain. Elder-berries.
Caor-theine. A firebrand.
Caothruadh. Mildew.
Caorthuin. Quicklime.
Caorrann. Service or mountain afh.

6   Cap.

Cap. A cart, tumbrel.

Cap. Cup, an old person.

Capa. A cap.

Capull. A horse or mare.

Capull-coille. The mountain cock, Caper-cailly.

Capam. To renounce.

Capat. The head.

Capflaith. Commander in chief.

Car. Brittle, smart; a twist, bending.

Car-neamhuin. A string of pearls.

Car. Care, the jaw, a trick, movement.

Car. A bar in music, a part.

Car. } A friend, nigh to.
Cara.

Carach. Meandring, deceitful, terrible.

Caradach. Befriended.

Carachdich. Wrestling.

Caradam. To befriend.

Carach-ullamh. An upper garment.

Caradas. Friendship, alliance.

Carac. Faithful.

Caraid. A friend.

Caraidd. Twain, a defence.

Carachadh-ceille Infanity.

Caraidhe A wrestler.

Caraigham. To move.

Caraingal. A guardian-angel.

Caraidheachd. Debate, dispute.

Caraidham. To wrestle.

Carachdach. Athletick.

Carachdidh. Wrestling.

Caradh. Mending, usage.

Caram. To love, to mend.

Caraisteacb. A carrier.

Caran. Crown of the head.

Carantach. Kind.

Caraois. Lent.

Caras A first-rate ship.

Carb. A basket.

Carb. A chariot, a ship.

Carb. A plank.

Carbad. A chariot, coach, litter, bier.

Carbad. A jaw.

Carbadoir. A charioteer, driver.

Carbal. Roof of the mouth.

Carban. An unlucky body.

Carbh. A ship.

Carbhan. A little ship.

Carbanach. Master of a ship.

Carbhanach-uisge. A carp.

Carbhodach. A sailor, clown.

Carbhus. Intemperance.

Carcar. A prison, a coffer.

Carchaillam. To destroy.

Card. Sending, a card to comb wool.

Cardaigh. Flesh.

Cardais. To set or lay.

Cardam. To send, to comb.

Carfhocal. Antiphrasis.

Carghus. Lent.

Carinuigham. To separate things mixed.

Carla. A wool-card.

Carlach. A cart-load.

Carlachan. A wool-carder.

Carlag. Floccus.

Carlaire. A carder.

Carlamh. Excellent.

Carmhogal. A carbuncle.

Carn. A province, a heap of stones, a sledge.

Carnan. A little carn.

Carnan-caochain. A molehill.

Carnan-aolaich. Dunghill.

Carn-cuimhne. A monument.

Carn. } Flesh.
Carna.

Carna. A booty, prey.

Carnaid. Red, carnet.

Carnach. A heathenish priest.

Carnadh. Heaping, a pile, riddance.

Carnam. To heap, pile, to rid.

Carnal. A mote of stones.

Carfhuilach. Having rolling eyes.

Carnfadadh.

Carnfadadh. Hoarfe.

Carnta. Piled up.

Carpat. Corrupted.

Caroid. Penitent.

Carr. A cart, dray, waggon.

Carr. A fpear.

Carra. A fcabby head.

Carra-meilghe. Wild liquorice, wood-peafe.

Carra. Bran.

Carrach. Scabbed, ftoney.

Carracan. A model.

Carrthadh. An erect ftone, a pillar.

Carraid. Diftrefs.

Carraidach. Diftreffed.

Carraig. A rock.

Carraidhin. The thick part of butter-milk.

Carrfhiodh. A knot in timber.

Carrfhiadh. A hart.

Carran. A weed, a fickle, fillabub.

Carran-creige. A conger, a prawn.

Carridh. Seeking.

Carrudhe. A fcab.

Car feal. For a while.

Carruigag. A fort of pancake.

Carfan. Hoarfenefs.

Carfanacb. Hoarfe.

Carfughadh. Punifhment.

Cart. A quart. Vide Cairt. Bark.

Cirtam. To cleanfe, purge, tan.

Carthanach. Charitable.

Carthan, carthanachd. Charity, friend-fhip.

Cartach. Of bark, a cart-load.

Cartacha. Deeds, charters.

Cartoit. Devout.

Caltal. Mint.

Cart-iuil. A mariner's compafs.

Cas. The plague, concern, fear, pity, dif-ficulty.

Cas. A foot, hair of the head, a cafe.

Cas. Money, a fhaft, handle.

Cas. Hafty, wreathed, fteep, paffionate.

Cafag. A coat.

Cafach. An afcent.

Cafachdaich } Coughing, cough.
Cafachdas.

Cafachdaighe. The herb coltsfoot.

Cafan. A path.

Cafmhor. Difficult, arduous.

Cafam. To bend, wreathe, to turn upon, to be angry, to twift.

Cafadh. Twifting, wreathing, gnafhing.

Cafaid. An accufation, complaint.

Cafaidam. To accufe, complain.

Cafaidach. Apt to complain.

Cafar. A little hammer, a path.

Cafbaladh. Obvious.

Cafbanach. Side by fide, parallel.

Caf-choifgach. Anti-peftilential.

Cafg. Stopping, a ftop.

Cafgchuing. Antafthmatick.

Cafgthuitamas. Antipopleàic.

Caifg. Eafter.

Cafair. A glimmering light from old tim-ber in the dark ; it is called teine ghealain.

Cafair. A thorn, buckle, clafp.

Cafair. A fhower, hail.

Cafair, cafarach. Slaughter, carnage.

Cafceim. A ftep, pace.

Cafaoid. Vide Cafaid.

Cafaidaiche. Complainant.

Caifain-uchd. A bit cut off a fheep from the lip along the belly to the tail, three inches broad.

Cafarmanach. Free.

Cafarnach. Lightning.

Cafbheart. Shoes and ftockings, leg ar-mour.

Cafbhairneach. A limpet, a cunner.

Cafcar. A cup.

Cas-cuirn. Draught-tree.

Cafda. Twifted, wreathed.

Cafdlaoidh.

Casdlaoidh. Curled hair.

Casgairam. To slaughter, cut and hew.

Cas-chrom. A sort of Hebridian hoe or plough.

Casla. Frizzled wool.

Caslach. Children.

Casrach. Slaughter.

Casnaid. Split wood, chips.

Cas-moidhaich. The herb haresfoot.

Cassal. A storm.

Cast. Pure, undefiled.

Castearbhan. Succory.

Castearbhan-nam-muc. Dandelion.

Castum.

Casthor. } A curled lock.

Cas-urla.

Cassarach. Branchy.

Casruisg. Barefooted.

Cat. Erroneously for Ciod.

Cat. A cat.

Cataidh. Generosity, noble.

Cataigham. To honour, reverence, to tame, to try.

Cataighte. Tamed.

Cat-crainn A rat-trap.

Catadh Taming.

Catanach. Freezy, rough, shaggy.

Cath Battle, companies.

Cath. Pollard, husks.

Catham. To fan, winnow.

Catham.

Cathaigham. } To fight, tempt.

Cathadh. Winnowing, a breach, defile.

Cathadh-cuir. Falling snow.

Cathadh-mara. Spoondrift.

Cathag. A jackdaw, jay.

Cathair. A chair, bench, city.

Cathairaiche. A citizen.

Cathair-thalmhuin Barrow.

Cathair-rioghal. A throne.

Cathair. A guard, centinel.

Cathaiseach Brave, stout, quick.

Cathan. A wild goose with a black bill.

Cathbhar. An helmet.

Cathbruith. Sowens, flummery.

Cathbharun. A commander, officer.

Cathan-aodaich. A web.

Cathfhir. Warriors.

Cathaighoir. A tryer, tempter.

Cathaghadh. Temptation.

Cathfam. I must.

Cathfuire. A caviller.

Cathlabhra. A general's speech.

Cathmhilidh. A colonel, chief officer.

Catholach.

Catolice. } Catholic, universal.

Cathruichoir. Citizen.

Cathlun. A corn.

Cathreim. Triumph.

Catluibh. Cudwort.

Ca trath. When?

Cathris. Watching.

Cathriseach. Watchful, quick.

Ce. The earth; night, a spouse.

Ceach. Each, every.

Ceachaing. Hard to march, inaccessible.

Ceachair. Dirt, filth, penury.

Ceachardha. Dirty, stingy.

Ceachardhachd. Stinginess, penury.

Ceachlam. To dig, hackle, destroy.

Ceachlath. Spent, worn.

Ceacht. Power, a lesson.

Ceachlar. Either, or.

Ceachta. A plough.

Ceachtlach. Coal black.

Cead. Leave, permission, licence.

Ceadaigham. To permit, dismiss.

Cead. First. Vide Ceud.

Ceadach. Talkative, cloth.

Ceadaighte.

Ceaduigthach. } Permitted, lawful.

Ceadacht. Permission.

Ceadaidh. A fitting.

Ceadaghadh. Dismissing.

Ceadal. A story, narrative.

Ceadal. Malicious invention.

Ceaddaoine. Wednesday.

Ceadamas. In the first place.

Ceadhfadh. A sense, faculty, opinion.

Ceadfadhach. Of the senses, sensual.

Ceadfaidheas. Sensuality.

Ceadhal. Full of sores, blistered.

Ceadhlaidh. Blistering.

Cheadbhilich. Centaury.

Ceadhna. Same.

Ceadthuifmeadh. Firstling.

Ceadnabhar. } An element.
Ceadthus.

Ceadthuightheach Venial

Ceadtomailt. A breakfast.

Cead-uair. First time

Ceal. Stupidity, heaven.

Ceal. Death, concealing.

Ceal. Fine flour, use, forgetfulness.

Cealadh. Eating.

Cealam. To eat.

Cealairm. A hiding place.

Cealchobhar. A sanctuary.

Cealfhuath. A private grudge.

Cealg. Treachery, hypocrisy, malice.

Cealgach. Crafty, treacherous, hypocritical.

Cealgaire. Hypocrite, cheat.

Cealgaireachd. Hypocrisy.

Cealgam. To beguile, deceive.

Cealgonadh. Dissimulation.

Cealgaiche. More crafty, spiteful.

Ceallach. Contention, war.

Ceall. A church, cell.

Cealladh. Custody.

Ceallghaoid. Sacrilege.

Cealloir. Dung, muck.

Cealloir. Superior of a monastery.

Ceallmhuin. An oracle, prophecy.

Geallphort. A cathedral church.

Ceallfhlaid. Sacrilege.

Cealftol. A close-stool.

Cealt. Apparel, clothes.

Ceallach. A Celt, a Gaul.

Cealltair. A cause, a spear, a castle.

3

Cealtmhuilleoir. A fuller.

Cean, ceana. Favour.

Ceanadh. Favouring, cherishing.

Cean, cion. Debt, fault, crime.

Ceana. Alike, the same.

Ceana. Even, lo, already. Achd ceana, howbeit.

Ceanail. } Kindness, mildness.
Ceanaltachd.

Ceanalta. } Kind, mild, gentle, clean.
Ceanamhail.

Ceanfolaidh. Unreserved but virtuous love.

Ceandail. Lice.

Ceandachd. Identity.

Ceann. The head.

Ceann-achra. Epiphany.

Ceannach. A reward, a covenant.

Ceannachd. Buying, purchasing.

Ceannaigham. To buy.

Ceanair. } An hundred.
Ceanan.

Ceannfhionn. White-headed, name of a cow.

Ceannfine. Chief of a tribe.

Ceangail. A bond, restraint.

Ceangailte. Bound.

Ceangalach. Obligatory.

Ceangalam. To bind.

Ceannghraimh. Motto, title.

Ceanngharbh. Rough, rugged.

Ceannachtrach. Upper part of the throat.

Ceannphort. A founder, author.

Ceann-adhairt. A bolster.

Ceanndubh. Vide Canach.

Ceannfath. Cause, reason.

Ceannaich. Strife.

Ceannaiche. } A merchant.
Ceannaide.

Ceann-aimsir. A date.

Ceannair. A driver.

Ceannairc. Rebellion, perverseness.

Ceannaireach. Rebellious, perverse.

Ceannadhairceim. A plowman.

Ceannaircam.

Ceannaircam. To rebel.
Ceannardach. Arrogant.
Ceannardachd. Arrogance.
Ceannas. Chieftainry, superiority.
Ceanasach. Haughty, mighty.
Ceannbhar. A hat.
Ceannbheairt. A helmet.
Ceannbhrat. Canopy.
Ceanncaol. }
Ceannbirach. } Bow of a ship.
Ceannbhriathar. Adverb.
Ceannchlaon. Headlong, steep.
Ceann-cinaidh. A chief of a tribe.
Ceannchun. A goad.
Ceann a cheile. Together.
Ceandeargan. A red-start.
Ceanndan. Pertinacious.
Ceannafg. The forehead.
Ceanndanadas. Pertinaciousness.
Ceannfeadhna. A leader, commander.
Ceannfiodha. The end of a ship-timber.
Ceannglachan. A bundle.
Ceanlaidir. Headstrong.
Ceannmaide. Blockhead.
Ceannrach. A tether, halter.
Ceannrithach. Headlong.
Ceannruadh. Celandine.
Ceannphurgaid. A gargle.
Ceannsa. }
Ceannsach. } Continent, bashful, mild, gentle.
Ceannsachd. Continence, mildness.
Ceannsgalach. A chief leader, active.
Ceannsgriobhin. Motto, title.
Ceansuigheadh. Subduing, reducing.
Ceannsuigham. To subdue, manage, suppress.
Ceannsuighte. Subdued, conquered.
Ceann-simide. A tad-pole.
Ceannurradh. A captain, chief.
Ceannsal }
Ceannsalachd. } Rule, government.
Ceannsaliche. A governor.
Ceannsuigeachd. Merchandise.

Ceanntreun. Obstinate.
Ceanntrom. Drowsy, sluggish.
Ceanntire. A peninsula, promontory.
Ceanntar. Side of a country, cantred.
Ceannuaisgineach. Rash, precipitate.
Ceannsrait. Capitation.
Ceannstuaighe. An arch.
Ceann-uighe. End of a journey, goal.
Ceap. A block, stocks, shoemaker's last.
Ceap. A sign set up in time of battle.
Ceap. A head, stock.
Ceapan. A stump, or pin.
Ceapanta. Niggardly, stiff.
Ceapsgaolam. To propagate.
Ceapadhrann. Scanning.
Ceapaire. A piece of bread and butter.
Ceapairam. To spread upon, daub.
Ceapam. To stop, intercept.
Ceapal. Stopping.
Cear. Offspring, progeny.
Cearam. To press.
Cear, ceara. Blood, red.
Cearachadh. Wandering, straying.
Cearb. Money, silver.
Cearb A cutting, slaughtering.
Cearb. A rag, lappet, excrescence.
Cearbach. Ragged, aukward.
Cearban-feoir. A healing herb.
Cearbchnaid. A severe reflexion.
Cearbhal. Massacre, carnage.
Cearc. A hen.
Cearc-fheancach. Turkey-hen.
Cearc-fhraoich. Heath-hen.
Cearc-thomain. A partridge.
Cearcach. Having hens.
Cearcal. A hoop, circle.
Cearclach. Circular, like a hoop.
Cearchal. A bolster, pillow.
Cearchiall. Madness.
Cearcloch. A hen-roost.
Cearcmhanrach. A hen-coop.
Ceard. A tinker, tradesman, mechanic.
Ceardach. A forge, smith's shop.

Ceardaiche. A mechanic.
Ceardachd. Tinker's trade.
Ceardamhuil. Well-wrought, artificial.
Ceardamhlachd. Ingenuity.
Ceardcha. A fhop.
Ceard-dhearg. Oker, keel.
Cearachur. A grave.
Cearla. A clue.
Cearlam. To conglomerate.
Cearmnas. A lye.
Cearlach. Round.
Cearn. A man, victory.
Cearn. Expence, a corner.
Cearnabhan. A corner.
Cearnach. Four fquare, victorious,
Cearn-airrdhe. A trophy.
Cearn-duais. Athletick laurel.
Cearnag-ghloine. Pane of glafs.
Cearnfearnadh. Deftroying.
Cearnluach. Prize.
Cearr. Left-handed, wrong.
Cearraich. Mafter of his art.
Cearracan. A carrot.
Cearram. To kill.
Cearrbhach. A gamefter.
Ceart. Juft.
Ceart. Little, fmall.
Ceartachadh. Adjufting.
Ceartaigham. To adjuft, cut, prune.
Ceart. ⎫
Ceartas. ⎬ Juftice, equity.
Ceartbhreith. Birthright.
Ceartchreidmhach. Orthodox.
Ceartfgriobhadh. Orthography.
Ceartughadh. Paring, pruning, rebuking, amendment.
Ceartuighois. A corrector, regulator.
Ceartlann. A houfe of correction.
Ceartlar. Center, middle point.
Ceas. Obfcurity, fadnefs.
Ceas. Irkfomenefs.
Ceafadh. Vexation, punifhment.
Ceafla. Oar.

Ceaflach. Fine wool.
Ceafda. Punifhed.
Ceafachd. Grumbling, difcontent.
Ceafachdach. Difcontented, grumbling
Ceafadh. Crucifying, paffion.
Ceafam. To crucify, to fuffer.
Ceafadoir. Tormentor.
Ceafd. A queftion.
Ceafgam. To afk, enquire.
Ceaflach. Coarfe wool on the legs
Ceaflaid. Sacrilege.
Ceafna. Neceffity, want.
Ceafnughadh. Queftioning.
Ceafnach. Complaining.
Ceafnuigham. To queftion, interrogate.
Ceafnuighacht. Complaint.
Ceafnughadh. Correction.
Ceaftuigham. To correct, amend.
Ceatam. To fing, celebrate.
Ceata-cam. The feven ftars.
Ceatal. Singing.
Ceatain Month of May.
Ceatfadhach. Judicious, fenfible.
Ceatfadh. Conjecture.
Ceatfadacht. Luft.
Ceatha. A fhower.
Ceath. A fheep, cream.
Ceathair. Four.
Ceathairchearnach. ⎫ Square, quadrangu-
Ceathaircuinnach. ⎬ lar.
Ceathairchofach. Quadruped, four-footed.
Ceatham. To fkim.
Ceatharfhliofnach. Four-fided.
Ceathramh. ⎫
Ceathro. ⎬ Fourth.
Ceathair-deug. Fourteen.
Ceathro-deug. Fourteenth.
Ceathrachad. Forty.
Ceathrachado Fortieth.
Ceathardha. Belonging to four.
Ceatharbh. A troop.
Ceatharnach. A foldier, fatellite, tory.
Ceathnaid. A fheep.

Ceathra. Four footed beasts.

Ceathramanach. Cubical.

Ceathramh. Fourth, fourth part, stanza, lodging, quarter.

Ceathramha. A trencher.

Ceathramhan. A quadrant.

Cearthrar. Four.

Cecht Power, might, a lesson, lecture.

Cedas. At first.

Cedudh A bed.

Cedach. Stripes.

Cedaidh. To sit down, rest.

Cedghin. First-born.

Cedludh. Beginning.

Cedluth. First, shout, applause.

Ceibe. A spade.

Ceibhin A fillet.

Ceid. First, former.

Ceide. A market, fair.

Ceide. A green, plain.

Ceide. A hillock.

Ceid-ghrinneacht. Ripeness of age.

Ceidhche. Till night.

Ceidiol. A duel, conflict.

Ceigh A wharf, quay.

Ceigainach. Thick, stout.

Ceilt. Concealing, concealment.

Ceill. Sense, reason, expression.

Ceile. A spouse, husband.

Ceile. A servant.

Ceile-de. The Culdees.

Ceile. Together, each other.

O cheile Asunder.

Ceileabhradh. Leave, farewel.

Ceilabhram. To bid farewel, to celebrate.

Ceilabhradh. Festivity, solemnization.

Ceilg. Deceit.

Ceilgheallam. To betroth.

Ceilam To conceal.

Ceilidh. Visiting.

Ceiliubhra. A concealment.

Ceilidham. To visit.

Ceill, cill. Church, cell.

Ceileir. Chirping of birds.

Ceille. Of sense, reason.

Ceiliram. To chirp, warble.

Ceillidh. Wise, sober.

Ceilgrunach. Litigious, deceitful.

Ceilt, ceilte. Hid, concealed, secret.

Ceiltin. Hiding, covering.

Ceilt-ienntin. Equivocation.

Ceim. A step, degree.

Ceim-toisaich. Precedence, pass.

Ceimhdhealg. Hair-bodkin.

Ceimhin. ⎫
Ceimhleog. ⎬ A fillet.
Ceimhionn. ⎮
Ceimhmhileach. ⎭

Ceimheasas. Geometry.

Ceimnigham. To step, go.

Cein. Whilst that.

Cein. Foreign, remote, ann ceinn.

Ceiniol. Children.

Ceinmhaer. O! happy!

Ceinmotha. Besides, except, without.

Ceinnliath. Grey-headed.

Ceinnsacham. To appease.

Ceip. A shoe-last.

Ceip-tuislaidh. A stumbling-block.

Ceir. Wax.

Ceir-bheachan. Bees-wax.

Ceirbhadh. Carving.

Ceire. A buttock.

Ceird Trade.

Ceird-thomhsaighe. Sorcery.

Ceirin. A poultice.

Ceirtighte. Conglomerated.

Ceirnin. A place.

Ceiriocan. Water-elder-tree.

Ceirgham. To cere.

Ceirgha. Waxen.

Ceirn, ceirnin. A dish, platter.

Ceirt. A rag, an apple-tree.

Ceirt. Justice.

Ceirtach. Ragged.

Ceirtag. A ragged girl.

Ceirtle.

Ceirtle. } A bottom of yarn.
Ceirtlin. }

Ceirtmheadhoin. A center.

Ceirnine. Small difhes, plates.

Ceis. A bafket, hamper.

Ceis. Lance, fpear.

Ceis. Loathing, want of appetite.

Ceis. Grumbling, murmuring.

Ceis. A furrow, a fow, pig.

Ceifchrainn. Polypody.

Ceifin. A fmall bafket, hurdle.

Ceifeog. A flip, youngling.

Ceifneamh. Whining, complaining.

Ceifnam. To complain of poverty.

Ceifd. A queftion, problem.

Ceifdeil. Sufpicious.

Ceifduigham. To queftion.

Ceifdughadh. Examination.

Ceifte. Dear.

Ceitam. A vehicle of rods.

Ceitain. May.

Ceitainach. Of the fummer.

Ceithaircearnam. To fquare.

Ceithre. Four.

Ceithreamhna. Lodgings.

Ceithairfhliofnach, Quadrilateral.

Ceithairramhach. Four-oared.

Ceithairfillte. Four-fold.

Ceithairghobhlanach. Four-pronged.

Ceithearnach. Sturdy fellow, foldier.

Celchin. A fine.

Cenel. Children.

Ceo. Mift, fog, vapour.

Ceo. Milk.

Ceo, fceo. And.

Ceothach. } Dark, mifty.
Ceothmhor. }

Ceathmhorachd. Darknefs.

Ceobanach. Small rain.

Ceobbach. Drunkennefs.

Ceo-bhraon. Mifling rain.

Ceobhran. Dew.

Ceol. Mufick, melody.

Ceolan. A little bell.

Ceolrimham. To modulate, play mufick.

Ceolmhor. Mufical, harmonious.

Ceoloifleifi. Dropping mifts, rain.

Ceolraidh. Muficians.

Ceolchuirm. Concert.

Ceomilteach. Mildew.

Ceor. A mafs, lump.

Ceos. Hip.

Ceothran. A fmall fhower.

Cerbheach. A gamefter.

Cerbufair. Banker.

Ceren. A poultice.

Cet. The mouth, prophecy.

Ceuchd. A plough.

Ceud. The firft.

Ceud. A hundred.

Ceudach. Centuple.

Ceudghin. Firft-born.

Ceum. A ftep.

Ceumal. Stately.

Ceufam. To crucify, torture.

Ceudmheas. Firft-fruit tax.

Ceutach. Elegant.

Ci. To lament.

Cia. How?

Cia mar. How? in what manner?

Cia as. Whence?

Cia dho. To whom?

Cia. A man, hufband.

Ciaban. A gizzard.

Ciabh. } A fide lock.
Ciabhag. }

Ciabhag-choille. A wood-lark.

Ciabharthan. A fhower.

Ciabh-cheanndubh. Deers hair.

Ciabh chafda. Curled lock.

Ciad. Firft, a hundred.

Ciadan. Height.

Ciadlus. Curiofity.

Ciabhach. Bufhy.

Ciaddhuillach. Centifolious.

Ciach. Mift, fog, forrow, concern.

Ciall.

Ciall. Death, reason, sense, meaning.
Ciall-chogair. A watchword.
Cialdha. Rational, prudent.
Cialluighach. Significant.
Ciallachadh. Signifying.
Cialluicham. To signify, interpret.
Cialtradh. A sentence.
Ciamhair. Sad, weary.
Ciabhbhachlach. Curl-haired.
Cian. Long, tedious, far, distant.
Cian. Long since.
Cianal. Lamentable, solitary.
Cianfhulang. Perseverance, invincible.
Ciapul. Strife.
Cianmharthanach. Continual.
Ciapam. To vex, torment.
Ciapalach. Contentious.
Ciapalam. To encounter, to quarrel.
Ciapalaiche. A quarrelsome person.
Ciar. A comb.
Ciar. A dark brown.
Ciarach. A young black girl.
Ciaralach. Perverse, froward.
Ciarail. A quarrel.
Ciaran. Grey.
Ciarog. A chafer.
Ciarsain. Grumbling.
Ciarsin, ciarsuir. A kerchief.
Ciarta. Waxed.
Ciasail. A dispute.
Ciata. An opinion.
Ciatach. Graceful, esteemed.
Ciatfadh. Admiration.
Ciatuichad. Gracefulness.
Ciatfach. Honest.
Cib. A hand.
Ciben. The rump.
Cibharg. A rag, a little ragged woman.
Cich. A greyhound.
Cidh. A sight, a view.
Cidham. To see.
Cidhis. A mask, a vizard.

Cigh. A hind.
Cigilte. Tickled.
Cigiltach Difficult, ticklish.
Cigiltam.
Cigilam. } To tickle.
Cigilt. Tickling.
Cil. Ruddle.
Cill The grave, death, a chapel, cell.
Cill. Partiality, prejudice.
Cilfin. The belly.
Cim. A drop, money.
Cimcheartuigham. To rifle.
Cimeach, cimidh. A captive.
Cimam. To captivate.
Cinbeirt. A ruler, governor.
Cinnbheirtas. Dominion.
Cincighis. Whitfuntide.
Cine. A race, tribe, family.
Cineadh
Cineal. } An offspring, progeny.
Cineadh. Determining, decreeing.
Cineal. Dainty.
Cinealta. Kind, gentle, extraction.
Cinadal. Fond of the name.
Cinnealtus. Kindness, affection.
Cinel. A sort, kind, sex, gender.
Cinfideadh. Conception.
Cing. Strong.
Cingeach. Brave.
Cingeachd. Bravery.
Cinid. Belonging to a family.
Cinmheath. A consumption.
Cinmhiol. Colours.
Cinmhioladh. A picture, image, art of painting.
Cinmhiolam. To paint.
Cinn. Inflection of Ceann, headlong.
Cinmhiolthoir. A painter.
Cinadas. Kindred.
Cinneachdin. Encrease.
Cinnam. To encrease, to happen, agree to.
Cinneadh. Preparing, happening.

[T]   Cinneamhna.

Cinneamhna. Accidental.
Cinneamhnach. Fatal.
Cinneamhuin. Chance, fortune, fate.
Cinni. A megrim.
Cinnine-cartach. A carter.
Cinnlitir. A capital letter.
Cinnmhiolam. To paint.
Cinnmhire. Broken down, frenzy.
Cinnte. Certain, certainty.
Cinntachd. Certainty.
Cinntach. Positive.
Cinntach. Positive.
Cinntreun. Obstinate.
Cinteagal. A coarse cloak.
Cinnseach. Want.
Cintigham. To appoint.
Cintin. Happening.
Ciob. A fort of grafs, hards, tow.
Ciobh. Vide Ciabh.
Ciobhal. The jaw-bone.
Ciocar. A hungry creature.
Ciocarach. Long after, greedy.
Cioch. Pap, breaft.
Cioch a mhuinail. The uvula.
Ciocht. A carver, engraver.
Ciochtadh. Engraved work.
Ciocht. Children.
Ciocras. A longing after.
Ciochran. A fuckling.
Ciocrafan. A hungry fellow.
Ciochan. A titmoufe.
Ciochtam. To rake, fcrape.
Ciod ? Ciodh ? What ?
Ciod chuige ? Why ?
Ciodar ? Wherefore ?
Ciodh. A maid.
Ciodhfa. } Wherefore, how many.
Ciodhfar. }
Ciogal. A diftaff.
Ciorbhadh. Taking away.
Ciol. Death.
Ciol. Inclination, propenfity.
Ciolarn. A veffel.
Ciolcach. A reed.

Ciolog. A hedge-fparrow.
Ciollach. Superior.
Ciolrathadh. Chattering.
Ciolratham. To chatter.
Cioman. Carding, combing.
Ciomam. To card, comb.
Cioma. A fault.
Ciomach. A prifoner.
Ciombal. A bell.
Ciomhas. A border, brim.
Cion. A fault, defire.
Cional. Guilty.
Cionaftam. To bear.
Cionchoran. A hook.
Cionda. Vide Ceadhna.
Cionfath. Occafion, quarrel.
Cionmhar. Becaufe.
Cionmhalcam. To bear.
Cionn, chionn. Becaufe.
Cionnas. How.
Cionnacha. The face.
Cionnfir. A cenfer.
Cionta. Guilt, crime.
Ciontach. Guilty.
Ciontaigham. To fin.
Ciontire. Tribute
Cionag. A kernel.
Cionradharc. Fate.
Cionradharcach. Stingy, narrow.
Cionthar. Mufic.
Ciopain. Vide Ceapan.
Cior. A comb, cud, jaw.
Cior. Hand.
Cior-mheala. Honeycomb.
Cioram. To comb.
Cioradh. Combing.
Ciorcal. A circle.
Ciorbham. To take away, mutilate.
Ciorbtha. Hurt.
Ciordhubh. Coal black.
Ciorghal. Brave.
Ciormairc. A fuller.
Ciormam. To wear out.

Ciorrbam.

Ciorrbam. To mangle, mortify; to become black.

Ciorthamach. Lame, maimed.

Cios. Rent, tribute, revenue.

Cios. Sin.

Ciosachadh. Restraining.

Ciosach.
Ciosachdach. } Importunate, slovenly.

Ciosal. Wages of a nurse

Cioschain. Tribute, tax

Ciotach. Left-handed, awkward.

Ciotag. The left-hand.

Cioth. A peal, heavy shower.

Ciotfar. Seems meet.

Ciothromach. Mean.

Cip. A rank, file in battle.

Cir. A comb, key

Cii. Joined, united.

Cirain. A cock's comb, crest.

Cirachan. A comb-cafe.

Cirb. Fleet, swift.

Cirbfire. A brewer.

Cireib. A tumult, insurrection, foul-house.

Cirin. A crest.

Cirainach. Crested.

Cirthanach A kitchen.

Cis. Rent, tribute, tax.

Cischain. A poll-tax.

Cischear. A shepherd's crook.

Cisain. A little chest, basket, pannier.

Cisde. A chest, treasure, a cake.

Cisdeamhuil. Capsular.

Cisdeag. A little chest.

Cismhangair. Engrosser.

Ciseal. Satan.

Cistineach. A kitchen.

Cisel. Low, as between two waters.

Cisteanadh. Rioting.

Cisire. A romancer.

Citear. It seems.

Cith. A shower, mist.

Cithi. Ye see.

Cithurach. Showery.

Ciucaltoir. A hearer, auditor.

Ciuchaing. To walk.

Ciuchair. Beautiful, dimpling.

Ciuchlaitham. To hear.

Ciuil. Music.

Ciuleabhar. A greyhound.

Ciuin. Meek.

Ciuin. A gentle gale.

Ciuine, ciuinas. Meekness, calmness.

Ciuinam.
Ciuinigham. } To appease

Ciumhas. A selvedge, border.

Ciura. Merchantable.

Ciuird A trade.

Ciuirin. A covering.

Ciuirinuigham. To cover.

Ciuram. To buy.

Ciurtha. Bought.

Ciuirt. A rag.

Ciurthamach. Maimed.

Ciuthramaicham. To hurt, harm.

Ciuthrach. A bird having a red head.

Ciurrar. Hurting.

Ciuirtach. Ragged.

Clab. An open mouth, a lip.

Clabach. Thick-lipped, wide-mouthed.

Clabaire. A babbling fellow.

Clabar. Clay, dirt, filth.

Clabarach. Dirty, filthy.

Clabh. Vide Claimh.

Clabhair. Mead.

Clabog. A scoff, blubber-lipped woman.

Clabhstur. A cloyster.

Clabsal. A column of a book.

Clach. A stone.

Clachair. A mason.

Clachadairachd. Masonry.

Clachan. A village, hamlet, burying-place.

Clach-oisin. Corner-stone.

Clich-thochailtaiche. A quarrier.

Clach na suil. Apple of the eye.

Cladach. The fhore, dirt, clay.

Cladan. A bur, flake of fnow.

Cladrin. Wreck, diforder.

Cladh. A bank, dike, burying-place, wool-comb.

Cladhach. Digging.

Cladhaigham. To dig.

Cladhaire. A coward, villain, rogue.

Cladhairachd. Cowardice.

Clag. A bell, clapper of a mill.

Clagan. A little bell, noife.

Claghartha. Sluggifh.

Claghartas. Sluggifhnefs.

Clagarnach. Noife.

Clagun. A flagon, a lid.

Claibhe. Vide Claimh.

Claibin. A top, fpigot.

Claigeog. Deceit.

Claigeach. A fteeple.

Claigiunn. The fkull.

Claig. A dimple

Claighe. A burial.

Claiguinnach freine. Headftall of a bri-dle.

Claidham. To dig, lay foundation.

Claidhamh. A fword.

Claidheamhairachd. Fencing.

Claimh. Mange, itch.

Claidhamhal. Enfiform.

Claimheach. Mangy, fcorbutic.

Clain. Engendering, children.

Clair. Boards, tables.

Clairbheil. A lid, cover.

Clairaodanach. Beetlebrowed.

Clairam. To divide.

Clarin. A fmall board, cripple.

Clairineach. Crippled.

Clairfhiacla. The fore-teeth.

Clairfeach. A harp.

Clairfeoir. A harper.

Clairthe. Dealt, divided.

Clais. A furrow, pit, dike.

I

Clais. A ftreak, ftripe.

Claifeach. A fword.

Claifceadal. Singing of hymns.

Claifdachd. } Hearing.
Claiftine. }

Claiftinam. To hear.

Claithe. A jeft, ridicule, a game.

Claithe. A genealogical table.

Clamhan. A buzzard.

Clamhan-gobhlach. A kite.

Clamhfa. A court, clofs.

Clamh. Mange.

Clampar. Wrangling.

Clamhradh. Scratching.

Clamhuin. Steel.

Clamhram. To fcratch as for the itch.

Clamhdair. A lazar.

Clamharach. Litigious, wrangling.

Clamras. Brawling, chiding.

Clanach. Virtue, fruitful perfons.

Clannmhar. Having iffue.

Clann. Children, tribe, clan.

Clannar. Shining, fleek.

Clannach. Hanging in locks, bufhy, fruit-ful.

Clannadh. Thrufting.

Clanntar. Was buried.

Claochladh. Alteration.

Claochlaigham. To change, alter, die.

Claoidham. To conquer, defeat.

Claoidhte. Defeat, overthrown.

Claoidhadh. Oppreffing, defeating.

Claoidhaire. A fugitive, filly fellow.

Claon. Partial, inclining.

Claonadh. Inclination, bending.

Claonam. To incline, bend.

Claonad. Proclivity.

Claonard. An inclining fteep.

Clapfhollus. Twilight.

Clar A board, trough, table, defk, flave.

Clar-ainmughaidh. Title-page.

Clarach. Bare, bald , the floor, a ftory.

Clar-

Clar-innfaidh, ammais. Index.
Claradh. Familiarity.
Clarchofach. Splay-footed,
Claragan. The fore-teeth.
Claraineach. Flat-nofed.
Clarag. Wattled-work on a fledge.
Clar-aodain. The forehead.
Claraodanach. Broad-browed.
Clarfhiacuil. Foretooth.
Claridh. Dividing.
Clarfeach. A harp.
Clarfair. A harper.
Clas. A play, craft, pit, furrow.
Clas. Melody, harmony.
Clafach. Crafty.
Clafaidheachd. Subtilty,
Clafba. A clafp.
Clafbam. To button, tye.
Clathe. Genealogy.
Clathnaire. Bafhfulnefs.
Cle. Partial, prejudiced.
Cle. Left-handed.
Cleachach. Thick, cluftering.
Cleachd, cleachda. A cuftom.
Cleachdach. Accuftomed.
Cleachdam. To accuftom.
Cleach-boid. A good ftick.
Cleachdin. Accuftoming.
Cleamhnas. Affinity, copulation.
Clearadh. Familiarity.
Clear an chaine. Poet of the tax.
Cleas. A play, trick, feat.
Cleafach. Playful, crafty, full of feats.
Cleafachd.
Cleafachdich. } Performing feats, plays.
Cleafuigham. To perform feats, plays.
Cleafuighachd. Craft, fubtilty.
Cleafaidhe. An artful man, juggler.
Cleath. A wattled work, the body of any thing.
Cleath. Concealing, a fecret.
Cleathairachd. Rufticity, boldnefs.

Cleatha. A goad, a rib.
Cleathard. Steep.
Cleathar-fed. A milch-cow.
Cleathchur. Relation by blood.
Cleathramh. Partiality, prejudice.
Cleibh. Vide Cliabh.
Cleibhin. A little bafket.
Cleir. Clergy.
Cleirachd. The church, clerkfhip.
Cleireach. A clergyman, clerk, writer.
Cleirgha. Of the clergy.
Cleite.
Cleitean. } Penthoufe, eaves of a roof, a quill, down.
Cleitadh. A ridge of rocks in the fea.
Cleith. Concealing. Vide Cliath.
Cleitach. Full of rocks, feathery.
Cleithach. Private, feathery.
Cleitham. To conceal.
Cleithachd. Lurking.
Clelamhach. Left-handed.
Cleaffa. Feats, tricks.
Clethe. An oar, ftake.
Cleitog. A little quill.
Cleithmhiofgas. A private grudge.
Clemhana. Mifchief.
Cleoca.
Cleocan. } A cloak.
Cleocam. To cloak, cover.
Cli. Left.
Cli. Succeffor to an epifcopal fee.
Cli. The body, ribs, ftrength.
Cliabh. A bafket, a man's cheft.
Cliabhan. A fmall bafket, cage.
Cliabhach. A wolf.
Cliabhrach. Side or trunk of the body.
Cliabh-fgeathrach. A vomit.
Cliadan. A bur.
Cliadh. Antiquaries.
Cliamhach. A fox.
Cliamhuin. A fon-in-law.
Cliamhnas. Vide Cleamhuas.
Cliar. Vide Cleir. A fociety, gallant, brave.

Cliaraidhe.

Cliaridhe. A fongfter.

Cliaraidhachd. Singing.

Cliaranach. A bard.

Cliath. Breaft, man's cheft, bafket, hurdle, harrow, darning of a ftocking.

Cliath chliata (or) fhoirfidh. A harrow.

Cliathan. The breaft.

Cliatham. To harrow, to tread as a cock the hen.

Cliath. Vide Gliath.

Cliathach. A battle, conflict.

Cliathag. A hurdle, the chine.

Cliath-iarruin. A trivet.

Cliath-fheanachais Genealogical table.

Cliathrach. Breaft-high

Clibain. A little piece, dewlap.

Clibog. A filly.

Clibis. A tumult.

Clibhifachd. Peevifhnefs.

Clichidh. To affemble.

Clifing. A bottle.

Clibhach. Curled, rough.

Cliobam. To tear in pieces.

Clilamhach. Left-handed.

Cliobhguna. A rug.

Cliobog-eich. A fhaggy colt.

Cliobain. The dewlap.

Clioc. A hook.

Cliogar, cliogartha. Croaking.

Cliocam. To hook.

Cliolunta. Stout, potent, hearty.

Clipe. A hook to catch fifh, fraud, deceit.

Clipam. To hook.

Clis. Active.

Clifgach. Skipping, ftarting.

Cliotach. Left-handed.

Clifgam. To ftart, fkip.

Clifte. Active, fwift.

Clifteachd. Activity, dexterity.

Clith. Vide Cli.

Clith. Clofe, true.

Cliu. Fame, renown.

Cliucach. Hooked.

Cliudan. A little ftroke with the fingers.

Cliutach. Famous, renowned.

Cliudh. Squint-eyed.

Clo. A nail, pin, peg, print. Vide Clodh.

Clo. Raw cloth.

Cloch. A ftone, the herb henbane.

Clochach. Stony.

Clochanam. To refpire.

Clochan. A pavement, caufeway, ftone fteps to crofs a brook. Vide Clachan.

Clochar. An affembly, convent, wheezing in the throat.

Clochara. Set with ftones.

Cloch-chinn. Tombftone, topftone.

Clochlain. The bird ftonechatter.

Clochfhuail. The gravel.

Clochfhneachd. ⎱ Hail.
Clochmheallan. ⎰

Cloch-theine. A flint.

Cloch-reathnach. Polypody.

Cloch na fuil. Apple of the eye.

Cloch-mhulainn. A millftone.

Cloch-fhaobhair. A hone whetftone.

Cloch-liobharain. A grindftone.

Cloch-chrocaidh. A fort of mortar.

Clochbhalg. A watchman's rattle.

Cloch-fhreathal. A free-ftone.

Cloch-uafal. A precious ftone.

Cloch-neart. The putting ftone.

Clochbheimnaich. Stamping.

Cloch-iuil. A load-ftone.

Clod. A clod, turf.

Clodach. ⎱ Full of clods.
Clodanach. ⎰

Clodam. To clod.

Clodan. A little clod.

Clodairachd. Cafting clods.

Clodh. A print, impreffion, tongs, prefs.

Clodh. Variety, change.

Clodhair.

Clodhair. A printer.

Clodhghalar. A vertigo.

Clodhlain. A piece of raw cloth.

Clodhbhualam. To print, stamp.

Clodhbhuailte. Printed.

Clodhbhualadh. Printing, stamping.

Clodhughadh. Drawing close together, making up.

Clodhuigham. To approach, draw close to.

Clog. A bell, clock.

Cloga. Tares.

Clogachd. Bellfry.

Clogad. A helmet, a cone, pyramid.

Clogam. To found as a bell.

Clogan. A little bell.

Clogas. A bellfry.

Clogarnach. Tinkling.

Cloichran. A stonechatter.

Cloidheam. To punish, subdue.

Clogshnathad. A gnomon.

Cloiche. Of stone, stone.

Cloichead. A passport.

Cloichreach. A stony place.

Cloidhe. A ditch, moat, rampart.

Cloigin. A little bell.

Cloigineach. Curled, frizzled.

Cloigmheur. The pin of a dial.

Cloigtheach. A steeple, bellfry.

Cloistin. Vide Claistin.

Cloisam. Vide Claistinam.

Cloithear. A champion.

Cloithag. A shrimp, prawn.

Clomh. A pair of tongs, an instrument to dress flax.

Clomham. To dress flax.

Clonn. A pillar, chimney-piece. Vide Columhan.

Clos. Hearing, report, rest.

Closach. A carcase.

Cloth. Noble, generous.

Cloth. Fame, praise.

Clotha. Was heard.

Clothach. Famous, illustrious.

Clothar. Chosen.

Closaid. A study.

Cluain. Deceit, a remote field; lawn, a bower, intrigue.

Cluaineorachd. }
Cluaineoras. } Flattery, deception.

Cluainaire. A flatterer, seducer, hypocrite.

Cluaise. Of the ear.

Cluaisin. A porringer.

Cluas. The ear, a handle; joy.

Cluas an fheidh. Melancholy-thistle.

Cluasach. Having ears, or handles.

Cluasag. A pin-cushion, a pillow.

Cluasmhaothan. The tip of the ear.

Cluasliath. Coltsfoot.

Cluaisain. A box on the ear, a pillow.

Cluan. }
Cluanag. } A secret field, a lawn.

Cluantaireachd. Crookedness, deceit.

Cluanaisach. Fond of going alone.

Cluaran. A spunge, a sort of daisy.

Cluaranach. A thistle.

Cluasdoille. Deafness.

Cluasfhaine. }
Cluasheud. } Earring.

Cluaisoil. Loud.

Cluais ri Claistin. Character in a romance.

Clubadh. A winding bay.

Clud. A patch, clout.

Cludam. To patch, cover up warm, to cherish.

Cludaire. A botcher, cobler.

Cludhamhuil. Famous.

Cludach. Ragged.

Cluiceog. Fraud, deceit.

Cluich. A play, game, battle.

Cluicheog. A little play.

Cluid. A rag, nook.

Cluigain. A pendent, little cluster.

Cluigainacb. Clustering.

Cluig, cluigin. A little bell.

Cluigain-cluaise. Ear-ring.

Cluimh.

Cluimh. Down, wool.

Cluimhealta. A Royſton crow, flock of birds.

Cluin. Fraud; an encloſure.

Cluinam. To hear.

Cluintin. Hearing.

Cluinte. Heard.

Cluinteorachd. Craftineſs.

Cluinteoir. A hearer, auditor.

Cluiſam. To hear.

Cluiteach. Vide Cliuteach.

Cluithe. A game, play.

Cluitheadh. Gaming.

Cluitham. To game, play.

Clnmh. Down, feathers, wool, plumage.

Clumham. To pluck feathers.

Clumtheach. Feathered, hairy.

Cluthuigham. To chace, run down.

Cluthar. Cloſe, ſheltered.

Cna. Good, gracious, bountiful.

Cnabar. Drowſineſs, heavineſs.

Cnadaire. A prating jeſter.

Cnadar-bharca. Ships.

Cnadan. A frog.

Cnag. A knob, peg, wrinkle, crack or noiſe, a knock.

Cnagach. Having knobs.

Cnagachd. Knottineſs, ſternneſs.

Cnagadh. Knocking down.

Cnagam. To knock down.

Cnagaid. A rap.

Cnagaidh. Bunchy.

Cnaid. A ſcoff, jeer.

Cnagaire. A gill.

Cnagh, cnaoi A conſumption.

Cnaib. Hemp.

Cnaidteach. Fretted.

Cnaigtheach. Sluggiſh

Cnaimhfhiach. A rook.

Cnaimhgheoidh. A bird between a gooſe and duck.

Cnaim-gobhail. The ſhare-bone.

Cnaire. A buckle.

Cnaimſeach. A midwife.

Cnamh, cnaimh. A bone.

Cnamhan. Continual talking.

Cnamhach. Waſting.

Cnamham. To waſte.

Cnamharlach. A ſtalk.

Cnamhmhargadh. The ſhambles.

Cnamhnaireach. Demure.

Cnamhruighadh. A cubit.

Cnaoi. A conſumption.

Cnaoigheadh. Gnawing.

Cnaoighte. Conſumed.

Cnaoidheam. To conſume, languiſh.

Cnap. A button, bump, knob, little hill.

Cnapach. Full of knobs, &c.

Cnapan. A little bump, knob, boſs, &c.

Cnarra. A ſhip.

Cnead. A ſigh, groan.

Cneadam. To ſigh, groan.

Cneadh. A wound.

Cneadhach. Full of wounds.

Cneamhaire. An artful fellow.

Cneas. Neck, the ſkin, the waiſt.

Cneaſmhuir. A ſtrait of the ſea.

Cneaſda. Modeſt, meek, fortunate, ominous.

Cneaſgheal. White-ſkined, white-boſomed.

Cneaſdachd. Mildneſs.

Cneaſughadh. Healing.

Cneaſuigham. To heal, cure.

Cneatrom. A kind of horſe-litter.

Cneidh. A wound.

Cneidhſhliochd. A ſcar.

Cneidham. To wound.

Cneidhſhliochdach. Full of ſcars.

Cneimam. To erode.

Cneim. Eroſion.

Cniocht. A ſoldier, a knight.

Cniopaire. A poor rogue.

Cniopaireacht. Acting the rogue.

Cno. Famous, excellent, a nut.

Cnoc. A hill, the herb navew.

Cnocan. A little hill.

I

Cnocaireachd.

Cnocaireachd. Walking abroad.

Cnocach. }
Cnocanach. } Hilly.

Cnomhuine. A wood of hazles.

Cnorachas. Honour.

Cnod. A piece joined to strengthen another.

Cnodhaire. A nut-cracker.

Cnomh A nut.

Cnopstarra. A ball at the end of a spear.

Cno-spuince. Molucca nuts.

Cnu, cnumh. A nut.

Cnuaiste. Gathered.

Cnuas. A collection, acquisition.

Cnuasachd. A collection, recollection, pondering.

Cnuasam. To gather together, assemble.

Cnuasaigham. To ponder, review, reflect, ruminate.

Cnuasaighte. Pondered, reflected upon.

Cnuasapuigh. Fruitful.

Cnuastoir. A gatherer.

Cnudhaire. A nut-cracker.

Cnuig, cnumh. }
Cnuimhag. } A maggot, worm.

Cnuimhagach, cnuimhach. Full of worms.

Cnuimhithach. Infectivorous.

Cnumhsor. Fruitful.

Co Who? which?

Co. As.

Co. Vide Comh.

Cho. Not, whose.

Coach. A violent pursuit.

Cho mhor. Almost.

Coan. Agreeable, well-seasoned.

Coard. A husbandman, a clown.

Caorde. Husbandry.

Cob. Plenty.

Cobh. Victory, triumph.

Cobhach. A tribute, stout, brave.

Cobhail. An inclosed place.

Cobhair. Assistance.

Cobhaltach. Victorious. *

Cobhar. }
Cobhragach. } Froth, foam, sillabub.

Cobhartigh. A prey.

Cobhla. A breach, cataract.

Cobhra. A shield, target.

Cobhthach. }
Cobhsach. } Victorious.

Cobhartha. }
Cobharthach. } Assisting, relieving.

Cobhtach. A creditor.

Coc. Manifest.

Coca. A boat, a cook.

Cocaire. A cook.

Cocaireachd. Cooking.

Cochar. Order, œconomy.

Cochdurn. A buckler.

Cochal. A husk, shell, mantle, a nut.

Cochallach. Capsular, having husks, coated.

Cochma. The parity of one thing to another.

Cochcaire. A strainer.

Cochcifoide. Corn-poppy.

Cochmiche. Keys.

Cocleisteise. Dropping rains.

Cocroth. A shield, target.

Cod, coda. }
Codach. } A piece, part.

Codaicham. To help, add.

Cod. Victory.

Codach. Invention, friendship.

Codadh. A mountain.

Codaille. A supping-room.

Codal, comhdal. Convention, assembly, friendship.

Codalta, codaltach. Sleepy.

Codaltachd. Drowsiness.

Codal. Sleep.

Codana. }
Codcha. } Parts.

Codalian. Mandrake.

Codarsna. Contrary.

Codhbhradh. A sacrificing, offering.

Cobhnach. A lord, great man.
Codhlam. To sleep.
Codlainean. Poppy.
Codeis. Indifferent.
Codhairteach. Barking.
Codramach. A rustic, a clown.
Codramacht. Equality.
Codromtha. Uncivilized, foreign.
Coemh. Little, small.
Coemh. Soon as, as swift as.
Cofra. A chest, box.
Cofrin. A little box.
Cogadh. War, warlike.
Cogach. Rebellious.
Cogaidh. Just, lawful.
Cogair. }
Cogairseach. } Suggestion, whisper.
Cogal. The herb cockle.
Cogamhuil. Warlike.
Cogar. An insurrection.
Cogaram. To whisper, conspire.
Cogarsnach A whispering.
Cogaras. Peace, amity.
Cochale. A wash-ball.
Cognam. To chew the cud.
Cognadh. Chewing, ruminating.
Cognamh. Gnashing.
Cogoirse. A well-ordered system.
Cograchal. Foreign.
Cogthach. A warrior, rebellious.
Coguis. Conscience.
Cogul. Rubbing off, chaffing.
Cogullach. Filings.
Coi. A poem.
Coib. A company, a copy.
Coibche. A dowry.
Coibchichte Purchased, procured.
Coibchichidh. Procuring, purchasing.
Coibchicham. To buy, purchase.
Coibhdean. A troop.
Coibhgioch. Fierce.
Coibhreocham. To comfort.
Coibhfeana. Confession, exorcism.
Coibhthe. A hire.

Coic. A secret, mystery.
Coice. A mountain.
Coicme. An udder.
Coid. Sticks, brushwood.
Coidhche, choidhche. Ever.
Coidhe. Chastity.
Coidhean. A barnacle.
Coig. Five.
Coigar. A five, or the number five.
Coigbhad. Fifty.
Coigeamh. A fifth, a province.
Coigmha, coigo. Fifth.
Coigeamhach. Belonging to the five pro-
vinces of Ireland.
Coigealta A conference.
Coigalam. To preserve, spare, to cover
the fire.
Coigalta. Spared.
Coigeal. A noise, clap.
Coigeart. Judgment, a question.
Coigeartam. To judge.
Coigeas. Five ways.
Coigaladh. A sparing, keeping alive.
Coigbhilach. Quinquefoliated.
Coigul. Vide Cuigal. A distaff.
Coigbliannach. Five years old.
Coigill. A thought, secret.
Coigle. A companion, a secret.
Coigleachd. A train, retinue.
Coigligham. To accompany.
Coigne. A spear, javelin.
Coigrich. A bound, limit.
Coigreach. A stranger.
Coigreachal. Strange, foreign.
Coigshliosnach. A pentagon.
Coigrinn. Five parts or divisions.
Coilbhin. A small shaft.
Coil. A corner.
Coilce. A bed, bed-clothes.
Coileasadh. A lethargy.
Coileir. The neck, collar.
Coileir. A quarry, a mine.
Coileach. A cock. Vide Caolach.

Coileach-

Coileach-ruadh. A heath-cock.

Coiligin. The cholick.

Coileain. A whelp, pup.

Coilis. Cabbage.

Coill, coille. A wood.

Coilleadh. A hog.

Coill. Sin, iniquity.

Coillag. A cockle.

Coilleam. To blindfold, trefpafs.

Coillearnach. A woody place.

Coillmhin. A young pig.

Coillte, coillteach. Woods, forests.

Coillmhias. A wooden-difh.

Coilt. A young cow.

Coillteachal. }
Coillteamhuil. } Woody, wild.

Coillte. Gelded.

Coilpen. A rope.

Coimh, comh, fometimes Co. Equal to the Latin Con.

Coimhchrioflach. The confines of a country.

Coimde. Practice, cuftom, ufe.

Coimde. A tub, keeve.

Coimhde. A landlord.

Coimear. Short, brief.

Coimeas. Equality, comparifon.

Coimeafam. To compare.

Coimeafg. Mixture.

Coimeafgam. To mix

Coimheach. Foreign, carelefs, fecure.

Coimheas. Coolnefs of affection.

Coimhead. A watch, ward.

Coimheadach. A warden, keeper.

Coimheardachd. Waiting, attending.

Coimheadam. }
Coimhdam. } To watch, keep, hold.

Coimheafda. Of equal worth.

Coimhaire. Without forewarning.

Coimhbheurla. A conference

Coimhbheiram. To contribute.

Coimhcdeangal. A joint, league, confpiracy, conjugation

Coimhcheanglam. To unite, couple, league.

Coimhcheafa. A protection.

Coimhcheimnigham. To accompany.

Coimhchliamhuin. Son-in-law.

Coimhchreapam. To contract.

Coimhdeach. Safe, fecure.

Coimhdheantacbd. A compofure.

Coimbdhreimeachd. A competition.

Coimhdhreachta. Conformed.

Coimheach. Like, alike.

Coimheafgar. A conflict.

Coimheignigham. To force, conftrain.

Coimheirge. Affociates.

Coimheirgam. To join with auxiliaries.

Coimhfeadhan. A company, troop.

Coimhfhear-cogaidh. A fellow-foldier.

Coimhfhiofrach. Confcious.

Coimhfhreagarach. Correfponding.

Coimhficham. To difpofe, fet in order.

Coimhfhreagaram. To correfpond, fit.

Coimhghleic. A conflict, ftruggle.

Coimhghne. Hiftorical knowledge.

Coimhghlinnam. To faften, adhere to.

Coimhghreamaicham. To adhere, cling to.

Coimhiathach. Compatriot.

Coimhidhach. Strange, foreign.

Coimhioc. A comedy.

Coimhionnan. Equal, alike.

Coimhleapach. A bed-fellow.

Coimhlionga. A race.

Coimirc. Mercy, quarter.

Coimhlighe. Coupling.

Coimircidh. Guarding.

Coimhligham. To lay together, couple.

Coimhlinn. An affembly.

Coimhlionam. To fulfil, perform.

Coimhlionta. Performed, fulfilled.

Coimhliontachd. Completion.

Coimhmeartas. Comparifon.

Coimhmeas. Equality, co-equal.

Coimhmeas. A confideration.

Coimhmeafam. To compare.

Coimhmeafda.

Coimhmeafda. Compared, of equal worth.

Coimhmortas. A comparifon.

Coimhneartuigham. To confirm, strength-en.

Coimhneartuighte. Confirmed.

Coimhneartughadh. Confirmation.

Coimhneas. A neighbourhood.

Coimhneafam To approach.

Coimhreidh. Plain, even.

Coimhreach. Affiftant.

Coimhrealt. A conftellation.

Coimhrainnam. To divide.

Coimhreimnigham. To affemble.

Coimhreir. Syntaxis, conftruction.

Coimhriachdanas. Diftrefs, great want.

Coimhriatuin. Engendering.

Coimhfheafamh. Equilibrium.

Coimhfeacach. Confequent.

Coimhfeacachd. Confequence.

Coimhfeacamhuil. Confequential.

Coimhfigham. To perceive.

Coimhfighte. Provident.

Coimhfhreagadh. A connection, rela-tion.

Coimhtheachas. A living together.

Coimhtheachaidhe. One that lives in the fame houfe.

Coimhthighafach. Cohabiting.

Coimhthional. An affembly, congrega-tion.

Coimhthiorthach. A compatriot.

Coimhthreunadh. A confirmation.

Coimhuc. A comedy.

Coimin. A common, fuburbs.

Coimire. A brief, abridgement.

Coimpreadh. Conception.

Coimric. Protection, fanctuary.

Coimpreamham. To conceive.

Coimfeach. Indifferent; deliberate.

Coin. Hounds, dogs.

Coinbheadh. A feaft, entertainment.

Coinbheadhach. A gueft at a feaft.

Coinbhearfaid. Converfation.

Coinbhile. The dogberry-tree.

Coinbhliocht. Conflict, battle.

Coinbhraghad. A difeafe in the throat.

Coince. Hafte, expedition.

Coinchinn. The brain.

Coinchinneafadh. Vertigo.

Coinchrioche. Gag-teeth.

Coindealg. Counfel, comparifon, fimili-tude, criticifing.

Coindealgam. To perfuade.

Coindiur. As ftraight as.

Coindhreach. Mifchief.

Coindreach. Inftruction.

Coindreacham. To direct.

Coindreagam. To feparate, divide.

Coindreamhan. Rage, madnefs.

Coindris. A dog-briar.

Coineadh. Reproof.

Coinneal. A candle; loan.

Coinnealbhathaidh. Excommunication.

Coinnalbhatham. To excommunicate.

Coinneo. The dogberry-tree.

Coinfeafgar. The evening.

Coinfheafgarach. Late.

Coinfhodhairne. Otters.

Coingiol. A qualification, condition, a pafs.

Coingir. A pair.

Coineadh. Reproving.

Coineaghadh. Reftraining.

Coingialldha. Conditional.

Coiniofg. Furze.

Coinnin. A rabbit.

Coinniceir. A warren, a rabbit-burrow.

Coinfhiacal. Canine madnefs.

Coingeabhadh. Retaining.

Coinnleoir. A candleftick.

Coinnlin. A ftalk, a bud.

Coinngiollach. A complaint.

Coinne. A meeting, rendezvous.

Coinne, coinneamh. Oppofite.

Coinne. A woman.

Coinnigham

Coinnigham. To meet, to face.

Coinneas. A ferret.

Coinnim. A gueſt.

Coinolachd. Vide Caomhnalachd. Kindness.

Coinreachda. Hunting laws.

Coinnathair. A father-in-law.

Coinſas. Conſcience.

Coint. A woman.

Cointin. A controverſy.

Cointinneach. Contentious.

Coinntine. A contentious man.

Cointinoidach. Cuſtom.

Coip. A tribe, troop, a copy.

Coip. Froth.

Coir. Juſt, right.

Coir. Juſtice, right, property.

Coir. Solitary.

Coir, coithre. Sin, fault.

Coir. An air, buſineſs.

Coirce. Oats.

Coirceach. Abounding in oats.

Coirceog. A bee-hive.

Coirdin. A ſmall cord.

Coirdeas. Agreement.

Coire. A kettle, cauldron.

Coire togabach. A brewer's cauldron.

Coire. Juſtice, right.

Coire. An invitation.

Coireaman. Coriander.

Coirgniomh. Satisfaction.

Coirigh. Ranges.

Coiriabhuin. Copulation.

Coiraiſach. Important, with an air of buſineſs.

Coirighte. Softly, delicately.

Coirigham. To ſin.

Coirm. Vide Cuirm. A feaſt.

Coiripeadh. ⎫
Coiriptheachd. ⎬ Corruption.

Coiripam. To corrupt.

Coiripthe. Corrupted.

Coirm. Ale.

Coirme. A pot-companion.

Coirmeog. A female goſſip.

Coirneach. A part, the kingsfiſher.

Coirrioll. Noiſe.

Coirriollach. Noiſy.

Coirneul. A corner.

Coirninach. Frizzled, curled.

Coirnſdial. A cupboard.

Coirrcheannam. To make round at top.

Coirrſcreachag. A ſcreech-owl.

Coirceann-ciogal. A whirlgig.

Coirrdheabham. To fight with a ſpear.

Coirt. Bark, a cart.

Coirteoir. A carter.

Coirthe. A ſin, fault.

Coirtheach. Faulty.

Coirthigham. To ſin, to blame, cen-
ſure.

Cois. A foot, near to.

Coiſagach. Snug.

Coiſbheart. Shoes and ſtockings, armour
for the feet.

Coiſceim. A ſtep, pace.

Coiſceimnigham. To ſtride, walk.

Coiſeamhan. A ſhoemaker.

Coiſeanuigh. Preſervation, deliverance.

Coiſeanuigham. ⎫ To conjure, to bleſs one's
Coiſunam. ⎬ ſelf.

Coiſde. A coach, a jury of twelve men to
try according to the Engliſh law.

Coiſeona mi. I will prove.

Coiſgam. To ſtill, quiet, quell.

Coiſglidh. Still, quiet, diligent.

Coiſidhe. ⎫
Coiſaiche. ⎬ A footman.

Coiſaigham. To walk.

Coiſin. A ſtem, ſtalk.

Coiſinam. To win or gain, earn.

Coiſir. A great feaſt.

Coiſiunta. Earned.

Coiſleathann. Broadfoot.

Coiſliathroid. A football.

Coiſreacam. To bleſs, conſecrate.

Coifreacan. Confecration.

Coifreactha. Confecrated.

Coifridh. Foot-forces.

Coifrioghan. Sanctification.

Coifriomhadh Scanning of a verfe.

Coifteachd. Hearing.

Coifteoir. A coachman.

Coifteonaigh. Vide Coftas.

Coit, coite. A coracle, fmall boat, canoe.

Coitcheadh. Public.

Coitchion.
Coitchionta. } Common, public, general.

Coitcheannachd. Community.

Coiteoran. A limit, boundary.

Coitair. A cottager.

Coitit. An awl.

Coitaicham. To prefs, perfuade.

Col. An impediment, prohibition.

Colach. Wicked, impious.

Colagag. The firft finger.

Colaim. To hinder.

Colaighneachd. A colony.

Colaifde. A college.

Colam. To plaifter.

Colamoir. The fifh called hake.

Col. Inceft.

Colamhuin.
Colbh. } A bed-poft.

Colamna. A cow-hide.

Colann. The body, flefh, fenfe.

Colbh. A poft, pillar, ftalk of a plant.

Colbhidh. Having pillars.

Colbha. Scepter.

Colbha. Love, friendfhip, efteem, regard.

Colbham. To fprout, fhoot.

Colbhtach. A cow-calf.

Colcach. A flock bed.

Colg. A prickle, fting, beard, awn, fword.

Colgach. Prickly, fcaly, bearded, fretful.

Colgag. The fore-finger.

Colgan. A falmon.

Colganta. Lively, martial.

Colgthroidam. To fight with a fword.

Colgbhruidhim. Butcher's broom.

Colgrafach. Prickly.

Coll. A head, hazel-tree, name of the letter C.

Colis. Cabbage.

Coll. Deftruction, ruin.

Collach. A fat heifer, a boar.

Collaim. To fleep.

Colladh. Sleep, reft.

Collaidh. A two-year old heifer.

Collaidh. Carnal, venereal.

Collaidheachd. Carnality.

Colladar. They lodged.

Collag-lion. An earwig.

Collbhuine.
Collchoille. } A wood of hazel.

Collchnu. A filbert.

Collotach. Soporific.

Coll-leabaidh. A bedftead.

Colltach. A fleet.

Colm, colum. A dove.

Colmh. A pillar.

Colma. Hardnefs.

Colman-cathaich. A whoop.

Colman-coille. A queeft, ring-dove.

Colmcha.
Colmlan. } A pigeon-houfe.

Colog. A fteak, collop.

Colpa. A fingle cow, horfe.

Colpa. Vide Calpa. A leg.

Colpach. A heifer, bullock, fteer, colt.

Colt. Meat, victuals.

Coltach. Likely, probable.

Coltair. Plowfhare.

Coltas. Likelihood, appearance.

Coltra. Dark, gloomy.

Coltraighe. A razor-bill.

Colubhairt. Cabbage.

I

Colinn. A collection of dressed victuals made all over the country on the new year, by the poor people.

Colum. } A dove, pigeon.
Columan. }

Columhan. A prop, pillar, pedestal.

Com. The waist, middle, body.

Coma. Indifferent.

Comach. A breach, defeat.

Comadair. A romancer.

Comadairachd. A feigned story.

Comain. An obligation, debt.

Comairce. Protection.

Comaircam. To protect, defend.

Comairam. To liken, compare.

Comann. Communion, society.

Comar. The nose, a way, meeting.

Comarc. A part, share.

Comamar. Comparison.

Comarćthoir. A protector.

Comart. To kill.

Comaoine. A benefit.

Comaontaoir. A benefactor.

Comaradh. Helping.

Comas. Power.

Comasdan. A commissary.

Comasdairachd. Commissariot.

Comasach. Powerful.

Comasg. Mixture.

Comasgachd. A composition, mixture.

Commasgghnumh. } A chaos, confused
Comasgmhiol. } mass.

Combach. A breach, defeat.

Combaidhe. Assistance, friendship.

Combrughadh. Oppression.

Combrugham. To oppress.

Combrughte. Crushed.

Comeirce. Dedication.

Comh Sometimes. Coimh & eo, equal to the Latin Con. The mh is omitted properly, when the word begins with a consonant.

Comhachag. An owl.

Comhad. An elegy, a comparison, the two last quartans of a verse.

Comhadh. Preservation, a groan, a bribe.

Comh. To keep, preserve.

Comhachd. Vide Cumhachd.

Comhachdach. Powerful

Comhacmach. A circuit.

Comhagal. A conference.

Comhaidh. A keeper, a reward.

Comhaille. Pregnancy.

Comhaillam. To bear, carry.

Comhailtam. To join.

Comhaimsirach. A cotemporary.

Comhaimseardha. Cotemporary.

Comhainm. A surname.

Comhair. Opposite.

Comhairmham. To number.

Comhaire. A cry, outcry.

Comhairce. Mercy, quarter.

Comhaircam. To cry out, bewail.

Comhairle. An advice, counsel, synod, council, convocation.

Comhairleach. A counsellor.

Comhairligham. To counsel, advise.

Comhaicheadh. Competition.

Comhaitcheas. A neighbour.

Comhairp. } Emulation, strife.
Comhairpas. }

Comhaisdreach. A fellow-traveller.

Comhal. A waiting-maid.

Comhalla. A foster-brother or sister.

Comhal. The performance, execution of a thing.

Comhal. Bold, courageous.

Comhal. To heap, join together.

Comhailam. To discharge an office, duty.

Comhaitaiche. A townsman.

Comhailtach. Fulfilled, performed.

Comhaltam. To join.

Comhan. A shrine.

Comham. To defend.

Comhaolachd. A college.

Comhaontuigham. To consent.

Comhaontughadh.

Co nhaontughadh. } Confent.
Comhaonta. }

Comhaontachd. Agreement, unity.

Comhaois. One of equal age.

Comhaofda. Of equal age.

Comhar. Oppofite.

Comhartha. A mark, fign, print.

Comharba. Protection, a partner in church-lands, a fucceffor, a vicar.

Comharbachd. A vicarage.

Comharbuigham. To fucceed.

Comhardachd. Agreement, correfpondence in poetry.

Comharnais. Emulation.

Comharguin. A fyllogifm.

Comharfan. } A neighbour.
Coimharfanach. }

Coimharfanachd. Neighbourhood.

Comhbhaidh. A fellow-feeling.

Comhtharuighte. Marked, diftinguifhed.

Comhbhrathair. A fellow.

Comtharuigham. To mark, fign.

Comhatheach. Competition.

Comchorbadh. Deftroying.

Comhbhith. Co-exiftence.

Comhbhithach. Co-exiftent.

Comhbhruach. The marches or confines of a country.

Comhbhualam. To contact.

Comhbhruachach. Bordering upon.

Comhbhagaram. To comminate.

Comhchaidreach. Correfponding.

Comhbhrioguchadh. Confubftantiation.

Comhchairdreachd. Commerce, traffic.

Comhchaidream. To traffic.

Comhchaint. A conference.

Comhchaochlaidhachd. Commutability.

Comhchaoidham. To condole.

Comhchaochlaidach. Commutable.

Comhcharaidhachd. Mutual ftruggling.

Comhchomhairlaicham. To confult.

Comhcharnta. Heap together.

Comhcheolraiche. A chorifter.

Comhcheangal. A confederacy.

Comhchiallach. Synonymous.

Comhchoigrich. A border, or limit.

Comhchongbhail. Honour.

Comchuan cogaidh. Theatre of war.

Comhchorp. A corporation.

Comhchuibhrigham. To concatenate.

Comhas. Good-fellowfhip.

Comhdach. A refuge, fhelter.

Comhdachadh. Refuge, fheltering.

Comhdaicham. To cover, fhelter.

Comhdhail. A meeting, an affembly.

Comhdailam. To coincide.

Comhdhoieh. As foon as.

Comhdhala. A ftatute, a law.

Comheas. Society.

Comhchnuafachd. Collection.

Comhchofmhuil. Alike.

Comhchoflas. Equality.

Comhchraite. Sprinkled, conquaffated.

Comhchratham. To conquaffate.

Comhchras. Good-fellowfhip.

Comhchraoidheachd. Agreement.

Comhchretoir. Fellow-creature.

Comhchruinnigham. To affemble, convoke.

Comhchruinnughadh. Congregation.

Comhchruth. Equiformation.

Comhchruinnighte. Affembled.

Comhchuiram. To difpofe, fet in order.

Comhchudthromigham. To equalize, proportion.

Comhchudthrom. Equilibrium.

Comhchuifnigham. To congeal.

Comhdaigham. To build, prove, quote.

Comhdachadh. Quotation, proof.

Comhdhaingnigham. To confirm, ftrengthen.

Comhdhealradh. Corradiation.

Comhdhalta. A fofter-brother.

Comhdhaltas. Relation of foftering.

Comhdhas An equal right.

Comhdhlutha. A compact.

Comhdhluthadh. Contribution.

Comhlutham.

Comhdhlutham.   To frame, join.
Comhdhuanadh.   Confirmation.
Comhdhunam.   To conclude.
Comhdhunadh.   Conclusion.
Comhdhuthchais. } Of the same coun-
Comhdhuthchasach. } try.
Comheud.   Rivalship.
Comnfasgaim.   To embrace.
Comfhogus.   Consanguinity.
Comhfhasam.   To concrete.
Comhfhuighleadh.   A conference.
Comhfhuil.   Consanguinity.
Comhfhurtachd.   Comfort.
Comhfhurtaichoir.   Comforter.
Comhfhurtigham.   To comfort.
Comhfhuirmam.   To compose.
Comhfhoghar.   A consonant.
Comhfhaghrach.   Consonant.
Comhfhoghair cluig.   A chime of bells.
Comhfhadthrath.   Equinox.
Comhfhreagradh.   Conformity.
Comhfhulangas.   Sympathy.
Comhghaol.   Consanguinity.
Comhghabhal.   Harmony, love.
Comhgharach.   Near to.
Comhghair.   Conclamation.
Comhghairdachas.   Congratulation.
Comhgaram.   To furnish.
Comhghairdaigham.   To congratulate.
Comhgusach.   Kindred.
Comhghluasachd.   Fermentation.
Comhiadhadh.   Shutting up together.
Comhfhlaithachd.   Democracy.
Comhfhlaith.   A demagogue.
Comhghiol.   Condition.
Comhghloir.   Consonance.
Comhghnas.   Genteel.
Comhghnathughadh.   Conversation.
Comhghnumtha.   Heaped together.
Comhghothach.   A consonant.
Comhghuilam.   To condole.
Comhlach.   A comrade.
Comhitham.   To eat together.

Comhla.   Guards.
Comhla.   A horn.
Comhlamh.   Together.
Comhlan.   A young hero.
Comhabhairt. } A conference, dialogue.
Comhlabradh. }
Comhlabhraim.   To confer, converse.
Comhlachtuighte.   A foster-brother.
Comhladh.   A door, sluice.
Comhlaim.   To rub.
Comhlair.   Quiet, even-tempered.
Comhlan.   A duel, combat.
Comhleaghadh.   Coliquefaction.
Comhleaghan.   Amalgama.
Comhleagham.   To amalgamate.
Comhlionam.   To fulfil.
Comhloin.   Obligation.
Comhlofgadh.   Conflagration.
Comhluadar   Conversation, company.
Comhluadaram.   To accompany.
Comhluath.   As swift, as soon as.
Comhluchd.   Partners.
Comhluidhe.   Alliance.
Comhmaoidheamh.   A common joy, or boasting.
Comhmaoidheam.   To congratulate.
Comhbhrathairachas.   Consanguinity.
Comhbhrughadh. } Contrition.
Comhbhrughteachd. }
Comhbhrughte.   Contrite.
Comhbhrugham.   To bruise.
Comhbhuaireadh.   Tumult, uproar, war.
Comhnasgam.   To join, compact together.
Comhnadh.   Help, assistance.
Comhnaighe.   A dwelling, habitation, rest.
Comhnard.   Even, level.
Comnuighe.   Always, perpetually.
Comhnuigham.   To stand still.
Comhnuightheach.   Continuing.
Comhnuigham.   To dwell, continue.
Comhoibruicham.   To co-operate.
Comhoglach.   A fellow-servant.
Comhoibrach.   Co-efficient.

Comhoigre. A fellow heir.

Comholthoir. A pot-companion.

Comholcas. Defpite.

Comhortas. Emulation.

Comhortuis. Comparative.

Comhra. A companion, a coffin.

Comhphais. Compaffion.

Comhphriofunach. Fellow prifoner.

Comhrac. A fight, battle.

Comhracam. To fight.

Comhracoir. An encounterer.

Comhrachadh. Affembling together.

Comhracham. To affemble.

Comhradh. A dialogue, converfation.

Comhraidham. To converfe.

Comhraidhteach. Converfable.

Comhrangach. Wrinkled.

Comhrochdam. To meet.

Comhrogain. Election, choice.

Comhroigham. To choofe.

Comhrionn. A fhare, a meal, portion.

Comhr.tham. To concur.

Comhrunaigham. To communicate.

Comhrunaghadh. A confpiracy.

-Comhfaighidh. Peace among you, quiet, reft.

Comhfhugraiche. A play-fellow.

Comhfanach. Everlafting, perpetual.

Comhfgolair. A fchool-fellow.

Comhfhiorruidh. Co-eternal.

Comhfhiorridhachd. Co-eternity.

Comhfhliofnach. Equilateral.

Comhfheidam. To conflate.

Comhfmugam. To vomit.

Comhfheirbhaifach. A fellow-fervant.

Comhfhruadh. } Confluence of rivers.
Comhfhruth. }

Comhfhrutham. To converge, conflux.

Comhfhollus. } Conftellation.
Comhfhoillfe. }

Comhfhuanam. To fleep, repofe.

Comhfpairnam. To wreftle.

Comhfanuidhe. A refidenter.

Combfhe rm. Harmony.

Comhfheomraiche. A chum.

Comhfhuireach. A rival.

Comhftrith. Strife, broil, quarrel.

Comhfhaighdair. A fellow-foldier.

Comhthathadh. Articulation, fyntax, joining together.

Comhthatham. To join, articulate.

Comhthaincaghadh. Congratulation.

Comhthoifga. As early as.

Comhthrom Juftice; even, equal.

Comhthromach. Juft, upright, even.

Comhhoghu. A coufin-german.

Comhuidh. A prefent.

Comult. Scratching.

Comultam. To fcratch.

Comircidh. A guard.

Comhtha, comhthach. A companion, comrade, fidelity.

Comhtbaite. A compact.

Comhtharangte. Contracted.

Comhtharuingam. To contract.

Comhthathuighte. A mutual old acquaintance.

Comhthional. Congregation.

Comhthionolam. To affemble.

Comhthoilaigham. To agree to.

Comhthogam. To conftruct.

Comhthoimhfach. Commenfurable.

Comhthras. } Sweet fmell.
Comhthrachd. }

Comhthra. Sweet-fcented.

Comhthromuigham. To weigh even, to
make even, level.

Comhthruaighe. Compaffion.

Comhthruaigham. To compaffionate.

Comhthruacanta. Compaffionate.

Comhthrufam. To contract.

Comhthuaram. To co-indicate.

Comhua. Vide Comhogha.

Comhuibhneoir. A pot-companion.

Comhmhaim. A wife.

Commairce. A riding together, friendfhip.

Commaithchcas.

Commaithcheas. Neighbourhood.

Commas togha. Conge d'elire.

Comhmheadh. Free quarters.

Commor. The nose.

Commain. A thing agreeable, a gratuity, obligation, favour.

Communn. Society.

Communaghadh. Communion.

Comon. But.

Comora. Comparing, kemping.

Comoradh. An assembly, congregation.

Comoraim. To gather together.

Companach. A companion.

Compantas. Fellowship, society.

Compluchd. A set, gang.

Comraighas. A form, fashion.

Compartuicham. To partake.

Compas. A ring, circle.

Compailt. A company.

Compraid. Comparison.

Comsuanadh. Rest.

Comthach. A companion.

Commuisgam. ⎱
Commeasgam. ⎰ To mix, mingle.

Comhursa. A neighbour.

Comuiltam. To rub.

Con   Sense, meaning.

Con. A dog.

Cona. Cat's-tail or mofs-crops.

Conablach. A carcase.

Conach. A shirt, murrain.

Conach. Prosperity, affluence.

Conachlon. An equal, companion, fellow; a kind of Irish versification.

Conadh   Prosperity, a greedy appetite.

Conadhaire. Therefore.

Conail. A plague that raged in Ireland.

Conailbhe. Friendship.

Conailbheach. Friendly, upholding.

Conair. A way.

Conairde. As high as.

Conairt   Hunting with dogs, a rout of wolves.

Conalach. Brandishing.

Conaisleach. Busy.

Conall. Love, friendship.

Conairtam. To hunt with dogs.

Conaltradh. Conversation.

Conas. A dispute, a carcase.

Conbach. Hydrophobia.

Conbhaidh. Stopping, withholding.

Conbhaigheas. Abstinence.

Conbhail. Holding.

Conbhaigham. To hold, stop, stay.

Conbhaiscne. The dogberry-tree.

Conbharsaid. Behaviour, conversation.

Conbhuidhean. A guard.

Conchliud. A conclusion.

Concubhar. A proper name.

Conasg. Whins, furze.

Conbhair. A dog-kennel.

Conbhalas. A support, stay.

Conclan. A comparison.

Concobhar. Help, assistance.

Condasach. Furious.

Condaighais. A countess.

Condasachd. Rage, fury.

Condreagadh. A separation.

Condualadh. Embroidery, sculpture.

Confadh. Roaring, howling.

Confuadach. A vulture.

Congantach. Helpful.

Congasach. A kinsman.

Congnamh. Help, assistance.

Congraidhe. A relation.

Conga. The antlers of a buck.

Conga. A cotemporary.

Congbhail. A house, habitation.

Congbhalas. A stay, help.

Congbhuisgam. To restrain.

Congcais. A conquest.

Conghaireadh. Roaring.

Conghaiream. To roar, shout.

Conghail. Gallantry, bravery.

Congnam. To help, assist.

Congnamh. Help, assistance.

Congra.

Congra. A narrative, relation.

Congraidhe. A relator, rehearser.

Congraim. Cunning, craft; apparel, cloth-ing.

Congraidham. To occupy.

Conla. Witty, sensible, prudent, chaste.

Conlach. Straw.

Conlan. An assembly.

Conn. A meaning, sense, reason.

Conn. The frame, the body.

Connadh. Wood, fuel.

Connaidhneas. Ratiocination, argumenta-tion.

Connail. Prudent.

Connail. A civil farewel.

Connaircam. To see, behold.

Connaircle. Indulgent.

Connaoi. A preserving, protecting.

Connartha. Earnest.

Conchas. Visum est tibi.

Connsachadh. Dissention.

Connspoid. A dispute, disputing.

Connspair. A disputer.

Conspeach. A wasp.

Conspoidche. A disputant.

Conspoidam. To dispute.

Contairismhe. A prince's court.

Conntoirbhram. To allege, maintain.

Conoidam. To heed, regard.

Conra. An agreement, compact.

Conradoir. A bearer at a funeral.

Consain. A consonant.

Constal. Counsel, advice.

Constairseach. Stiff, opinionate.

Contabhairt. Chance, peril, peradventure, danger.

Conntabhairtach. Doubtful, dangerous, fortuitous.

Contagram. To affirm, allege.

Contagairt. Affirming.

Contar. A doubt.

Contas. Vide Cuntas.

Contrail. Opposition.

Contrachd. Misfortune, a curse.

Contrardha. Contrary.

Contrardhachd. Contrariety.

Contruadh. Lean, poor.

Copan, A cup.

Copan-freine. Boss of a bridle.

Copag. Dock-leaf, dock.

Copagach. Abounding with dock.

Copchaille. A coif.

Cor. A state, condition, circumstance.

Air Chor. So that.

Cor air bith. At all, by no means.

Cor. Music.

Cor. A twist, turn.

Cor. A cast, throw, a circular motion.

Cor. Surety, a corner.

Cor. Near, neighbourhood.

Cora. Peace, a wier, dam.

Cora. A quoir.

Corach. Justice.

Coranach. The Irish cry.

Corag. A finger.

Coragadh. Neatness, trimness.

Coraid. A pair, cheese-rennet.

Coraidh. A champion, hero.

Coraidheachd. Recognizance.

Coraig. Although.

Coraise. A curtain.

Coraim. To turn.

Corb. A coach, waggon.

Corba. Lewdness.

Corra, corba. Lascivious, lewd.

Corbadh. A cast, throw.

Corbaidhe. The cramp.

Corbaire. A cartwright.

Corboire. A coachman.

Corc. A large pot, cauldron; a knife.

Corc. Children.

Corcach. A moor, marsh.

Corcuir. Red, purple, a red dye.

Corcuirach. Red.

Corcan. A pot.

Corcach. Hemp.

Corc. A little knife.

Corcan-coille. A fort of flower.

Corcog. A bee-hive.

Corda. A cord or line.

Cordadh. Agreement.

Cordam. To agree.

Cordaidhe. Spafms.

Corghas. Lent.

Corn. A drinking-cup or horn.

Cornchlar. A cupboard.

Cornadh. A folding, rolling, a fkirt, corner.

Cornam. To fold, plait.

Cornta. Folded.

Corog. A faggot, bavin.

Coron. A crown, chaplet.

Coroin-mhuire. A rofary of beads.

Corplein. A winding-fheet.

Corp Chriofd. The Eucharift.

Corp. A body, corpfe.

Corpanta. Bulky, folid.

Corpordha. Bodily, corporeal.

Corr. A fnout, bill.

Corr. A corner.

Corr. Odd, not even.

Corr. A pit of water.

Corra-margaidh. The rabble.

Corr-mheur. An odd finger. Cho chuir
mi mo chorr-mheur air. I will not touch
it.

Corrlach. Overplus, remainder.

Corr. ⎫
Corrghridhin. ⎬ A heron, crane.
Corrghlas. ⎭

Corrach. Steep, a fetter, fhackle, a marfh.

Corran. A fickle, prickle.

Corrach. Wavering, inconfiftent.

Corr-caigailt. Green and blue luminous
particles, obferved at raking the fire at
night, refembling glow-worms, faid to
forebode froft.

Corra-bhan. A ftork.

Corranach. ⎫
Corranta. ⎬ Barbed, hooked.

Corrachofach. A cheeflip, millipedes.

Corraghil. Gefture, ftirring about.

Coribham. To carve, grave.

Corrocadh. To perfuade.

Corrtha. Weary, fatigued.

Corrughadh. A motion.

Corruigham. To ftir, move.

Corruigheadh. ⎫
Corruigh. ⎬ Injury, anger.

Corfa. A coaft.

Corfaicham. To cruize.

Corfair. A coafter, cruizer.

Cortas. Debt.

Corthoir. A border, fringe.

Corudhadh. Coral.

Corughadh. An ornament, armour.

Cos. The foot, leg.

Cos. Confideration.

Cofach. Footed, having feet.

Cofaidham. To teach, inftruct.

Cofaint. A reply, defence.

Cofair. A feaft, a banquet.

Cofair. A bed.

Cofmhuil. Alike.

Cofamhuilachd. Similitude, comparifon.

Cofan. A foot-path.

Cofainam. To keep off, defend, to preferve, to avouch, to maintain.

Cofanta. Kept off, defended.

Cofanta. Perplexed, entangled.

Cofantach. ⎫
Cofantoir. ⎬ The defender in a procefs.

Cofaracha. Fetters.

Cofboir. An object.

Cofc, cofg. A ceafing, failing, giving
over.

Cofc, cofg. An impediment, hindrance.

Cofcim. A ftep, pace.

Cofdam. To coft, expend.

Cofdas. Expence, coft.

Cofdafach. Rich, coftly.

Cofgar. A flaughter, havock.

Cofgaram. To flaughter, cut and hew.

Cofcar. A triumph, rejoicing.

Cofcarachd. } Victorious, triumphant.
Cofgara.

Cofgrach. Slaughter, mafiacre.

Coflach. Like.

Coflom. Bare-foot.

Cofleathan. Web-footed.

Cofluath. Swift-footed

Cofmhuil. Like.

Cofmhuilachd. Imitation, fimilitude.

Cofmhuilachdidh Figurative.

Cofnadh. Defence, prefervation.

Cofnadh. Gain, earning, gaining. Vide Coifinam.

Cofnam. To defend, maintain.

Cofnamh. Defence, battle, war.

Coftol. A footftool.

Cofnamh. Swimming.

Cofpanach. Vide Cafpanach. Parallel.

Cofrach. Slaughter.

Coftag a bhaile gheamhridh. Coftmary.

Coftafach. Expenfive.

Cofuifge. Wild chervil.

Coffumach. } Rubbifh.
Coffumail.

Cot. A part, fhare, portion.

Cota. A coat.

Cotaigham. To cover.

Cotaig. A good correfpondence, harmony.

Cotaigham. To be afraid.

Cotchanibh. } In parts.
Cotchaibh.

Cotan. A little coat, piece, a part.

Coth. Meat, victuals.

Cota preafach, ingheain an riogh. The herb ladies mantle.

Cothacha. Debate, difpute, obftinacy.

Cothaigham. To contend, ftruggle, feed, fupport.

Cothadh. A fupport, preferving, protection.

Cothan. A cough, anhelation.

Cothlon. Viaticum, victuals for a journey.

Cothughadh. A ftay, fupport.

Cothon. Frothy.

Cotta. A cottage.

Cottud. A mountain.

Couthartach. Plunder.

Crabhadh. } Devotion, religion.
Crabhachd.

Crabhach. Devout, religious.

Crabham. To worfhip.

Crac. A crack.

Crabhdiadn. Mortification.

Cracal. Cracking.

Cracan. A hill fide, a cracking noife.

Cracaireachd. Converfation.

Cradhgheadh. Vide Cnamhgheadh.

Cradh. Pain, anguifh.

Cracaire. A talker.

Cradham. To pain, torment, vex.

Cragh. Sleek.

Craibhdhigh. Mortifying people.

Crag. Vide Cnag.

Craidhte. Tormented, vexed, afflicted.

Craidhal. A cradle.

Craidhlag. A bafket.

Crag. A paw.

Craidhteachd. Mifery, vexation, pain.

Cragairam. To paw, to handle indelicately.

Cragairt. } Pawing, handling.
Cragairachd.

Craig. A rock.

Craigeach. Rocky.

Craimhor. Corpulent.

Craimpiafg. The torpedo.

Crain. A fow.

Crainam. To gnaw.

Craintfeile. Tough phlegm.

Crait. A fmall farm, field, glebe.

Craite. Shrunk.

Cramhor. Gross.

Cramhag. Caput mortuum.

Crampa. A knot.

Crampaid. A ferril.

Cranadh. Choosing by lots.

Cranaghlach. A carpenter.

Cranaidhe. An old decrepid man.

Cranachur. Lot, casting of lots.

Cranchust. The bark of a tree.

Crandolbh. Lottery.

Cranfaistine. Sorcery.

Crann A tree, a mast, a bar, bolt, a plough.

Crannag. A pulpit, hamper, round top.

Crann-critheach. The aspen-tree.

Crann-ola. Olive-tree.

Crannchu. A lapdog.

Crann-dordain. A kind of music made by putting the hand to the mouth.

Crann-gail. Lattices before the altar.

Crannda. Decrepid.

Crannlach. Boughs, branches.

Cransaor. A carpenter.

Cranntarraing. A wooden pin.

Crannchuiram. To ballot.

Cranngasan. The herb henbane.

Crannam To bar, bolt, barricade.

Crannlacha. Teal.

Crannlochan. A churn.

Crannarbhair. A plough.

Crannphiosan. Some missive weapon.

Crannteach. An arbour.

Cranntarach. Hoar-frost.

Crann-taisuing. A cross-bar, a diameter.

Crannteante. A press, a printer's press.

Crann-tabhuil. A sling.

Cranntogalach. A crane.

Cranntoisaich. The foremast.

Crannmeadhoin (mor). The main-mast.

Crann-denaidh. The mizen-mast.

Crann-riaslaidh. A sort of plough.

Crahn-uisge. } The boltsprit.
Crann-spreoide. }

Crann-seunta. Sacred wood.

Crann-sgoide. The boom.

Crann-apricoc. Apricot-tree.

Crann-siris. Cherry-tree.

Crann-sitron. The citron-tree.

Crann-cennel. The cornel-tree.

Crann-pailm. The date-tree.

Crann-fioguis. The fig-tree.

Crann-calltin. The hazel tree.

Crann-limoin. The lemon-tree.

Crann-maoldhearc. The mulberry-tree.

Crann-neochdair. The nectarine-tree.

Craobh-orainis. An orange-tree.

Crann-pheitseog. A peach-tree.

Craobh-pheur. A pear-tree.

Craobh-phlumbis. The plum-tree.

Crann-grainabhuil. The pomegranate-tree.

Crann-cuinnse. The quince-tree.

Crann-airnag. The sloe-tree.

Crann-gallchno. The walnut-tree.

Crann-fearna. The alder or arn-tree.

Crann-uinsionn. The ash-tree.

Crann-labhrais. The bay-tree.

Crann-faidhbhile. The beech-tree.

Crann-beitha. The birch-tree.

Crann-bucsa. The box-tree.

Crann-sedair. The cedar-tree.

Crann-airce. The cork-tree.

Crann-canaich. The cotton-tree.

Crann-cuphair. The cypress-tree.

Crann-eboin. Ebony-tree.

Craobh-dhromain. An elder or bore-tree.

Craobh-leamhain, no ailmog. An elm-tree.

Crann-giubhais. A fir-tree.

Crann-tuise. Frankincense-tree.

Crann-cuilinn. The hollin-tree.

Cranndearg-labhrais. The laurel-tree.

Crann-teile. The lime-tree.

Crann-mhalpis. The maple-tree.

Crann-meidil. The medlar-tree.

Crann-

Crann-daruich. The oak-tree.

Crann-tuilm. The holm-oak.

Crann-pion. The pine-tree.

Crann-pobhuil. The poplar-tree.

Crann-feilaich. The fallow-tree.

Craobh-chaorthuin. The service-tree.

Crann-fice. The sycamore-tree.

Crann-feilaich-fhrancaich. The willow-tree.

Craobh-iubhair. The yew-tree.

Craobh. A tree, branch.

Craobh-caoimhnas-fgeoil. A genealogical tree.

Craobham. To branch, sprout.

Craobh chofgair. Laurel, trophy.

Craobhin chno. A clufter of nuts.

Craobhfgaolam. To publifh, promulgate.

Craobhin. A bufh, bunch.

Craochadh. Withering, blafting.

Craoidhte. Shod.

Craoifin. A glutton.

Craos. Excefs, gluttony, a wide mouth.

Craos-fhotharguin. A gargarifm.

Craofghlanam. To gargle.

Craofan. } A glutton.
Craofaire. }

Crofach. Gluttonous.

Craoifeach. } A fpear.
Craoifneach. }

Craoifeach dhearg. A burning fpear.

Craofol. Drunkennefs.

Crapadh. Shrinking, crufhing, contraction.

Crapara. One that crufheth, ftrong.

Craptha. Warped.

Crapluigham. To fetter, bind.

Crapfuifgil. The twilight.

Cras. } The body.
Crafan. }

Crafgach. Corpulent.

Crafgach. A box, coffer.

Crathadh. Shaking.

Cratham. To fhake, fprinkle.

Crathrach. A plafhy bog.

Cre. A creed.

Creabille. A garter.

Creabhach. Dry brufh-wood.

Creabhag. A twig, a young woman.

Creabham. To crave, dun.

Cre, creadh. Clay, duft, a body, being.

Creach. Plunder, an hoft, a wave, ruin.

Creach. Blind, grey.

Creach, creachan. A fcolloped-fhell, a cup.

Creacham. To plunder.

Creachach. Rapacious, having fhells or cups.

Creachadoir. A plunderer.

Creachan. Rocks.

Creachar. A veftry.

Creachd. A wound.

Creachdam. To wound.

Creachdach. Full of wounds.

Creachairas. Sculpture.

Creachdlorgach. Full of fcars.

Creachram. To ftigmatize, mark, to fear.

Cread. What ? a creed.

Creadal. Religious.

Creadha. Clerkfhip.

Creadhla. Clergy.

Creadhach. Wounded.

Creadhal. Religious, worfhipping.

Creadmhail. Faith.

Creadradh. A chariot.

Creafog. Powder, duft.

Creag. A rock.

Creagach. Rocky.

Creagan. A rocky place.

Creagag. A fort of perch.

Creagag-uifge. A perch.

Creamam. To gnaw, corrode, pluck.

Creamh. Wild garlick.

Creamh-garaidh. A leek.

Creamh-

Creamh-muice-fiadh. Hart's tongue.

Creamh-nual. The noise of people carousing.

Creadhoule. A lamprey.

Crean. A buying, purchasing.

Creanait. A market-place.

Creanam. To consume, remove.

Creanadh air. Suffering for it.

Creanair. Sedition.

Creannas. Neat-handed.

Creapal Entangling.

Creapalam. To stop, hinder, stay.

Crearadh. Bending, crooking.

Crearal. A retaining, withholding.

Creas, crios. A girdle.

Creasam. To set or lay, to tire.

Creas. Narrow, straight.

Creaschas. A narrow house.

Creasgoinam. To wound.

Creasmhuir. A strait of the sea.

Creas. A shrine.

Creasughadh. A girding.

Creat. The form or figure of one's complexion.

Creat. Terror.

Creat. A science, knowledge.

Creata. Earthen.

Creatach. A hurdle.

Creatachan. A churning-stick.

Creatar. Faithful, religious, holy.

Creatar
Creatairair. } A sanctuary, shrine.

Creatoir. A creature.

Creath. A swan.

Creathadh. Trembling.

Creatham. To cause to tremble.

Creathan. A shaking, trembling.

Creathair. A sieve.

Creathnaigham. To tremble, shake.

Creathnughadh. Trembling, shaking.

Creath-thalmhuinn. An earthquake.

Creatrach. A wilderness.

Creatuir. A creature.

Crechdach. Sinful.

Cred. Wherefore.

Credh. Ore.

Credh-umha. Ore of brass.

Creic. A prey.

Creideamh. Faith, belief.

Creidam. To believe, credit.

Creidas. Credit.

Creidmhach. Faithful, believing, a believer.

Creidmhasach. Creditable.

Creidte. Believed.

Creidsin. Believing.

Creidteoir. A believer.

Creidhmh. A disease.

Creidhmheach. Full of sores.

Creidhmam. To gnaw, chew.

Creig. A rock.

Creigach. Rocky.

Creigag. A conger.

Creigair. A grapple.

Creimam.
Creinam. } To gnaw.

Creimadair. A carper.

Creisineamh. A scar.

Creithir. A cup, a sieve.

Creithrin. A little cup or sieve.

Crennaighte. Terrified.

Creithul. A cradle.

Creodhar. A rail or sieve.

Creopam. To seduce.

Cresan. A girdle.

Cresean. Old earth, clay.

Creseam. Religious, pious.

Creuchd. A wound.

Creuchdach. Full of sores.

Creuchdam. To wound.

Creumhach. A rock.

Creun. The body.

Creug. A rock.

Creugan. A rocky place.

Creugach. Rocky.

Creud fa. Wherefore? why?

Cri. The heart.

Criach, for crithach. Trembling, shaking.

Criadh. Earth, clay.

Criadhcheanglam. To cement.

Criadh loifge. A potfherd.

Criadhaol. Mortar.

Criadha. Earthen.

Criadhadair. A potter.

Criadhluch. A mole.

Criadhuire. A hufbandman.

Criapach. Rough.

Criathar. A fieve.

Criathar-meala. A honeycomb.

Criathram. To fift.

Criathradh. Sifting.

Criathrach. A wildernefs.

Crib. Swiftnefs, hafte, fpeed.

Crich. A territory, country.

Crilidh. A buying, purchafing.

Cricein. Vide Lus nan ruiteachan.

Crimtheart. Second-milking.

Crimag. A morfel, bit.

Crimchaig. Grumbling, reflecting.

Crindreas. A bramble.

Crinlin. A box, coffer.

Crine, crineachd. Rottennefs, withering.

Crineamh, cloch na crineamh. The fatal, or coronation ftone, of the Scotch kings; it is commonly called Lia fail. It is at this day preferved as a monument of antiquity in Weftminfter-abbey.

Crineamh. To fall.

Crinlin. A writing-defk.

Crinmhiol. A wood-loufe.

Crinam. To gnaw, bite.

Crintach. Fretting.

Criobh. A jeft, trifle.

Crioch. Preferment, confines, territory, a brier.

Crioch. An end, conclufion.

Criochnaigham. To finifh, end, conclude, die.

Criochnuighte. Finifhed.

Criochnuighach. Finite.

Criochnuichoir. Finifher.

Criochnuighachd. Finitude.

Criochan. Striving.

Criochdairan. The gag-teeth.

Crioch-fgeoil. An epilogue.

Criochfearainn. A land-mark.

Criochfmachd. A government.

Criodaigham. To pat, ftroke.

Criodaire. A fondler.

Criodh, criodhe. The heart.

Criodhamhuil. Hearty, cheerful.

Criodhar. A leech, a woodcock.

Criol. A cheft, coffer.

Criomhthan. A fox.

Criomadan. Bits.

Crion. Dry, withered.

Crionach. Dry fticks, faggots.

Crionam, crionaigham. To dry, wither, fade.

Crionaghadh. Withering, fading.

Crioncan. Strife.

Crioncanam. To ftrive.

Crioncanadh. ⎫
Crioncanachd. ⎬ Striving.

Crionlach. Touchwood.

Crionmon. A collection.

Crionna. Old, antient, fage, prudent, wife.

Crionnachd. Prudence, wifdom, wit.

Crios. A belt, girdle, cingle.

Criofach. Tight, having girdles.

Criofach, for griofach. Embers.

Criofd. Chrift.

Criofdaighe. A chriftian.

Criofdachd. Chriftendom.

Criofduigh. Chriftian.

Criofd. Swift, quick, nimble.

Criofd-athair. A god-father.

Criofleach. A limit, border, bofom.

Crioflachadh. Girding the loins.

Crioflaigham. To gird.

Criofluighte. Girded.

Crioftal. Cryftal.

3

Crioftalamhuil.

Criostalamhuil. Tranfparent.

Criotamhuil. Earthen, made of clay.

Crioth. A fhaking, trembling.

Criotham. To fhake, tremble, fhiver.

Criothanach. Quaking.

Criothchumadair A potter.

Criothnuigham. To tremble.

Criothfdabhaire. A potter.

Criothfhuileach. Purblind.

Crifcheangal. A fwaddling-band.

Criflion. Sinews.

Criplach. A cripple.

Criotacham. Vide Crioduigham. To hug.

Criplaicham. To maim.

Criplachd. Decrepitude.

Cripagaicham. To rimple, wrinkle.

Cripag. A wrinkle.

Crit. The back.

Criteagan. A dwarf.

Crith, crioch. A region, country.

Crith. Trembling.

Crith-thalmhunn. Earthquake.

Crith. Fit of an ague, fhaking.

Critheach. Shaking, quaking.

Critheagal. Terror, aftonifhment.

Critheaglach. Aftonifhed.

Crithean. The afpen-tree.

Crithghalar The palfy.

Crithide. Caufe of fear and trembling.

Crithidh. Terrible, horrible.

Crithir. A drinking-cup.

Crithneal. A fhower.

Cithre. Sparks of fire from the clafhing of arms, fmall particles of any thing.

Cithreothadh. Weak ice or froft.

Crindarnach. The hickup, yexing.

Criun. A wolf.

Cro, croth. A hut, cottage, hovel.

Cro. Death, an iron bar.

Cro Children, the eye of a needle.

Cro. Straight, narrow, clofe.

Croan. Correction.

Crobh. A hand, a paw.

Crobh-priachain. The herb cranes-bill.

Crobhall. Genitals.

Crobhungaibh. Clufters.

Croc. Horns.

Crocach. Horned.

Croc. An earthen veffel.

Crocad. Barley-broth.

Crocam. To beat, pound.

Croch. Saffron.

Croch. Red.

Crochadair. A hangman.

Crochadan. A pendulum.

Crocham. To hang.

Crochadh. Hanging, depending, grief, vexation.

Crochadairachd. Hovering about, the office of hangman.

Croch, croich. Gallows, a crofs.

Crochaire. An idle fellow, hangman.

Crochaid. Cockernony.

Crochaodach. Hangings.

Crochar. A body, a bier.

Crocharfach. A fheepfold.

Crochruaidh. A certain Irifh idol.

Crocharb, crocharbachd. A bier.

Crodh. Cattle, cows, a dowry, portion.

Crodha. A flipper.

Crodha. Valiant, brave, fmart.

Crodhachd. Valour, bravery, prowefs.

Crodhaidhe. An heir.

Crodhbhoinn. A bunch of berries.

Crodhghuta. The gout in the hand.

Crodhmhain. The wrift.

Crogan. A pitcher.

Crodhain. Hoof of a cow or fheep.

Crodhall. The crocodile.

Crog. A paw, clutch.

Crogach. Having claws and clutches.

Croibheal. Coral.

Croic. Difficulty; a venifon feaft.

Croich. A gallows.

Croichde. Hanged.

Croicionn. The fkin, hide.

Croideach.

Croideach. A portion.

Croidhe. The heart.

Croidhfhionn. White-hoofed.

Croidheachd. A portion, dowry.

Croidhean. A gallant, lover, sweetheart.

Croidhil-bais. Knell.

Croidhebhrugh. Contrition.

Croidheog. A mistress, sweetheart.

Croilighe an bhais. The pangs of death.

Croimsgiath. A sort of crooked target.

Croinic. An annal.

Croinicam. To colour, paint, to try, pull, to correct.

Crois. A crofs, a market-place.

Crois-thochrais. A reel, or yarn-windles.

Croisfighil. A crofs prayer, i. e. with hands acrofs.

Croisford. A rail, barrier.

Croiflin. A diameter.

Croit. A hump on the back, a little eminence.

Crois-fhlighe. A by-way, road.

Croiftara. A signal to take up arms in the Highlands, by sending a burning stick from place to place with great expedition.

Croithte. Waved, toffed.

Croitheamh. An infect.

Croloc. A place where malefactors are executed.

Croloitam. To wound mortally.

Croloitighte. Dangeroufly wounded.

Crom-Conal. A plague in Ireland.

Crom. Stooping, bending, crooked.

Cromam. To ftoop, bend, bow.

Cromadh. Bending, bowing, the fide of a hill.

Croman.
Croman-lachdan. } A kite.

Croman-luath. A fire-fhovel.

Croman-loin. A fnipe.

Croman. The hip, hip-bone.

Cremh. A worm.

Cromhchruach. A famous Irifh idol.

Cromleac. An altar for heathenifh worfhip.

Cromaig. Gallows.

Cromnofg, gormrofg Grey-eyed.

Cromlus Poppy.

Crom nan duilleog. The woodcock.

Crom nan gad. A fort of Hebridian plough.

Cromfhlinainach. Hump-backed.

Cron. A fign, mark.

Cron. Brown, dun-coloured, red, fwarthy.

Cron. Time.

Cronach. A mournful elegy at funerals.

Cronam, cronaigham. To bewitch, to blufh for fhame, to rebuke, reprove.

Cronan. The bafs in mufick, any dull note, the buzzing of a fly, purring of a cat.

Cronnog. A kind of bafket or hamper.

Cronntaigham. To loath, abhor, deteft.

Cron-feanachais. An anachronifm.

Cros. A crofs, hindrance.

Crofach. Streaked.

Crofadh. Hindering.

Crofam. To ftop, hinder.

Crofanach.
Crofanta. } Perverfe, crofs, obftinate.

Crofog.
Crofantachd. } Perverfenefs, obftinacy.

Crofanachd. A kind of verfification.

Croftal.
Crotal. } A mofs, the dye feuillemorte.

Crofra, crofrian. A crofs-road.

Crotach. Hump-backed.

Crotach-mara. A curlew.

Crotal. An awn, hufk, cod, a cymbal, rind of a kernel.

Crotan. Purple dyer's lichen.

Crottal. A kernel.

Crothadh, crathadh. Sprinkling.

Crothnigheadh. Miffing.

Croth. A form, or fhape.

Crotham. To coop, houfe.

Crotha. A cymbal.

Crothait. A gravel.

Crothar. A bier, any vehicle.

Crottag. A fort of plover.

Cru. Blood, gore.

Cruabairam. To crunch, chew.

Cruach. A rick, or heap of any thing.

Cruachdadh, Heaping, hardening or drying

Cruacham. To heap, dry, harden.

Cruachdalach. Coarfe.

Cruachan. A heap, a drying, toafting.

Cruach phadruic. The herb plantain.

Cruad. A ftone

Cruadail. Danger, courage, covetoufnefs.

Cruadh, cruaidh. Hard, difficult, firm.

Cruadhach. Steel, of fteel.

Cruadhail. Hardfhip, diftrefs, difficulty,
ftinginefs.

Cruadhalach. Hard; ftingy, poor, puzzling.

Cruadhcuing. Rigour, flavery.

Cruadhchuifeach. Difficult.

Cruadhmhuinalachd. Stiff-necked, obftinate.

Cruadhnafgtha. Entangled.

Cruadhagach. Strict.

Cruadhoige. Diftrefs.

Cruaghadh. A ftrengthening.

Cruaidh. Steel, hard.

Cruaidhcheifd. A riddle.

Cruaidheadh. Hardening.

Cruaidcheanglam. To tye faft.

Cruaidhte. Hardened.

Cruaidhaicham. To harden.

Cruaidhchriodhach. Hard-hearted.

Cruaidh-lus Sneeze-wort.

Cruan. Red.

Cruas Hardnefs, rigour

Crub ⎱ A horfe's-hoof, a claw, fang, the
Crubh ⎰ nave of a wheel.

Crubach. Lame; difficult.

Cruban. A crab-fish, a crooked creature.

Crubam. To contract, creep.

Crubha-fithainn. A haunch of venifon.

Crubin na faona. Dwarf mountain bramble.

Crubghoin A floodgate.

Crubhaic. A crimfon-colour.

Crubog. A knot or contraction of a thread
in weaving.

Cruca. A crook or hook.

Crucach. A heap.

Crudh Milking.

Crudham. To milk.

Crudath. A belt or fword-girdle.

Cruimheachta. A crow.

Crughalach. Hard, difficult.

Cruidheata. Hard.

Cruidhearg. Of a fcarlet-colour.

Cruidin. A king's fifher.

Cruighneachd. ⎱
Cruithneachd. ⎰ Wheat.

Cruim. Thunder.

Cruimaodanach. Whole, entire, a down-
looking perfon.

Cruimam. To thunder.

Cruimfhlinean. A bunch on the back.

Cruimthear. A prieft.

Cruinn. Round, circular.

Cruineafadh. A giddinefs.

Cruinne. The globe of the earth, round-
nefs.

Cruinnughadh. An affembly.

Cruinnuigham. Gathered, affembled.

Cruinnam. To wrangle.

Cruinnlin. Orbit.

Cruinnioc. Dew, mift.

Cruinneog. A little round woman.

Cruinneolas. Addrefs.

Cruifcea. ⎱
Cruifgin. ⎰ A lamp.

Cruit. A harp, a fiddle, a cymbal, a hump
on the back.

Cruiteog. A female fiddler, harper.

Cruitire. A harper, fiddler, crowder.

Cruital. Pleafant, fprightly.

Cruith Ingenious, lively.

Cruithe.

Cruithe, cruitheachd. Prudence.

Cruitheocham. I shall mention, prove.

Cruithin Tuath. The old Irish name for the Land of the Picts.

Cruithneach. A Pict.

Cruithneachd. Wheat.

Cruitin. A hump-backed man.

Crum. Vide Crom.

Cruma. Half a quarter of a yard.

Crumba. A bowl.

Crumam. To bow, bend, to worship.

Crumh. A maggot.

Cruman. The hip-bone.

Crumhe. A hoof, shoe.

Cruman. A sort of instrument used by chirurgeons.

Crumag. A skirret.

Crumanaidhe. A turner.

Crumhar. Bloody.

Crumshuileachd. Sourness of look.

Crun. A crown, diadem, five shillings.

Crunam. To crown.

Crun na h airte. Ornaments in the description of a shield.

Crunnan. A group.

Cruog. Need, necessity.

Crupam. To contract.

Cruphutog. A blood-pudding.

Crupag. A wrinkle.

Crusgaoileadh. The bloody-flux.

Crutaire. A musician, crowder, harper.

Cruth. A form, figure, shape, countenance.

Crut. The hand.

Cruthaigham. To prove, aver, assert, to create.

Cruthaighoir. A creator.

Cruthaighte. Created, discovered, experienced.

Cruthughadh. A proof, creation, creating.

Cruthuigheachd. The creation.

Cruthlachd. A belt, sword-girdle.

Crutbchaochlaigham. To transfigure, metamorphose.

Cruthchaochladh. Transfiguration, metamorphosis.

Cu. A dog.

Cu allaidh. A wolf.

Cua. Flesh, meat.

Cu-eunaich. A spaniel.

Cu-luirg. A slow-hound.

Cu-uisge. A water-dog.

Cuamhargadh. The flesh-market.

Cuabhacan. A flesh-hook.

Cuabhruid. Itch, lechery.

Cuac. Narrow.

Cu-dubh. The name of a dog.

Cuacca. Empty.

Cuach. The cuckow.

Cuach, cuachag. A bowl, cup.

Cuachfholt. Curled hair.

Cuachach. Curled, frizzled.

Cuach-Phadruic. Plaintain.

Cuachan. The work of a bird's nest.

Cuach-bhleothain. A milk-pail.

Cuacham. To fold, plait.

Cuachanach. Cupped.

Cuachshrann. A vehement snorting.

Cuadh. To tell or relate.

Cuagan. The hinder part of the head.

Cuaghran am feoil. A kernel in the flesh.

Cuaicheanach. Curly-headed.

Chuaidh. Went Vide Racham.

Cuail. Coal; an impediment to marriage.

Cuailain. A lock, curl, wreathe.

Cuailain amalach. A curled lock.

Cuaill, cuaille. A pole or stake.

Cuain. A corner.

Cuainte. Able.

Cuairealta. Curious.

Cuairt. A visit, sojourning, circulation, tour.

Cuirtachas. A visiting, gossiping.

Cuairsgeadh. A volume.

Cuairtair,

Cuairtair. A visitant.

Cuairgean. A wrapper, felly of a wheel.

Cuairsgein. The core, the heart.

Cuairsgam. To roll, wreathe, to twist, wrap.

Cuairsgte. Rolled, wrapped up.

Cuaith. The country.

Cual. Faggot.

Cualin. A bundle.

Cuala, chuala. I heard. Vide Cluinam.

Cuallach. Herding.

Cuallachd. Following, dependants, a colony.

Cuallaidhe. A companion.

Cuallaidheachd. Society.

Cuallas. An assembly

Cuamhor. Fat, gross.

Cuamhargadh. The shambles.

Cuan. A bay, harbour, haven.

Cuauar. Soft.

Cuan. The sea.

Cuanna. Handsome, neat, fine.

Cuanna. A hill.

Cuar. Crooked, perverse.

Cuar cumaisg. A tour.

Cuara. A vessel.

Cuaran. A sock, a bandage.

Cuaroga. Shoes or brogues made of untanned leather.

Cuarsgeach. Twisted.

Cuart. Vide Cuairt.

Cuartag shluganach. A whirlpool.

Cuartuigham. To surround, search out.

Cuartan. A maze, labyrinth.

Cuartughadh. Surrounding, a diligent search.

Cuas. A cave, hollow of a tree, a cavity.

Cuasach. Concave, full of holes.

Cuasachdach. A cough.

Cuasag. Honeycomb in hollow trees.

Cuasan. A hole, cavity.

Cua-uinne. Worm-eaten nuts.

Cub. A bending of the body.

Cubet. Joking, sporting, ridiculing, fraud.

Cubam. To stoop, bend.

Cubhachail. A bedchamber.

Cubhad. A cubit.

Cubare. A black cock.

Cubair. A cooper.

Cubhaidh. Decent, becoming, honour.

Cubhais. An oath.

Cubhaing. Strait.

Cubhag A cuckow.

Cubhag-ghliogarach. A snipe.

Cubhal. A religious habit.

Cubhar. A corner, foam, froth.

Cubhruinn. A coverlet.

Cubhas. A tree.

Cucca, chucca. To them.

Cucclaidhe. A narrow way.

Cucamhar. A cucumber.

Cucht. A colour, kind, image.

Cuchraidh. A maker, former.

Cuchtair. A kitchen.

Cuclaidhe. A residence, habitation.

Cudaim. To fall.

Cudaimeasadh. The falling sickness.

Cudal. Bad, wicked.

Cudachd. Also, likewise.

Cudam. A scar on the head, a fault in the hair, an eruption on the side of a mountain.

Cudamach. Frail, corruptible.

Cudarman. The vulgar.

Cudarun. A cap or hood.

Cudh, A head.

Cudinn. A little fish called a cuddy.

Cudthrom. Weight.

Cudhnodh. Haste.

Cudshaoth. An apology.

Cudthromach. Weighty, important.

Cueirt. An apple-tree.

Cufar. } A cypress-tree.
Cufrog. }

Cugadsa, chugadsa. To you.

Cuguin, chugin. To us.

2   Cugann.

Cugann. Rich standing milk.

Cuib. A cup.

Cuibh. A dog, greyhound.

Cuibhid. Worthy.

Cuibhe. Meet, competent.

Cuibheis. So much, enough.

Cuibhet. Fraud.

Cuibhiosach. Passable.

Cuihhreach. Bands, bonds.

Cuibhrigham. To fetter, shackle.

Cuibhrighte. Bound, fettered.

Cuibhrionn. A portion, share.

Cuice. Until.

Cuid. A part, share, a supper.

Cuid an trath. A meal.

Cuid-alaich. A litter.

Cuid-oiche. A night's lodging.

Cuid ri. Along with.

Cuidalachd. Pride.

Cuidarun. A cowl.

Cuideachd. A troop, company, likewise, also.

Cuideachdaigham. To accompany.

Cuideachadh. Help, helping.

Cuidachal. Assisting.

Cuidaigham. To help, assist.

Cuideamhail. An intruder.

Cuideamhuil. Meet, fit, decent.

Cuidamhlachd. Decency, meetness.

Cuibheachd. Decency.

Cuidbheachdach. Parted, severed.

Cuidhal. A wheel, a spinning-wheel.

Cuidhealam. To wheel.

Cuidhalairachd. Wheeling, rolling, spinning.

Cuidigh. A midwife.

Cuidigham. To help, succour, aid, assist.

Cuidighteach. } An assistant, helper.
Cuidaiche. }

Cuidughadh. Aid, help, assistance.

Cuidmheadh. A scoff, jeer, a flout, ridicule.

Cuidridh. Common.

Cuife. A pit.

Cuig. Five.

Cuigeadh, cuigo. The fifth, a province.

Cuige. Therefore; chuighe so, for this purpose; chuige agus uaidhe, to and fro.

Cuigeal. A distaff.

Cuigealach. As much flax or wool as is put on a distaff at a time, a task.

Cuil, cuileog. A fly.

Chuile. Every.

Cuil. A couch, a corner, a closet.

Cuil. Lead, wicked, prohibited.

Cuilas-dighthoir. An eaves-dropper.

Cuilc. A reed.

Cuiltach. Corners, a place full of corners.

Cuilche. Any clothes.

Cuilbhar. A fowling-piece.

Cuilbheirtidh. Wiles.

Cuilcheann. The noddle.

Cuilcheannag. A bribe.

Cuilceach. A veil, cloth, hood; a steeple.

Cuileach. Party-coloured.

Cuilc-chrann. Cane.

Cuilctharnach. A place where reeds grow.

Cuildubh. A beetle.

Cuilag-shionnachain. A glow-worm.

Cuilean. A whelp, pup, kitten.

Cuileann. }
Cuilfhionn. } Holly.

Cuilear. A quarry.

Cuileasg. A jade, a horse.

Cuileog A gnat.

Cuilfhinn. Handsome, lovely.

Cuiliosal. Vile, little worth.

Cuilidh. A cellar, storehouse.

Cuille. A quill, black cloth.

Cuilioch. Flea-bitten.

Cuilleasga. Hazle *rods* or twigs.

Cuilm. A feast.

Cuilmhionnachadh. Abjuration.

Cuilmhionnuigham. To abjure.

Cuilog. A pair.

Cuilfean.

Cuilfean. The quilt or tick of a bed.

Cuilfe. Beating.

Cuilfheomar. A bedchamber.

Cuilfinnteas. Delay, negligence.

Cuilt. A bed-tick, a bed.

Cuilteach. A bakehouse.

Cuim. Entertainment.

Cuim. Mercy, protection, a shirt.

Cuimeir. Neat, proportioned.

Cuime. Hardness.

Cuimeoladh. Wiping.

Cuimhealta. Bruising.

Cruimheamhachd. A competency.

Cuimhlan. A wheel.

Cuimhne. The memory, remembrance, a memorial, record.

Cuimhneach. Mindful.

Cuimhnachan. A memorandum, keep-sake.

Cuimhnam. ⎱
Cuimhnigham. ⎰ To remember.

Cuimhnughadh. Remembering, memorial.

Cuimhnighthoir. A recorder, chronicler.

Cuimhre cuir. Said to be hart's horn.

Cuimhrean. A portion, share, eating together, messing.

Cuimhleadh. Intermeddling.

Cuimin. A little coffer or chest.

Cuimim. Cummin seed.

Cuimide. An appointed time.

Cuiminibh. Suburbs.

Cuimir. Neat.

Cuimne Protection.

Cuimseach. Mean, little, indifferent.

Cuimse. A mark, an aim.

Cuine. When?

Cuinneog. A churn, can, pail.

Cuineadh A coin, mourning.

Cuineam To coin.

Cuineag. A copy.

Cuineang. Narrow.

Cuineas. Rest, silence, quietness, a calm.

Cuiniochthaoi. Ye shall keep.

Cuing. A yoke, band, duty, obligation.

Cuing analach. An asthma.

Cuingeach. A pair, couple.

Cuinge. A folicitation, an entreaty.

Cuinge, cuingad. Narrowness, straitness.

Cuingir. A couple.

Cuingis. Penticost.

Cuingam. To desire, solicit, request, demand.

Cuingcheangal. Subjugium.

Cuingdis. They used to keep or retain.

Cuinghid. A request or petition.

Cuingreach. A cart or waggon.

Cuingcear. A rabbit-burrow.

Cuinuigham, cuinigham. To assuage, mitigate.

Cuinneire. Nostrils.

Cuinin. A rabbit.

Cuinion froine. A nostril.

Cuinrein. A snout.

Cuinseal. A face, countenance.

Cuinsgeallan. A stable.

Cuintearcham. To render.

Cuinn, from Conn. Quintius, a king of Ireland.

Cuinne. A corner.

Cuinnse. Quince.

Cuip. Froth, foam; A whip.

Cuirbeachta. Birds claws.

Cuiraidach. Cunning.

Cuirc. A knife.

Cuirc. A whittle, a swathe.

Cuirce. Oats.

Cuirceog. A hive.

Cuird. A trade. Vide Ceaird.

Cuire. A cauldron. Vide Coire.

Cuireadh. An invitation.

Cuiram. To put, send, to sow, plant, to invite.

Cuire. A multitude, or throng.

Cuiram air lagh. To prepare, adjust, aim.

Cuireat. The knave at cards.

Cuirsam. To tire, fatigue.

Cuirin. A small cauldron, or kettle.

Cuirm. A kind of beer or ale amongst the old Irish, a feast, banquet.

Cuirnain. The head of a pin, or any such thing, a ringlet.

Cuirnainach. In ringlets.

Cuirpidh. Wicked, impious, corrupt.

Cuirpeachd. Wickedness, corruption.

Cuirpeoir. A carper.

Cuirt, cuirteog. An apple-tree, a wilding.

Cuirt. A court or palace, a yard.

Cuirteamhuil. Courtly, courteous.

Cuirtamhlachd. Courtliness, courteousness.

Cuirtais. Courtesy.

Cuirtaisach. Ceremonious.

Cuirteag. A kind of cup.

Cuirtin. A curtain.

Cuirtir. An eunuch.

Cuis. A matter, affair, a thing, a cause.

Cuisag. A stalk, a foot.

Cuiscle. A private affair.

Cuisdag. The little finger.

Cuisean. A crime.

Cuisbhurta. A buffoon.

Cuisle. A vein, a pipe.

Cuisleach. Full of veins.

Cuisleog. A lancet.

Cuislean. A castle

Cuisleanach. A piper.

Cuisne. Ice, frost.

Cuisnigham. To freeze, congeal.

Cuisle-mhor. An artery.

Cuislin. A pole.

Cuisneamhuil. Frosty.

Cuisnighte. Congealed, frozen.

Cuison. Wise, prudent.

Cuiste. A couch.

Cuit. The head.

Cuite. Sound, healthy, well.

Cuiteach. That recompenseth.

Cuite. Quit.

Cuitam. To quit.

Cuitigham. To recompense, render, reward, requite.

Cuiteach. A denial, revenging.

Cuitughadh. A requital.

Cuithbheirt. An helmet, head-piece, hat, bonnet.

Cuithe. A trench.

Cuitheach. Foam, froth; rage, fury.

Cul. Custody, guard, defence.

Cul. The back of any thing.

Cul. A chariot, coach, waggon.

Culag. Turf, peat, the cheek-teeth

Culaidh. Apparel, a suit of clothes, a tool, instrument, a boat.

Culaidh-shiuil. Canvas.

Cul-taic. A defence, redoubt.

Culam. To thrust or push back

Culantas. Bashfulness.

Cularain. Cucumbers.

Culb. An artist.

Culbhoc. A wether-goat, a buck.

Culchaint. ⎫
Culchainadh. ⎬ Backbiting, calumny.

Culchainam. To backbite, slander.

Culdich. Retired, set apart.

Culchainteoir. A backbiter.

Culchoimeid. A rear-guard.

Culcheimnuchadh. Tergiversation.

Cul-earalais. A corps de reserve.

Culmhutairachd. Mutiny.

Culmhutaire. A mutineer.

Culidh-fanoid. A laughing-stock.

Culidh-bhrostidh. An incentive.

Culidh-mheallaidh. A dupe.

Culghairm. Recalling.

Culghairmam. To recall.

Cul-ithe. Backbiting.

Culla. A hood, a cowl.

Cullach. A boar.

Cullin. Holly.

Culloid. A great noise, rattling, splutter.

Cullordeach,

Culloideach. Noify, brawling, quarrelfome.

Culmhaire. A wheelwright.

Culmhionnuigham. To abjure.

Culradharcach. Circumfpect.

Culfleamhnaigham. To backflide.

Cultharruinguicham. To retract.

Culuigheach. Apparel.

Culthaideach. Prepofterous.

Culuran. A cucumber.

Cum. Form, fhape, trunk of the body.

Cum, chum. To, for, therefore.

Cum. A combat, fight, duel, battle.

Cuma. Indifferent. Vide Comma.

Cumadh. A model, form, pattern, forming.

Cumach. A breach, derout.

Cumachda. A command.

Cumadh Vide Camadh.

Cumadoir. A framer, fhaper, fafhioner.

Cumadoirachd. Device, invention.

Cumam. To fhape, form, frame.

Cumam. To hold, to faften, keep.

Cumagach. Curling.

Cumal. Holding.

Cumailam. To touch, wipe, rub off.

Cumailt. Wiping, rubbing.

Cumal. The price of three cows.

Cumaineach. The communion.

Cumaifc. Mixture.

Cumaifcam. To mix, mingle, blend.

Cumaifgte. Mixed, blended.

Cuman. A fkimmer, a fort of difh, a pail.

Cumann. Affection. Vide Communn.

Cumannach. Affectionate.

Cummanta. Common.

Cumaoin. Obligation.

Cumar A point or place where ftreams, roads, or any thing elfe meet, confluence, interfection.

Cumarra. A proper name, a fea-hound.

Cumafgadh. Mixing.

Cumafgam. To mix.

Cummaraice. A valley; a people living in a country full of valleys and hills.

Cumas. Strength, power.

Cumafach. Strong. Vide Comafach.

Cumafg. A mixture.

Cumhadh. Mourning, forrow.

Cumha. A bribe, reward, condition.

Cumhac. Narrow.

Cumhag. A cuckow

Cumhag-bhogadh-toine. A wagtail.

Cumhachag. An owl.

Cumhachd. Power, force.

Cumhachdach. Powerful, mighty.

Cumhachdaiche. Mightier.

Cumhadhach. Sad, forrowful.

Cumhaing. Narrow, ftraight.

Cumguim. Daring, adventuring.

Cumhainge. Narrownefs.

Cumhaingam. To ftraighten, to narrow.

Cumhais. A felvage.

Cumhal. A handmaid, a bondmaid.

Cumhal. Obedience, fubjection.

Cumhaldha. Belonging to a fervant.

Cumhang. Power, ftrength.

Cumhan. Mournfulnefs; a ftrait.

Cumhdach. A defence, veil, covering, cover of a book.

Cumhdach. An ouch, cumhdach oir, an ouch of gold.

Cumhdachda. Fenced.

Cumhduigham. To fence, maintain, fupport.

Cumhgach. Straightnefs, diftrefs.

Cumhladh. Rubbing, wiping.

Cumhlam. To rub, fcrape.

Cumhnanta. A covenant.

Cumhnantgha. Federal.

Cumhnantuigham. To bargain, covenant.

Cumhra. Sweet-fmelling, fragrant.

Cumhrachd. Fragrance.

Cumhrog. Sweet apple-tree.

Cumraicham. To cumber, encumber.

Cumhfgtha.

Cumhfgtha. Moved, provoked.

Cumhthach. Bribery.

Cumhfgughadh. Marching, journeying.

Cumhul. Vide Cumhal.

Cumtha. Shaped, formed.

Cumthadh. Dear, coftly.

Cumus. Power, ability.

Cumufg. A mixture.

Cumfgadh. Ringing.

Cun. A body.

Cunablach. A carcafe.

Cunabhaireas. Slothfulnefs.

Cunganta. Helpers, affiftants.

Cungantach. Helpful.

Cunghas. Co-operating.

Cunbhalam. To hold, faften.

Cunbhailtach. Firm, durable.

Cunbhailteachd. Firmnefs, durablenefs.

Cungaidh. Materials, tools, ingredients.

Cunghnamh Help, fuccour, aid.

Cungarach. Exigent.

Cungir. A couple.

Cunna. Friendfhip.

Cunnairc, chunnairc. Saw.

Cunnarthach. Betrothed, a cheap bargain.

Cunnla. Modeft.

Cunnradh. A covenant.

Cunnrathach. Agreed upon.

Cunntabhairt. }
Cunntairt. } Doubt, danger.

Cunntabhairtach. }
Cunnartach. } Dangerous, doubtful.

Cuntaidh. A county.

Cuntas. Account, counting.

Cuntafach. Keen, fharp, narrow.

Cuntam. To reckon, tell.

Cunnuil. Objection.

Cupull. A cupple or rafter.

Cupuil. Shrowds.

Cup. }
Cupan. } A cup.

Cupar. Conception.

Cupla. A pair, couple.

Cuplam. To couple, pair.

Cuphair. Cyprefs.

Cur. Sowing, fending, putting, throwing, raining, fnowing, prefenting ; as, Cur fiol, cur air fhiubhal, cur as, cur cloich, cur fneachd, cur failm amach. Vide Cuiram.

Cur-romham. Purpofing.

Cur. Power.

Cur. Wearinefs, defeat.

Cur. Difficult.

Cur air. A defeat.

Cur as. Extinction.

Cur as. leath. Afcribing, imputing.

Cur ann. Encreafing, preferring.

Cur ann ard. Elevating.

Cur amach. Addrefs, converfation.

Curtha. Tired, fatigued.

Curach. A bog, marfh.

Curach. A coracle, a little boat.

Curachan. A fkiff.

Curach na cuaig. Small-leafed bell-flower

Curadh. An obftacle, fevere diftrefs.

Curaideach. Frifky, cunning.

Curaideachd. Frifkinefs, cunning.

Curaidhe. A champion.

Curaighir. A mug.

Curaidhe na craoibh ruaidhe. The heroes of the Red Branch. A certain band of warriors in the fervice of the king of Ulfter.

Curaighean. A cann, mug, tankard.

Curaighean. Cheefe-rennet.

Curam, care. A prey, prize.

Curamach. Careful, folicitous.

Curamas. Care, diligence.

Curanta. Courageous.

Curufan. A milk-pail or firkin for butte.

Curantachd. Bravery, courage.

Curbifeach. Additional.

Curcag. A fand-piper, a bud.

Curcais. Hair, a bullrufh.

Cuir. A corner, end, a pit.

Curn. Vide Corn. A cup.

Currach. A bog, fen where fhrubs grow.

Curra. } Sowing, a little farm.
Currachd. }

Currac. A cap, a woman's head-drefs.

Currac-conlaich. A bon-grace.

Curracaig. A lapwing, a cock of hay.

Currac na cuaig. Blue-bottle.

Curagh. A burying-place.

Curran. A root of the carrot, or radifh kind, daucus.

Curran-buidhe. A carrot.

Curran-dearg. A radifh.

Currghalan. A bucket, a didapper.

Currtha. Wearied, fatigued.

Curthigham. To tire, fatigue.

Currel. Plain, manifeft.

Curfa. A courfe or manner, row, rank, order.

Curfaigham. To courfe, traverfe.

Curfachd. Traverfing.

Curfach. Winding, folding, meandring; Brat-curfach, a loofe robe.

Curfachadh. A curfe, malediction.

Curfon. A learned man.

Curta. Bad.

Curftabha. A bucket.

Curfuir. A courier, meffenger, attendant.

Cus. A fubfidy, tribute.

Cus. Enough.

Cufadh. Bending, inclining.

Cufag. Wild muftard.

Cufal. Courage.

Cufbair. } An object, mark to aim at.
Cufpair. }

Cufmunn. Cuftom, impoft.

Cufmafc. Diverfity.

Cufpoirachd. An objection or argument, throwing, cafting at a mark.

Cufpoiraidhe. An opponent.

Cufpoiraidham. To object; to aim at a mark.

Cufp. A kibe, mouls.

Cufpach. That hath kibes.

Cuftaire. A tanner.

Cuft. Skin.

Cutach. Bobtailed.

Cutag. Any fhort thing of feminine gender, a fhort fpoon.

Cutal, cuthal. Bafhful.

Cutallaidhe. A companion, comrade, partner.

Cuth. A head.

Cutha. } Rage, fury, fiercenefs.
Cuthach. }

Cuthach. } Raging, furious.
Cuthaichte. }

Cuthaileachd. Bafhfulnefs.

Cutharlan. An onion, earth-nut, pig-nut.

Cuthdarun. A fort of cap, a Monteio-cap.

Cuthbhar. An helmet.

D.

D, Called Duir, oak, is the fourth letter of the alphabet, and is founded foft, as in the French.

Da. Two.

D'a. Off, or to, his, her, it.

Da. If.

[E e]   Da-adharcach.

Da-adharcach. Bicornous.
Dabhach. A tub.
Dabheothach. Amphibious.
Dabhlianach. A two-year old.
Dabhoch. A farm that keeps sixty cows.
Dabhan. A pitcher, a bucket.
Dachruthach. Biformed.
Dacheannach. Bicipitous.
Dachorpach Bicorporal.
Dachofach. Biped.
Dachbheurla. An idiom.
Da-dheug. Twelve.
Dadadh. ⎱ A jot, whit, a trifle, somewhat,
Dad. ⎰ any thing.
Dadhas. The buck of the fallow deer.
Dadum. Something, any thing, a mote.
Dadhuilleach. Bifoliated.
Dadmun. A mote.
Dae. A man, a person.
Dae. A high dyke, a wall, a house.
Dae. A hand.
Dafhoghair. Two vowels, a diphthong.
Dafhilte. Twofold.
Dafhiaclach. Bidental.
Dagh. Good. Vide Deagh.
Daga. A pistol.
Dagach. Armed with a pistol.
Daga-diolaid. A holster.
Dagham. To singe, burn.
Daghte. Singed, burned.
Daghadh. An empyreuma.
Daghar. Wind.
Daibhi. David.
Daibhliag. A church.
Daice. Belonging to a tribe.
Daicheil, dathamhuil. Likely, well-look-
    ed.
Daicheilad. Likeliness.
Daibhbhir. Needy.
Daif. Drink.
Daigh. Fire, pain.
Daigh. Hope, confidence. Vide Doigh.

Daighbhiorasg. Fuel.
Daidhbhras. Poverty.
Daighchinnmhiol. Enamelling.
Daigheadh. Giving, delivering.
Daigham. To give.
Daighnigham. To establish.
Daighedh. Great odds.
Dail. A delay, decree.
Dail. Near, within reach, conjunction;
    'N a dhail, towards him.
Dail. A share, portion.
Dail. A separate tribe.
Dail. Desire, willingness.
Dail. A meeting, convention.
Dail-chath. A pitched battle.
Daileadh. Tradition, affiance.
Dail-chuach. A fort of herb.
Dailag A date-tree.
Dailein. A scoff.
Dailam. To give, deliver.
Daille. Night, darkness, blindness.
Dailthe. Dealt, parted, divided.
Dailthe. After.
Dailtin. A jackanapes, puppy of a fellow,
    rascal.
Dailtinnas. Scurrility, impertinence.
Daimh. A house, friend, connection, con-
    sanguinity.
Daimh. Assent, free-will.
Daimh. Translated by Mr. Macpherson,
    stranger.
Daimh. A poet, a learned writer.
Daimhal. Connected, allied, syb.
Daimheach. A companion, associate.
Daimhaodann. A frontispiece.
Daimhfheoil. Beef.
Daimhiach. Of a powerful clan.
Daimhliag. A church.
Daimsin. A damson-plum.
Dain. The gen. of Dan. A poem.
Daindeoin. Against will, in spite of.
Daingeann. Strong, firm.

Daingean

3

Daingean. An aſſurance, contract.

Daingneach. }
Daingneachd. } A fortification, ſtrength.

Daingnuicham. To fortify, faſten, eſta-
bliſh.

Daingnuchadh. Fortifying, a ratification.

Dainoide. A ſchoolmaſter.

Dair. An oak.

Dair, daireadh. Bulling.

Dairam. To bull, take the bull.

Dauibh. A kind of worm, a little perſon.

Dairbhre. An oak, a nurſery of oaks.

Dairbag, A tadpole.

Dairghe. An oak-apple.

Dairt. A clod, a heifer.

Dairteach. Full of clods.

Dais. A mow.

Daiſgin. A writing-deſk.

Daithte. Coloured.

Daith Quick, nimble, active, ſupple.

Daitean }
Daiteamhla. } A foſter-father.

Daithe. }
Daitheadhadh. } Revenge.

Daitheamhuil. Likely, comely, handſome.

Daitheamhlachd. Comelineſs, grandeur,
majeſty.

Daitheaſc. Eloquence, a ſpeech, remon-
ſtrance.

Daitheaſc. Unanimouſly.

Daitheoir. An avenger.

Daithle. After.

Daithnid Sorry.

Dal A ſhare, diviſion, lot.

Dal. An aſſembly; a tribe.

Dal. A plain field, a dale.

Dala. News, an oath, eſpouſals, a meeting.

Dala. A relation, hiſtorical fact.

Dala. As to, as for.

Dalaigham. To aſſign, appoint.

Dalaighidh. Aſſignment.

Dalan-de. A butterfly.

Dallan. A great bulk.

Dallan-cloich. A large ſtone, a monument
ſtone.

Dalladh-eun. Purblindneſs.

Dallan. A fan to winnow with.

Dalbh A lye, contrivance.

Dalba. Impudent, forward.

Dalbhdha. Sorcery.

Dalgaol. Affinity.

Dall. Blind, puzzled.

Dalladh. Blindneſs.

Dallam. To blindfold, blind, puzzle.

Dallaigeantach. } Dull-witted, fooliſh, hea-
Dallintinneach. } vy.

Dallog. A leech, a buffet, a mole.

Dallog-an-fhraoich. A ſhrew.

Dallog-fheoir. A dormouſe, a mole.

Daltach. Betrothed.

Daltan. A foſter-child, diſciple.

Dallta. Like, likeneſs, in manner of.

Daltin. A ſtripling.

Dam. A conduit, reſervoir.

Damh. An ox.

Damh. Learning.

Damh dhamh. To me.

Damanta. Condemned, damned.

Damnam. To condemn, damn.

Damnadh. Condemnation.

Damhan-eallaidh. A ſpider.

Damhach. A vat.

Damhadh. Permiſſion, liberty.

Damham. To permit, ſuffer, allow.

Damhair Earneſt, keen.

Damh-feidh. A buck or red deer.

Damhlann. An oxſtall.

Damhoide. }
Damhphupa. } A ſchoolmaſter.

Damhna. The matter out of which any
thing is or may be formed, Riogh damhna,
king elect.

Damhnadh. A band or tye.

Damh-nartaidhe. A bullock.

Damhſadh.

Damhſadh. Dancing.

Damhſadh deiſe. A Strathſpey dance.

Damhaſam. To dance.

Damhſair. A dancer.

Damhaſaire dubh an uiſge. Water-ſpider.

Damhamhuil. } A ſtudent.
Damhtha. }

Damtha. Scholaſtic.

Damnuigham. To condemn.

Damnughadh. Condemning.

Damuinte. Condemned, damned.

Dan. Work.

Dan. Fate, deſtiny, bha e 's an dan do, it was his fate.

Dan. A poem; poetry.

Dan, dana. Bold, impetuous, impudent.

Dan-argaid. Money worth, goods.

Dana-loingais. A fleet, ſquadron.

Danachd. } Boldneſs.
Danadas. }

Danaigham. To dare, defy.

Dannartha. Impudent, ſtubborn.

Dannarthachd. Stubbornneſs, frowardneſs.

Danair. A ſtranger, foreigner.

Danat. A nurſe.

Dandha. Fatal.

Dant. A morſel, portion, ſhare.

Dantuigheachd. Poetry.

Daoch, daochag. A periwinkle, ſea-ſnail.

Daochal. A morſel, a bit.

Daochan. Anger.

Daochanach. Angry.

Daoi. A man; wicked.

Daoil. A leech.

Daoine. Men, people.

Daoineach. Populous.

Daoin. Thurſday.

Dainnas. Manlineſs.

Daoirfhine. A ſubjected people.

Daoirmheaſdach. A taſkmaſter.

Daoirſe. Dearth, ſcarcity.

Daoirſe. } Captivity, bondage.
Daoirſin. }

Daol. A bug, beetle, chafer.

Daolair. A lazy man.

Daolagach. Abounding with beetles.

Daolag-bhreac. A lady-cow.

Daolag. A lazy ſneaking female.

Daomhaiſam. To ruin, demoliſh.

Daon. To raiſe up, aſcend.

Daonna. Human, humane.

Daonnachd Humanity, civility.

Daonnachdach. Civil, liberal.

Daonnan, for do ghna. Always.

Daonchon. The moral of a fable.

Daonfhuil. Akin, related.

Daonghaoidhile. Moral philoſophy.

Daor. Dear, precious.

Daor. Guilty, condemned.

Daoram. To condemn, ſentence.

Daortha. Condemned, convicted.

Daoradh. Condemning.

Daorich. Drunkenneſs.

Daorara. } A ſlave.
Daoranach. }

Daorbhodach. } A ſlave.
Daoroglach. }

Daorſe. Slavery.

Daoſgarſluaigh. The populace, mob.

Daothain. Sufficiency.

Dar. By, through, whoſe, whereof.

D'ar. Unto our, your; from off our, your.

D'ar. To our, your.

Dara. Second.

Dara ait. Second place.

Darab. *Improperly* whoſe.

Darach. Oak.

Darag. A ſtone as large as a man can caſt.

Darag-talmhuin. Germander, the name of a bird.

Darabhall. Oak-apples, galls.

Dararich. Slapdaſh.

Darcan. An acorn.

Darcan,

Darcan, na lagan.   The hollow of the hand.
Darargnegheadh.   Thought.
Darairgnegham.   To think.
Daras.   A home, a dwelling.
Darb.   A worm, a reptile.
Dabbh.   A coach or chariot.
Darcain.   A maft or acorn.
Darcanam.   To gather acorns.
Dardal.   Bad weather, fevere time
Darn.   A fchool.
Darna.   The fecond.
Darriogha.   Above or beyond kings.
Daraidh.   Rutting.
Dart   To bull a cow.
Dartan.   A herd, drove.
Dars.   A habitation.
Dartluich.   Impoffible.
Das.   A defk.
Dafachd.   Fiercenefs.
Dafachdach.   Fierce.
Dafhioladh.   A diffyllable.
Dafan.   Binocular.   Vide Dafhuilach.
Dafan.   To him.
Dafidh.   Furious.
Data.   Pleafant.
Datan.   A fofter-father.
Dath.   Colour.
Dathach.   Coloured, chromatick.
Dathadh.   Dying, a tincture.
Dathadh.   A prefent, a favour.
Dathadoir.   A dyer.
Dathag.   A worm in the human body.
Dathagmhortach.   Anthelmintick.
Datham.   To dye, to colour.
Dathamhlachd.   Honour, decency, refpect, comelinefs.
Dathamhnas.   Decency.
Dathamhuil.   Pleafant, decent, comely.
Dathan.   Colour, paint.
Dathchlodhach.   Parti-coloured.
Dathigh, dhathigh.   A home, home.
Dathnaid.   A fofter-mother.
Dathughadh.   A dying, colouring.

Dathe.   Agility.
De.   Whence? from whence? thereof.
De.   Of God, genitive cafe of Dia.
De.   Genitive of Dia, a day.
De, ande.   Yefterday.
Deabhadh.   Hafte, fpeed.
Deabhadh.   A fkirmifh, a battle, encounter.
Deabham.   To haften, to battle, encounter.
Deabhlach, deabhthach.   Contentious, litigious.
Deaccair.   Strange, wonderful.
Deaccair. }   Hard, difficult.
Deaclach. }
Deach.   Better.
Deachadh.   Paft tenfe of Racham, to go.
Deachair.   A feparating, following, brightnefs.
Deachairam.   To follow.
Deachain.   Vide Feuchin.
Deachdam.   To dictate, debate, teach.
Deachdadh.   Dictating, a law.
Deachdoir.   A dictator.
Deachmhaidh.   A tenth, tythe.
Deachmhugham.   To tythe.
Deachnamhar.   A decade.
Deacmhoradh.   Courtefy, affability.
Deachra.   Separated.
Deachra.   Anger, indignation.
Deachd.   Divinity, Godhead.
Deachda.   Dictates.
Deachduighte.   Dictated.
Deachtoir.   A dictator, teacher.
Deacmaic.   Hard, difficult.
Deacrachd.   Difficulty, hardfhip.
Dead.   A jaw, fet of teeth.
Deadith.   The tooth-ach.
Dead.   Meet, proper, decent.
Deadhachd.   Godlinefs, religion.
Deadhan.   A dean.
Deadhanachd.   Deanery.
Deadhail.   A releafing, weaning.
Deadhbheachd.   A civility.
Deadhbhal.   Wretched, woeful.

[F f]   Deadhair.

Deadhair. Swift.

Deadhmann. A moth.

Deaghchruthach. Shapely, handfome.

Deadhoil. The feparation of night and day.

Deadla. Bold, confident.

Deadlas. Confidence.

Deafhogharach. A diphthong.

Deaganach. A dean.

Deadhbheufach. Virtuous.

Deathbholtanas. ⎫
Deadhbholadh. ⎬ A fweet fmell, odour.

Deaghbhaltram. To perfume, to cenfe.

Deaghbholtrach. Aromatick.

Deadhbhuil. Well-difpofed.

Deagh. Good, and is often prefixed in compofition.

Deaghallam. To recal.

Deaghainm. Good name.

Deagharfgair. A chronicler.

Deaghbhuilachadh. Frugality.

Deaghbheus. Good habit, morality.

Deaghbheufach. Moral.

Deaghfhuin. Good-will.

Deaghghean. Favour.

Deaghla. Salutation.

Deaghmhuinte. Well-bred.

Deaghtheis. ⎫
Deaghtheifdas. ⎬ A good report.

Deaghthrial. A good gait.

Deadughadh. Accoutring.

Deagailt. A difcharge, divorce.

Deaghnach. Laft.

Deaghbhlas. Flavour.

Deaghbhlafda. Dainty, well relifhed.

Deaghfhoclach. ⎫
Deaghlabhartha. ⎬ Well fpoken.

Deaghiomchar. Good comportment.

Deaghghuth. Euphony.

Deaghalbharthach. An orator.

Deaghmhaifeach. Handfome, comely.

Deaghmhaifaigham. To adorn.

Deaghmhaifughadh. An ornament.

Deaghmhifnachal. Confident.

Deaghmhifnach. Confidence.

Deaghnad. Froft.

Deaghoibbra. Good works.

Deaghoideafach. Difcreet.

Deaghorduighte. Prudent, provident.

Deaghorduigham. To methodize.

Deaghraidham. To love fincerely.

Deaghthoil. Benevolence.

Deaghthoileach. Favourable, friendly.

Deaghuair. An opportunity.

D' eagal gu. For fear that, left.

Deaith. Wind, air.

Deaitheach. Windy.

Deala. Kindred, friendfhip.

Deala. A refufing, denying.

Deala. A cow's udder.

Deala. A leech.

Dealachd. ⎫
Dealaghadh. ⎬ A divorce, feparation.

Dealaigham. To feparate, divorce.

Dealan. A coal.

Dealan doruis. A latch.

Dealanach. Lightning.

Dealan de. ⎫
Dealbh ande. ⎬ A butterfly.

Dealbh. The countenance, face, form, image, frame, figure, ftatue.

Dealbham. To form, frame, make, contrive, to feign.

Dealbh. Poor, miferable.

Dealbhach. Refembling, ingenious, inventive, fpecious.

Dealbhadan. A mould.

Dealbhchluith. A ftage-play.

Dealbhthach. Pleafant.

Dealbhadoir. ⎫ A ftatuary, framer, inDealbhthoir. ⎬ ventor.

Dealbhliobhoir. A painter.

Dealbhthoireachd. Delineation.

Deallas. Zeal, quicknefs, hurry.

Deallafach. Hafty, quick, zealous.

Dealbhas. Mifery, poverty.

Dealg. A thorn, wire, skewer, prickle, pin, needle.

Dealgach. Prickly, stinging.

Dealgcluaise. An ear-picker.

Dealc-fuilt. A hair-pin.

Dealghionadh. Laying waste.

Dealgnaidhe. Unjust, unlawful.

Dealradh. Brightness.

Dealradhach. Bright.

Dealraidham. To shine, brighten.

Dealt. Dew.

Dealuigham. To divorce, separate.

Dealughadh. Separation, divorce.

Dealuigheach. Separable.

Dealuighte. Separated, divorced.

Deamal. } A demon, evil spirit.
Deamhon. }

Deamh. Want, lack.

Deamharruin. A mystery.

Deamhas. Scissars, sheers.

Deamhra. Vide Diomhair.

Dean. } Colour.
Deann. }

Deann. Force, impetus, haste.

Deanachdach. Vehement, keen.

Deanadh, deanamh. An action.

Deanadh, deanasach. Active.

Deanam. To do, act, work; come away, go on.

Deanamh. Doing.

Deanas. A space, a while.

Deanbha. An effect.

Deanchoire. A cauldron.

Deanchlodhach. Of changeable colours.

Deanmhasach. Prim.

Deannag. A little quantity of any comminuted matter, a pinch.

Deannal. Stir, hurry, flash.

Deanmhusach. Coy.

Deangan. Vide Seangan.

Deantog. A nettle.

Deante. Done, finished.

Deanmhas. An effect.

Deannam. To colour.

Deantach. Practical.

Deantus. Rhyming, poetry.

Deantanas. Doings, deeds.

Deantasach. Active.

Dear. Great.

Dear. A daughter.

Dear. A denial, refusal.

Dear. Vide Deur. A drop, tear.

Deara. Notice, remark.

Dearadh se. Vide Deiram.

Dearaornteach. Despairing.

Dearbairde. Signs, tokens.

Dearbh. Sure, certain, true, fixed.

Dearbh. Peculiar, particular.

Dearbh. A churn or milk-pail.

Dearbhach. Sure of.

Dearbhadh. Experience, trial, proof.

Dearbham. To prove, confirm, try, experience.

Dearbhag. } A touchstone.
Dearbhliag. }

Dearbharasc. A proverb.

Dearbheachd. Certainty, assurance.

Dearbhchliamhuin. A son-in-law.

Dearbhghniomh. } An axiom.
Dearbhann. }

Dearbhtha. Confirmed, proved, tried.

Dearbhrathair. A brother.

Dearbhrathair-athair. An uncle.

Dearbhbhrathair-mathair. An uncle by the mother.

Dearbhbhrathaireachd. Society, brotherhood.

Dearbhphiuthar. A sister.

Dearbhthachd. Experiment.

Dearbhughadh. Alleging, protesting, affirming, swearing.

Dearc. An eye.

Dearc. A berry; a lizard.

Dearc. A cave, grave, grotto.

Dearcabhal. An oak-apple.

Dearc-bhallach. A speckled serpent.

Dearcam.

Dearcam. To fee, behold, to look ftedfaft-ly at.

Dearcadh. Looking, beholding.

Dearcnach. Goodly, likely, handfome.

Dearca-francach. Currants.

Dearca-fiaich. Blackberried heath.

Dearca-roide. Bilberries.

Dearca-eidhuin. Ivy-berries.

Dearca-fraoich. Blue-berries.

Dearca-iubhair. Juniper-berries.

Dearc-luachrach. A lizard, efk.

Dearcach Berried, having berries.

Dearg, deargan. Crimfon, red.

Deargam. To redden, to paint crimfon, to blufh, to kindle, burn.

Deargam. To make, prepare.

Dearganta. A plea.

Deargan. The fifh called bream.

Deargan. Crimfon, red dye, purple, rouge.

Dearganach. A red-coat foldier, a whig, or one loyal to the Hanoverian houfe.

Dearglafadh. Flaming, red hot.

Deargan-alt. A keftrel.

Deargan-fraoich. A goldfinch.

Deargchriadh. Ruddle.

Deargliagh. A furgeon.

Dearmad. Forgetfulnefs.

Dearmail. Anxiety.

Dearmadach. Forgetful.

Dearmhail. Huge, very great.

Dearmhair. Very great, exceffive, violent.

Dearmhara. Wonder.

Dearna. Palm of the hand.

Dearnam. To do, act.

Dearnad. A flea.

Dearnadaireachd. Chiromancy, palmiftry.

Dearal. Beggarly, poor, wretched.

Dearalachd. Want, defeat.

Dearrafan. Hurry, ruftling.

Dearfach. A ray, beam, beaming.

Dearfam. To ray, fhine, beam.

Dearfaigham. To watch.

Dearfaigh. Watching.

Dearfaigheachd. Vigilancy, watchfulnefs.

Dearfgam. To polifh, file, burnifh.

Dearfguithe. Complete, finifhed, bright, polite.

Dearfgaithe. Science.

Dearfnughadh. Making polite, complete.

Dearfgnuidheachd. Politenefs, excellence.

Dearthach. The apartment in a monaftery calculated for prayers.

Deas. South.

Deas. Right.

Deafadan. A repofitory.

Deaflamh. Right hand.

Deaflamhach. Neat-handed.

Deas. Neat, pretty, ready, elegant.

Deas. Order.

Deafaigham. To prepare, get ready, to bake, drefs, adorn, mend, correct.

Deafal. Round with the fun.

Deafam. To ftay, remain.

Deafcadh. The laft.

Deafcheumach. Stately gait.

Deafcadh. }
Deafguin. } Lees, dregs, yeft.

Deafghabhail. Afcenfion-day.

Deaflabhradh. Elocution, addrefs.

Deaflamhach. Neat-handed, dextrous.

Deafughadh. Mending, dreffing, preparing.

Deaflamhachd. Ambidexterity.

Deasfhoclach. Ready-witted.

Deafalan. A buffet.

Deafpoireachd. Difputing, arguing.

Deafpoiream. To difpute.

Deafgaram. To pluck off the ears.

Deafghnath. A ceremony.

Deafmas. }
Deafmiras. } Curious.

Deafoireach. Spicy.

Deafuighte. Prepared, ready, adorned.

Deatach. Smoak, vapour, exhalation.

Deatach-thalmhuin. Fumitory.

Deataigham. To fmoak.

Deatamhuil.

Deatamhuil. Full of fmoak.

Deachofa. Lo! there! fee! behold.

Dechealt. Cloth.

Dechedfaidh. War, battle.

Dedhbhel. Poor, miferable.

Dedhel. A calf.

Dedla. Bold, impudent, prefumptuous.

Defordal. Error.

Deiade. Care, diligence, circumfpection.

Deibheadh. A debate, fkirmifh, battle.

Deibheadh. Hafte, fpeed, expedition.

Deibhidhe. The firft fort of *Dan direach*, a kind of verfe which requires that the firft quartan fhall end with a minor termination, and the fecond with a major.

Dethabha. Jehovah.

Deich. Ten.

Deichach Decuple, tenfold.

Deichmhadh. ⎫
Deicho. ⎬ The tenth, decimal.

Deichmhigham. To decimate.

Deichbhrighte. The Decalogue.

Deichmhios. December.

Deichnar. A decade.

Deich fithbhe. Decurio, a ferjeant, corporal.

Deichfhliofnach. A decagon.

Deiccir. Difficult.

Deicfin. To fee, behold.

Deidag. Baubles.

Deide. Obedience, fubmiffion.

Deidh. Defire, longing, a protector, defender.

Deideadh. The tooth-ach.

Deidhe. Two things, a double proportion.

Deidhal. Defirous, fond of, addicted to.

Deifir. Hafte, fpeed, expedition.

Deifirach. Hafty, in hafte.

Deifruigham. To haften, hurry.

Deifreadh. Difference.

Deifrimhearachd. Want.

Deigh. Ice.

Deigh. After.

Deigh laimh. Afterwards, too late.

Deigheanach. Laft, hindermoft.

Deigheanuighe. Later.

Deighlean. A quire of paper.

Deighthiodhlaicthe. Goods.

Deil. ⎫
Deilag. ⎬ A lath, a rod.

Deilbh. A figure. Vide Dealbh.

Deilbh. Fine, fair, fprightly.

Deile. A deal, or plank.

Deilbhealach. The meeting of two ways.

Deilbhin. A little image, picture.

Deilchead. Ill, bad, fad.

Deilcheannach. Biceps.

Deilaodannach. Double-faced.

Deileadoir. A turner.

Deileala. The fpace of two days.

Deileang. A two year old pig.

Deileas. Grudging through covetoufnefs.

Deiloidhche. Space of two nights.

Deilethorc. A hog of two years.

Deilf. A dolphin.

Deilgionnadh. Wafte, havock.

Deilgionnam. To lay wafte.

Deilgne. Thorns, prickles.

Deilgneach. Thorny.

Deilgneach. Spear-thiftle.

Deilam. To turn with a lathe.

Deilgreine. The name of Fingal's ftandard.

Deilin. A little deal or plank.

Deilidham. To lean upon.

Deillam. To feparate. Vide Deolutgham.

Deilm. A found, noife, trembling.

Deiligheadh. Accufing.

Deilfag. A box on the ear.

Deiltre. Druid-idols.

Deiltreadh. Gilding.

Deiltharruinn. A trigger, or iron nail.

Deim. Lack, want.

Deimheas. A pair of fheers.

Deimhe. Darknefs.

Deimhin. True, certain.

Deimhne. Affurance, certainty.

Deimhnigham. To affirm, prove.

Dein, *fa dhein.* Even as.

Dein. Clean, neat, strong, close.

Deine. Cleanness, neatness.

Deineachdach. Rude, vehement, violent, urgent.

Deineachd. Keenness, violence.

Deinas. Rudeness, violence.

Deineasach. Violent, forcing, fierce.

Deineasaighe. Lightning.

Deinmeas. Vanity.

Deinmheach. Void, vain, frivolous.

Deinmheacha. Toys, trifles.

Deinmheachoir. A pedlar, a toyman.

Deinmhigham. To vanish.

Deinmhin. }
Deinmheachin. } A vain fellow.

Deinmne. Swift, active, nimble.

Deir. Say thou.

Deiram. To say, speak.

Deir, i. e. Teine fiaidh. St. Anthony's fire, the shingles.

Deirbh. A churn. Vide Dearbh.

Deire. The deep, abyss.

Deirc. Alms ; Thor deirc dhamh air ghaol De, Give alms for the love of God.

Deircach. Poor, penurious.

Deircag. A narrow penurious woman.

Deirdas. They say. Vide Deiram.

Deireadh. The end, rear, stern.

Deireannach. Last, hindmost.

Deirge. Redder.

Deirge. }
Deirgad. } Redness.

Deirgheine. He made.

Deirginnladh. Red cattle.

Deirglidh. A buying, purchasing.

Deirgliaigh. A surgeon.

Deirid. A secret, mystery.

Deireannan. A desert.

Deiridh. Of the last, hindmost.

Deirli. A present, reward.

Deirmide, i. e. Dith-oirmidin. Disho- nour.

Deirrideach. Secret, hid, private.

Deis. After.

Deis. Gen. of Dias. An ear of corn.

Deisad. Neatness, exactness.

Deise. Of the right-hand.

Deise. Of the two. Vide Dual.

Deise. Neater, handsomer, fitter.

Deisceart. The southern point or quar- ter.

Deisciobal. A disciple.

Deiscreide. Discretion. Not Galic.

Deise. A suit of clothes.

Deisachd. Convenience, ornaments.

Deisad. Neatness, elegance.

Deiseach. Towards the south.

Deisibh. Lands.

Deisidh. He sat or rested.

De.sidham. To stay, remain.

Deisidhocca. They agree, or consented.

Deismigheadh. Dress, ornament.

Deisean. Ugly.

Deisearrach. Sunny, southern aspect.

Deistean. Dislike, squeamishness, disgust.

Deisteanam. } To hate, abhor, detest,
Deistinaigham. } make squeamish.

Deisteanach. Disgustful, squeamish.

Deistin. Numbness.

Deithbhir. Legal.

Deithbhreachadh. Haste, making speed.

Deithbhrigham. To hasten, make speed.

Deithide. Separation ; care, diligence.

Deithineach. Dainty.

Deithneamhar. A decade.

Deithneas. Haste, speed.

Deithneasach. Keen, hasty.

Deithneasaigham. To make haste.

Dennadh. Variation.

Deabhronnta. Consecration.

Deo. Breath, air ; go deo, for ever.

Deoch. A drink.

Deoch an doruis. The parting drink, bon aller.

Deoch-eiridin. A potion.

Deoch-

Deoch-uasal. A costly drink, foreign drink.

Deocham. To embrace tenderly.

Deochair. A difference, distinction.

Deoch slainte. A health, toast.

Deochal. Grudging.

Deoig. Always.

Deoigh. Therefore, for the sake of.

Deoghbhaire. A cup-bearer.

Deoin. Accord, will, purpose.

Deoirseach.
Deoirseoir. } A slave, a porter.

Deoir. A tear, drop. Vide Deur.

Deoir. Will, pleasure, inclination.

Deoirseoneachd. Going about from door to door.

Deolaidh. Aid, help, succour; a dowry.

Deolchar. A present.

Deonach. Agreeable, willing, granting.

Deonachd. Pudendum.

Deonaigham. To voucasafe, grant, allow, approve, consent.

Deontas. Willingness.

Deontach. Voluntary.

Deonnightheach. Willing.

Deoradh.
Deoraidhe. } An alien, fugitive, stranger, outlaw.

Deor. A tear, drop.

Deoraidh. Strong, stout.

Deoraidb. A surety that withdraws himself.

Deoraidh. Disobedience.

Deoraidheachd. Banishment.

Deoraidham. To banish, expel.

Deoral. In tears, wretched.

Deoranta. Strange, cashiered, banished.

Deorata. Otherwise, foreign.

Deothadh. Henbane.

Deothal. Suck, sucking.

Deothalam. To suck.

Deothalagan. Honeyfuckle.

Deothafach. Desirous, desirable.

Dern. A box, buffet.

Des. Land, pl. Deisibh.

Des. A spot, speckle.

Dese. A number, multitude, troop.

Descuidh. Godly.

Det. Victuals, food.

Detiach, deteigheach. The weasand, larynx.

Deugaidhe. Wish, wou'd to God.

Deunam. To do.

Deud. A jaw, set of teeth.

Deudidh. Toothach.

Deunach. Sad.

Deur. A tear, drop.

Deurach. That sheddeth tears, sad, mournful.

Deurghe. Quitting, leaving.

Deusin. An aspect..

D'i. To her, it, from her, it.

Di. Little, Di am, a little while.

Di. Want.

Dia. God.

Dia. A day.

Dia-domhnuich. Sunday.

Dia-luain. Monday.

Dia-mairt. Tuesday.

Dia-ceadaoine. Wednesday.

Dia-ceadaoine an luathraich. Ash-wednesday.

Dia-daoirne. Thursday.

Dia-aoine. Friday.

Dia-sathuirne. Saturday.

Diabail. Without fire.

Diabhal. The devil.

Diabhlaidh. Devilish.

Diabheum. Blasphemy.

Diabladh. Twice as much, double.

Dia-aithadh. Atheism.

Diachair. Sorrow, grief.

Diacharach. Sorrowful.

Diadha.
Diadhamhuil. } Godly, godlike, divine.
Diadhidh.

Diadhachd.

Diadhachd. Godhead, godlinefs, theology.

Diadhair. A divine.

Diadhairachd. Divinity.

Diadheanamh. Apotheofis.

Diadhuigham. To deify.

Diaigh. An end, after.

Diail. Quick, foon, immediately.

Di-airmhe. Innumerable.

Diall. Submiffion.

Diall. The arfe, breech.

Diallaid. A faddle.

Dialon. A diary.

Diallog. A bat.

Diamann. Food, fuftinence.

Diamain. Unfpotted, untainted.

Diamhaoin. The fubftance of a church.

Diamhain
Diamhainach. } Idle, vain, lazy.

Diamhanas. Idlenefs, vanity.

Diamhar. Huge, enormous.

Diamhar. diamhair. Dark, occult, fecret, hid.

Diamhaireachd. A fecret place.

Diamhafladh. Blafphemy.

Diamhafluighoir. A blafphemer.

Diamhafluigham. To blafpheme.

Diaimhladh. A place of refuge.

Diamlughadh. To make dark or coloured.

Dian. Sad, vehement, violent, nimble, brifk.

Dianas. Vehemence, violence.

Dianairm. A place of refuge or fafety.

Dianathchuinge. An importunate requeft.

Dianchomhla. An aid de camp, an officer of the life-guards.

Dianlorgaireachd. Indagation.

Diarath. Daily.

Diardan. Surlinefs, anger.

Diarmuid. The name Dermid.

Dias. Vide Dis.

Dias.
Diafag. } An ear of corn.

Diafach.
Diafdach. } Full of ears of corn.

Diafada.
Diafadach. } Long-bladed.

Diafradh. Gleaning.

Diafram. To glean.

Diathraimh. Defert, defolate.

Dibheach. An ant.

Dibheal. Old.

Dibhealach. Unpaffable.

Dibhearadh. Confoling.

Dibhearam. To confole.

Dibeadach. Negative.

Dibeoil. Dumb, mute.

Dibeartha. Banifhed.

Dibearthach. A fugitive, exile.

Dibiram. To rout, banifh.

Dibirt. Banifhment, banifhing.

Dibh. From or off you.

Dibhe. Of a drink.

Dibhe. Refufing, feparating.

Dibheargach. A robber; vindictive.

Dibheirt. Vide Dibirt.

Dibhfheirge. Indignation, wrath, vengeance.

Dibhir. Private.

Dibhirce. An endeavour.

Dibhirceach. Diligent; fierce, violent, unruly.

Dibhridh. Driving out.

Dibine.
Dibineachd. } Extremity.

Dibir. Forgetfulnefs, neglect.

Diblidh. Vile, drooping, wretched.

Diblighachd. A drooping ftate, wretchednefs.

Dibligham. To make or become vile, drooping, wretched.

Dibrigh. Contempt.

Dicheal. Forgetfulnefs.

Dicheal.

Dicheal. Attempt, endeavour, diligence.
Dicheallach. Diligent.
Dichealltair. The shaft of a spear.
Dichealtair. A deer-park.
Dicheann. A man beheaded.
Dicheannam. To decapitate.
Dicheannadh. Decapitation.
Dicheannta. Beheaded.
Dicheilam. To forget.
Dichreidamh. Disbelief.
Dichreidmheach. An unbeliever, credulous.
Dichreidthe. Incredible.
Did. A pap, diddy.
Dideann. A fort, sanctuary, protection, defence.
Dideannaigham. To defend, protect.
Didein Haste.
Dioliochdadh. Delight.
Didil. Great love, kindness.
Didionnoir. } A protector, guardian.
Didnighoir. }
Difeadacha. Forward.
Difir. Difference.
Difhulang. Intolerable.
Dighe. Gen. of Deoch. A drink.
Dighe. Succour, satisfaction.
Dighe. Condign, adequate.
Dighdhe. A commendation, blessing.
Dighdhe. Gratitude.
Digham. To come, to arrive at a place.
Dighinam. To fuck.
Dighiona. Morose.
Dighreana. Bald.
Digam, diugam. To cluck as a hen.
Dige. A ditch.
Digeach. Full of ditches.
Diic. Sorrow.
Dile. } A deluge, inundation.
Dilionn. }
Dile-ruadh. The deluge.
Dile. Love, friendship.
Dileach. Beloved.

Dileachd. } An orphan.
Dileachdan. }
Dileaghadh. Digesting.
Dileagham. To digest food.
Dileagradh. Address.
Dileaglam. To reverence, revere.
Dileamain. } Love, kindness, affection.
Dileamhaon. }
Dileas, dilios. Dear, beloved, faithful.
Dileaschoimhadh. Protection.
Dilse. } Love, affection, lovingness,
Dilseachd. > faithfulness.
Dilsad. }
Dilghionn. Destruction, plundering.
Dilgion, dilgionadh. Emptying.
Diliadhadh. Boiling, concoction.
Dilmain. Meet, proper, fit.
Dillain. Illegitimate, not in wedlock, unmarried.
Dillanas. } Fornication.
Dillantas }
Dilib. A legacy.
Dilbiche. A testator, legator.
Dille. Dill.
Dilin. For ever.
Dilte. Nutriment.
Dimchisin. To see, behold.
Dimbrigh. Contempt.
Dimbuaigh. A crime.
Dimeas. Contempt, a bad name.
Dimeasam. To undervalue, despise.
Dimeasal. Contemptuous.
Dimeasda. Despised.
Dimeasdachd. Disrespect.
Dimhe. Protection.
Dimhin. Vide Deimhin.
Dimhinachd. Confidence.
Dimnidhachd. Sadness.
Dimhnigham. To affirm.
Dimnidhach. Sad.
Dimreas. Need, necessity.
Din. Pleasant, delightful, agreeable, sucking.

Dinaitam.

Dinaitam. To diflocate.

Dine, cine. A generation, age.

Dine. A beginning, the firft.

Dineart. The power of God.

Dineart. Imbecility.

Dineartuigham. To weaken, to flank.

Ding. A wedge.

Dingam. To urge, thruft, pufh.

Dinafgadh Untying

Dingadh. Thrufting, pufhing.

Diniath. A helmet.

Dingir. Cuftody.

Dingthe. Wedged in, preffed, fqueezed.

Dinam. To drink, imbibe.

Dinib. Drinking.

Dinmhiach. Idle.

Dinn, dinne. From, off us.

Dinn. A hill, fortified hill.

Dinnis. An oath.

Dinnis. Contempt.

Dinneir. A dinner.

Dinnfair. A wedge, ginger.

Dioach. For Diadhach. Divine.

Dioachd. Divinity.

Diobadh. A prick, a point.

Diobain. To die without iffue.

Diobbar. Difrefpect, omiffion.

Diobh. Of them. Vide Dibh.

Diobhadh. Deftruction, death, inheritance.

Diobhadh. A portion, dowry.

Diobhaidh. Impious.

Diobhaighidh. Confuming.

Diobhail. Lofs, defeat.

Diobhaidham. To deftroy, confume.

Diobhal. Old, antient.

Diobhalach. Robbed, fpoiled, the ablative.

Diobhanach. Lawlefs.

Diobhargadh. Captivity, enflaving, perfecution.

Diobhargach. Keen, fierce.

Diobhlacha. Material, of moment.

Diobhartha. Exiled, banifhed.

Diobhratha. Difcovered.

Diobhratham. To difcover.

Diobhuidhe. Ingratitude.

Diobhuidhach. Ungrateful.

Diobram. To forfake.

Diobradh. Forfaking, failing, wanting.

Diochioll. Endeavour.

Diochiollam. To endeavour.

Diochairtam. To peel, decorticate.

Diochmaire. Theft.

Diochoifguidhach. Implacable.

Diocholna. Without body.

Diochuimhne. Forgetfulnefs.

Diochuimhnach. Forgetful.

Diochonaire. Without any way or paffage.

Diochra, diochur. Diligence.

Diochron. Immediately, without time.

Diochuidh. Small.

Diocfa. Lofty.

Diodhailin. An atom, a mite.

Diodhaoineadh. Depopulation.

Diodhaoinam. To depopulate.

Diodhatham. To difcover.

Diodhma. A fort, fortification.

Diodhnadh. To fatisfy.

Diodhuille. Without leaves.

Diofhulang. Intolerable.

Diofhlain. Exanguious, pale.

Diofhochain. A mulct paid for not marrying.

Diog. A ditch, dyke, pit.

Diogg. A breath, life.

Diogam. To ditch, enclofe, entrench.

Diogan. Revenge, fpite, feverity.

Dioganta. Fierce, cruel, revengeful.

Diogantachd. Revenge, cruelty.

Dioggladh. Sucking clofe.

Diogha. The worft.

Dioghaltas. Revenge.

Dioghaltach.   } Vindictive, revengeful.
Dioghaltafach. }

Dioghbhuth.

Dioghbhuth. Deſtruction.

Dioghmhalach. Hurtful.

Dioghrabham. To leſſen, diminiſh.

Dioghadh. Miſchief.

Dioghann. Plentiful.

Dioghais. High, tall, ſtately.

Dioghalam. To revenge.

Dioghalt. Revenge.

Dioghalta. Revenged.

Dioghaltoir. An avenger.

Dioghartham. To behead.

Dioghbhail. Damage, deſtruction.

Dioghbhalach. Hurtful, noxious.

Dioghiona. Moroſe.

Dioghla. Revenge, injuſtice.

Dioghluim. To glean.

Dioghna. Contempt.

Dioghnas. Rare.

Dioghradha. Moroſe, rude.

Dioghrais. Conſtantly, frequently.

Dioghrogam. To belch.

Diogras. Uprightneſs.

Dioghraiſach. Beloved.

Dioghuin. Forcing, compelling.

Diograis. Diligence, a ſecret.

Diol. Worthy, ſufficient.

Diol. An object.

Diol-deirc. A beggar.

Diol. Selling, uſe, pay, ſatisfaction.

Diol. An end.

Diolabiche. A legator.

Dioladh. Paying, filling, ſatisfying, ranſoming.

Dioladhmhail. A receipt, diſcharge.

Diolacht. Blameleſs.

Diolachtchomh. Protection.

Diolaidheacht. Payment.

Diolam. To pay; renew, change, recompenſe

Diolaim. To glean, leaſe, write.

Diolaimhnighthoir. A weeder.

Diolathairachd. Abſence

Diolaithram. To pillage.

Diolantas. Manhood.

Diolbhrugh. A ſhop.

Diolcomhan. Confederacy.

Diolchuan. A ſhop.

Diolgadh. Diſmiſſion, forgiveneſs.

Diolgam. To diſmiſs.

Diolmain. Faithful.

Diolamhnach. ⎫
Diolmhanach. ⎬ A hireling, a ſoldier, a brave ſtout man.
Diolunach. ⎭

Diolanas. Fornication.

Diolaſchoimhed. Patronage, protection.

Diolaſchoimhadaiche. Protector.

Diolas, diolis. Faithful, loyal, true, dear.

Diolta. Repaid.

Diolſan.

Dioltoir. A ſeller.

Diollaid. A ſaddle.

Diollaidair. A ſaddler.

Diolughadh. Conſumption, deſtruction.

Diollait. Apparel, raiment.

Diollmhanach. A hired ſoldier.

Diolunta. Valiant, ſtout, brave, generous.

Dioluntas. ⎫
Dioluntachd. ⎬ Hoſpitality.

Diom, dhiom. From or of me.

Diomadh, diombuaidh. Diſpleaſure, anger, indignation.

Diombagh. Grief, ſorrow.

Diombaghach. Sorrowful, mournful.

Diombuan. Fading, tranſitory.

Diomgha. Diſpleaſure.

Diomdhach. Diſpleaſed.

Diomhalach. Profuſe, hurtful.

Diomhaltas. Caution, notice.

Diomhaonach. Idle, vain, lazy, trifling.

Diomhaonas. Idleneſs, vanity.

Diomharr. Secret. Vide Diamhir.

Diomhargam. To quench, ſuppreſs.

Diomhagad. Enfranchiſement, liberty, freedom.

Diomhagam. To make free.

Diomh-

Diomhothaigheach. Stupid.

Diomhoileadh. A demolishing.

Diomhillam. To destroy utterly.

Diomhrachd. Obscurity, darkness.

Diomhran. A mystery, a hermit's cell.

Diomaltoir. A glutton.

Diomoladh. Dispraise.

Diomoltam To dispraise.

Diomolta. Dispraised, blamed.

Diomoltoir. A slanderer.

Diomrac. A temple.

Diomasach. Proud, haughty, arrogant.

Diomus. Pride, arrogance.

Dion. A shelter, protection, covert, fence.

Dion. The second semimetre or *leathrann* of a verse, consisting of two quartans; it is more commonly called Comhad.

Dionach. Close joined, water-tight.

Dionachadh. }
Dionadh. } Security.

Dionadair. A fender.

Dionam. To defend, protect.

Dionairm. }
Dionait. } Refuge.

Dionaigham. To secure, make water-tight.

Dionasgadh. Disjoining, loosening, undoing.

Dionasgam. To disjoin, loosen.

Dionasgtha. Dissolved.

Dionbhreid. An apron.

Dionchosnam. To garrison.

Dionchaint. A defence

Diongam. To match, equal, overcome.

Diong. Worthy.

Diongmhalta. Perfect, effectual, worthy, meet, proper, suitable.

Dionn. A hill.

Diongbhalar. Worthy.

Diongbhalta. Firm, fast, fixed.

Dionnal. A shot.

Dionnan. A little hill.

Dionlongphort. A garrison.

Dionnsoighidh. Even to.

Dionsuighe. Unto.

Dionnta. Turning about.

Dionuighoir. A patron, protector.

Dionte. Defended.

Diopal. Severe.

Dior. Meet, proper, decent.

Dior. A law.

Diorachrach. Lawless.

Diorach, direach. Just, right, equitable erect.

Diorain. A dropping.

Diorgadh. Directing.

Diorgham. To direct.

Diorangam. To belch.

Dioradaim. To annihilate.

Diorgas. Uprightness.

Diorma. A troop, company, crowd.

Diormach. Numerous, infinite.

Diorna. Quantity.

Diorrasg. Suddenness, fierceness.

Diorrasach. }
Diorrasgach. } Froward, rash.

Diorsan. Bad new .

Diorusimeach. An atom, a mite.

Diosc. }
Diosgadh. } Barren, dry, not giving milk.

Diosgan. A gnashing of the teeth.

Diosgam. To gnash the teeth.

Diosgadh. A noise.

Diosgar. }
Diosgarnach. } The mob, rabble.

Diosmugam. To snuff a candle.

Diosnaidhm. Smooth, without knots.

Diospoireachd. Vide Deaspoireachd.

Diot. Of thee, from thee.

Diot. A meal of meat, a dinner.

Diotadoir. An assistant.

Dioth, dith, di. Want.

Diothchuiram. To force away, drive off.

Diothach. Destruction.

Diothlathairughadh. Destruction, consumption.

Diothreamh.   A wilderneſs, a deſert.

Diothruaillam.   To unſheathe.

Dipinn.   A net.

Dire.   A tribute.

Direach.   Straight, upright, juſt, frugal.

Dearachan.   A perpendicular.

Direadh.   Aſcending.

Direadham.   To aſcend, go up.

Direachdas.   Uprightneſs.

Direachdam.   To geld.

Direadh.   A panegyric.

Direagadh.   A direction.

Direme.   Without way or paſſage, out of the way.

Diribe.   Bald.

Dirigham.   To make ſtraight, direct, guide.

Dirim.   Numerous, plenteous, great.

Dirisgleam.   To ſtrip bark.

Dis.   Two, both, a pair, brace.

Dis.   Chilly, poor, miſerable.

Diſbeagam.   To contemn, deſpiſe.

Diſbeirt.   Twofold, double.

Diſcir.   Fierce, nimble, active, quick.

Diſgir.   Sudden.

Diſgreitſia.   A diſeaſe.

Diſle.   Dearer, more loyal.   Vide Dilas.

Diſle.   } Love, eſteem, friendſhip, fide-
Diſleach. } lity, loyalty.

Diſle.   Property.

Diſle.   A die, dice.

Diſlean.   A dice-box.

Diſligheach.   Uncouth, ſtraggling, impervious.

Diſleachd.   Faithfulneſs, propriety.

Diſliogam.   To hide, conceal.

Diſread.   The aſpergillum uſed at maſs to ſprinkle the holy water on the people.

Dit, do dhit.   It remains.

Dith.   Want, defect.

Dith.   To ſuck, give milk.

Dithbhir.   Difference.

Diteadh.   Condemning, ſentencing.

Diteam.   To condemn, ſentence.

Dithche.   Eating.

Dithcheal.   Induſtry, endeavour.

Dithcheallach.   Diligent.

Dithchealtoir.   A necromantic veil or covering that worketh charms.

Dithcheannam.   To behead.

Dithchioll.   Induſtry, attempt, endeavour.

Dithchiollach.   Induſtrious, diligent.

Dithchiollam.   To endeavour.

Dithchuir.   Forcing.

Ditheach.   A beggar, empty.

Dithein.   Darnel, corn-marygold, tare.

Dithlachdach.   An orphan.

Dithimh.   A heap.

Dithinge.   Dumb, mute.

Dithiſd.   Two.

Dithleach.   Forgetful.

Dithreabh.   An hermitage.

Dithreabhach.   An hermit, anchoret.

Dithreachdach.   Lawleſs.

Diu.   A long time, the worſt.

Diugh.   To-day.

Diubhracam.   To caſt, fling, throw, brandiſh.

Diubladh.   Refuge.

Diuc.   The pip, a ſickneſs of fowls.

Diuc.   A duke.

Diucam.   To cry out, exclaim.

Diudan.   Giddineſs.

Diudanach.   Giddy.

Diugaighil.   A ſobbing, ſighing.

Diughailfainn.   Sucking.

Diugam.   To cluck, cackle.

Diugam.   To drink off.

Diughe.   The worſt, extreme, bad.

Diucain.   The eyes.

Diucair.   A bladder to keep up fiſhing nets.

Diuid.   } Tender-hearted, flexible.
Diuideach. }

Diulam.   To ſuck.

Diultam.   To deny, refuſe.

Diultadh.   A denial, refuſal, negative.

Diunach.   Vide Deonach.

Diunlaoch. A young hero.

Diur. Difficult, hard.

Diurnam. To gulp, fwallow.

Dius. Protection.

Diuthadh. Worft.

Dlaidh, dlaoigh. ⎫ A lock of hair, hand-
Dlagh. ⎭ ful.

Dlaimh. Darknefs.

Dlaoigh. A handful.

Dleachd. A law.

Deafdanas. Duty.

Dleafdanach. Dutiful.

Dligead. A feparation.

Dlighe. A law, ordinance, rights, dues.

Dligheach. Lawful.

Dlighidh. ⎫
Dlighthar. ⎭ Perfect, excellent.

Dlightheach. Lawful, juft.

Dlightheamhuil. Juft, fkilled in law.

Dlightheamhnach. A lawgiver.

Dlightheoir. A lawyer.

Dlighthinoir. A magiftrate, juftice of the peace.

Dligam. To feparate.

Dlifteanach. Lawful.

Dlochd. ⎫
Dlodan. ⎭ A ftrainer.

Dlochram. To prefs.

Dloige. Loofing.

Dlomh. To tell.

Dlomhadh. A denial, refufal.

Dlomham. To make plain or manifeft.

Dlomhaifin. Deftruction.

Dludh. A retribution.

Dluige. A loofing, releafing.

Dluigh. Active, nimble, prepared.

Dluimh. A cloud, darknefs, a blaze of fire.

Dluithin. A little ftudy or clofet.

Dlumh. Much, plenty.

Dluth. Near, clofe, tight, confined.

Dluth. Warp of a web.

Dluth-ftol. A clofe-ftool.

Dluth. Near.

Dluth. An inclofure.

Dluthas. Nearnefs.

Dlutham. ⎫ To make clofe, to pack, to
Dluthaigham. ⎭ approach, draw near, to enclofe.

Dluthcharcair. A labyrinth.

Dluthuighte Knit, compacted.

Do. The fign of the dative, and fometimes put before the infinitive, do dhuine, to a man; do fgriobhadh, to write.

Do. Not properly a fign of the paft tenfe. Vide Analyfis.

Do. Thy, the genitive of thou, and become the poffeffive thy, thine.

Do, for da. Two.

Do. A prepofitive particle of negation, as do-rannfuighte, infcrutable.

Doacal. Affliction.

Do-aighneafach. Indifputable.

Do-airmheach. Innumerable.

Do-aomidh. Inexorable.

Do-atharruighte. Immutable.

Dob. A plafter, a gutter.

Dob, or do b', do, the fign of the paft tenfe, and b' for bu, the fubftantive verb, as do b' eigin, it was neceffary.

Dob. A river, ftream.

Dobadh. ⎫
Dobail. ⎭ Daubing over.

Dobam. To daub, to plafter.

Dobhais. Immortal.

Dobair. A plafterer.

Do b' eidir. Perhaps, it was neceffary.

Dobholadh. A rank fmell.

Dobheirt. Mifchief, harm, the devil.

Dobhar. Dark, obfcure.

Dobhar, and dur. Water.

Dobhar-chu. ⎫
Dobhran. ⎭ An otter.

Dobhar. The border of a country.

Dobharfhoidheach. A pitcher, bucket.

Dobhart. Vide Dobheairt.

Do bhrigh. Becaufe.

Dobhran-

Dobhran-leaflathan. A beaver.

Dobh.
Dobhidh. } Boifterous, fwelling, raging.

Dobron. Sorrow, grief, fadnefs.

Dobronach. Sorrowful, fad.

Dobronam. To be fad, forrowful.

Docamhuil.
Docamhlachd. } A difficulty, hardfhip.

Docamhlach. Difficult, hard.

Doch. One's native country.

Docha. More likely, probable.

Dochad. Rather.

Dochann.
Dochar. } Harm, hurt, damage.
Dochaireas.

Dochannach.
Docharach. } Hurtful.

Dochannam. To hurt, injure.

Dochas. Hope, confidence.

Dochafgidh. Unruly.

Docheannfuighte. Unappeafable.

Dochma Weak, incapable.

Dochoruighte. Immoveable.

Dochoimeafgte. Immifcible.

Dochraith. Luft.

Dochlaoidhte. Infuperable, indefatigable.

Docht. Strait, narrow, clofe.

Dochlaoidtheachd. Infuperability.

Dochta. Inftructed, taught; documents.

Dochreidfin. Incredible.

Dochtam. To ftrain, bind hard.

Dochtrail. Luxury.

Do chum. To the end that.

Dochuid.

Dochuingeadh. Disjoining.

Dochum. An arbour.

Docra. Sadnefs.

Docran. Anguifh.

Docrach Noxious.

Docuracha. Carelefs.

Do d'. To thy.

Dodhaing. Difficult, hard.

Dodha. Of two, binarius.

Dodhealuighte. Indiffoluble, unalienable.

Dodhail. Bad news.

Dodhealbhach. Unlikely.

Doeth. Sicknefs, difeafe.

Dofhaicfinach. Invifible.

Dofhaghail. Hard to find.

Doghailfi. Anguifh, perplexity.

Doflainn. Without blood.

Dofhuafgladh. Inextricable.

Dogadh. Mifchieving, fingeing, fcorch-ing.

Dofhulangte. Intolerable.

Doghadh. Singeing, fcorching

Dogaladh. Revenging.

Dogaltach. Revengeful.

Doghaltas. Revenge.

Do ghna. Always.

Dogham. To burn, finge.

Doglacte. Impregnable.

Doghte. Singed, burnt.

Doghra. Sorrow, fadnefs, dullnefs, ftupi-dity.

Doghran.
Doghruin. } Anguifh, perplexity, danger.

Doganta. Fierce.

Doghruinach. Dangerous.

Doghartadh. Beheading.

Doghiulan. Infupportable.

Doghluaifte. Immoveable.

Doghraineach. Painful.

Doib. A plafter.

Doibealadh. Daubing.

Doibh, dhoibh. To them, dative of tu.

Doibhear. Rude, uncivil.

Doibheas. Vice.

Doibhre. Sacrifice.

Doibrith. Sowens or gruel.

Doich. Swift, quick.

Doiche. The former, foremoft, hope, con-fidence.

Doicheadhfadh. War, ftrife.

Doicheannfa. Contumacious.

Doicheallach. Churlifh.

Doicheall.

Doicheall. Churlifhnefs.

Doicheidhe. Rather

Doichidh. Haftening.

Doicham. To haften.

Doichme. Ill-fhaped.

Doid. The hand.

Doidgheal. White-handed.

Doid. A few acres of land, a little farm.

Doiddeach. Fond of drefs, ftrong.

Doidheanta. Impoffible.

Doidhche. By night.

Doidhreann. A duel.

Doigheagla. Individual, indivifible, fpoken of a fpirit.

Doif. A potion.

Doigh. Hope, confidence, truft.

Doigh. Ways and means, a guefs, fuppofition, good order, condition, manner, a teftimony.

Doigh. Sure, certain, doubtlefs; gu bu doigh an t fleagh, the fpear was fure.

Doigheadh. Confuming.

Doighal. Well appointed, in good condition.

Doigheadh. Hoping, fingeing, adjufting.

Doigheam. To hope, confide.

Doighear. A fpear.

Doighliag. A touchftone.

Doichthe. Pangs.

Doighthe. Adjufted.

Doighniomh. Injury.

Doilain. An eddying wind.

Doilainach. Eddying.

Doilleir. Dark, obfcure, myftical.

Doilbh. Dark, gloomy, obfcure, dufky.

Doilbheas. ⎫
Doilgheas. ⎭ Sorrow, mourning.

Doilghe. Sore, hard, troublefome.

Doilgheafach. Grievous, forrowful, fad.

Doilidheachd. Frowardnefs.

Doilig. ⎫
Doiligh. ⎭ Difficult, doleful, grieved.

Doille. Blindnefs.

6

Do-imchar. Intolerable.

Doimh. Poor.

Doimheis. Infinite.

Doimhal. Stormy.

Doimhann. Deep, profound.

Doimhnaicham. To deepen.

Doimhne. ⎫
Doimhneachd. ⎭ Depth.

Do-impoichte. Inconvertible.

Doineann. ⎫ Inclement weather, a tem-
Doinnfhionn. ⎭ peft; melius, don-fhion.

Doineannta. Stormy.

Doinne. ⎫
Doinnad. ⎭ Brown.

Do-innfidh. Unaccountable.

Dointe. A fmall black infect.

Doindearg. Of a reddifh-dun.

Doineimh. Deep.

Dointe. Intelligible.

Doirb. An attempt.

Doirbh. Peevifh, diffatisfied, quarrelfome

Doirbhcheiram. To frame, model, fafhion.

Doirbhachd. Peevifhnefs.

Doirbhas. Anguifh, grief, forrow, adverfity.

Doire. A wood, grove, thicket.

Doireach. Woody.

Doi-reama. Bye-paths, impaffable places.

Doiriardha. Difficult, ungovernable.

Doiriata. Lewd.

Doirmidhafadh. Lethargy.

Doirling. An ifthmus, beech.

Doirneag. Handle of an oar, a large ftone to caft.

Doirfa. The plural of dorus a door.

Doirneagach. Full of round ftones.

Doirfeoir. A porter.

Doirfeoirachd. The office of a porter.

Doirfach. Full of doors, open, expofed.

Doirfin. Folding-doors.

Doirt. Spilled, poured out.

Doirteal. A fink.

Doirteach. Spilling, that fpilleth.

Doirtam.

Doirtam. To fpill, fhed.

Doit. A grain of inebriating quality that grows amongft corn.

Doite. Burned, finged. Vide Dagham.

Doite, daith. Quick, nimble, active.

Doith. Soon.

Doithcheall. Niggardlinefs, churlifhnefs.

Doithcheallach. Churlifh, grudging, niggardly.

Doithir. A covenant.

Doitham. Vide Dogham.

Doithir. Dark, gloomy, obfcure.

Dol. A kind of fifhing-net.

Dol. A fpace, diftance.

Dol. Going. Vide Racham. Analyfis.

Dolabhartha. Ineffable.

Dolaidh. Lofs, detriment, defect.

Dolaidh. Impatient, intolerable.

Dolaimhgen. A two-handed fword.

Dolas. Grief, mourning, defolation.

Dolas. Abhorrence, difdain, loathing.

Dolafach. Sad, melancholy, fick, mournful.

Dolbh. Sorcery.

Dolbhad. Fiction.

Doleabhtha. Illegible.

Doleanmhuin. Inimitable.

Do-leighas. Immedicable.

Dollidh. Damage.

Doleafuighte. Irreparable.

Dolfa. Hefitancy, flownefs.

Doleirfin. Inexplicable.

Dolmha. Delay, loitering.

Dolidh Difficult.

Dolubtha. Stubborn, inflexible.

Doluaidh. Unfpeakable.

Doluigheadh. Falling down.

Dolum. Surly.

Dom. A houfe.

Do'm. To my.

Doma. Scarcity, want.

Do m'aice. Near me.

Domain. Tranfitory.

Domairm. Speech.

Domairm. An armoury, magazine.

Domharbhtha. Immortal.

Domharbhthachd. Immortality.

Domblas. The gall on the liver; anger, choler, difguft, bile.

Do m' dheoin. Of my own free will.

Domblafda. Unfavoury, difguftful, biliary.

Domburdheach. Unthankful.

Domhadh. The fecond.

Domhail. Bulky.

Domhain. Deep, hollow.

Domhaithte. Irremiffible.

Domhan. The world.

Domhan-fgriobhadh. Cofmography.

Domhoin, doimhoin. Bad, naughty, idle.

Domhar. Water.

Domhghnas. Hereditary; patrimony, inheritance.

Domhghnas. Propriety.

Domhlios. A houfe furrounded by a moat or watered trench, for a fortification.

Domhlas. Bulk, a crowd.

Domhl. Bulky, thick.

Domhnach. A great houfe, a church.

Domhnach. Sunday.

Domhnach. Lamentable.

Domnach-inid. Shrove-funday, Quinquagefima.

Domhnach Cingcis. Whitfunday.

Domhnon. The Firbolg.

Domhothuigheach. Imperceptible, unfeeling.

Domhothuighachd. Imperceptibility.

Domnafcam. To bind.

Domhuchaidh. Inextinguifhable.

Domhuin. Deep.

Domhuinte. Intractable.

Don. Mifchief, evil.

Donadh. Evil, bad, awkward.

Do'n. Of the, to the.

Donas. Mifchief, harm, hurt, ill-luck.

         Donaigham.

Donaigham. To make bad, to hurt.
Donamharc. Naughtiness.
Donn Dun, brown.
Donn. Pregnant.
Donnog. A fish so called.
Donnam. To grow brown.
Donnalaich. Howling.
Donnaghadh. Destroying.
Donnaladh. }
Donnalach. } Howling like a dog.
Doradh. A line, a rule.
Doraidh. Intricate, strife, dispute.
Doraingeachd. Frowardness.
Dorainnte. Indivisible.
Dorar. A battle, conflict.
Doras. A door, gate.
Dorala. It happened.
Doran. Pain, torment.
Dorangach. Pain, frowardness.
Dorannsughidh. Inscrutable.
Dorbruadhar. Rough, rushing.
Dorcha, dorch. Dark, black, dusky.
Dorchadas. Darkness.
Dorchadh. An eclipse.
Dorchaigham. To darken, incloud.
Dorchchaint. Ambilogy.
Dorchchaintach. Ambilogous.
Dord. }
Dordal. } A humming, muttering.
Dordam. To hum like a bee.
Do reir. According to.
Dordan. A humming noise, buzzing.
Doreitighte. Irreconcileable.
Dordhuille. Folding doors.
Dorga. Despicable.
Dorga. A fishing-net.
Do-riartha. Insatiable, surly, peevish.
Do-riarthachd. Surliness, peevishness.
Doriaghlighte. Ungovernable.
Dorlach. A bundle, handful.
Dorling. A neck of land, isthmus.
Dorn. The fist, haft, handle, a box, blow,   5

Dorneag. A round stone that a man can cast.
Dornan. A small bundle, handful of flax, straw, or the like.
Dorn-dighe. A finger-sucker.
Dornchur. }
Dornchul. } The hilt of a sword.
Dornam. To box.
Dornadair. A bruiser.
Dorr. Anger, wrath.
Dorr. Harsh, rough.
Dorrach. }
Dorrda. } Rough, rugged, austere.
Dorrdha. Fierce, cruel.
Dorram. To grow angry.
Dorrsprocht. Stirring to anger.
Dorruighe. Surly, grim.
Dorseir. A porter, door-keeper.
Dorsan. A grashopper.
Dorseirachd. Keeping a door.
Dortam. To pour out, spill.
Dortadh. Spilling.
Doruigsin. Unattainable.
Doruin. Pain, torment, danger.
Dorubha. A line.
Doruingeach. Uneasy, dangerous.
Dorus. A door. Vide Doras.
Dos. A bush, a cockade, a bramble, thorn, thicket.
Dos. Froth, scum.
Dosach. }
Dosrach. } Bushy.
Dosal. Slumber.
Dosan. A little bush, as of hair or the like.
Dosan, dhasan. To him.
Do-sgartha. Inseparable.
Do-sgrudadh. Unsearchable.
Do-sdiuridh. Intractable.
Dosgeul. A romance.
Dosguidhachd. Extravagance.
Dosharta. Troublesome, difficult.
Do-sheachanta. Inevitable.
Do-shasuighte. Insatiable.

Do-fheallta. Invifible.

Do fhior. Always, continually.

Dofgaidha, Evils of the year.

Do-fhiubhal. Impaffable.

Dofgidhachd. Morofenefs.

Dofin. Thereunto.

Do-fmachdidh. }
Do-fmachdighte. } Obftinate, incorrigible.

Do-fpionnta. Unfearchable.

Do-fmuintighte. Incomprehenfible.

Do-fpriochte. Stubborn, intractable.

Dofraich. Buffeting of water. Dofraich nan ton fuidh fron.

Dot. Vide Dod.

Dothadh. Vide Daghadh.

Dothar. A river.

Dotharchlais. A conduit.

Dothchus. Hope.

Dothchufach. Confident, hopeful.

Dothchufam. To hope, truft, confide.

Do-theagaifgte. Indocile.

Do-thomhaifde. Immenfurable.

Do-thomhas. Immenfurability.

Do-thogtha. Rejected, hard to rear.

Do-thuigfin. Unintelligible.

Drab. A fpot, ftain.

Drabag. A dirty woman, flattern.

Drabaire. A dirty fellow.

Drabafda. Dirty, indelicate.

Drabafdachd. Dirtinefs, indelicacy.

Drabh. A cart.

Drabh. Grains.

Drabhag. Dregs, lees.

Drabhagach. Dreggy.

Drabhin. Idle.

Drabhlin. Trifles, idlenefs.

Drag. Fire, anger, a thunderbolt.

Dragaighean. A fire-fhovel.

Dragbhod. The leffer bear-ftar, i. e. a fiery tail.

Dragart. A flint.

Dragon. }
Draic. } A dragon.

Dragh. Trouble.

Draghal. Troublefome.

Draghalachd. Troublefomenefs.

Dragham. To peel, tug.

Draghadh. A pulling, dragging.

Draghair. A dragger, puller.

Draghairachd. Pulling, tugging, dragging.

Draigheann. Thorn.

Draigh-bhiorafg. Fewel.

Draighneach, draigneog. A black thorn, floe.

Draighneach. A great rattling noife, as of thunder.

Draighionn. A dog-rofe bufh.

Draillfain. A fparkling light.

Drain, draint. }
Drainnafcoradh. } Grinning.

Draillfainach. }
Drailfante. } Twinkling, fparkling.

Drainn. A hunch, a hump-back.

Drainneaforam, drainntam. To grin.

Drainc. A fnarling.

Draincanta. Snarling.

Dram. Much, plenty.

Dram. }
Dramaig. } A dram of fpirits.

Dram. Vide dream.

Dramaig. A dirty mixture, crowdy.

Dramhabtam. }
Dramhaim. } To kick, fpurn, tread.

Dramham. To grin.

Dramhdaim. To mutter, grumble.

Dran, dranog. Rhyme, metre.

Drandan. The whiftling of wind or ftorm; humming noife or finging.

Drand. Leaft bit, a fmall quantity.

Drannt, dranntan. Snarling of a dog, grumbling.

Dranutanach. } Snarling, envious, grudging,
Drandanach. } complaining, humming.

Drandannachd. Singing, humming.

Draoi, draoith. A druid, augur, charmer, magician.

Draoitheache.

Draoitheachd. Magic, forcery, enchantment ; properly the Druidical worfhip and facrifice.

Draolin. Tedioufnefs, inactivity.

Draoithneach. Vide Draoi.

Draoighnionn. Thorn.

Diafda, ann-drafda. Hitherto, now, not yet.

Draos. Trafh.

Draofda. ⎫
Draofdal. ⎬ Obfcene, fmutty.

Draofdachd. Obfcenity, fmut.

Dre. A fled.

Dreach. Form, figure, image.

Dreachach. That dreffeth, polifheth ; drawn, figured, delineated.

Dreachamhuil. ⎫
Dreachal. ⎬ Comely, well-looked.

Dreachamhuil. A ftatuary.

Dreachadan. A mould.

Dreachadh. A portraiture, polifhing, adorning.

Dreachadair. A painter, houfe-painter.

Dreacham. To figure, delineate, adorn, polifh.

Dreachda. A troop.

Dreachdam. To fignify.

Dreachfhompladh. A platform, ichnography.

Dreacht. A poem, draught, pattern.

Dreachd. An article ; office, employment.

Dreachta. Weaknefs.

Dreagadh. Advertifement.

Dreaghuin. Prickles.

Dreagam. To fight, wrangle ; to certify, give notice.

Dream. A tribe, family, thofe, folk.

Dream. ⎫
Dreamag. ⎬ A handful of hay, or the like.

Dreamanach. Fanatical, mad, frantic.

Dreaman. Madnefs, furioufnefs.

Dreamhnach. Perverfe, foolifh, a coxcomb.

Dreamhnam. To rage, fret.

Drean. Bad, naughty.

Drean. Strife, debate.

Drean. A wren.

Dreanad. ⎫
Dreann. ⎬ Good.

Dreandha. Repugnant, contrary, oppofite.

Dreann. Contention , grief, forrow, pain.

Dreannad. Rafhnefs.

Dreannam. To fkirmifh, encounter.

Drean comhac. A leg.

Dreangcuid. A flea.

Dreanor. A prophet.

Dreapam. To climb, clamber.

Dreapairachd. Climbing, clambering.

Dreas. Place, ftead.

Dreas, dreafag. A briar, bramble.

Dreaf-nan-fmiar A bramble.

Dreafail. Small pieces.

Dreafchoill. A thicket.

Dreafgidh. ⎫
Dreafamhuil. ⎬ Prickly.
Dreafamhuil. ⎭

Dreafarnach. A place where brambles grow.

Dreathan, dreathlan donn. A wren.

Drechd. A tale, ftory.

Drecheng. Three perfons.

Dreibhfe. A fpace.

Dreibhfe o fin. A little while ago.

Dreige. A meteor, a candle put out.

Dreigaifach. Peevifh.

Dreim. An endeavour, attempt.

Dreim le h anal. Gafping.

A dreim. Comparing with.

Dreimineach. A gradation, degree.

Dreimam. To climb.

Dreimire. A ladder, ftair.

Dreimire-muire. The herb centaury.

Dreimhne.

Dreimhne. Warfare.

Dreogham. To rot, to wear out.

Dreollan. A wren.

Dreollan-teasbhuidh. A grasshopper.

Dreoighte. Rotten.

Dres. News, a story, rehearsal.

Dresbheartach. A tale-bearer.

Dreasdh. A rehearsal, relation.

Driachadaich. ⎱ Stiffness, inflexibility, ob-
Driachairachd. ⎰ stinacy.

Dricc. A dragon.

Dricc. Angry.

Driamlach. A fishing-line.

Dril. A drop.

Drillam. To drop.

Drillseach. Dropping.

Drim. The back, a ridge of mountains.

Drim a' chrainn. The beam of a plough.

Drim luinge. The keel of a ship.

Drim uachdaran a'chairain. The upper pa-
late.

Driodar. Dregs, lees; gore, corrupt matter.

Driodartha. Mixed with dregs.

Driogam. To drop, distill.

Driopam To climb.

Drip. Affliction, a snare.

Dris, drisle, drisleach. ⎱ A bramble, briar.
Driseag, drisleag. ⎰

Driseach. ⎱ Fretful.
Driseanta. ⎰

Drithle. ⎫
Drithladh. ⎬ A sparkle.
Drithlag. ⎭

Drithlean. A rivet.

Drithligham. To sparkle.

Dribhlach. A cowl.

Driuch. A beak, snout; fretfulness, anger.

Driuchal. Angry.

Driuchalachd. Anger.

Driucham. To stand on end as the hair on
the head.

Driuchadh. A standing on end.

Driuchd. Dew.

Driuchdal. ⎱ Dewy.
Driuchdach. ⎰

Dro. A mason's or fisher's line.

Droblas.

Drobhlasach. Miserable, pitiful.

Droch. Evil, bad; a prepositive word.

Droch. Right, straight, direct.

Droch. A coach-wheel.

Drochaid. A bridge.

Drochaid-thogalach. A draw-bridge.

Droch-anfais. Mistrust, jealousy.

Droch-airidh. Unworthy.

Drochaistan. Idle naughty tricks.

Drochaisteach. Idle, mischievous.

Drochbhail. Lavishing.

Droch-anfaiseach. Jealous.

Drochbholtan. ⎱ A bad smell.
Drochbholadh. ⎰

Droch-bharal. Prejudice.

Droch-bhlas. A bad taste.

Droch-bhriathar. Evil expression.

Drochbheart. Vice, evil deed.

Drochbheusach. Immoral.

Drochbheartach. Vicious, evil doing.

Droch-chomhairlaicham. To misadvise.

Drochd. Black, dark, obscure.

Drochchuinsachadh. Mal-administration.

Droch-fhocal. A malediction.

Droch-imchar. Ill-behaviour, malapert.

Droch-ghuidhe. An evil wish.

Droch-iomradh. Evil report.

Drochmharbhadh. Murder.

Drochmhunadh. Bad breeding, insolence.

Drochmhuinte. Insolent, saucy.

Droch-mhifnachal. Faint-hearted.

Drochmhisnach. Pusillanimity.

Drochmhaoineas. Idle.

Droch-fhuil. An evil eye.

Drochthead. A bridge.

Droch-thoiltanas. Demerit.

Droch-thuar. An ill omen.

Droch-thuarafgbhal ⎱ An ill report, misin-
Droch-fhaiftin. ⎰ formation.

Droch ghniomh. Mifdeed, crime.

Droch-mhein. Ill-will.

Drog. The motion of the fea.

Drogaid. Drugget.

Drogha. A fifher's line.

Droibhal. Difficult, hard.

Droich. A dwarf.

Droichal, droichanta. Dwarfifh

Droicham. To wrong, abufe, do evil.

Droichdhe. Taken up.

Droichliam. Shortnefs of breath.

Droicheoin. Deep waters.

Droichtheiftam. To defame.

Droidheachd. Vide Draoitheachd.

Droigheal. Active, affecting.

Droighean. The deep, depth.

Droighionn. A floe.

Droighneach. Thorns.

Droimlin. Diminutive of Dromain.

Droing. Vide Dream.

Droinn. To make, do, be.

Drol. A bay, plait, loop, quirk, ftrata
gem.

Droinnop. Tackle.

Droltha. ⎱
Drolla. ⎰ A pair of pothooks.

Drom. A back. Vide Druim.

Dramadoir. A drummer.

Droma. A drum. Vide Druma.

Droman. A dromedary.

Droman. The bore-tree.

Dromain. The back.

Dromana. Declaring for, renouncing a
thing or perfon.

Dromchla. A furface.

Dromhaoineach. Idle.

Dron. Right, ftraight.

Dron. Sure, ftedfaft.

Dronadh. Direction.

Dronain. A throne.

Dronam. To affirm, avouch.

Dronchruichte. Perpendicular.

Drondunadh. Stopping, fhutting.

Drondunam. To fhut, ftop.

Drongadh. A troop, company.

Dronnach. White backed, name of a cow

Dronnan. The back.

Dronnag. Higheft part of the back, furi-
mit.

Dronuille. A right-angle.

Dronuillinach. Rectangular.

Drothanfais Fear.

Drothan. A breeze of wind.

Drothla. A rafter, a wain-beam.

Drothloir. A carpenter.

Drothloireachd. The trade of a carpenter.

Druadh. A charmer, magician.

Druaip. Lees, fediment.

Druathadh. Fornication.

Druatham. To commit fornication.

Drubh. A chariot.

Drubh. A houfe, habitation.

Drubhoir. A cart-wright, or coach-ma-
ker.

Druchd. A hearing; a rifing up.

Druchd. Vide Driuchd.

Druchd na muine. ⎱ An herb ufed for dy-
Druchdan monadh. ⎰ ing hair.

Druchdan. Whey, a drop.

Druchta De. i. e. Ioith & bliochd. Encreafe of corn and cattle.

Drud. An enclofure.

Drugaire. A flave or drudge.

Drugairachd. Slavery, drudgery.

Druibhal. A dark place or recefs.

Druichdin. Dew.

Druid. ⎱
Druidag. ⎰ A ftare, thrufh. Vide Truid.

Druid. Shut thou.

Druidam. To fhut.

Druidte. Shut.

Druidhean. Black-thorn.

Druidheam. To pour out, diftill, ooze,
drop; to operate upon.

Druidheadh.

Druidheadh. Dropping, diftilling; a drop.

Druidhidhte. Dropped, diftilled, poured out.

Druimleach Vide Driamlach.

Druim. The back, ridge of a hill or houfe.

Druimineach. Speckled.

Druimbota. ⎫ A vault.
Druimbogha. ⎭

Druin. Needlework.

Druinneach. An artift, one that works with a needle.

Druinneachas. Practice in needlework, embroidery, artifice.

Druis. ⎫ Luft.
Druifamlachd. ⎭

Druifeach. Lecherous, a lecherous perfon.

Diuifeamhuil. Lecherous.

Druifalachd. Moifture.

Druifam. To play the wanton.

Druiflann. A bawdy-houfe.

Druifteoir. A fornicator.

Druiteach. Feeling.

Druma. A drum.

Druman. Ridge, back, fummit.

Drumadair. A drummer.

Druman. The back band of a cart-horfe.

Drumchla. A houfe-top.

Drunhac. A baftard fon.

Drunan. The back, ridge of a hill

Drung. Vide Droing

Drus. Vide Druis.

Druth. A harlot.

Druth. Foolifh, lafcivious.

Druthanog. A bawd.

Druthlabhram. To blab out.

Druthlabhradh. Babbling, blabbing.

Druthmhancair. ⎫ A pimp, pander.
Druthbhofgair. ⎭

Druthmhac. A baftard.

Druthlan. A bawdy-houfe.

Drutoir. A fornicator.

Dtheodha. Henbane. Vide Deothadh.

Du. Meet, juft, proper, fit.

Du. A land, country.

Duach. A proper name of Irifh princes.

Duad, duadh. Labour, hardfhip.

Duadh. Eating.

Duadhmhal. ⎫ Laborious, hard, difficult.
Duadhmhor. ⎭

Duadhamhlachd. Hardfhip.

Duadhobair. A handicraft, hard labour.

Duae. A dwelling-houfe.

Duaichniugham. To disfigure.

Duaichnidh. Disfigured, ugly.

Duaigh. Evil.

Duailc. Propriety.

Duaimh. Evil.

Duaillbhearta. A dialect.

Duairc. Surly, ftern, ill-humoured.

Duairc. A furly ftern perfon.

D'uairibh. At times.

Duais. A reward.

Duaifeach. Giving a reward.

Dual. A duty, law.

Dual. Hereditary.

Dual. A loop, a fold, plait, a lock of hair.

Dualach. In locks, thick.

Dualadh. Carving.

Dualaidhe. A carver, engraver.

Dualaideas. Sculpture, engraving.

Dualan. A trefs, lock.

Dualgas. Hire, wages, duty.

Dualphurtich. Shrieking, howling.

Dualadoir. An embroiderer.

Dualam. To fold, plait, carve.

Duam. A city.

Duan. ⎫ A poem, canto, rhyme.
Duanag. ⎭

Duan-mordha. An epic poem.

Duanaire. A canter, chanter.

Duanaireachd. Canting.

Duantachd. Verfification, poetry.

Duantach. Full of poetry.

Duanarteach.

Duanarteach. A senator.

Duanchruitheachd

Duangaois. } Policy.

Duar, duara. A word, a saying.

Duaridh. A dowry.

Dubadh. A pond.

Dubam. To dip, duck.

Dubham. To blacken, condemn.

Dubairt. An earnest prayer.

Dubh, dubhach. Ink, a black dye.

Dubh. Black, dark.

Dubh. Great.

Dubhach Vide Dabhach.

Dubhach. Sad, sorrowful.

Dubhachas. Sadness, sorrow.

Dubhdan. An empyreuma, soot.

Dubhdanach. Having an empyreuma, sooty.

Dubhadan. An inkholder, standish.

Dubhadh. Mourning.

Dubhagan Blacking, ink.

Dubhaigein. The deep, ocean.

Dubhailce Vice.

Dubhailceach. Vicious, wicked; a wicked person.

Dubhalladh. Want.

Dubhatai. Doubtful, uncertain.

Dubhan A hook, a snare.

Dubhan-iasgaich. A fishing-hook.

Dubhan. A kidney.

Dubhan. Darkness.

Dubhan alla. Vide Damhan eallaidhan.

Dubhar. Darkness.

Dubhchosach. The herb Maidenhair.

Dubhlachd. Wintry weather.

Dubhlidh. Wintry, dark.

Dubhradh. A shade.

Dubhradhach. Shady.

Dubhrachd. Earnestness, sincerity.

Dubhrachdach. Earnest, sincere.

Dubhbhreac. A smelt.

Dubhcheist. Motto, superscription.

Dubhchios. A tribute.

Dubhchosach. Name of a dog, blackfoot, melampus.

Dubhchraige. A ring ouzel.

Dubhchuil.

Dubhdhaol. } A beetle.

Dubh-Eirionnach. A wild Irishman.

Dubhghormadh. Making black and blue.

Dubhghlas. Dark grey, Douglas.

Dubhghorm. Dark blue.

Dubhfhocal. A riddle, dark saying, parable.

Dubhith. A pudding.

Dubhlan.

Dubhshlan. } A challenge, defiance.

Dubhghall. A foreigner, Englishman.

Dubhlochlanaich. The Danes.

Dubhliath. The spleen.

Dubhloith. Melancholy.

Dubhneulam. To obnubilate.

Dubhadh.

Dubhogh. } A lake.

Dubh-feddidh seamh leathann. One of the horses to Cuchullin's chariot.

Dubhshnamham. To dive.

Dubshnamhaiche. A diver, didapper.

Dubhfraith. A foundation.

Dubuilte. Double, cunning, false.

Dubuluigham. To double, fold, to distill a second time

Dubladh. Covering, lining, a sheath, case.

Dubhram. I said.

Dubhras. A house, room, habitation.

Dubhairt. He, &c. said.

Dubhron. Grief.

Dubhronach. Grieved.

Dubhshiubhal. Black stream.

Dubhthoill. Hemorrhois.

Duchan. War.

Duchas. A visage, countenance.

Duchas. Vide Dutchas.

Dud. Tingling of the ear, the ear, a rag

Dudich.

Dudach. Ragged.

Dudag. A hunting horn, war trumpet.

Dudaire. A trumpeter.

Dudaireachd. Noise of horns and trumpets.

Duda. Steel.

Dudag. A little stroke on the ear, a small cup.

Dudlach. } The stormy part of the year.
Dudlachd. } Vide Dubhlachd.

Dughachtadh. A bequeathing.

Duibeal. Quick, nimble, active.

Duibh, dhuibh, dhuibhsa. To you, ye.

Duibhchios. Tribute.

Duibhe. Darker, blacker.

Duibhe } Blackness, ink.
Duibhad. }

Duibheagan. Depth, abyss.

Duibheartha. Vernacular.

Duibhgeann. A sword, dagger.

Duibhgeinte. The Danes, i. e. the black nations.

Duibleaid. A doublet.

Duibhir. Anxious, melancholy.

Duigham. To cluck as a hen.

Duil. An element, a creature.

Duil. Delight, desire, hope.

Duil. Partition, distribution.

Duileachd. Doubt, suspicion.

Duilbhir. Anxious, sad.

Duilbhirachd. Sadness, gloominess.

Duile. A poor creature.

Duille. } A leaf, a fold, a scabbard.
Duilleag. }

Duilleach. Foliage.

Duille-sgeinne. The sheath of a knife.

Duilleach. } Leafy, full of leaves.
Duilleogach. }

Duileamh. God.

Duileamhuil. Skilled.

Duileamhanachd. The godhead.

Duileamhanta. Of the godhead.

Duilleoga. Folding-door.

Duilgne. Wages, hire.

Duilam. To take pleasure, delight.

Duilleabhra. The leaf of a book.

Duilleabhrach. Full of leaves.

Duilleachan. A book or pamphlet.

Duilleur. Belonging to a leaf.

Duillean. A spear.

Duilliasg. Palmated fucus, dilse.

Duilliasg-nam-beann. Mountain laver.

Duilleog-bhaite. White water-lily.

Duillughadh. Bearing leaves.

Duilluigham. To flourish.

Duillmhiol. Caterpillar, convolvulus.

Duilich. Difficult.

Duilidh-tionsgnaidh. The elements.

Duilin. Elements.

Duilinne. Tribute.

Duiliomaral. Error.

Duillthaobh. A page.

Duim. Poor, needy.

Duine. A man.

Duine-gan-diughe. Raca.

Duineamhuil. Manly.

Duinamhlachd. } Manliness.
Duinamhlas. }

Duinan. A manikin.

Duineabhadh. Manslaughter.

Duinn, duinne. To us.

Duinoircneach. An assassin.

Duinte, dunta. Shut.

Duir. Oak, the letter D. Vide Darach.

Duirce daraich. Acorns.

Duire. A wood, grove. Vide Doire.

Duire. Harder.

Duire. } Hardness, stupidity.
Duirad. }

Duirmeabhraghadh. Caballing.

Duis. A crow.

Duis. A present, a jewel.

Duischill. A sanctuary.

[M m]   Duiseal.

Duiseal. A spout.

Duisgiolla..
Duisoglaoh. } A client.

Duisighe. Awaked.

Duisughadh. Awaking

Duisgam. To awake, rouse up.

Duisleog. Dilse.

Duit, dhuit. Unto thee.

Duithbhair. Deformed, ugly.

Duithir na h oiche. The morning.

Dul. A snare, trap, gin.

Dul. The terraqueous globe.

Dul. A satirist.

Dul. Going. Vide Dol.

Dula. A pin, peg.

Dulam. To hook or catch with a loop.

Dulbhar. Doleful, unpleasant, gloomy.

Dulbharachd. Dolefulness, gloominess.

Dulchanach. Dirty, miserable, pitiful.

Dulchan, dulchanachd. Avarice, covet-
ousness.

Dulchaon. A lamentation.

Dulchaointeach. Mournful.

Dumha. A place of gaming.

Dumhl. Bulky.

Dumhlas, dumhlad. Bulkiness.

Dun. A strong or fortified house or hill, a
fortress, fastness, strength.

Dun-aolaich. A dunghill.

Dunan. A little hill or fort.

Dunadh. Shutting, buttoning, lacing.

Dunadh. A camp, dwelling.

Dunam. To shut, barricade, button,
lace.

Dunaras. A habitation.

Dunbhallach. A mere fellow.

Dunfhoilsighte. A manifesto.

Dunfuigheadh. Stopping.

Dunlios. A palace.

Dunmharbham. To commit homicide.

Dunmharbhadh. Homicide, massacre.

Dunmharbhthach. A manslayer.

Dunn. A doctor, teacher.

Dunte. Shut.

Dur. Dull, hard, stupid, obstinate.

Durain A dull obstinate fellow.

Dur. Water.

Duras. A house, room.

Durain. Affable.

Durachd. Good-will, luck's penny, diligence, sincerity. Vide Dubhrachd.

Durachdach. Diligent, sincere.

Duraicne. A cabal.

Durain. Cooling in water.

Durb. A distemper, disease.

Durbhath. A cell.

Durbhodach. A dunce.

Durdal. Cooing; Bhith-durdal, to coo

Durdan. A humming noise.

Durdan. A bit of dust, a mote.

Durga.
Durganta. } Surly.
Durragha.

Durlus. Water-cresses.

Durn. A fist, a hand.

Durrog. A maggot.

Dursa, dursan. A crack, noise.

Durtheach. A foundation, a cell, hut,
cabbin.

Dnrtheach. A pilgrim.

Durunta. Rigid, morose.

Dus.
Duslach. } Dust.

Dus. In order to, to the end that.

Dus. A fort.

Dusait. A place of refuge, safety.

Dusal. Dusty.

Dusara.
Dusoglach. } A client.

Dusacht.
Dusas. } Watchfulness.

Duscumhal. A woman client.

Dusgam. To awake.

Dusgairm. A calling, appellation.

Dusling.

Dufling. Duft.

Duthchas. The place of one's birth, an hereditary right.

Duthchafach. Of one's country, natural to one by his family, hereditary.

Duthaidh. A land, country.

D   n. A nation.

D   chamhuil. Of a good family.

Duthcha. Genuine.

Duthith. A pudding.

Duthrachd. Vide Durachd.

Duthrachdach. Vide Dubhrachdach.

E.

EAB

E Is the fifth letter of the alphabet, it is one of the fmall vowels, and founds like epfilon in the Greek, or ee in Englifh. In Irifh it is called Eabha or Eadha, from Eadha, the afpen-tree, commonly called crann crithach, and is not unlike the Greek name Eta, and Hebrew Heth.

E. The pronoun *he,* or *it,* and is founded broad, as the Greek Eta.

E ! An interjection of furprife.

Ea. A diphthong, in which both vowels are heard.

Ea. A negative particle ufed indifcriminately with ei. The negative particles are enumerated in the following verfe:

    Neimh & an, amh, eag, fas,

    Ei, e, do, di, *ni h ord dimheas.*

    Ing mi, *ni modh ceilge.*

    Deich diultadh na Gaoidhlige.

Eaban. ⎱
Eabar. ⎰ Mud, mire.

Eabha. The name of the letter e, the afpen-tree.

Eabha. The firft woman, Eve.

Eabhra. The Hebrew tongue.

Eabhrach. An Hebrew, Jew.

Eabhrach. Hebrew, Jewifh.

EAC

Eabradh. Iron.

Eabron. A pan, cauldron.

Eabur. Ivory.

Eacceart, eiceart. Iniquity, injuftice.

Eacartha. Stupid. –

Eaccomhlan. Injuftice, oppreffion.

Eaccomhlaim. To omit.

Eacconnach. Mad, doting, abfurd.

Eaccon. Rage, madnefs, want of fenfe.

Eaccon-duine. A filly foolifh man.

Eaccofg. The face, countenance, likenefs.

Eaccofg. A degree.

Eaccofg. A framing or building.

Eaccofmhuil. Unlike.

Eaccofmhuileachd. Difparity.

Each. A horfe.

Each. Any.

Eachach. Abounding in horfes.

Eachan. A wheel, an inftrument to wind yarn.

Eachan-gaoithe. A blaft of whirlwind.

Eachanach. Of blafts, ftormy.

Eachann. Hector.

Eachaodach. Caparifon

Eachchior. A horfe-comb.

Each-freine. A courfer.

Eachdaire. An hiftorian, chronicler.

Eachdairachd. Hiftory, chronicle.

Eachd.

Eachd. A condition. Vide Achd.

Eachda. Clean, pure, neat, decent.

Eachdam. To do, to act.

Eachlann. A stable.

Eachlach. A servant, post-boy, news-carrier, a soldier's boy.

Eachlasg. A rod, a goad, horsewhip.

Eachleigh. A farrier.

Eachmac, eachmong. To happen, fall out, come to pass.

Eacnach. Blasphemy.

Eachradh, eachri. Horses.

Eachrais. Rowing.

Eachrais. A fair.

Eacht. An accident that moves sorrow or compassion.

Eacht. An atchievement, feat, exploit. Vide Eibhachd.

Eacht. A condition.

Eachtamhuil. Conditional, doing great things.

Eachtradh. An adventure.

Eachtran. ⎱
Eachtranach. ⎰ A foreigner.

Eacradh. A pen, fold, pound, cincture.

Eatrocair. ⎱ A prey, spoil, unmerciful-
Eatrocairachd. ⎰ ness.

Eatrocairach. Unmerciful.

Ead. Jealousy, zeal.

Ead. Obloquy, reproach.

Eadach, aodach. Clothes.

Eadaigham. To clothe, dress.

Eadail, eadal. Profit, advantage, treasure; prey, spoil, booty.

Eadailach. Having treasure, rich.

Eadailleach. An Italian.

Eadailt. Italy.

Eadaingionn. Weak, defenceless.

Eadaingneachd. Weakness, defencelessness.

Eadaire A jealous person.

Eadairmeas. The art of invention.

Eadann, aodann. The forehead

Eadnan. A frontlet.

Eadar, eidar. Between.

Eadaradh. ⎱ Division, interest, rest at
Eadarthrath. ⎰ noon.

Eadarghaire, eadarsgaradh. Divorce, separation.

Eadarghna. Ingenuity.

Eadarghnaim. To know, distinguish.

Eadarghuidhe. Supplication, intercession

Eadarnaidh. Fraud, malice, deceit.

Eadarsgain, eadargain. Interposition, parting, quieting.

Eadaoirsuigham. To naturalize.

Eadoimhann. Shallow.

Eadochas. Despair.

Eadochasach. Despairing, desponding.

Eadochasaigham. To despair, despond.

Eadfhulang. Intolerable.

Eadh. Time, opportunity, season.

Eadh. Yea, yes.

Eadhadh. An aspen-tree.

Eadhoin. Namely, to wit.

Eadmhor. Jealous, zealous.

Eadmhorachd. Zealousness, jealousy.

Eadmheadhonach. Immediate, mediate.

Eadoighigham. To despair.

Eadram. Between me.

Eadrad. Between thee.

Eadrinn. Between us.

Eadribh Between you.

Eadrochd. Plain, manifest.

Eadtairiosiochd. Alienation, ill-will.

Eadtairsiogham. To put out of doors.

Eadtlaith ⎱ Courageous, strong, un-
Eadtlathach. ⎰ daunted.

Eadtreoir. Imbecillity, irresolution.

Eadtreorach. Irresolute, weak, ignorant.

Eadtorra. Between them.

Eadtorras. Mediocrity.

Eadtrom. Light, brisk, nimble, giddy.

Eadtromachan. ⎱ Lightness, ease, com-
Eadtruime. ⎰ fort.

Eadtromaghadh. Alleviating, alleviation.

Eadtromuigham.

Eadtromuigham. To alleviate.

Eadtroman. A bladder.

Eadtualang. Incapable, unable.

Eadturlabhradh. A folecifm.

Eadurchamh. Of old.

Eag, eafga. The moon.

Eag. Death.

Eaga. Ice.

Eagach. Deep.

Eagal. Fear.

Eagalach. Fearful, timid.

Eaglam. To fear, frighten, deter.

Eagan. A bottom. Vide Dubhhaigan.

Eagan. A gizzard.

Eagar. Order.

Eagar. A row, bank, bin.

Eagaram. To fet in order, or in rows.

Eagbroth. A carrion.

Eagcaoine. A fob, dying groan, a complaint.

Eagchaor. A founding line.

Eagcruas. Sicknefs.

Eagcoir. Injuftice.

Eagcofmhuil. Various, unlike.

Eagfamhuilachd. The ftate of not being like a thing.

Eagcofg. Likenefs, face, countenance, figure.

Eagceart. Unjuft, incorrect.

Eagcruaidh. Sick, weak, feeble.

Eagcubhidh. Unfit, improper.

Eaglais. A church.

Eaglaifeach. Of the church, a churchman, clergyman.

Eaglaifamhuil. Belonging to the church, or clergy.

Eglais chathuighidh. The church militant.

Eaglais neamhlcha· Church triumphant.

Eaglan A biting.

Eaglafda. Ecclefiaftical.

Eagmhais. Without.

Eagmhais. Reputation, fame.

Eagmhuifach. Very great.

Eagmin. About, a winding circuit, meander.

Eagmin mall. A flow meander or winding of a river.

Eagnaidh. Prudence, wifdom.

Eagnaidhach. Prudent, wife.

Eagnaidhe. A philofopher, wife man.

Eagnach, eacnach. Blafphemy.

Eagnach. A complaint, refentment, caufe of grief.

Eagnaidham. To complain, accufe.

Eagnairc. Love.

Eagnairc Querulous, complaining.

Eagnais. Without.

Eagnarcaire. A mediator.

Eagcruaidh. Impotent, fick, feeble.

Eagraigham. To fet in order.

Eagfamhuil. Singular, matchlefs, ftrange; various, diffimilar, mixed.

Eagfamhlachd. Strangenefs, variety, diverfity.

Eagfamluigham. To diverfify.

Eagfamhlughadh. Varying, diverfifying.

Eal, for neal. A fwoon.

Eala, ealadh. A fwan.

Ealach. A pin to hang any thing on, as a hat-pin.

Ealadhain. Learning, fkill, an art, fcience.

Enladhanta, Artificial, curious, ingenious, alert, quick, ready.

Ealaidham. To fteal away, defert, to ftalk.

Ealaidhtheach. A revolter, deferter.

Ealang. A fault, flaw.

Ealar. Salt.

Ealbha. A herd or drove.

Ealc Malicious, fpiteful, envious.

Ealcmhar. Envious, fpiteful, lazy, fluggifh.

Ealg. Noble, excellent.

Ealoghadh, ealughadh. Sneaking, ftealing away.

Ealuigham. To fneak off, fteal upon.

Eall. A trial, proof, effay.

Eallabhair. } A vaſt number, a great mul-
Eallagair. } titude.
Eallach. A hearth; rather Teallach.
Eallach. Cattle.
Eallach. A burden, load.
Eallach. An artful trick.
Eallog. A log, bracket.
Eallach. A battle.
Eallaighe. Houſehold ſtuff, furniture.
Eallamh. Wonder, aſtoniſhment.
Eallamh. Cattle given as a portion.
Ealſcadh. Cozineſs.
Ealta. Repentance.
Ealt, ealta. } A flock, herd, covey, drove,
Ealtuin. } trip, rout, pace, ſownder.
Ealta eun. A covey or flock of birds.
Ealta mhuc. A herd of ſwine.
Ealta dhamh. A drove of bullocks.
Ealta ghabhar. A trip of goats.
Ealta maduidhe alta. A rout of wolves.
Ealta aſſail. A pace of aſſes.
Ealta fiadh-thorc. A ſownder of wild boars.
Ealta marcach. A troop of horſe.
Eallach. Gregarious.
Eallaidhe. White.
Ealltin. A razor, ſword.
Eamhain. } Double.
Eamhanta. } Double.
Eamhainſe. Wiſdom.
Eampaid. A kind of ſtone.
Ean. A bird, a fowl.
Ean fionn. An oſprey, a kite.
Ean, an. Water.
Ean uiſge. } An aquatic bird.
Ean ſnamh. } An aquatic bird.
Ean, aon. Any.
Eanchon. Any wiſe, at all.
Eanda. A ſimple in medicine.
Eang. A year.
Eang. A track, footſtep.
Eang. Point of land, a guſſet.
Eangach. A fiſhing net, a chain of nets for
ſalmon or herring fiſhing.

Eanghach. A bladder.
Eanghlor. Of one voice or ſpeech.
Eangla. An anniverſary feaſt.
Eanglaim. A lining.
Eanghlais. Small mixed drink.
Eanghnamh. Generoſity; dexterity at
arms, prudence.
Eanghobhrag.
Eangſad. They went forward or moved
Eanluireachd. Fowling.
Eanluith. Birds.
Eannec. Innocent.
Eanſathadh. At once.
Eantog, feantog. A nettle.
Eantoiſg. On purpoſe, in one bulk.
Eantort. In any manner or ſort
Eanuair, aonuair. One hour, at once.
Eanuair, an-uair. Bad weather.
Eanuc. An eunuch.
Eaondachd. Unity.
Ear. A head.
Earadh. Refuſal.
Earadh. Fear, diſtruſt.
Earadham freine. Reins of a bridle.
Earaim. Riding.
Earal. An exhortation, caution.
Earalach. Cautious, provident.
Earalas. The virtue of being provident.
Earaligham. To exhort.
Earam. To refuſe, deny.
Earais. The end.
Earb, earbog. A roe.
Earba. To tell, relate.
Earb. An offer, command.
Earba. An occupation, employment.
Earbail. A truſt.
Earbull. A tail.
Earbam. To truſt, rely, confide, bid, com-
mand.
Earbſa. Confidence, reliance, truſt.
Earbſach. Confident, relying, truſting.
Earc. Speckled, red.
Earc. A cow.

7   Earc.

Earc. A falmon.

Earc. A bee, honey.

Earc. A tax, tribute.

Earc. Heaven.

Earcam. To fill.

Earcamhuil. Pleafant, fweet, agreeable.

Earcın Delicacies.

Eearcdhath. Coloured red.

Earchaill. A prop, poft, pillar.

Earchaillam. To eraze.

Earchaille. A bairing, hindering.

Earchaomh. Noble.

Earcluachrach. A lizard, emmet.

Earcra. A deficiency, eclipfe.

Eardach. A feaft, folemnity.

Eardanal. A piper, trumpeter.

Earfhlaitheas. ⎫
Earfhlaithachd. ⎭ Ariftocracy.

Earfhloith. A noble perfon, grandee.

Earghabhail. A miferable captivity.

Eargaim. To build, frame, make up.

Earghabham. To apprehend, make prifoner.

Farghaire. Prohibition.

Earghairam. To congratulate; to forbid, prohibit.

Earghalan. A piper.

Earghalan. Noify, clamorous.

Erghnaidh. Magnificent, worthy, virtuous.

Earghnamh. To prepare a feaft.

Eargna. Conception, quicknefs of apprehenfion.

Earlamh. Noble, grand, auguft.

Earma, earmaidheafa. Galloping.

Earmadh Arms.

Earn, eorna. Barley.

Earnagh. Iron.

Earnnail. A part, fhare.

Earnnede. To watch, take care of.

Earr End, conclufion, tail, limit, boundary.

Earr A champion, noble, grand.

Earach. The fpring.

Earradh. Drefs, habit, military fuit, com-

plete armour.

Earradha. Wares, commodities, accoutrements.

Earraidham To fpring.

Earradhreas. The dog-briar.

Earraid. A miftake, fault.

Earilinn. ⎫
Earrinn. ⎭ The end.

Earraithear. To be ferved or attended.

Earrunn. A fhare, portion, divifion.

Earrufaid. A fort of loofe wrapper wore by women in the Highlands of Scotland till very lately, without fhift or any thing elfe.

Eafadh. Sicknefs, difeafe.

Eafafnadh. Expulfion, banifhment.

Eafaidham To expel, banifh.

Eafag. A pheafant, a fquirrel.

Eafaille. Difpraife, difparagement.

Eafailuigham. To debafe.

Eafaituigham. To diflocate.

Eafam. To make, to do.

Eafamlair. An example, copy, pattern, fample.

Eafal. A tail.

Eafaontach. Diffenting, repugnant, difobedient, rebellious.

Eafaontas. ⎫
Eafaontachd. ⎭ Difagreement, difobedience.

Eafaontughadh. Schifm.

Eas. ⎫
Eafar. ⎬ A cataract, fall of water, cafcade.
Eafaid. ⎭

Eafard. A quarrel, foul houfe.

Eafarguin. A tumult.

Eafarluighachd. Incantation.

Eafba. Want, fcarcity, defect, abfence.

Eafba broghad. The king's-evil.

Eafbaigham. To want, lack.

Eafbain. Spain.

Eafbaloid. Abfolution.

Eafbarta, eafporta. Evening-prayers.

Eafbhuidh. Want.

Eafbhuidheach In want, poor, empty.

Eafbog.

Eafbog, eafbuig. A bifhop.

Eafbuigachd. A fee, prelacy.

Eafc. Water ; old.

Eafgaich. A quagmire.

Eafgaire. A warning.

Eafgair. A ftorm, bluftering wind, furprize.

Eafcar, eafgor. Shooting into ears.

Eafcar. A fall.

Eafcara. } An adverfary, enemy.
Eafaraid. }

Eafchriodhachd. Difagreement.

Eafcoman. Dirty, filthy, nafty.

Eafcomata. Satisfied.

Eafcomlam. To die, depart life.

Eafcong. Water.

Eafcongra. A cry, proclamation.

Eafconn. An old man, an elder.

Eafconn. The moon.

Eafcra. A cup, drinking-veffel.

Eafcradh. Walking, ftepping, marching.

Eafg, eafga. The moon.

Eafgaidh. Eafy, fenfible, nimble, ready,
active, officious.

Eafgaine. A curfe, malediction.

Eafgal. A found, noife.

Eafgan. }
Eafga. } An eel.
Eafcu. }

Eafgbhaineach. Lunatick.

Eafgleafadh. Confufion.

Eafgnaim. To climb up, afcend.

Eafgud. The hough, ham.

Eafgul. A wave.

Eafidhe. Confpicuous, remarkable.

Eafionnracas. Difhonefty, faithleffnefs.

Eafionnruic. Difhoneft.

Eaflabhra. Bounty, courtefy, affability.

Eaflain. } Sicknefs, infirmity.
Eaflainte. }

Eaflainteach. } Infirm.
Eaflan. }

Eaflach. A lake, pool.

Eafmail. A reproach, reproof.

Eafmail. Power of, dependence.

Eafmailteach. A reproachful perfon.

Eafnadh, eafnamh. Want of web for the
loom.

Eafnadh. Mufic, fong, melody.

Eafnadh. Time.

Fafmaigh. A lath, fparr.

Eafog. A weafel.

Eafoman. A welcome.

Eafomoid. Difrefpect, difhonour.

Eafomoideach. Difrefpectful, difobedient

Eafonoir. Difhonour, abufe.

Eafonorach. Difhonourable, abufive, ill-
bred.

Eafonoraigham. To difhonour, abufe.

Eafontach. Rude.

Eafordach. Factious.

Eafordugh. Diforder, confufion, anarchy

Eafordughadh. Wifhing things different
from what they are.

Eaforduigham. To wifh things different
from what they are, to confufe.

Eaforgain. Contrition.

Eaforgaim. To hurt, offend.

Eaforgnadh. Squeezing, crufhing.

Eafpuig-fpeain. The herb ox-eye-daify
Latin, belles major.

Eafrannait. The world.

Eafraoite. Loofe.

Eafruadh. A cataract on the river Earn,
county of Donnegal in Ireland.

Eaffaoth. Health.

Eaflarruing. Extraction.

Eafuainam. To fcum, fkim.

Eafumhal. Difobedient, irreverent.

Eafumhlachd. Difobedience, obftinacy

Eafumhluigham. To difobey.

Eafurrudhas. Prefumption.

Eafurrudhafach. Prefumptuous.

Eafurram. Difrefpect.

Eafurramach. Difrefpectful, ftubborn, a
rebel.

Eafurramaigham. To revolt, difobey.
Eafurramaghadh. Difobedience, rebellion.
Eata. Old, ancient.
Eatach. An elder, aged perfon.
Eatal. Pleafure, delight.
Eatal. Flight.
Eatal. The world.
Eatha. Gone, fent.
Eathar. A veffel, fhip, boat.
Eathla. Prayers, fupplication.
Eatla. Sadnefs.
Eatlaim. To fly.
Eatorra. Between them.
Eatrathach. Late.
Eatroman. A bladder.
Eatrom. Light.
Eatruime. Lighter.
Eatruime. } Lightnefs, levity.
Eatruimad. }
Eatromuigham. To relieve, lighten, alle-
 viate.
Eatrocair. Cruelty.
Eatrocaireach. Unmercitul.
Ebar. Mire, dirt.
Ebrach. Miry, dirty.
Ebeirt, ebirt. Topography.
Ebhadh. The afpen tree, the letter E.
Ebhling. To fpring off or on.
Ebhlingadh. Skipping, leaping.
Ebhladh. A kilt.
Ebhladh. } Burning coal.
Ebhlag. }
Ebhlach. Full of burning coals.
Ebhrionta. A young gelded goat.
Ebron. A kettle, cauldron.
Ebhul. Vide Ebhlog.
Eccnech. Reproof, reprehenfion.
Eccnairc. The time paft.
Eccnairc. A prayer, interceffion.
Eccofg. Vide Eagcofg.
Eccradach. Spiteful, unfaithful.
Eccraide. Enmity, fpite.

Ece. Clear, evident, manifeft ; ece an ta-
 lamh, fee the land.
Ecna. Eating.
Ecfidhe. Apparent, manifeft.
Ed. Vide Ead.
Ed. Gain, profit, advantage.
Ed. To make, receive, to handle.
Ed. Defence, protection.
Ed, eid. Cattle.
Edal. A treafure.
Edalach. Rich, having a treafure.
Edaoigh. Uncertain.
Edreimam. To catch at.
Edean. A receptacle.
Edearbh. Falfe, uncertain.
Edeighneach. Gelded.
Edel. Prayers, orations.
Edhon, eadhon. To wit, namely, that is.
Edidh. Ugly, deformed.
Edim. To catch, apprehend.
Edir. Vide Edar.
Edire. Hoftages.
Edirghlimam. To endure, fuffer.
Edirmheadhontoir. A mediator.
Edmhar. Jealous.
Efeachd. Effect, great things.
Efeachdach. Effectual, that hath done great
 things.
Egmhil. Handfome.
Eibhligham. To fparkle.
Eiblit. An interjection.
Eid. Tribute, tax, fubfidy.
Eiddighe. Ingratitude.
Eide, eideadh. Cloth, apparel, raiment,
 armour.
Eidadh-gairdain. A bracelet.
Eidadh-uchd. A breaft-plate.
Eidadh-muineil. A gorget.
Eidadh-droma. A back-piece.
Eeidadh-calpa. Greaves.
Eideam. To drefs, attire, arm.
Eideadhach. Harneffed.

Eidarbhtha. Diſſolute, loose.

Eidarſgaram. To ſcatter, diſperſe.

Eidheann. Ivy, genitive Eidhne of ivy.

Eidhneach. Full of ivy.

Eidhnean.
Eidheanog. } An ivy branch or bough.

Eidhnen-thalmhuinn. Ground-ivy.

Eidhliomh, eidhliodh. A plea, a caſe; claim, demand of debt.

Eidhre.
Eidhreagach. } Ice.

Eididheach. A cuiraſſier.

Eidimhin. Doutful, uncertain, fluctuating.

Eidinte. Doubtful.

Eidarſhollus. Twilight.

Eidar. Muſt.

Eidir. A captive, priſoner, hoſtage.

Eidarcheart. An equal diſtributive right.

Eidirceart focal. An interpretation.

Eidirdhealughadh. A difference, ſeparation, diviſion, diſtinction.

Eidirdhealuigham. To ſeparate, divide, diſtinguiſh.

Eidirdilgin. A devaſtation, ravaging.

Eidirgin. Interpoſition.

Eidirghleo. A decree, judgment.

Eidirghlaodham. To judge, decide.

Eidirghuidham. To intercede.

Eidirghuidhe. Interceſſion.

Eidirghuaille. Regio dorſalis.

Eidirlen. Captivity.

Eidirmheadhonach. Indirectly, mediately.

Eidirmheadhontoir. A mediator.

Eidirmheadhonairachd. Interceding.

Eidirmhinuigham. To interpret.

Eidirmhinughadh. Interpretation.

Eidirfallamh. Space.

Eidirſhollus. Twilight.

Eidirthriath. Inter-regnum.

Eifeacht. Effect, ſenſe, conſequence.

Eifeachdach.
Eifeachdamhuil. } Effectual.

Eifeaſach. Serious.

Eigmhuis. Want, defect.

Eeigceart. Injuſtice, iniquity.

Eigciallidh. Abſurd, ſilly, fooliſh.

Eigcinnte. Heſitancy, doubt.

Eigcinntach. Uncertain, innumerable, unreſolved, undetermined.

Eigeas.

Eigcneaſda. Rude, impolite.

Eigcinte. Uncertain, doubtful.

Eigcneaſdachd. Frowardneſs, rudeneſs

Eigcrionna. Imprudent, impolitic.

Eigcrionnachd. Imprudence, folly.

Eigean.
Figintas. } Force, violence, compulſion,
Eigin. } neceſſity, a rape, need.

Eige. Web.

Eigin. Neceſſary, certain, ſome.

Eigin. Truly, ſurely.

Eigean. Lawful, rightful, juſt.

Air eigin. Scarcely, with difficulty.

Eigintach. Neceſſary, indiſpenſable, needful, needy.

Eigeas. A learned man.

Eigipteach. An Egyptian.

Eigipht. Egypt.

Eigcordadh. Jarring.

Eigcordam. To jarr.

Eigha. A file.

Eighamh. A cry, ſhout, call.

Eigham. To cry, ſhout, call.

Eighamhthoir. A cryer.

Eighi. Science.

Eiglidhe. Mean, abject.

Eiglidheacht. Abjectneſs.

Eigne. A ſalmon.

Eignidham. To force, conſtrain, compel, raviſh.

Eignighte. Forced, raviſhed.

Eignughadh. Forcing, raviſhing, a rape.

Eigſeach. A ſchool, ſtudy.

Eigſi. Art, ſcience, learning.

Eill, iall. A thong, latchet.

Eill. An ell.

Eileam. To rob, fpoil.

Eile. Other.

Eile. A prayer, oration.

Eileachdam. To alienate, part with, pafs away.

Eilighthoir. A creditor, accufer.

Eiligham. To accufe, charge.

Eilughadh. Accufing, accufation, charging, calling to account.

Eilid. A hind.

Eilain. An ifland.

Eilair, eilair an fheidh. Walk of deer.

Eilimh. A plea.

Eillgheadh. A burial, interment.

Eilne, eilnead. Uncleannefs, pollution.

Eilnigham. To corrupt, fpoil, violate.

Eimh. Quick, active, brifk.

Eimhe, eighamh. A cry, call.

Eimheachd. Obedience, compliance.

Eimham. Vide Eigham.

Eimhleog. A live coal.

Ein, ean. One. Vide Aon.

Eineach. A face, countenance.

Eineachas. ⎫ Bounty, goodnefs, courtefy,
Eineach. ⎬ affability.

Eineachlan. Protection, defence, fafeguard.

Einfeachd. At once.

Einghin, aonghin. Only begotten.

Einmheid. Of equal fize.

Einread. One thing, any thing.

Eipelam. To die, perifh.

Eipiftil An epiftle, letter.

Eirag. A pullet, a young hen.

Eirbhearnam. To tranfgrefs, break.

Eirbhir Afking indirectly.

Eirbhirach. That afketh indirectly.

Eirbheirtam. To move, carry.

Eirbheirt. Moving, ftirring.

Eirbheach. A wafp.

Eirceach. An heretick.

Eireachdal. Fair, beauteous.

Eireachd, eireachdas. Congregation.

Eirceachd. Herefy.

Eirerich. Night-waking of the dead; alfo drying of corn in a pot for grinding, as is done in the Highlands, the grain and bread fo prepared

Eirghe ⎫ A rifing, mutiny
Eirigh ⎬

Eirgham. To arife, pafs on, advance.

Eirghachd. The act of rifing.

Eirigh. A viceroy, chief governor.

Eiric. An amercement, or fine for blood-fhed, a ranfom or forfeit, reparation.

Eiridin Nurfing a fick perfon, the perfon nurfed

Eirige. ⎫ A command, or government.
Eirigeachd ⎬

Eirgionnach. Purfuer.

Eiram. To ride, go on horfeback.

Eirim. A fummary, abridgment.

Eirin. Ireland, i. e. iar-inn, weftern ifland, or according to an ingenious writer, I-iarruin, *ifland of iron*, becaufe Ireland abounded in mines of iron, tin, and copper.

Eirionnach. Irifh, Irifhman.

Eiris. An æra, or account of time.

Eiris. A friend.

Eiris. Miftruft.

Eirle. ⎫ A fragment.
Eirne. ⎬

Eirlioch. Deftruction.

Eirneadh. A gift, prefent, favour.

Eirnam. To require, call for.

Eirr. A fhield.

Eirr, earr. End.

Eirr. Snow, ice.

Eirrfce. A trunk, ftump.

Eirfam. To arife.

Eis. A band, or troop.

Eis. A footftep, trace. Vide Tar-eis.

Eifc, eifg. Of fifh.

Eifceach. Exception, exclufion.

Eifcam.

Eifcam. To cut off, except, exclude.

Eifdeachd. Hearing, attention.

Eifdam. To hear, liften, be filent, attentive.

Eifeadh. Seeking, hunting after, refearch.

Eifean. He, himfelf.

Eifeaftar. He prayed.

Eifeirghe, aifeirghe. Refurrection.

Eifeirgham. To arife again.

Eifir.
Eifeiridh } An oyfter.

Eifgin, eifglinn. A fifhpond.

Eifgir. A ridge of mountains.

Eifibham. To drink.

Eifidam. To fit.

Eifil, eifeolach. Rude, ignorant, unfkilful.

Eifam. To trace.

Eifimh. Near, clofe at hand.

Eifinnil. Weak, infirm.

Eifiodhan. Unclean.

Eifiomal. Valour, courage, bravery, power of.

Eifiomlair, eifiomplair. Example, pattern, copy.

Eifiomlaireach. Exemplary.

Eifith. Debate, difagreement.

Eiflain. Sicknefs, forrow. Vide Eaflan.

Eiflinn. Weak, infirm.

Eiflinneach. Pregnable.

Eiflis. Neglect, miftake, forgetfulnefs.

Eifmeach. Lying, falfe.

Eifmeach. Unready.

Eifreacht. An orphan.

Eifredheadh. To loofe, untie.

Eifteachd. Death.

Eiftam. To hear.

Eite.
Eiteog. } A quill, feather, wing.

Eiteach. Wings, fins.

Eitireach. Winged.

Eite. An addition to the ploughfhare when worn.

Eitire. Vide Oittir. A ridge or bank jutting into the fea.

Eiteaccal. Volatile.

Eiteach. A refufal.

Eiteag A fort of white ftone; I fuppofe rather a feather.

Eitachadh. Refufing.

Eitaigham. To refufe, deny, forfwear.

Eitallach. Flying.

Eitheach. A lye, untruth, miftake.

Eitheor. A liar.

Eitheach. An oak.

Eithigham. To abjure, refufe, deny.

Eithreach. Wildernefs.

Eithre. An end, conclufion.

Eithre. A burden.

Eitam. Danger, hazard.

Eitleadh. Flight.

Eitleog. A bat.

Eitlam.
Eitalam. } To fly.

Eitleorachd. Flying.

Eitre. A trench, furrow.

Eitreorach. Feeble, weak, ungirded.

Ela. A fwan.

Elc, eaelc. Bad, naught, vile, malicious.

Elchaire. Grief, forrow, pain.

Eleathraim. An election.

Eleathrain. A bier.

Eleathrach. One that carries a bier, a bearer.

Ell, iall. A flock, multitude.

Ell. Hazard, danger.

Ell. Battle.

Ellea. Elecampane.

Elteafaidheachd. Warmth, heat.

Elton. Steep, up-hill.

En, eun. A bird.

En. Vide Ein, ean, the fame as Aon.

Encheannaigh. The comb of a cock.

Eneach. A fhirt, fmock.

Eneaclann. Reparation, amends.

Enne. Behold! fee!

Eo. A falmon.

Eo. A peg, pin, bodkin, nail, thorn, point.

Eo. Praife, good, worthy, refpectable.

Eo, The yew-tree.

Eo. A grave, place of interment, tomb.

Eobhrat. Head-drefs, coif, cap.

Eocha. Name of a man. Lat. Euchadius.

Eochair, iuchair. A key.

Eochair. Brim, brink, edge.

Eochair. A tongue.

Eochair. The rann of fifh.

Eochair. A young plant, fprout

Eogan. Owen, the name of feveral great men in Ireland.

Eoghunn. Youth.

Eoin. John.

Eoin. Of a bird.

Eoinfhiadhachd. Fowling.

Eoin-fhealgair. A fowler

Eol. } Knowledge, fcience, art; chaim,
Eolas. } noftrum.

Eolach. Knowing, acquainted, fkilled, expert.

Eolchaire. Sorrow, mourning, grief, concern.

Eolchaireachd. Sad, forrowful.

Eolgagh. Knowing, fkilful.

Eoluidhe. A guide, director.

Eolus. Vide Eolas.

Eonadan. A cage, aviary.

Eondraoitham. To divine by the flight of birds.

Eonfhaigam. Idem.

Eoibhrat. A coif, cap.

Eorna. Barley.

Eos, ad eos. It was faid.

Er. Great, noble.

Era A denial, refufal.

Eraidh. Apparel.

Ercheallan. A pole, ftake.

Ercheannchaidhe. Moft certainly, affuredly.

Erchrethe. Tranfitory.

Erebeut. A burden, carriage.

Erin. Ireland.

Erinnach. Irifh, Irifhman

Ernail A fign, prognoftication, foretoken.

Erog. } Ice.
Erogach. }

Erlamh. A faint, holy perfon.

Err, earr. An end, tail, fin.

Earraid. An erior, miftake.

Efceptus. Oppofing.

Efreimeach. Deviating.

Efs. A fhip or veffel.

Efs. } Death.
Etfeacht. }

Etenge. A mute.

Ette. Age.

Ettionach. An eunuch.

Ettreifigham. To awake a perfon.

Ettuachail. Unhandy.

Ettualang. Incapable, unable.

Eud, ead, eada. Jealoufy, zeal

Eudach, aodach, eadach. Cloth, clothes.

Eudadh, eidadh. Clothing, dreffing.

Eudmhor. Jealous, zealous.

Eudmhorachd. Zealoufnefs.

Eudal. Treafure, wealth, riches, lucre.

Eudolach. Rich.

Eudann, aodann. The forehead.

Eug. Dying, death.

Eugam. To die, perifh.

Eugcoir. Wrong, injuftice.

Eugcorach. Injurious, unjuft.

Eugcruaidh. An infirm perfon, fick, weak.

Eugcruas. Sicknefs, infirmity.

Eugnaidh. } Irrational.
Eucconaidh. }

Eugfamhuil. Matchlefs, various. Vide Eagfamhuil.

Eugas, eugafg. Likenefs, image.
Eugfhaoghar. Diffonance.
Eugfhaogharach. Diffonant.
Euladh, eulaghadh. Efcape.
Eulaigham. To efcape, fneak off.
Eulaightheàch. A deferter.
Eulfartadh. Slumbering.
Eulogh. An efcape.
Eun. A bird, fowl.
Eun-fionn. The kite.
Eunlaith. Fowls, birds.

Eunadan. An aviary.
Eunadair. A fowler, bird-catcher.
Eunadair-malluichte. The devil.
Eunadairachd. Fowling.
Eunbhrith. Broth, gravy.
Eunlion. A fowler's net.
Eun-uafal. A foreign bird.
Eunchriodhach. Timid, hen-hearted.
Eurmaireachd. Galloping, riding.
Eurn. The lake of Ern in Ulfter.
Eutrom. Vide Eattrom.

F.

F Is the fixth letter of the alphabet, and is called Fearn, the alder-tree. It has the fame power and found as in other languages, but is filent before h.

Fa, fo, fuidh. Under.
Fa chul. ⎫
Fa dhruim. ⎬ Backwards.
Fa leath. ⎫
Fa feach. ⎬ A part, one by one.
Fa chomhair. Before.
Fa thuairam. Towards, about.
Fadheoidh. Finally.
Fa dheireadh. At length.
Fa dho. Twice.
Fa re cheile. Together.
Fa-thri. Thrice.
Fa. Sometimes unto, as
Fan choill. Unto the wood.
Fa. Sometimes for bu, ba, was, were.
Fabhal. A fable, romance.
Fabhal. An expedition, journey.
Fabhaltas. Profit, benefit, gain, income.
Fabhar. Favour, friendfhip.

Fabharach. Favourable.
Fabhram. To favour, befriend.
Fabhra. A veil, curtain, eye-lid, fringe.
Fabhranta. The eye-lids, eye-lafhes.
Fabhrantacb. Ciliary.
Fabhra. February.
Fabhthoirfe. Negligence.
Fabhthoirfeach. Carelefs, negligent.
Facal. A word.
Faclach. Full of words.
Fach The hole of a lobfter.
Fachaim. Matter, caufe, reafon, motive.
Fachach. A puffin.
Fachain. A calling, temptation.
Fachain. Fighting, engaging.
Fachail. Strife.
Fachaill. Full of woods.
Fachtnach. Juft.
Facht. A battling or fighting.
Fad, fada. Long, tall.
Fad. Length.
Am fad. Whilft.
Fadaigham. To ftretch, lengthen

Fadachadh.

Fadachadh. Stretching, lengthening.
Fadadh. Kindling, lighting.
Fadaidham. To kindle.
Fadadh-cluaife. Priming of a gun, a match
Fadadh-cruaidh. Part of a rainbow in bluftering weather, which failors call a dog.
Fadadh-fpuince Touchwood, tinder.
Fadail. Delay, prolixity.
Fadail. Lingering.
Fadalach. Tedious, lingering.
Fadalam. To linger, procraftinate.
Fadh, fadhb. A mole, opportunity.
Fadchluafach. Long-eared.
Fadchofach. Long-legged.
Fadfhulang. Longanimity.
Fadfhulangach. Long-fuffering.
Fadh. Cut.
Fadh Science.
Fadhb A queftion, riddle, a knot.
Fadhb A fault, a widow.
Fadhban. A mole-hillock.
Fadhlaidh. Loofing.
Fadhlaim. To diftinguifh.
Fadht. Breath.
Fadog. To provoke.
Fadfhaoghlach. Long-lived.
Faetham. To kill.
Faethe, faetheadh. Laughter.
Fafa ! O ftrange !
Fagam. To leave, quit, wreft.
Fagal Leaving, quitting.
Fagha, fogha. A fpeai, an attempt, offei.
Faghal. Getting, finding, obtaining.
Faghal. Power.
Faghaim. To get, obtain, find.
Faghaltach. }
Faghaltaifeach. } Profitable, advantageous.
Faghaltas Gain, profit, advantage.
Faghraim. To favour, befriend.
Faghbham To ftrip.

Fagifg, fogafg. Near
Faic. A fpaikle.
Faicam. To fee
Faicin, faicfin. Seeing.
Faice. A ftitch.
Faicealach. Evident, manifeft.
Faicealachd. Evidence.
Faiceamhuil. Important, of a moment, in a trice.
Faiche. A field, green.
Faiche-bhula. A bowling-green
Faicheachd. Walking in the fields.
Faicheal. Wages, reward, falary.
Faicheallach. A lamp, light, candle, luminous.
Faichios. Fear.
Faicfinach Vifible.
Faicil. Caution, guard, watch.
Faicilach. Cautious.
Faide. Longer.
Faide mach. Remoteft, utmoft.
Faide. Length.
Faideocham. To deceive.
Faideog. Lot, chance.
Faidh. He went.
Faid, faidh. }
Faidheadoir. } A prophet.
Faidheadoirachd. Prophecying, prophecy.
Faideamhuil. Prophetic, critical, witty.
Faidham. To find; to give up, to yield
Faidhbhile. A beech.
Faidhidin. Patience.
Faidid. Diftance.
Faidhir. A fair.
Faidhirin. A fairing.
Paidfeach. Lumpifh.
Faigheoladh. Day.
Faig. A prophet.
Faighle, faighleadh. Words, converfation.
Faighleadh. Ivy.
Faigin. A fheath, fcabbard.
Faigham. To fpeak, talk.

I   Faighidin.

2

Faighidin. Patience.

Faighidinach. Patient.

Faighleadh. Converfation, taking hold of.

Faigh. Begging by patent or leave; in Scotland a thickftei.

Fail. The hickup.

Fail. A ring, wreath, ouch, a ftall.

Fail-fheula. Motto, fuperfcription.

Fail, fial Generous.

Fail. Company, fociety.

Fail. Fatal.

Failbhe. Lively.

Failbheas. Livelinefs.

Failbeim. Blafting as of corn.

Failbhigham. ⎱
Failbham. ⎰ To quicken.

Failbheadh. Vegetation.

Fail-mhuc. A hog-ftye.

Fail-chuach. Violet

Fail-chon. A dog-kennel.

Faile. A gap, opening, a hair-lip mouth.

Failce. Bathing.

Failceam, falceam. To bathe.

Failce-teth. Hot-baths.

Failcis. A pit.

Failceann. A lid.

Faile. Scent, fmell. Vide Aile.

Faile-cumhra. A fweet fmell.

Failam. To fmell.

Failais. A fhadow.

Faileachan. An ear-ring.

Faileog. A hump or hillock, hickup.

Faileabadh. Death.

Failgeach. Poor.

Failgam. To beat.

Failidh To exhale.

Failnughadh. A failing.

Failnigham. To fail.

Faill. ⎱
Fail n. ⎰ A kernel, a hard lump of flefh.

Faill. Ra her Aill. A cliff, precipice.

Faill. Advantage, opportunity.

Faill, foill. Leifure.

Faillbhe, faillbhachd. Emptinefs.

Faille. Danger, decay.

Faillean. Sucker of a tree, root, root of the ear.

Faillol. Deceitful.

Failm The tiller of a fhip.

Failnich. Trifling.

Faillfuigham. To fweat, perfpire.

Faillfeach. Sudorific.

Failleadh. Neglect, failure, omiffion.

Faillighe. Lapfe.

Failligham. To fail, neglect, delay.

Failligheach. Drowfy.

Failte. A welcome, falutation, hail.

Failteach. Welcome.

Failtigham. To welcome, greet, falute.

Failtughadh. Saluting, greeting.

Failthin. An intermeddler.

Faime. Border, hem.

Faimeam. To hem.

Faine. A ring

Faine. A wart. Vide Foine.

Fainne. Weakening, leffening, languifh-ment.

Faing, fang. A certain Irifh coin.

Faing, fang. A raven.

Fainge. An infignificant.

Fainnadh, fionnadh. The hair of the body.

Fainne. Ignorance.

Fair. Watch thou.

Fairam. To watch, guard.

Fair. The rifing or fetting of the fun.

Fairb. Weeds.

Fairbre. A notch, impreffion; a fault, ftain, blemifh.

Fairce. Extent.

Fairche. Diocefe, epifcopal fee.

Fairceal. A reward.

Fairdhreis. A bramble.

Faire, fairadh. A watching, watchfulnefs, a watch-hill, height.

Faire-ch.

Faireach. Watchful.

Faireog. A hump, hillock; a wax kernel, gland.

Fairfonadh. Warning.

Fairegach. Glandular.

Faire! Fie! behold!

Fairigan. An interjection of admiration.

Fairge. The sea, a sea or wave.

Fairgseoir. A spy.

Fairigh. A parish.

Fairiogsionach. A brave champion.

Fairigham. To watch, perceive.

Fairughadh. Perception.

Fairmheadh. Position, situation.

Fairmam. A train, retinue.

Fairnicam. To obtain, get, invent, devise.

Fairspeag. A large gull.

Fairrigeoir. A sailor.

Fairseang. Wide, large, spacious.

Fairsinge. Plenty, largeness, extent.

Fairsingam. To enlarge.

Fairsion. Upon.

Fairthe. Soon, quickly.

Fairthe. A feast.

Faisce. Cheese, pressure, violence.

Faisceadh. A penfold.

Faiscre. Compulsion, violence.

Faiscre. }
Faisgre. } Cheese.

Failg, faisgeadh. A fold.

Faisgeadh. A squeezing.

Faisgeamhuil. Flat, compressed.

Faisgam. To squeeze, wring, compress.

Faisgte. Squeezed, compressed.

Faisgain. A press, a spunge.

Faisigham. To remain.

Faisneis. Speakable.

Faisneise. Intelligence, rehearsal, relation.

Faisneigham. To certify, prove, tell, relate.

Faisteanoir. A soothsayer, augur, prophet.

Faistine. An omen, prophecy.

Faistineach. A wizard, soothsayer.

Faiteas }
Faitcheas } Fear, apprehension.

Faital. Light.

Faiteach. Fearful, timorous, shy.

Faiteal. Music.

Faithche, faith. A field.

Faitcheachd. Stalking gait, walking in the fields.

Faitchal. Stately.

Faith. Heat, warmth.

Faith. Apparel, raiment.

Faithe. The hem of a garment.

Faitheimid. A field, green.

Faithne. A wart.

Faitighios. Reluctance, dread of bad consequence.

Faithim, faime. The hem or border of a garment.

Faithioltoir. A broker.

Faithirleog. A swallow, a lapwing.

Faithlios. A wardrobe.

Faithliosoir. The yeomen of the robes.

Faithneam. A liking.

Faitse. The south, southern point.

Faitseach. Southward, southern.

Fal. A fold, penfold, circle.

Fal. Wall, hedge.

Fal-dos. A thorn hedge.

Fal. A scythe, spade.

Fal mhonadh. A peat spade.

Fal. A king, great personage.

Fal. Much, plenty, a trifle.

Fal. Guarding, tending cattle.

Fala. Spite, grudge, malice, fraud, treachery.

Falach. A veil, covering, a case.

Falachadh. Hiding.

Falachda-fionn. Places in the fields, according

cording to Keating, where Fingal and his son ufed to light fires.

Faladair. Orts.

Faladh. Hatred.

Falaigham. To hide, cover, keep clofe, conceal.

Falain. A whale.

Falaifg. Moorburn.

Falamh. Empty.

Falamhnughadh. Dominion, fovereignty.

Falaightheoir. One who covers or hides.

Falaid. A glofs, polifh, meal put on a cake to make it look white.

Falarafa. ⎤ Pacing, ambling, horfeman-
Falarachd. ⎦ fhip.

Falaire. An ambler, pacer.

Falatas. Chaftifement.

Falbhach. One troubled with the hickups.

Falbham. To go away.

Falam. To hedge, inclofe.

Falc. Barren, fteril.

Falc. Froft, fterility from drought.

Falc. A flood.

Falcare. A fcoffer, cheat.

Falcam. To bathe.

Falcadh-teth. Hot baths.

Falcus. A fhade, fhadow.

Falgha. A jeft.

Falgleuta. A hedge.

Falidh. Softly.

Falla. Dominion.

Fallam. To come.

Fallamh. Empty.

Fallamhachd. ⎤
Fallumhe. ⎬ Emptinefs.
Fallamhad. ⎦

Fallamhuigham. To empty.

Fallaimhe. Emptier.

Fallamhaichoir. Emunctory.

Fallain, fallan. Healthy, wholefome.

Fallaineachd. ⎤ Wholefomnefs, healthinefs,
Fallaine. ⎦ health.

Fallamhnachd. Rule, dominion.

Fallamhnam. To govern, rule as a king.

Fallamhnas. A kingdom, dominion.

Fallan. Sound, healthy.

Fallanachd. Health, foundnefs.

Falluinn. A mantle, cloak, a hood.

Fallofgadh. Setting on fire, burning, combuftion.

Falloifgam. To burn.

Fallfa. Deceitful.

Fallfachd. Deceit, fallacioufnefs, philofophy.

Fallus. Sweat, perfpiration.

Fallufuigham. To fweat, perfpire.

Falmadair. A tiller.

Falmuir. A hole.

Falra, falarachd. Pacing, ambling.

Falraigham. To pace, amble.

Falfa. Falfe, deceitful.

Falfachd. Deceit, falfhood.

Faltan. A welt, belt, ribbon for the head, fnood.

Faltanas. An occafion, pretence, quarrel, enmity.

Falumhain. A fort of coarfe garment.

Fa'm, fo'm, fu'm. Under me.

Famh. A mole.

Famhair, fomhait. A giant.

Famhthorr. A mole-hill.

Fa'n. Under the.

Fan, fana. Prone, propenfe.

Fan. ⎤ A declivity, fteep, inclination,
Fanadh. ⎦ defcent, headlong.

Fan. Stay thou, wait thou.

Fanachd. Staying.

Fanam. To ftay, wait.

Fanam. To precipitate.

Fan. A wandering, ftraying, peregrination.

Fan. A church, chapel, fane.

Fanear.

Fanear. Obfervation, notice, heed.

Fan-Lobuis. Name of a church in the county of Corke.

Fanaictheach. Mad, frantic, fanatic.

Fang, faing. A raven, vulture.

Fang. A pound to catch cattle in.

Fangam. To drive to a fold.

Fang, faing. An Irifh coin, gold or filver leaf.

Fan-leac. An altar of rude ftone, a ftone in an inclined pofition.

Fanlonta. Slender.

Fann.
Fannanta. } Faint, weak, infirm.

Fannad. Faintnefs, weaknefs.

Fannthath. Ignorant.

Fannlag. Weak.

Fanntais. Weaknefs, languifhing.

Fanntaifeach. Fainting, inclining to faint.

Fannuighe. Away.

Fannuidhideach. Negligent, carelefs.

Fannuigham. To faint.

Fanoid. Mockery, ridicule, derifion.

Fanoidaiche. A mimick, mocker.

Fanoideach. Derifive, mocking.

Fanntaloch. Waiting, refting.

Fanntin. Remaining, ftaying.

Faobhar. Edge of a tool or weapon.

Faobham. To rob.

Faobharach. Sharp, keen-edged, active, nimble.

Faobhairt. Edge, temper.

Faobharam. To whet, fharpen.

Faoch. A field.

Faochadh. Crifis in ficknefs.

Faochag-thuachaill. A whirlpool.

Faochag. A periwinkle, the eye.

Faodalaiche. A foundling.

Faodal. Waif.

Faodh, faoi. The voice.

Faoighle. Words, expreffion.

Faodhbham. To fhout, cry aloud, proclaim.

Faogh. Punifhment.

Faoghaid. Game, men that ftart game.

Faoghaidaiche. Carnivorous birds.

Faoghar. A found, voice, confonant.

Faoi, fuidh. Below, beneath.

Faoi. A vice or turn.

Faoi dho. Twice.

Faoi fin. For that reafon.

Faoibh. Dead men's cloaths.

Faoichearbaire. An ufurer.

Faoichearbam. To lay out money at interest.

Faoidh. Departing.

Faoidheamh. A meffenger.

Faoidham. To fleep, reft; ro faoidh for leic, flept on a rock.

Faoidham. To go, to fend.

Faoidh. A voice, noife, found.

Faoileach, faoilidh. Glad, joyful, thankful.

Faoiligham. To rejoice, be glad.

Faoilidh. Generous, hofpitable.

Faoileann.
Faoileag. } A fea-gull.

Faoill. Deceit.

Faoilleach. } February, half of February
Faoillidh.   } and January, bad weather.

Faoileach. Holydays, carnival.

Faoimh-chial. Interpretation.

Faoin. Weak, mean.

Faoin. Sloping.

Faoinam. To indulge.

Faoinbleghan. Gentlenefs, mildnefs.

Faoine.
Faoineachd. } Vanity, idlenefs.
Faoinas.

Faoineachd. Enquiring, enquiry.

Faoineadh. Indulging.

Faoinealach. Foolifh, filly.

Faoifdin.
Faoifide. } Confeffion, confeffing.

Faoifeadh.

Faoifeadh. Helping, recovering, aid, recovery from ficknefs.

Faoifgeog. A filbert.

Faoifneadh. Burfting from the hufk.

Faoite. Sending.

Faol. Patience, forbearance.

Faol. Wild.

Faolchu. A wild dog, wolf.

Faoladh. Learning.

Faoladh. Learned.

Faolam. To teach.

Faolchon. The falcon.

Faolfhulang. A prop.

Faoloch. A bird of prey.

Faolfcadh. Burning, fetting on fire.

Faolfhnamh. Swimming.

Faomaidhteach. Submiffive, humble.

Faomh. Confent, permiffion.

Faomham. To affent, to bear with.

Faomhar. Harveft.

Faomhathair. A predeceffor.

Faon. Void, empty, feeble.

Faondra. Wandering.

Faofamh. Protection, relief.

Faofaid. Confeffion.

Faoitin. Finding, obtaining.

Far. For.

Faradh. A ladder.

Farachdach. A mallet, beetle.

Fardh. Freight, naulage.

Faradail. Greater part.

Faram. To freight.

Faradh. Litter put in a boat to receive horfes.

Farall. A fample, pattern.

Farallam. To bear, carry, offer, prefent.

Faran. Wild garlick.

Faran. A turtle.

Faraon. Together, at once.

Faraor! Alas!

Farafda. Solid, fober, eafy, foftly.

Farbhonn. Upper-fole of a fhoe.

Farbhalla. Buttrefs.

Farbhuilladh. A back blow.

Farainm. A nick-name.

Farcluaifam. To eaves-drop.

Farcluais. Eaves-dropping.

Farchroicionn. Epidermis.

Fardach. Quarters, lodgings, an houfe.

Fardin. Farthing.

Farca teintidhe. A flaming thunderbolt.

Fardail. The major part of any thing.

Fardorus. The lintel of a door.

Faredrum. A faddle-back.

Fargam. To kill, deftroy.

Farghbhais. That leaves behind.

Fari. Reins of a bridle.

Farlaicam. To caft, overcome.

Farmad. Envy.

Farmhala. Eyelids.

Farnaicam. Vide Farnicam.

Farrach. Violence, force.

Farradh. Comparifon.

Farradh. } In company with, along with.
Far ri. }

Farraidam. To enquire.

Farraid. Enquiry, queftion.

Farran. Force, violence, anger.

Farranta. Tombs.

Farranta. Great, ftout, generous.

Farrantas. Power.

Farfan. Explication.

Farfing. Wide, large.

Farfneachd. Width.

Farfnigham. To widen, increafe.

Parruineog. A lattice.

Farufcag. Artichoke.

Farfpag. A gull.

Faruifg. Lees, dregs.

Faruin na beine. Opening between mountains.

Farthadh. Hen-rooft.

Fas. Growing, increafe, growth.

Fas. Grow thou.

Fas. Empty, vacant, hollow.

Fas na h aon oich. A mushroom.

Fasach. A desert, wilderness.

Fasag, feusag. A beard.

Fasam. To grow, increase.

Fasaicham. To desolate.

Fasamhuil. Growing, increasing, wild desert.

Fasan. Fashion.

Fasanta. Decent, fashionable.

Fasbhuin. Stubble.

Faschoill. A young grove.

Fasd. Yet.

Fasfhallamh. Ruinous.

Fasg. A prison.

Fasgadair caise. A cheese vat.

Fasgadh. Shelter, lee, refuge, sparks from red hot iron.

Fasgadh. Wringing, squeezing.

Fasgadan. A sconce, umbrella, shade.

Fasgidh. Sheltered.

Fasgam. Vide Faisgam.

Fasgan. A muscle.

Faslaich. Vacuities.

Faslairt. Encampment.

Faslomairt. An expeditious way of dressing victuals in the stomach of an animal amongst the Highlanders.

Fasnam. To cleanse, winnow.

Fasgnam. To purge.

Fasmhor. Lonely, solitary, desolate.

Fasnag A fan to winnow.

Fasne. }
Fasneog. } A wheal, pimple, measle.

Fassach Stubble.

Fassradh. Harness.

Fastuigham. To stop, stay, make fast, to hire.

Fastughadh. Fastening, securing, seizing.

Fasuicham. To destroy, lay waste.

Fath. Cause, reason, opportunity.

Fath. Skill, knowledge.

Fath. A poem.

Fath. A mole, a field.

Fath. Heat.

Fath. The breath, breathing.

Fathach. Prudence, knowledge.

Fathach, athach. A giant.

Fathan. A journey.

Fathas. Skill, poetry, prudence.

Fathfhaim. The hem of a garment.

Fathast. Seasonable, as yet.

Fathbhan. Mole-hill.

Fathdhorus. A small door, wicket.

Fatche. A green.

Fathoide. A school-master, usher.

Fathsgriobham. To subjoin.

Fathsgriobhadh. Subjoining.

Fathsgriobhte. Subjunctive.

Fatseach. Southward.

Fatuaim. Law.

Fe, fo, fa, fuidh. Under.

Fe. A measuring-rod, a rod to measure graves.

Fe. A hedge, pound, penfold, park.

Feab. Good.

Feab. A widow.

Feabh. As if.

Feabh. A conflict, skirmish.

Feabh. Means, power, faculty.

Feabhal. Loch Foyle in Ulster.

Feabhas. }
Feabhus. } Goodness, beauty, comeliness, decency.

Feabhdha. Goodness, honesty, knowledge.

Feabhra. February.

Feabhsa. Rent.

Feabhsa. Science.

Feabhsach. Cunning, skilful.

Feac, Feach. The handle of a spade, shaft.

Feach. A journey.

Feacadh. A turning.

Feacidh. They put, set.

Feacam. To bow, bend.

Feacc, focc. A tooth.

Feach. See, behold.

Feacham. To see, behold, to try.

Feachadh. A pick-ax, mattock.

Feachadair. A wizard, a seer.

Feachain.

Feachain. A view, fight, trying.

Feachd. Time, turn, vice, alternative.

Feachd. Journey, expedition.

Feachd. Danger.

Feachd. Forces, trained-bands, levy.

Feachda. Crooked.

Feachdadh. Bending, moving.

Feachdnan. On a certain time.

Feachte. The cramp.

Feachfaithar. They fhall be fent.

Feachtha. ⎱
Feachna. ⎰ Was fought, fent.

Feadam. To tell, relate, amhuil ad fead leabhar Glinn da Loch, as the book of Glen da Loch relates.

Fead. ⎱ a. Whiftle, or fhrill noife.
Feaduighiol. ⎰

Feadalach. ⎱
Feadaireachd. ⎰ Whiftling, hiffing.

Feadam. To whiftle.

Fead. A bulrufh.

Fead A fathom.

Fead. An ifland.

Feada coile. Bulrufhes, wild forrel.

Feadadh. A relation, rehearfal.

Feadag. A flute, a plover.

Feadaim, Feudam. To be able.

Feadan. A pipe, reed, flute, a fpout, hollow place through which the wind eddies.

Feadanach. ⎱
Feadaire. ⎰ A piper.

Feadanam. To pipe, whiftle.

Feadarlaigh. The Old Law or Teftament.

Feadarthachd. Poffibility.

Fead ghuile. Lamentation.

Feadghaile. A noife the belly of fome horfes make as they ride.

Feadh. Extent.

Feadh. Whilft, during.

Feadh, fiodh. Timber, woods.

Feadha. A calm.

Feadhaireachd. A gift or prefent.

Feadhaireacht. Strolling, idling.

Feadhaim. To rehearfe, relate.

Feadhain. A band, troop, company.

Feadhan. ⎱
Feadhanfanach. ⎰ Wild, favage.

Feadhb. A fault, defect.

Feadhb. A widow.

Feadh-chua. Venifon; an extenfive country.

Feadhanach. A breeze.

Feadhmach. Potent.

Feadhmadoir. He that hath the ufe of a thing.

Feadhmam, feimam. To make ufe of, to ferve, adminifter.

Feadhmanach. A governor, overfeer, fteward, fervant.

Feadhmantas. ⎱
Feadhmantachd. ⎰ Superintendence.

Feadhmanta. Official.

Feadhmghlacam. To make one's own by poffeffion.

Feadhmghnathughadh. Ufurpation.

Feadhna. A captain.

Feagha. A beech tree.

Feag. A tooth, offence.

Feagadh. To fee. Vide Feacham.

Feagh. A fathom.

Feagadh. Perhaps.

Feal. Bad, naughty, evil.

Feal. Treafon, fubtilty.

Fealb. A kernel, lump in the flefh.

Fealcaidh. Auftere, harfh, deceitful, knavifh

Fealcaidheachd. Sharpnefs, fournefs, knavery.

Fealcaidheas. A debate, difpute.

Feall. Treafon, treachery, confpiracy, murder.

Feallam. To deceive, fail.

Feallan. Felon, nefcock.

Feallghniomh. A vile action.

Feallduine. A bad man.

Feallmhian. A confpiracy.

Feallfamh. } A philofopher.
Feallfanach. }

Feallfa. } Philofophy.
Feallfamhnachd. }

Feallfamhnach. A fophifter.

Feallmhac. A learned man.

Fealltamhuil. Murderous, traitorous.

Fealtoir. A traitor, villain.

Feamach. Grofs, fuperfluous, dirty.

Feamachas. Superfluity, groffnefs.

Feamain. Bladder fucus.

Feamnach. } Sea-ore, fea-weed.
Feamuin. }

Feam. } A tail.
Feaman. }

Feancadh. Wreftling, wreathing, crook-ednefs.

Feanchas. Genealogy.

Feanndag Ghreugach. Fenugrek.

Feanndag. Nettles.

Feannam. To flay.

Feannog. A Royfton crow, a whiting.

Feannta. Full of holes.

Fear. Good.

Fear. A man, a hufband.

Fear n'a bainnfe. } A bridegroom.
Fear nuadh pofda.. }

Fear, feur. Grafs.

Fear tirim. Hay.

Farachas. Manhood.

Feirachas-tighe. Hufbandry.

Fear na cairn. An outlaw.

Fear-ceaird. A tradefman.

Fear-ancheairt. A droll.

Fear-brataich. Fnfign-bearer.

Fear-drabhlinn. Jefter.

Fear-cuiridh. Inviter.

Fearam. To act like a man, to fight.

Fearachafbaile. Œconomy.

Fearairm. A hay-loft, hay-yard.

Fearadhachd. } Force, might, power, man-
Fearamhlachd. } linefs.

Fear-fuiridh. Suitor.

Feart-foirneart. A robber, violent man.

Fear-oibre. Workman.

Fear-aifaig. Feriyman.

Fear-labheirt. Speaker.

Fear-lagh A lawyer.

Fear-iafachd. Borrower.

Fear-breige. A puppet.

Fear faire na h aon fuil. A character in an Irifh novel.

Fear-leathfgeoil. Excufer.

Fear-fearcluais. Eaves-dropper.

Fear-inntleachd. Engineer.

Fear-dana. A poet.

Feara-feoirna. Cheffmen.

Fearamhail. Manly, brave.

Fearan. Wild garlick

Fearan. A queeft, ring-dove.

Faran-eidhion. A turtle.

Fearanda. A countryman, a boor, farmer.

Fearann. Ground, land, country.

Fearann ban. Lay land.

Fearafadh. Imitation.

Fearafoir. Imitator, mimick.

Fearb. A cow.

Fearb. A word.

Fearb. A wheal, pimple, any excrefcence.

Fearb. Goodnefs.

Fearbam. To kill, deftroy, maffacre.

Fearbhan. The herb crow-foot.

Fearbhaire. A herdfman.

Fearboc. A roebuck.

Fearbholg. A fcabbard, fheath, budget.

Fearchuidreadh. Threefold.

Fearchur. A champion, manhood, courage.

Feardha. Male.

Feardhachd. Manhood.

Fearg. Anger.

Fearg. A champion, warrior.

Feargach. Angry, paffionate.

Feargachd. Anger, paffion.

Feargam. To vex, fret.

Fearmhaic. Strong, able man.

Fearmhar. Graffy.

Fearn. The elder-tree ; the letter F

Fearn.

Fearn. Good.

Fearn. A shield.

Fearna. Town of Ferns in Ireland.

Fearna. The mast of a ship.

Fearnaidhe. Masculine.

Fearr Better.

Fearradha. Vide Fearadha.

Fearradhachd Manhood.

Fearsa. A verse.

Fearsaid. A spindle.

Fearsaid. A strand-pit, ulna brachialis, or cubit.

Fearfud. A wallet.

Fearsan. A short verse.

Fearscal. A man.

Fearsda. A pool, standing water.

Feart. A good or virtuous act.

Feart. Virtue, attribute, repute.

Feartal. Reputable.

Feart A miracle.

Feart. A grave, tomb.

Feart. Country, land.

Feartamhuil. Miraculous.

Feartaigham. To bury.

Feartaille. A funeral oration.

Fearthuin. } Rain.
Fearshion. }

Feartuinach. Rainy.

Feartmholladh. } A funeral oration, pane-
Feartghraimh } gyrick.

Feas, fios. Knowledge.

Feafach. Knowing, skilful.

Feasag, feusag. A beard, fibre.

Feascartha. Late in the evening.

Feascar. The evening.

Feofcorluch. A dormouse, field-mouse; a buzzing infect that flies about in the evening.

Feascarach. Late.

Feasd, am feasd. Never, ever.

Feasda. A feast, entertainment.

Feasda. A festival, festivity.

Feasda, feasd. Hereafter, henceforward.

Feasfhothargadh. } A gargarism.
Feasghlanadh. }

Feasgalaidhe. A herald.

Feasgor. A separation.

Feasog. A beard, feelers, a herd.

Feaftreach. A muzzle.

Feat, feadam To whistle, hiss.

Feat. Music, harmony.

Feath. Learning, skill, knowledge.

Feathadh. The sight.

Feath A calm, tranquillity, a bog.

Feathamhuil. Calm, still, quiet.

Feathamhlachd. Calmness, stillness.

Feathaigham. To quiet, calm, still, be calm.

Feathal. The face, countenance.

Feathal. A bowl, cup, a fur.

Feathan. Fur, hair.

Feathmaith Sinewy.

Feathsgartleadh. The palsy.

Feb. Whilst, as long as.

Febhasaigam. To correct, amend.

Fec. Weakness, feebleness.

Fed. A narrative, relation.

Fedaim. To tell, relate.

Fed. Hard, difficult.

Fedh. Calm, respite.

Fedhan. Flight.

Fedoil. Cattle.

Feibh. As.

Feibh. A long life.

Feibh. Good.

Feicam. To be in a continual motion, to fidget.

Feich, feith. A sinew.

Feitheamhnach. } A debtor
Feichnean. }

Feidhil. Just, true, faithful, chaste.

Feideog. A green-plover.

Feidhlidhe. A follower.

Feidhlidham. To continue true and faithful.

Feidhm, feim. Use, employment.

Feidhmcheus

Feidhmcheufam. To ufurp.

Feidhmghlic. Provident.

Feidmfhealbhaigam. To make a thing one's own by long poffeffion.

Feidhmal. Needful, neceffary.

Feidhmalachd. Need, neceffity.

Feidil. Faithful.

Feidir, feadar, Able, poffible.

Feigh. Bloody.

Feigh. Sharp.

Feigh. Deer.

Feighe. A warrior, champion, flaughterer.

Feighe. The top of a houfe, hill, mountain.

Feighligh. Long.

Feighligham. To catch, apprehend.

Feil. Secretly.

Feil, feile. ⎫ Vigil of a feftival, holiday,
Feighhil. ⎬ market.

Feil. Long.

Feil-Michail ⎫ Michaelmas.
Feileoinrod. ⎬

Feil-Martuin. Martinmas.

Feil-Eoin. St. John's day.

Feil an riogh. Epiphany.

Feile. ⎫ Generofity, liberality.
Feileachd ⎬

Feile. Arrant, bad in a high degree.

Feile-flaith. A bad mafter.

Feilfios. The fecond-fight.

Feiliocan. A May-bug.

Feilios. Vanity, trifle.

Feilin. A fea-gull. Vide Faolann.

Feiliofach. Frivolous, trifling.

Feilioflathrair. A wheedler, a fmall talker.

Feillmhian. Vide Feallmhiann.

Feilirg. A feftilogium, calendar.

Feille. A market-day, feftival, holiday.

Feilteachd. ⎫ Feafting, keeping holidays.
Feillughadh. ⎬

Feilteog. A cod

Feim. Need, ufe.

Feimal. Needful, neceffary.

Feimalachd. Neceffity, need.

Feimalach. A needy perfon.

Feimam. To need, require.

Feimglic. Providential.

Feimdheadh. Denial, refufal.

Feimean. The feminine gender.

Feimineach. Feminine, effeminate.

Feir. A bier, coffer.

Fein. Self.

Feine. A farmer, boor, ploughman.

Feinne. The celebrated militia of Ireland.

Feinfhiofrach. Confcious, experienced.

Feinfhios. ⎫ Confcioufnefs, experi-
Feinfhiofrachd. ⎬ ence.

Feinorioflachd. Condefcenfion.

Feinfhoghintach. Self-fufficient.

Feinoriofal. Condefcending.

Feinfhoghaintas. Self-fufficiency.

Feinghluaifair. Automaton.

Feinghluafach. Automatical.

Feinmhort. Suicide.

Feinfpeis Self-conceit.

Feir. Of hay or grafs.

Feirdhris. A bramble, briar.

Feiread. A ferret.

Feirge. Anger, indignation.

Feirn-feoil luinge. The lower end of a maft.

Feirrfi. Strength, courage.

Feirfde. The pits or lakes of water on the fand at low ebb, whence beul na fearfde, Belfaft.

Feis. A convention, convocation, fynod.

Feis. ⎫ An entertainment, feaft.
Feifd. ⎬

Feifdam. To feaft.

Feis. A pig, fwine.

Feifain. ⎫ A young cat.
Feifag. ⎬

Feis. Carnal communication.

Feifte, feifteas. Entertainment, accommodation.

Feifteas oiche. A night's lodging.

Feith. Honey-fuckle.

Feith. A finew.

Feithchrupadh. Spafm.

Feith. Tranquillity, filence, calmnefs.

Feitham. To wait, attend, ftay.

Feithach. } Sinewy.
Feithanach. }

Feithamh. Waiting, attending.

Feithide. A beaft.

Feithis. To gather, affemble, keep, preferve.

Feithleog. The hufk, pod of beans, peas, &c.

Feitheamhaoir. An overfeer.

Feithin. A tendon.

Feitheomh. A creditor.

Fel. Strife, debate.

Feleacan. A butterfly.

Feleaftar. A flag.

Felin. } Honeyfuckle.
Felog. }

Fem. } A wife.
Femen. }

Fen. A wain, cart, waggon.

Fencheap. The ring of a waggon.

Feneoir. A carter, waggoner.

Feneul. Fennel.

Feneul-athaich. Fennel-giant.

Feocham. To droop, fade, decay.

Feocullan. A pole-cat.

Feodaidh. Hard.

Feodhas. Better.

Feodhradh. A manner, fafhion.

Feoghain. Folks.

Feoghaicham. To fade.

Feoil. Flefh.

Feoildhatha. Carnation colour.

Feoilchroidhog. A flefh-worm.

Feoirling. A farthing.

Feoirna. Chefs.

Feoite. Faded.

Feol, feoil. Flefh.

Feolghabhal. Incarnation.

Feoladair. A butcher, flefher.

Feoladairachd. Bufinefs of a butcher.

Feoilithach. Carnivorous.

Feolmhar. Flefhy, carnal.

Feolmhorachd. Luft, carnality.

Feolmhach. Flefh-meat.

Feorag. I fuppofe a fquirrel.

Feoran. A green, a mountain-valley, land adjoining to a brook.

Feoraigham. To afk, enquire.

Feorachadh. Afking, enquiring.

Feornan. A pile of grafs.

Feorlan. A meafure containing four pecks.

Feotham. To wither.

Feothan. } A thiftle.
Feothanan. }

Feothas. Goodnefs, better.

Feren. A thigh.

Feren. A cingle, girth.

Fes. A mouth, an entry.

Fefam. To kill, deftroy; fes am milidh, he fhall kill the champion.

Feth. A finew.

Feth. Science, knowledge, inftruction.

Fetha. Fur, hair.

Fethlen. } Honeyfuckle.
Fethleog. }

Feubham. To wait.

Feuch ! See ! behold !

Feucham. To fee, vifit, behold, try, tafte.

Feuchadoir. A wizard.

Feuchain. Trial, feeing, vifiting, a look, afpect.

Feud. Can, able.

Feudam. To be able.

Feuddam. To whiftle.

Feudd. A whiftle.

Feudag. A flute, a plover.

Feudan. A flute. Vide Feadan.

Feudairachd. } Whiftling.
Feudalach. }

Feudin. Being able.

Feudmach. Potent.

Feudhmantach,

Feudhmantach. Superintendent.

Feudhmantachd. Superintendence.

Feugmhas. Abfence, want.

Feum. Need. Vide Feim.

Feur. Grafs.

Feurach. Graffy.

Feuran. Sives.

Feurigham. To feed, graze.

Feurachadh. Feeding.

Feurithach. Graminivorous.

Feurcha. A hay-loft, hay-yard.

Feurdris. A bramble.

Feurmhor. Graffy.

Feurlochan. A lake that dries.

Feurthan. A graffy field.

Feufog. A beard.

Feufgan. The fhell fifh called a mufcle.

Fi. Fretting, anger, indignation.

Fi. Bad, naughty, corrupt.

Fia. Land.

Fiabhras. An ague, fever.

Fiabhrafach. Feverifh.

Fiabhrafchafg. A febrifuge.

Fiacail. A tooth.

Fiacla-carbaid. Cheek-teeth.

Fiacal-leoghain. Dandelion.

Fiacla-forais. Late grown teeth; dentes fapientiæ.

Fiaclach. Having teeth.

Fiaclaigham. To grin, fhew the teeth, be angry.

Fiaclaghadh. Growing angry.

Fiacla-collaic. Boar's tufks.

Fiaclan a dhrannidh. Grinning.

Fiach.
Fiachan. } Price, a debt, news.

Dfhiachadh. Incumbent.

Fiach. A raven.

Fiach-mara. A cormorant.

Fiach.
Fiachach. } Worthy, worth, valuable.

Fiach, fiadhachd. Hunting.

Fiadha. A lord.

Fiadh. Land.

Fiadha.
Fiadhidh. } Savage, wild.

Fiadha.
Fiadhidhad. } Savagenefs, wildnefs.

Fiadh. Meat, food, victuals.

Fiadh. A deer.

Fiadhach. Venifon.

Fiadhach. Detefting, hating.

Fiadham. To tell, relate.

Fiadhaighe. A huntfman.

Fiadhachd. Hunting.

Fiadhaile. A weed.

Fiadhain. Wild, favage.

Fiadhadan. A witnefs.

Fiadhair. Lay land.

Fiadhanta. Fierce.

Fiadhantachd. Fiercenefs.

Fiadhchullach. A wild boar.

Fiadhfhal. A deer-park

Fiadhath. A hunting-fpear.

Fiadhfionn. A roe-buck.

Fiadh-lorg. A hunting-pole.

Fiadhleana. Wild glens.

Fiadhmhuc. A wild boar or fow.

Fiadhnuis. A witnefs, teftimony, prefence.

Fiadhnuifadh. Bearing witnefs.

Fiadhroidhis. Wild radifh.

Fiadhnuifam. To bear witnefs.

Fiadhta. Froward.

Fiafrach. Inquifitive.

Fiafruigham. To enquire, afk.

Fiafrughadh.
Fiafrich. } Enquiring, afking.

Fiaile. Weeds.

Fiail-theach. A houfe of office.

Fial. The veil of a temple.

Fial.
Fialidh. } Generous, liberal, bountiful.

Fial. A ferret.

Fialachd. Bounty, hofpitality.

Fialai.

Fialai. Confanguinity.

Fiallach. A hero, champion, knight-errant.

Fialmhar. Bountiful.

Fialmhuire.
Fialmhuireachd. } Liberality, bounty.

Fialteagh. A place where ferrets are bred.

Fiamarach. A glutton.

Fiamh. A footftep, trace, track.

Fiamh. Fear, reverence.

Fiamhidh. Fearful, timid.

Fiamh. Ugly, horrible, abominable.

Fiamh. A chain, hue.

Fiamhadh. A tracing, purfuing.

Fiamhach. Modeft, fhy.

Fiamhachd. Modefty, fhynefs.

Fiamhlochd.
Fiamhan. } A heinous crime ; fear.

Fiamharrachd.
Fiamchoir. } A monfter.

Fian-bhoth. A tent, hut, booth, cottage.

Fiann Eirin. A kind of militia or trained bands in Ireland, to defend their coaft againft invaders, of whom Fionn mac Cumhail, or Fingal was the commander, concerning whom many fables have been written in fucceeding ages, and on which now the poems of Fingal and Temora are founded.

Fiannach. A giant, Fingalian hero.

Fiannachal. Gigantick, auguft, grand.

Fiar. Crooked, inclined, wicked, perverfe.

Fiaradh.
Fiarach. } Inclining, twifting, wreathing, flanting.

Fiaram. To incline, bend, twift, wreathe, wry.

Fiarfoirinn. Impetuous.

Fiaras. Crookednefs.

Fiarogha. Great-grandchild.

Fiarfuighe, fiafruighe. A queftion.

Ffarghtorach. Diffembling.

Fiarfhuileach. Squint eyed.

Fiartha. **Wreathed, twifted.**

Fias. I will tell, relate. Vide Fiadham.

Fiafdar. Anger.

Fiatail. A weed.

Fiatghail. Vetches.

Fibhras. Confufion, fever.

Fich, fiudhuch. A fee-farm.

Fich. A country village or caftle.

Ficham. To put or fell, to break.

Ficham. To fight.

Fichad. Twenty.

Ficheall. A buckler.

Fideog. A fmall pipe, reed.

Fideog. A fort of bird, a fmall diminutive worm.

Fidgheis. A fpear, lance.

Fidgheadh. A cuftom, manner, fafhion.

Fidhigham. To weave, knit.

Fidhlin. A fmall fiddle.

Fidhal. A fiddle.

Fidhalach. Of a fiddle.

Fidhalair. A fiddler.

Fidhalairachd. Playing on the fiddle.

Fidir. Confider thou.

Fidirachdin. Confideration, compaffion.

Fidir. A teacher.

Fidiràm. To confider, weigh, try.

Fig. A flit.

Fighil. A prayer.

Fige. A fig-tree, a fig.

Figheacban. A garland, wreath.

Figham. To weave, plait, twift.

Figheadh. A weaving, knitting.

Figheadoir. A weaver.

Figheadora. The woof, weft.

Figheadora. Of a weaver.

Figiodh. A fig.

Filbin. A lapwing.

File. A bard, poet.

Filin. A little bard, poetafter.

Filidheachd. Poetry.

Fileamhuil. Poetical.

Filead. A fillet.

Fileata. Poetic.

Fileon. A spruce jemmy fellow, a crafty man.

Filam. I am. For Bheilam.

Filleadh. A fold, plait, a cloth.

Fillag. A shawl or wrapper, a little plaid.

Filleadh-beg The kelt or petticoat part of the highland dress.

Fillam. To fold, plait.

Fillas. That betrayest.

Fillam, pro Pillam. To return, imply.

Fillte. Folded, plaited, implied.

Fim. Drink, wine.

Fimineach. An hypocrite.

Fimineachd. Hypocrisy.

Fine. A tribe, family, kindred, nation.

Finneal-cumhthra. Sweet-fennel.

Finneal-fraide. Sow-fennel.

Fineachas. An inheritance.

Fineadhas. A nation.

Fineamhuin. A twig, ozier, a rod; a vine, vineyard.

Fineur. A stock, lineage.

Fineag. A mite.

Fineagachadh. Growing full of mites.

Fineon. A buzzard.

Finiche. Jet.

Finideach. Wise, prudent.

Finn, fionn. White; milk.

Finndhabhaigh. A counterfeit fight.

Finne. Attendance, testimony.

Finnel.⎫
Finnen.⎬ A shield.
   ⎭

Finngheallam. To profess.

Finnfhoilsuigham. To protest.

Finnreicam. To proscribe, enslave.

Finnreicadair. Enslaver.

Finndiolam. To enslave.

Finngheinte. The Norwegians.

Finnidheach. Vigilant, prudent.

Finnidheachd. Care, vigilance.

Finnsgeul. A romance, story.

Fiobhar, faobhar. An edge.

Fioch. Land.

Fioch. Wrath, anger, choler, ferity.

Fiochal. Angry, fierce.

Fiochgha, fiochmhar. Angry, fierce, froward.

Fiochmhorachd. Anger, fierceness.

Fiochra. Anger.

Fiochuil. Vigesiangulus.

Fiodadh. Laughter.

Fiodam. To laugh.

Fiodhan. A cheese-vat.

Fiodh. A wood, wilderness.

Fiodhach.⎫
Fiodais. ⎬ Shrubs.
    ⎭

Fiodhain A witness.

Fiodhbhai. Hollowness.

Fiodhbhadh. A wood, thicket, wilderness.

Fiodchat. A mouse-trap.

Fiodchonnadh. Cord-wood, brush-wood.

Fiodhnach. Manifest, plain.

Fiodhghual. Charcoal.

Fiodhrach. Encrease.

Fiodhradh. Fashion.

Fiodhrubha. A wood, thicket.

Fiog. A wall.

Fiogh. A braid or wreath.

Fiogha. The weather or windward-side.

Fioghait. A four-square figure.

Fioghair. A figure, sign.

Fiogis. ⎫
Fiogog.⎬ A fig-tree.
    ⎭

Fiolidh. Vide Fialidh.

Fiomhalach. A giant, big fellow.

Fion. Wine.

Fion. Truth; old, small.

Fion fionn. White wine.

Fionach. Antique.

Fionas. Presence of, a witness.

Fionaiseach Manifest.

Fion dearg. Red wine.

Fiongeur. Vinegar.

Fion. Small, little, few.

Fionabhal. } A grape.
Fiondearc. }

Fionach. Old, antient.

Fionail. A fine.

Fionaghail. The Fingallians, inhabitants of Fingal.

Fionbhoth. A tent, booth, fcenery.

Fionchaor. A grape.

Fionda. Cœruleous.

Fionduille. A vine-leaf.

Fioneamhuin. A vine, vineyard.

Fioneamhnach. Full of vines.

Fionfhaifgain. } A wine-prefs.
Fiondlos. }

Fionfadh. } The beard, fine fur, hair.
Fionnadh. }

Fionnfhuar. Cool.

Fionnfhuaireachd } Coolnefs, a gentle gale,
Fionnfhuaire. } frefhnefs.

Fionnfhuairuigham. To refrigerate.

Fionfuirmeadh. A maxim.

Fionghal. Treafon, murder of a relation, parricide.

Fiongalach. A murderer, parricide.

Fionghort. A vineyard.

Fionlabhram. To verify.

Fionmhor. Abounding with wine, a wine-bibber.

Fionn. White, pale, fair; truly.

Fionn. Sincere, true, certain.

Fionn. Little, fmall.

Fionnlochlunach A Norwegian.

Fionnachdin. Experience.

Fionnad. A waggon, carriage.

Fionnadh. Hair, fur.

Fionnadhmach. Hairy, rough.

Fionnfirthean. Long coarfe grafs.

Fionnam. To look upon, behold, fee; to flay.

Fionnan-feoir. A grafshopper.

Fionnaobh. Neat, clean, clear.

Fionna-fada. The middle finger.

Fionealta. Fine, whitened.

Fionealtachd. Finenefs.

Fionnaolta. White-wafhed.

Fionnafga. Bands wherewith vines are tied

Fionnfadhach. Fine, fmooth, fenfible.

Fionnfhuaradh. A cooling, refrefhing.

Fionnfhuaram. To cool, refrefh.

Fionnchofmhuil. Probable.

Fionnchofmhuileachd. Probability.

Fionnmheug. Whey.

Fionn-obthaidh. Sober, abftemious.

Fionns. A well.

Fionnfgoch. A flower.

Fionnfgiathach. White-fhielded, a firname.

Fionntach. Having hairs on the body.

Fionnua. A grandfon's grandchild.

Fionuir. The vine-tree.

Fior. True, notable, perfect.

Fioram. To make certain, to verify.

Fioraidheachd. Veracity.

Fioran. Salutation, welcome.

Fioreun. The eagle.

Fiorchofmhuileachd. Probability.

Fiordha. Sincere, true, righteous.

Fiorghlan. Pure, clean, fincere.

Fiorghloine. Sincerity, quinteffence.

Fior-iochdar. The loweft part, bottom.

Fiormameint. The firmament.

Fiormhath. Perfectly good.

Fior-ordha. Illuftrious.

Fiorraideach. Frivolous, trifling.

Fiorraidheacht. Truth, veracity.

Fiorraidheach. } That fpeaks truth.
Fiorraithris. }

Fiorfa. Neceffity.

Fiorthan. Long coarfe grafs.

Fioruigham. To juftify.

Fioruifge. Spring-water.

Fiorthobair. A fpring well.

Fios. Art, knowledge, fcience, meffage, vifion, underftanding.

Fiofach.

Fiosach. } Knowing, expert.
Fiosal.

Fiosaigham. To know.

Fiosaiche. A forcerer, foothfayer.

Fiosaich mac Faiftin. Character in an Irifh novel.

Fiogfaigheachd. } Sorcery, occult fcience.
Fiosachd.

Fiofrach. } Inquifitive, bufy, pry-
Fiofraightheach. } ing.

Fiofraigham. To know, examine, enquire, afk, vifit.

Fiofiaghadh. Enquiring, afking.

Fiothnaife. Sorcery, poifon.

Fir. Of a man. Vide Fear.

Firb. Swiftnefs.

Firbolg. The third colony, according to Keating, that came into Ireland before the Milefians.

Firbhreige. Puppets.

Firdhileas. Genuine, true, fincere.

Firdhris. A bramble.

Fire, fireachd. Truth, event.

Fireach. Hill, moor, a hill with a plain at top.

Fireadh A bottom, truth; a flower.

Firead. A ferret.

Firean, fireanach. Vide Firineach.

Firean. An eagle.

Fireann. Male, mafculine.

Fireann. A chain, a garter.

Fireannach. A male.

Fireannachd. Male kind, manhood.

Fireanta. True, juft, righteous, loyal.

Fireantachd. Integrity, righteoufnefs, loyalty, faithfulnefs.

Fireunam. } To juftify, verify.
Firinuigham. }

Firinughadh. Juftification.

Firiomal. The utmoft coaft or limit.

Firin A manikin.

Firineach. Juft, righteous, faithful.

5

Firinne. } The truth.
Firin. }

Firineach. A juft, righteous, faithful perfon.

Firineachd. Truth, verity.

Firinfce. The mafculine gender.

Firionadach. A lieutenant.

Firlionam. To multiply.

Firlionadh. Multiplying.

Firmeoir. A farmer. Not Galic.

Firochtrach. Innermoft, loweft.

Firniamham. To purify.

Firfi. Strength, power.

Firthean. Bound, obliged.

Fireun. An eagle.

Fis. Colour, dying, tincture.

Fis. A dream, vifion.

Fis, fife. Of knowledge, vifion, a vifionary.

Fifag. A young cat.

Fit. A collation, breakfaft.

Fitag. A kind of grafs.

Fith. Land.

Fithe, fighte. Woven, wreathed, twifted, braided.

Fitheam. Vide Figham.

Fitean. A quill.

Fitheach. A raven. Vide Fiach.

Fithean. A hog.

Fithchiod. Twenty.

Fithchiodo. Twentieth.

Fithchioll. A complete fuit of armour.

Fithil. A poetafter.

Fitchill, fitchille. Tables, chefs-board.

Fithir. A doctor, teacher.

Fithreach. A fort of alga called duilleafg, or dilfe, which people eat.

Fiu. Worth, worthy.

Fiu. Edible, fit to eat.

Fiu. Like, alike.

Fiubhas. Dignity, worth.

Fiuchach. That boileth.

Fiuchadh.

Fiucham. To boil up, spring forth, simmer, estuate.

Fiuchadh. Heat, boiling, a boiling up, scatebra

Fiughan. A cheese-vat.

Fiughar. Earnest expectation.

Fiudhe. Good stuff.

Fiughantas. Generosity.

Fiughantach. Generous.

Fiughan. Memory.

Fiughanach. That hath good memory.

Fiughidh. A hero.

Fiun, fiunas. A price, value.

Fiuntach. Worthy, deserving.

Fiuntas. Merit, worth, dignity.

Fiuran A sapling, a certain rank weed that cattle eat, metaphorically a young man.

Fiusach. Earnest.

Fiuthidh. Perhaps an arrow.

Flaiche. A sudden blast or gust of wind.

Flaichach. Windy, blustering.

Flaindearg. Sanguine, murrey, a staynard colour in heraldry, used to express disgrace or blemish in the family.

Flaindeargthachd. The bloody-flux.

Flaith. A lord, a prince, a flower.

Flaith. A kind of strong ale or beer amongst the old Irish.

Flaithbhearta. Proper name of a man.

Flaithchiste. A royal treasure.

Flaitheachd Government.

Flaitheamhuil. Princely, generous.

Flaitheamhlachd. Princeliness, generosity, shew, pomp.

Flaitheas. } Sovereignty, dominion, a
Flaithammas. } kingdom.

Flaitheas. ⎫
Flaithamhnas. ⎪ Heaven, the sky, abode of
Flaithanas. ⎬ the blessed.
Flaithinnis. ⎭

Flamhnaidhe. A heathen priest.

Flan, flann. Blood; red.

Flann. The name of some Irish chiefs.

Flanfgaoileadh } The bloody-flux.
Flannbhuineach. }

Flanshuileach. That hath red eyes.

Flath, flaith. A prince, hero.

Flathamhuil. Princely, generous, shew, elegant.

Flatha. A sitting, session, a court.

Fleachdal. Folt or fleachdal air an suidh.

Fleadh. A banquet, feast, entertainment.

Fleadham. To feast, banquet.

Fleadhachas. Feasting. banqueting.

Fleasg. A rod, wand.

Fleasg. A wreath or rundle, ring, cha

Fleasg Moisture.

Fleasg. A sheaf.

Fleasgan. A treasure.

Fleasgach. A fiddler, clown, rascally fellow, bachelor.

Fleasgachan. A rustic, mean fellow.

Fleasglamha. Land, a field, farm, tenement.

Fleisdam. To slaughter as a butcher, to flay.

Fleisdair. A flesher, butcher.

Fleisdairachd. The business of a butcher

Fleoidhte. Flaccid.

Fleodruin. A buoy.

Fliche. Phlegm, moisture.

Flicidheachd. Humours.

Fliche, fliuch. Water, more wet.

Flicheachd. Moisture, ooziness.

Flichmeadh. Any measure for liquids

Flichne. Sleet.

Flidh, fliodh. } Chickweed.
Flig. }

Flochd. The second dram taken before breakfast.

Fliodhan. An excrescence, wen.

Flios. Vide Flaith.

Fliream. To water.

Fliuch. Wet, moist, oozy.

Fliucham. To wet, water.

Fluchadh. Wetting, rain.

Fluchlachd. Wet, wet weather.

Fluchfhuileachd. A running of water from the eyes.

Fluchbheulach. That ships water, that spits much.

Fluchfhneachd. } Sleet.
Flithfhnachd. }

Floch. Lax, foft.

Flochas, flocas. A lock of wool.

Flur. Meal, flower, bloffom.

Fluth. A wen.

Fo. Under, towards.

Fo. A king, prince, fovereign.

Fo. Good.

Fo. Eafy, quiet, unconcerned.

Fo. In compofition implies rarity.

Foairm. A great number.

Fobhille. A fmall ftroke.

Fobhadh. Swift.

Fobhar. Vide Foghmhar.

Fodbuine. A little man.

Fo. Honour, efteem, regard.

Foachd, fiafruigh. Enquiring, afking.

Foairn. A fwarm ; fairn foghlomtha, fwarms of learned men. Keating.

Fobair. Begun, commenced.

Fobhaidh. Quick, fwift, nimble.

Fobhailte. Suburbs.

Fobhaoile. A town without the walls, fuburb.

Fobhair. Sick, infirm, weak.

Fobhair. A falve, ointment.

Fobhith. Becaufe, becaufe that.

Fobhuidhe. Tawny, yellowifh.

Fobhualam. To beat gently.

Fobhthan. A thiftle.

Foc. Obfcure.

Focal. A word, a vowel, a promife.

Focalaiche. A good fpeaker.

Focal magaidh. A fcoff, taunt, bye-word.

Focalfreumhachd. Etymology.

Focalfreimhuighe. An etymologift.

Focas. Profufe, prodigal.

Fochaid· Scoffing.

Fochaidhe. A difeafe, diforder

Fochain. A caufe, motive, reafon.

Fochain. Difturbance, quarrelling.

Fochair. Prefence, company, near to, before.

Aochall. Dirt, filth, corrupt matter.

Fochan. Food, fodder, provender.

Fochan. Young corn in the blade, a plant.

Focheimnigham. To fucceed.

Fochla. A den, a cave; the worth, an offering.

Fochmhad. Scorn, contempt.

Fochrac. A reward, recompence.

Fochradh. Banifhing, routing.

Fochraic. Happinefs, blifs, felicity.

Fochras. The bofom.

Fochras, a feart ann. Her grave was dug there. Chron. Scotor.

Focht. Interrogation, afking a queftion.

Fochuidhe. } A flout, jeer, derifion,
Fochuidmheadh. } fcorn

Fochuidmham. To fcoff, fcorn.

Fochuidmheach. Joking, fcoffing; a mocker.

Focla. A propofition, maxim.

Foclan. Vide Feoculan.

Focloir. A vocabulary, dictionary.

Fod. Art, fkill, fcience.

Fod. A clod of earth, glebe, foil, land, a peat.

Fodar. Straw, hay, provender, fodder.

Fodram. To give provender.

Fodach. Wife, prudent, difcreet.

Fodaghadh. Obftruction.

Foduighoir. Obftructor.

Fodhalam. To divide, diftinguifh.

Fodhbhruid. } Fiends, furies.
Fodhchnumh. }

Fodh. Knowledge, fkill.

Fodhail. A divifion, releafing, diffolving.

Fodhailam. To loofe, untie, divide

[U u]   Foidnb.

Fodhb. A cutting down.

Fodhin. Vide Fonn.

Fodhord. The humming of bees; a loud noise; a conspiracy, plot.

Fodhorous. A wicket.

Fodhuine. A plebeian, servant.

Fodruair. Perceiving.

Fodurluasach. Busy.

Fofiadha. A yard, park, inclosure.

Fogailam. To teach, instruct, dictate.

Fogairam. To command, publish.

Fogairam. To chace, pursue.

Fogairt. Chasing, pursuing, driving away, banishing.

Fogh. Entertainment, hospitality.

Fogarach. An exile.

Fogartha. Gracious.

Fogha. A dart, an attack, a rape.

Fogh marach. A pirate.

Foghail. An inroad into an enemy's country, robbery, offence.

Foghailam. To plunder, spoil.

Fogaluidhe. A robber.

Foghal. The whole.

Foghanam. } To do good, to suffice, to
Foghnam. } serve.

Foghanta.

Foghaintach. Good, prosperous, serviceable, generous.

Foghantachd. } Goodness, prosperity, suffi-
Foghaintas. } ciency, generosity.

Foghannan. A thistle.

Foghaoth. A gentle gale, blast.

Foghar. A sound, noise, voice, tone, accent, vowel.

Fogarach. Echoing, resounding, loud, noisy, clamorous.

Foghard. Tingling.

Foghairam. To make a noise, to tingle.

Foghbhanan. A thistle.

Foghladh. Trespass.

Foghlam. Learning, instruction, discipline.

7

Foghlumtheach. } A novice, apprentice,
Foghluinte. } scholar.

Foghlamta. Learned, ingenious.

Foghlasam. To grow pale.

Foghlamam. To learn.

Foghlughadh. A ransacking, robbing.

Foghluigham. To ransack.

Foghluigheachd. Rapacity.

Foghluidhe. A robber.

Foghmhar. The harvest.

Foghmharach.
Foghluidhe fairge. } A sea-robber, a pirate.

Foghnaidh. Enough.

Foghnam. To suffice, to do good.

Foghnamh. Servitude, slavery.

Foglaim. To loose, untie.

Foghnas. Profit.

Fogradh. } A warning, charge, caution, a
Foghraimh. } proclamation, decree, ordinance, declaration.

Fogradh. Exile.

Fograim. To warn, caution, order, decree.

Fogus. }
Fogusg. } Near, at hand.

Foi. The name of a place.

Foi, fuidh. Under.

Foiche. Under her, it.

Foicheall. A day's hire, wages, salary.

Foicheimnughadh. A series.

Foichillam. To provide, prepare.

Foid. A turf, peat.

Foidhbiun. Quick, smart, ready.

Foideastar. Is sent, gone.

Foidheach. A beggar.

Foidhreach. A little image.

Foidhreachda. Likeness.

Foige. Topmost part.

Foigeasge. Next, proximate.

Foigseachd. Proximity.

Foighid. } Patience, forbearance.
Foighidin. }

Foighidinach. Patient.

Foighidam. To bear patiently.

Foighin.

Foighin. A green plat, a mead.

Foigfe. Nearer, next.

Foil. A while.

Foill. Deceit, fraud.

Foill. Slowly, softly.

Foill. Leifure.

Foilbheuma. Fierce, cruel, terrible; fcandal.

Foilcheadradh. Abjuration, conjuring.

Foilcheadraod· To conjure.

Foilcheadtoir. A conjurer.

Foileaba. A truckle-bed.

Foilead. A fillet, coif.

Foileanam. To follow, go after, hang after.

Foilearbadh. Death.

Foileafan. An afp.

Foilleachdach. A refearch.

Foilleachd. A track, footftep.

Foilleamhna. Proper, expedient.

Foilcanam. To follow.

Foilearbha. Death.

Foileafan. An afp.

Foillear. The bud of a flower.

Foilligheach Negligent, fluggifh.

Foillligh. Hidden, latent, that does not externally appear. The old parchments on medicine ufe it frequently in this fenfe.

Foilllfigham. To reveal, publifh, fhew, difcover, exprefs, declare, manifeft.

Foiluirm. A fea-gull.

Foilfighte. Manifefted, declared.

Foilfughadh. Declaring, manifefting; a manifeftation, declaration, difcovery.

Foilfughadh an tigharna. Epiphany.

Foilmean. A bad drefs.

Foimeal. Confumption.

Foimhdin. In expectation of, againft.

Foine. A wart.

Fo' inn. Under us.

Foineach. A demand.

Foinneamh. Genteel.

Foinneafach. Sightly.

Foinnighte. Tempered.

Foi-neul. A little cloud, a gleam.

Foinnaigham. To temper.

Foinfe. } The afh-tree.
Foinfeog. }

Foinfi. Wells, fprings, fountains.

Foir. Help, deliver thou.

Foiram. To help, deliver, fave.

Foir. A fhip's crew, a number of people ftowed together.

Foirailluigham. } To deck, adorn.
Foirbham. }

Foirbham. To be prefent.

Foirbhailligh. Acceptable.

Foirbhriathar. An adverb.

Foirbhreathnuigham. To divine, conjecture.

Foirbhrioch. Force, power.

Foirceadal. Inftruction, exhortation, admonition.

Foirceadalam. To teach, inftruct, admonifh.

Foirceannach. White-faced.

Foirceann End, conclufion.

Foirchroicionn Forefkin.

Foircin. Application, fomentation, embrocation.

Foircnuigham. To apply embrocations.

Foirchcimnigham. To proceed.

Foirciobal. A reinforcement.

Foirdheirc. More excellent.

Foirdhealbh. Scheme.

Foirdhealbhadair. Schemer.

Foireamhuil. Steep, headlong.

Foirdiis. Sweet-briar.

Foireidam. To prevent.

Foireagantoir. Obftructor.

Foiregean. Violence, conftraint.

Foireignadh. Oppreffion.

Foireignam. To opprefs, obtrude.

Foirfe. Old, ancient, perfect.

Foirreach. An elder.

Foirfeachd. Perfection, old age.

Foirfhiaclu

Foirfhiacla. The fore-teeth.

Foirghealla. Witnefs, teftimony.

Foirghiol. A declaration, manifeftation.

Foirghiol na firin. Manifeftation of the truth.

Foughiollam. To prove, declare.

Foirghlacam. To occupy.

Foirghlidhe. Nobility, truth.

Foirglidhe. True, certain.

Foirglidis. They ufed to fwear.

Foirgneamh. A building.

Foirgnigham. To build.

Foirgnaghadh. Building.

Foirghe. Taught.

Foiriarach. Prepofterous, eccentric

Foiridinam. To prevent.

Foirifighin. To perform.

Foirigham. To ftay, wait, delay.

Roirighthin. Aid, help, relief, fuccours.

Foirim To blefs, make happy, relieve, aflift, heal, fave.

Foirimeal. The utmoft part, or limit.

Foirimalach. A front; extrinfic, on the outfide, outward.

Foirin. Supply, aid, help, ftrength.

Foiriomradh. A ceremony.

Foiriomraidhteach. Ceremonious.

Foiriongantach. Prodigious.

Foiriongantas. Prodigy.

Foirithin. Vide Foirin.

Foirleathad. Expanfe.

Foirleathann. Extenfive, large, general.

Foirleathnughadh. Periphrafe.

Foirleathanuigham. To extend.

Foirlion. Much, great many.

Foirlionadh. A completion, fupplement, reinforcement, appendix.

Foirlionam. To complete, make perfect.

Foirlionta. Complete, perfect.

Foirm. A manner, form, image.

Foirmal. Formal, clever.

Foirmalachd. Formality.

Foirmheangam. To prevaricate.

Foirne. Dwellers, inhabitants, a brigade.

Foirneadh. Inclination; air foirneadh, headlong, defcent.

Foirneart. Oppreffion, high-hand, violence, mifchance.

Foirneartach. Oppreffive, violent.

Foirrril. Manifeft, apparent.

Foirfcith. Reft.

Foirfeadh. Harrowing.

Foirfair. An officer, fearcher, conftable.

Foirfairachd. Rummaging, fearching.

Foirfeam. To harrow, rummage, fearch.

Foirfhiolam. To propagate.

Foirfhioladh. Propagating.

Foirfgeamham. To deck, adorn.

Foirtbe. A cutting off, a cut.

Foirtbhreathnughadh. Divination.

Foirtchi. Black, fwarthy; a fhoe.

Foirchi. A fhoe.

Foirthir. Remote, eun foirthir, a bird of paffage.

Foirthoin. Enough.

Foirthoil. Bold, ftout, active.

Foirtheagafg. Rudiments, introduction

Foirtible. Slaughter, maffacre.

Foirtil. Able, ftrong, hardy.

Foirtile. More hardy.

Foirtile. ⎫ Patience, greatnefs of foul,
Foirtileach ⎬ courage, fortitude.

Fois. Leifure, reft.

Foifcionnach. Backbiting, malice, a cry.

Foifeamh. Recovery.

Foifgigham. To approach.

Foifam. To ftop, reft.

Foifte, foifte. A refting, refiding.

Foifteadh. Hiring, wages.

Foifteanach. Serious; arranged, in good order.

Foifteochoir. A hireling.

Foith. About.

Foithal. Plundering, prey.

Foithre. Woods.

Foithreith. Hunger.

Fola. A fhort day, a little while.

Fola. A garment

Fola, fuil. Of blood.

Folabh. Going, moving, departing.

Folobham. To go, depart, move.

Folabhan. Stirring or continual motion.

Folabhair. A mover, follower, creeper.

Folabhach. Moving, that provides for itself.

Folabradh. A good speech, pleading, reasoning.

Folach. Covering, hiding.

Folachan. A concealment, hidden treasure.

Folach, am folach. Hid, secret, private.

Folachd. Bloodiness, a feud.

Folachtain. Toleration, forbearance.

Folachtain. Water-fallad, water-parfnip.

Foladh. A cover, covering.

Foladh. Power, ability.

Foladha. Cattle.

Foilaid. A wimple, muffler. If. iii. 23.

Folaidham. To hide, cover, secret.

Folaightheach. Secret, private, hid.

Folamh. Empty, void, vacant.

Folamhaigham. To empty, void.

Folaram. To command, offer, proffer,

Folaramh. An offer, order.

Folarnaidheachd. Equality, parity.

Folarnaidheach. Equal.

Folarthoir. An emperor.

Folartnidh. A sufficiency, enough.

Folartnaigham. To satisfy.

Folas. A shoe, sandal, slipper.

Folcadh. A cleansing of the hair by bathing, bathing.

Folcam, falcam. To bathe, cleanse.

Foldath. Generous.

Folfaidh. Whole, entire.

Folg. Active, nimble, quick.

Folabham. To go away.

Folabh. Going, departing.

Folabham. Going about, motion.

Follach. A kind of water-gruel, a covering, garment.

Folladh. Government.

Follam. To make hollow.

Follamhan. A grace, ornament.

Follamh. Ancestors.

Follamnuighadh. A ruling, governing as a prince.

Follamhnuigham. To rule, govern, sway.

Follaine. Better.

Follas. Plain, evident, manifest, kindred.

Follscadh. A scalding,

Follsigham. Vide Foillsigham.

Follasdiol. An action.

Follusglan. Clear, loud,

Folmhach. That makes hollow, or emptieth.

Folmhaigham. To make empty.

Folofcain A tadpole.

Folofg. A moor-burn, or mountain brook.

Folofgadh. Burning of heath. Vide Fothlofgam.

Folt. The hair of the head, a tail.

Foltchib. A leek.

Folthath. Grey hairs.

Foludham. To be active, nimble.

Foluaimneach. Stirring, active, nimble, prancing.

Foluaimain. A giddy motion, running away, flying, skipping.

Foluar. A footstool.

Foluigheach. Hid, secret.

Folumain. Bad clothes.

Fo m'. Under me.

Fo d'. Under thee.

Fomas. Obedience.

Fomafam. To obey.

Fomhaol. A king's slave.

Fomhumaghadh. Obeisance, humiliation.

Fomhar. Harvest, autumn.

Fomhardha. Autumnal.

Fomhifgeach. Half-drunk.

Fomhor. ⎤ A pirate, a sea-robber, a
Fomhorach. ⎦ giant.

Fomofach. Month of August.

Fomifgeach. Half-drunk.

Fonadh. Quantity, fufficiency.

Fonuigham. To fuffice.

Fonamhad. Jeering, mockery.

Fonal. Cold, rigour.

Fonamhadach. A jeering perfon; that mocketh.

Fonamhadam. To jeer, fcoff, mock.

Fonn. Land, earth.

Fonn. Delight, pleafure, defire, longing.

Fonn. A tune, fong.

Fonn diadhidh. Hymn.

Fonn. Inclination, defire.

Fonnadh. A journey, proficiency.

Fonnmhor. Tuneful, melodious, willing, defirous, meek, difpaffionate.

Fommhorachd. Melody, inclination, propenfity, meeknefs.

Fonnomham. To jeer, hifs.

Fonnfa. ⎱
Fonfa. ⎰ A troop, band.

Fonfair. A cooper.

Fontabram. To rejoice, be glad.

For. Before, beyond, fore in compound words.

For. Over, upon.

For. Difcourfe, converfation.

For. Protection, defence.

For. Enlightening, illumination.

Fora. ⎱
Foradha. ⎰ A feat, bench.

Forabaidh. Early, ripe, before the time.

Forach. A difpute, controverfy.

Forachair. A watchman.

Foraich. Wages.

Foraidheach. Fierce, cruel.

Foraidheachd. Fiercenefs, cruelty.

Foraigham, fairam. To watch, guard.

Foraighis. A foreft, a fox-kennel, the haunt of a wild beaft.

Forail. Excefs, fuperfluity.

Foraoil. Imperious.

Foraileachd. Imperioufnefs.

Forailaim. To command.

Forailaimh. Imperative.

Foraillam. To offer.

Foraimh. A journey.

Foraimheam. To remember.

Forainm. A pronoun, a nickname, an epithet.

Forair. A watch by night.

Foraire. A watch, ward.

Foraitmheadh. Remembrance.

Foran. Anger, wrath.

Forann. A fhort verfe, verficle, fong.

Foranta. Angry, refolute, prefumptuous.

Foraofaglach. Old, ancient; an old man.

Foras. Knowledge, underftanding.

Foras. Ford of a river.

Foras. Old, antique, ancient.

Foras. Increafe, augmentation.

Foras. A law, foundation.

Foraos. A foreft.

Foras, focal. An Etymologicon.

Forafda. Grave, fedate, fenfible.

Forafdachd. Gravity, fobriety.

Forafna. Illuftrated.

Forb. A landlord.

Forba. Land, glebe-land.

Forba. A tax, contribution.

Forbadh. Cutting, flaying, flaughtering.

Forbiltigh. Acceptable.

Forbairam. To grow, increafe.

Forbairt. Increafe, profit, emolument.

Forbais. A conqueft.

Forban. Banns of marriage, proclamation of an edict.

Forban. Excefs, extravagance.

Forbhas. A fnare, ambufh.

Forbhriathar. An adjective.

Forbhrat. A cloak, the upper garment.

Forbhruach. A pinnacle.

Forbhfaoileadh. Mirth, rejoicing.

Forc. Firm, ftedfaft.

Forc. A fork.

Forcam. To teach, inftruct; to pitch with a fork.

Forcach.

Forcach. Forked.

Forcar. Violence, a wooden hook.

Forchagra. A command, decree.

Forchalmaigham. To prevail.

Forchathreacha. Suburbs.

Forchaoin. A catch or quirk in words.

Forchinntachd. Predeftination.

Forchongradh Perfuafion, advice, inftigation, command.

Forchongram. To bid, command.

Forchoimheadh. Watching, lurking for.

Forchroiceann. The forefkin, fcurf.

Forcmaidh. } Superfluity, excefs.
Forcaidh. }

Forcomal. A binding together.

Forcaidh. Rifing or dawning of day.

Forcuth. The fore part of the head.

Fordall. Erring, ftraying.

Fordhabh. A lid, cover.

Fordharc. The light.

Fordharc. Plain, manifeft.

Fordhorus. A porch.

Fordhroin. A loin, the womb.

Fordul. Error.

Fordulach. Erroneous.

Foreidam. To prevent.

Foreigean. Force, a rape, violence.

Foreigneach. Violent, ravifhing.

Forf. A guard.

Forfaire. A watch, guard.

Forfhaireach. Watching, a watchman.

Forfairam. To watch, guard, lay in ambufh, to affemble.

Forfhocal. A byeword, proverb.

Forfhogradh. Advertifement.

Forfuinneog. A window-fhutter, lattice.

Forgairm. A convocation.

Forghairam. To provoke, call together, fummons.

Forgan. Keennefs, anger.

Forghal A lye, fable, romance.

Forghalam. To tell, relate.

Forghart. The fore part of the head.

Forghlacam. To prevent.

Forgla. For the moft part.

Forgla. Election, choice.

Forghuin. A wound.

Forgnuicham. To build.

Forgo. Jewels, precious things.

Forige. Sincere, true.

Foriorg. A rudiment, trial of fkill.

Forlan Force, power, pain, fuperfluity, excefs, conqueft.

Forlaimh. Leaping, bounding.

Forlamhnuigham. To poffefs.

Forlamhas. Poffeffion.

Formach. An increafe, fwelling.

Forma. A feat.

Formad. Envy.

Formadach. Envious.

Formalach. An hireling.

Formamhuil. Of a good form or figure, fightly.

Forman. A type, mould.

Formna. Much, great deal.

Fornaidhach. A glutton.

Forneart. Violence.

Forneal. Appearance, colour.

Fornaire. A command, offer.

Forngabhail. Hardnefs.

Foroideas. A rudiment.

Forordh. Renowned, famous.

Forodughadh. Predeftination.

Foroduigham. To predeftinate.

Forrach. An angling-rod, a perch.

Forraid. Near to, hard by, towards.

Forreilam. To fhine forth, manifeft, difcover.

Forrogheana. Served, did fervice or good.

Forroicam. To prevent.

Forrumha. Fringes.

Forrumha. Sent.

Forfanam. To fhine.

Forfaoiltam. Divination, forefight.

Forfgaite. Fore-knowing.

Forfhaothach. A bafon.

Forfhuigham.

Foirfhuigham. To preſide.

Forfhuighoir. A preſident.

Forſmuaintuigham. To premeditate.

Foirſmuintughadh. Premeditation.

Fortamhuil. Strong.

Fortan, firthean. Tied, bound up.

Fortan. Fortune, bound.

Fortanach. Fortunate.

Foirtartnaidheach. A glutton.

Fortas. Straw, litter.

Fortha. A ſeat.

Forthach. A baſon.

Forthan. Plenty.

Forthan-ſpreidh. Much cattle.

Forthunnach. Fruitful.

Forthan graidhe. A ſtud or breed of horſes.

Fortheagaſg. Rudiments.

Fortil. Strong, hardy, patient.

Fortil la ſaoth. Strong for labour.

Fortheachdair. An uſher, or gentleman, 'ſquire.

Fortraigh. A riſing.

Fortraigh maidne. Riſing of day.

Foruadh. A baſtard red, reddiſh.

Forugaire. A command.

Forus. Knowledge.

Foruinneog. A balcony.

Forus fios air Erin. Notitia Hibernia, the name of an Iriſh book.

Fos. Yet, ſtill, alſo; achd fos, moreover, but yet.

Fos, foſadh. A delaying, ſtaying, reſting, fixing, pitching, a prop, buttreſs, wall, or ditch.

Foſadh. An atonement.

Foſaidh. Ceſſation.

Foſadh. Sloping, reſting.

Foſam. To ſtay, reſt, pitch, lodge.

Foſcalam. ⎫
Foſgalam. ⎬ To open, unlock.

Foſcuilte. ⎫ Open, unlocked, publicly, open-
Foſgailte. ⎭ ly.

6

Foſgam. To approach. Vide Foiſge.

Foſgadh. A ſhadow, ſhelter. Vide Faſgadh.

Foſgriobhadh. Poſtſcript.

Foſlong. A manſion, dwelling-houſe.

Foſlongphort. An encampment, a camp, harbour; rinn iad foſlongphort, they encamped, ag treigſin am foſlongphort, raiſing the ſiege, decamping.

Foſra. Releaſing, diſſolution.

Foſrolaic. Heavenly, ſuperior.

Foſt. Gold.

Foſtam, faſtaigham. To hire, to ſtop.

Fot. A giant.

Fot. Raging, ſtorming, violent.

Fotha. A foundation.

Fotha. Taken away or out of.

Fotha. Under them.

Fothach. A cough, a diſeaſe in horſes.

Fothamas. A warning.

Fothach. A lake, pond.

Fothanan. A thiſtle.

Fothannan-beannuighte. Bleſſed-thiſtle.

Fothchathreacha. Suburbs.

Fothlainteach. An apprentice, novice.

Fothorgadh. Cleanſing.

Fothorgadh. ⎫
Fothragfhoin. ⎬ A bath, well of purifica-
Fothragthobair. ⎭ tion.

Fothragam. To cleanſe, bathe, purify.

Fothram. A great noiſe, ruſtling.

Fothughadh. A beginning.

Fotrus. Orts.

Four, foghair. Diphthongs.

Frach. Bleakneſs.

Frag. A woman, wife.

Frag. A hand.

Frag. A ſhield, buckler.

Fraidreaghadh. A floating.

Fraigal. Oſtentatious of ſtrength.

Fraigalachd. Shew of perſonal ſtrength.

Fraigam

Fraigain. A little man with a martial erect gait.

Fraigaifach. Of, belonging to a fraigain.

Fraigh. A bufh of hair.

Fraigh. The fea, an arch.

Fraileach. Sea-weed.

Frainc. France.

Fraincis. The French tongue.

Francach. A Frenchman, French.

Francachal. Frenchman-like.

Franclus. Tanfy.

Fraoch. Heath, ling, hadder.

Fraoch. Anger, rage, hunger, fury.

Fraochach. Heathy.

Fraochal. } Angry, furious, fretful.
Fraochaidhe. }

Fraochag. A wortle-berry.

Fraochan. A patch put on the toe or point of a fhoe, anger, fome part of a deer.

Fraochanach. Angry, rippling.

Fraochchearc. A heath-poult, groufe-hen.

Fraoidh. Skirts.

Fraon. Places of fhelter in mountains.

Fraoidhnaifeach. Waving, flourifhing.

Fras. A fhower.

Fras. Hail, fmall fhot, feed.

Fras. Ready, active.

Frafach. Fruitful, fhowery.

Frafrach. Like a fhower, fhowery.

Fraf-luaighe. Shot.

Fras-caol. Small feed or fhot.

Fras-linn. Flax-feed.

Frafam. To fhower, rain.

Fras-cainab. Hemp-feed.

Freacadan. A guard, watch.

Freacadanach. Watching, hovering about.

Freacadan dubh. The black-watch, or forty-fecond regiment of highlanders fo called.

Freacadanaiche. A fentry.

Freacair Ufe, practice, frequency.

Freac. Crooked, bending.

Freacar. Witnefs, teftimony.

Freacaran. } A wreftling-fchool, place
Freachnughadh. } of exercife.

Freachruigham. To exercife, accuftom, difcharge an office or duty.

Freacnairc. The prefent time.

Freadh. A pillaging, plundering.

Freagar. } An anfwer.
Freagaradh. }

Freagairt. Anfwering.

Freagaram. To anfwer, make anfwer.

Freagarthach. Anfwerable, accountable.

Freagarthoir. A refpondent, defendant.

Freagnam. To work, labour.

Freagnairc. Converfation.

Freagnamh. Labour.

Freagnaircam. To converfe.

Freagram. To anfwer.

Freagradh. An anfwer.

Freamh. } A root, ftock, lineage; found
Freamhach. } fleep.

Freamhachd. An original.

Freamhuigham. To take root, radicate.

Freamhrollam. To extirpate.

Freamhughadh. Taking root.

Freamhuinean. A fucker.

Freamhamhuil. Radical.

Freamhfhocal. An etymology.

Freancam. To make crooked, to bend.

Freancach. Winding, bending, turning.

Freapadh. Medicine.

Freapadh. Running, bouncing, fkipping, kicking.

Freafc. Upwards.

Freafabhra. Oppofition, reluctance.

Freafdal. Serving, waiting, attending, providence, lot, fate.

Freafdalach. Provident, providential.

Freafdalam. To provide, ferve, wait, or attend upon.

Freafghabhal. Afcenfion into heaven.

Freafgam. } To climb, afcend.
Freafghabham. }

Frechoimheadam. To referve.

[Y y]   Freitach.

Freitach. Vow.

Freituigham. To vow, refufe.

Fremhach. Fundamental.

Frefci. A reflection, fuppofition.

Frefcre. Brittle, withered.

Frefgadh. Climbing, waiting.

Frefligh. Anger, refentment.

Freunaidhe. A foundation.

Freunaidham. To found, eftablifh.

Fri, fria. The fame as re, air.

Fri. Vide Frith.

Frialta. Free, fried.

Fride. A tetter.

Fridhan. A briftle.

Friochnamh. Care, diligence, circumfpection.

Friochnamhach. Diligent, careful, circumfpect.

Friochtalam. To fry, parch.

Friochtan. } A frying-pan.
Friochtail. }

Friolifgam. } To turn down and open
Friofaodham. } the mouth of a fack or bag.

Friofgram. To anfwer.

Friotal. A word, interpretation.

Friotalach. Fretful, angry.

Friothbhruth. A refufal, denial.

Friothbharamhuil. } A paradox.
Friothcheadfaidh. }

Friothchantaireachd. Recantation.

Friothchoidheas. Antipathy.

Friothlanna. Streamers.

Friothoibruigham. To wriggle.

Friothola. A covenant.

Friotholamh. } Service, attendance.
Friotholadh. }

Friothalam. } To ferve, attend, admi-
Friothalaigham. } nifter.

Friotholaghadh. Attending, adminiftering.

Friotholochal. Subfervient.

Friothradham. To contradict.

Friothfailfidhear. That fhall be ferved.

Frifcart. An anfwer.

Frifcam. To hope.

Frifcis. Hope, expectation.

Frifmbeartam. To betray, deceive, kill, murder.

Frifneidh. Be told or faid.

Frifninnle. Attendance.

Friogcabhfam. To ftand up, arife.

Fritham. To find, to behave, act.

Frith. Mouth of a river, fate.

Frith. A wild mountainous place, a foreft, furly look.

Frith. Small, little.

Frith. Profit, gain, advantage.

Frithbhachd. Barb of an hook.

Frithbhaile. Suburbs.

Frithbheartam. To object, contradict.

Frithbhualadh. Palpitation, pulfation, pit-a-pat.

Frithbhuaillam. To palpitate, ftrike back.

Frithbhuille. A back ftroke, a little ftroke.

Frithbhuailteach. In mfs. on medicine, repercuffiva, healing and repelling medicines.

Frithchoille. Underwood.

Friththeitham. To fcuddle.

Frithchedfidh. A witneffing, a teftimony.

Fritheilain. A floating or fmall ifland.

Fritheoilte. Servants, attendants.

Fritheagal. Surprife.

Fritheoladh. Difpenfation.

Frithighidh. Attending, ferving, waiting.

Frithiafg. Bait for fifh.

Frithir. Earneft, eager, fervent.

Frithing. A relapfe.

Frithirach. } Fretful, peevifh.
Frithire. }

Frithleim. A quick leap.

Frithleimam. To leap, bound.

Frithne.

rithne. An uninhabited wood or mountain.

rithneasach. Fretful.

rithoigheann. A warming-pan.

rithreasa. Contradiction, peevishness.

rithshearc. A return of love, mutual regard.

rithsheasam. To resist.

ritheachd. A returning back.

rog. A fen.

rogan. Anger.

rogach. Fenny.

rogganta. Pert, lively.

roghim. Wrong, injury.

roghain. Injury.

rointhadh. A tugging or plucking.

roithlin. A whirl.

romham. To try, taste, examine, enquire.

romhadh. A trial.

romhidh. Hoarse.

romhtha. Tried, experienced.

ros. Dark, obscure.

rothal. } A whirl.
rothlan. }

u, fo, fa. Under.

uach. Word.

uachd. Cold.

uachaid. A jilt, tricking harlot.

uachas. A cry, outcry.

uachasach. A den, cave, hole.

uachda. An engraver.

uachdan. A sore or kibe on the heel.

uadh. A bier.

uadach. } A running away with, a
uadaigham. } rape.

uadachd. Robbery, depredation.

uadaigham. } To elope with, run away
uadaim. } with, to force away, impress.

uadaigheach. Ravenous.

uadh, fuath. Hatred.

Fuadhmhar. Odious, hateful.

Fuadhmhaireachd. Abomination, detestation.

Fuadar. Haste, preparation to do a thing.

Fuadarach. Active, diligent.

Fuadram. To cross or hinder.

Fuaduighte. Taken or snatched away.

Fuaghail. Sewing, stitching.

Fuaghala. A ring, thimble.

Fuagham. } To few, stitch.
Fuaigham. }

Fuagaitha. Proclaimed, published.

Fuagra. A proclamation, edict.

Fuagraim. To admonish, proclaim.

Fuaid. A remnant.

Fuaidhlean. Anger, fury.

Fuaidram. To stagger, reel.

Fuailfeadh. Leaping, skipping.

Fuailfheadan. The ureter.

Fuaim. Sound, rebounding noise, echo.

Fuaimir. Sounding.

Fuaimnach. Great noise, frequent noise, noisy.

Fuaimamhuil. Resounding, rebounding.

Fuaimnachal. Noisy.

Fuaimeturaig. Herb fumitory.

Fuairchritham. To shiver with cold.

Fuaire. Colder.

Fuaire. Coldness.

Fuairad, fuairghreadadh. A cold blast.

Fuairam. To find, discover.

Fuair, fhuair. Found.

Fual. Urine, water.

Fualachtam. To boil.

Fualan. A chamber-pot, a pimp.

Fualas. A tribe, family.

Fualascaidhe. Oziers, small twigs.

Fualbhrostach. A diuretic.

Fualiosg. The stranguary.

Fual-losgadh. Heat of urine.

Fuaman. A shade, shadow.

Fuaman. Whiteness.

Fuaman.

Fuaman. A rebound.

Fuamnain. }
Fuamnigham. } To rebound, refound.

Fuamfe. Under me.

Fuan. Cloth, a veil.

Fuanam. To cover, clothe.

Fuar. Cold, chilly.

Fuara-cluaifa. A fhip's earring.

Fuaradh. A cooling, making cold.

Fuaradh. The breeze, blaft, the windward, the weather-fide.

Fuarag. Meal and water mixed, croudy.

Fuaram. }
Fuairaigham. } To cool.

Fuaraighte. Cooled.

Fuaragham. To nourifh, cherifh.

Fuaraghadh. Cooling; eafe, relief.

Fuaralach. Cold, chilly.

Fuaralachd. Chillinefs.

Fuaran. A fpring, fountain, a water for cattle to ftand in to cool themfelves.

Fuaranta. Grown cold.

Fuarafdair. Judicious.

Fuarbheann. A cold bleak mountain.

Fuarbholadh. An ungrateful fcent, ftench.

Fuarbhodradh. Benumbing.

Fuarchrabhadh. Hypocrify, indevotion.

Fuarchraibhtheach. An hypocrite.

Fuarchrapadh. Benumbing.

Fuardachd. Coldnefs.

Fuarlite. A cataplafm.

Fuarmharbham. To ftarve with cold.

Fuarnadh. A controverfy.

Fuafcradh. Fright, terror.

Fuafcraim. To put to flight.

Fuafgaladh. A ranfom, redemption, liberty, untying.

Fuafgalam. To redeem, fet at liberty, loofe, untie.

Fuafgailte. Untied, diffolved.

Fuafgluithoir. The Redeemer, Saviour.

Fuafgailteachd. Loofenefs, eafe, opennefs, fimplicity.

Fuafnam. To aftonifh.

Fuafnuidhtheach. Tumultuous.

Fuath. Hatred, averfion, abhorrence.

Fuath a' mhaddaidh. Wolf's bane.

Fuath-muic. Hare bells.

Fuathas. }
Fuath. } An image, fpectre, apparition.
Fuaths. }

Fuatham. }
Fuathaigham. } To hate, abhor, diflike.

Fuathach. Hateful, hated.

Fuathadh. }
Fuathaghadh. } A deteftation, abhorrence.

Fuathais. A den, a cave.

Fuathafach. Dreadful, horrible, frightful.

Fuathog. Armour, a coat of mail.

Fuathmhor. Hateful.

Fubal, pubal. A general's tent, pavilion.

Fubha. A hurt or fcar.

Fubtadh. Threats, menaces.

Fucam. To full or mill cloth.

Fucadh. Fulling.

Fucadair. A fuller.

Fud. Among; air-fud, amongft.

Fufaireachd. The Irifh cry or howling at funerals.

Fug, fuigham. To find.

Fughog. A thrum, a loofe thread or end in weaving cloth.

Fugufg. Patience, perfecution, fteadinefs.

Fuibige. An argumentator, difputant.

Fuicheachd. Luft, lechery.

Fuicheal. Reward.

Fuidbh. A knob, bunch.

Fuidheach. With joy or thanks.

Fuidheal. }
Fuidhlach. } Remainder, remnant, relick.

Fuidhir. Gain, profit.

Fuidhir. A word, an hireling, a veil.

Fuidhre.

Fuidhir. A hireling.

Fuidhre. Attendants, servants.

Fuidhreach. Naked, exposed.

Fuidradh. Paste.

Fuidreachd. Mixing.

Fuidram. To mix.

Fuigheall. Judgment.

Fuigheall. A word.

Fuigham. To get, obtain.

Fuigam. To leave, forsake, abandon. Vide Fagam.

Fuighle. Words, expressions, language.

Fuighlam. To say, speak, tell, relate.

Fuil. Blood, gore.

Fuileach.
Fuileachdach. } Bloody, cruel.
Fuilteach.

Fuilchionnta. Bloodguiltiness.

Fuilchiontach. Bloodguilty.

Fuildhortadh. Bloodshed.

Fuileachd. Bloodiness, bloodshed.

Fuileadh. Encrease, profit, gain.

Fuileasan. An asp.

Fuiliat. Bloody.

Fuilidhe. Blood-red.

Fuilam. To be. Vide Bheilam.

Fuilangach. Enduring, patient.

Fuilingeach. Armed with a shield or spear.

Fuilmain. A bleeding toe, by striking it against a stone.

Fuilleadh. A reward.

Fuilsiofri. Pumice.

Fuin. The end or termination of a thing; will, purpose.

Fuineam. To kneed, bake.

Fuineadh. Baking, boiling.

Fuingeall. An idiot.

Fuinneog. A window.

Fuinnliuchath. A leaver.

Fuinnsedn.
Fuinnseann. } An ash-tree.
Fuinnseog.

Fuinnseog coille. The herb virgo pastoris.

Fuinte. Kneaded, baked.

Fuinteoir
Fuinadoir. } A baker.

Fuinteoirachd.
Fuinadoirachd. } The trade of baking.

Fuirbirneach. A strong man.

Fuireachd. Delay, staying, waiting, tarrying.

Fuirean. Croud, multitude.

Fuiras. Entertainment.

Fuirnaisaigham. To furnish, provide.

Fuirnaisaighadh. Providing, furnishing.

Fuirnam. To precipitate.

Fuireachair. Deliberate.

Fuiraigham. To stay, wait, tarry, delay.

Fuireadh. A preparation, feast.

Fuireanal. An urinal.

Fuiridhthe. Ready, prepared, sensible, antient, old.

Fuirion. Furniture, the crew of a ship, an association or body of men.

Fuirlicham. To overcome, defeat.

Fuirlughadh.
Fuirluchdin. } Overcoming.

Fuirm. A form, manner, fashion.

Fuirmeadh. Travelling, going.

Fuirmeadh. Humiliation, lessening.

Fuirmheadh. A feat, foundation.

Fuirmheal. Tired, fatigued.

Fuirmhidh. Hard.

Fuirneis. A furnace, stove.

Fuis. Active, thrifty.

Fuiscog. Vide Uiseog.

Fuite. A sound, reiterating noise.

Fuithe, fuiche, foiche. Under her, it.

Fuith. A rag of cloth.

Fuithir. Good land.

Fulair. Satis est, opus est, Cho'n fhulair, I must.

Fulang. Patience, passion, forbearance, feeling;

feeling; foundation, fhore, prop, buttrefs, a ftud, bofs.

Fulangas. Patience, endurance.

Fulangam. To bear, fuffer, endure.

Fulanga na h aigne. Affections, paffions of the mind.

Fulangach. Patient, enduring, fuffering.

Fulangaiche. A fufferer, patient.

Fulla. A lie, falfhood, untruth.

Fulla. A leaping, fkipping.

Fullon. An ornament.

Fulpanach. Articulation, or joining of things together.

Fulra. } Corruption, gore.
Fulfhruth. }

Fu'm'. Under me.

Fun. Land. Vide Fonn.

Funn. Defire.

Funfada. Lands.

Furachas. } Expectation, watching.
Furachras. }

Furachar. Watching, watchful.

Furachar mac an Ealaigh. A character in an Irifh novel.

Furail. } An offering, command, in-
Furaileamh. } citement.

Furain. Plenty, abundance.

Furas. Able.

Furafda. Eafy to do.

Furchoimheadam. To beware.

Furailam. To offer, incite, provoke.

Furan. A welcome, falutation, entertainment.

Furanach. Saluting, courteous, civil, cautious.

Furbi. } A ftrong ftout fellow, a
Furbarneach. } clown.

Furfhogradh. Precaution.

Furbaidh. Wrath.

Furmuir. A prompting, exciting.

Furm. A ftool, feat, form.

Furnaidhe. A dwelling, refting, ftaying.

Furfannam. To kindle.

Furtachd. Comfort, relief, eafe, help.

Furtaigham. To help, relieve, comfort.

Furtaighthoir. A comforter, helper.

Furtughadh. Helping, relieving, comforting.

Furthain. Satiety, fufficiency.

Furthanach. Plentiful.

Futamhuil. Foppifh.

Futha. Under them.

G.

G Is the feventh letter of the Irifh alphabet, and is called Gort, i. e. an ivy-tree, and fometimes Gath, a fpear or javelin. In the Irifh dialect it is frequently commutable with c. Before the afpirate h it forms a combined found or power, nearly like y in yellow, you, your, young. Thus ghabh is nearly yabh, and gheall, yeall. In other refpects the fame as in Englifh.

Ga. Sometimes for ag, a fign of the prefent participle.

'G a. For ag a, as 'g a thogal, raifing it.

3

Ga.

Ga. For ca, whence.

Ga, gath. A spear, javelin.

Gabaifde. Cauliflower, cabbage.

Gabh. Take thou.

Gabha. A smith. Vide Gobhadh.

Gabhach. Dangerous, perilous.

Gahhadh. Want, danger, need, occasion.

Gabhail. Taking, catching, making prisoners.

Gabhail-fhearain. A bit of land, little farm.

Gabhail. Spoil, booty, conqueft.

Gabhal-cine. The antient law of Gavel-kind, by which the lands of a house were divided amongft its branches.

Gabhal. A fork. Vide Gobhal.

Gabhal. Taking, burning into a flame.

Gabhal. A day's labour, a yoking.

Gabhal. Regio perineum. Vide Gobhal.

Gabhal. Folding; gabhal nan caorach, folding the fheep.

Gabhaltas. Land obtained by conqueft; a farm rented from a landlord.

Gabhaltuidhe. A farmer.

Gabhagan. The bird called Titling, which attends the Cuckow.

Gabhad. An artful cunning trick.

Gabhadaire. A cunning fellow.

Gabhadach. Cunning, artful.

Gabhadan. A receptacle, ftore-houfe.

Gabham. To take, receive, enlift, burn, require, to go, fing.

Gabhail. A courfe, direction.

Gabhaltach. Capable, infectious.

Gabham air. To beat.

Gabham trid. To go through.

Ghabh an teine. The fire burned.

Gabham oran. To fing.

Gabh romhad. Get you gone.

Gabhidh. Dangerous, ftrange, wonderful.

Gabhann. A gaol, prifon, a pound, flattery.

Gabhar. A gaol.

Gabhar-oiche. A fnipe.

Gabharlann. A goatfold.

Gabhar-bhreac. A bucky fnail.

Gabharach. Skipping, bouncing.

Gabhla. A fpear, lance.

Gabhlach.
Gabhlanach. } Forked, divided.

Gabhlam. To fpring, fhoot out.

Gabhlan. A branch, fork of a tree or branch.

Gabhlag. Any forked piece of timber.

Gabhlughadh. Propagation, genealogy.

Gabhlas. Hate.

Gabhluigham. To fprout.

Gabhtha.
Gabhte. } Taken, caught.

Gabhuin. A calf.

Gabhnach. A ftripper.

Gabhuin ruadh. A yearling deer.

Gabla. A cable.

Gach. Each, every.

Gad. A withe, twifted twig, or ozier.

Gadachd. Thieving, theft.

Gadam. To fteal, take away.

Gada. A bar of any thing, as iron, an ingot.

Gadtha. Stolen.

Gadaidhe. A thief.

Gadan. A voice, noife.

Gadh, gath. An arrow, dart.

Gadh. A fkirmifh, fight.

Gadh. Peril, want.

Gadham, guidham. To pray, intreat.

Gadhar. A dog, maftiff.

Gadluine. A flender feeble fellow, falmon after fpawning.

Gaduighe. A thief.

Gaduigham, gaidam. To fteal.

Gaf.
Gafa. } A hook, any crooked inftrument.

Gafann.

Gafann. Henbane.

Gag. A cleft, chink.

Gagach. Leaky, full of chinks.

Gagadh. Growing into chink.

Gagam. To grow into clefts and chinks, to split, to notch.

Gaggan. Cackling, a knot in timber.

Gaggach. Stammering in speech.

Gagganach. Noisy speech, cackling.

Gai, gaoi. A lie, untruth.

Gaibhne. Of a smith.

Gaibhneachd. A smith's trade.

Gaibhtheach. A person in want, a constant craver, complainant.

Gaid. A father.

Gaid. Theft.

Gaid. Withes.

Gaidhbhin. A little study, closet.

Gaidin. A little withe.

Gaige. A proud coxcomb.

Gaige. Stammering, stuttering.

Gail, gal. Smoke, vapour, fume.

Gail. Slaughter.

Gaile. The stomach.

Gaileach. Extraordinary.

Gailebhein. A great rough hill.

Gailbhinn. Storm at sea.

Gailbhach. Stormy at sea.

Gailchin. A fine for manslaughter.

Gailam. To evaporate, boil, seethe.

Gailin. A parasite.

Gailineach. Flattering.

Gailmheachd. Flattery, soothing.

Gaill. A sulky look.

Gaille. A chop, cheek.

Gailleach. That hath large chops.

Gaillag. A cuff, a blow on the cheek.

Gaill, adgaill He spoke to.

Gailchearc. A duke or drake.

Gailleach. The gum.

Gailleamhuin. Offence.

Gaillean. A strange or foreign bird.

Gaillian. A dart, arrow.

Gaillshion, gaill-shion. A storm.

Gaillshionnach. Stormy.

Gaillian. Leinster, a tribe of the Fir bolg.

Gailliafg. A pike.

Gaillam. To hurt.

Gaillimh. Galway.

Gaillseach. An earwig, a nimble infect dangerous to go near a person's ears.

Gaimhean. A skin, hide.

Gaimhgin. A skillet.

Gain.
Gainneach.
Gainmh.
Gainmhach. } Sand.

Gain. Clapping of hands, applause.

Gaincheap. A pillory, stocks.

Gaine. Hunger, scarcity.

Gaine. A shaft, sand.

Gaineamhait. A sandy stone.

Gaineoir. An archer.

Gaing. Jet, agate-stone.

Gainmhein. Sandy.

Gainne. Scarcer, poorer.

Gainne.
Gainnad. } Hunger, scarcity, fewness.

Gainne. A reed, cane, arrow, fin.

Gainneach. A place where reeds grow.

Gair. An outcry, rejoicing, laughter.

Gair-chath. Shout of battle.

Gair na fairge. Noise of the sea.

Gair-theas. The glittering reflection of the sun from the sea, or a rock or luminous body.

Gairbhe.
Gairbhachd.
Gairbhad. } Roughness, harshness, tartness, coarseness.

Gair-chreug. Echo.

Gairbh-aodach. A coarse garment.

Gairbhall. Big-limbed.

Gairbheoil. Big-lipped.

Gairbhin creugach. A sort of plant growing on rocks by the shore good for bruise

Gairbhfhios

Gairbhſhion. Rough weather, tempeſt, ſtorm.

Gairde. Sooner.

Gairde. Joyfulneſs.

Gairdeachas. A rejoicing, pleaſure.

Gairdain. The arm, guardian.

Gairdaingha. Brachial.

Gairdughadh. Rejoicing, congratulating

Gairduigham. To rejoice, be glad.

Gairdin. Garden.

Gaire. A laugh.

Gaireachdidh Laughter.

Gaireal. Free-ſtone.

Gaiream. To laugh.

Gaire. Reparation, amendment, good luck, uſpces

Gairedh. Laughing, bawling, calling.

Gaireadh. A vault.

Gairfecc. A dimple.

Gairg. } A diver, cormorant.
Gairgeann. }

Gairge. Fierceneſs.

Gairghean. A niece.

Gairghala An outcry.

Gairgin. Dung, ordure.

Gairgun. Stale urine.

Gairgere. A diver.

Gairgre. } A pilgrim's habit.
Gairgin. }

Gairid. Short, lately.

Gairleog Garlick.

Gairom. To extol, rejoice, laugh. Vide Gaiream.

Gairam. To call, bawl, ſhout.

Gairmam. To call, qualify, dub.

Gairm. A title, name, calling, qualification, proclamation.

Gairm-chaolaich. Cock-crowing.

Gairm poſaidh. Banns of marriage.

Gairmghille. A cryer.

Gairmſcoille. An aſſembly of bards.

Gairm-ghallan. Howling of dogs at hunting.

Gairingean. A niece.

Garraim. A ſhort form, compendium.

Gairmionnach. Nominative.

Gairrfhiach. A raven, vulture.

Gairre. Next, nearer.

Gairrigeach. Rocky, full of rocks.

Gairiſneach. Lewd, idle, naſty, terrible.

Gairſeamhuil. Wanton.

Gairſeamhleachd. Lewdneſs, debauchery.

Gairſen. Horror, ſhuddering with fear.

Gairſeicle. A ſhort life.

Gairſneach. Horrible.

Gairte. A narrow path.

Gairtein. } A garter.
Gairteil. }

Gais. A torrent, ſtream.

Gais. A ſurfeit.

Gaiſde. A gin, trap, ſnare.

Gaiſde. Armed, accoutred.

Gaiſe. A flaw.

Gaiſe. Boldneſs, valour, chivalry.

Gaiſdidhas. Painting.

Gaiſdidhe. A painter.

Gaiſge. Bravery, feats of arms.

Gaiſgeamhuil. Valiant, brave, warlike.

Geiſgeamhlachd. The doing valiant actions.

Gaiſdidheach. A champion, warrior.

Gaiſgeachd. Feats, heroiſm.

Gaiſgeanta. Brave.

Gaiſin. Scanty crops.

Gaiſam. To flow.

Gaiſte, gaiſteag. A ſnare, gin, trap, wile.

Gaiſtam. To trepan, deceive.

Gaiſtin. A crafty fellow

Gaiſtincloch. A little bird of the ſize of a wren.

Gaitin. A brief, an abridgment.

Gaithean. A ſtraight branch.

Gal, gail. Smoke, vapour.

Gal. A puff, gale, a blaſt or flame of ſtraw.

Gal. Warfare, battle.

Gal, gaol. Kindred, relations.

Gal. Weeping.

Galabhas. A paraſite.

Galach. Valour, courage, fortitude; valiant, brave.

Galan. A gallon; a noiſe.

Galann. An enemy.

Galanach. Noiſy.

Galar. A diſeaſe, diſtemper.

Galar-fuail. The gravel.

Galar-gaſda. The flux.

Galar-goilleach. The mort.

Galar-plocadh. Squinzy.

Galar-milighteach. Green-ſickneſs.

Gallidh. Hot.

Galar-teth. The rot.

Galaſtair. They ſpoke to.

Galba. Rigour, hardneſs.

Galbhaigham. To be hot or warm.

Gallbholgach. The French-pox.

Galgadh. Stout, valiant, a champion.

Galia. An helmet, a military cap, a hat.

Galic. Vide Gaoidhealg.

Gall. A ſtranger, foreigner; an Engliſhman, or Low Country Scotchman.

Gall. A rock, a ſtone, pl. gailleacha, ſtones.

Gall. A cock, a ſwan.

Gall. Milk.

Gallda. Belonging to an Engliſhman or Low Countryman; ſtrange, foreign, ſurly, poor-ſpirited.

Galldachd. Low country of Scotland.

Galoban. A dwarf.

Galltrumpa. A trumpet, clarion.

Galla. Brightneſs, beauty.

Gallchno. A walnut.

Gallad. A laſs, little girl.

Galla. A bitch.

Galluch. A rat.

Gallunach. Soap.

Galltach. A Gaul.

Gallan. A branch.

Gallan-greannchair. Tuſſilago.

Gallan-mor. Butter bur.

Gallmhuileann. A mill-wheel.

Galloglach. A cuiraſſier, ſervant.

Galldruma. A kettledrum.

Gallubh. Caithneſs.

Galopam. To galop.

Galma, galba. Hardneſs.

Galmas. A pledge.

Galrughdach. Divination.

Galoig. A ſhoe.

Galruigham. To puniſh.

Gamaineach. Scarcely, hardly.

Gamainighe. Scarcity.

Gamal A fool, ſtupid perſon.

Gamal. A camel.

Gambun. A leg.

Gamh. Winter, corn.

Gamhann. A ditch.

Gamhchogus. A dent, notch.

Gamhnach. Unbulled, of a ſtripper cow.

Gamhuin. A calf, yearling, ſtirk.

Gan. Without.

Ganail. A rail, fold.

Gangaid. Falſehood, deceit, a buſtle, light-headed creature.

Gangaideach. Falſe, deceitful, light-headed, pitiful, narrow-hearted.

Gangaideachd. Craft, knavery, deceit.

Gann. Scarce, little, ſhort, difficult.

Gannail. Lattices.

Ganndas. A grudge.

Ganra. A gander.

Gantan. Hunger.

Gantir. A priſon, dilemma.

Gaod. A ſwan.

Gaoi. Prudence, wiſdom.

Gaoi, go. Untruth, a lie.

Gaoid. Wind, blaſts, flatulence.

Gaoidbhein. A mountain in the iſle of Arran.

Gaoideanta. Idle, ſlothful.

Gaoidheann.

Gaoidheann. Falfe colour, counterfeit.

Gaog. Evaporation, flatnefs; air dol a ghaog, dead.

Gaoidhal. An Irifhman, Highlander of Scotland.

Gaogan. Part of a thread fpun finer than it ought to be

Gaoil A family, or kindred; love.

Gaoidhleag. The Irifh, Gaelic, or old Celtic tongue.

Gaoidhealtachd. The Highlands of Scotland

Gaoilam. To boil, feethe.

Gaoil. Boiling, anger.

Gaoilach. Boiling.

Gaoine. Good.

Gaoine. Goodnefs, honefty.

Gaoirbh. The paunch of a deer.

Gaois, gaos. Wifdom, prudence.

Gaoifid. Hair of beafts.

Gaoifnain. A fingle hair.

Gaoith, gaoth. Wind.

Gaoithreog. A blaft, or blowing.

Gaol. Love, liking, fondnefs.

Gaolin. Sweetheart.

Gaolach. A dear, mo ghaolach, my dear.

Gaolbhola. Confanguinity.

Gaolam. To break.

Gaolach. Lovely.

Gaorfte. A whirlwind.

Gaorr. Dirt, dirt contained in the inteftines.

Gaoiram. To cram, glut.

Gaoran. A little glutton.

Gaofmhor. Prudent, fkilful, occafion.

Gaofneach. Hairy.

Gaoth. A dart, a ftitch, fhooting pain.

Gaoth. The wind.

Gaothruadh. A blafting wind, mildew.

Gaoth ghuartain. A whirlwind.

Gaoth. The fea.

Gaoth. Wife, prudent.

Gaoth. Pains.

Gaoth. Theft.

Gaotha. Streams left at low water.

Gaoth-near. Eaft-wind.

Gaoth-niar. Weft-wind.

Gaoth-deas. South-wind.

Gaoth-tuath. North-wind.

Gaothach. ⎫
Gaothanach. ⎬ Windy.
Gaothmhor. ⎭

Gaothmheigh. Anemometer.

Gaothmhor. Painful.

Gaothinnifan. Anemofcope.

Gaothmhar. A painful wound.

Gaothmhaireachd. Pain, great anguifh, flatulence, ftorm.

Gaothraigham. To winnow.

Gar. Defert, merit, accommodation.

Gar, car. Near, nigh to, foon, ann gar, at hand.

Gara, garach. Ufeful.

Garab. Not clofe.

Garabhan. Bran.

Garachdal. Huge.

Garach. A brawl.

Garachdalachd. Hugenefs.

Garadan. A regifter, note-book.

Garadh. A gratuity.

Garadh. A garden, hedge, dyke.

Garadh. A hiding place for wild beafts, den, cave.

Garaileamhathair. The great-grandfather, fifter, abamita.

Garam. To gratify.

Garam. To warm.

Garamhuil. Near, neighbouring, warm, fnug, comfortable.

Garan. An underwood, foreft, thicket.

Garan, guirain. A blotch.

Garathair. A great-grandfather, tritavus.

Garbanach. Rude, raw, unexperienced.

Garbhag-garaidh. Savory.

Garbh. Rough, coarfe, rugged, boifterous.

Garbhanach. A tall ftout fellow.

Garbhthonn.

Garbhthonn. A boisterous wave.

Garbhshion. A tempest.

Garbhach. A grandson.

Garbhait. A rough place.

Garbhchludach. A coarse blanket, coverlet.

Garbhchulaidh. A frieze-coat.

Garbhchrioch. A rough country, the Highlands of Scotland.

Garbhghaineamh. Gravel.

Garbhan. Bran.

Garbhleass. A shout.

Garbhlocc. A crag, a thicket.

Garbhleach. The rugged part of a country.

Garda. A guard, garden.

Gardrich. A troop, company.

Garg. Austere, fierce, cruel, rough, firm; sore.

Gargachd. ⎫ Rudeness, roughness, cruelty;
Gargad. ⎬ soreness.

Gargin. Dung.

Garidh. A cave.

Garlach. A young infant because it screams; a naked starving child; a bastard.

Garluch. A mole.

Garmadh. A calling.

Garmadair. A cryer, proclaimer.

Garmain. A post, pillar, a beam.

Garman. A gallows.

Garmhathair. A great-grandmother.

Garnaloir. A gardener.

Garneal. An ark, or magazine to hold meal in.

Garoid. A splutter, noise.

Garoighe. The next.

Garrach. Gorbellied.

Garran. A strong or hackney horse. Vide Gearran.

Garran. A grove, or wood.

Garran. A glutton, gorbelly.

Garran gainmhaich. A certain little fish.

Garrbhuaic. A noise, clamour.

Garrbhuaiceach. Clamorous, noisy.

Garrdha. Of a garden.

Garrfhiach. A glutton.

Garrthoir. A cryer, bawler.

Garruicam. To prattle, prate.

Garruicachd Prating.

Garrunnach. Dirty, shocking, horrible.

Gart. Liberality, bounty.

Gart. A head, a threatening posture

Gart. Standing corn.

Gartan. A bonnet, cap, hat.

Gartghlanam. To weed, examine.

Gartha. ⎫
Garthaich. ⎬ A shout or great cry.

Garthal. Warm, snug.

Gartlann. A corn-yard.

Garua, garogha. A great-grandchild's grandchild. Adnepos.

Gas. A bunch, bough, stalk, stem of an herb, a military servant, a boy.

Gaspidam. A hornet.

Gasach. Bushy.

Gasra. ⎫ A band of domestic troops, anciently mercenary soldiers.
Gasradh. ⎬

Air gasradh. Proud, hot as a bitch.

Gas. Strength, anger, wrath.

Gai sguabaidh. A besom, broom.

Gas, gus. Unto, to.

Gasam. To shout, sprout, to look.

Gascorbhthach. A midwife.

Gasg. A tail.

Gasgan. A puppy.

Gasganach. Petulant.

Gasgara. The posteriors.

Gast. A snare, wile.

Gast. An old woman.

Gasda. Clever, neat, ingenious, skilful

Gastachd. Ingenuity, cleverness, neatness.

Gastog. A wile, trick.

Gasun. A boy, a little sorry fellow, garçon.

Gath. A spear, javelin, a ray or beam, a sting.

Gath-dubh. A weed, the beard of corn.

Gath-cuip. A medical tent.

Gath-bolg. A trunk for blowing darts.

Gath-muinne. A mane.

Gath-greine. A fun-beam.

Gath-fruigh. A poifoned arrow.

Ge, ce. The earth.

Ge, gedh, Geadh. A goofe.

Ge. As, whence.

Ge as air bith. Whence foever.

Ge, for ce. Who? which? what?

Ge. Though, although.

Geabhaire. } A carper.
Geabhfaire.

Geabham. To find, behave.

Geabhthaigheas. Fear, dread.

Geachdaidheachd. A debate.

Gead. A buttock, haunch.

Gead. A fpot, a ftar in the forehead of a horfe.

Geada. A ridge, bed, or fmall fpot of ground.

Geadh. A goofe, a taylor's iron.

Geadhlann. A goofe quill.

Geadh-dubh. A fpecies of goofe.

Geadha. A pole, a boat-hook.

Geadus. A pike.

Geag, geug. A bough, branch, limb, member.

Geagach. Having branches.

Geagamhuil. Branched, having boughs or branches.

Geagam. To branch, bud, fprout forth.

Geal. Fair, white, bright.

Gealadhairc. An animal with a white horn, the name of a cow.

Gealadhairceach. White-horned.

Gealchos. White-foot, name of a dog.

Gealan. The white of the eye.

Gealacan. The white of an egg.

Gealach. The moon.

Gealaigham. To whiten, bleach.

Gealaighte. Whitened, bleached.

Gealadh. Whitenefs.

Gealairgidh. A prickle.

Gealbhhunn. } A fparrow, a common
Gealun. } fire.

Gealbhan lion. A linnet, lintwhite.

Gealcadh. Whitenefs.

Gealcam. To whiten.

Geall } A pledge, mortgage, bet,
Geall-barantus. } defire.

Geal-daingnuchidh. Earneft-money.

Gealladh. A promife.

Geallam. To promife, devote.

Geallamhna. A promifing, promife.

Geallmhor. Defirous.

Geallmhorachd. Defire.

Geallamhuin. Promife, vow.

Geallag-bhuachair. The bird called bunting.

Geallog. A falmon-trout, a white-falmon, an eel.

Gealfhuileach. Moon-eyed.

Geallta. Promifed.

Gealta. Whitened.

Gealltin. Promifing.

Gealtach. Timorous, fearful, jealous, aftonifhed.

Gealtachd. Timoroufnefs, fear.

Gealtaighe. Jealoufy

Gealtanas. Act of promifing.

Gealtuigham. To dread, fear.

Gealta. A bleecher, fuller.

Gealtuire. } A coward.
Gealtran.

Gealltholl. A horfe-leech.

Geam. A jem, jewel.

Geamanach. A fervant, lacquey.

Geamhar. A blade of corn, corn in grafs or blade.

Geamh. } A branch, flip.
Geamhag.

Geamhladh. A chain, fetter.

Geamhlag. A crow of iron, lever.

Geamhloch. Sandblind.

Geamhradh. Winter.

Geamhrachal. Wintry.

Gean. Fondness, love, favour, approbation.

Gean. A woman.

Geanach. Of a pleasant humour.

Geanach. Greedy, covetous. Vide Gionach.

Geanachd. Chastity.

Geanaidham. To deride.

Geanair. January.

Geamhshuileach. Pink-eyed.

Geanair. Was conceived, or born.

Geanamhlachd. Grace, beauty, comeliness.

Geanamhuil. Graceful, comely, acceptable.

Geanamhna. Chaste, pure.

Geanas. Chastity.

Geanasach. Chaste, modest.

Geangam. To strike, beat.

Geanmchnu. A chesnut.

Geanmhaidhe. Pure, chaste, incorrupt.

Geanmnaidheachd. ⎫
Geanamhnachd. ⎬ Chastity.
Geanasachd. ⎭

Geangam. To strike, beat.

Geangachd. Comeliness.

Geanmath. Good-will.

Geannaire. A hammer, mallet.

Geannaireachd. Hammering, sharpening.

Gearr. Short, shortly.

Gearaghadh. A soliciting, enticing.

Gearbhreac. A guillemot.

Geraigham, rather geuraigham. To sharpen.

Gearait. Holy, a saint.

Gearait. Wise, prudent.

Gearait. A virgin.

Gearam, geuram. To whet, sharpen.

Gearan. A complaint, supplication, groan, sigh.

Gearanaicham. ⎫
Gearanam. ⎬ To complain, condole.

Gearanach. Accusative, complaining.

Gearb. A scab.

Gearba. Bran, the itch, a tumour.

Gearbach. Scabbed, rugged.

Gearbam. To grieve, hurt, wound.

Gearblasda. Tart, sour.

Gearcaiseadh. Smartness, briskness.

Gearchuise. Subtilty, sagacity.

Gearchuiseach. Ingenious, shrewd, subtile

Geardhearc. A birberry.

Gearg. A botch, bile.

Gearg, garg. Fierce, cruel.

Geargha. A short dart, javelin.

Gearghlais. A gloss, short note.

Gearleanam. To pursue, eagerly, persecute.

Gearleanmhuin. Persecution.

Gearmhagadh. A sarcasm, bitter jest.

Gearmheasach. Neat.

Gearradh. A tax, tribute.

Gearradh. A cut, rent.

Gearrchumhain. A pack-saddle.

Gearr. Short, a ware for catching fish.

Gearradair. A cutter.

Gearram. To cut, bite, gnaw, shorten.

Gearachoileir. Assassin, cut-throat.

Gearradh-guirt. A quail.

Gearghath. A short javelin.

Gearran. A work-horse, hack.

Gearcuig. A brood.

Gearrearballach. Bobtailed.

Gearchuisle. Venesection.

Gearrchosach. Short-footed.

Gearran-ard. A hobby.

Gearrasgian. A dirk, stilletto.

Gearrfhiadh. A hare.

Gearrfhoirm. An abstract, abridgment.

Gearrghuin. A horse-leech.

Gearrmhagadh. A sarcasm.

Gearrog. Fortune, fate, destiny.

Gearrshaoghlach. Short-lived.

Gearr-sporan. A cut-purse.

Gearrshuileach. Short-sighted.

Gearsmachd. Severity, wrath.

Gearsom. Entrance-money.

Geart.

Geart. Milk.

Gearthach. A flux.

Gearthoir. A carver, hewer.

Gearuigheachd. Railing, satirizing.

Gearuigham. To whet, sharpen, to scold, exasperate.

Gearun. A gerund.

Geasa. A conjecture, guess, religious vow, oath, enchantment, charm.

Geasa droma draoitheachda. A kind of Druidish sorcery, explained at large by Dr. Keating.

Geasadan. A shrub.

Geasadair. A wizzard, charmer.

Geasadoirachd. Divination, sorcery.

Geasam. To divine, foretell.

Geasan. An oath.

Geasrogadh. Superstition, superstitious ceremonies.

Geast, giost. Barm, yeast.

Geastal. A deed, fact.

Geastal. Want, need, necessity.

Geat. Milk.

Geata, geatadh. A gate.

Geatram. To adorn, make neat.

Ged. But.

Gedal. A reed.

Gedas. A pike-fish.

Gedh A goose.

Geibheal, geall. A pledge.

Geibheal, geimhal. Chains, fetters.

Geibham. To get, obtain.

Geibhion. Fetters, prison, any great distress.

Geibleid. A sloven.

Geibleidach. Slovenly.

Geibleidachd. Slovenliness.

Geibhis. A valley.

Geibhligham. To fetter, put in chains; to pledge, mortgage.

Geideal. A fan.

Geilfhreagradh. A stipulation, a reply.

Geilios. Traffic.

5

Geil. Meaning, sense, expression, for ceill, from ciall; cuiram ann geill, I will declare.

Geille. Gives, fetters.

Geille. }
Geill. } Submission, obedience.

Geilligham. }
Geillam. } To serve, obey, do homage.

Geillachdin. Obeying, reverencing, humbling.

Geillios. Kindness, friendship

Geillsine. Submission, homage.

Geilmin. A pilchard.

Geill, ingeilt. Pasture.

Geilt. Terror.

Geilt. A wild man or woman, a silvestrous person.

Geilt. Mad.

Geimhean. Restraint, bondage.

Geimhleachd. A bond or chain.

Geimhre. Of winter.

Geimhream. To winter, to take winter-quarters.

Geimeam, geimneam. To low, bellow.

Geimreach, geimneach. Lowing, bellowing.

Gein. A conception, offspring.

Geinn. A wedge.

Geinnam. To press, squeeze.

Geinnamhuil. Cuneiform.

Geinadh. Generation, springing forth.

Geinealach. A genealogy, pedigree, family.

Geineamhuin. A birth.

Geineamhuineach. Genitive.

Geinearalta. General.

Geineog. A gem.

Geinam. To beget children, to generate.

Geiniolach. A family, stock, generation.

Geinmotha. Except, save only.

Geinnag. A pundle.

Geinteoir. A sower, planter.

Geintilach A Gentile, Pagan.

Geintileachas.

Geintileachas. }
Geintileas. } Paganifm, idolatry.

Geir. Suet.

Geire. More fharp, harfh.

Geire, geirad, geiraichad. Sharpnefs, fournefs, tartnefs.

Geireach. Greafy.

Geiram, geirgham. To whet, greafe.

Geirintleachd. Sagacity, fubtilty.

Germhinughadh. A glofs, or fhort comment.

Geirneal. A granary.

Geirre A brief, abridgment.

Geirnin. A fnare.

Geirrfeach. A girl.

Geirrfgiath. A fhort fhield.

Geis. A cuftom, an order; geifa na Teamhra, the cuftoms of Tara.

Geis. A vow, protefting againft a thing, a prohibition or injunction.

Geis. A prayer.

Geis. A fwan.

Geifas buar namhad fri fhleagha. That obtains the cattle of his foes by his fpear.

Geifeadh. Intreaty.

Geifg. A creaking noife, creak, roar.

Geifgal. }
Geifgadh. } Creaking.

Geifgam. To creak, roar, clung.

Geifneach. Enchanted.

Gen. A fword.

Gen. A hurt, wound.

Genchrios. A fword-belt.

Gendeabham. To fence.

Gendreanaire. A fencer.

Gendreanam. To fence, fcuffle.

Generalta. General, univerfal.

Gentlidhach. A Gentile, heathen.

Geocach. A ftroller, vagabond, glutton.

Geocachd. Gluttony.

Geocaigham. To ftroll, gormandize, devour.

Geochd. A wry-neck.

Geochdach. Having a wry-neck.

Geocamhail. Strolling, gluttonous.

Geocaire. A debauchee.

Geocthoir. A reveller, debauchee.

Geodhlann. A goofe-pen.

Geoidh. Geefe.

Geogna. A hurt, wound.

Geolach. Shoulder-bands put on dead men in the highlands.

Geolach ort. A common highland imprecation.

Geolthadh. A yawl.

Geoin. A confufed noife.

Geoin. A fool, foolifh perfon.

Geoilrean. }
Geolan. } A fan.

Geofadan. A fmall ftalk, fhaft, arrow.

Geofan. The belly.

Geoth, gaoth. Wind.

Geoth. The fea, ocean.

Geothadh. A bay or creek.

Getar. To hurt, wound.

Geuga. A branch, a man's arms.

Geugach. Branchy.

Geugam. To branch out.

Geulran. A fan.

Geurfhocal. Witticifm, gibe.

Geurfhocalach. Full of repartee.

Geurainachd. Paffing wit.

Geurachdach. Sharp.

Geuraigham. To fharpen, four, to whet.

Geuraghadh. Souring, fharpening.

Geufchuireach. Strict, rigorous.

Geur. Sharp, four, edged.

Geurad. Sharpnefs, fournefs.

Geurchaifeadh. Sharpnefs.

Geurag-bhilach. The herb agrimony.

Geurchluais. Short notice, quick hearing.

Geurchuife. Subtilty.

Geurchuifeach. Subtle.

Geure. Sharper.

Geurg. A bile.

Geurgach

Geurgath. A dart, javelin.

Geurinntleacbd. Subtilty.

Geurinntleachdach. Subtle.

Giabhair. A proftitute, a whore.

Gial, giall. The jaw, cheek.

Giallbhrat. A neckcloth.

Gialla. Softnefs.

Giall, gialla. Hoftages, a pledge.

Giamh. A defect.

Giamhach. Defective.

Gianach. Lazy.

Gianaire. A lazy perfon.

Gibbach. Rough, hairy.

Gibbaichad. Roughnefs.

Gibbog. A little fheaf, bundle.

Gibbogan. A fringe.

Gibhis, geibhis. A glen, valley.

Gibne. Thread.

Gibne. A cupping-horn.

Gibne. A greyhound.

Gidh. Who, what.

Gidh b'e air bhith. Whofoever.

Gidh, Giodh. } Although, though.
Gidheadh. }

Gidhrean. A barnacle.

Gigill. Tickling.

Giglam. To tickle.

Gighis. A mafquerade.

Gighifairachd. Mafquerading.

Gil. Water.

Gilab. A chifel.

Gilabam. To chifel.

Gilaid. A little creek.

Gile. }
Gileachd. } Whitenefs.
Gilead. }

Gile. Whiter.

Gille, giolla. A man-fervant, a ftripling, a male.

Gillagan. A doll.

Gille mu leann. A fea-weed like a rope.

Gille-boidhre. A fox.

Gille-mirain. A whirlgig.

Gille-bride. An oyfter-catcher.

Gille-gorman. Corn fcabious.

Gillefuinbrinn. A periwinkle.

Gilleachafionn. } A periwinkle that dyes
Gillefionntruin. } purple.

Gilmeinach. Dainty.

Gilm. A buzzard.

Gilnemhog. A water-adder.

Gimleach. One fettered.

Gimlaid. A gimlet.

Ginn. A wedge.

Ginealach. A genealogy, pedigree, family, race.

Gineamhuin. A bud, fprout, birth.

Ginel. Species, race, ftock, lineage.

Ginnel. An order of battle in the form of a triangle, or wedgewife.

Ginan. To beget, bud, fprout.

Gintin. Begetting, growing.

Giob. The tail, rug.

Giobach. Rough, hairy.

Giobaichad. Roughnefs.

Giobal. A garment, canvas, caft clothes; fur, hair, a rag, clout.

Giobalach. Full of hairs, ragged.

Giobam. To tear, tug, pull.

Giobadh. A pull, tug.

Giobag. A rag, a little fheaf or bundle.

Giobogach. Ragged.

Giodal. Flattery.

Giodar. Dung, ordure.

Giodh. Although, though.

Giodhran A barnacle.

Giodheadh. However.

Giodhtrachd. Neverthelefs, howbeit; ufed when the thread of a ftory is refumed; jam vero.

Giofach. Dutiful, officious.

Giofachd. Officioufnefs.

Giofaire. A client.

Giofog. A female client, a gipfey.

Giogach. A bag, budget.

I

Giogadh.

Giogadh. Cringeing.

Giogailam. To follow, purfue.

Gioghram. A plain.

Giogun. A thiftle.

Giole. A broom, reed, cane.

Giolcamhuil. Made of broom, reed, or cane.

Giolcanach. Reedy.

Gioleog. A reed.

Gioladh. Leaping nimbly.

Giolcair. A flippant fellow.

Giolcanachd. Flippancy.

Giolbheifd. A Naiad.

Giolam. ⎫
Giolaman. ⎬ Tattling.
Giolmanachd. ⎭

Giolmanach. Tattler.

Giolam-goilam. Tittle-tattle.

Giolla. A man-fervant, lacquey.

Giolla-coife. A footman, runner, forerunner.

Giolla-carbaid. A coachman, poftillion, charioteer.

Giolla-copain. A cup-bearer.

Giolla-graidh. A fecretary, confident, chief fervant.

Giolladha an t fluaigh. An army's baggage, alfo the fervants of the army.

Giolla-fguain. A train-bearer.

Giolla-each. A groom, oftler.

Giolla-botin. Boot-catcher.

Giolla-brog. A fhoe-black.

Giolla-muchain. A chimney-fweeper.

Giollamhuil Belonging to fervants.

Giollachd. Service, management of an affair, conduct.

Giollas. Service.

Giolmham. To folicit.

Giomach. A lobfter.

Giomanach. A hunter.

Giomh. A fault, a lock of hair.

Giomhreann. A part.

Gion. Will, defire.

Gion. The mouth.

Gionach. Hungry, keen, gluttonous, voracious.

Gionachd. Hunger, gluttony.

Gionaire. A greedy-gut.

Gionbhair. January.

Giorac. Noife, talking.

Gioracach. Noify, talkative.

Gioracam. To prattle, chat.

Giorradain. A periwinkle.

Giorag. Dread, fear Vide Giorac.

Gioraman. A hungry fellow.

Gioramhach. Greedy.

Gioramhachd. Greedinefs, covetoufnefs.

Giorra. Shorter.

Giorrach. Short and dry heath or hair.

Giorraide. ⎫
Giorta. ⎬ A buttock, haunch.

Giorruifge. Inconfiderate.

Giortolam. To patch, mend.

Giofcan. The noife of a wheel or door, gnafhing.

Giofcan-fhiacal. Gnafhing of teeth.

Giofg. ⎫
Giofgain. ⎬ Barm, yeaft.

Gioftairas. Old-age.

Gioftal. A fact, deed.

Giota. An appendage, dependance.

Girt. A girth, cingle.

Girtam. To tie a girth, lace.

Gifeil. A line.

Giubhas. Fir, pine-tree.

Giubhal. Chirping noife of birds.

Giubhafach. Fir-wood.

Giuban. A fly.

Giucram. Complaining noife, moaning

Giuig. A drooping chilly attitude

Giugach. Drooping, starved.

Giulan. Bearing, carrying, a burial, funeral.

Giulan. Conduct, converfation, comportment.

Giulam. To follow.

Giulanam.

Giulanam. To bear, suffer, carry; to comfort, behave.

Giullachadh. Cherishing.

Giurrad. Shortness.

Giuran. The gills of a fish.

Giurre. Shorter.

Giusta. A cann, tankard.

Giustal. The games or athletic exercises used formerly by the Irish at their aonachs, or aontheachd, or public meetings.

Glac. The palm of the hand, a prong, fork, quiver.

Glac   } A narrow glen, glacag nam fea
Glacag.   } dan, the valley of blasts.

Glacach. A strain in the hand, a disease in the hand so called.

Glacan. A prong, fork.

Glacanach. } Forked.
Glacach.   }

Glacadan. A repository.

Glacadoir. A receiver.

Glacadh. Acceptance, receiving, feeling

Glacam. To accept, take, receive, seize, apprehend, feel.

Glacaireachd. An impress.

Glaclach.   } A handful, bundle.
Glacallach. }

Glacleabhar. A pocket-book.

Glacoin. A bundle, a faggot.

Glactha. Handled, taken, seized.

Glacal   } Seizing, handling, taking.
Glacin }

Gladaire. A gladiator.

Glaedh. Vide Glaodh.

Glaedh. Broad.

Glafaire. A babbler.

Glafar.   }
Glafarnach.   } Noise, din, prating, chatting.
Glafoide.   }

Glagan. The clapper of a mill.

Glagan-doruis. The knocker of a door.

Glagaitha. Flowing, slowly, sluggish.

Glagaire. } A talkative person.
Glaigin.   }

Glaib. Dirty water, puddle.

Glaic. A handful, grasp, little glen.

Glaidineachd. Gluttony.

Glaicais. Wrestling.

Glaicaisach. Athletic.

Glaimh. } A great noise, clamour, pitiful
Glaim.   } complaint, a common report, a yelling, howling.

Glaimhin. A spendthrift

Glaimm. A large mouthful, gobbet.

Glaimsair. A voracious eater, muncher.

Glammam. To eat voraciously, cry out, bawl.

Glamham. To catch at greedily.

Glamhaire. One that catcheth at greedily.

Glamhaireachd. Catching at with greediness.

Glamhfan. Murmur.

Glamhfoir. Murmurer.

Glaimhnigham. To roar, cry out.

Glaine. Cleanness, brightness.

Glaine. Cleaner, more bright.

Glaineachd. } Clearness, neatness.
Glainad.   }

Glaineadoir. Vide Gloinadoir.

Glainne. Glass

Glainne-cian-amharc. A telescope.

Glainfiach. A glutton.

Glaise. Poverty.

Glaise.   } Greyness, a shade, eclipse,
Glaiseachd. } greenness, verdure.

Glaise. More green.

Glaisain. A sort of fish.

Glaisain-daraich. A green-finch.

Glais-leun. Pepper-grass, lesser spearwort.

Glaisain-scalaich. A willy-wagtail.

Glait. Prepared.

Glam. An outcry, a shout, noise.

Glamaire.

Glamaire. A noify, filly fellow.

Glamaireachd. A conftant babbling.

Glamhin. A fpendthrift.

Glan. Clean, pure, fincere.

Glanam. To cleanfe, purge, purify.

Glanadh. Wafhing, cleanfing.

Glanamhuil. Abftergent.

Glang. A fhoulder.

Glanlabhradh. Clearnefs of expreffion.

Glanlach. A fence, dike.

Glanlaigham. To fence, enclofe, intrench.

Glanmhan. Clean wheat.

Glanbhar. A good head of hair.

Glanta. Clean, wafhed.

Glantaibhreadh. Clearnefs of expreffion, evidence.

Glantoireachd. Cleanfing, weeding.

Glanthoileach. Curious.

Glaodh. Birdlime, glue.

Glaodn. A call.

Glaodham. To call, bawl out, to glue.

Glaodhach. Calling out, bawling.

Glaodh a chaolaich. Cock-crow.

Glaodhan. Pith of wood.

Glaoidh. A heap, a pile.

Glaoghan. Pipes, tubes.

Glaoidheamhin. A wolf.

Glaoine. Glafs, cleannefs.

Glaoran. Flower of wood-forrel.

Glaothar. A noife, prating.

Glaotharanta. Noify, prating.

Glaothran. A rattle.

Glas. A lock.

Glas. Grey, green, pale, wan, poor.

Glafdidh. Pale, wan.

Glafaire. A prattler.

Glafam. To lock, fetter, become green.

Glafamhuil. Greenifh, pale, wan, greyifh.

Glafan. A fort of edible alga, fea wrack, any fallad.

Glafbhan. Pale.

Glafghort. A green plot.

Glafliath. Greyifh.

Glafmhaigh. A green field.

Glafneulach. Pale.

Glafog. A water-wagtail.

Glafruighe. Greens to eat.

Glafruigham. To make green, to prepare green thread for ufe.

Glaf-uaine. Green.

Glasfheur. Grafs.

Gle. Pure, clean.

Gle. Open, plain.

Gle. Good.

Gle. Enough, perfectly, a compofitive particle.

Gleac. A fight, conflict.

Gleacam. To wreftle, ftruggle.

Gleacaidhe. A combatant.

Gleachas. A gallery.

Gleadh. } Tricks, fham, humour.
Gleadhna. }

Gleagham. To bear leaves; to keep, fave.

Gleaghadh. Induftry.

Gleaghtach. Frugal, faving.

Gleghlan. Bright, clear, immaculate.

Gleghlanam. To purify, fpiritualize.

Glegheal. Exceeding fair, or white.

Gleghrach. A loud cry, fhout.

Gleair. Neat, clean, tair.

Gleal. Exceeding white or clear.

Gleghealaigham. To blanch or whiten.

Gleamhfach. Tedious.

Gleamhfa. A flow long draught of liquor.

Gleamhfan. Continual fpeaking.

Gleanam. } To adhere, to ftick clofe
Gleannam. } to.

Gleann. A valley, vale.

Gleangarfach. Tinkling.

Gleannach. } Of or belonging to a valley,
Gleanntamhuil. } ley, fteep, fhelving.

Gleannan. A little valley, defile.

Glearam. To follow.

Glearthach.

Glearthach. Pliable, flexible.

Gleas. A manner, order, condition, lock of a gun, key or gamut, inftrument.

Gleafam, gleufam. To prepare, make ready, to tune.

Gleafann A ftorehoufe.

Gleafta. Provifion.

Gleafta. Prepared, tuned, provided, good-humoured.

Gleafdachd. Neatnefs, readinefs, order, good-humour.

Gleaftoir. A farrier.

Gleic. Wreftling, joftling,

Gleicein. A fhuttlecock.

Gleicam. To wreftle.

Gleicair. A wreftler.

Gleigheal. Vide Glegheal.

Gleile. } Whitenefs, purenefs.
Gleileachd. }

Gleile. Much, plenty, a great deal.

Gleire. Choice, election.

Gleirmeifi. A commiffioner.

Gleitham, gleagham. To keep, fave, to clear up, manifeft, cleanfe.

Gleithaire. A gadbee.

Gleithe. Grazing.

Gleith. Pure, neat.

Gleo. A fight, uproar, tumult, difturbance.

Gleogh. A figh, groan.

Gleodh. Cleanfing, fcouring, polifhing, flumber.

Gleodham. To cleanfe.

Gleodhamanachd. Drowfinefs.

Gleodhman. A drowfy fellow.

Gleoid. A floven.

Gleoidal. Slovenly.

Gleoite. Handfome, curious, tight, pretty, neat.

Gleofathach. Expert, clever.

Gleorann. Creffes.

Gleofg. A'vain fil'y woman.

Gleofgaire. A vain ftupid fellow.

I

Gleogairachd. Stupid geftures.

Gleothan. A clue.

Gleten. Glue.

Glethe. Clean.

Gleus. Order, lock of a gun, key or gamut. Vide Gleas.

Gleufam. To prepare, tune.

Gleufta. Prepared, tuned.

Gliadh, gliath. War, battle.

Gliadrach. A drab.

Glib. A lock of hair, flut.

Glib. Slippery.

Glibfhleamhin. Slippery with fleet.

Glic. Wife, prudent, cunning, crafty.

Glidduicham. To move, ftir.

Glifid. A noife.

Glifram. To prate, make a noife.

Glin. A generation. Vide Glun.

Glingin. Drunkennefs.

Glinam. To follow, to cling.

Glinn. Light, the fky.

Glinn. A fort, fortrefs, garrifon.

Glinn. Clear, plain.

Glinn. Of a valley, vallies.

Glinnach. Full of vallies.

Glinne. A habit, cloak.

Glinneaftar; le neart De do ghlinneaftar. Hoc virtus Dei præftitit. Brogan in vita S. Brig.

Glinnigh, glinn. Manifeft, clear.

Glinnuigham. To obferve clofely, fee clearly.

Glinntheach. Flexible, pliant.

Gliocas. Prudence, ingenuity, craft, cunning.

Gliogar. }
Gliogarfnach. } A tinkling ringing noife.
Gliofgarnaich. }

Gliogar. Slownefs.

Gliogaram. To ring, tinkle.

Gliomach. A lobfter, a long-limbed fellow.

Gliomach-fpaintach. A craw-fifh.

Gliongam.　A jingling noife, chink.

Gliofaire.　A prattling fellow.

Glioftaire.　A clyfter.

Gliugal.　Clucking of a hen.

Gliumh.　Glue.

Gliuftachd.　Slownefs.

Glocan.　Vide Glacan.

Glochar.　｝Breathing, refpiration with

Glocharnach.　｝difficulty, wheezing.

Glocaire.　A lubberly coward.

Glocnid.　The morning dram in bed.

Glochdan.　A wide throat.

Glogluinn.　Rolling of the fea in a calm.

Glog.　A foft lump.

Gloine.　Glafs.

Gloilionta.　Crammed.

Gloinadoir.　A glazier.

Gloich.　An ideot.

Gloichal.　Ideotical.

Gloichalachd.　Ideotifm.

Gloir.　Glory, talk.

Gloirais.　Boafting talk, prating.

Gloiraifach.　Boafting, babbling, verbofe.

Gloraigham.　To glorify.

Gloirmhiann.　Ambition.

Gloirmhiannach.　Ambitious, proud, vain-glorious.

Gloir-reim.　Pomp, triumph, pageantry

Gloiflionta.　Full-ftuffed, crammed, thick-fet.

Gloitireachd.　Gluttony.

Glomuin.　The evening.

Glomhar.　An inftrument tied to the mouth of a lamb to prevent its fucking.

Glonaid.　A multitude.

Glonnmhar.　Loathing.

Glonn.　A fact, deed

Glonn.　A loathing, qualm.

Glonnra.　Glittering.

Glor.　A noife, voice, fpeech.

Glor.　Clear, neat, clean.

Glorach.　Noify, clamorous.

Gloram.　To found, make a noife.

Gloramas.　Boafting talk.

Glormhar.　Glorious, famous, celebrated.

Glormhaoidham.　To boaft.

Glormheid.　Boafting.

Glotain.　A bofom.

Gloth.　Wife, prudent, difcreet.

Gloth.　A veil, covering.

Glothagach　Frog-fpawn.

Gluair.　Pure, clean, clear.

Gluaireachd.　Brightnefs, neatnefs.

Gluais.　A device, invention.

Gluais　Move thou.

Gluaifmhinughidh.　Gloffes, explications.

Gluaife.　Cleannefs, neatnefs.

Gluaifam.　To go, pafs, move, march.

Gluaifdeach.　Affecting, moving, pathe-tick.

Gluaifte.　Moved, ftirred, provoked.

Gluafachd.　Gefture, motion, pathos, ftir-ring, difturbing, provoking.

Gluafog, glafog.　A water-wagtail.

Glug.　The motion and noife of water con-fined in a veffel.

Glugan.　Rolling like a fhip at fea.

Glugaire.　One that has an impediment in his fpeech.

Glugach.　Stammering.

Gluganach.　Rolling, unfteady, totter-ing.

Gluine.　The knees.

Gluineafadh.　The gout in the knee.

Gluineach-bheg.　Knot-grafs.

Gluinfheacam.　To bend the knee.

Gluinein.　A garter.

Gluing.　The fhoulder.

Gluifgheagach.　Full of green leaves.

Glumagan.　A deep hole.

Glun.　A knee, a generation, ftep, or de-gree.

Glunam.　｝To kneel.

Glunlubam.　｝To kneel.

Glunlubadh.　Genuflection.

Glundos.　Bandy-legged.

Glus. Light, brightnefs.

Gna, gnath. Manner, fashion, cuftom, ftature.

Gnabhlus. Cudweed.

Gnae. A woman.

Gnais. The female privity.

Gnamhan. A fea-fnail, periwinkle.

Gnamhuil. Peculiar, proper.

Gnaoi. The countenance, a grin.

Gnaoifhiofaiche. A phyfiognomift.

Gnaofhiofachd. Phyfiognomy.

Gnas. A cuftom.

Gnath. A manner, fashion, cuftom, ftature.

Do ghnath. Always.

Gnathbheurla. Vernacular tongue.

Gnathach. Cuftomary, common, continual, conftant

Gnathachadh. Practice, cuftom, manner.

Gnaithaigham. To accuftom, ufe, inure, exeicife, practife.

Gnathuichoir. A practitioner.

Guathas. Experience.

Gnathchaoi. A beaten path.

Gnatheolas. Experience.

Gnath-cuimhne. Tradition.

Gnathfhocal. A proverb, phrafe, bye-word.

Gne A kind or fort, natural temper, manner, form, appearance.

Gne. An accident, or outward fenfible fign.

Gnedhail. Shapely, mannerly, kindly.

Gneghalachd. Tendernefs, kindnefs.

Gneath. Was born.

Gnemhillam. To deform, disfigure.

Gni A voice.

Gnia. Knowledge.

Gnia. A tree.

Gnia. A fervant.

Gnia. A judge, a knowing perfon.

Gniadh. A doing fervice.

Gnic. Knowledge.

Gnidham. To effect, bring to pafs, to do, make.

Gniomh. A parcel, divifion of land; twelfth-part of a ploughland.

Gniomh. A fact, deed, an action, pl. Gniomhthara.

Gniomh-ingneach. A griffin.

Gniomhnach. Active, actual, bufy.

Gniomhachd. Efficiency.

Gniomhadh. Acting, doing.

Gniomham. To atchieve.

Gniomhchomafach. Powerful.

Gniomhthoir. An actor, agent.

Gnifgam. ⎫
Gnifam. ⎬ To bring to pafs, effect.
Gnifigham. ⎭

Gnithe. Tranfactions, deeds.

Gnodhan. An angry groan, noife, moan.

Gno. ⎫ Bufinefs, affairs.
Gnothach. ⎭

Gnothach. ⎫ Winning, gaining, pur-
Gnothachadh. ⎭ chafing, profit

Gnothaigam. To win, gain, purchafe, get, obtain.

Gnothaigheach. Bufy, active.

Gno. Famous, remarkable, notable.

Gno. Jeering, mockery.

Gnoig. Sulky frown.

Gnogach. Sulky.

Gnoigag. A little fulky woman.

Gnuach. Leaky.

Gnuis. The face, countenance

Gnuis. Hazard, danger, jeopardy.

Gnuis. A notch.

Gnuifmheallam. To counterfeit.

Guifnaire. Bafhfulnefs.

Gnumh. A dent, notch.

Gnumh. A heap, pile.

Gnumham. To heap up, pile, amafs.

Gnufadh. A notch.

Gnufadh. ⎫ The lowing of a cow to
Gnufachdich. ⎭ her calf.

Gnufgulach Grunting.

Go, gu. To, unto, until.

Go.

Go. Put before any adjective forms the adverb of that adjective; luath, quick, go luath, quickly.

Go. The sea.

Go, ga. A spear.

Go. A lye, deceit.

Gob. A bill, beak, snout.

Gobach. Prating

Gobag. A dogfish.

Gobam. To bud, sprout forth

Gob-labhartha. } A redshank.
Gobhlan-bhartha. }

Goban. A muffle; any external hindrance to speech.

Gobanach A prattler.

Gobel. The harbour's mouth.

Gob-easgidn. Snapping.

Gobha. A smith.

Gobha-dubh. A water ousle.

Gobha-uisge. The king's fisher

Gobham. To lessen, diminish

Gobhal. A post, pillar, prop, shore.

Gobhal. Regio perineum.

Gobhlach. Forked, pronged.

Gobhlacan. Astride.

Gobhlan. A prong, fork, weedhook.

Gobhlanach. Pronged, forked.

Goblan-gaoith. A swallow.

Gobhlan-gainmhaich. A sand-martin.

Gabhar. A goat, formerly a horse.

Gobhar oiche A snipe.

Gobharr. A periwig.

Gobhacan. The tilting.

Gobhireong. } Compasses.
Gobhalian. }

Gocman. An usher, or gentleman.

Gochadh. Quality.

Gochdmun. A watchman.

Godach. Giddy, coquettish.

Gog. A tittle, syllable, nod.

Gog-gheadh. A small goose.

Gogach. Wavering, reeling.

Gogshuileach. Having wandering eyes.

Gogam. To nod, gesticulate.

Gogaidach. A coquette.

Gogaidachd. Coquetry.

Gogailleachd. Dotage.

Gogcheannach. Light-headed, whose head shakes.

Gogallach. The cackling of a goose, duck, or hen.

Gogal. } Cackling, prating.
Gogan. }

Gogor. Light.

Goibin, gobag. A little bill; a sand-eel.

Goibhin. A little hill.

Goibhneachd. Smith trade.

Goibhrios. A false colour.

Goic A scoff, taunt, a cocking up of the head.

Goical. Scoffing with an erect head.

Goid. Theft.

Goidheal. An Irishman, or Scotch Highlander.

Goidhealg. The Gaelic tongue.

Goidhealach. Irish, Highland.

Goiglis A tickling.

Goil Prowess, chivalry.

Goile. The stomach, appetite.

Goileamnuin. Grief, sorrow.

Goilam. To grieve, cry, chatter.

Goill. A swollen angry face.

Goill. War, fight, or whatever causes grief.

Goilline. The devil.

Goilmin. A chatterer.

Goimh. Anguish, vexation, a grudge.

Goin. A hurt, wound.

Goin. A chapter, paragraph.

Goin. Delusion.

Goinad. Painfulness.

Goinam. To wound, hurt.

Goinnach. Voracious, that stingeth, prickly.

Goinnanta. Keen, wounding.

Goire. Near, pro Car.

Goind.

Goirid. A short space.

Goir. Call thou.

Goiram, gairam. To call.

Goireil. Snug, convenient.

Goirmin. Woad.

Goirgain-garaidh. Garlick.

Goirnead, guirnead. A gurnard.

Goireas. Apparatus, tools.

Goirrige. A dolt, a fool.

Goirrifeadh. Convenient.

Goirfeadh. A target.

Goirrfgeatham. To retch.

Goirt, genitive of gort. A corn-field.

Goirt. Sore.

Goirt. Sour, bitter, salt.

Goirt. Famine, hunger, starving.

Goirt, gortach. Poor-spirited, narrow, mean.

Goirtbhrifeadh. Mifery, calamity.

Goirthe. Warm, warmed.

Goirtain. A little field of corn.

Goiftidh. A goffip; the father of a child to which one is godfather, is called that godfather's goiftigh.

Goifte, gaoifde. A halter, fnare.

Goithne. A lance or fpear; a quick gait.

Gola. Gluttony.

Golghair. Lamentation.

Golog. A budget.

Gona. With, along with.

Gonadh. ⎫ A lancing, flinging, flabbing,
Gonadhaire. ⎬ darting.

Gonadhairefin. Therefore, from whence, whereupon.

Gonais. A prick, a wound.

Gonam. To wound, fling, flab.

Gont. Wounded, flabbed, hurt.

Goor. Light.

Gor. Advantage, profit.

Gor. Short.

Gor. Laughter, pleafure.

Gorach. Foolifh.

Goram, garam. To heat, warm.

Goraiche. ⎫
Gorachd. ⎬ Folly, foolifhnefs.
Goraichad. ⎭

Goraiclais. Croaking.

Goraiceadh. A croaking fhout.

Goraical. Screeching, croaking.

Goraman. A hungry fellow.

Goramhach. Greedy.

Goramhachd. Greedinefs.

Goran. A pimple.

Gorg, garg. Fierce, cruel.

Gorge. Dotage, fretfulnefs.

Gorgeach. Peevifh.

Gorgeachas. Dotage.

Gorgaicham. To hurt, annoy.

Gorghlantoir. A weeder.

Gorm. Blue.

Gorm. Noble, illuftrious, excellent.

Gormam. To make blue or red.

Gormghlas. Of an azure or blue colour.

Gormmhac. A brave fturdy domeftic or fervant.

Gormfhuilach. Blue-eyed.

Gormrod. A paffage through the fea.

An gorman. Woad.

Gorn. An ember, firebrand.

Gorn. The force of poifon.

Gorrgeachas. Dotage, peevifhnefs, furlinefs.

Gorfaid. A cuirafs.

Gort. The ivy-tree; the letter G.

Gort, gart. Standing corn, a field, garden.

Gort, goirt. Famine, hunger..

Gortach. Hungry, greedy, ftarving; fparing, ftingy.

Gorteog. A hungry ftingy woman, a four-apple-tree, a crab-tree.

Gortaladh. Patching, mending.

Gortan. A hungry ftingy fellow.

Gortghlanam. To weed corn.

Gortughadh. Hurt, oppreffion, wrong, fouring.

Gortughadh.

Gortuigham. To hurt, oppreſs, wrong, to ſour.

Gortighean. The univerſal language before the confuſion of tongues. Vide Keat.

Gortreabhadh. Miſery.

Goſda. A ſpirit, ghoſt.

Goſtaois. Old age.

Goth. Straight, even.

Goth. A ſpear.

Goth. }
Gothadh. } A vowel.

Gothanach. Opprobrious.

Gothadh. An appendix, tendency to bend.

Gothadh. }
Gojhnadh. } A ſmart gait.

Gothnadh. }
Gothneid. } A ſpear to fight with.

Grabach. Notched, indented.

Grabadh. A let, hindrance, impediment.

Grabaire, grabog. A jeſter.

Grabajrachd. Gibble gabble.

Grabbam. To ſtop, hinder.

Grabhaladh. Engraving.

Grabhalam. To engrave.

Grabhalaiche. An engraver.

Grablochd. }
Grabhſhorb. } A fault, error, blot.

Grad. Sudden, quick.

Grada. Vide Granna, Granda.

Gradh. Love, charity.

Gradh. A degree, gradation.

Gradhduine. Philanthropy.

Gradan. Parched corn.

Gradhach. Loving, beloved, dear.

Gradcharach. Nimble.

Gradleiman. To leap quick.

Gradaigh. Of a ſudden.

Gradhdan. The complaining noiſe of hens.

Gradhmbor. Loving.

Gradhmhorachd. Fondneſs, lovingneſs, lovelineſs.

Gradhuigham. To love.

Gradhughadh. Loving.

Graduighte. Beloved, dear.

Grafam. To write, inſcribe, grub, ſcrape.

Grafan. A grubbing-ax.

Grafchur. Grafted.

Grafchuiram. To engraft.

Grag. The noiſe of crows, croaking, a ſhout.

Gragaire. A glutton.

Gragallach. The clucking of a hen, or crow.

Gargam. To cry out, bawl, ſqueal, ſhriek.

Gragan. A manor, village, diſtrict.

Gragan. The boſom.

Gragh, graigh. A ſtud of horſes, breed of mares.

Graibh. An almanack.

Graibhchriolach. The archives, or repoſitory of records.

Graibhri. A title.

Graidal. A girdle to toaſt bread with.

Graigh. A herd, flock, a ſtud of horſes, breed of mares.

Graidhag. A beloved female.

Graigheach. }
Graighaire. } A ſtallion.

Graidheoir. A lover, ſweetheart.

Graifne. }
Graifneaghadh. } Riding, horſemanſhip; an alarm.

Graige. }
Graigeachd. } Superſtition.

Graigin. A glutton.

Graigineas. Gluttony.

Graigham. To love, regard, eſteem.

Grain. Deformity, loathing, abhorrence, nuiſance.

Graince. Diſdain, loathing.

Graincigham. To diſdain.

Graineamhuil. Abominable, deteſtable.

Graineamhlachd. Abomination.

Graine. A grain, corn.

Graine-mulaich. The top grain on a ſtalk.

Grainein

Grainein. A grain, a pinch.

Grainithach. Granivorous, phytivorous.

Grainuigham. To deteft, abhor, deform.

Graineog. A hedge-hog; cruafachd na graineoig, a proverb, expreffing the folly of worldly people, who part with all at the grave, as the hedge-hog does with his crabs at his narrow hole.

Grainnad. Uglinefs.

Grainfeach. A grain farm, grange.

Graineach. Abounding in grain, granulous.

Grainfeoir. An overfeer.

Grainte.
Graintheachd. } Hoarinefs.

Grain-abhal. A pomegranate.

Graifg. The common people, mob, canaille.

Graifgeamhuil. Vulgar.

Graifgamhlachd. Vulgarity.

Gramadach. Grammar.

Gramaifg. The mob.

Gramafgar. A flock, company.

Grammaiche. A flefh-hook.

Gramog. A buffoon, jefter.

Gran, granalach. Dried corn.

Gran. Hail, fhot.

Granna.
Grannda } Ugly.

Granni. Long hair.

Granfhobaire. The glanders.

Granlach. Corn, grain.

Grant. Grey.

Graoina. Joyful, chearful, bright.

Graoinachas. Joyfulnefs, chearfulnefs; brightnefs.

Graoinagaicham. To provoke, irritate, incenfe.

Graofda.
Graofdachd. } Filthy, obfcene.

Graoltas. Obfcenity.

Grapach. A dung-fork.

Gras, grafa.
Grafan. } Grace, favour, aid, help.

Grafda. Compaffionate.

Grafamhuil.
Grafmhor. } Gracious, merciful.

Grafare. Arable ground.

Grata. Excellent, noble, diftinguifhed.

Gratarnach. Noify, clamorous.

Grathun. Awhile.

Gre. Vide Goirt.

Gre. Grey.

Greabhailte. A helmet.

Gread. A ftroke, blow.

Greadam. To burn, fcorch, to torment, whip feverely.

Greadan. Parched corn, fnuff, creaking.

Greadanach. Babbling, chattering, clamorous, obftreperous.

Greadanta. Hot, warm, fcalding.

Greadh. Horfe.

Greadhanachd. Drolling.

Greadhaire. A ftallion.

Greadhairachd. Covering a mare.

Greadog. A griddle.

Greadtha. Scorched, parched, burnt.

Greadhuin. A great number, a band, troop.

Greadhdach. Vide Graoinach.

Greallach. Dirty.

Grealloigh. Clay.

Greallag. A fplinter-bar, a fwing.

Grealfach. A fort of fifh.

Greag. Greece.

Greagach. Greek, Grecian.

Greagam. To deck, adorn.

Greamaigham. To hold, faften, adhere to.

Gream, greim. A bit, morfel, piece; pl. Greamana.

Greamana. Gripes, ftitches.

Greamughadh. Faftening, holding, cleaving to.

Greamuighte.

Greamuighte. Faſtened, clinched.

Grean. Gravel.

Greannach. Long-haired, rough, uncombed, briſtly.

Greann. A rough uncombed look, a beard, fair hair.

Greann. Love, friendſhip.

Greann. Hue, a joke.

Greanaghadh. Exhortation.

Greannughadh. The hair ſtanding on end.

Greannuigham. To defy, to be angry. Horreo.

Greanghairbhas. Hairineſs.

Greanmhar. Lovely, facetious, witty.

Greannadh. Graving.

Greanta. Carved, engraved.

Greantaſan. Graving.

Greas. A gueſt.

Greas. A manner.

Greas. Protection, preſervation.

Greaſach, greas. Uſually.

Greaſam. To prepare, haſten, dreſs, adorn, accoutre; to encourage, promote.

Greaſachadh. Haſtening.

Greas, gen, greis. Fine clothes, gold embroidery, furniture, needle-work.

Greaſachd. Haſtening.

Greaſailt. An inn.

Greaſaire. An inn-keeper.

Greaſan. A web.

Greaſaidhe. A ſhoe-maker, embroiderer.

Greath. A noiſe, cry, ſhout.

Greatham. To dreſs victuals, winnow.

Greathadair. A dreſſer, winnower.

Greathadairachd. Winnowing, dreſſing.

Greathlach. The inwards, inteſtines, purtenance, pluck.

Grech. A hound.

Grech. A nut.

Grech, a. Salt.

Greithte. Winnowed.

Greibhel. A gift, fairing.

Greidal. A gridiron, griddle, a baking-iron.

Greig. Greece.

Greigais. The Greek tongue.

Greillain. A dagger, old ruſty ſword.

Greim. A bit, morſel, taſk, hard word, difficult expreſſion, a hold; pl. Greimani.

Greim. A ſtitch, bite, throb, pang.

Greimaigham. To hold faſt, take hold.

Greimaire. A grappling, pincers.

Greimughadh. Taking hold.

Greimailteach. Firm, faſt holding.

Greim-fola. The pleuriſy.

Greimhric. Samphire.

Greimiſg. Old garments, traſh, trumpen, lumber.

Greine, of the ſun. Solar.

Greinbheachd. }
Greinferen.   } The zodiac.

Greis. Needlework, embroidery, furniture, fine clothes.

Greiſam. To fringe.

Greis. Awhile, ſpace of time.

Greis-comairc. Protection.

Greis. A champion.

Greiſchill. Sanctuary.

Greiſeachd. Soliciting, enticing.

Greiſeach. Enticing.

Greiſghiolla. A client.

Greiſg. Greaſe.

Greiſteoir. A carter.

Greit. A champion, warrior.

Greith. Dreſs, ornaments, a jewel, precious ſtone.

Greliath. Grey hairs.

Greth. A gift, preſent.

Greſach. Common.

Greus. Embroidery.

Greus-obair. Needlework.

Griaſda. A great warrior, champion, hero.

Grian. The ſun.

Grian.

Grian. The ground, bottom of the sea, lake, or river.

Grian. Land.

Grian-bille. Glebe-land.

Grianach. ⎫
Grianmhor. ⎬ Sunny, warm.

Grianan. A summer-house, a walk arched or covered over on a hill for a commodious profpect; a palace or royal feat.

Grianannta. Sunny.

Grianchloch. ⎫
Grianarc. ⎬ A dial.

Griangamhftad. The winter folftice.

Grianfhamhftad. The fummer folftice.

Grianchoinamh. Oppofite.

Grianmhuine. Blackberries.

Grianchrios. The zodiac.

Griandeatach. An exhalation.

Grianraigham. To dry or bafk in the fun.

Grianfgarradh. A cranny.

Grianftad. A folftice.

Grib. An impediment.

Grib. Dirt, filth.

Grib. A hindrance.

Gribadh. A manger.

Grib. The feathers on the feet of hens, &c.

Gribh. A finger.

Gribh. A griffin, a fierce warrior.

Gribhag. Hurry.

Gribhagach. Timorous.

Gribhingneach. A griffin.

Gribeach. A hunting nag.

Gridadh. Chillinefs.

Grifach. The meafles.

Grigag. A pebble, bead.

Griglachan. A conftellation.

Grim. War, battle.

Grim. A grey fubftance growing on trees.

Grimchliath. Hurdles ufed in fieges, a kind of penthoufe.

Grimcharba. A female giant, an apparition.

Grimcharbad A war-chariot, fuch as the Britons ufed

Grimamhuil. Warlike, martial, fkilful.

Grimifgeoir. A pedlar.

Grin. A piece, morfel.

Grinn. Workmanlike, artificial, neat, clean.

Grinn. A fort, garrifon.

Grinn, greann. A beard.

Grinn, gen. of Greann. Love, facetioufnefs.

Grinn. Deliberately, ferioufly, profoundly.

Grinnachadh. An effort.

Grinnas. Neatnefs, gentility.

Grinneach. A young man.

Grinnach. Shaggy.

Grinneadh. Dying, perifhing.

Grinneal. ⎫
Grinniol. ⎬ The bottom, bed of the fea or river, channel.

Grinnidham. To gather, to pierce.

Grioblas. Clofenefs.

Griogchan. A conftellation.

Griollfam. To ftrike or flap.

Griomchallaire. A herald, one that pro claims peace and declares war.

Griomcharbad. A war-chariot, currus falcatus.

Griomh. A man's nail, a claw, talon.

Griomhaighil. Motiuncula.

Griomhfhronach. Hawknofed.

Grionach. Vide Grianach.

Griongal. ⎫
Griongalachd. ⎬ Care, affiduity, forrow.

Griongalach. Induftrious, careful.

Grirongnach. A griffin.

Griofam. To entreat, befeech, to abet.

Griofach. Hot, burning embers.

Griofta. Stirred, provoked.

Griofuicham. To ftir the fire, to provoke.

[F f f]   Grioth,

Grioth. The fun.

Gris. Grey.

Gris. Fire, inflammation from heat, pimples.

Grisdhearg. A colour mixed with red and grey.

Grisfhionn. A fort of brindled colour.

Grisgin. Broiled meat.

Grith. Knowledge, fkill.

Grithail. The grunting of young pigs.

Gritheach. Learned, wife, difcreet, prudent.

Griuthlamhach. Quick.

Griun. A hedge-hog.

Grobach. Serrate.

Groban. The top of a rock.

Grod. Smart, proud.

Grod. Rotten.

Grodam. To rot.

Grod. Foam.

Grod. Vide Grad.

Grodan. A boat.

Grodh-iarruinn. An iron crow.

Grog, gruag. The hair of the head.

Groibleach. Long nailed, having large talons.

Groigh. A ftud of horfes, breed of mares.

Groghach. Vide Gnothach.

Groifaid. A goofeberry.

Groifair. A goofeberry-bufh.

Groifeanach. Mouthed.

Groifgeach. A droll.

Gron. A ftain, blot, blemifh.

Grontach. Corpulent.

Gropadh. A gulley, fewer.

Gropis. Mallows.

Gros. Snout.

Groffach. Having a large fnout or mouth.

Groffal. }
Groffairachd. } Grunting.

Groffaire. A grunter.

Grothal. Sand, gravel.

Grothan. Complaining, moan, noife, purring.

Grothlach. Gravelly, a gravel-pit.

Grotonach. Corpulent.

Gruadh, gruaidh. The cheek.

Gruag. The hair of the head.

Gruag-bhreige. A periwig.

Gruag. A woman, wife.

Gruagach. A woman giant, a ghoft, apparition, fuperftitioufly fuppofed to haunt houfes, called in Scotland a Browny, alfo a girl; the chief of a place.

Grugach. Hairy.

Gruaidh. A brow, cheek.

Gruaim. A furly look, gloom.

Gruaimin. A filly fellow.

Gruama. } Obfcure, fullen, dark, gloomy,
Gruamach. } morofe.

Gruamag. A fullen little woman.

Gruamachd. Gloominefs.

Grubhan. The liver.

Grudaire. A brewer, diftiller.

Grudairachd. Brewing, diftilling.

Grug. A lie, untruth.

Grug. Morofe, a wrinkle.

Grug. Weak, feeble.

Grugach. Wrinkled, morofe.

Grugare. Having long hair, noble.

Grufam. To engraft.

Gruid. Grains, malt.

Gruig. Churlifhnefs, inhofpitality, a drooping look.

Grullan. A cricket.

Grum. }
Grumach. } Grim, furly, fevere.

Grumachd. Surlinefs.

Grunaigham. To ground, to found.

Grunnachadh. Grounding, founding.

Grunnadh. Gathering in heaps.

Grunnafg. Groundfel.

Grunnt. The ground, bottom, foundation.

Grunfgigh. A truce, ceſſation of arms.

Gruntal. Having a foundation, ſolid, ſenſible.

Gruntalachd. Solidity, ſenſe.

Gruntas. Dreggs.

Gruth. Curds.

Gruthach. Curdled, having curds.

Gu, go. That, to the end that.

Guall. Low.

Guag. A light, giddy, phantaſtical fellow; an unſettled capricious perſon.

Guaillaigham. To go hand in hand.

Guaillighe. } A companion.
Guaillair. }

Guaillfhionn. Name of a cow, a cow with ſpeckled ſhoulders.

Guamaiſeach. Quiet, comfortable.

Guairtain. A whirlwind.

Guaire. The hair of the head, noble, a briſtle.

Guairſgeach. That hath hair on the head.

Guais, guas. Danger.

Guaiſbheartach. Enterprizing, adventurous.

Guaitam. To leave off, let alone, be quiet.

Guailain. } A burnt dead coal.
Gualain. }

Gual. A coal, coals, fire.

Guala. } A ſhoulder.
Gualluin. }

Gualgha. Of coals.

Guala. Vide Gola.

Gualabhran. A firebrand.

Guallam. To blacken, burn.

Guallach. Cords tying the ſhoulders of dead men; hence the imprecation of geolach ort.

Guamach. Thick, plentiful, ſmirking.

Guanach. } Light, active, nodding, wav-
Guanaiſach. } ing.

Guanalais. Wavering, ſtrolling.

Guarthag-bleothain. Milch-cows.

7

Guas. Peril, danger.

Guaſachd. Danger, jeopardy, adventure.

Guaſachdach. Dangerous, dreadful; painful, in mſs. on medicine.

Gubha. Mourning, lamentation.

Gubha. A battle, conflict.

Gubhthach. Mournful, ſorrowful.

Gucag. A bud, ſprout, bell, bubble.

Gucagach. Cluſtering.

Gudham, guidham. To pray, wiſh.

Gudhb. A ſtudy or ſchool-houſe, armory.

Gudhbach. Studious, aſſiduous.

Gufurghoill. Falſe teſtimony.

Gugail. }
Gugullaigh. } Clucking.
Gugarnaigh. }

Gugan. A bud, flower, a daiſy.

Guga. A St. Kilda gooſe, a fat fellow.

Guibheirneoir. A governor.

Guidbhain. England.

Guidhe. A prayer, entreaty, interceſſion.

Guidhachan. An imprecation.

Guidham. To pray, entreat, beſeech.

Guidhuighoir. A prayer, ſwearer.

Guilam. To weep, cry, bewail.

Guillag. Chattering of birds.

Guilimne. Calumny.

Guilimneach. Calumnious.

Guilimnigham. To calumniate, reproach.

Guilneach. A curlew.

Guilugag. A cry of joy.

Guimionn. A holy relick.

Guin. Points, darts, pain.

Guincheap. A pillory.

Guinneach. Sharp-pointed, prickly, keen.

Guinam. To prick, ſting, wound.

Guinnaire. The falling-ſickneſs.

Guinn. Vide Cruth.

Guinſcead. A ſcar.

Guinſcidin. A little ſcar.

Guirbhriſam. To exulcerate.

Guirin. A ſpot, blain, wheal, pimple.

Guirm. Of blue.

Guirme. Blueness, more blue.

Guirme. An inn.

Guirmeachd Blueness.

Guirmin. Any blue dye.

Guirnead. A gurnard.

Guisag. A straw, stalk.

Guiseach. Leaky, full of chinks.

Guiscad. A gusset, clock of a stocking.

Guiseir. A stocking.

Guiscead. A scar.

Guisam. To flow.

Guitair. A gutter, conduit, gully-hole.

Guiteas. Denial, refusal.

Guite. A fan, sieve.

Guitineach. Bashful.

Gul. Weeping, crying out, lamentation.

Gulam. To weep.

Gulba. The mouth.

Gulbroin. }

Guldeur. } Eyedrop.

Gulfa. Narrow.

Gumha. A battle.

Gun. For Gan, without.

Gu'n. For Gu an, thus, Gu'n rachadh se, that he might go

Gun. A breach.

Gunbhuine. A spear, javelin.

Gunlann. A prison.

Gunn. A prisoner, an hostage.

Gunncha. A prison.

Gunn. A gown.

Gunna. A gun.

Gunna-glaic. }

Gunna-caol. } A fusee, fowling-piece.

Gunna-mor. A cannon.

Gunnair. A gunner.

Gunnairachd. Engineering, firing guns.

Guntabhart. Vide Cuntabhart.

Gunragadh. Erring, straying.

Gunta. An experienced, skilful, prying man.

Gunta. Prepared.

Gunta. Wounded.

Guntach. Costiveness.

Gur. That; Gur maith-e, that it is good.

Gur. A blotch, a wheal.

Gur. A brood of birds, incubation

Guram. To incubate, hatch.

Gur Sharp, valiant

Guraiceach. A blockhead.

Gurchliathach. A pallisadoe.

Gurna. A cave, den.

Gurt. Pain, trouble, fierceness.

Gurtach. Fierce.

Gus. Until, as far as.

Gus. Weight, force, strength.

Gus. Death.

Gus. Anger.

Gus. A deed.

Gus. Sharp, keen.

Gusar. Sharply.

Gus. A desire, inclination.

Gusmhar. Valid, strong, powerful.

Gustal. A burden.

Gusgul. Roaring, making lamentations.

Gusgan. A hearty draught.

Gusgurlach. A keen sharp fellow.

Guta. The gout, puddle.

Gutach, cutach. Bobtailed.

Gutam. To gut fish.

Guth. A voice, a vowel.

Guth. Ill-name, calumny.

Guthach. Noisy, that hath a voice.

Gutolaidhe. A cuckold-maker.

Gutturrdhusach. Confident.

H.

H.

H, Although now admitted into the Galic alphabet, is more an aspirate than a letter, for there are no words in the language beginning with h. After a consonant, different combinations, new sounds or letters are formed, as may be seen in a scheme laid down in the Analysis of the Galic Language, to which I refer the reader. The name of this letter or aspirate is Uath, the white thorn-tree. H, between two words, is a euphonic, thus, dheisd e ri a h oran, he listened to her song.

I.

IS the eighth letter of the alphabet, sounds as in Latin, French, and Italian, and is called Iodha, vulgo, iubhar, the yew-tree. The Galic admits of no (I) consonant any more than the Greek, and it appears that the Latins did not use it as a distinct character, for they wrote peius for pejus, and eius for ejus. Joined with the other vowels several diphthongs are formed. Vide Analysis.

I. An art, science.

I, or si. She.

I. Low, shallow.

I. Erroneously in.

I. An island, hence.

I Cholum Cille. Icolmkill, or the island of St. Columbus.

I-fein. Herself.

Iach. A salmon.

Iach. A yell, scream.

Iachdar. The bottom, foundation, lower part, nether.

Iachdar-chanus. The bassus-cantus in music.

Iachdaruighe. Lower, lowest, inferior.

Iachadh }
Iachal. } A noise, cry, howl.

Iacham. To scream, yell, howl.

Iad. They, them.

Iad-fan. They, themselves.

Iadsa. These.

Iaddsin. }
Iadsud. } Those.

Iadhadh. Shutting, joining, binding.

Iadham. To shut, join, bind.

Iadhte. Shut, closed, joined.

Iagh. An island.

Iadhshlat. Honeysuckle.

Iarbhreith. After-birth.

Iaircheann. The noddle.

[G g g]   Iarchair

Iairegair. Confequence.

Iarfheur.

Iairfceart. The Weft.

Iairtreabh. An habitation.

Ial. Light.

Iall. A latchet, thong.

Iall. God forgive you.

Iall. Vide Ealt.

Iallachrann. Shoes.

Iallin. ⎫
Iallag. ⎬ A thong, fhoemaker's thread.

Iallach. Full of thongs.

Ialtog leathair. A bat.

Ian. A veffel.

Ian. Blade of a fword.

Ian. A weafel.

Iar. Weft.

Iar. Dark, black.

Iar. A bird.

Iar. After.

Iar-fin. After that, afterwards.

Iar, for air. At, upon.

Iar, fiar. Back, backwards, the weft.

Iarbel. ⎫
Iarbheo. ⎬ Still alive.

Iarbhleothan. After-milk.

Iarchuimhe. After-game.

Iarcheann. The hind-head.

Iarrum. To afk, feek, look for, enquire.

Iarunn. Iron.

Iardhonn. A brownifh-black.

Iardhraoi. A remnant.

Iarfaidhe. Ward, cuftody.

Iarflath. A feudary lord, or one depending on a greater; hence Earl.

Iarflaithachd. Ariftocracy.

Iarculta. Churlifh, backward.

Iargan. Groans of the dying, forrow, pain.

Iarganach. Uneafy, in great pains, afflictive.

Iarghaoth. Weft-wind.

Iarguil. A fkirmifh, battle, ftrife.

Iarguileach. Warlike, contentious.

Iarla. An earl.

Iarlus An earneft-penny.

Iarlaithruighadh. A preparation.

Iarmort. Riches.

Iarmbreith. After-birth, fecundine.

Iarmart. Confequence, iffue of an affair.

Iarmart. ⎫
Iarmad. ⎬ Offspring, pofterity.

Iarmbeurla. A pronoun; indeclinable particle.

Iarmair. Remnant.

Iarmailte. The fkies.

Iarmbuille. An after-clap, a back-ftroke.

Iarmbunudhas. Derivation.

Iarmheirge. Mattins, morning prayer, rifing early.

Iarmfna. A remnant.

Iarna. ⎫ A chain of thread, a fkain, confufion.
Iarnan. ⎬

Iarnachan. An iron tool.

Iarnaidhe. Irons, of or belonging to iron.

Iarndo. A fawn.

Iarnaoifa. After-ages.

Iarog. A weafel.

Iarag. Vide Eirag.

Iarog Anguifh, grief.

Iarraigh ⎫
Iarratas. ⎬ A requeft, petition, inftance.

Iarrataiche. A probe.

Iarrataichan. Feelers.

Iarratoir. A beggar.

Iarram. To afk, feek, look after.

Iarrunn. Iron.

Iarrun-eafidh. Crifping iron.

Iarrunaigham. To fmooth or iron linen.

Iarfceart. The weft.

Iarfceartach. North-weft.

Iarfin. Afterwards.

Iarrunach feifaraigh. Plough-irons.

Iarfpealadh. After-grafs.

Iartaracha. Weft.

Iarfma. A relick, remnant, an incumbrance, burden; a new year's gift.

Iartaighe. Defcendants, pofterity, domefticks.

Iarthar. The weft, weft country.

Iarthoir. A beggar.

Iafachd. Loan; advantage, profit.

Air Iafachd. In loan, borrowed.

Iafachdaiche }
Iafaid.   } A creditor.

Iafalach. Eafy, feafible.

Iafalachd. Facility.

Iafan. Saucinefs.

Iafatach Squeamifh.

Iafc. }
Iafg. } A fifh.

Iafg air chladh. Fifh at fpawning.

Iafgachd. Fifhing.

Iafgair. A fifher, fifherman.

Iafgairachd. Fifhing, the art of fifhing, fifhery.

Iafgair-cairneach. An ofprey.

Iafgan. A little fifh, a mufcle.

Iafgloch. A fifh-pond.

Iafg-fliogach. Shell-fifh.

Iafgithach. Pifcivorous.

Iath. Land.

Iatlu. A little feather or fin.

Iatham. To furround, move round.

Iathadh. Surrounding, moving round.

Ibh. A country, tribe of people.

Ibh. Drink thou.

Ibh Ye, you.

Ibhear. Marble.

Ibhric.

Ibham. To drink.

Ibhtheach. Soaking, that imbibes water.

Ic. A cure, remedy; a fupply, eek.

Ic. Balm.

Icam. To heal, cure; fupply, eeke.

Iceadh. Healing, curing; fuffering, paying for.

Iclus. Healing by herbs.

Iclufam. To heal by herbs.

Ichd air neachd. At any rate.

Id. Good, juft, honeft.

Id. A ring.

Idars. Towards.

Iadarfalamh. }
Idarfas.   } A fpace, diftance of time or place.

Idarghuaille. Space between the fhoulders.

Idears. Towards.

Idearumnas. A diftance.

Idh. A wreathe or chain; a ridge.

Idh. Ufe.

Idhad. Chafte, clear.

Idhal. An idol.

Idho. The yew-tree, the letter I.

Idid. Cold.

Iddir. At all.

Idir. Between, betwixt.

Idirgeanas. Diftance.

Iddarmanachd. Hydromancy.

Iddirrioghachd. Inter-regnum.

Idirchur. Interpofition.

Idireug. Change of the moon.

Idirgeanas. }
Idirdreas. } Diftance.

Idirdhealughadh. Diftinction, difference.

Idirmhinuigham. To expound.

Idirmeadhonoir. A mediator, interceffor.

Idirtheangthoir. An interpreter.

Idarthamul. Interval.

Idna. Arms, weapons.

Ifin. A goofeberry.

Ifrionn. Hell.

Ifrionnach. Hellifh, a hellifh fellow.

Ifrionda. Hellifh, of hell.

Igh. A ring.

Igh. Tallow.

Il, ile. Much, plenty, great; well, a compofitive particle.

Ilbheufach. Arch, of varous ways and humours.

Ilcheardach. }
Ilcheardaighe. } A Jack of all trades.

Ilcheoimeafgte. Mifcellaneous.

Ilchumafg. Mifcellany.

Ilchearnach.

Ilchearnach.   Multangular.

Ildealbhach.   Well-featured.

Ildheanadh.   Variation.

Ildheannam.   To vary.

Ildheanmudh.   An emblem.

Ile.   A great number of people.

Ile, ileas.   Diverfity, difference.

Ileach.   Vide Aoileach.

Ilghnitheach.   Of all forts, diverfe, various.

Ilghraineach.   Very horrid, ugly.

Ilgneach.   Skilful.

Ilgnetheca.   Strange, unufual.

Ilghreafach.   An inn, lodging.

Ilguidham.   To vary, alter.

Illafan.   The very fame people, themfelves.

Illeabhar.   A volume, or tome.

Illeabhrach.   Voluminous.

Ilphaifd.   A ferpent, fnake, adder.

Ilrincadh.   A ball, promifcuous dance.

Ilrincam.   To dance in a promifcuous dance.

Ilfheafamh.   Diftance.

Im.   Butter.

Imgha.   Of butter, buttery.

Im, for uime.   About.

Imad.   Many.

Imaduigham.   To multiply.

Imadaghadh.   Multiplying.

Imaithighidh.   Ufe, cuftom, experience.

Imarbhas.   Tranfgreffion.

Imarbhadh.   Strife, contention, fkirmifh.

Imairg, imairc.   Plundering, devaftation, ranfacking.

Imcheimnigham.   To walk round.

Imchian.   Far, remote.

Imchill.   About.

Imcham.   To refcue.   Vide Imthigham.

Imchubhuidh.   Fit, proper.

Imchomhradh.   Thefis.

Imchubhidhachd.   Fitnefs, propriety.

Imdheagal.   Protection.

Imdheal.   A league, covenant.

Imdhearbhadh.   A proof.

Imdhearbham.   To prove.

Imdhearbhtha.   Proved, maintained.

Imdheargadh.   A reproof.

Imdheargam.   To reprove, rebuke, reproach, difpraife.

Imdheargtha.   Reviled, reproved, rebuked

Imdhiol.   A feaft.

Imdiol.   Guile, deceit.

Imdhorus.   A back door.

Imeachtraigh.   Plough-bullocks.

Imead.   Jealoufy.

Imeadmhor.   Jealous.

Imdeadaire.   A zealot.

Imeagal.   Fright, fear.

Imeaglach.   Fearful, terrible.

Imeaglam.   To fear.

Imeal.   Edge, border, coaft.

Imeaforgain.   A ftriking on all fides.

Imeocham.   We will go.

Imfheadan.   A draught.

Imhoicheadh.

Imfidh.   A petitioner.

Imghaoth.   An eddying wind.

Imhear.   A marble.

Immarcach.   Many, exceffive.

Imiadhag.   A coupling, or joining together.

Imileadadh.   Unction.

Imileadam.   To anoint.

Imligham.   To lick.

Imiradh.   A ridge of land.

Imirc.   A journey, removing from a place.

Imircam.   To remove, change refidence

Imirtlan.   A gaming-houfe.

Imirighe.   An emigration.

Imlan.   Full, perfect.

Imlanachd.   Fullnefs, perfection.

Imlad.   Motion, ftirring.

Imladam.   To change, move, alternate.

Imleabhar.   A tome, volume.

Imlinn. }
Imleag. } The navel.
Imliocan.}

Imlioc.   Bordering on a lake.

Immain.

Immain. Driving.

Immainam. To drive.

Immeal. Skirt, an end, border, limit, boundary.

Imne. Thus.

Immalach. Remote, fequeftered.

Immairt. Gaming, play.

Immiram. To row.

Immram. Rowing.

Immradh. Mention.

Immradham. To mention.

Immradhteach. Famous, noted.

Imneifigham. To bind, tie.

Imnidhe. Care, diligence.

Imnidheach. Careful, anxious, folicitous.

Imnifi. Contention, difunion.

Imnifam. To yoke.

Impidh. A twig, rod.

Impidhe. A prayer, petition, fupplication, converfion.

Impidheach. An interceffor, petitioner, converter.

Impidham. ⎰ To befeech, entreat, pray, re-
Impuigham. ⎱ queft, convert.

Impire. An emperor.

Impireachd. An empire.

Impoighte. Converted.

Imreaccuibh. It happened, fell out.

Imreas. ⎰
Imreafan. ⎱ Difpute, controverfy, ftrife.

Imreafam. ⎰
Imreafanam. ⎱ To ftrive, difpute, contend.

Imreafanuidhe. A difputant.

Imreafanadh. Striving, difputing.

Imreimnigham. To go about.

Imram. To play, divert.

Imram. A riding.

Imfcin. A bed-room, clofet.

Imfeach. Revengeful.

Imfeachan. Rage, fury.

Imfeachtrach. A project.

Imfeargna. Strife, contention.

Imfhniomh. Heavinefs, fadnefs.

Imfhniomh. Care, diligence.

Imfhniomhach. Anxious, folicitous, un-eafy.

Imfhiuth. Countertide.

Imfhiubhlam. To walk about, ramble.

Imtheachd. A progrefs, migration; Exodus.

Imtheachd. An adventure, feat, expedition.

Imthigham. To go, emigrate, remove.

Imtheachdaighe. One about to depart.

Imthreafcram. To wreftle.

Imthus. A progrefs, expedition.

Imthufa. Adventures, feats.

In. Formerly ufed for Ann, in.

In. Fit, proper, ufed in compound words.

In. A country.

Ina, inas. Ufed in old mfs. for Na.

Inaituighte. Habitable.

Inbhe. Quality, dignity, rank.

Idbheach. Eminent, forward, in high rank.

Inbhear. For Ann mhuir. The mouth of a river.

Inbheirt. A perfect birth.

Incheannuigh. That may be bought, mercable.

Inchinn. The brain.

Inchomharuighte. Notable.

Inchreachadh. Blame, reproach.

Inchreachadh. Gleaning or leafing corn.

Inchreacham. To confider.

Inchruinighte. Leviable.

Indeanta. What may be done.

Indine. A fight, engagement.

Indiola. Vendible, fit for fale.

Indioluighe. One able to pay.

Indiongbhala. Matchable.

Indlios. A court.

Ineach. The lining of cloth in weaving, woof.

Ineach. Hofpitality, generofity, good houfe-keeping.

[H h h]   Ineachthreas.

Ineachthreas. A fair or public meeting.

Ineagnuidhe. Deplorable.

Inealta. Neat, well made.

Inealtachd. Neatneſs, being well done.

Infeatham. To meditate.

Infhaicſin. Notable.

Infheadhma. Manlike action.

Infheatha. Meditations.

Infhir. Fit for a huſband, marriageable.

Infhiochas. Choice, election.

Infiſi. A ſwelling.

Infaſda. Obnoxious.

Ing. A negative particle.

Ing. Force, compulſion.

Ing. A ſtir, move.

Ingaire. Herding.

Ingear. A level, perpendicular.

Ingedthe. Of twins in the womb; what comes to perfect birth.

Ingiul. Conſequence, concluſion.

Ingglain. Uncleanneſs.

Ingglan. Dirty, filthy, unclean.

Ingill. Feeding, grazing, paſture.

Ingillam. To feed.

Ingin. ⎫
Ingean. ⎬ A daughter.
Inghin. ⎭

Inghin-cheile. A daughter-in-law.

Ingnidham. To nip, pinch.

Inghreim. Ravening, perſecuting.

Ingir. A carpenter or maſon's line.

Ingir. An anchor.

Ingir. Affliction, grief, ſorrow.

Ingleid. A hook.

Ingne. Pl. of Ionga. Nails.

Ingreimtheach. A perſecutor.

Iniatar. A bowel or entrail.

Inid. Shrovetide.

Inidhe. ⎫
Inida. ⎬ Bowels, entrails.

Iniltam. To feed, graze.

Inirte. Weakneſs, feebleneſs.

Inis. An iſland.

Inis. Diſtreſs, miſery.

Inis. Tell thou.

Iniſam. To tell.

Iniſce. A reproach.

Iniſiol. A ſervant.

Iniſcighin. A garden.

Inithte. ⎫
Inite. ⎬ Edible, eatable.

Inleadh. Making ready, preparing.

Inleighais. Incurable.

Inleathſgeula. Excuſable.

Inlam. To prepare, make ready.

Inlaochtadh. Fit to bear arms.

Inmhe. Rank, dignity; an eſtate, patrimony, land.

Inmheach. Eminent, high, ripe, advanced.

Inmheallta. Deceivable.

Inmheaſda. Commendable.

Inmheadhonach. Mean, moderate, inward, inmoſt.

Inmheadhonas. Temperance.

Inmhillein. Blameable.

Inmhuin. Affable, courteous, loving, beloved.

Inmhianna. Deſirable.

Inn. Us, we.

Inn. For Ann, in.

Inn. A wave.

Innainadh. A want, deficiency.

Inne, innidhe. A bowel, entrail.

Inneach. Woof.

Inneal. Reſtraint.

Inneal. Service, attendance.

Inneal. An inſtrument, ſtate, condition; mean, carriage, deportment, order or diſpoſition of a thing, dreſs, attire.

Innealta. Well-adorned, neat.

Innealtradh. Paſturage.

Innealtram. To feed cattle, graze.

Inneamh. Increaſe, augmentation.

Innealladh. An inſtrument, tool.

Inneidham. To tell, certify.

Inneir. Dung.

Inneiridh. Sitting up, watching.

Inneoin. An anvil, the middle of a pool or pond.

Inneoin. In spite of.

Inneoinadh. Striking, stamping.

Inneonam. To strike or stamp.

Innighe. Entrails, bowels.

Innil. } Active, prone to, ready.
Inniolta. }

Innil. A gin, snare, instrument.

Innile. Cattle.

Innill. A fort, garrison.

Innilt. A handmaid.

Innis. Distress, misery.

Innis. An island, a field to graze cattle.

Innis-ealga. A name of Ireland.

Innisam. } To tell, say, relate.
Innsam. }

Innsadh. } Telling, relating.
Inniudh. }

Inioc. A blow.

Iniochadh. Agitating.

Iniochas. Choice.

Innliugham. To aim, purpose.

Innlis. A candle.

Innlidh. Forage.

Innorcam. To kill, destroy.

Innocain. Murder.

Inneaca. Vendible.

Innreachtain. A pudding.

Innriomh. Preparation.

Innseaga. Scattered little fields of corn, as in the Highlands of Scotland.

Innsgin. A pronoun.

Innte. A kernel.

Innte. In her, it, therein.

Innteach. A way or road, a gate.

Inntile. A budget, wallet, satchel.

Inntin. The mind.

Inntineach. High-minded, sprightly, sensible, hearty, jolly, merry.

Innthomh. Treasure.

Innthomhcha. A treasury.

Inntradh. Entrance, beginning.

Inntram. To begin, enter.

Inntras. Entry-money.

Inoibrighte. Malleable.

Inphosda. Marriageable.

Insce. } Sex, gender, a speech; fir-insene,
Inscne. } masculine gender, bean-insene, the feminine gender.

Insgineach. Sprightly.

Insiubhal. Passable.

Inte. Therein. Vide Innte.

Intleachd. Ingenuity, invention, contrivance.

Intleachdach. Ingenious, witty, sagacious, subtle.

Inthomhaiste. Measurable, artificial.

Intreabh. Want.

Intruagh. Miserable, pitiable, poor.

Intuite. Apt to fall.

Iobadh. Death.

Ioc. Payment, rent.

Ioc-eiric. Kindred-money, ransom.

Iocaidhe. A tenant, farmer, tacksman.

Iocam. To pay; to suffer, endure; to heal, cure.

Iocas. Payment.

Iochd. Clemency, humanity, confidence, good-nature.

Iochd. Children.

Iochdamhlachd. Clemency, mercy.

Iochdar. The bottom.

Iochdarach. Lower, lowest, nether.

Iochdaran. A subject, inferior, underling.

Iochdmhoi. Merciful, clement.

Iochdmhoire. Mercifulness.

Iochroidheachd. Discord.

Ioclus. A healing by herbs.

Ioclusam. To cure by herbs.

Iocshlainte. A healing-draught, nectar, cordial.

Iocshlainteach. Healing, benign, cordial.

Iodallach. An Italian.

Iodalt.

Iodalt. Italy.

Iodarchur. An interjection.

Iodarfolamh. Area, court-yard.

Iodarmhala. Space between the brows.

Iodras. Towards.

Iodarthamul. Diftance.

Iodh. } The cramp or any fort of pain,
Iodha. } rheumatifm.

Iodh. A chain, collar.

Iodh-Mhoruin. A collar or neck-chain, fo called from the Irifh judge Moran, who wore it.

Iodha. The yew-tree, the name of the letter I.

Iodhaladhradh. } Idolatry.
Iodhalachd. }

Iodhal. }
Iodhaladhraidh. } An idol.

Iodhaladhraghoir. An idolator.

Iodhan. Sincere, pure, clean, undefiled.

Iodhana. Pangs, torments.

Iodhat. Diet.

Iodhbairam. To facrifice, offer.

Iodhbairt. A facrifice, offering.

Iodhbeirthach. A facrificer.

Iodhlan. A leap, fkipping.

Iodhlanadh. Leaping, fkip.

Iodhlanam. To leap, fkip.

Iodhna. A fpear, lance.

Iodhna. Protection, fafeguard.

Iodhnach. Valiant, warlike, martial.

Iodhnaidhe. A ftaying, dwelling.

Iodhon. Vide Eadhoin.

Iogan. A bird's craw.

Iogan. Deceit, fraud.

Ioganach. Deceitful.

Ioghaile. The pylorus, or lower orifice of the ftomach.

Ioghlactha. Tractable.

Ioghlaithruigheam. To confume.

Iogras. Uprightnefs.

Iol. Signifies variety, and is a compofitive particle.

Iolach. Mirth, merriment, fhouting.

Iolach. Lofs, damage.

Iolagall. A damage.

Iolam. }
Iolaram. } To vary, change.

Iollahach. Brifk, fprightly, perk.

Iolan. Sincere.

Iolar. An eagle.

Iolar-tiomchiollach. }
Iolar-ghreagach. } A gier eagle.

Iolar. }
Iolardhas } Variety, diverfity.

Iiolairam. To annumerate.

Iolar. Much, plenty.

Iolardha. Diverfe, various.

Iolbheufach. Multifarious.

Iolbhuagach. Victorious, triumphant, allconquering.

Iolchroidhach. Inconftant.

Iolchruthach. Comely, well-featured, inconftant, various, multiform.

Iolchuire. Sadnefs, lamentation.

Ioldanach. Ingenious.

Ioldathach. Of diverfe colours.

Ioldamhfadh. A ball, promifcuous dance, country-dance.

Iolga. Tongs.

Iolghillach. Complex.

Iolgha. }
Iolghuth. } Of various tongues.

Iolgneathach. Heterogeneous.

Iollan. Expert, mechanical.

Iolghleufach. Manifold, complicated.

Iolicheachd. Contentment.

Iolmhadhach. Manifold, various.

Iolmhaoina. Much goods and chattels.

Iolphofadh. Polygamy.

Iolradh. Plural.

Iolfhliofnach. Polygon.

Iolfhioladh. Polyfyllable.

Iolthilgte. Amphibolus.

Iolforcas. Variance, debate.

Iomachar. A bier.

Iomad. Much, plenty, a multitude.

Iomadach. Numerous, infinite.

Iomadachadh. Multiplication.

Iomadaigham. To multiply, encreafe.

Iomadamheachd. Abundance, plurality, multiplicity.

Iomadamhuil. Multipliable.

Iomadhall. Guilt, fin, iniquity.

Iomadh. Many.

Iomaduigh. Superfluity, too much.

Iomagan. Flitting.

Iomagal. A dialogue.

Iomaguin. Anxiety.

Iomaghuinach. Anxious, diftracted.

Iomagallaimh. Counfel, advice.

Iomaidfi, iomhadh. Envy.

Iomaigh. A border.

Iomaigh. Champaign ground.

Iomaille. Together.

Iomaine. For Uiminne, over us, about us.

Iomainam. To drive, to tofs; whirl.

Iomain. Driving before it.

Iomaire. A ridge.

Iomairachd. Courting.

Iomaire. Removing, changing refidence.

Iomaircam. To migrate.

Iomairam. To play, game ; to require, need.

Iomairt. Playing, gaming.

Iomairtaiche. A gamblei.

Iomairtach. Gameful.

Iomaitham. To check, rebuke.

Iomaithfhear. One that checks or rebukes.

Iomall. A border, frontiers.

Iomallach. Remote, external.

Iomaltar. A center.

Iomarafg. Deverbium.

Iomairaidfheachd. Decency.

Iomairaidhe. Decent, becoming fit.

Iomarbhadh. A lie, deceit, ftrife.

Iomarbhaidh. A debate, controverfy.

Iomaibhaighe. Comparifon.

Iomarbhas. Sin, banifhment.

Iomarcach. Very numerous, fuperfluous.

Iomarcaidh. Superfluity.

Iomarchur. Rowing, fteering with oars.

Iomarchui. Tumbling, wallowing.

Iomartas. Induftry.

Iomarfgal. Wreftling.

Iomafcrach. An inn or lodging-place.

Iomarull.

Iombath. The adjoining fea, fea encompaffing an ifland.

Iombathadh. Overwhelming, fwooning.

Iombatham. To overwhelm, fall into a fwoon.

Iombbhuaillam. To hurt or ftrike foundly.

Iombbholgadh. Filling.

Iomchaifin. A looking, obferving.

Iomchaomhnas. A queftion.

Iomcharmhail. A tribute, cuftom, toll.

Iomchafam. To murmur, complain.

Iomcharam. ⎱ To carry, move, ftir, deport,
Iomchram. ⎰ behave.

Iomchar. Carrying, moving, comportment.

Iomcharag. A female porter.

Iomchaoire. Reflection.

Iomchaoireach. Reflective.

Iomchlaidheamh. Sword-fighting.

Iomchlaidheamhoir. A fword-fighter, fencing-mafter.

Iomchomairc. A petition, requeft.

Iomchomharc. A gift, prefent, favour.

Iomchoiie. Complement.

Iomchomhineait. Strong, able.

Iomchomhradh. A thefis.

Iomchuidh. ⎱ Fit, meet, proper, de-
Iomchubhidh. ⎰ cent.

Iomchubhidhachd. Fitnefs, meetnefs, propriety.

Iomdha. Anger.

Iomdha. A fhoulder.

Iomdha. A bed or couch

Iomdha. For Iomadh, much, many.

Iomdhathach. Parti-coloured.

Iomdhorus. The lintel of a door.

Iomdhran. A drawing to.

Iomdhruidam. To enclose, shut in, to siege.

Iomdhruidadh. A siege, enclosing, impaling.

Iomfhorail. Superfluity, excess, extravagance.

Iomfhorran. A skirmish, battle.

Iomfhorran. A comparison.

Iomfoicheadh. A bawling, crying out.

Iomfoicham. To cry out, to bawl, squall.

Iomfhuasgailteach. Nimble.

Iomfhuasglach. A-propos, good at a pinch.

Iomfhulang. Patience, long-suffering.

Iomghabhail. Erring, straying.

Iomghaoth. An eddying wind, whirlwind.

Iomghnuis. Wonder.

Iomghuim. A battle.

Iomghuin. Pangs, agony.

Iomhadh. Envy.

Iomhaidh. An image, statue.

Iomhog. Ivory.

Iomhas. Knowledge, judgment, erudition.

Iomlaine. Maturity, perfection.

Iomladach. Moving, fickle.

Iomladam. To move, exchange.

Iomlaineachd. Fulfilling, accomplishment.

Iomlaiteadh. A rolling, turning, winding.

Iomlan. Full, complete.

Ioml.sgadh. Anxiety.

Iomlat. Gesture.

Iomlat, iomlad. Exchange, moving, stirring.

Iomligham. To lick, lambe.

Iomluadham. To talk much.

Iomluagal. Wandering, straying.

Iomluaimneach. Inconstant.

Iomluas. Fickleness.

Iomluasgadh. Commotion.

Iomne. As this, thus.

Iomnuachar. Polygamy.

Iomoill. Polygonous.

Iomoltoir. An altar.

Iomoi. Between.

Iomorach. A border.

Iomorran. A comparison.

Iomoidadh. A reproach, expostulation.

Iomoireascar. A wrestling, throwing down each other.

Iomorro. But.

Iomorthaigh. Comparison.

Iompoidh. An exhortation towards a conversion.

Iompoigheadh. A turning, a reeling, staggering.

Iompoigham. To turn, convert, rout, reel.

Iompoighte. Turned, converted.

Iompol. An error.

Iomradh. Fame, report.

Iomradhadh. Thinking, musing.

Iomradham. To muse, make mention.

Iomradhteach. Famous, eminent, renowned.

Iomramh. } Rowing.
Iomram. }

Iomram. } To row.
Iomramham. }

Iomramhaidhe. A rower.

Iomroil. Wandering, an error.

Iomraidheadh. Moving, stirring.

Iomraidheam. To publish, divulge, report, repeat.

Iomrolladh. Going off or away, departing.

Iomrollam. To go off, depart.

Iomruagadh. An invasion, routing, persecution.

Iomruagam. To invade, rout, disperse, persecute.

Iomruagaire. An invader, persecutor.

Iomruinam.

Iomruinam. To affign, appoint.
Iomfgaoilam. To difperfe.
Iomfgaoladh. Difperfion.
Iomfgarthadh. Separation.
Iomfhniomhach. Ghaftly.
Iomfgoltadh. Superfluity, excefs.
Iomtha.
Iomthach. } Envious.
Iomthaireag. A getting, finding.
Iomthnuth. Zeal, envy.
Iomthnuthoir. A zealous lover.
Iomthoineadh. A digreffion, a year.
Iomtholtaim. Free, voluntary.
Iomtothaidh. Wifdom, prudence.
Iomthus.
Iomthachd. } Departure, migration, Exodus.
Iomthufa. Adventures, feats.
Iomthus. Chance.
Iomthufa. As to, with regard to.
Iomuinne. About us, concerning us.
Iomuireadh. Excefs, exacting.
Ion. In compound words fignifies fitnefs.
Iona. For Ann a, whereof, in which.
Ionach. A dirk.
Ionad. For Annad, in thee.
Ionad. A place, or room.
Ionadh. Admiration, wonder.
Ionaid. A vicegerent, viceroy.
Ionailgham. To wafh, cleanfe.
Ionaire. The decenteft word for convey-
  ing the idea of the privities, male and
  female.
Ionaiteghte. Habitable.
Ionaithionta. Knowable.
Ionaltradh Pafture.
Ionaltram. To pafture, feed, graze.
Ionamhuil.
Ionnann. } Equal, the fame.
Ionaolam. To white-wafh.
Ionar. Whither.
Ionar. A kind of mantle.
Ionar. Bowels.
Ionaram. To clothe.

Ionaradh. Clothing.
Ionarbhadh. Banifhment, expelling.
Ionarbham. To banifh, expel, exile, thruft
  forth.
Ionarbtha. Banifhed, exiled.
Ionarbirdheil. A fluice.
Ionas, ionnas. Treafure.
Ionbhaidh. The time of a woman's bear-
  ing.
Ionbholgadh. Filling, fwelling, extending.
Ionbholgam. To fill, fwell, extend.
Ioncamos. Ufury, intereft.
Ioncamoir. An ufurer.
Ionchoibhche. Saleable.
Ionchoimeas. Comparable.
Ionchoimhead. Confervable.
Ioncholnadh. Incarnation.
Ioncholnaighte. Incarnate.
Ioncollnuigham. To become incarnate.
Ionchomharaighte. Remarkable.
Ionchonfpoideach. Debateable.
Ionchofg. Inftruction, doctrine.
Ionchofgam. To teach.
Ionchofgthoir. A teacher.
Ionchofanta. Defenfible.
Ionchraffal. Excrement.
Ionchreimgha. Corrodible.
Ionchuibh. Bowels.
Ionchuir. Capable, comparable, engraft-
  ing.
Iondaortha. Condemnable.
Ionditalta. Indictable.
Iondiola. Vendible.
Iondheanta. Feafible.
Ionduile,
Ionduileamhuil. } Defireable.
Iondus So that, infomuch.
Iondran. Miffing.
Iondranam. To mifs.
Iondula. Fit.
Ionduthras. Negligence.
Ionfhoinn. Defireable.
Ionfhorran A fkirmifh, battle.

7   Iunga.

Ionga. A nail, claw, talon, hoof; pl. Ingne.

Ionghabhail. Circumfpection.

Ionghlacta. }
Ionghabhala. } Acceptable.

Iongabhras. Without queftion, doubtlefs.

Iongabhail. Management, conduct.

Ionghabham. To manage, conduct, regulate, guide, lead; to attack, fubject, reduce.

Iongantach. Wonderful, furprifing, ftrange.

Iongantas. }
Iongnadh. } Wonder, furprize, miracle.

Iongnadh do ghabhail. To wonder.

Iongnadh do ghlacail. To be aftonifhed.

Iongbhal. Gefture.

Iongglan. Unclean.

Iongar. Matter, pus.

Iongaraigham. To fuppurate.

Ionghuiram. To feed cattle, to herd.

Iongnatha. The dead.

Ionladh. Wafhing; a thing acceptable.

Ionlaid. Wafhing.

Ionlam. To wafh.

Ionlaighte. Wafhed.

Ionlaighthoir. A wafher, an accufer, informer.

Ionleathfgeulgha. Excufeable.

Ionlad. A wafhing.

Ionlaoghas. Encreafe.

Ionmhall. Heavinefs, fatigue.

Ionmhaithte. Ignofcible, pardonable.

Ionmhagaidh. Ridiculous.

Ionmhas. }
Ionnas. } Treafure.

Ionmheallta. Fallible.

Ionmholta. Commendable, praife-worthy.

Ionmhathuighte. Perceptible.

Ionmhuin. Kind, loving, courteous, debonair.

Ionmhuinach. Beloved.

Ionmhuinachd. Courteoufnefs, ftate of being beloved.

Ionn. Upper part, the head.

Ionnad. For Annad, in thee.

Ionnuinne. For Anninne, in us.

Ionnaltoir. A bath.

Ionnan. Equal, fame.

Ionnanas. Equality.

Ionnarachd. A gift.

Ionnaradh. A reward.

Ionnaram. To reward.

Ionnarbham. To confine, deftroy.

Ionnus. So that, infomuch that.

Ionnchuireadh. Grafting.

Ionnduras. Chaftity.

Ionnlaigh. Accufation.

Ionnlaigham. To accufe.

Ionnlaighthoir. Accufer.

Ionnoir. The bowels.

Ionolta. Potable, drinkable.

Ionphianafda. Punifhable.

Ionnrach. A medical tent.

Ionnraic. Honeft, upright, chafte, faithful.

Ionnracas. Integrity, uprightnefs.

Ionnracan. An honeft, upright perfon.

Ionnradh. Deftroying, plundering, laying wafte.

Ionnradhach. That deftroyeth, plundereth, layeth wafte.

Ionnradham. To lay wafte, plunder, deftroy.

Ionnran. An account, reckoning.

Ionnranam. To reckon.

Ionnrofg. A word.

Ionnfa. Grief, forrow.

Ionnfach. Sorrowful, fatal.

Ionnfaidh. An approach to, an attack, affault, fally.

Ionnfaigham. To approach, attack, affault.

Ionnfaigheach. An aggreffor.

Ionnfmuaintighte. Imaginable.

Ionnfamhuil. Such like.

Ionnfhorchughadh. Illuminating, enlightening.

Ionnfgathmhach

Ionnſgathmhach. A looſeneſs of the ſkin.
Ionnſuigh. An invaſion, attack, aſſault.
Ionnta. Unawares.
Ionntabhartha. Allowable.
Ionntlas. Long.
Ionntodham. To roll, turn, tumble, wallow, to wind, to ſcorn, flight.
Iontuite. Fallible.
Iorails. }
Iorailtachd. } Ingenuity.
Iorailteach. Ingenious.
Iorbal. A tail. Vid. Earball.
Iorcallach. A robuſt, ſtrong fellow.
Iorchadach. Evil.
Iorchaire. Poſterity.
Iordhalta. Certain, continual.
Iorgadh. Guiding, directing.
Iorguil. Fray, ſtrife, tumult, ſkirmiſh.
Iorghuilach. Quarrelſome.
Iorghuis. Prayer, entreaty.
Iorlann. A cellar, buttery, larder.
Iorna. }
Iornan. } A haſp, or ſpindle of yarn.
Iorpais The dropſy.
Iorrtaoiſeach. The captain of the rearguard.
Iorrlaochra. Tiiarii.
Iorſubhaiſgeith. The handles of a buckler.
Ios. For Sios, down; Anios & ſios, to and fro.
Ioſa. Jeſus.
Ioſadh. Eating.
Ioſal. Low.
Ioſam. To eat.
Ioſcad. Vid. Eaſgud.
Ioſda. A houſe, habitation.
Ioſda nam bochd. The poor's houſe.
Ioſdan. A college.
Ioſdas Entertainment, accommodation.
Ioſdail. Convenient, meet.
Ioſlaigham. To humble, lower, degrade.
Ioſlaghadh. Lowering, humbling.
Ioſle. Lower.

Ioſlad. Lowneſs.
Ioſlann. A ſtorehouſe, larder, buttery.
Ioſoip. Hyſſop.
Iota, iotan. Thirſt.
Ioth. Corn.
Iothchruinuigham. To forage, purvey.
Iothghaireach. Fertile.
Iothghaireachd. Fertility.
Iothlann. A granary, barn, corn-yard.
Iothloſgadh. A blaſting of corn.
Iothros. Cockle.
Iotmhor. Thirſty.
Iphin. The gooſeberry tree, name of the diphthong io.
Ir. Anger.
Ir. A ſatire, lampoon.
Ircilt. Side poſt of a door.
Ircra. Scarcity.
Irchiullach. A monſter.
Ire. Ground, land.
Ireas. Occurſion.
Irial. An anſwer, reply, ſalutation, greeting.
Irionn. A field, land, ground.
Irioſal. Humble.
Irire. A cure, malediction, blame, anger.
Iris. Braſs.
Iris. A hen-rooſt.
Iris. A friend, lover.
Iris. An aſſignation.
Iris. A deſcription, diſcovery, a record, chronicle.
Iris. An æra, epoch.
Iriſeas. A preſent.
Iriſeach. Juſt, judicious, equitable.
Iriſich. Lawful.
Iriſlaigham. To humble.
Iriſeal. Humble, lowly.
Iriſleachd. Humility.
Iriſleabhar. A diary, day-book.
Iriſlachadh. Humiliation.
Iriſneartughadh. A confirmation.
Irr. An end, concluſion; a fiſh's tail.

Irrſithbhe.

Irrfithbhe. } Commander of the rear-
Irrthreoruidhe. } guard.

Irt.

Is. The fubftantive verb Am.

Is. Contracted improperly for Agus, and.

Is. Under.

Ifa. Whofe, whereof.

Ifa. } She.
Ife. }

Ifben. A faucer.

Ifean. A chicken, young fowl.

Ifeal. Low, privily, foftly.

Ifgeas. Doubt.

Ifi. She herfelf.

Ifiol. Low.

Iflain. A humble, poor perfon.

Ifle. Lower.

Ifliughadh. Humiliation.

Ifraeldha. Ifraelitifh.

Iffa. In that, in that place.

Ite. } A feather, wing, fin.
Itag. }

Itagach. Feathered.

Itachan. A bobbin for yarn.

Itach. Winged.

Italaich. Flying.

Italaicham. To fly.

Ite. In like manner, alfo, to wit.

Itche. A petition, favour, requeft.

Ith. Corn.

Itheadh. Eating.

Itham. To eat.

Ithchomla. A file.

Ithdhias. An ear of corn.

Ithfen. A carr, or dray for corn.

Ithiomradh. A murmuring, grumbling, backbiting.

Ithiomraidhteach. Slanderous, abufive, backbiting.

Ithiomradham. To flander, backbite.

Ithir. Corn-field, foil.

Ithte. Eaten.

Itropa. A head.

Itros. A headland.

Iubhar. The yew tree.

Iubhar-talamh. } Juniper.
Iubhar-beinne. }

Iuchair. A key, fpawn.

Iucharag. The female fifh.

Iuchar. The dog-days.

Iudh. A day, An iudh, to-day.

Iudiceachd. Judgment.

Iudach. A Jew.

Iul, eol. Knowledge, a guide, a fea compafs, way, fervice, attendance.

Iul. Month of July.

Iulmhor. Wife, judicious.

Iullagach. Light, fprightly, cheerful.

Iullagaiche. Cheerfulnefs.

Iumarach. Removing, changing place.

Iumhrach. A boat.

Iun. A naughty creature.

Iuna. Vid. Ionadh.

Iundran. Vid. Iondran.

Iunaras. Face of the fky; hurricane.

Iunnfachadh. Learning, education.

Iunnfaigham. To learn.

Iunnfaighte. Learned.

Iur. The yew tree.

Iur. Plunder, flaughter.

Iuran. A fort of luxuriant plant which cattle eat; metaphorically a handfome youth.

Iuarram. Fidgeting; the oar fong, a long libel or rhime.

Iurpais. Reftlefs, neftling.

Iufan. Levity.

L.

Is the ninth letter of the Gaelic alphabet, and is called Luis, from Luis, vulgarly Crithan, the quicken-tree. It, as also N, R, never admits the aspirate h after it in the inflection of nouns or verbs, but is founded in such situations as if a ll. Thus labhair e, he spoke, is not as with the other letters lhabhair e, but llabhair e, although never written so. Vide Analysis.

La, lo, laoi. A day; pl. Laethe.

La le Muire. Lady-day.

La, lia. In old mss. for Le, with.

Laban. Mire, dirt.

Labanach. A plebeian, day-labourer.

Labanta. Of a plebeian or labourer.

Labaonadh. Dissimulation.

Labhairt. }
Labhradh. } A speech, speaking.

Labhar, labeir. An ewer, laver.

Labharam. }
Labhram. } To speak.

Labhartha. Said, spoken, loud, noisy.

Labragan. Perhaps a walking-stick.

Labhras. A bay-tree.

Lach A duck, drake.

Lachach. Abounding in ducks.

Lacha-ceannruadh. The herb celandine.

Lacha-lochlannach. A dunter-goose.

Lach a' chinn uaine. A mallard.

Lachadh. Diving like a duck.

Lacham. To dive, duck.

Lachadair. }
Lachaire. } A diver.

Lachmhor. Comely.

Lachd. Milk.

Lachd. A family.

Lachdan. }
Lachtna. } Homespun, grey, dun.

Lad. A water-course, a lade.

Lad. A load.

Ladh. A sending, mission.

Ladham. To send.

Ladhar. A fork, prong, toe.

Ladharg. A thigh.

Ladhg. Snow.

Laddar. A ladle.

Ladhgan. Flummery.

Ladhna. Dumbness.

Ladhgrach. Hasty.

Ladhgraith. Rashness.

Ladorn. Bold.

Ladornachd }
Ladornas. } Boldness.

Ladhuilgne. A day's wages.

Ladron. A thief, highwayman.

Laethamhuil. Daily.

Lag. Weak, feeble, faint.

Lag. A hollow, cavity.

Laga. Praise, fame, honour.

Lagaigham. To weaken, diminish, lessen.

Lagaghadh. Weakening.

Lagan. A little cavity.

Lagan-meachaire. A dimple.

Laganal. A gasp, asthma.

Lagatrag. The thigh.

Lagchuisach. }
Lagchriodhach. } Faint-hearted.

Lagh. Law, order; Cuiram air lagh bogha, to bend or prepare a bow.

Laghamhuil. Legal, lawful.

Laghamhlachd. Legality.

Laghairt. A lizard.

Laghar,

Laghar, lagharog. A prong, toe.

Laghrach. Pronged, forked.

Lagſaine. Diminiſhing.

Lagſaine. Freedom, liberty, remiſſion.

Lagthaiſde. An abatement in a bargain.

Lagrachar. Debility.

Laibh. Clay.

Laibhin. Leaven.

Laibhreach. A coat of mail.

Laidheachan. An ambuſcade, ſnare, lying in wait.

Laidham. To lay down.

Laidionn. Latin.

Laidionnoir Latiniſt.

Laidh-ſhiubhla. Childbed.

Laidireas. } Strength.
Laidreachd. }

Laidir. Strong.

Laidre. Stronger.

Laidraigham. To ſtrengthen.

Laige. Weaker.

Laige. } Weakneſs, debility.
Laigſe. }

Laighe. A ſpade, ſhovel.

Laigbhigheach. Weakened, diſmayed.

Laighean. A ſpear, javelin, halberd.

Laigheann. The province of Leinſter.

Lailt. Mould, clay.

Laimh, lamh. A hand.

Laimh-ri. Nigh to, near.

Laimhbhaſbam. To fence.

Laimhcheard. A handycraft, any mechanic trade.

Laimdeachus. Captivity.

Laimhdia. A domeſtic god.

Laimheadh. Handling, preſuming.

Laimhuigham. To handle, take into cuſtody, preſume.

Laimhfhoillead. A handkerchief.

Laimhſgiath. A target.

Laimhſigham. To handle, finger, diſcuſs.

Laimhrig. A pier, ford.

Laimhthionnach. Deſirous, eager, given to chiromancy.

Lain }
Lainad. } Fulneſs.
Laine. }

Lainbhliaghanach. Perennial.

Laincheatharn A guard.

Laincheimnigham. To wander.

Lainchriochnuigham. To complete, perfect.

Laindeanta. Complete, finiſhed.

Laine. Fuller, more full.

Laine. Chearfulneſs, merriment.

Laineachd. Glad, joyful, merry.

Lainne. Gen. of Lann, a ſpear, blade.

Lainneach. Armed with a ſpear.

Lainnal. Handſome, buxom.

Lainneoir, laidionnoir. A Latiniſt.

Lainmheirleach. A ſacrilegious perſon.

Lainreidham. To complete.

Lainſhoillſe. Tranſparency, diaphanity.

Lainſiubhlam. To traverſe.

Laiphaid. An inſtrument uſed to form horn ſpoons.

Lair. A mare.

Lair-aſſal. A ſhe aſs.

Laire. } The thigh.
Lairge. }

Lairge. Rather than.

Lais. Vide Leir.

Lais. A hand.

Laiſde. A latch.

Laiſe. A flame, flaſh.

Laiſceanta. Fierce.

Laiſeadh. Throwing, caſting.

Laiſeam. To throw, caſt down.

Laith. A multitude.

Laith. Milk.

Laithe. Scales to weigh gold and ſilver.

Laitheamhuil. Daily.

Laithgheur. Verjuice, acetum.

Laithigh. Dirt, mire.

Laithilt. Weighing with scales.

Laithre. A cow.

Laithreach. Ruins of an old house.

Laithrigham. To appear, be present.

Laithreachd. Presence.

Laithreach. Present.

Laitis. Lattice.

Lalach. A giant.

Lamais. A poet.

Lamanta. Menstruous; Mna lamanta, mulieres menstruatæ.

Lamh. A hand.

Lamh an uachdar. Upper or whip hand.

Lamhach. Having hands, active.

Lamhach. Report of guns or cannon, warlike manœuvres.

Lamhachas. Idem; Luchd lamhachais, bowmen, slingers, artillery

Lamhadh. }
Lamhagan. } Handling, groping.

Lamham. To dare, presume.

Lamhainn. A glove.

Lamh-laidir. Strong hand, force.

Lamh-dheas. Right-hand.

Lamh-chli. Left-hand.

Lamhainn-iaruinn. A gauntlet.

Lamhainneoir. A glover.

Lamhanart. A towel.

Lamhannan. A bladder.

Lamhairt. Handling.

Lamhcheard. A mechanic.

Lamhcheardamhuil. Mechanical.

Lamhcharam. To handle.

Lamhchomhart. A clapping of the hands.

Lamhchoille. A cubit.

Lamhdeanas. A restraint.

Lamhdhroithachd. Chiromancy.

Lamhdhraoith. Chiromancer, palmistry.

Lamhliaigh A surgeon.

Lamhmhuilleann. A hand-mill.

Lamhrod. A bye-road, foot-path.

Lamhrachdidh. A handling, large dealing.

Lamhrachan. A handle, shaft.

Lamhragan. Fingering, handling.

Lamhsgriobhadh. Manuscript.

Lamhsgriobhaidh. Amanuensis.

Lamhspeic. A handspike.

Lamna. A space of time.

Lampa. A lamp.

Lamprog. A glow-worm.

Lamrag. An ignorant silly woman.

Lamruig. A black-bird with white spots, supposed to be an Allen-hawk.

Lan. Full, in composition signifies perfection, enough, well.

Lan-mara. The tide.

Lan. A church.

Lan, lann. A scale, fin.

Lan. Before, in comparison of.

Lana. A lane or walk.

Lanamhuin. A couple, married couple.

Lanamhnas. Carnal copulation.

Lanbhuidheann. A garrison.

Lanchoire. A cauldron-full.

Lanchomhlam. To perform, finish, accomplish.

Lanchriochnuighte. Fully accomplished.

Lanchrodha. Courageous.

Lanchumhachdach. Plenipotentiary.

Lanchumhachd. Plenipotence.

Landaingneachd. Perseverance.

Lang. Falshood, treachery.

Langa. A sort of fish.

Langan. Noise, lowing of deer

Langan-braghad. The weasand.

Langach. Slim, slender.

Langaiche. Slimness.

Langaid. Fetters for horses.

Langaire. Soam.

Langfethir. Fetters, chains.

Langhuin. A period.

Langerilach. A lamprey.

Lanluach. Full-price.

Lann. Land.

Lann. A house, repository, church.

Lann. A veil, a vizard.

Lann. A fword, knife, blade.

Lann. A gridiron.

Lann. A ftud, a bofs.

Lann. A fcale.

Lanngan. The lowing of the hind after the deer.

Lannam. To cut, put to the fword.

Lannadh. Peeling.

Lannadha. Studded.

Lanngleuta. An inclofure.

Lannoir. A cow.

Lanntoir. A pantry, partition.

Lanphunc. A full period or ftop.

Lannuir. Gleaming, glitter, fplendor, radiance.

Lannruicham. To gleam, glitter, fhine, emblaze, befpangle.

Lannruchadh. Gliftening, gleaming, glittering.

Lannrach. A vaft flame.

Lanfaidhe. A pike-man.

Lanfgrudadh. Perpenfion.

Lanfhoilleir. Evident, clear.

Lanfhuileach. Full eyed.

Lantlachd. A perfect liking.

Lantoileach. Perfectly fatisfied.

Lantoil. Satisfaction.

Lanthurbha. A guard.

Lantolladh. Perforation.

Laobh. Partial, prejudiced.

Laobhdha. Bending, inclining.

Laoch. A hero; pl. Laochra.

Laochamhuil. Brave, heroic.

Laochan. A little hero.

Laochra. Militia.

Laodh. Vide Laogh.

Laodhan. Pith of wood, pulp, marrow.

Laodag. The little-finger.

Laogh. A calf, a fawn.

Laoghach. Abounding in calves.

Laogh-allaidh. A fawn.

Laoghar. A claw, toe.

Laoghfheoil. Veal.

Laoghrach. Pronged, forked, having toes.

Laogh. Snow.

Laoi, la, lo. A day.

Laoidh. An hymn, a poem.

Laoidheadh. An exhortation.

Laoidham. To exhort.

Laoileabhar. A diary.

Laoimheadhan. Mid-day, noon-tide.

Laoireult. Morning-ftar.

Laoinneach. Fine, ftately, fhewy.

Laom. A blaze of fire.

Laomdha. Bent, bowed, crookened

Laomhdhachd. Curvature, crookednefs.

Laomfguire. Great, prodigious.

Laofboc. A wether goat.

Lapach. Froft-bitten, benumbed.

Lapadh. A paw or fift.

Lapadan. A kind of fea-fifh.

Lar. The ground-floor, middle, center.

Larach. A field of battle, fite of a building, veftige.

Larach. A filley.

Larum. An alarm.

Las. Light thou.

Lafach. Slack.

Lafachadh. Slackening.

Lafach. That burneth, fiery, flammable.

Lafadh. Lighting, kindling, fhining, flaming.

Lafair. Flame.

Laffag. Faggots, combuftibles.

Lafair-choille. A goldfinch, a woodpecker.

Lafam. To light, kindle, burn.

Lafan. Anger, paffion.

Lafanta. Paffionate.

Lafantacht. Habitude to anger.

Lafarach. Flaming, burning

Lafd. Ballaft, lading.

Lafar teintigh. A flafh of lightning.

La-fodhain. Therefore, by fo much as.

Laffaire. A flafhy young fellow, a fpark.

Laftain. Hem, edge.

Lat. A foot.

Lath. A youth, champion, dog.

Lathach. Mud, puddle.

Lathair. Prefence.

Lathreach. Prefent.

Lathairamhuil. Immediate.

Lathairce. A thigh.

Lathar. An affembly.

Lathar. A private ftory, or narrative.

Lathar. Strength, vigour.

Lathar. Near.

Lathroid. An affembly.

Lathuilgne. A day's wages.

Lauba. An eye-brow.

Le. With.

Lea. With her.

Leab, leabog. A piece, fragment.

Leabe. A bed, pl. Leapacha.

Leabe-chul-beinc. A bed formed by the wall on one fide of a highland houfe, the trunk of a tree on the other, between which is placed enough of heath or ftraw, and fome blankets, whither, as a public bed, the whole family and guefts, when there are any, are promifcuoufly admitted.

Leabe-chluimh. A feather-bed.

Leabe-fhloccuis. A mattrafs.

Leabe-fheiftior. A couch, pallet.

Leabe-thogalach. A folding bed.

Leabag. A flounder.

Leabag-chearr. A foal.

Leabar. Smooth.

Leabhach. Awry, ftaring.

Leabhadh. Reading, a lecture.

Leabham. To read.

Leabhadair. A reader.

Leabhadoirachd. Reading.

Leabhar. A book.

Leabhar. Long, trailing.

Leabhar-chlar. Pafteboard.

Leabhar-reicadair. A bookfeller.

Leabharagan. } A library.
Leabharlann· }

Leabhar, libhearn. A fhip.

Leabhrach. Bookifh.

Leabharan. A little book.

Leac. A flat ftone, a flate.

Leacach. Flat ftones, full of flat ftones.

Leacadh. Deftroying.

Leacam. To flay, deftroy.

Leacanta. Rigid, precife, neat.

Leac-oidhre. A flake of ice.

Leac-lithe. A grave-ftone.

Leacain. Side of a hill, the cheek.

Leacht. A grave, a pile of ftones in memory of the dead.

Leacht, leachtfa. With thee, thine.

Leacht. A leffon.

Leachta. Flattened, molten.

Leachtam. To fpread.

Leachtan. A lecture, inftruction.

Leachtuighe. A fepulchre.

Lead. Breadth, extent.

Lead, lead fe. He faid.

Leadan. Teazle.

Leadan-liofta. Burrdock.

Leadan. Mufical notes, litany.

Leadan. A head of hair.

Leadanach. Precife, mufical, that hath fine hair.

Leadhman. A moth.

Lead-boife. A hand-breadth.

Leadurra. Elegant.

Leadh, leath. Alternate.

Leadram, liodram. To tear, rend, mangle, maim.

Leagh. Melt thou.

Leag. Vide leicc.

Leagam. To throw down, fall.

Leagadh. A fall.

Leaghad. A band, bandage.

Leaghadair. A founder, fmelter.

Leagham. To melt, thaw, diffolve.

Leaghach.

Leaghach. Colliquant.

Leagham. To read.

Leaghan. Liquor.

Leaghthoir. A reader.

Leaghte. Melted.

Leaglaidh. Rufhes.

Leagaim. To lick, to clip, fhear.

Leagail. Clipping, fhearing, throwing down.

Leam, leamfa. With me.

Leam leat, rium riut. A falfe perfon.

Leamam. To nip.

Leamh. Foolifh, fimple, infipid, mealy-mouthed.

Leamh. A rower.

Leamhachas. }
Leamhadas. } Simplicity, foolifhnefs.

Leamhan. The elm tree, the inner rind of a tree.

Leamhan. A moth, night butterfly.

Leamhdhanachd. Fool-hardinefs.

Leamhdanach. Fool-hardy.

Leamhnachd. Sweet milk.

Leamhnachadh. Stopping.

Leamhnaireach. Coy.

Leamhragan. A pimple on the eye.

Lean, leun. Sorrow, ruin.

Leana. A meadow, fwampy plain.

Leanam. To follow, adhere, purfue.

Leanabh. A child.

Leanabh-liughach. A puppet, doll.

Leanabh-altram. A fofter-child.

Leanaban. A little child.

Leanabanachd. Infancy.

Leanabas. } Childifhnefs, pufillani-
Leanabidhachd. } mity.

Leanabidh. Pufillanimous.

Leanag. A little meadow.

Leanaill. }
Leantin, } Following, adhering.

Leanailtach. Following, perfevering, adhering.

Leanmhain. Following, adhering.

Leanamhain. Goods, fubftance.

Leann. Humours of the body.

Leann. Ale.

Leann. A coarfe caffock, coat of mail.

Leann-loifg. Dregs from which ale is brewed.

Leannan. A favourite, fweetheart, pet, concubine.

Leannan-fith. A familiar fpirit, fuccubus.

Leannantachd. Whoredom, fornication.

Leanartuch. The herb tormentil.

Leanghobhrag. A fnipe.

Leanta. Paffions, humours.

Leaptha. Belonging to a bed.

Leapthach. Bedding.

Lear. For Le ar, with our.

Lear. The fea.

Lear. Clear, evident.

Lear. Much, a great deal.

Leardhromain. The ridge of a hill.

Learfhaicfin. Seeing clearly.

Learg. The rain goofe, it is grey, neftles within reach of the water, and never rifes during incubation—A fmall brown fort of fcarth or cormorant.

Learg. A little eminence, a beaten path.

Leargaidh. The floping fide of a country.

Leargan. The fteepnefs of a fmall hill.

Leargach. Steep.

Learmhaddadh. A dog-fifh.

Learfgail. A map.

Learfinach. Acute, fharp-fighted.

Learthaod. A fpring tide.

Learthoid. A foot-ball.

Lear-uinuin. A fea onion, fquill.

Leas. A blifter, a blotch, a fpot.

Leas. The light.

Leas. A reafon, motive, caufe.

Leas, lios. A court.

Leafach. Full of blifters.

Leafaigham. To blifter.

Leafachadh. Bliftering.

Leafachail. Epifpaftic, efcharotic.

Leafainm.

Leafainm. A nickname.

Leafmhathair. A ftepfather.

Leafluan. ⎫
Leafgoth. ⎬ A ftepfon.
Leafmhac. ⎭

Leafluidh. Leaning upon.

Leafmhurfaid. A galoon.

Leafs. Good, profit, advantage.

Leaffachadh. Correcting, amending, repairing, manure.

Leaffaigham. To rectify, correct, amend; to manure, clean fhoes.

Leaffaighte. Rectified, repaired, manured.

Leafrach Thighs.

Leaftair. An arrow-maker

Leaftar. A cup, ftale butter.

Leaftar. A fmall boat.

Leaftar. The veffels and furniture of a houfe.

Leiath-fiar. America.

Leat, leatfa. With thee.

Leatadach, Wide, large.

Leath. Half, apart, feparate.

Leatha. Gain, profit.

Leath-taice. A prop.

Leathach. Half, divided.

Leathad. Breadth.

Leatham. To half, divide.

Leathadaigham. To augment, encreafe, enlarge.

Leathan. Broad.

Leathanach. A page of a book.

Leathainm. A nickname.

Leath-amach. ⎫ External, outward, out-
Leath-amuigh. ⎬ fide.

Leath-aftigh. Internal, infide, inward.

Leathar. Leather.

Leathbhrith. Parboiled.

Leathbhritham. To parboil.

Leathbhreac. Mate, fellow, marrow, correlate.

Leathcheann. Side of the head.

Leathchearcal. A femicircle.

Leathchodlam. To dofe, fleep ill.

Leathchruinne. A femicircle, hemifphere.

Leathchuid. Half fhare; partiality.

Leathfhad. A declivity, flope.

Leathghrabal. A halfpenny.

Leathid. The like, fuch.

Leathlagfa. Somewhat weak and feeble.

Leath-leann. Small beer.

Leathluidhe. Leaning.

Leathmhas. A buttock.

Leathniche. A rolling pin.

Leathnuigham. To enlarge, fcatter.

Leathog. A flounder, plaice.

Leathphunt. Eight ounces.

Leathrach. Leather.

Leathrann. Half, a hemiftich.

Leathrannach. Partial.

Leathre. Towards.

Leathrofg. Purblindnefs.

Leathrofgach. Purblind.

Leathchomalta. Half eaten.

Leathriogh. A copartner in government.

Leathruadh. Somewhat red.

Leathrod. A bye path.

Leathfgoiltain. A plank, joift.

Leathfgeul. An excufe.

Leathfgeulach. Excufatory.

Leathfgeulaiche. A mediator.

Leathfhuileach. Monocular.

Leath-taobh. One fide, a flitch.

Leathtromach. Oppreffive, partial; pregnant.

Leathtruime. Oppreffion, counterweight, pregnancy.

Leathuiluinn. Half fitting; acute angle.

Legaid. A legate, ambaffador.

Legaide. A legacy.

Leibeann. A long ftretch, ftride.

Leibheann. The deck of a fhip, a fcaffold, gallery; fide of a hill.

Leibh, leibhfe. With you.

Leice. Neglect.

Leicc, leug. A precious ftone, diamond. In the highlands a large cryftal of a figure

[M m m]   fomewhat

fomewhat oval, which priefts kept to work charms by. Water poured upon it, at this day, is given to cattle againft difeafes. Thefe ftones are now preferved for the fame purpofes by the oldeft and the moft fuperftitious in the country.

Leicead. Neat, elegant.

Leiceanta. Exact, neat, precife.

Leidmach. Strong, robuft.

Leidmhighe. An appetite.

Leigiun. A legion.

Leigeadh. Permitting, letting, difcharging.

Leigadair. A fpigot.

Leigam. To let, permit, difmifs.

Leigal. Letting.

Leigam gunna. To fire a gun.

Leigam orm. To pretend.

Leigam as. To loofe from the yoke, difmifs.

Leigheadh. Permiffion.

Leigh. A phyfician.

Leighean. Inftruction, erudition.

Leighas. A cure, remedy, medicine, healing.

Leighafam. To cure, heal.

Leighafta. Cured, healed.

Leigheoir. A mender.

Leighionn. Vide Leigheann.

Leighin. A ftudent.

Leighlofgadh. Cautery.

Leighloifgam. To cauterize.

Leighthoir. A reader.

Leighthoirachd. Reading.

Leigteal. Any thing melted.

Leim. A leap.

Leim (Chuchullin). Loop's head at the mouth of the Shannon.

Leimhe. Simplicity, folly.

Leimadoir. A dolphin, a leaper, jumper.

Leimam.
Leimnigham. } To leap, jump.

Leimneach. Leaping, defultory.

Leimfgian. A razor.

Leine. A fhirt, fhift.

Leine-aifrionn. A furplice.

Leingean. A ftepdaughter.

Leinne. By or with us.

Leinbhbhreith. Childbirth.

Leinbhluafga. A cradle.

Leir. Sight, perception.

Go leir. Altogether.

Leir. Wife, prudent, clofe, managing.

Leirg. A plain, a road, or way.

Leirg. A reafon, motive.

Leirgam. To counterfeit, pretend.

Leireadh. Tormenting, paining, pain.

Leiram. To pain, torment, thrill, pierce.

Leirighe. Being in fight.

Leirfholach. A canopy.

Leirfin. Sight, feeing.

Leirfinach. Seeing, intelligent.

Leirfgrios. Utter deftruction.

Leiriftin. A mallet, hammer.

Leirfmuine. Confideration, reflection.

Leirmheas. Ballancing, confidering.

Leirte. Earneftnefs.

Leis. With him, it, wherewith, to the leeward.

Leis, leife. Of a thigh. Vide Leafs.

Leis. Apparently.

Leifbheart. Armour for the thighs.

Leifdhear.
Leifinghean. } A ftep-daughter.

Leife. Happinefs.

Leifg. Sloth, lazinefs.

Leifg, leifgeamhuil. Lazy, flothful.

Leifgeul. An excufe.

Leite. Water-gruel.

Leithe, leithad. More grey, greynefs.

Leithe. Mouldinefs.

Leithe. The fhoulder-blade.

Leitheach. A kneeding-trough.

Leitheach, leitheag. A flounder, plaice.

Leith, leath. A half.

Leithbhe. Partiality.

Leithdrechdam,

Leithdrechdam. To excufe.

Leithead. Breadth.

Leitheis. Derifion, Mockery.

Leithid. The like, a peer, paragon.

Leitheolach. A novice.

Leithiomal. A border, partial.

Leithimalach. Bordering, fuperficial.

Leithinnife. A peninfula.

Leithghlin. Denmark and Norway.

Leithneachd. Breadth.

Leithreachas. Separation.

Leithreachas. Unjuft dealing.

Leithreadh. Of a fide, together.

Leithleach. } Partial.
Leithridheach. }

Leithridhachd. Partiality.

Leithrigham. To appear, be in fight.

Leithrinn. Fetters.

Leithfgeul. An apology.

Leithfgeulam. To excufe, apologize.

Leithfe. This fide.

Leithtir. Side of a country.

Le m'. With my.

Lemhne. Fatnefs.

Lenne. Faces, complexions.

Lentog. A little fhirt or fhift.

Leo. With them.

Leo. } A lion.
Leoghan. }

Leobhar. Long, tawdry.

Leod. A cutting, mangling.

Leog. A marfh.

Leogach. Marfhy.

Leoghadh. Flattery.

Leogham. To flatter, footh.

Leoghanta. Lion-like.

Leoghantachd. Inconftancy.

Leoir. Enough.

Leomach. Flirting, prudifh.

Leomachas } Prudery.
Leom. }

Leomhan. } A moth.
Leomain. }

Leomaire. A fop.

Leon. Affliction, wound, mouth.

Leonam. To wound.

Leonadh. A wound, fprain.

Leonta. Wounded, fprained.

Leontachd. Brave actions, keennefs of morals.

Leor. Enough.

Leor-ghniomh. Satisfaction.

Leos. Reproof.

Leos. Light.

Leofam. To give light.

Leofchnuimh. A glow-worm.

Leofghath. } A ray of light.
Leofmheur. }

Ler. With which, whofe.

Lere. Religion.

Les. A bladder.

Les-lafgtha. A clyfter.

Lefimob. The ureter.

Lethe, letheachd. Hoarinefs.

Leud. Vide Lead.

Leug. A diamond, gem. Vide Leicc.

Leuga lomhar. Brilliant gems or diamonds.

Leum. A leap, leaping.

Leumam. To leap. Vide Leim.

Leumfgar. Clever.

Leur. Seeing.

Leurgus. Sight.

Leus. Light.

Leus. A fpot. Vide Leas.

Leufach. Having light.

Leufchnuimh. Vide Leafchnuimh.

Leufgath. Vide Leafgath.

Li, ligh, lithe. Colour, tinge.

Li. The fea.

Lia, le, ri.

Lia. For Leathane, broader.

Lia. A hog, pig.

Lia. Hunger.

Lia. A ftream, flood.

Lia. A great ftone.

Lia fail. The fatal ſtone, called Cloch na cineamhna, on which the Scottiſh kings were wont to be crowned, now in Weſt-minſter-abbey.

Liabhran. A little book.

Liachac. Hog's dung.

Liach. A ſpoon.

Liach. Bad news.

Liachd. Great many, a multitude.

Liachlan. A ſpoonful.

Liachro. A hog-ſtye.

Liadh. A ladle.

Liadhbhog. A flounder.

Liag. Vide Leag.

Liagan. An obeliſk.

Liaghdhealg. A bodkin, claſp, button adorned with cryſtal.

Liagh. A phyſician.

Liagh. The blade of an oar.

Liaphutog. A hog's pudding, ſauſage.

Lias. Vide Lios.

Lias. A hut for lambs.

Liath. Grey, grey-haired.

Liathag. A fiſh of the ſalmon kind.

Liathghath. A violent dart.

Liathchearc. The hen of the black cock.

Liathdrus. Muſtineſs.

Liathach. Pale, blank.

Liathadh. Making grey, a grey tinge.

Liatham. To tinge grey.

Liathluachaid. ⎱
Liathreothadh. ⎰ Hoar-froſt.

Liathlus. Mugwort.

Liathradh. Sliding, rolling.

Liathram. To ſlide, roll, ſprinkle on.

Liathroid. A ball, roller, a knob, chaff.

Liatis. Mouldy.

Liatruiſg. A fieldfare.

Libh. Vide Leibh.

Libar. A lip.

Libheadhan. A dowry.

Libhearn. A ſhip, houſe, habitation.

Li-dealbhtha. Painted.

Li-dealbhthoir. A painter, limner.

Lic. Gen. of Leac.

Licag. A little flat ſtone.

Liclith. A grave-ſtone.

Licnean. A wedge.

Lide. A little bit.

Lideach. Stopped.

Lig, leig. Allow, let thou.

Ligach. Sly.

Ligham. To lick.

Lil. A following, purſuing.

Lile. A lily.

Lilam. To follow.

Liltheach. Flexible, pliant.

Lin, lion. Flax, linen.

Linn. A line, thread, ſeries.

Lingeadh. A ſkipping, fly off, flinging, darting.

Lingam. To ſkip, go away, to fling, dart.

Linigham. To delineate.

Linighthoir. A delineator, deſigner.

Linleanta. An ill habit.

Linn, linne. With us.

Linne. A pool, the ſea, water.

Linn. An age, period.

Linngineach. Roundiſh.

Linnin. Linen of clothes.

Linnſgearadh. Genealogy.

Linſeach. One clothed in linen.

Linaodach. Linen cloth.

Linte, lionta. Full.

Liobor. A lip, a ſlovenly perſon.

Liobarnach. Slovenly, awkward.

Liobaſda. Slovenly.

Liobhadh. Smoothing.

Liobham. ⎱
Liobhram. ⎰ To ſmooth, poliſh, file.

Liobhan. A file.

Liobhan. Vide Leamhan.

Liobhtha. ⎫
Liobhte. ⎬ Poliſhed, filed.
Liobthara. ⎭

5

Liobhagach

Liobhagach. A floating weed common in standing water.

Liobhghruag. A wig.

Liobharam. To deliver.

Liobhairt. Delivery, delivering.

Lioboidach. Slow, lingering.

Liobrach. Thick-lipped.

Lioca. A cheek.

Liocadan. A chin-cloth.

Liocard. A leopard.

Liodan. A litany.

Liodart. Tearing in pieces.

Liodaram. To tear in pieces, bruife.

Liodha. Strong, able.

Liod. Lifping.

Liodach. That lifpeth.

Liodaiche. A lifper.

Liodhraimhe. } The blade of an oar.
Liogh. }

Liog. Vide Leug.

Liogam. To whet, edge.

Liogar A tongue.

Lioghais. Power, ability.

Lioghan. A trowel.

Lioghdha. Fair, fine, foft.

Liomhadh. Smoothing, polifhing.

Liomham. To polifh.

Liomhan. A file.

Liomhtha. } Polifhed, burnifhed.
Liomhara. }

Liomfa. Vide Leamfa.

Lion. Flax.

Lion. A net, fnare.

Lion. A parcel, number.

Lion an damhain allaidh. A cobweb.

Lion fear 'us fear. One by one.

Lionadh. Filling.

Lionadh-mara. The tide.

Lionam. To fill.

Lionaighe-tighe. } Cieling, tablature.
Lionigeadh. }

Lionta. Full.

Liontach. Satiating.

Liontachd. Satiety.

Lionadair. A funnel.

Lionchar. That which delighteth, pleafes.

Lionmhor. Numerous, plenty.

Lionmhorachd. Plenty, multiplicity.

Lionmhoire. More plenty.

Lion-obbair. Net-work.

Lionn. Ale. Vide Leann.

Lionn. A humour in the body.

Lionn-dubh. Melancholy, gloomy fits.

Lionnughadh. Growing in humours.

Lionradh. A web.

Lionradh. A thin mixed unfubftantial draught.

Lionta. Nets.

Lios. A houfe, habitation ; a palace, court, a fortified place ; now the name of the Danifh forts to be feen in Ireland.

Lios. Enclofures or ftalls for cattle.

Lios. The longing of a woman with child.

Liofair. A garden.

Liofda. Slow, lingering, tedious.

Liofdachd. Slownefs, tedioufnefs.

Liothadh. Frightening, difmaying.

Liothra. Hair.

Liothradharc. Pomp.

Lipin. A fmall meafure in Scotland called a lippie.

Lipin. Trufting to, confiding in.

Lis. Mifchief, evil.

Lifam. To mean, imagine, think of.

Lifg. Feelers.

Lit. Activity, celerity.

Lite. Porridge.

Lith. Happinefs, profperity.

Lith. Solemn, feftival.

Lithadh. That part of a river where the water ftagnates.

Litheas. Solemnity, pomp.

Lithiughadh. Aftonifhment, furprife.

Litimhaire. A diffembler.

Litir. A letter, epiftle. Pl. Litreacha.

Litir-dhealaghaidh. A bill of divorce.

Litir-ghrinnich. A challenge.

Liu. To follow, pursue.

Liuc. A shout, noise.

Liugadh. Creeping.

Liugach. Sneaking, creeping.

Liug. A contracted sneaking look.

Liumh. A cry, noise.

Liumhadh. Crying out.

Liumham. To cry out, shout.

Liun. Slothful, sluggish.

Liunaidheas. Idleness, sloth.

Liunchlos. Rest.

Liur. A prating noise.

Liurach. Noisy, prating.

Liuram. To beat, strike.

Liuth, liuthad. As many, so many.

Lo, la. A day.

Lo. A lock of wool.

Lo. Water.

Lobaircin. A dwarf.

Lobais. Craft, ingenuity.

Lobhadh. Rottenness, rotting.

Lobh. Rotten.

Lobhadas. Rottenness, fulsomness.

Lobham. To rot.

Lobhar. A leper.

Lobhgach. A cow with calf.

Lobhradh. The leprosy.

Lobhtha. Rotten, putrified.

Lobhthachd. Rottenness.

Loc. A stop, hindrance.

Locam. To refuse, hinder.

Locar. A place.

Locaram. To plane.

Locarsgathaich. Shavings.

Loc. A place.

Locc. A filthy mire.

Loch. A lake; lough, arm of the sea.

Loch. Black, dark.

Loch. Every, all.

Lochag. Vide Loth.

Lochain. Sea-grass or wrack.

Lochan. Chaff.

Lochan. A little pool or lake.

Locharman. A pigmy.

Lochafair. A shower of rain.

Lochd. A fault.

Lochd, lochdain. A wink of sleep.

Lochbhleine. The region under the short ribs.

Lochdach. Faulty, criminal.

Lochdaigham. To blame, reprove.

Lochdaighte. Blamed, censured.

Lochdughadh. Blaming, censuring

Lochlonnach. A Dane.

Lochran. A lamp or torch.

Lochrannach. Lighted with lamps.

Lochthomhaidhan. A sudden bursting of water from mountains.

Locuist. A locust.

Lod. Puddle.

Lodan. A light puddle.

Lodaigham. To stagnate.

Lodam. To arrive at, contrive, seduce.

Lodain. The flank or privy members.

Log. A pit or dike of water, a dungeon, a place.

Logan. A small pit, hollow of the hand.

Logaidhe. A fool.

Logha. } An indulgence, remission, jubilee.
Loghan. }

Loghadh. A rotting, putrefaction.

Logham. To rot, putrify.

Loghaimhlachd. Foolery.

Loghda. Allowance.

Loghdha. Indulgence.

Loghmhar. Excellent, famous.

Loghtha. Rotten.

Loghthachd. Rottenness.

Loiceamhlachd. Dotage, foolery.

Loibain. One that toileth in foul and fair weather.

Loich. A place, a dirty hussey.

Loichead. A light, lamp.

Loicheadaire. A chandler.

Loige. Vide Laige.

Loigeic. Logic.

Loilgheach. A new calved cow, a milch-cow.

Loimdioghbhall. Poverty, want.

Loime. Barenefs, poverty.

Loimic. A plaifter for taking off hair.

Loin, gen. of Lon. Provifions.

Loin. A rivulet.

Loinear. Light, a gleam or flafh of light.

Loinag. A lock of wool.

Loineardha. Bright, fhining.

Loineardhachd. Brightnefs.

Loingeas. Shipping, a fleet.

Loingbhrifeadh. A fhipwreck.

Loingfhaor. A fhip-carpenter.

Loingfeoir. A mariner, pilot.

Loingfigham. To fail, fet fail.

Loini. The fciatica.

Loinn. A corn field or pen.

Loinn. Good condition, fatnefs, joy, glad-nefs.

Loinnel
Loinneach. } Elegant, becoming.

Lonneis. Wavering, rambling.

Loinnream. To gleam, fhine, lighten.

Loirc. A gammon.

Loirgaireachd. Searching, enquiry.

Loirgairam. To enquire, look for.

Loirgbheirt. Leg-armour.

Loirghniomham. To requite, make a-mends.

Loirgnadh. A ftalk.

Loife. A flame.

Loifceanta. Fierce, fiery, blafting.

Loifcionn. A locuft.

Loifge.
Loifg. } Burnt.

Loifgeadh.
Loifgneas. } Burning.

Loifgeam. To burn, finge.

Loifgach. That burneth.

Loifgain. A burnt pimpernel.

Loifi. A flame.

Loifi. A fox.

Loifgrean. Burned corn.

Loifteamhuil. Slothful.

Loiftin. A lodging, a booth, tent.

Loiftich fuinidh. Kneading troughs.

Loit. A wound, wounding.

Loitam. To wound.

Loitmhille. To candy.

Loiteog. Nettles.

Loitfhealgaire. A rioter, debauched fel-low.

Lom. Bare, lean.

Lomadh. Baldnefs, fhaving.

Lomam. To fheer, fhave, make bare, chafe.

Lamadoir. A fhaver, fheerer, plunderer.

Lomain. A fhield.

Loman. An enfign, banner.

Lomaifteach. Bare, bald, fhorn.

Lomanach. A bald man.

Lomartha. Bald, bare, fhort, fhaven.

Lomchofach. Bare-footed.

Lomcoidh. To carry.

Lomar. A fleece.

Lomargain. Devaftation.

Lomeigin. Tearing, ftripping by force.

Lomna. A cord, rope.

Lomnochd. Nakednefs, naked.

Lomnochduighe. Nakednefs.

Lomnoir. A harper.

Lomhar. Brilliant, tranfparent, ftately.

Lomhair-chon. A pack of hounds.

Lomlan. Quite full.

Lomoigh. A fhorn fheep.

Lompas. Sparing, niggardly.

Lomradh. A fleece.

Lomram. To fheer, clip.

Lomtha. Peeled, ftripped.

Lomthoir. A barber, fheerer.

Lon. Food, provifion.

Lon, londubh. An ouzle, blackbird.

Lon. An elk.

Lon. A marſh, pond, moraſs.

Lon, lonadh. Hunger, voraciouſneſs.

Lonach. Voracious, greedy.

Lonan. Boaſting.

Lonid. A frothing ſtick, a churn ſtick.

Lonaigh. A ſcoff, jeſt.

Lonaidh. He grew red, coloured.

Lon lairge. Hip and thigh.

Loncha. A larder, buttery.

Long. The fiſh called ling.

Long. A ſhip.

Long. A cup.

Long. A bed.

Long. The breaſt.

Long. A houſe, reſidence.

Longadh. Supper.

Longadh. Caſting, throwing, devouring.

Longain. A ſhip's crew.

Longam. To devour, deſtroy, worry.

Longas. Baniſhment.

Longbach. Shipwreck.

Longbhraine. The prow of a ſhip.

Longphort. A palace, royal ſeat; a fort, garriſon, tent, a camp; a harbour.

Lonloingean. The gullet, throat; any pipe.

Long-chogaidh. A man of war.

Longſhaor. A ſhipwright.

Long-ſpuilin. A pirate.

Longthogal. Ship-building.

Longfhada. A galley.

Lonin. A lane or paſſage for cattle.

Lonn. Strong, powerful.

Lonn. Anger, choler.

Lonn. High ſwelling of the ſea.

Lonn. Timbers laid under boats in order to launch them the more eaſily.

Lonn. To be ſtrong, powerful; to reſide, dwell, ſojourn.

Lonnogain. A paſſionate youth.

Lonrach. A blaze.

Lonrach. Shining, bright, brave.

Lonnraigham. To ſhine, brighten.

Lonnughadh. An abiding, continuance, a dwelling, ſojourning.

Lor. Vid. Leor.

Lorc. Murder.

Lorc. Fierce, cruel.

Lorc. The cramp.

Lorcchoſg. Antiſpaſmodic.

Lor-daothain. Sufficiency.

Lorg. Progeny, offspring.

Lorg. A footſtep, trace, tract, print.

Lorg. Blind.

Lorg. A troop, band; a walking ſtaff.

Lorga. A leg, ſhin, ſtalk of a plant.

Lorgadh. ⎱ Searching, tracing.
Lorgairachd. ⎰

Lorgam. ⎱ To trace, ſearch, enquire.
Lorgairam. ⎰

Lorgaire. One that traceth.

Lorgaire mac luirg. A novel character.

Lorganach. A ſluggard.

Lorgbheirt. Foot-harneſs.

Lorgim. To wound.

Los. The point or end of a thing.

Los. A tail.

Los. Sake of, intention, purpoſe.

Loſaid. A kneading trough.

Loſg. A cripple, lame, blind.

Loſgadh. A burning, ſcalding.

Loſgadh-braghad. The heart-burn.

Loſgan. A frog, childhood; a ſort of dray without wheels.

Loſt. Vide Loſaid.

Lot. A wound, hurt, bruiſe.

Lot. Wool.

Lot. A whore, proſtitute.

Lotam. To wound, bruiſe, commit forni-cation.

Lotadh. Gallery, a ſcaffold, loft; forni-cation.

Lotar. A ruining, mangling.

Lotar, lodar. They went.

Loth, lothag. A colt, filley.

Lothal. The plant brooklime.

Lothar. A congregation, affembly.

Lothar. A cauldron.

Lothar. Cloth, raiment.

An Lothair. Lavender.

Lott. A drinking party, compotation.

Lu Little, fmall

Lua. A foot, a kick.

Lua. An oath.

Lua. Water.

Luach. Price, wages.

Luacha. Froft.

Luachair. A bulrufh.

Luachairneach. A place full of rufhes.

Luacham. To hire

Luacharman. A pigmy.

Luacharn. A light, lamp.

Luachmhor. Precious, excellent.

Luachmhoire. More precious.

Luachra.
Luachrach. } Of rufhes.

Luada.
Luaidicin. } The little finger.

Luadh. Mention.

Luadham. To mention.

Luadhairl. Motion, exercife.

Luadhraidham. To report.

Luag. A doll.

Luaga. Lefs.

Luaghair. A reward.

Luaghlais. Fetters.

Luaghuta. The gout.

Luaidhe. Coition, copulation.

Luaidreannuidhe. A vagabond.

Luaidreann Vagary.

Luaigh. Pleafant, cheerful.

Luaighe. Lead.

Luaigheachd. A reward.

Luaighthe. As foon as.

Luailleach. A mimic.

Luailteach. Full of geftures.

Luaimaireachd. Volubility of tongue.

Luaimh. An abbot.

Luaimhnighthe. A wave-offering.

Luaimneach. Leaping, ranging, fickle.

Luaimnithe. Waved.

Luaintin. Nephritical.

Luain-eafadh.
Luan-ghalar. } Nephritick pains.

Luaith. Duft, afhes.

Luaithre.
Luaithreach. } Afhes.

Luaithreamhuil.
Luaithreanta. } Dufty.

Luaithreadh.
Luaithrean. } Afhes.

Luaithe. Quicker, fafter, fwifter.

Luaithad. Quicknefs, faftnefs.

Luamain. A veil.

Luamh. An abbot, prior.

Luamhire. A pilot.

Luamhnaic Vide Luaimneach, volatile.

Luamhnachd. An abbotfhip.

Luan. A loin, kidney.

Luad. A warrior, champion, fon, a lad.

Luan. A greyhound.

Luan. The moon, Monday.

Luanaifg. Fetters, chains.

Luanafgbha. Fettered, chained.

Luarach. Fetters.

Luardha. Vulgar, common.

Luas. Swiftnefs.

Luafcadh. Moving, rocking.

Luafgach. Wavering.

Luafgam. To fwing, jolt, rock, drive away.

Luafgan. A cradle.

Luafganach. That rocketh, fwingeth.

Luafganachd. Rocking.

Luafganaidhe. A rocker, fwinger.

Luath. The foot.

Luath. Afhes.

Luath. Swift, quick, fleet.

Luath. Activity, agility.

Luathadh. Hafting, making hafte; fulling, milling; moving.

Luatham. To haften, make hafte, move; to full, mill cloth.

Luatha. Belonging to ashes.

Luathas. Swiftness, fleetness.

Luatharan. A sea lark.

Luathghaire. Joy, gladness.

Luathghaireadh. Rejoicing.

Luathghairam. To rejoice, be glad.

Luathlamhach. Covetous.

Luathmhor. Swift, active.

Luathmharc. A race-horse.

Luathmharcach. A messenger express.

Luathmhire. Boasting.

Luathrigham. To hasten.

Luathradh. Hastening.

Luathrighte. Hastened.

Lub. A loop, inclination, bow, a thong; a maze, meander, winding; cunning, craft.

Lubach. Crooked, winding, serpentine, meandring; cunning, crafty, subtle.

Lubaire. A crafty fellow.

Lubam. To bend, incline.

Luban. A hoop, bow.

Lublinnach. Curvilinear.

Lutha. The body.

Lubcheangal. A hinge.

Lubhar. Vide Lobhar.

Lubhghort. A garden.

Lubhra. Leprosy, infirmity.

Lubhra. Work.

Lubhrach. Leprous.

Luch. ⎫
Luchag. ⎬ A mouse.
      ⎭

Luch-fhrancach. A rat.

Luch. A captive, prisoner.

Luchair. A glittering colour, brightness.

Luchaire. A mouser.

Lucharman. A pigmy.

Luchairt. A palace, retinue.

Luchbhru. A white head of hair.

Luchd. Folks, people; equal to the French Gens.

Luchd. A pot, kettle, cauldron.

Luchd. A cargo, burden, lading.

Luchdaigham. To load, laden.

Luchdaghadh. Loading.

Luchd-coimhaidachd. Retinue, servants in waiting.

Luch-fheoir. A field-mouse.

Luchlann. A prison.

Luchdmhor. Full, loaded, rapacious.

Luchidh fhairge. Small black birds resembling swallows, with crooked bills and webbed feet. They go into holes like mice. When they are taken, a quantity of yellow oil drops from their bills. They are found upon the island of Staffa, of which Mr. Penant and Mr. Banks take so much notice. The man who lives on that island, as I am informed, says, that they hatch their eggs by sitting on the ground, at the distance of about six inches from it, and turning their face towards it, continue repeating Gur le gug, i. e. Hatch with a song, day and night, till it is hatched. This bird seems to be a species of Pettrill, or what sailors call Mother Cary's chickens.

Luchmhaire. Abundance.

Luchthaire. A gulph, whirlpool.

Luchram. To rummage.

Lud, lod. A pond.

Ludh. Appearance.

Ludairt. Waddling in dirt.

Ludnan. A hinge.

Ludram. To dip and besmear with dirty water.

Luddartha. Sluggish, slovenly.

Ludragon. A shambling fellow.

Ludusach. Powerful.

Lugach. Bow-legged.

Lugain. A short crooked fellow.

Lugha. Less, least.

Lugha. An oath.

Lugadh. Thirst, want.

Lughad. Littleness.

Lugh To leap.

Lughadaigham. To lessen, diminish.

                      Lughadaghadh.

Lughadaghadh. Diminiſhing.

Lughaird. Retinue. Vide Luchairt.

Lugham. To ſwear.

Lughadh. Swearing by.

Lughadag. The little finger.

Lui. Bow, branch.

Luibh. }
Luibhean. } An herb.

Luib. A corner, little glen.

Luibheanchoſach. Having toes, finger, and legs

Luithne. A dart, ſpear.

Luibhne. The fingers, toes.

Luibhre. A coat of mail.

Luibhreagham. To put on a coat of mail.

Luithreach. Belonging to a coat of mail.

Luibhphiaſt. A caterpillar.

Luibin. A crafty fellow.

Luibineachd. Craftineſs.

Luid. A rag.

Luidag. A little rag.

Luidach. }
Luidagach. } Ragged.

Luidh. An herb. Vide Luibh.

Luidh. A word of endearment.

Luidh an liugair. Lovage.

Luidh. He went, he died.

Luidh nan tri bheann. Plant of three leaves or corners.

Luidhe. A lying, ſituation, poſition, going, death.

Luidhid m'inntin. I am content, pleaſed.

Luidham. To lye, lay.

Luidham. Vide Lugham.

Luidhachan. An ambuſh.

Luidhaſam. To permit, allow.

Luidhaſachadh. Permitting, allowing.

Luidheolach. Skilled in plants.

Luidheolas. Botany.

Luidin. The little finger.

Luig. Gen. of Lag, a pit.

Luighe. A proof.

Luighe. A cauldron, kettle.

Luighe. Lying.

Luigham. To tear, rend, encourage, to abet.

Luighioch. Lying.

Luilgheoch. A milch-cow.

Luim, leim. Milk.

Luimain. A target, ſhield.

Luimlinn. A ſtream of milk.

Luimneachda. An enſign-bearer.

Luin. A ſword or ſpear.

Luingbriſeadh. A ſhipwreck.

Luingbhriſam. To ſuffer ſhipwreck.

Luingios. A fleet, navy.

Luingſeorachd. A voyage by ſea.

Luiniaſg. A ſword-fiſh.

Luinne. Anger.

Luinneach. Merry, jovial.

Luinneag. A chorus, a highland catch.

Luinneagach. Friſking, ſkipping.

Luinneinich. Toſſing.

Luinnſeach. A watch coat.

Luinnſaire. One that goes about idly, a watchman.

Luireach. A coat of mail.

Luirgne. Legs.

Luis. The quicken tree, the letter L.

Luis. A hand.

Luis. Drink.

Luis. Weeds, herbs.

Luiſam. To dare, adventure.

Luiſam. To drink.

Luiſiot. Bad, naughty, evil.

Luiſne. A flame, flaſk, a bluſh.

Luithe, luaithe. Swifter.

Lulgach. A ſoldier.

Lumain. A veil, coarſe cover, ſackcloth; a large great coat.

Lumhaire. A diver.

Lunaſd. Lammas.

Lundach. Lazy.

Lundaire. A drone, ſluggard.

Lundaireachd. Lazineſs.

Lung, Long. A ſhip.

Lung. An houſe, the handle of an oar.

Lunn. A bond.

Lunnach. An active youth.

Lunnacha. Helved.

Lupait. The name of that ſiſter of St. Patrick who was brought to Ireland along with him, and ſold into captivity in the county of Lowth, then called Magh-murteinne.

Lurach. Pretty

Lurachan. Ramps.

Lurag. A pretty female.

Lurg. The end.

Lurga ' Behold! ſee !

Lurga.
Lurgann. } A leg, ſhank, ſtalk.

Lurginach. A ſhaft, long-legged.

Lus. Pith, ſtrength.

Lus. An herb or plant, a leek.

Luſan.
Luſin. } A little herb.

Luſach. Of or belonging to herbs, herbaceous.

Luſairnach. A place where herbs grow.

Luſca. Space of five years, a luſtrum.

Luſca. Infancy.

Luſca. A cave, ſubterranean vault.

Luſca. Blind.

Luſchuach. A caterpillar.

Luſmhaoth. Bearing virtuous and ſoft herbs.

Lus mhic Cummin. Cumin.

Lus a'cholmain. Columbine.

Lus a' choire. Coriander.

Lus an t ſlanughaidh. Ribwort.

Lus a' chromchinn. Daffodill.

Lus nan leac. Eyebright.

Lus a' phiobair. Dittany.

Lus an t ſaoidh. Fennel.

Lus leath an t ſamhraidh. Gillyflower.

Lus na ſiothchaint. Looſeſtrife.

Lus an liagaire. Lovage.

Lus-Mairi. Marygold.

Lus na h oiche. Nightſhade.

Lus an fhucadair. Teazle, fuller's thiſtle.

Lus mhic riogh Brettuin. Wild thyme.

Lus an fhograidh.
Lus mhic Raonail. } Chaſe the devil.

Lus Cholum-cille. St. John's-wort.

Lus nan laogh. Orpine.

Lus nan cnamh. Samphire.

Lus a 'chrois. Dwarf honeyſuckle.

Lus a Chrubhain. Gentian.

Lus an leaſaidh. A plant that raiſeth bliſters when applied.

Lus cneas Guth-ullin. Meadow-ſweet.

Lus nan eithreag. Cloud berries.

Lus na fearnaich. Sundew.

Lus mor. Spearwort.

Lus mor. The herb fox-glove.

Lus nam broilag.
Lus nan geira bornigh. } Bear whortle-berries.

Lus na ſtalog. Berry-bearing heath.

Lus mhic bethaig. Betony.

Lus an t ſiucair. Succory.

Sus na Spain. Pellitory of Spain.

Lus a' bhalla. Pellitory of the wall.

Lus phoinc. Piony.

Lus nan laoch. Roſewort.

Lus nan gorm dhearc. Blaeberry-plant.

Luas na mealla. Honeyſuckle.

Lus a' chorrain.
Lus na ſeilge. } Spleenwort.

Lus nan tri ballan. Valerian.

Lus gan mhathair gan athair. A plant reſembling lintſeed, found on the ſurface of ſprings, with roots not touching the ground.

Luſdradh. A proceſſion.

Luſcaire. A troglodite.

Luſgam. To lurk.

Luſradh. Herbage.

Luſra nan ſcor. Clown's all-heal.

Luſrag. A charm with herbs.

Luſtaire. A flatterer.

Luſtram.

Luſtram. To flatter.
Luth. Longing, earning.
Luth. Strength, power.
Luthmhor. Strong, nimble.
Luthmhorachd. Strength, nimbleneſs.
Luthmhoire. More active.

Luthach. The ſinews or veins.
Luthghair. Vide Luthghaire.
Luth-chleaſa & gaiſga. Athletic exerciſes.
Luthaire. Cuchullin's driver.
Luthais. Ludovick.

M.

M Is the tenth letter of the Gaelic alphabet, and is called Muin, a vine. It ſounds the ſame as in other languages, only that before h aſpirate a new combination or letter is formed nearly as v. Thus Mathair, a mother, do mhathair, to a mother, is Do vathair. Vide Analyſis.

Ma, madh. If.
Ma. A breach.
Ma-reir. Looſe, at liberty.
Ma, uime. About, near about.
Mac. A ſon; pl. Macra, mic.
Macan. A young or little ſon, the young of beaſts.
Mac-mic. A grandſon.
Mac an abar. The ring-finger.
Mactire. A wolf.
Macleabhair. A copy of a book.
Mac. Clean, pure.
Macſamhailt. ⎱ The like, equal, em-
Maca.   ⎰ blem.
Mac an dogha. Burdock.
Macadh. Bearing, carrying
Macaim. To bear, carry, to fondle.
Macamh. A youth, a lad.
Mac-choinne. A daughter-in-law.

Macamh-ballaich. A boy.
Macamh-mna. A girl, a young girl.
Macamhuil. ⎱ Filial.
Machanta. ⎰
Macha. A Royſton crow.
Machaire. A field, plain.
Macanta. Meek, mild.
Macantachd. ⎱ Meekneſs, mildneſs.
Macantas.   ⎰
Machlag. The womb, matrix.
Macht. A wave or ſurge.
Machdual. A ſponge.
Machtnadh. Deliberating on.
Machtre ! A Highland interjection.
Machtaim. To deliberate, conſider on.
Machtnamh. Wondering, deliberating.
Machuil. A ſpot, ſtain, defect.
Mac-muirigheach. The eſcallop-fiſh, the ſcolloped ſhell-fiſh.
Macmemna. The fancy, imagination.
Macnas. Licentiouſneſs, wantonneſs, kindneſs, fondneſs.
Macnaſmemna. The fancy.
Macnaſach. Wanton, merry, tender.
Macne. A tribe, clan.
Macoirh. A ſtranger.
Macraidh. A diſeaſe, diſtemper.

Macra. Young men, a band of young men, males.

Macramhuil. Like as.

Macrafach. Peevifh, faucy.

Macras. Sighing, fobbing, peevifhnefs.

Mactach. Pernicious.

Mactadh. Slaughtering, flaughter.

Mactalla, mactulloch. Echo.

Mactam. To flaughter, butcher.

Mactadh. A wondering, furprife.

Macthoghadh. Adoption.

Mad. A hand.

Maddadh. A dog.

Maddadh-allaidh. A wolf.

Maddadh-ruadh. A fox.

Maddadh-donn. An otter.

Madh. An extafy, trance.

Madh. A plain, field.

Madh. Be it, if it were.

Madha. Unlawful, unjuft.

Madhana. Meadows.

Madhanta. Coy.

Madhm. A breach, battle, derout.

Madhm. Any large round mountain.

Madhm. As much grain, or any thing comminated, as may be taken up between both the hands.

Madhmadh. An eruption, fally.

Madhmam. To overthrow.

Madhman. A fkirmifh.

Madhm-feic. A rupture.

Madhm-fleibhe. A fudden eruption of water from mountains.

Madh-beag. Few, little, a fmall fhare.

Madhramhail. July.

Madduin. The morning.

Maddra. Dogs.

Maddar. The herb madder.

Maddrach-alla. Wolves.

Madramhuil. Belonging to a dog, doglike, doggifh.

Mag. A paw.

Magan. A little paw, a toad.

Magairt. Creeping, pawing, fingering.

Magairam. To creep, paw, finger.

Magaran. Creeping on all fours.

Magaranam. To creep, go on all fours.

Magadh. Mocking, jeering, fcoffing.

Magamhuil. Jeering, fcoffing.

Magarle. A tefticle.

Magh. A plain, level country.

Magh-adhraidh. A plain or field of adoration, where an open temple, confifting of a circle of tall ftrait ftone pillars, with a very large flat ftone called Cromleac, ferving for altar, was conftructed by the Druids for religious worfhip. Thefe Druidical temples, whereof many are ftill exifting in Ireland and Scotland, were built in the fame manner with that which was built by Mofes, as it is defcribed Exod. xxiv. 4. confifting of twelve ftone pillars as an altar. Whether the object of the Druidifh worfhip was the true God, I cannot affirm. Several places in Ireland at this day wear thefe names. There is one in the county Clare, where the kings of the O'Brien race were inaugurated. Another, about four miles north of Corke, now called Beal atha magh-adhoir, from which the valley called Gleann magh-adhoir, derives its name.

Maghair. Plowed land.

Maghar. Fifh-fry, bait to catch fifh.

Maghach, moidhach. A hare.

Maghar. A word, expreffion.

Maghfhal.
Maghlann.   } Barracks.

Maglidh. Soft.

Maghuifge. A winter lake.

Maglothuin. He cherifhed.

Maibhin. Pouring forth.

Maicne. Kindred, relations.

Maide. Wood, timber, a ftick.

Maide-milis. Liquorice.

Maidain. A little ftick.

Maideog. The fhell called Concha veneris.

Maide-brifde. The tongs.

Maide-fdiuraidh. A pot-ftick, a thivel.

Maide-finglaidh. A fwingle-ftaff.

Maide-fniomh. A diftaff.

Maidheog. A midwife.

Maidhdean. A maid, virgin.

Maidhdeanas. Virginity, maidenhead.

Maidhin. A battle, fkirmifh.

Maidhm. A breach, eruption, fally, flight.

Maidhmam. To tear, burft.

Maidham. To be broke in battle, to be routed.

Maidham. To upbraid or boaft againft a man the favours he has conferred upon him.

Maidheanach. Slow.

Maiddin. Morning.

Maiddinughadh. Dawning.

Maiddinag. The morning ftar.

Maighean. A place.

Maigain. A toad, a little fat fellow.

Maighifdir. A mafter.

Maighiftriochd. Maftery.

Maighifdir-fcol. A fchoolmafter.

Maighne. Great.

Maigneas. A field.

Maighre. A falmon.

Maighreleun. A falmon trout.

Mailis. Malice. I doubt this to be Galic.

Mailifeach. Malicious.

Maill. Delay.

Maillachan. The young of fprites, in Scotland called Browny. It is a good-natured being, and renders good offices to favourites.

Maille. Together with.

Maille ribh. With you.

Maille riut. With thee.

Mailligham. To flacken, delay.

Main. The morning, day.

Main. The hand.

Maineag. A glove.

Mainobair. Handicraft.

Mainbhitheach. Crafty.

Mainchille. A fleeve.

Maineachna. Negligence, inattention.

Maineachtnach. Indevout, negligent in devotion.

Maineas. A miftake.

Mainneir. A fold, prifon, pen.

Mainigh. Madnefs, foolifhnefs.

Mainis. A lance, fpear.

Mainneafach. Sluggifh.

Mainnis. Drawling, trifling.

Mainnifdair. A monaftery.

Mainnrach. A booth, hut, fold.

Mainneamhuil. Early.

Mainfe. Maintenance.

Mainfair. A manger.

Mairbhghreim. The morphew.

Maircairn. Cots.

Maireafail. Life.

Maireun. A fmall falmon.

Mairg. Woe.

Mairgeach, mairgneach. Woeful, forrowful.

Mairgnigham. To groan, bewail.

Mairthachdin. Laft, continuance, lafting.

Mairtham. To live, continue.

Mairthann. Being, life.

Mairthionnach. Long lived, lafting.

Mairthinnach. Lame.

Mairlam. To bruife, crumble.

Mairnam. To betray.

Mairnealach. A pilot, mariner.

Mairneal. A let, delay.

Mairnealach. Dilatory, tedious.

Mairtirach. A martyr.

Mais. A lump, heap.

Mais, meas. An acorn.

Maifcaor. A lump.

Maife. An ornament, bloom, beauty, grace.

Maife. Food, victuals.

Maifeach. Beautiful, graceful, handfome.

Maifeachd.
Maifeamhlachd. } Elegance, handfomenefs.

Ma is feadh. If fo be, then, therefore.

Maifeamhuil. Handfome.

Maifigham. To adorn, deck.

Maifteog. The maftich-tree.

Maiftir. Urine.

Maiftirradh. A churning.

Maiftiram.
Maiftiruigham. } To churn.

Maith. Good, excellent.

Maith.
Maithe. } Chieftains, nobles.

Maitheachas.
Maithmheachas. } Forgivenefs, pardon.

Maitheamh. An abatement, flackening.

Maitheas. Goodnefs, bounty.

Maitham. To forgive.

Maithrean. An aunt by the mother's fide.

Mal, mall. Slow, dilatory.

Malis. A delay, let, hindrance.

Mal. Rent, tribute, tax, fubfidy.

Mal. A king, prince.

Mal. A poet.

Kal. A champion, foldier.

Mala. A bag, budget, mail.

Mala. The eye-brow.

Malaid. A bag, budget.

Maladair. A farmer, renter.

Malair. A merchant.

Malairt. Exchanging, bartering; exchange, barter.

Malairtach. Mutual, reciprocal.

Malairtam.
Malairtaigham. } To exchange, barter.

Malairtughadh. Exchanging.

Malairtain airgaid. A banker.

Malcair. A porter, bearer of burthens.

Malcaireachda. Of or belonging to the market.

Malcaireas. Sale.

2

Malcam. To bear, carry, to rot.

Malcadh. Rottennefs, rotting, bearing, carrying.

Mallchodach. One that fups late.

Malcthaire. A porter.

Mallbheurlach. Slow fpoken.

Mall. Slow, dilatory.

Malldromach. Saddle-backed.

Malla. Modeft.

Mallachd. Modefty.

Mallachd. A curfe.

Malluighte. Curfe.

Malluigham. To curfe.

Mallughadh. Curfing.

Malltriallach. Slow travelling.

Maloid. A flail, fcourge, thong.

Malraidham. To exchange, barter

Malratoir airgaid. A banker.

Maloigheagh. To grow dull.

Mall-fmuainteadh. Deep mufing or ftudy.

Malta. Mild, foft.

Mam. A hand or fift; a handful, vide Madhm.

Mam. Vile, bafe.

Mam. A mother.

Mam. Might, power.

Mam. A hill, mountain, a gap, a pafs.

Mamm. A breaft, pap.

Mama. Alone.

Mamas. Might, ftrength, power.

Mam-fioc. A rupture.

Man. The hand.

Ma'n. Before, ere.

Mana. A caufe, condition.

Manach. A monk, friar.

Manachdal. Conventual.

Manachan. The groin.

Manadh. Fate, lot, Cur air mhanadh, foretelling.

Manadhis. A fpear.

Manama. A glove.

Manchach. Of or belonging to monks.

Mancuairt. About.

Manchnumh

Manchnumh. A cheefe-mite.

Mandach. That maunteth.

Mandracach. A mandrake.

Mang. Morofenefs, fournefs.

Mang. A bag, budget.

Mang. Deceit.

Mang. A fawn.

Mangach. Like a fawn.

Mangaire. A taverner.

Mann. Wheat, food, bread.

Mann. A wedge, an ounce.

Mannar. Loofening.

Mann. A fin.

Mann. Bad, naught.

Manntach. Tongue-tied, maunting, ftut-tering.

Manrac. A gift.

Manrach. A fheep-fold.

Manrachd. Happy.

Manradh. Deftruction.

Manran. Amorous difcourfe.

Manranach. Noify.

Manras. Motion.

Manta. Demure, bafhful.

Mantacht. Bafhfulnefs.

Mantaire. A lifping perfon.

Maoidhm. A hard word.

Maoithmheach. ⎫ Vain-glorious.
Maodhmheach. ⎬

Maoidheadh, maoidheamh. Boafting, pro-claiming.

Maoile. ⎫ Baldnefs
Maoilad. ⎬

Maoilin. The fummit, brow of a ridge or hill.

Maoilaodannach. Bald-pated.

Maoin. Love, efteem.

Maoin. Worldly fubftance.

Maoirfeachd. Stewardfhip.

Maois. A pack or bag.

Maois-eifg. Five hundred fifh.

Maoifeog. A little pack or bag.

Maoifeach, maoifleach. A fhe deer, doe.

Maoitheach. Vain-glorious, boafting.

Maoitham. To boaft.

Maoithmheachas. Boafting.

Maoithmheach. An objection.

Maodal. Stomach, paunch, tripe.

Maodhadh. Boafting, reproaching, pro-claiming.

Maodhfeachlach. Apt to boaft.

Maol. Bald, blunt, without horns, hum-ble.

Maol. A promontory, cape.

Maol. A fervant, a fhaved perfon devoted to fome religious order.

Maolan. A beacon.

Maolaodanachd, Baldnefs.

Maol-Cholum-cille. Colum-cille's fervant.

Maol-feachluin. St. Seachluin's fervant.

Maol-aigeantach. Dull-witted, ftupid.

Maol-Iofa. A Highland faint.

Maolchluafach. Tame, gentle, inactive.

Maoluigham. To become dull, ftupid; to allay, calm.

Maoldorn. A fword-hilt.

Maoldorn fhionn airgaid. Silver-hilted fword.

Maolchair na mailin. The fpace between the eye-brows.

Maoldhearc. A mulberry.

Maolfhaobhrach. Blunt.

Maolluin. A mule.

Maom. Fear, terror.

Maom fleibhe. A torrent.

Maon. Dumb, mute.

Maonas. Proper name of a man.

Maor. A fteward, officer, a fervant; for-merly a baron. Vide Mormhaor.

Maor-eaglais. Apparitor.

Maor-ftriopaich. A pimp.

Maorach. Shell-fifh.

Maoth. Tender, foft.

Maothalach. Emollient.

Maothalachd. Emollients.

Maothan. A twig, ofier, bud; a carti-lage,

lage, griftle; any thing tender, foft. The Xiphoides, or griftle in the fcrobiculum cordis.

Maothla matha. Acorn and fruit.

Maothmhuadh. Nice, delicate.

Maothfhuileachd. Watrinefs of the eyes

Maothughadh. Moiftening.

Maothuigham To moiften, irrigate.

Mar. As, like, where.

Mar-fo. Thus.

Mar gu. As if.

Mar-fin. So, in that manner.

Mara. Belonging to the fea.

Marach. To-morrow.

Marachd. Error, miftake, marine.

Marag. A pudding.

Maran. Entertainment.

Maraon. Together.

Marafgal.
Marafglachd. } Subjection.

Maras. Ten thoufand, a myriad.

Marbh. Dead, heavy, benumbed.

Marbhadh. Slaughter, maffacre.

Marbham. To kill, flay.

Marbhan. A corpfe, dead body, margin of a book.

Marbhach. Deadly.

Marbhchras. A carcafe.

Marbhdhraoithachd. Necromancy.

Marbhdhraoth. A necromancer.

Marbhla. A ftill day.

Marbhnach. An elegy.

Marbhlapam. To be benumbed, to be froft-bitten.

Marbhphaifg. Dead men's fhrouds and drefs; alfo an Irifh and Highland imprecation.

Marbhortaliche. Lethargy.

Marbhthach. Mortal, cruel.

Marbhrann. An elegy, death fong, epitaph.

Marbhranntach. Elegiac.

Marbhfhruth. Wake of a fhip.

3

Marbhthoir. A murderer, flaughterer.

Marbraid. A fort.

Marc, marcan. A horfe.

Marcach. A horfeman, rider.

Marcachd.
Marcaidhachd. } Riding, horfemanfhip.

Marcuigham. To ride.

Marc-choimhliong. A horfe-race.

Marclach. Any provifion of victuals.

Marclann. A ftable.

Marcreil. Mackerel.

Marcfhluagh. Cavalry.

Marg. A mark in money.

Marg fearainn. A markland.

Margadh. A market.

Margal. Marketable.

Margadhluidh.
Marfonta. } A merchant.

Margha. Marine.

Maighan. A margin.

Marla. Rich clay, marl.

Marmur. Marble.

Marros. Rofemary.

Marri. With, along with.

Marris. Along with him, it.

Marria. With her, it.

Marrium. With me.

Marriut. With thee.

Marrinn. With us.

Marribh. With you.

Marriu. With them.

Marrifd. A match, hufband.

Marruigham. To moor, anchor.

Marrughadh. Mooring.

Maron. Sound.

Marfontachd. Merchandize.

Mart. A cow.

Mart. Month of March.

Mar ta. Even, fuch as.

Martfheoil. Beef.

Marthain. Being, life.

Marthanach. Lafting, durable

Marthannachd,

Marthannachd. Duration, eternity.

Martham, mairtham. To laſt, continue, live.

Marthuigh. Changing.

Martram. }
Martraigham. } To maim, lame.

Martartha. Maimed.

Martineach. A cripple.

Marunno. Steady.

Ma is, ma's. If.

Mas. A buttock, thigh, breech.

Mas. Excellent, handſome.

Maſan. Delay.

Maſanach. Slow, tedious.

Maſdidh. A maſtiff.

Maſeadh, ma is e. If it be ſo, then, therefore.

Maſgam. To infuſe, ſteep malt for brewing.

Maſladh. Reproach, ſlander.

Maſcan. A lump.

Maſlach. Reproachful, ignominious.

Maſlim. Maſtlin.

Maſlughadh. Reproaching, ſlandering.

Maſluigham. To reproach, ſlander.

Maſſadh. Spiteful.

Ma ta If ſo be, nevertheleſs, however.

Mata. Great, dark, gloomy

Mata A mattraſs.

Math. Good.

Math. Fruit.

Math. A hand.

Matha. Matthew.

Mathadh. A pardon, pardoning.

Mathaim. To forgive, pardon.

Mathain. Mercy, diſpoſal.

Mathair A mother, cauſe.

Mathair. Gore.

Mathair-abhair. }
Mathair-ail. } A cauſe, primary cauſe.

Mathair-uiſge. A reſervoir of water, ſource of water.

Mathair-iongair. The cauſe of ſuppuration.

Mathair na lughadaig. The ring-finger.

Mathaudha. Of, belonging to a mother.

Mathaudhachd. The right of a mother.

Mathaudhas. Motherhood.

Mathairorn. Matricidium.

Mathairornoir. Murderer of his mother.

Mathairamhuil. Motherly, tender.

Mathairamhlachd. Motherlineſs, tenderneſs.

Mathamhnas. Forgiving.

Matham. To meliorate, manure.

Mathdheanamh Beneficence.

Mathas. Goodneſs, bounty.

Mathfadh. Doubt.

Mathghabhuin. }
Maghghamhuin. } A bear, i. e. wild calf.

Mathan. The ſucker of a tree.

Mathfam. To doubt.

Mathon. A bear.

Mathſlogh. A congregation.

Mathte. Forgiven, pardoned.

Me. Me, the accuſ of Mi, I.

Meabhal. Shame, fraud, deceit.

Meabhalach. Deceitful, fraudulent.

Meabhair. The memory.

Meabharach. Mindful.

Meabhrigham. To ſcheme, plan, plot.

Meabhra. A fiction, lie.

Meabhrach. Chearful, merry.

Meacan A parſnip.

Meacan-uillionn. Elecampane.

Meacan-buidhe. }
Meacan-raidigh. } A carrot.

Meach. Hoſpitality.

Meactroig. The ox next the plough.

Mead. Encreaſe, bigneſs, bulk.

Meadaigham. To encreaſe, enlarge, improve

Meadaighte Augmented, enlarged.

Meadar. A churn, an anſated veſſel, milk-pail,

pail ; the Irish is four-cornered, and hollowed with a chissel ; the Scotch round and hooped.

Meadar, meadarachd. Verse, metre.

Meadbhronn. Dropsy.

Meadh. A ballance, scale.

Meadh. Metheglin, mead.

Meadhach. A stallion.

Meadhach. Fuddled with mead.

Meadhachan. Force.

Meadhaigham. To weigh, ballance, consider.

Meadail, maodal. A belly, paunch.

Meadhair. Talk, discourse, mirth.

Meadhair. A forewarning of future events.

Meadharach. Chearful, lively.

Meadhon. The midst, middle, center ; a mean instrument.

Meadhonach. Mid, middle, intermediate, instrumental.

Meadhon-la. Noon, mid-day.

Meadhrach. Glad, joyful.

Meadhg, meidhg. Whey.

Meag. The earth.

Meall. A ball, lump, knob.

Meall. A hill, hillock, eminence.

Meala, mealgha. Of honey.

Meala. A reproach.

Meala. Grief, sorrow.

A' mheali. Broom.

Mealb, mealbhog. A satchel, budget, knapsack.

Meall, meallach. Good, pleasant.

Meall. An heap, lump.

Mealladh. Deceiving, defrauding.

Meallag. The milt of a fish.

Meallcair. Hasty-pudding, pap.

Meallam. To deceive, defraud.

Meallam. To enjoy, brook.

Mealltin. Enjoying.

Meallta. Deceived, defrauded.

Mealltoir. A deceiver.

Mealltoireachd. Deceit, fraudulence.

Meam. A kiss.

Meamam. To kiss.

Meambra. A shrine.

Meamrum. Parchment.

Meamhair. Memory.

Meamhairam. To remember, consider.

Meamhraigham. To mention, put in mind of.

Meamhairaighte. Studied, considered of, mentioned.

Meamnaicam. To think.

Meanadh. An awl.

Meanadh. }
Meanan. } Gaping, yawning.

Meanadh. Foretelling, fate.

Meanuir. He thought of.

Meanan. Plain, clear.

Meanbh. Small.

Meanbhchuilag. A gnat.

Meanbhchuisach. Curious.

Meanfach. }
Meanfagadh. } Yawning.
Meanfuigheal. }

Meang. Craft, deceit.

Meangach. Crafty, deceitful.

Meangan. }
Meanglan. } A branch, bough, twig.

Meangraidhte. Sophistry.

Meanma, meanman. Courage, vigour

Meanmach, meanamnach. Chearful, in spirits, elate.

Meanmaradh. Thought.

Meanmlaige. Dullness, laziness, weakness.

Meanmnaigham. To regale, gladden.

Meanmughadh. An exhortation.

Meanmuin. Joy, gladness.

Meann. Manifest.

Meann. Famous, illustrious, celebrated

Meann. Dumb.

Meann. }
Meannan. } A rib.

Meannath-athar. A snipe.

Meannad. A place, room.

Meanrachd. Happinefs, blifs, good-luck.

Meantail. Deceit.

Meanntus. Spearmint.

Mear. Quick, fudden, merry, wanton.

Mear. A finger, toe.

Mearachd. Miftake, error.

Mearachd-ceille. Madnefs, wrong in judgment.

Mearaigham. To miftake, err.

Mearagan. Fingering, handling.

Mearaighe. A fool.

Mearaithne. A flight doubtful knowledge of one.

Mearardhachd. Sobriety.

Mearaghadh. Miftaking, erring.

Mearbha. A lie, fiction.

Mearbhal. A miftake, random.

Mearbhallachd. Erring.

Meardhana. Foolhardy.

Meardhanachd. Rafhnefs.

Mearghradh. Fondnefs.

Meargranta. } Brifk, obftinate.
Mearnighte. }

Mearle. } Theft.
Mearlachd. }

Mearlach. A thief.

Meas. Fruit, particularly acorns.

Meas. Meafure, a rod to meafure graves.

Meas. A weapon, edge or point.

Meas. A pair of fhears.

Meas. A fofter-child.

Meas. A falmon.

Meas. Refpect, opinion, advice, conceit.

Meafa. Worfe, worft.

Meafamhuil. Refpected, efteemed.

Meafan. } A lap-dog.
Meafchu. }

Meafaire. Juft weight or meafure.

Meafardha. } Temperate, frugal.
Meafartha. }

Meafam. To efteem, think, or fuppofe.

Meafardhachd. } Temperance.
Meafarthachd. }

Meafchaor. A plummet, founding-line.

Meafchraobh. A fruit-tree.

Meafchruinigham. To gather acorns, to gather in corn.

Meafg. Among, amongft.

Bhur Meafg. Amongft you.

'*Nar* Meafg. Amongft us.

'N am Meafg. Amongft them.

Meafgadh. A mixture, mixing.

Meafgam. To mix, ftir about, to move, mingle.

Meafghort. An orchard.

Meafog. An acorn.

Meafraigham. To temper.

Meafuim, meafam. To prefume, fuppofe, confider, obferve, efteem, to lay a tax, to rate.

Meata. Cowardly, fearful.

Meatachd. Cowardice.

Meath. Decay.

Meatha-dhala. At leaft.

Meath-challtin. Southernwood.

Meathach. Perifhable, a degenerate perfon.

Meathach. Fat.

Meathadh. Withering, fading, fhrinking.

Meathaigham. To grow fat.

Meathaim. To fade, decay, wither.

Meathas. Fat, fatnefs.

Meathligham. To faint or die of cold.

Meathufradh. Fatlings.

Meaththinnas. A confumption.

Meathlughadh. Sinking under cold.

Meid, mead. Bignefs, magnitude.

Meide. The neck.

Meideach. A ftallion.

Meidil. A medlar.

Meidhe. A ftump, ftock, trunk.

[R r r]   Meidhg,

Meidhg, meadhg. Whey.

Meidghamhuil. Serous.

Meidhife. The middle, midft.

Meidhleach, meilach. Bleating of fheep.

Meidhlam. } To bleat.
Meilam. }

Meigh. A ballance, fcale.

Meigiollach. } Bleating of a goat.
Meigiodach. }

Meigiollam. To bleat as a goat.

Meile. A hand-mill.

Meileadh. Bleating.

Meilam. To grind.

Meilg. Death.

Meilg. Milk.

Meill. A cheek.

Meilliach. The globe.

Meilt. Grinding.

Meilt. Cafting, hurling.

Meillig. Rind.

Meimeadh. A poem.

Mein. The mind.

Mein. Oar, a mine.

Meinn. Quality, mien, clemency, mercy.

Meinneamhuil. Affable, well - difpofed, kindly.

Meir. Gen. of Mear.

Meirbh. Slow, tedious, weak.

Meirbhe. Weaknefs, dullnefs.

Meirbhe. A lie.

Meirceann. A finger.

Meirdreach. A whore, harlot.

Meirdreachas. Fornication.

Meire, mire. Mirth, madnefs.

Meirg. } Ruft.
Meifd. }

Meirge. An enfign, ftandard, banner.

Meirgeach. Rufty, full of ruft.

Meirgeall. Roughnefs, ruggednefs.

Meirghe. A band, troop, company.

Meirin nam magh. Agrimony.

Meirleachas. Treafon, rebellion.

Meirleach. A thief, rogue, rebel.

Meirneal. A merlin.

Meirtneach. } Feeble, fatigued.
Meirthnidhe. }

Meis. Gen of Mias.

Meis. Bad, wicked.

Meifchcolam. To fing, modulate.

Meifde. Worfe.

Meifeamhnigham. To judge.

Meifge. Drunkennefs.

Meifi. A judge.

Meifi. Fairies.

Meifin. A little difh.

Meifneach. Courage.

Meifneamhuil. Courageous.

Meifnigham. To encourage, nourifh, cherifh, refrefh, enliven, exhort.

Meifriobhar. A bufhel.

Meiffi. Ghofts, apparitions.

Meith. Fat, corpulent.

Meitheallach. A fatling.

Meithle. Reapers.

Meithrios. Fatnefs.

Meithreas. Kitchen-ftuff.

Mele. A woman's coif.

Mele. A fluggard, cowardly foldier.

Melg. Death.

Melghi. Point of death, death-bed.

Meligham. To bleat as a fheep.

Melinich. An ewe.

Men, mein. Oar.

Men. A mouth.

Mennan-athar. A fnipe.

Menm-ara. A whale.

Menighi. Lame, gentle.

Meodhan, meadhon. A means.

Meodhanach, meadhonach. Middlemoft, fmall.

Meogal. A medley, mixture.

Meomhrachan. } A memorandum, record, minutes.
Meomhranach. }

Meomhair. The memory.

Meomhairach. Mindful, having a ftrong memory.

2   Meomharaigham.

Meomharaigham. To remember, mention.

Meor, meur. A finger.

Meorad.
Meoracan. } A thimble.
Meuran.

Meothal. Help.

Mertnigham. To weaken.

Mether. A veil, covering.

Methle. A reaping.

Meud, mead. Greatnefs.

Meudal. Vide Maodal.

Meug. Whey.

Meugach Having much whey.

Meugamhuil. Serous.

Meunan. Gaping, yawning.

Meur. A finger, prong.

Meurag. A pebble, a little clue of yarn.

Meuran. A thimble.

Meuthas. Fatnefs. Vide Meathas.

Mi. I.

Mi, mio. A compofitive and negative particle.

Mi, mios. A month.

Mi. A mouth.

Miach. A bag, budget.

Miadh. Honour, refpect.

Miadhmhor. Honourable, noble.

Miaduigh. A hog, fwine.

Miadhach.
Miadhal. } Precious.

Miadadh. Shutting.

Miamhal. Mewling as a cat.

Miann. The will, defire, love.

Mianach. Oar, a mine.

Mianfhaolidh. A gaping.

Miannach.
Miannmhor. } Defirous, longing.

Meannmhorachd. Appetibility.

Miannghas. Inclination, favour, longing, flavour.

Miannghafach. Defirous.

Mianndiultadh. Abnegation.

Mias. A difh, platter.

Mias. An altar.

Mic. Of a fon; fons.

Michadhas. Ingratitude.

Michadhas. An affront.

Micelmhe. An ill omen.

Micheadfa. Indignation.

Micheadfach. Difpleafed, vexed, difcontented.

Micheill Madnefs, folly.

Micheillidh. Foolifh, imprudent.

Micheilligham. To rave, date.

Micheineamhuin. Mifadventure.

Michneafta. Inhumane, uncivil; perilous, ominous.

Michreadamh. Unbelief.

Micheir.
Michearta. } Kind, gentle.

Midh. The fight, afpect.

Midheamhaltach. Frugal.

Midheamhuin. Meditation.

Midheang. Slender-waifted.

Midhiomhalta. Doubtful.

Midhion. Ill-coloured.

Mi-effeachdach. Vain, ineffectual.

Mighniomh. Iniquity, lewdnefs.

Mighreann. Difdain, loathing.

Migheur. Blunt.

Mil. Gen. Meala. Honey.

Mil.
Mileadh. } A foldier, champion.
Milidh.

Milanta. Brave.

Milbhir. Mead, metheglin.

Milcaire. A parafite.

Milcheo.
Milchruimheog. } Mildew.

Mildeoch. Mead.

Mile. A thoufand, a mile; pl. Milta.

Milneach.
Mineach. } A thorn, bodkin.

Milighe. The point of death.

Mileanta. Soldierly.

Milightheach. Pale, wan.

Milis. Sweet.

Mill. Pl. of Meall.

Millein. Blame, tax.

Milleadh. Ruining, spoiling.

Millam. To spoil, marr, ruin.

Milliudh. An ill eye, a fascinating look.

Milse.
Milsad. } Sweetness.
Milseachd.

Milsean. Any sweet thing, sweetmeat, cheesecurds.

Milsainan. Dainty dishes.

Milsean-mara. A sort of sea-weed.

Milseanta. Sweetened.

Milshliosneach. A chiliagon.

Millte. Ruined, spoiled.

Millich. Tufts of good grass.

Millteoir. An oppressor.

Milltne.
Milltneachd. } Bravery, gallantry.

Milmheacan. A mallow.

Milse. More sweet.

Milsuigham. To sweeten, mull.

Milta. Pl. of Mile.

Mimheasam. To undervalue, despise.

Mimheasta. Mean, vile, despised.

Minheisnigham. To despise, terrify.

Min. Fine, tender, delicate, soft, smooth.

Min. A plain, a field.

Min. Meal, flower.

Minanach. A minikin.

Minan. Small of coal and other things.

Minaois. Minority.

Minbhrisam. To bruise, comminate.

Mindreach. A little image.

Mine. Smoother.

Mine.
Minad. } Smoothness.

Minad. Smallness, fineness.

Minag. A gentle meek woman.

Minagach. Tender, meek.

Minbhean. A wife.

Minchruth. Miniature.

Mine. Pusillanimity.

Mineite. A small feather.

Mineach. Mealy.

Mineachd. Softness, gentleness.

Mineaghadh. Politeness.

Minadurtha. Unnatural, ill-natured.

Minchagnam. To mump.

Min-eallach. Small cattle.

Minfheur. Soft grass.

Mingheal. Soft and fair.

Minghearram. To hash, mince.

Minghaduighachd. Pilfering.

Minidh. An owl.

Minicthi. Tame, gentle.

Minn. Kids. Vide Meann.

Minnain. A little kid, fawn.

Minnaid. A minute.

Minnaidach. Careful, steady.

Minneighadh. Adjuring.

Minic. Frequent, often.

Miniasg. Small fish.

Minughadh. Taming, smoothing, explaining.

Minuigham. To explain, smooth, polish, paraphrase.

Minneach. A lye.

Minisdair. A minister, servant.

Minisdralachd. Serving, administering, ministration.

Minearghnas. Ignorance.

Minlach. The finest of grass.

Minmhear. Hemlock.

Min-iaruinn. The filings of steel.

Minrosgach. Meek-eyed.

Minos. Unchasteness.

Minuach. The herb Millmountain, purging flax.

Minnsag. A young she-goat.

Mio-adh. Bad fortune.

Mio-adhmhor. Untowardly, awkward, unfortunate.

Miobhal. Unthriftiness.

Mioboile. Scab.

Miobheusach.

Miobheufach. Impolite.
Miobhuidhachas. Ingratitude.
Miobhuineadh. Defpair, diftruft.
Miobhuileadh. Loathing.
Miobhuilughadh. Mifapplying.
Miobhuiluigham. To mifimprove.
Miobhuidhach. Ungrateful.
Miochaine. A prefent.
Miochaire. Loving, affable.
Miochairthe. A monfter.
Miochas. Ingratitude, difefteem.
Miochadhafach. Ungrateful.
Miochean. Difguft.
Miocheart. Unjuft.
Miochuinas. Difquiet.
Miocheill. Folly.
Miochliu. Difpraife, reproach.
Miochliutach. Infamous.
Miochoingioll. Deceit, treachery.
Miochoingiollach. Treacherous.
Miochoirteach. Monftrous.
Miochomhghair. Difappointment.
Miochreidafach. Difcreditable.
Miochreidas Difcredit.
Miochriodhal. Heartlefs, difheartened.
Miochriodholachd. Difpiritednefs.
Miochomhthrom. Unjuft, unequal.
Miochreidamh. Unbelief.
Miochumas. A donation.
Miochuifeach. Bewitching.
Miodadh. Confidering.
Miodal. Flattery, fair fpeeches.
Miodalach. Flattering.
Miodar. Good pafture.
Miodh. Metheglin.
Miodhbhaidh. Protection.
Miodhchuairt. A whirlpool.
Miodhilis. Unfaithful.
Miodhiadhidh. Ungodly.
Miodhealbhach. Unlikely.
Miodhealbham. To misfhape.
Miodhuileadh. A loathing.
Miodhreach. A bad look or appearance.

Miodhreacham. To disfigure.
Miodhuiligham. To deteft, abhor.
Miodhuthrachd. Negligence.
Midrach. An anfated difh.
Miodag. A knife.
Mio-eudmhor. Cold, difloyal.
Miofhallan. Healthlefs.
Miofhoighid. } Impatience.
Miofhoighiden. }
Miofhoighidinach. Impatient.
Miofhortun. Misfortune.
Miofhortunach. Misfortunate.
Miog. A fmirk, fmile.
Miogfhiule. Laughing eye.
Miogfhuileach. Having laughing eyes.
Miogach. Sparkling.
Mioghean. Difaffection, diflike.
Miogheamnidh. Lewd.
Miogheamnidhachd. Lewdnefs.
Miogheur. Blunt.
Mio-iomchubhidh. Unfit.
Mioghlic. Foolifh.
Mioghleatham. To hufband badly.
Mioghleatbadh. Bad management.
Mioghnaitham. To abufe, mifapply.
Mioghnamhach. Lewd, mifchievous.
Miol. A loufe.
Miol-caorach. A fheep-tick, a ked.
Miol-balla. A wall loufe.
Miol-monadh. An animal that fwims on the furface of ftanding water, like a flea.
Miol-mor. A whale.
Miol-crion. A moth.
Miol-gaile. A belly-worm.
Miol-ingneach. A crab.
Miolabhartha. Froward, fullen, fnailing.
Miolach. Brutifh; loufy.
Miolag. Any fmall thing; a melon.
Miolaineach. Thoughtful, melancholy.
Miolafgach. Reftiff.
Miolboidhe. A hare.
Miolc. Whey.

       Miocladh.

Miolcadh. Flattering, flattery.

Miolcam. To flatter, smooth.

Miolcaireachd. Flattery, soothing.

Miolchomhlan. A park.

Miolchu. A greyhound.

Miolscoiteachd. Eloquence.

Miolscoithe. Eloquent, affable, debonair.

Mioltag. A fly, gnat.

Mioltag-leathair. A bat.

Miollach. Devouring.

Miomasg. A lancet, spear.

Miamhacanta. Dishoneft.

Miomhacantachd. Dishonefty.

Miomhinuigham. To misinterpret.

Miomhisnachal. Dispirited, irrefolute.

Miomhisnuigham. To discourage.

Miomhisnughadh. Discouraging.

Miomheas. Disrespect.

Miomheafal. Disrespectful.

Miomhiannuigham. To disanimate.

Miomhisnach. Discouragement.

Miomhadh. Scandal, reproach, uncivility, bad manners.

Miomhodhal. Rude, uncivil, ill-bred, ruftick.

Miomhodham. To reproach, revile, prophane.

Miomhara. Impudent, mean.

Miomhuinighin. Diffidence, diftruft.

Mio-onorughadh. Dishonouring.

Mio-onoruigham. To dishonour.

Mion. Vide Miann.

Mion. A diadem.

Mion. Small. Vide. Min.

Miun. A letter.

Mionach. Bowels.

Mionach. Metal.

Mionaire. Impudence, affurance, effrontery.

Mionaireach. Shamelefs, impudent, frontlefs.

Mionaiteach. Particular.

Mionnan. A kid.

2

Mionadurtha. Unnatural.

Mionbhughmhann. A haggefs, minced meat.

Mionca. Oftener, ofteneft.

Mioncas. Atoms.

Mionaomh. Prophane.

Mionaomhaigham. To prophane.

Mionbhaile. Suburbs.

Mionbhar. Hemlock.

Mionbhradach. Light-fingered.

Mionbhruigham. To mince, crumble.

Mionchloch. A pumice.

Mionchuileog. A gnat.

Mionduine. A manikin.

Miongraim. To gnaw.

Mionn. A bell.

Mionn. The crown of the head, the fkull.

Mionn. An oath.

Mionn riogha. A royal diadem.

Mionnaigham. To fwear.

Mionrann. A fhort verfe.

Mionnughadh. Vowing, fwearing.

Mionnlachd. Gentlenefs.

Mionofach. Morofe.

Mionos. Diftraction; a jug.

Mionriogh. A petty king.

Mionfhuileach. Pink-eyed.

Miontan. A fmall bird, a titmoufe.

Miontas. Mint.

Mionaurach. A fmall pitcher.

Miophairt. Ingratitude.

Miorbhadh. To kill, deftroy.

Mior. A bit. Vide Mir.

Miorag. Vide Mirag.

Miorbhuile. A prodigy, miracle, wonder.

Miorbhuilleach. Wonderful.

Miorun. Ill-will, malice.

Miorunach. Malicious.

Mioriaghailt. Confufion.

Mioriaghailteach. Rebellious, turbulent, irregular.

Miortal. Myrtle.

Miortalnach.

Miortalnach. A place where myrtle grows.

Mios, A month.

Mais-buidh. July.

Moisach. The plant purging-flax.

Miosachan. An almanack.

Miosasta. Displeased.

Mioscais. Spite, hatred.

Moiscaiseach. Spiteful.

Mioscaith. A curse.

Miosdiuram.
Miosheolam. } To mislead.

Moisgan. A small vessel full of butter.

Miosgus.
Miosgin. } A grudge, spite.

Mioshamh. Rough, rugged, hard.

Mioshiofhalta. Uncivil, impolite.

Miosin. A little dish.

Moishuaimhnach. Restless, uncomfortable.

Mioshuaimhnas. Disquiet.

Miosheamhsor. Unlucky, ominous.

Miosheamhas. Ill fortune.

Misheun. Ill fortune, infelicity.

Miosneach. Courage.

Miosneachal. Couragious.

Moistuama. Immoderate, intemperate.

Mioshonadh. Unfortunate, unbless'd.

Miosur, A measure.

Miosurachd. Mensuration.

Miotal.
Miotailte } Metal.

Miothag. A bite, pinching.

Mithagaicham. To pinch.

Moithaitnam. To displease.

Miothaincol. Ungrateful.

Miothainc.
Miothaincolachd. } Ingratitude.

Miothur. Little, narrow.

Miothurasa. An ill omen.

Miotag. A mitten.

Miothaitnamhach. Disagreeable, unpleasant.

Miothapadh. Mishap.

Miothaibhach. Unprofitable.

Miothairbhe. Disprofit.

Miothlachd. Contempt, disrespect.

Miothlachdor. Disagreeable, contemptible.

Miothoil. Ill will, unwillingness.

Miothoileach. Unwilling,

Miothoilaicham. To dissatisfy.

Miothoilichte. Dissatisfied.

Miothuigam. To misunderstand.

Miothuigsin. Misunderstanding.

Mir. A bit, part, piece.

Mir. The top, summit.

Mirain. Frolicksomeness.

Mirag. Play, frisking.

Miragach. Sportful, frisking.

Mire. Levity, madness.

Mireanach. The bit of a bridle.

Mireann. A portion, share.

Mireannuigham. To shatter.

Mireusonta. Unreasonable, irrational.

Mireusontachd. Unreasonableness.

Miriaghalta. Untractable, unruly.

Miriaghaltach. Irregular, informal, excentric.

Miriaghalachd. Untractableness.

Miriaghuil. Rebellion, transgression.

Mirle. A ball, a globe.

Mirra. Myrrh.

Mirtail. A myrtle-tree.

Mis, mios. A month.

Miseach. A young kid.

Miseamhnach. Agreeable, pleasant.

Misgeul. A calumnious story.

Mise. I myself.

Misheun. Adversity, ill luck.

Misimin-dearg, Bogmint.

Misimirt. Foul play.

Misge.
Misgad.
Misgeamhlachd. } Drunkenness.

Misgeamhuil.
Misgach. } Drunken.

Misgair.

Mifgair. A drunkard.

Mifleanach. Springing up.

Mifneach. Courage.

Mifneachal. ⎫
Mifnamhal. ⎬ Courageous.

Mifnachadh. Encouraging, abetting.

Mifnuigham. To encourage.

Mifnuighoir. Encourager.

Mifte. Worfe, worft.

Miftiri. A fly creeping fellow.

Mitailte. Metal.

Mitailteach. Mettled, keen, fmart.

Mitailtaiche. A mineralift.

Mitheir. Weak, crazy.

Mithfir. Weak, ignorant.

Mithich. ⎫
Mithidh. ⎬ Time, proper feafon.
Mithis. ⎭

Mithlachd. Difguft, difcord.

Mithlachdoi. Difgufted.

Mithlufor. Cruel.

Mithluforachd. Cruelty.

Mithur. Niggardly.

Miug. Whey.

Miuran. A carrot.

Miuran geal. A parfnip.

Mligh. The point of death.

Mna. Inflected cafe of Bean, a woman.

Mnamhal. Womanifh, effeminate.

Mnamhalachd. Effeminacy.

Mnigh. An epitaph.

Mo, mogh. ⎫
Modh. ⎬ A man.

Mo. My, mine.

Moa. Greater, greateft.

Moch. Early, foon.

Mochabuidh. Early ripe.

Mochd. Promotion.

Mochd. Great.

Mocheirigh. Early rifing.

Mochthrath. The dawning of the day.

Mod. A court.

Modh. A manner, fashion, breeding.

Modh. Work.

Modhaidheas. Hufbandry.

Modhamhuil. Mannerly, well-bred.

Modhamhlachd. Mildnefs, gentle behaviour, good breeding.

Modhan. Child-birth, travel.

Modhanach. Moral.

Modhdhamh. A plough-ox.

Modhluinin. Tabernacle, tent.

Modhmhargadh. A flave-market.

Modhfaine. Slavery, bondage.

Mogach. Shaggy.

Mogal. A hufk, fhell of any fruit; a
mafh, a clufter, branch.

Mogan. A young hero.

Mogan. A boot-hofe.

Mogul na fuil. Apple of the eye.

Mogulach. Full of hufks, plenteous, like
net-work.

Mogh, modh. A manner, fashion.

Moghaighe. A hufbandman, clown.

Moghna. A-falmon.

Moghur. Soft, mild.

Moghfuine. Slavery.

Moguidh, maggadh. Mocking.

Moiche. Earlier.

Moichad. State of being early.

Moid. ⎫
Moidghealladh. ⎬ A vow.

Moid. A court, judgment-feat.

Moid, moid meanman. The height of
courage.

Moidaigham. ⎫
Moidam. ⎬ To vow, fwear, afcertain.

Moide. Greater, bettered.

Moideach. A votary.

Moidheach. A hare.

Moidheamh. Boafting, bragging.

Moidh, amuigh. Abroad.

Moidthe. Devoted.

Moigh, muigh. At moft.

Moigh, magh. A plain.

Moigheanar. Happy, feftive.

Moil. A kind of black worm.

Moil. A heap caft up.

Moill, maill. Delay, hindrance.

Moiltin, molt. A hogrel.

Moim. The eruption of water from a mountain, torrent.

Moin. A mountain.

Moinmhor. A mountain in Ireland.

Moine. Turf, mofs, a bog, peat.

Moinfheur. A meadow, mountain grafs.

Moingrealt. A comet.

Moinfe. A peat pit.

Mointeach, A peat-mofs.

Moipal. A mop, brufh.

Moir. In compound words for Mor, great.

Moirb. An ant, pifmire.

Moircheart. Juftice, clemency.

Moireafadh. The falling ficknefs.

Moireal. A borer.

Moireis. Haughtinefs.

Moirfhearthunnach. Very rainy.

Moirghnithachd. Magnificence.

Moirinntinach. Magnanimous.

Moirmheafam. To magnify, efteem.

Moirneis. Great ftreams of water.

Moirfheifar. Seven.

Moirt. } Dregs, lees.
Moirteadh. }

Moirteal. A cripple.

Moirteal. Mortar, plaifter.

Moirteur, A pounding mortar.

Moirtis. } A mortife, tenon.
Mortis. }

Mois. A cuftom, manner.

Moifleabhar. An Ethick-book.

Moit. A fhort neck crefting up, fulkinefs.

Moitamhuil. Pettifh, fulky.

Mol. An affembly, flock, number.

Mol. Loud, clamorous.

Mol muiluinn. The beam that fets a mill in motion.

Mol olla. A ball of wool.

Moladh. Praife, praifing.

Molam. To praife.

Molan, mulan, A fmall hill, heap.

Molaibh a ghabhail. To coin.

Molc. Fire.

Molcha. An owl.

Molfa. Great.

Moll. Chaff.

Mollachd. Vide Mallachd.

Molrach. A giant.

Molt. A wether.

Moltair. Moulter.

Moltach. That praifeth.

Molta. Praifed, extolled.

Moltfheoil. Mutton.

Momhar. } Stately, noble.
Momharach. }

Mo'n, mu'n. If not, before that.

Mon. A trick, a wile.

Monadh. Money.

Monadh. A mountain, extenfive common.

Monaifach. Sedate, mild, applied to the female fex.

Monaiftir. A monaftery.

Monar. Work.

Monar. Murmuring, purling noife.

Monaran. A certain berry growing on mountains.

Monarcha. A fhop, workhoufe.

Monathar. The inwards.

Mong, muing. Mane or creft of a horfe.

A'mhongach mhear. Henbane, or hemlock.

Mong-fteudach. A fine crefted horfe.

Mongar. Roaring.

Monlach. Rough, brufhy.

Monmhar. Murmuring, detraction.

Monuar. Alas ! woe is the day.

Mor. Great, noble, bulky, many.

Moracthachd. Rottennefs, corruption.

Moral, Moramhuil. Majeftic, great, magnificent.

Moraigham. To magnify.

Moramhlachd. }
Mordhachd. } Majesty, greatness.

Moraigantach. }
Morchriodhach. } Magnanimous.
Morinntinach. }

Moraigantachd }
Morchriodhachd. } Magnanimity.

Moralta. Moral.

Moraltachd. Morality.

Moran. A great number, multitude, many.

Moraonach. A great assembly, market-place.

Morc. A hog, a sow.

Morc. Great, huge.

Morchlais. }
Morgantachd. } Magnificence.

Morchoinneal A torch, link.

Morchoind. A fleet.

Morcholnach. Corpulent.

Morcroid. A highway.

Morchuis. Pomp.

Morchuisach. Pompous.

Morchuisle. An artery.

Morcshaoth. }
Morcthuit. } The falling sickness.

Morcthas. }
Morgadh. } Corruption.

Morchuairt. Grand tour, visitation of a bishop.

Morchuidhtheach. Corrupt.

Mordha. Worthy, noble, magnificent, epic.

Mordhachd Greatness, majesty.

Mordhail. }
Mordhalach. } Majestic, vain-glorious.

Mordhail An assembly, convention, parliament.

Mordhail Droma-ceit. The parliament of Dromceit, county Derry, at which were present Aodhgan king of the Scots, and Collum Cille, abbot of I.

Mordhraidheann. Agrimony.

Moreisioch. Gay.

Morfhairge. The ocean.

Morfhas. Train oil.

Morfhliogh. Masterwort.

Morfleadh. Epulation.

Morfhlath. Great chief.

Morgantach. Magnificent.

Morgha, muiramh. A spear to kill fish.

Morghniomh. An exploit.

Morghrain. Abomination.

Morleaththiomach. Advanced in pregnancy.

Moiluaigh. }
Morluach. } Precious, valuable.

Morlibh. Lees.

Mormhaor. A lord-mayor, high steward, an earl, lord.

Moimhuigheamh. A brag.

Mormor. Especially, moreover.

Mormonta. Wormwood.

Mort. Murder, murdering.

Mortair. A murderer.

Mortam. To murder.

Mortla. Devastation by fire.

Morshluagh. A multitude.

Morthir. The continent, main land.

Morthorach. Very fruitful.

Mortis. A mortice or tennon.

Mortus. Gasconade, insolence.

Moruasal. Noble.

Moruaisle. Nobility.

Moruigham. To extol, exalt.

Morughadh. Magnificence, exaltation.

Moruadh, moruach. A mermaid, a sea-monster.

Mos. A manner, fashion.

Mosach. Of, belonging to manner, fashion.

Mosach. Rough, bristly.

Mosan. Rough trash, such as chaff, &c

Mosgalam. To awake.

Mosgaltach. Watchful.

Mosgaltachd.

Mofgaltachd. Watchfulnefs.

Mota. A mount, mote.

Moth. Male of any creature.

Mothach Fertile, fruitful, pregnant.

Mothaigham. To feel, perceive, know.

Mothughadh. Feeling, fenfibility, touch.

Mothuigheach. } Senfible.
Mothughal.

Mothar. A park.

Mothar. A high fea, loud noife.

Mothar. A tuft of trees.

Mothchat. A he-cat.

Muadh, muaidh. A cloud.

Muadh. An image.

Muadh. Middle, midft.

Muadh. Noble, good.

Muadh. Soft, tender.

Muadhaire. A rogue.

Muadham. To form, fhape.

Muadhbhlofg. Very loud, noify.

Muadhbhraidh. A platform.

Mual. Summit, top of an hill.

Muc. Sow, hog, pig.

Mucir A little fow.

Muc amidhe. A fow with young.

Muc-alla. Echo, i. e. pig of the cliff, potius Mac alla.

Muc. An inftrument of war whereby befiegers were fecured in approaching a wall, like the pluteus of the Romans, covered over with twigs, haircloth, raw hides, and moving on three wheels.

Muca-meala. Something vegetative, which I do not know; the words I met with in a defcriptive poem of the ifland of Arran.

Muc-ghaine. A fhelf, quickfands.

Muc mhara. A whale.

Muc-bhirach A porpoife.

Mucag. The fruit called hip.

Mucag. A cup.

Mucair. A fwine-herd.

2

Mucfheoil. Pork; Lorc mucfheoil, a gammon of bacon.

Much. Smoke.

Mucha. An owl.

Muchadh. Extinguifhing, extinction.

Mucham. To extinguifh, fmother.

Muchadon Extinguifher.

Muchan. Chimney.

Muchna. Dark, gloomy.

Mucnach. Hoggifh, morofe.

Mucnachd. Grimnefs, morofenefs.

Mucraigh. A gammon of bacon.

Mucfhneachda. A fnow-ball.

Mucufg. Swine's greafe.

Mudhughadh. Dying, perifhing.

Mudan-croicin. A bit of fkin to cover the lock of a gun.

Mudha. Dying, perdition.

Mudharn. An ankle.

Mudidh. Dun-coloured.

Mudhladh. Killing.

Mudhlaim. To kill.

Muduighe. Cloyed.

Mugan. A mug.

Mugha. Perdition, deftruction.

Mughraidhe. Slavery.

Muicinnis. Ireland.

Mughaim. To kill, deftroy.

Mughard. Mugwort.

Mugart. A hog.

Muich. Sadnefs, dullnefs.

Muiche. Day-break.

Muiche-laoi. Dawning of day.

Muicidhe. A fwine-herd.

Muicineach. A plebeian.

Muidhe. A churn.

Muifled. A muffler.

Muigham. To fail, faulter, fall, be defeated.

Muigein. A furly little fellow.

Muilcionn. Pennygrafs.

Muileag. Cranberries.

Muilaid.

Muilaid. A mule.

Muill. Delay. Vide Moill.

Muillain.⎱
Muilnen.⎰ A particle of chaff.

Muilaidachd. An ill scent.

Muileann.⎱
Muilunn.⎰ A mill.

Muille. A mule.

Muilleadh. Preparing, to prepare.

Muillean. A little bell.

Muillair. A miller.

Muillair-luathaidh. A fuller.

Muillairachd. Grinding, the office of a miller.

Muilleathan. Flat-headed.

Muime. A nurse, stepmother, godmother.

Muin. The back.

Air muin. Upon.

Muin. The thorn-tree, the letter M.

Air do muin. Upon thee.

Muin. The neck.

Muince. A collar.

Muine. A thorn, bush, bramble, a mountain.

Muineach. Thorny.

Muineadh. Teaching, instructing.

Muinam. To teach; to pifs.

Muineal. The neck.

Muing. A mane.

Muingiall. I believe the headstall of a bridle.

Muinghin.⎱ Confidence, truft, hope, Dea-
Muinin. ⎰ nam muinghin ann, to confide.

Muinghinach. Confident.

Muiniughadh. Poffeffion.

Muinle. A sleeve.

Muinmhear. Hemlock.

Muintir. People, men, parents, family, clan, tribe.

Muinthead. A necklace, collar of effes.

Muinte. Taught, inftructed.

Muinteardha.⎱
Muintiral. ⎰ Kind, friendly.

Muintirdhas. Kindnefs, fervice.

Muinteoir. A teacher.

Muir. The fea.

Muir-teachd. Unnavigable fea.

Muiraidhe. Leprofy.

Muirbhleaghadh. Amazement.

Muirbhruchd. A high tide.

Muircheartach. An Irifh proper name of a man; i. e. expert at fea.

Muirchabhlach. A fleet, fquadron.

Muirchreach. A wave.

Muirchu. ⎱ Irifh proper name of a
Muireadhach.⎰ man.

Muirchudleadich. Afterfall.

Muireadhach. A fovereign.

Muireach. A failor, mariner.

Muirean. A woman.

Muireann. A dart, fpear; a woman's name.

Muirfeachd. A fleet.

Muirfidh. Will kill. Vide Marbham.

Muirgeag. A frith, narrow fea.

Muirgheilt. ⎱
Muirimhgach.⎰ A mermaid.

Muirginach. Dull, ftupid.

Muirgineas. Dullnefs.

Muirighin. A great noife.

Muirighin. A burden, charge, a family.

Muirghinneach. Burthenfome, poor, many.

Muirgrim. A naval engagement.

Muirn. A troop, company.

Muiririn. A fort of alga that is eaten, it confifts of very long ftalks, and long narrow leaves.

Muirn. Natural affection.

Muirne. Fondnefs, careffes.

Muirneach. Fond, affectionate, careffed.

Muirneamh. An overfeer.

Muirnigham. To burden, load.

Muirnineam. To fondle, dandle.

Muirnin,

Muirnin. } A dearly beloved per-
Muirnineach. } fon.
Muirfcionn.   A fpout-fifh.
Muifcin   An Englifh pint.
Muirt.   Riches.
Muifeag.   Threatening.
Muifean.   Primrofe.
Muifiall.   A curb.
Muite.   Mute, dumb.
Muith.   Without, on the outfide; fouth-
ward.
Mul.   An axle-tree.
Mul.   A congregation, multitude.
Mulach. } A fea-calf.
Mulbha. }
Mulach.   A top, fummit, hill.
Mulachan.   A cheefe, cheefe-curds.
Mulad.   Melancholy, fadnefs.
Muladach.   Sad, melancholy.
Mulag.   A mule.
Mulan.   A ftack, little hill.
Mulcan, mulcha.   An owl.
Mulghart. }
Mulcheann. } The pole.
Mulchuth. }
Mul-mhagan.   A kind of large toad.
Mull, maol.   Top or extremity of a thing,
a promontory.
Mulla, mullog.   The patine of a chalice.
Mullach.   A top, height, hill.
Mulladh.   A mould.
Mullan.   Vide Mulan.
Mulurt.   Dwarf-elder.
Mumhuin.   Munfter in Ireland.
Mun.   For, fake of.
Mu'n.   Before that.
Mun.   Urine, pifs, piffing.
Muna.   Unlefs, if not.
Munadh.   Inftruction.
Munam.   To make urine, pifs.
Munar.   A fact, deed.
Munata.   A champion.

Munbhar.   A backbiting, grudging, mur-
muring.
Mung, muing.   A mane, hare.
Munloch.   Puddle, dirty-water, mire.
Muntorc.   A neck-chain, collar.
Mur.   A wall, bulwark, a houfe.
Mur-ollamh.   An academy.
Mur.   Unlefs.
Mur.   Many, much.
Murac.   Murex or purple-fifh.
Muraim.   To wall in.
Muran.   Rents.
Muran.   A carrot, fea-reed grafs.
Murbhuachile.   A diver.
Murcach.   Sad.
Murcas.   Sadnefs.
Murdhraidhan.   Agrimony.
Murdhuchan.   Sea nymphs.
Murgabhal.   An arm of the fea.
Murlan.   A rough top or head.
Murrtha.   Succefsful.
Murfanach.   A fubject.
Murfantachd.   Subjection.
Murthaidhe.   Men of the fea.
Murufc.   Sea-fhore, fea marfh.
Murthuila.   A tide, flood.
Murthoradh.   Product of the fea.
Murtill.   Dull.
Mus, mas.   Pleafant, agreeable, hand-
fome.
Mufgalam.   To awake.
Mufgaltach.   Watchful.
Mufgallachd.   Watchfulnefs.
Mufg. } A mufket.
Mufgaid. }
Mufgam.   To be mouldy, mufty.
Mufgan. } Muftinefs.
Mufganachd. }
Mufgladh.   Awaking.
Mufla.   A mufcle.
Mut.   Any fhort thing.
Mutaiche.   Mouldinefs.

[U u]   Mutach,

Mutach. That is fhort, thick, and blunt.

Muthairne. An ankle.

Mutan. An old mufty rag, any thing worn by time or difeafe.

N.

N Is the eleventh letter of the Irifh alphabet, and like L is never afpirated. It is called Nuin, from Nuin, the afh-tree. N, when fingle, founds hard, nearly as in Englifh, but doubled becomes fofter, or more nafal, as may be feen from Bean, a woman; Beann, a mountain; Cean, affection; Ceann, an head.

Na. Than.

Na. Not; equal to the Latin Ne.

Na, no. Or, Nor, Neither.

Na, 'n a. In his, in her.

Na. Of the; gen. fem. of the article An the.

Na. The pl. of the article.

Nabadh. A neighbour.

Nach. Not. An interrogative and negative particle, is Beag nach do thuit mi, I had almoft fallen.

Nad. The arfe, buttocks.

Nad, i. e. Ann do. In thy.

Nada. Nothing.

Nadh. No, not.

Nadhmairdhe. } An earneft penny.
Nadhmchomhthara. }

Nadluga. Formerly, antiently.

Nadur. Nature.

Nadurtha. Natural.

Nae, nai, nui. A man, woman.

Nae, a nae, ande. Yefterday.

Naebh. A fhip.

Naebhog. A little fhip.

Naid. A lamprey.

Naidhe. Who? which?

Naidhme. A bargain, covenant.

Naidhmcheanglam. To confederate.

Naidhm na Borumha. Obligation of paying the mulct, called Borumha.

Nail. Another.

Nailbheal. } A bridle-bit.
Nall. }

Naimhdal. } Hoftile, inimical.
Namhaidach. }

Naimhdalachd. Hoftility.

Naimhde. Pl. of Namhaid.

Naimhdean. An enemy.

Naimhdeanas. Enmity, hoftility.

Naimhdeas. Enmity.

Naindean. Valour, chivalry.

Naing. A mother.

Naingmhor. A grandmother.

Naird, An aird. Up.

Naire. Shame, bafhfulnefs.

Naire. Clean, neat.

Naireach. Bafhful.

Naireachd. Bafhfulnefs.

Nairaighe. More bafhful.

Nairaigham. To fhame, make afhamed.

Nairne. Sure, certain.

Naifair. The old inhabitants of a country.

Naisc. A ring.

Naistin. Care, warineſs.

Nalb. Long.

Nall. Towards us, from the other ſide; Nall & anunn, hither and thither.

Nallana. The time paſt, anciently, formerly.

Nallod. Formerly.

Nallus, fallus. Sweat.

Nama, namadh. Only, alone.

Namh. ⎫
Namha. ⎬ An enemy.
Namhad ⎭

Namhadas, vide Naimhdeas. Enmity, fierceneſs.

Nan, nam. Gen plural of the article.

Naochad. Ninety.

Naochado. Ninetieth.

Naoi. A man, perſon; Noah.

Naoi. Nine.

Naoi. A ſhip.

Naoidhe. ⎫
Naoidheachan. ⎬
Naoidhenan. ⎪ A babe, infant, ſuckling.
Naoidhan. ⎭

Naoidheachdha. The golden number.

Naoidheachdha. The nineteenth.

Naoidheachda. A chief, principal.

Naoidheantachd. ⎫ Infancy.
Naoidheanachd. ⎭

Naoidheanta. Infantine, like an infant.

Naoidho. Ninth.

Naoidhideadh. An hoſpital.

Naoidhin. An infant.

Naoimh, naomh. Saints.

Naoimhghlinigham. To ſanctify.

Naoimhi. ⎫
Naoimhios. ⎬ November.

Naoimhioſdadh. A ſanctuary.

Naoineal. Proweſs, chivalry.

Naoitheachdha. Chief, principal.

Naomh. A ſaint.

Naomhaithis. Blaſphemy againſt the Saints.

Naomhaithiſach. Blaſphemous.

Naomhartadh. To ſanctify.

Naomhaithiſam. To blaſpheme.

Naomhmhallughadh. Blaſpheming, blaſphemy.

Naomhmhalluighoir. A blaſphemer.

Naomchiſd. A ſacriſty.

Naomhchoiſreagadh. Conſecration.

Naomhdheanam. To canonize.

Naomhghoid. Sacrilege.

Naomhreachd. The divine law.

Nacmhoran. An anthem.

Naomhtha. Sanctified, holy.

Naomhthachd. Holineſs.

Naomhthaiſc. A veſtry.

Naomhthreigſin Apoſtacy.

Naomhthreigach. Apoſtate.

Naomhaigham. To ſanctify.

Naomhughadh. Sanctification, ſanctifying.

Naon Certain.

Naomnhar. ⎫
Naonar. ⎬ The number nine, nine.

Naoſga. ⎫
Naiſgach. ⎬ A ſnipe.

Naoſgaire. An inconſtant.

Naoſgaueachd. Inconſtancy.

Nar. That not, Ionnuſnar, ſo that not.

Nar. For Naire, ſhame.

Nar. Good, happy.

Narab. For Nar bu; ut non fit.

Narach. Shameful, baſhful.

Naraigham. To ſhame, affront.

Narachadh. Affronting, cauſing ſhame.

Nard. Skill, knowledge.

Nardaim. To know, be ſkilled.

Narr. A ſerpent.

Nas. A band, tye, death.

Nas. An anniverſary.

Naſadh. A fair.

Naſadh. Fame.

Naſadh. Noble, famous.

Naſc. A tye, band.

Naſc.

Nafc. A collar, chain.

Nafc. A ring.

Nafgad. An obligation.

Nafgam. To bind, tye, to develope.

Nafgthte. Bound, tied down.

Nafgaire. A surety.

Nafcar. A defence, fortification.

Nafgidh. Freely, without price, also a treasure, gift; potius Afgidh; Ann afgidh, in a gift.

Nath. Science.

Nathach. Dark grey.

Nathair. A snake, adder, viper, serpent.

Nathair nimhe. A viper.

Nathan. Noble, famous.

Nathrach. Of a serpent.

Ne. Yesterday.

Nenar, i. e. An e nar. Whether or no.

Neabhan. A Royston crow.

Neach. Any one, one, some one, he.

Neach. A spirit, apparition.

Neachtar. Neither.

Neachtar. Outwardly, without.

Nead. A nest.

Neadaghadh. Nestling.

Neadaigham. To nestle.

Neag. A notch, indent.

Neagam. To jagg, indent.

Neal. A cloud.

Neal. Noble.

Neal. A trance, extafy.

Neallaire. A rogue.

Neambaoghal. Safety, security.

Neambaoghalach. Secure.

Neamh. Heaven, gen. Neaimh.

Neamhabbuidh. Immature.

Neamhach. A heavenly being.

Neamh. A compofitive and negative particle, pronounced Neo, except when a vowel follows——Neo is fometimes written in this Dictionary.

Neamhgha. }
Neamhidh. } Heavenly, divine.

Neamhain. Pearl.

Neamhaidhal. Unfortunate.

Neamhaife. Terrible, cruel.

Neamhaireach. Heedlefs.

Neamhaire. Inadvertence.

Neamhaitheanta. Unknown.

Neamhaithghinte. Heterogeneous.

Neamhaltach. Smooth.

Neamhamhrafach. Indubitable.

Neamhaobhin. Joylefs.

Neamhathreachas. Impenitence.

Neamhan. A raven, crow.

Neambhig. Agreeable.

Neamhbhog. Hard.

Neamhbriogh. Contempt, infignificance.

Neamhbhunaitach. Groundlefs, unfixed.

Neamhbuaigh. Worthlefs, incapacity.

Neamhbhriogh. Infignificance, contempt.

Neamhbrioghman. Adjective.

Neamhbhrathairal. Unbrotherly.

Neamhbhith. Non-exiftence.

Neamhbheathal. Lifelefs, fpiritlefs, inanimate.

Neamhbheachdidh. Indeterminate, dubious.

Neamhbheufach. Immoral.

Neamhbhlafta. Taftelefs, infipid.

Neamhbheartuighte. Unyoked.

Neamhbhuairte. Undifturbed.

Neamhbhuan. Tranfitory.

Neamhchnagach. Without knots.

Neamhchoigilt. Unthrifty.

Neamhchoigilteach. Profufe, lavifh, liberal-minded.

Neamhchoimhtheach. Free, generous, hofpitable.

Neamhchoingeallach. Ill-natured, perfidious.

Neamhcharrthanach. Uncharitable.

Neamhchomhdach. Negligent.

Neamhchoruighte. Unfhaken.

Neamhchoruigheach. Immoveable.

Neamhchordach. Disjunctive.

Neamhchordadh. Difcord.

Neamhchordam.

Neamhchordam. To difagree.

Neamhchoruigheachd. Immobility, fteadinefs.

Neamhchriochnuighach. Infinite.

Neamhchriochuighte. Unfinifhed.

Neamhchubhidh. Improper, unbecoming.

Neamhchuid. Poverty.

Neamhchuideach. Poor, indigent, improvident.

Neamhchuimhne. Forgetfulnefs.

Neamhchuimhnach. Forgetful.

Neamhchoimeafgte. Unmixed, pure, uncompounded.

Neamhchuramach. Carelefs.

Neamhchuram. Carelefsnefs, fecurity.

Neamhcheanalta. Indelicate.

Neamchean. Difrefpect.

Neamhcheannfuighte. Unbridled, diffolute.

Neamhcheannfa. Immodeft.

Neamhchinta. Uncertainty.

Neamhchiontach, Innocent.

Neamhchiontas. Innocence.

Neamhchinntach. Uncertain, precarious.

Neamhchiallach. Imprudent, unadvifed.

Neamhcheadaigham. To difallow.

Neamhchearbach. Not aukward.

Neamhchuimfeach. Infinite, incomprehenfible.

Neamhchofruigte. Inconfecrated.

Neamhcheartuighte. Incorrected.

Neamhchuirtal. Uncourteous.

Neamhchruthighte. Increated.

Neamhchealgach. Undefigning, unaffected.

Neamhchnuafaighte. Indigefted.

Neamhchomhthrom. a. f. Unjuft, uneven, difproportion.

Neamhchomhthromuigham. To difproportion.

Neamhchomhnard. Uneven, not level.

Neamhchomharluighte. Unrefolved, unadvifed.

Neamhchumonta. Unufual.

Neamhchruinuighte. Uncollected.

Neamhchruadalach. Unconcerned.

Neamhchompanta. Infociable.

Neamhchrabhach. Indevout.

Neamhchreidmhach. Difbeliever.

Neamhchoimhdheas. Incommodious.

Neamhchoimhdheafachd. Inconveniences.

Neamhchoithreach. Inculpable.

Neamhchomafach. Incompetent.

Neamhchomas. Impotence.

Neamhchuranta. Unwarlike, immartial.

Neamhcheaduighte. Illicit.

Neamchofmhuil. Diffimilar.

Neamhchaochlaideach. Immutable, unchangeable.

Neamhchaochlaidachd. Immutability.

Neamhchleir. The laity.

Neamhchleirach. Lay, a layman.

Neamhchleachdte. Unaccuftomed.

Neamhdha. Heavenly.

Neamhdhaicholachd. Improbability.

Neamhdhlightheach. Unlawful.

Neamhdheanam. To undo.

Neamhdhubhrachd. Negligence, infincerity.

Neamhdhubhrachdach. Infincere, negligent.

Neamhdhiadhidh. Ungodly.

Neamhdhiolte. Unpaid.

Neamhdhleafdanach. Undutiful.

Neamhdhleafdanas. Undutifulnefs.

Neamhdhilis. Unfaithful.

Neamhdhiomalach. Frugal.

Neamhdhuinal. Unmanly.

Neamhdhuinalachd. Unmanlinefs.

Neamhdhiongbhalta. Infufficient.

Neamhdhaonna. Inhumane.

Neamhdhearbham. To difprove.

Neamhdheas. Homely, not neat.

Neamhdhifle. Faithleffnefs.

Neodhuine. A nobody.

Neamheagalach. Bold, unappalled.

Neamheidam.

Neamheidam. To difarray.

Neamhefeachdach. Ineffectual.

Neamhefeachd. Inefficiency.

Neamhealladhanta. Inartificial.

Neamheolach. Unacquainted.

Neamhfhalfa. Unfeigned, fair.

Neamhfhailigheachd. Care, vigilance.

Neamhfhas. A grudge.

Neamhfhaicfinachd. Invifibility.

Neamhfhaicfinach. Invifible.

Neamhfheimal. Needlefs.

Neamhfhabharach. Unfavourable.

Neamhfhallan. Unhealthy.

Neamhfhoiftinach. Reftlefs.

Neamhfhoiftin. Reftlefsnefs.

Neamhfhoilfighte. Unrevealed.

Neamhfhirinach. Unrighteous, difinge-
nuous.

Neamhfhoghlumte. Illiterate.

Neamhfhafanta. Unfafhionable.

Neamhfhreafdalach. Difficult.

Neamhfhurafda. Unfavourable, improvident.

Neamhfhortunach. Unfortunate.

Neamhfhiofrach. Unconfcious.

Neamfhonnmhor. Jarring.

Neamhfhonnmhorachd. Jarr.

Neamhgharamhuil. Incommodious.

Neamhghean. Difaffection, hatred.

Neamhgheanmath. Difapprobation, difaffection.

Neamhghlan. Impure, unclean.

Neamhghlanas. ⎱ Uncleannefs, impurity,
Neamhghlaine. ⎰ pollution.

Neamghlic. Unwife.

Neamhghnathach. Unufual.

Neamhghnothach. Idle.

Neamhghealtach. Unappalled.

Neamhgheamnidh. Unchafte.

Neamhghaigham. To celeftify.

Neamhgheamnidhakhd. Inabftinence.

Neamhghluaifte. Unruffled.

Neamhghrafmhor. Ungracious.

Neamhghrafmhorachd. Ungracioufnefs.

Neamhiulmhor. Unfkilful.

Neamhiomchar. Abortion.

Neamhiomlan. Imperfect, incomplete.

Neamhiomlanachd. Imperfection, incom-
pletion.

Neamhiomchubhidh. Improper, unfit, un-
qualified.

Neamhionmhuin. Unbeloved, morofe.

Neamhionnan. Unequal.

Neamhionnanas. Inequality.

Neamhinntleachdach. Unartful.

Neamhinntleachd. Unartfulnefs.

Neamhthoilicheachd. Difcontent.

Neamhlaghal. Illegal.

Neamhlaghalachd. Illegality.

Neamhleaffuichte. Unreformed.

Neamhlochdach. Innocent.

Neamhloifgach. Not keen, afbeftine, in-
combuftible.

Neamblathairach. Abfent.

Neamhluchduigham. To difburthen.

Neamhmharbhthach. Immortal.

Neamhmharbhthachd. Immortality.

Neamhmhearachdach. Unerring, unerr-
able.

Neamhmheas. Contempt.

Neamhmheafardhachd. Excefs.

Neamhmhealltach. Undiffembling.

Neamhmheafardha. Intemperate, exceffive,
immenfe.

Neamhmheata. Fearlefs.

Neamhmhifgach. Sober.

Neamhmhothuighach. Infenfible.

Neamhmhothughadh. Stupidity, infenfibi-
lity.

Neamhurras. Unprofitable, difficult.

Neamhnuall. An anthem, hymn.

Neamhonn. A diamond.

Neamhni. Nothing, non-entity.

Neamhnithachd. Nothingnefs.

Neamhnitham. To annihilate.

Neamhonorach. Ignoble.

Neamhoireamhneach. Unbecoming, improper, inadequate.

Neamhrannphartuighte. Incommunicable.

Neamhphoitamhuil. Sober, abstemious.

Neamhriaghalta. Heteroclite.

Neamhshalach. Undefiled.

Neamhsharuighte. Unconquerable.

Neamhsheasmhach. Unstable, inconstant.

Neamhshailte. Unseasoned.

Neamstraoighamhuil. Frugal.

Neamhshant. Loathing.

Neamhshuilmhur. Churlish, morose.

Neamhshuidhichte. Diffuse, unsettled, unsteady, discomposed.

Neamhsgeaduigham. To undress.

Neamhsgathach. Undaunted.

Neamhshocruigheachd. Disquietude, unsteadiness.

Neamhshocruighach. Unsteady, disquiet.

Neamhsgarthamhuil. Inseparable.

Neamhshuimal. Negligent, indifferent.

Neamhshuimalachd. Indifference.

Namhshonruighte. Indefinite.

Neamhshoilleir. Indistinct.

Neamhshoillirachd. Indistinctness.

Neamhshollarach. Improvident, shiftless.

Neamhshoirbhidhach. Unsuccessful.

Neamhsgeaduighte. Unclothed, undressed.

Neamhsgithuighte. Unwearied.

Neamhsheargte. Undecayed.

Neamhsholasach. Indelightful.

Neamhthabhachdach. Ineffectual, futile, immaterial.

Neamhthabhachd. Futility.

Neamhthabhartach. Stingy.

Neamhthachd. Heavenliness.

Neamhtharbhach. Unprofitable, fruitless.

Neamhthairbhe. Unprofitableness, fruitlessness.

Neamhthorthach. Unfertile, unfruitful.

Neamhthorthaichachd. Infertility.

Neamhthaomha. A novice.

Neamhthrocairach. Unmerciful.

Neamhthrocairachd. Unmercifulness.

Neamhthruaillidhachd. Incorruption.

Neamhtharthalamh. A common field.

Neamhthruaillidh. Incorruptible.

Neamhthruaillighte. Unadulterated, undefiled.

Neamhthoil. Unwillingness, nolition, an inclination.

Neamhthoilach. Unwilling.

Neamhthoilalachd. Stubbornness.

Neamhthoiltinas. Demerits.

Neamhthoiltinach. Undeserving.

Neamhthreoruighte. Undirected.

Neamhthrathal. Unseasonable.

Neamthoidhrighte. Unseasoned, unaccustomed.

Neamhtheagaste. Untaught.

Neamhthoiluighte. Dissatisfied, disaffected.

Neamhthoilachasinntin. Disaffection, discontent.

Neamhthoirt. Indifference, negligence, contempt.

Neamhthoilaigham. To dissatisfy.

Neamhthuitamach. Infallible.

Neamhthoirt. Indifference, disinclination.

Neamhthoirtal. Indifferent.

Neamhthuigsach. Absurd, senseless, injudicious.

Neamhthuigse. Senselessness.

Neamhthaitne. Disapprobation, disgust.

Neamhthaitnach. Disagreeable, unacceptable.

Neamhthearinte. Insecure.

Neamhthearintachd. Insecurity.

Neamhthreabhte. Impenetrable.

Neamhthraighach. Inexhaustible.

Neamhthoirtfanearach. Inattentive, inconsiderate.

Neamhthortfanear. Inattention, inconsiderateness.

Neamhthimchiollghearradh. Uncircumcision.

Neamh-

Neamhthruacanta. Relentlefs.

Neamhthimchiollghearrte. Uncircumcifed.

Neamhuafal. Ignoble, ungenerous.

Namhuireafbhuidhach. Not poor.

Neamhullamh. Unprepared.

Neamhurchoidach. Harmlefs.

Neamhuallach. Not proud, humble.

Neamhurchoidach. Innocent, fafe.

Neamhuras. Ufelefs.

Nean. An inch, a fpan.

Nean. A wave, billow.

Neannaidh. ⎫
Neant.   ⎬ A nettle.
Neantag. ⎭

Neannaifg. That bindeft.

Near. A wild boar.

Near. Eaft.

Nearach. Lucky, happy.

Nearcluachra. A lizard.

Nearrdheas. South-eaft.

Nearaid. A place where wild boars are kept.

Nearnaim. To liken, compare.

Nearnadh. Likening, comparing.

Nearthuath. North-eaft.

Neart. Strength, power.

Neartaigham. To ftrengthen.

Neartmhor. Strong, powerful.

Neartughadh. Strengthening.

Neas. A fortified hill.

Neas. A weazle.

Neas. A hurt, wound.

Neas. Noble, generous.

Neafa. Next.

Neafachd. Contiguity.

Neafan. The next place.

Neafg. An ulcer, a bile.

Neafgaid. A bile, ulcer.

Neafgaidach. Full of fores.

Neafta. Juft, honeft.

Neathas. Manflaughter.

Neid. A fight or battle, a wound.

Neidhe. Wind.

Neillin. A fmall cloud.

Neim. ⎫
Neimh. ⎬ Brightnefs, fplendour.

Neimh. Poifon.

Neimh. Sometimes wrote for Neamh, the negative particle.

Neimheadh. A poem, fcience.

Neimhead, quafe, neimh-iath. Glebe land, confecrated ground.

Neimheach. Glittering, fhining.

Neimhedh. ⎫
Neimhidhacht. ⎬ Filth, dirt.

Neimheilnidhe. Uncorrupted, unviolated.

Neimhi. Ants eggs.

Neimhim. To corrupt, fpoil.

Neimhneach. ⎫ Sore, painful, paffion
Neimhal.   ⎬ ate.

Neimhalachd. Painfulnefs.

Neimhfeadh. Contempt.

Neip. A turnep.

Neith. A fight, battle, engagement.

Neithe. Pl. of Ni, things.

Neitheach. Falfe.

Neitheamhuil. Real.

Neimhain. Madnefs.

Nemhan. A vulture, Royfton crow.

Neo. The pronunciation of the compofitive particle Neamh.

Neo, or Air neo. Elfe, otherwife.

Neo. An.

Neoch. Good.

Neoid. Bad, naught.

Neoil. Pl. of Neal, neul, a cloud.

Neoni. Non-entity.

Neonithachd. Nothingnefs.

Neotheach. Cold.

Nefs. A promontory, peninfula.

Neul. A cloud; pl. Neoil, neulta.

Neul. Light, a glimpfe of light, colour.

Neul. A fit, trance, fwoon.

Neuladoirachd. Sneaking and gazing about.

Neuladoir. An aftrologer.

Neulfhurtadh. A flumbering.

Ngedal. A reed.

Ni. Not.

Ni. A thing, cattle; pl. Nithe, neithe.

Ni headh, i. e. Ni e. Nay, not fo, it is not.

Nia. A fifter's fon.

Niadh. A champion.

Niadhas. } Valour, bravery, chival-
Niadhchus. } ry.

Nial. Neil, name of a man.

Nial. A letter.

Niamh. The brightnefs, colour, appearance of a thing.

Niar. Weft.

Niardheas. South-weft.

Niarthuath. North-weft.

Niatal. A reed.

Niamham. To gild, colour over.

Niamhdha. Pleafant, bright.

Niamhachd. Brightnefs.

Niamhchuridh. Tenacious.

Niamhghlas. Greemfh.

Nic. A daughter, in oppofition of Mac.

Nid. For Gnid, they make.

Nid. Gen. of Nead, a neft.

Nid. Manflaughter.

Nidhe. Time.

Nigh, or ni. A daughter or niece.

Nighan. A daughter.

Nighanag. Pronounced Ninag, a little girl.

Nigham. To wafh.

Nighadh. Wafhing.

Nighte. Wafhed.

Nightin. Soap.

Nil. For Ni bheil, it is not.

Nilam. To be wanting, to be abfent.

Nim. A drop.

Nim. To do, make.

Nimdhergfadh. Reproving.

Nimh.
Nimhe. } Poifon, bitternefs, fournefs.

Nimghlic. Strong, impregnable.

Nimhneach. Poifonous, mortal, peevifh, paffionate.

Nimhneachan. Rheumatifm.

Nin. An image.

Ningir. Sore, fick, bitter.

Ninfci. One who interrupts another's dif-courfe.

Ninneach. Pleafant.

Niodha. Real.

Niomhdha. Bright, fhining.

Niomham. To fhine, glitter.

Niomhas. Brightnefs.

Niomfgaoilte. Scattered.

Nion, nuin. An afh-tree, name of the letter N.

Nion. A wave, a letter.

Nion. For Nighan, a daughter.

Nionach. Pleafant, fpeckled, forked, catching.

Nionadh. Prey, booty.

Nionag. For Nighanag, a little girl.

Nionaim. To prey, plunder.

Niopfam. I would not be.

Nior, nir. Not, comes before the paft tenfes.

Nios, anios. From below.

Nis. For Nior.

Nife. Gen of Neas, a wound.

Nis. For Ni is; as, Nis laidire, ftronger, that is ftronger.

Ni 's mo. No more, no longer.

Nis moa. Greater, that is greater.

Nitar. Shall be done; fut. of Deanam.

Nith. A battle, manflaughter.

Niuc. A corner, nook.

Niugh. To-day.

No. Noi, or.

No gu. Until that.

No. New.

Nobhaidh. Time, feafon.

Noch. Which? who? whofe?

Nocha, nochad. Ninety.

Nochd, nocht. To-night, night.

Nochd. Nakednefs.

Nochd. Naked.

Nochdam. } To make naked, uncover,
Nochdaigham. } difclofe, peel, to ftrip.

Nochduighte. } Uncovered, difclofed.
Nochta. }

Nod. An abbreviation, a difficulty.

Nod. Thus; Nod leat, Obferve, take notice.

Nodaire. An abridger.

Nodaireachd. Method of ufing abbreviations.

Nodam. To underftand.

Nodadh. Underftanding.

Nodaigham. To graff.

Nodughadh. Graffing.

Nodh. Noble, excellent.

Nodhlag. Chriftmas.

Noere. A feaman, mariner.

Noibhighis. Ordure, dung.

Noibhifach. A novice.

Noimhnidadh. A fool.

Noin. Noon, ninth hour of the day, according to the Roman calculation.

Noin-dorcha. An eclipfe of the fun.

Noinean. A daify.

Noinreult. The evening ftar.

Nois, nos. A cuftom, manner.

Nois & beachda. Carriage and behaviour.

Nois. Noble, excellent.

Noit. A church, congregation.

Noitheach. Noble.

Nollag. Chriftmas.

Nonn Beyond, to the other fide.

Nonn & annall. To and fro, hither and thither.

Norp. Houfeleek.

Nos. A fafhion, cuftom, manner.

Nos. Knowledge.

Nos luingas. A fhip-dock.

Nos. White, pureft white.

Nofadh. Liking, approving.

Nofa. Now, at prefent.

Nofaigham. To enact, approve.

Nofaire. Soft.

Notha. Difcovered.

Nua. Strong.

Nua, nuadh. New.

Nuacholla. Aftonifhing.

Nuachor, nodhchur. A companion, bride, bridegroom.

Nuacoinfeach. A harlot, proftitute.

Nuadh. New; it is often prefixed to words, as

Nuadhbhrioghughadh. Tranfubftantiation.

Nuadhtheachd. Tidings, news.

Nuadhfeinidhe. A novice.

Nuaidhmhilidh. An untrained foldier.

Nuaidhfhianuis. A new law.

Nuadhthionfgantoir. Innovator.

Nuail. A roaring, howling.

Nuailam. To howl.

Nuair, an uair. When, feeing that.

Nuall. Famous, noble.

Nuall. Lamentation, mourning.

Nuall. An opinion, a freak.

Nuall gan ghaoi. A true faying.

Nualladh. } Ualladh. Howling, roaring.
Nuallan. }

Nuallfurtach. } Howling, roaring.
Nuallgubha. }

Nuallfan. Noble, generous.

Nuamhanoir. Embroidery.

Nuar. Alas.

Nuas, anuas. From above, down.

Nuathaigh. Heaven.

Nuathar. A wedding.

Nuidhifeachd. A lonely journey.

Nuige, go nuige. Until.

Nuige fo. Hitherto.

Nuimhir. Number.

Nuimbruigham. To number.

Nuimhirughadh. Numbering.

Nuin. The afh-tree, the letter N.

Nuna. Hunger.

Nunn, nonn. To the other fide, beyond.

Nuridh, nuair-rith. Laft year.

O.

O Is the twelfth letter of the alphabet, and is called Oir, the spindle-tree. It is sounded sometimes short, and sometimes long. Vide Analysis.

O. From whence in the relative sense.

O ! An interjection.

O Since, seeing that.

O, ogh. An ear.

Oar. A voice.

Ob. Hops.

Obha, obhuin. A river.

Obadh. A denial.

Obaim. To refuse, deny.

Obainne. Swiftness, hastiness.

Obair Work, labour.

Obair ghreis. Embroidery, tapestry.

Obairuigham. To work, labour.

Obairaighte. Worked, wrought, done with art.

Obair-uchd. A parapet.

Obair-lionan. Network.

Obair-shnathad. Needlework.

Obair-uairadair. Clockwork.

Obair-ghloine. A glass-house.

Obair-theine. A fire-engine.

Ooair-uisge. A water-engine.

Obair-cheardamhuil. An engine.

Oban. A small bay.

Obann. Quick, soon, nimble.

Obar. Vide Obadh.

Obela. Open.

Obhan, uabhun. Fear, dread, terror.

Obhan. Froth.

Obhnach. Frothy.

Obo ! Interjection oho !

Obuinn. Rash.

Obuinne. Rashness.

Oc. A poet.

Ocaid. Business, an occasion.

Ocar. Interest, usury.

Ocaras. Hunger.

Ocarasach. Hungry.

Ocas. Interest, annual rent.

Och ! Oh !

Ochal. Moaning, complaining.

Ochd, uchd. The bosom, breast.

Ochd.
Ochdar. } Eight.

Ochdach. A good key of voice.

Ochdmhacadh. Adoption.

Ochdmhadh. Eighth.

Ochdmhad. Eighty.

Ochdmhado. Eightieth.

Ochdmhios. October.

Ochdshliosneach. Octagon.

Ochra. Shoes.

Ochras. Gills of a fish.

Ochus. Itch.

Ocoth. A shower.

Ocrasan. A glutton.

Ocrach.
Octasach. } Hungry.

Ocras.
Ocrus. } Hunger.

Od. From, thy.

Od, ud. There, yon, that there.

Odh, oidh. Music.

Odh. O strange !

Odh. The point of a spear, sharp end of any thing.

Odhall. Deaf.

Odhann. A pan, kettle.

Odhar. Pale, wan, dun; a mixture of white and red.

Odharog.

Odharog. A fcrat, young cormorant.

Odharan. Cow-parfnip.

Odharach mhullach. Devil's bit.

Odhmhos. Refpect, homage.

Odhmhofach. Refpectful, dutiful.

Offig. Office, officer.

Offraideach, offigach. A Druidifh prieft, offerer.

Offrail. An oblation, offering.

Offralam. To offer.

Og. Young.

Ogachd. ⎫
Oganachd. ⎬ Youth.
Oige. ⎭

Ogachda. Virginity.

Ogal. Youthful.

Ogalachd. Youthfulnefs.

Ogan. A bough, twig, branch.

Ogain. ⎫
Oganach. ⎬ A young man.
Oigair. ⎭

Ogbho. A heifer.

Ogchiern, ogthiarna. A young lord.

Ogchulloch. A grice.

Ogh. The ear.

Ogh. Whole, entire.

Ogh. A virgin.

Ogh. ⎫
Ogha. ⎬ Pure, fincere.

Ogha. A grandchild.

Oghar. Vide Odhar.

Oghdhachd. Virginity.

Oglach. A fervant, a youth, foldier, a vaffal.

Oglachas. Slavery, vaffalage, fervitude, a fort of Irifh verfe.

Oglofgain. A tadpole.

Ogmhart. A heifer, a young beef.

Ogmhadduin. The early dawn.

Ogmhios. June.

Ogluidh. Bafhful, afraid, awe-ftruck.

Ogluidhachd. Bafhfulnefs, awe, fear.

Ogri. The youth, young men.

2

Oi, ai, aoi. A fheep.

Oibne, obbainne. Quicknefs, fuddennefs.

Oibid. Obedience, fubmiffion.

Oibrigham. To work, to caufe, effect, operate.

Oibrighte. Wrought.

Oibrightheoir. ⎫
Oibruighe. ⎬ A workman.

Oibrughadh. An operation.

Oiche. The night, evening.

Oiche. A water.

Oide. A godfather.

Oideadh. A maffacre, death.

Oidean. Love, tendernefs, generofity.

Oide altram. A fofter-father.

Oideas. Inftruction, counfel.

Oidche. The night.

Oideachas. Inftruction.

Oidhchmhearleach. A night-robber.

Oidhe. A gueft, traveller.

Oidheacht. Entertainment, a night's lodging.

Oidheadh. ⎫
Oighidh. ⎬ Death.

Oidheas. Freeftone.

Oidhir. ⎫
Oighir. ⎬ Snow.

Oidhirp. Attempt, undertaking.

Oidhre. Ice.

Oidhre. ⎫
Oighre. ⎬ An heir, heirefs.

Oidhreachd. An inheritance.

Oidhreamail. Frofty.

Oidhreata. ⎫
Oighreata. ⎬ Frozen.

Oiffig. An office.

Oifigeach. Officer.

Oiffigeamhuil. Official.

Oifrionn. Mafs.

Oig. A champion.

Oigbhean. A young woman.

Oige. A web.

Oige. Younger.

Oigeach. A young colt.

Oigh A virgin, maid.

Oighcheoil. Virginals.

Oighe. Fullnefs, entirenefs.

Oighe A file.

Oigheann. A pan, cauldron.

Oighiramhuil. Icy, frofty.

Oighidh A fojourner, gueft.

Oigham. Obedience, homage.

Oigham. To behold, look upon.

Oighreir. A defpotic power, obedience.

Oighreachd. Inheritance.

Oighream. To freeze, fnow.

Orghreog Froft, ice.

Oigthiarna. Heir apparent

Oigimh A ftranger

Oil. A rock

Oil A reproach, infamy

Oilam To nurfe, cherifh.

Oilabhan. An elephant.

Oilbheim, Reproach, fcandal, offence.

Oilbheimam. To ftumble, take offence.

Oilbhreo. A funeral fire.

Oilcheas. A doubt.

Oilcheafach. Doubtful.

Oile, eile. Other, another.

Oileamhnach. Requifite, nourifhing.

Oileamhnach. A ftudent, fcholar.

Oileamhnam. To educate.

Oileamhuin. Nurture, food, honeyfuckle, education.

Oileain. An ifland.

Oilear.   } A pilgrim.
Oilearach. }

Oilearadh. A pilgrimage.

Oilearam. To go on a pilgrimage.

Oilearcha. A nurfery.

Oilathair. A fofter-father.

Oilem. Inftruction.

Oilicheadh. To frighten.

Oilthire. A pilgrim.

Oilithreach. A pilgrim, belonging to a pilgrim.

Oille, uille. Greater.

Oillmheadh. Ballances.

Oilltheud. A cable.

Oilt. Terror.

Oiltal. Terrible, fhocking.

Oin, on. A thing lent, loan.

Oineach. Mercy, liberality.

Oinicc. Liberal.

Oinigh. A harlot.

Oinme. With.

Oinmhidh. A fool, filly perfon, nidget.

Oinmhideach. Foolifh, filly.

Oinmhideachd. Folly.

Oinfeach A harlot, abandoned woman.

Oinninn A pebble, onion.

Oir. For, becaufe that.

Oir. Golden, of gold.

Oir. The fpindle tree. The diphthong Oi is fo called.

Oir, Air. Upon, over, above.

Oir. A hem, border.

Oirbheart. Good actions.

Oirbheartach. Great, precious.

Oirbhidin. Honour, veneration.

Oirbhidineach. Venerable.

Oirc A lapwing.

Oircain. A young pig.

Oirceadal. Inftruction, doctrine.

Oirceart. A hurt, wound.

Oircheas. Necefary, fit, proper.

Oircheafachd. Need, neceffity.

Oircheafachd. A mefs.

Oirchneis. The forefkin.

Oirchil. Provifion referved for the abfent.

Oirchill. Againft, in wait or expectation.

Oirchillam. To bear, or carry.

Oirchiabhach. Golden-haired.

Oirchios. Charity.

Oircifeach. A portion, fhare.

Oirchifde. A treafury or bank of gold, a precious magazine.

Oirchifdair. Treafurer.

Oirchrios. A belt, an ornament.

[Z z z]   Oirdhearcam.

Oirdhearcam. To flourish, be famous.

Oirdheirc. Noble, honourable, excellent, illustrious.

Oirdhearcas. Lustre, excellency.

Oirdnibh. Splinters.

Oireachdas. An assembly.

Oireachas. Preheminence, supremacy.

Oireachda. Statute, decree.

Oiread, uread. As much, so much, whilst.

Oireadh. Befitting, becoming.

Oiream. To befit, become.

Oireagha. Chief, excellent.

Oireagail. A waste-house, habitation.

Oireamhuil. }
Oireamhnach. } Meet, proper.

Oireamhuin. Pertinence.

Oireamhuineach. Pertinent.

Oireamhuin. Influence.

Oireamhnaim. To adapt, make fit.

Oirear. Pleasant.

Oirsid. }
Oirfideadh. } Music, melody.

Oirfideach. A musician, musical.

Oirghreas. Ornament, piece of embroidery wrought by a needle-woman.

Oiridh. Devices in gold.

Oiridh. Meet, deserving.

Oiriad. Vide Oiread.

Oirim. To serve.

Oirghios. Cheer.

Oirle. A piece, fragment.

Oirleach. An inch.

Oirleach. Slaughter, havock.

Oirleam. To cut off.

Oirlionam. To encrease.

Oirmhid. Credit, respect.

Oirmhine. Offence.

Oirne. Upon, over us.

Oirnealta. Neat, elegant, ornamental.

Oirneimham. To shine like gold.

Oirneis. Goods, chattels, instruments, tackling.

Oirneis. A qualm of stomach, nauseousness.

Oirnam. To ordain, put in authority.

Oirip, Eorp. Europe.

Oirpheal. Gilded.

Oirthir. The shore, coast, borders.

Oirthir-ghainmhaich. A sand-bank.

Oirthear. The east, eastern world.

Oirthearach. Eastern.

Oirthior. The day after to-morrow.

Oisbheas. An epicycle.

Oisbhreag. An hyperbole.

Oischreidamh. Superstition.

Oischeimnughadh. Eminence, superiority.

Oisg. An ewe, sheep.

Oisin. A corner.

Oissin. The son of Fingal and a poet.

Oisionair. A taberd, a habit formerly worn over a gown.

Oisire. An oyster.

Oisfgriobhin. A superscription.

Oissinam. To lie with the face upwards.

Oislin. Charms.

Oittir. A bank or ridge jutting into the sea.

Oitag. A blast.

Ol. Said.

Ol. Drinking, drink.

Ola. Oil, olive.

Olach. Given to drunkenness.

Olachan. Immoderate drinking.

Olam. To drink.

Olann. Wool.

Olart. A hone.

Olartar. An ungrateful smell.

Olc. Bad, naught, harm, damage.

Olcas. Naughtiness, badness.

Olclabaireach. Blubber-lipped.

Olchobhair. Pleasure, avarice.

Oldus. But.

Oleach. Soaking.

Oleasach. Usual, frequent.

Oll. Great, grand.

Olla, olgha. Woollen.

Ollamh. Vide Ullamh.

6

Ollamh. } A doctor, chief bard, gen. Ol-
Ollamhan. } lamhun.
Ollamhan re lagh. Doctor of laws.
Ollamhan re diadhachd. Doctor of divi-
nity.
Ollamhan re leighas. Doctor of Medi-
cine.
Ollamhain. The learned, literati, instruc-
tion.
Ollamhnuigham. To instruct, teach, so-
lemnize.
Ollabhar. A great army.
Ollanachadh. Burial.
Ollathach. Resentment.
Olldas. Than, more than, rather than.
Olldrag. A funeral pile.
Olleadh Affront, indignity.
Ollghloi. Bombast.
Ollmhucach. Plentiful of swine.
Ollmhathas. Great riches.
Olltuath. The great axe.
Olom. Crop-eared.
Oluidh. A cow.
Oluin. Of wool.
Omal. Vide Tomaladh.
Omar. } Amber.
Onab. }
Omh. Lonesome, unfrequented.
Omhan. Fear, terror.
Omhnach. Terrible.
Omhan. Froth, sillabub.
Omhnach. Frothy.
Omhnear. An embryo.
Omna. An oak, a lance.
Omna. A lance, spear.
Omoideach Obedient.
Omoidam. To obey.
Omrann. A division, share.
Qmur. A trough, cupboard.
On. Gain, profit.
On. A stain.
On. Sloth, laziness.
Ona. Slow, sluggish, inactive.

Ong. Clean, clear.
Ong. Sorrow, grief, a sigh.
Ong. Healing, curing; a groan.
Ong. A fire, hearth.
Ongadh. Anointing, unction.
Ongam. To anoint.
Ongbhron. A trespass.
Ongtha. Anointed.
Onnar. There is.
Onn. A stone.
Onn. A horse.
Onn. Furze, gorse, hence the letter O is
called Onn by the ancient Irish.
Onoir. Honour, respect.
Onorach. Honourable
Onoraiche. More honourable.
Onoraigham. To honour, reverence.
Onoruighte. Honoured.
Oi. Gold
Or, oir. For, because.
Or. A voice, sound.
Or. A border, coast.
Oracuil An oracle.
Oradh. Gilding.
Oragan. The herb organy.
Oraid. An oration, prayer, declamation.
Oraideach. An orator, declaimer.
Oraidaigham To declaim.
Oraim. To pray.
Oraiun. Writing tables.
Onnchon. A standard, ensign.
Oraisde. An orange.
Oram, orm Air me, i. e. Upon me.
Oran. A song.
Oranach. Full of songs.
Oranaiche. A songster.
Orbhaire Mercy, goodness.
Orbhann. A gold coin.
Orbit. Humble, mild.
Orbhuidheach. The pure yellow called
Or or Topaz, in the arms of an earl or
lord, or Sol in that of a prince or king.
Orcam. To kill, destroy.

Orcadh.

Orcadh.   Killing, deftroying.

Orc.   A hen egg.

Orc.   A falmon, a whale.

Orc.   Vide Oircain.

Orc.   The cramp.

Oic   A prince's fon.

Orcabhe.   Whales of the ocean ; Orkneys.

Oichaon.   A poetical incantation.

Oichoilier.   A gold collar.

Oichcard   A goldfmith.

Orchradh   Grief, forrow.

Orchoilen   A gold mine.

Orc-iafg.   The torpedo.

Orctreth.   A prince's fon.

Ord.   An order, feries.

Ord beannuighte.   Holy orders.

Ord.   A hammer, mallet.

Orda.   A piece, fragment.

Ordaigham.   To order, command, defire.

Ordan.   Love, generofity.

Ordha,   Golden, of gold.

Ordhuilleog.   Gold leaf.

Ordin   A mallet.

Ordamhuil.   Orderly.

Ordog.   A thumb, great toe.

Ordugh.   An order, decree.

Ordughadh.   Ordaining, decreeing, order-
ing.

Ordughal.   Set, ftudied, formal, regular.

Orduigham.   To order, fet in order, ordain.

Orduighte.   Ordered.

Orgain.   An organ.

Orgain.   Slaughter.

Orgham.   To gild.

Orghruagach.   Yellow-haired.

Orlafta.   } Shining like gold.
Orlaftamhuil. }

Orleathair.   An uncle by the father's fide.

Orleach.   An inch.

Orlughadh.   Befpewing.

Orm.   } i. e. Air me. Upon me.
Ormfa. }

Ormaidean.   The morning, break of day.

Ormheinach.   Gold ore, a gold mine.

Orn.   Slaughter, maffacre.

Orna.   Barley.

Ornaighe.   A prayer.

Ornaigham.   To adorn.

Orneach.   Bits.

Orneis.   A qualm, naufeoufnefs.

Orp.   Houfe-leek.

Oria, orrtha.   On them.

Orrar.   A porch.

Orrachda.   A widower

Orraghan   } Charms, enchantments.
Orruighachd. }

Ort.   On thee.

Orta.   Be gone.

Ortaigham.   To depart.

Ortha.   A collect, fhort prayer, a charm.

Orrtha.   On them.

Orthuigear.   After to-morrow.

Ortfa.   On thee.

Oruibh.   Upon you.

Orumfa.   Oramfa.   Vide Orm, Ormfa.

Os.   Above, over, upon, and is ufed in
compofition.

Os.   A deer.

Os aird.   Publicly, loudly.

Os iofeal.   Softly, privately.

Ofadh.   Defifting, ceffation.

Ofaim.   To defift, to ceafe.

Ofar.   The younger.

Ofbarr.   Befides, over and above, from the
whole.

Ofcach.   Eminent, fuperior.

Ofcar.   Motion of the hands in fwim-
ming.

Ofcar.   A leap, bound.

Ofcar.   A gueft, traveller.

Ofcar   A champion, the fon of Offian.

Ofcar.   A ruinous fall.

Ofcardha.   Renowned, famous.

Ofcarlann.   An hofpital.

Ofcarthachd.   Energy, emphafis, loudnefs,
Ofcartha.

Oſcartha. Loud, clamorous, emphatical, energetic.

Oſchomhaiſte. A meteor.

Oſceann. } Above, over.
Oſcionn. }

Oſcheimnigham. To exceed, excel.

Oſcheimnughadh. Superiority, pre-eminence.

Oſchrabhadh. Superſtition.

Oſcuilte. Open, manifeſt.

Oſcul. The arm-pit.

Oſda. An inn.

Oſdair. An inn-holder, hoſt, landlord.

Oſgarach Frail, brittle.

Oſglam. To open.

Oſgraibh. Superſcription.

Oſgriobhan. Epigram.

Oſmharthach Surviving.

Oſnadh A ſigh, groan, blaſt.

Oſnadhach. Sighing, groaning.

Oſnaidhe. } A groaning.
Oſnaidhal. }

Oſnaigham. To ſigh, groan.

Oſſag. A blaſt.

Oſſagach. Bluſtering, ſqually.

Oſſan. A ſtocking, hoſe.

Oſſanaiche. A hoſier.

Oſſar. A back, burthen.

Oſſaraidhe. } A porter, carrier.
Oſſaroir. }

Oſtoir. An oſtler.

Oſſraidhe Cow-dung.

Oſſruidhe. Oſlory in Leinſter.

Oſſadla A league.

O taim. Since that I am.

Otar. Labour.

Othar. Sick, weak, wounded.

Othar. Wages.

Otir. A ridge or bank jutting into the ſea.

Othrach. Vide Otrach.

Othras. A diſeaſe, diſorder.

Othraſach. Sick, diſeaſed.

Othraſcha. An hoſpital.

Otrach. Dung, a dunghill.

P.

P Is the thirteenth letter of the Galic alphabet——This letter is called by the Iriſh grammarians Peith-bhog, but they do not tell us from what tree, for the letters were commonly named after trees. It would, however, appear to be nothing elſe than Beith-bhog, or B ſoft, i. e. P is only a ſoft or mollifying way of expreſſing B, and the reaſon is, originally they were the ſame letter, and P was not uſed in the Iriſh language until our knowledge of the Latin, ſince the time of St. Patrick. In the old parchments theſe letters are indiſcriminately uſed, as Prutach, a boor or ruſtic, for Brutach, Peiſt for Beiſt, &c. With the aſpirate H which it bears, it is pronounced like the Greek Phi, and Ph in the Engliſh word Prophet.

Pabhail. A pavement.

Pac. A pack.

Pacair. A pedlar.

[4 A]   Pacaigham.

Pacaigham. To pack.

Paclach. An armful.

Pacairachd. Bufinefs of a pedlar.

Padruic. } Patrick.
Padhruic. }

Padhal. An ewer.

Padhadh. Thirſt.

Padhuilun. A tent, booth, hut.

Paganach. A heathen.

Paganachd. Gentiliſm.

Paidii. The pater-noſter.

Paidiruin. A rofary of beads to fay a pa-ter-noſter, a necklace.

Paidhadh. Pay, payment.

Paidhir. A pair.

Paidhiram. To pair, couple.

Paidham. To pay.

Pailchloch. Paving ſtones.

Paileiris. } Palfy.
Pairithis. }

Pailliunn. A tent, pavilion.

Pailm. The palm-tree.

Pailt. Abundant, plentiful.

Pailtas. Plenty, abundance.

Painachas. Bail, fecurity, infurance.

Painneal. A pannel.

Painidh. Strong.

Paintearam. To enfnare, trepan.

Painte. Lace, ſtring to lace clothes.

Paintair. A net, gin, fnare.

Paintairam. To enfnare.

Paintairadh. Enfnaring.

Paipair. Paper.

Pairc. A park, field.

Paircam. To enclofe.

Pairt. A fhare, portion, relation, kin-dred.

Pairtach. Having a fhare, related, free-hearted.

Pairtaiche. A partner, affociate, abettor.

Pairtaigham. To partake, to communi-cate.

Pais. Paffion, fuffering.

Paifde. A child.

Paifdin. An infant.

Paifonadh. A faint.

Paifgam. To ſtarve of cold.

Paifgte. Starved of cold.

Paiteach. Thirſty.

Paiteog. Butter.

Paitt. A hump.

Paitrifg. A partridge.

Palas. A palace, regal feat.

Palin. A winding-fheet, fhroud.

Palmare. A rudder.

Palluin. A tent, tabernacle, booth.

Panna. A pan.

Panna-fiolaidh. A dripping-pan.

Pannag. A pancake.

Pannal. A crew, a band of men.

Papa. The pope.

Par. Parchment.

Paralais. The palfy.

Paralus. A parlour, or room to enter-tain.

Parraifte. A parifh.

Parrathas. Paradife.

Partach. Partaking.

Partaidhe. A partner, partaker.

Partan. A crab-fifh.

Parn. A whale.

Pafcairt. A pannier.

Pafgam. To enwrap, fwaddle.

Pafgan. A bundle.

Pafgte. Enwrapped.

Paflaghadh A didapper.

Pata. A veffel.

Pata. A hare.

Patan. A leveret.

Patantachd. Thickneſs.

Patrun. A patron.

Peabhcach. Neat, fine.

Peabhchaolach. A peacock.

Peabhchearc. A peahen.

Peacach. Sharp-pointed, beautiful.

Peaccach. Sinful.

Peac, peuc, piac. Any fharp-pointed thing; the fprouting germ of any vegetable, a long tail.

Peaccadh. Sin, tranfgreffion.

Peaccaigham. To fin, offend againft.

Peaccthach. A finner, tranfgreffor.

Peall. A horfe.

Peall. A couch, pallet.

Peall, pealltog. A veil.

Peallam. To mat, cover; to teaze, pull afunder.

Peallaftair. A quoit, penny-ftone.

Peanas. Punifhment.

Peanafaigham. To punifh.

Peann. A writing-pen, a reed.

Peannagan A pen-cafe.

Peanfal. A pencil.

Peannfair. A fencer.

Peanfuir. Pincers.

Pearla A pearl, precious ftone.

Pearlach. Plaited, corrugant.

Pearlaigham. To corrugate.

Pearlughadh. Corrugating.

Pearlog. A partridge.

Pearfa. A perfon; pl. Pearfana.

Pearfa. A verb.

Pearfaigham To perfonify.

Pearfal Parfley.

Pearfanta. Perfonable.

Peas. ⎫
Peafan. ⎬ A purfe.

Peafan A punchy forry little fellow.

Peafghaduighe ⎫
Peafladron. ⎬ A pickpocket.

Peafgadh. A gafh, cut.

Peafgam. To cut and flafh.

Peatiuit. A halter.

Peic. A great tail.

Peick. A peck.

Peiciollach. That hath a long tail.

Peileir. A bullet, a bowl, a pillar.

Peileir-tarnainaich. A thunder-bolt.

Peillic. A hut or booth made up of earth and branches of trees, the whole covered at the top with fkins of beafts, antiently ufed in Ireland It is the name of different places in the county of Corke at this day.

Peliocan. A pelican.

Peinn, piann. Pain, punifhment.

Peindlighe. A penal law.

Peinnair. ⎫
Peinreachd. ⎬ A pen-cafe.

Peinteal. A fnare.

Peircioll. A corner, the lower part of the face, the jaws, the abdomen.

Peire. A pear, pear-tree.

Peireadh. Rage, fury.

Peiriacul. Urgent neceffity, danger.

Peirfe. A row, rank, a perch in length.

Peirfile. Parfley.

Peifchearbhaire. ⎫
Peifghearrthoir. ⎬ A cut-purfe.

Peift. A worm, beaft, monfter?

Peifteog. A little worm, infect.

Peit. A mufician.

Peiteadh. Mufic.

Peitag. A waiftcoat.

Peitain. A fhort jacket.

Peitarlaichte. Verfed in antient or facred hiftory.

Peitarlach. The old law or teftament.

Peitfeag. A peach.

Peithir. A forefter, a thunderbolt.

Pelag. A porpoife.

Peodar. Pewter.

Peodarair. A pewterer.

Pepog. A pompion.

Peffeir. Peafe.

Peffeir-chappul. Vetches.

Peffair-luchag. Lentils.

Peffrach. Of peafe.

Peffeir-tuilbhe. Heath-peafe.

Peithbhog. The letter P.

Petadh. A pet, a tame animal.

Peubar. Pepper.

Peubaram,

Peubaram. To pepper.

Peur. A pear.

Peurla. Vide Pearla.

Phairifneach. A pharifee.

Phairifnachal. Pharifaical.

Pharo. Pharaoh.

Piagham. To hang up.

Pian. Gen. Pein, pain; pl. Pianta, pangs.

Pianadh. Affliction, tormenting.

Pianam. To torment, to pain, punifh.

Pianair. The teaze.

Piantuighoir. A tormentor.

Piaft. A worm.

Piafgach. Rough, rugged.

Pib, piob. A pipe.

Pib-mhala. A bag-pipe.

Pibam. A pipe, the throat.

Pibbin. A lapwing.

Pibhar. A purfe.

Pic, pich. Pitch.

Pic-mheallach. A Lochabar axe.

Picil. Pickle.

Picilam. To pickle.

Pighe. A pye.

Pighe-feola. A pafty.

Pighaid. A magpye.

Pighaidachd. Pye-coloured.

Pighin. A penny.

A' phighin rioghal. Pennyroyal.

Pigadh. } An earthen pitcher.
Pigin. }

Pile. Vide Feille.

Pileir. A pillar.

Pillam. To turn, roll.

Pillin, pannel. A pack-faddle.

Pilliur. A pillar.

Pilfeir. A pilchard.

Pinchrann. A pine-tree.

Pincin. A gillyflower.

Pinn. For Binn, a peek or cliff.

Pinnadh. A pin, peg.

Pinnt. A pint; i. e. two quarts.

Pintealam. To paint.

2

Pintealta. Painted.

Piob. A pipe, flute.

Piobadoir. A pipe-maker.

Piobaire. A piper.

Piobaireachd. The pipe mufic, a march tune, piping.

Piobam. To pipe.

Pioban. A fmall pipe, the throat.

Piobar. Pepper.

Piobhar. A fieve, honeycomb.

Piob-leigidh. Cock of a barrel.

Piob-thaofgidh. A pump.

Piobfhionnaich. A pipe blown with bellows.

Piob-uifge. A conduit-pipe.

Piocaid. A mattock, pick-axe.

Piocam. To pick, nibble.

Piolaid. A prince's palace.

Piolaid. Pilate, a proper name.

Pioloid, pioloir. A pilloiy.

Pioloidach. A pilot.

Piollam. To pick.

Pion. } A pin, peg.
Pionnadh. }

Pionchrann. A pine-tree.

Pionas. Punifhment.

Pionofta. Punifhed.

Pioraid. A pirate.

Pioroide. A parrot.

Piorra. A pear.

Piorra. A fquall.

Piofa. A piece, a filver cup to drink whifgy.

Piofan. A little piece, any little engine or inftrument.

Pioftal. A piftol.

Piofreog. Vide Pifeog.

Piothan. A pye.

Pis, peffir. Peafe.

Pifarnach. Whifpering.

Pifeanach. Lentils.

Pifeog, pifeoga. Sorcery, witchcraft.

Pifeogaiche. A forcerer, wizard.

Pisfinain. Vetches.

Pisflach. Encrease, good luck, blessing.

Pip. Vide Pioban.

Pit. A hollow, pit, female privities.

Piteanta. Effeminate.

Piteantachd. Effeminacy.

Piuthar A sister.

Piutharal. Sisterly.

Piutharalachd. Sisterliness

Pla. A green plot, a meadow.

Placantachd. Coarseness.

Plaghaim. To plague.

Plaichid. A flagon.

Plaigh. A plague, pestilence, contagion.

Plaide A plaid

Plaighal Contagious, plaguy, pestiferous.

Plained A planet.

Plaitin. The skull, a little pate.

Plam. Curdled.

Plana. A plane.

Planta. A plant.

Plantaigham. To plant.

Plantaichoii. A planter.

Plaosg. A husk or shell.

Plaosgach. Of shell.

Plaosgadh A sound, noise.

Plaosgam. To burst, to sound, make a noise.

Plasda. ⎫
Plasdach. ⎬ A plaister.

Plasda. Feigned.

Plasdam. ⎫
Plasdruigham. ⎬ To plaister.

Plastrail. ⎫
Plastradh. ⎬ Plaistering.

Plata. A plate.

Platseadh. A squash.

Plath. A glance.

Pleadhag. A spade, dibble.

Pleaghan. A little oar.

Pleaghanachd. Rowing with a little oar.

Pleaghart. A buffet.

Pleasg, pleasgadh. A noise.

Pleasgam. To crack, break, burst, strike, beat.

Pleide. Spite.

Pliathroid. A flipper.

Plibin. A plover.

Ploc. A stopper, bung, a large stump, round head.

Plocach Having a round head, lumpish.

Plocam. To knock on the head, bruise.

Plod. A pool, a fleet.

Plodadh. Floating, buoyancy.

Plodmhor. Buoyant, a float.

Plodam. ⎫
Plodaigham. ⎬ To float.

Plodan. A small pool

Plodanachd. Paddling and rowing in water.

Plodhaisg. A bumpkin, looby.

Plaisg. Spungy, elastic, dry and spungy, inflammable.

Plosg. Quick.

Plosgail A sound, noise.

Plosgartich. Open, bold, panting.

Plosgartuigham. To pant, throb.

Plubam. To plump or fall as a stone in water.

Plubrach. Plunging.

Pluc. The rot among sheep, a knot, a bung.

Plucadh. Blowing the cheeks.

Plucis. The flux.

Plucam. To puff up the cheeks.

Plucaire. A fellow with large chaps.

Plucaireachd. Impertinence.

Plucmhalghach. Beetle-brow'd.

Plucham. To press, squeeze, constringe, smother.

Pluic A cheek.

Pluicach. Blub-cheeked.

Plumba. A plummet.

Plumbis. A plum.

Plur. Flower, meal, a flower.

Pluran. A flower.

Plurach.

Plurach. Full of meal.

Plutadh. A breaking down, scolding.

Pobul. A people, tribe, congregation.

Poc, boc. A he-goat.

Poc ruadh, Boc ruadh. A roe-buck.

Pocadh. A pocket, or little bag.

Pocan. A little he goat.

Pog. A kiss.

Pogadh. Kissing.

Pogam. To kiss.

Pobhuil. }
Poibleog } A poplar-tree.

Poiblioch. The common people.

Poiblighe. Public.

Poidin mearbhul. Jack with the lanthorn.

Poireaga. Hollow.

Poirse. A porch.

Poirsiun. A portion.

Poisgheallam. To betroth.

Poisam, To lug, haul.

Poit. Great drinking.

Poitam. To drink.

Poitairachd. Hard drinking.

Poitair. A drunkard.

Poitchriadh. Potter's clay.

Poitin A small pot.

Pota. }
Poite. } A pot.

Pola. A pole.

Polaire. A sign.

Polaire. A searcher of holes and corners.

Poll. A hole or pit.

Poll. Mire, dirt.

Pollaire. Nostrils.

Ponc. A point, article.

Poll-accairaidh. A bay to anchor ships.

Poll-iasgaich. A fish-pond.

Poll-marcachd. A road for ships.

Poncal. Distinct.

Ponair. Beans.

Ponair Fhrancach. French beans.

Poni. A little horse.

Pont. Austere, cruel.

Popa. A master.

Porc. A pig.

Por. Seed, or race for planting or propagating.

Por cochullach. Pulse.

Porcan. A small pig.

Porraisde. A parish.

Porraisdeach A parishioner.

Poit. Severe, fierce

Port. A tune, jig.

Port A port, harbour, a bank.

Ri poit. Wind-bound.

Poit A fort, garrison, the area of a place.

Port. A house

Portair. A waterman, ferryman.

Portin. A crab-fish.

Poitos The mass book.

Port-traithe. A stall-fed hog.

Porth. Severe.

Posadh Marriage, wedlock.

Posam. To marry.

Posda Married.

Posgha. Bridal, nuptial.

Posta. A post, pillar.

Postam. To trample with the feet.

Postanach. That hath stout legs.

Potaire. A toper, drunkard.

Potadoir. }
Potair. } A potter.

Potaim. To drink.

Potchriodh. Potter's clay.

Potfolach. A pot-lid.

Poth. A bachelor.

Prab. Quick.

Prab. Rheum, or the discharge from the
corner of the eyes.

Prabach. Having humours about the eyes,
blear.

Prabar. A worthless fellow.

Praidhin. Earnest business, great haste.

Praidhinach. Earnest, in great haste.

Prainsag. A haggess.

Prais.

Prais. Brafs, pot-metal.

Praiseach. A pot.

Praiseach. Broth, pottage.

Praiseach. A manger, crib

Praisaiche. A brazier.

Pramh. Sleep.

Prann. A wave.

Prantaire. A hammer.

Prafcan. A mob, a gang.

Preab. A kick.

Preabadh. Stamping, kicking

Preabam. To kick, ftamp, fpurn.

Preabsn. A court-yard

Preaban. A patch, a patch on a fhoe.

Preabanaiche. A botcher.

Preabuic. A hearty brave man.

Preabog A wincing horfe.

Preabraigh Patching, clouting.

Preabaireachd. Acting bravely or gallantly.

Preach Hold, ftand, ftay.

Preachan A crow, kite, or ravenous bird

Preachan nan cearr. A ringtail.

Preachan ingneach A vulture.

Preachan ceannan. An ofprey.

Preachoine A cryer.

Preacham. To punifh.

Prealaid. A prelate, bifhop.

Preas. A bufh, brier.

Preas nan ros. Rofe-bufh.

Preas nan fpiontag. The currant or rizar bufh.

Preas nan geardhearc The berberry-bufh.

Preas nim fiontag. Blackberried heath.

Preas. A wrinkle, plait.

Preafam. To plait, rimple.

Preafarnach. A fhrubbery.

Preas fubh craoibh. Rafberry-bufh.

Preat. Boggy.

Priacail. Danger.

Priceadh. Pricking.

Pribam. To wink, to twinkle.

Pribadh. Twinkling.

Pricam. To fting, prick.

Priginam To haggle.

Primh, priomh. Chief, great, prime, etymon

Priomhachd. A fource.

Priomhathair. A patriarch.

Priomharcal. The main beam.

Priomhadh. A primate.

Priomhbhlofgam. To prickle, fparkle.

Priomhchiall. Great underftanding.

Priomhchoflas Archtype

Priomhchlar. Autograph, original.

Priomhchleirach. Protonotary.

Priomhdha. Wifdom.

Priomhdhraoith. An arch-druid

Priomhfhaidh An ancient prophet.

Priomhlongphoit. A royal feat.

Priomhuachdaran. The chief ruler.

Prionnfa A prince.

Priomhghleus A beginning, foundation.

Priomhlaoch. A prime-foldier.

Priomhthus. A foundation

Priomhughdar. The original author.

Primidil. Firftlings.

Prine. A pin.

Prinachan. A pin-cufhion.

Priofan. A prifon

Priofonach. A prifoner.

Priofonachd. Imprifonment.

Priotchadh. Preaching.

Priotchaim. To preach, exhort.

Priotceach. A preacher.

Priofal. Precious.

Pris Price, value.

Prifealachd. Value.

Prifein. Bufhes.

Proantain. Provender.

Probhal. A conful.

Procadoir. A proctor.

Proghain. Care, anxiety.

Proimpfheillain. A drone, beetle.

Proinnuighadh. Dining.

Proinn,

Pronn, prainn. A dinner, a meal, voraciouſneſs.

Proinnuigham. To dine.

Proinnlios A refectory, dining-room.

Proinnteach Id. Vide Chron. Scot.

Proideal. A bottle.

Proidil Bold

Promhach. A proof.

Pronn. Pollard.

Pronn Smooth.

Pronnam. To pound, bruiſe, mince.

Pronnan Fragments.

Pronnog. Any thing minced.

Pronnfam. To bray, grind.

Pronnghloir. Loquacity.

Pronnghlorach. Loquacious, a ſmall-
talker.

Pronndol. A low noiſe.

Pronnuſc Brimſtone.

Prop. Vide Prab.

Proſda Strong.

Pruchlais. A den.

Pſailm. Vide Sailm.

Pubal. A tent, tabernacle, booth, marquee.

Publicanach. A publican.

Publigh. Public.

Pucan. Vide Pocan.

Pudar. Powder.

Pudarach. Powdered.

Pudhar. Hurt, harm.

Pudharacha. Suppuration.

Puiblighe. Publicly.

Puibligham. To publiſh, proclaim.

Puic. Pl. of Poc. He-goats.

Puichain. A little impudent ſtinking fellow.

Puicin. A veil or cover over the eyes,
blind-man's buff.

Puicne ſcreabhal. A ſpangle.

Puilpid. A pulpit.

Puinſion. Poiſon.

Puinſonaigham. To poiſon.

Puirleagach. Creſted, tufted.

Puirtin. A ſmall fort, turret.

Puirt. Ports for guns, tunes.

Puiſgam. To beat, whip.

Puiſin. A lip.

Puiſt. Of a poſt or pillar.

Puitric A bottle.

Pullog. The fiſh called Polluck, I believe
the porpoiſe, a pantry.

Punc. A point, article, jot, tittle, whit.

Puncal. Diſtinct, articulate

Punan. A ſheaf of corn, bundle of hay
or ſtraw.

Pun-glaſs. Purple melic-graſs.

Punnt. A pound.

Punnt ſaſgunnach. A pound ſterling.

Puntuin. Benumbing.

Pupal. Vide Pobul.

Pur. Neat, pure.

Purpi. Poppy, purſlain.

Purpair. Purple.

Purgaid. A purge.

Purgadoirachd. Purgatory.

Purt. A fort, tower, town.

Futadh. }
Purradh. } A puſh.

Purram. }
Putam. } To puſh.

Purraghlas. Name of a cat.

Pus. A lip.

Pus. A cat.

Putag. A pudding, a thowl or oar-pin.

Putan. A hare.

Puttrall. A lock of hair.

R.

R Is the fourteenth letter of the alphabet, and with L and N does not admit of the aspirate H. R in general sounds the same as in other languages. It is called Ruis from Ruis the elder-tree, anciently so called, but now Troman.

Ra. A going, moving.

Rabach. Fruitful, plentiful.

Rabhadh. Advertisement, caution, a precedent, example.

Rabhadar. They were.

Rabhagach. Vide Rabhach.

Rabhan. A long repetition, rhapsody.

Rabhladh. Boasting.

Racadh. A rake.

Racaire. A rake, prattler.

Rac. A king or prince.

Rac. A bag, pouch.

Racadal Horse-radish.

Racam. To rake.

Racam. To rehearse, repeat.

Racaireachd. Raking, repeating, romance.

Racan. Mischief, noise.

Racham. To go.

Rachdam. To arrive at, come to.

Rachdan. A bowling.

Rachgan. A harrow.

Rachin. I would go.

Rachoil. A winding-sheet.

Racht. He arose, got up.

Racht. A fit.

Racht, reachd. A law, ordinance.

Rachtaire. A law-giver, judge, a dairy-man.

Rachdmhor. Giving laws, legislative.

Rad. Vide Rod.

Radaim. To give up, deliver.

Radaireal. Wandering, strolling.

Radan. A rat.

Radh. A saying.

Radham. To say, relate.

Raha. A bidding.

Radharc. Sight, sense of seeing.

Radmuillam. To dream.

Rae. A field, plain.

Rae. Much, plenty.

Rae. A battle.

Rae. A salmon.

Rafta. A gallery.

Rag. A wrinkle.

Rag. Stiff.

Ragach. Stiff, wrinkled.

Ragaim, meacan ragaim. Sneezewort.

Raghait, i. e. Rangadar. They reached.

Ragairachd. Violence.

Ragmhuinalach. Stiff-necked.

Rai. Motion.

Rai, ad rai. He arose.

Raib. Rape.

Raibe. A turnip.

Raibh. Was.

Raicneach. A queen.

Raidh. Will.

Raidhe. Quarter of a year.

Raidhe. An umpire, arbiter.

Raidhmheas. A dream, romance.

Raidhmhaiseach. Fabulous, romantic, gasconading.

Raidhteachas. A saying, report.

Raidhteachas. A contest, trial of skill.

Raidhtionga. A comma in writing.

Raidhreach. A prayer, request.

Raidis. A radish.

Raittine. Laughter, laughing.

Raidolach. Craft.

Raigeamhlachd. Impetuosity.

Raigh. An arm. Vide Ruigh.

Raigh. Frenzy.

Raighbheirt. A fleeve, wriftband, bracelet.

Raidhmheis. A cubit.

Raidhthcoir. A peafant, boor.

Raighe. A ray.

Railge. A church-yard.

Raimhdeas }
Raimhre. } Fatnefs, being fat.

Raimhe. Fatter.

Raimh. Brimftone.

Raimhad. Fat, fatnefs.

Rainidham. To reach.

Rainmillam. To abrogate, abolifh.

Rainn, rinn. The point of a fpear or fword.

Rainnefidhe. Ranges, ranks.

Rainn. A divifion.

Rainn-ann-ruifg. Eyebright.

Rainn. Pl. of Rann.

Rainn-da-leath. Bipartition.

Rainnin. A fhort verfe.

Rainfgriofam. To abolifh.

Raiteachas. Pride, arrogance, conteft.

Raiteachas. Saying, fpeech.

Raitean. Pleafure.

Raith. He went.

Raith. On account of, for the fake of.

Raithneach. Fern, brake.

Raith. Entreaty, fpeech, interceffion.

Raithne. It fhined.

Raithe. Quarter of a year.

Raithal. Quarterly.

Raithe. An umpire.

Raithre. It pleafed.

Ralaim. To happen, to commit, to make.

Ramh. An oar.

Ramhaiche. A rower.

Ramhad }
Ramhadoir. } A way, road.

Ramhar. Fat, grofs, thick.

Ramhraigham. To fatten.

Ramhilleadh. Raving in ficknefs.

Ramhaim. To row.

Ramhdhraidheann. Buckthorn.

Ramhlong. A galley.

Ran. A crumb, morfel, truth.

Ran. Plain, manifeft, noble, nimble.

Rann. A verfe, ftanza, fection, a fong, poem.

Rannach. }
Ranntaiche. } A fongfter.

Ranaighe. A romancer, ftory-teller.

Ranaim. To make manifeft.

Ranca. A ftep

Ranc. Rank, order.

Ranntachd. Verfe, poetry, verfification.

Randach. A partizan

Randonaigham. To abolifh, abrogate.

Rang. }
Rangan. } The bank of a river.

Rang, rangan. A wrinkle.

Rangach. Wrinkled.

Rann. A part, divifion, fong, genealogy.

Rannach. Diftributive.

Rannadh. Beginning, commencing.

Rannan. The lowing of deer.

Rannaim. To divide, fhare.

Rannbhallardam. To proclaim.

Ranntuarchorthach. Fertile, fruitful.

Rannphairt. Participation, participle.

Rannphairteach. }
Rannphairtamhuil. } Partaking of.

Rannphartuigham. To communicate.

Rannphartuighe. A partaker.

Ranfughadh. Searching, rummaging.

Ranfuigham. To fearch, rummage.

Raod, rod. A thing.

Raogha. Choice.

Raoghnam. }
Raoghnaigham. } To choofe.

Raoimeadh. Depredation, plunder.

Raomadh. Phlegm.

Raonadh. A way, road, haunt.

Raon. A field, plain, a green.

Raona. Breaking, tearing.

Raonam. To turn, change.

Rap. Any creature that digs.

Rapal. Noife.

Ras. A fhrub.

Rafach. Full of fhrubs.

Raffaidhe. A rambling woman, gipfy, huffy.

Raffaidhid. A bile, blotch.

Rafan. Underwood, brufhwood.

Rafchrann. A fhrub-tree.

Rafcradh. To part, fcatter.

Rafdal A rake.

Rafdalam. To rake, gather.

Rafmhaol A fea-calf.

Rafmhaidhe. A fhrub.

Raftach A churl.

Rat Motion.

Rath. Good-luck, profperity.

Rath. A furety.

Rath. Fern.

Rath. Wages.

Rath A fortrefs, garrifon, a village, an artificial mount or burrow, a prince's feat.

Ratha. Quarter of a year. Vide Raithe.

Ratha. Running, racing.

Rathach. A hough.

Rathachadh. Profperity.

Rathadar. They ran.

Ratham. To make profperous, profper

Rathamhnas. Profperity, happinefs.

Rathmhor.
Rathoil. } Profperous, happy.

Rathfhollus. Between the fore and back doors.

Re The moon.

Re. For Le, with.

Re For Ri, ris, at, to, by, of, againft.

Re. Time, duration, life, exiftence.

Re Sign of the future participle to.

Re, ad re He arofe.

Reabadh, reubadh. Tearing.

Reabam, reubam. To tear.

Reabach. That teareth.

Reabalach. A rebel.

Reabalachd. Rebellion.

Reabh. A wile, craft, trick.

Reabhach. Subtil, crafty.

Reabhlangar. Skipping, playing, fporting.

Reabhlangam. To fkip, play.

Reabhradh. A fkipping, playing.

Reac, reic. Sell thou

Reacam. To fell Vide Reicam.

Reacadoir. A feller.

Reacar. Swift, hot, quick growirg.

Reachd. A law, ftatute, ordinance.

Reachdaire. A judge, lawgiver.

Reachdaire. A dairy-man.

Reachdairm. A court of judicature.

Reachdcheanglam. To article.

Reachdhaingneadh. A decree.

Reachdamhuil. Regular, lawful.

Reachdmhathair. A mother-in-law.

Reachdmhor. Subftantial.

Reachdfhaoirfeach. Licenfed, authorifed.

Reachfad. I will go.

Reacht. A man.

Reacht. He came.

Reacht. A juft law.

Reacht. Power, anthority.

Reachtaire. A lawgiver, king, judge.

Reachtach. Strong.

Reachtam, riachtam. To arrive.

Reachtfgoth. A fon-in-law.

Read. A thing.

Readan. A pipe, a reed.

Readchord. The reins of a bridle.

Readh, go readh. Yet.

Readh. Rage, fury.

Readhg. A mad bull or ox.

Readhlabhrachd. Eloquence.

Readhlabhra. Eloquent.

Readhfgaoileadh. A flux.

Reag. Night.

Reagdhall. Purblind.

Reaghlorach.

Reaghlorach. Refounding.
Reaghtghe. Juftice.
Reaith. A ram.
Reaithin. A little ram.
Reall, realt. A ftar.
Realtan. } An aftrolabe.
Realtangrais. }
Realtbhuidheann. A conftellation.
Realtchuirt. The ftar-chamber.
Realtchofgaire. An aftronomer.
Realtog. A fmall ftar, an afterifk.
Realtoir. An aftrologer.
Reamain. A beginning.
Reamaire. A traveller, wayfaring-man.
Reamh. For Roimhe, is ufed as a compo-
fitive particle.
Reamhain. Foretelling, prognoftication.
Reamhainmuighte. Forenamed.
Reamhar. Thick, fat, grofs, coarfe.
Reamhaithnuigham. To foreknow.
Reamhaithne. } Foreknowledge.
Reamhfhios. }
Reamheadradh. Forenoon.
Reamhoiduigham. To foreordain.
Reamhtheachdaire. A forerunner.
Reamhfhealladh. Forefight.
Reamhaithrifam. To forebode.
Reamhchroiceann. The preputium.
Reamhlon. A viaticum.
Reamhofeadh. Rheumatifm.
Reamhraigham. To fatten, clot, concrete,
coagulate.
Reamhrach. Coagulative.
Reamhrughadh. Grofnefs, fatnefs, grow-
ing fat.
Reambradhte. Forecited.
Reamhradh. A preface.
Reamhradhaim. To preface.
Reamhfmuinuigham. To foreimagine.
Reanga. Reins of the back.
Reanna. Stars.
Reannaire. An aftrologer.
Reannan. A ftar.

Rear. Provifion.
Rearacht. A rifing, rearing up.
Rearidh. A fenior, elder.
Reareidham. To go, proceed.
Reafan. To plead, allege.
Reafeach. Prattling, talkative.
Reafonta. Reafonable.
Reafonaigham. To reafon.
Reafort. Prefervation.
Reaftraim. To bring back, reftore.
Reafun. Reafon.
Reafunachadh. Ratiocination.
Reat. With thee.
Reatas. Enmity, hatred.
Reatha. Running, racing.
Reathadh. A ram.
Reathachas. Ramming, rutting.
Reathaim, ritham. To run.
Reataire. A clergyman, clerk.
Rec. A thing done in hafte.
Recail. Went down.
Recearnaim. To recreate, divert, pleafe,
delight.
Rech. Grief.
Recne. Sudden.
Red. To thy, with thy.
Redhealbham. To form again.
Redhe. The Fauns, or gods of the woods.
Re dhiol. To be fold.
Redhreim. } A climate.
Redhreimreachd. }
Regh. A crofs, gallows.
Reibh. With you.
Reichdcheadach. Licenfed, authorifed.
Reicam. To fell, vend.
Reicadoir. A feller, vender.
Reidh. A plain.
Reidh. Plain, level.
Reidhlain. A level field, green for play.
Reidh, Ready, prepared.
Reidh. A rope, wythe.
Reidheachd. Ready fervice, officioufnefs.
Reidheadh. Affent, agreement.
Reidhight.

Reidhighe. An agreement.

Reidham. To prepare, provide, agree.

Reidhreamhanach. Lunatic.

Reidhteach. A plain, level.

Reidhteach. Union, harmony, propitiation.

Reidh. Plain, open.

Reighdam. To judge.

Reighlios. A church, fhrine.

Reightioch. To fadge.

Reil A ftar.

Reil Clear, manifeft.

Reil Lawful, rightful.

Reileag. A church, church-yard.

Reiltin. An afterifk.

Reim. Power, authority, great fway.

Reim. A way, progrefs, feries.

Reim A calling out.

Reim. A troop, band.

Reim Evennefs of temper.

Reimamhuil. Bearing great fway or authority, perfevering, conftant, even, rampant.

Reimam. To ramp.

Reimhbhriathar. An adverb.

Reimhbhlaifam. To foretafte.

Reimhchinam. To affign, appoint.

Reimhe. Thicker, fatnefs, pride.

Reimheach. Arrogant.

Reimhamhuil. Belonging to the roads.

Reimheas. Time.

Reimhgheallam. To pre-engage, to promife.

Reimnigham. To go, to walk.

Reimhorthonn. Forefkin.

Reimfe. A club, a ftaff.

Reing
Reingach. } Timbers of a fh p.

Reir. Will, defire, pleafure, Ma reir, at liberty.

Reir, do reir. According to.

Reir, roir. Laft night.

Reis. A fpan, nine inches long.

Reifaid. A raifin.

Reifghiobhar. A harlot, proftitute.

Reifin. Sooner than, before that.

Reifidhe. A rehearfer, romancer.

Refiot. Congealed.

Reifineirdieach. A harlot.

Reite. An agreement, fettlement, contract.

Reiteach. Harmony, reconciliation.

Reiteach. A plain.

Reitaigham. To agree, fettle upon, ratify, reconcile.

Reithe. A ram.

Reithe raobcha. A battering-ram.

Reitheadh. Rammed.

Reitricoir. A rhetorician.

Rem. With my, to my.

Remfeuchadh. Forefeeing.

Remfheucham. To forefee.

Remhain. Pleafure.

Remhraidham. To foretel, proclaim.

Remhaithnuigham. To foreknow.

Reo. Froft.

Reoleach.
Reoghleac. } Ice.

Reoleacam.
Reoghleacam. } To freeze, congeal.

Reomham, romham. Before me.

Reomhad, romhad. Before thee.

Reomhinn, romhinn. Before us.

Reomhpa, rompa. Before them.

Reon. A fpan.

Reothadh. Froft, ice.

Reotham. To freeze.

Reothte Frozen.

Rer. With our, unto him.

Rerchearc. A heath-poult, or groufe.

Refealadach. By turns, alternate.

Refbaid. A beggar's brat.

Retlan. A fpark.

Retnughadh. To imagine.

Reubadh. Tearing.

Reubam. To tear, lacerate.

Reubair. A robber, violent perfon.

Reubin. Plundering.

Reudan. A timber-worm.

Reudanach. Full of worms.

Reuladh. A declaration.

Reulag. A ftar.

Reulagach. Starry.

Reulldhraoith. Aftrologer.

Reuleolas. Aftronomy.

Reultiafg. A fifh with fhining teeth.

Reult. A ftar; pl. Reulta.

Reult-buidheann. A conftellation.

Reuma. Phlegm.

Reumamhuil. Phlegmatic.

Reufun. Reafon.

Reufonaigham. To reafon.

Reufunta. Reafonable.

Ri, riogh. A king, fovereign prince.

Ri, ris. To, againft.

Ri! An interjection of furprize.

Ria. With her, againft her.

Riabhach. Brindled, greyifh.

Riabhaichad. Brindlednefs, greyifhnefs.

Riabhag. A lark.

Riabhag-monaidh. A titlark.

Riabhan. A handfome young fellow.

Riach. Grey, brindled.

Riach. He came, rippling up.

Riachan. Any thing grey.

Riachdailleas. Neceffity.

Riachdanas. Want, neceffity, duty.

Riachdanach. Needy, neceffitous, incumbent, dutiful.

Riadh. A running, racing.

Riadh. Correction, taming, fubduing, grief.

Riadhadh. Hanging.

Riadhach. Darkifh.

Riadhlann. A correction-houfe.

Riagh. A crofs, gallows.

Riagh. Religious.

Riaghaim. To hang, crucify

Riaghuil. A rule, government.

Riaghailt. A rule, directory.

Riaghailtchearnach. A fquare.

Riaghailtach. Regular, fober, peaceful.

Riaghalta. Ruled, governed.

Riaghlach. An old woman.

Riaghluicham. To rule, govern.

Riaghluichoir. } A ruler, governor.
Riaghalloir.

Riaghaire. A hangman, a rogue.

Riama. A victory.

Riamh. Ever, at any time, before.

Riamhach. Precious, valuable.

Rian. The road or way, a path, footftep.

Rian. A fpan.

Rian. The fea.

Rian cruinith-tuatha. The country of the Picts

Rianuighe. A wanderer.

Riar. Diftribution.

Riaradh. Pleafing, fatisfying, diftribution.

Riaraidhe An oeconome, difpenfer of meat and drink.

Riarachd-inntin. Contentment.

Riaram. } To pleafe, fatisfy, diftri-
Riaruigham. } bute.

Riartha. Content, ferved, diftributed

Riafg. A moor, fen, marfh, lay-ground.

Riafgach. Moorifh, ftiff.

Riafgal Indocile, rigid, wild, moorifh.

Riatha. Hire, rent, intereft, rib, a fnare

Ribe. }
Ribeog. } A hair, whifker, a doffil.
Ribin. }

Ribach. Rough, hairy.

Ribh. To you, againft you.

Ribeacha nan cuinnein. Hairs of the noftrils.

Ribhid. A reed, pipe.

Riblach. A line or long ftring.

Richead. A kingdom.

Richis. A flame.

Ridire. A knight.

Ridul. A fieve, a coarfe fieve.

Ridhail. A parliament.

Ridgileanach. A redfhank.

Rif. Bent.

Riglachan. A ridgling.

Rig. A spy.

Rigam. To reach.

Rigam a leafs. I need not.

Righ, ri. A king, fovereign.

Righ. ⎰ The arm from the elbow to the
Righe. ⎱ wrift.

Righeachd One's reach, attainment.

Righeadh. To need, reach at a thing.

Righam. To reach, ftretch, to confent.

Righchifte. A royal fifcus.

Righe. Reproof.

Righfheinnidh A generaliffimo.

Righin Tough, adhefive, fluggifh, drow-
ly, dilatory.

Righineachas. ⎰ Delay.
Roighneas ⎱

Righrinionn. A diadem.

Righneachd. A gift, favour, prefent.

Righnigham. To make ftiff, to delay.

Rightheach. An arm.

Rig heachd. An ambaffador, envoy.

Righthigham. To be wanting.

Rillean. A riddle, coarfe fieve.

Rilleam To fift with a riddle.

Rimh. Number.

Rimham. To number.

Rimhiadh
Rimheighe. ⎰ Pride.

Rimnfheinnam To play mufic.

Rimnin A conftellation.

Rincidh. Dancing.

Rinceoir. A dancer.

Rincam. To dance.

Rincne. A lance, fpear.

Riafheithiomh. Contemplation.

Ringeadh. Hanging.

Ringheibhionna.
Ringheimhleacha. ⎰ Chains.

Ringthe Torn, parted.

Rimmheas. Scanning of a verfe.

Rinn. The point of a weapon.

Rinn. Mufic, melody.

2

Rinn. A foot.

Rinn. The ftars.

Rinn. The perfect tenfe of the verb Deanam.

Rinne. Unto us, againft us.

Rinn na ruifg. Apple of the eye.

Rinnadoir. A carper, fpy-fault.

Rinnbhearthag. A hiftory.

Rinne. The underftanding.

Rinne Ireland.

Rinneach.
Rinngheur. ⎰ Sharp-pointed.

Rinnag A ftar.

Rinnag earbail A comet.

Rinnag fheabhais. A wandering ftar.

Rinnec. Grafs.

Rinnfeatham. To defign, intend, forecaft.

Rinnicne A graving tool.

Rinnimh. The heavenly conftellations.

Rinnreim. A conftellation.

Rinnmhor. Having fins.

Riobhar. A fieve, honey-comb.

Riobhlach. A rival.

Rioboid. A fpendthrift.

Rioboideachd. Prodigality.

Rioboideach Prodigal.

Rioboidam. To riot, revel.

Riochd, riuchd. The fhape, likenefs.

Riochuaidh. A plague, contagion, pefti-
lence.

Riodh. A ray.

Riodham To ray.

Riodhnachd. A gift.

Riogh, righ. A king.

Rioghachd. A kingdom.

Riogha.
Rioghamhuil. ⎰ Royal, kingly, princely.

Riogham. To reign.

Rioghan.
Rioghbhin. ⎰ A queen.
Rioghbhean.

Rioghcholbh. ⎰ A fceptre.
Rioghfhlat.

Rioghchoran.

Rioghchoran. A royal crown.

Rioghdhach. A palace, court.

Rioghdhail. A parliament.

Riogh-damhna. A king in fieri, a prince designed.

Rioght. A reign.

Rioghlaoch. A prince, a respectable old man.

Rioghlann. A palace, king's court.

Rioghnathair. A cockatrice.

Rioghphubal. }
Rioghbhoth. } A king's tent.

Riom. With me, against me.

Riomh. Number, reckoning.

Riomham. To number, reckon.

Riomhach. Precious, valuable, fond of.

Riomhaidh. Fondness.

Riomhaireachd. Arithmetic.

Riomhaiream. To reckon, count.

Rion, rian. A way, road.

Rionadair. A ruler, steward.

Rionaidhe. An engraver.

Rionaigham. To carve, engrave.

Rionaidheas. }
Rional. } Sculpture.

Rionghach. A strong man.

Rionluas. Career.

Rionnadh. Redness.

Rionnach. A mackerel.

Riofaithris. }
Riofalaigheadh } Mimicking.

Riot, riut, riutfa. Against thee, to thee.

Rioth. Running, racing.

Riotham To run, race.

Riotfa. With thee.

Rireadh. }
Do rireadh. } Serioufly, verily, true.

Ris. Unto him, it, against him, it.

Ris. Hiftory.

Ris. A king.

Ris. Intelligence, knowledge.

Ris, aris. Again.

Rifa. Bark.

Rifeach. A romancer.

Rifgineach. A brave foldier.

Rifion, rifean. An hiftorian.

Rifion. Againft him, to him, it

Rifteal. A fort of plough ufed in the ifland of Lewes.

Rith. A courfe, flight.

Rith. }
Ritheach. } Running.

Rith, righe. An arm.

Rithadh. A fhielding.

Rithleimnach. Quick.

Rithcadh. A grove.

Ritham. To run.

Rithlearg. An extemporaneous verfe

Riu. Unto them, againft them.

Riubh. Brimftone.

Rium. Unto me, againft me.

Riut. Againft thee, unto thee.

Riutha. Againft them, unto them.

Ro Very, too much, over much.

Ro. For Roimh, firft, before.

Ro. For Do, fign of the paft tenf..

Ro. To go to, reach a place.

Roba. A robe.

Robhaidheach. Very thankful, gracious.

Robhairidhe. A monument.

Robham, rabham. To admonifh, warn

Robhar. A fieve.

Robheag. Very fmall.

Robhro. Very ancient, very old.

Robuin Robbery.

Robuin-eaglais. Sacrilege.

Robuift. Cuftody.

Roc. Tops of fea weeds that appear abovt water.

Roc. A rock.

Rocach. Rocky.

Rocach. Curly.

Rocan. A cottage, hut.

Rocan. Rolling.

Rocan. A plait, fold, a wrinkle.

Rocan. A hood, mantle, furtout.

Rochaidheamhuil.

Rochaidheamhuil. Very decent, becoming, proper.

Rochairdeamhuil. Very courteous and obliging.

Rochar. A killing, flaughtering.

Rochdaim. To reach, arrive at.

Rochduin. An afcent, arriving at, reaching.

Rochdan. A thicket.

Rachora. The beft, the chief.

Rochtaire. A cuftomer.

Rochuaid. A lamprey.

Roclifde. Expert.

Rochuilleach. Terrible, very dangerous.

Rochuram. Anxioufnefs, exceeding care.

Rochuramach. Vigilant, over-careful.

Rocus. A rook.

Rod. A way, road.

Rod-mor. A highway.

Rodacht. A covering, fence.

Rodadh }
Rodail. } Lancing, fcarifying.

Rodamhuil. Profperous.

Rodh. Water edge or mark.

Rodhbadh. Was loft, undone.

Rodhbath. Breaking.

Rodheidh. Striving

Rodhoineanta. Very ftormy.

Rodhuil. Jealoufy.

Rodhuin. A commoner, a rogue.

Rodhubhrachdach. Very earneft, careful.

Ro-eolach. Familiar.

Ro-eolas. Familiarity.

Rodi. Shrunk, rotten.

Rodmuim. A fox

Rodruoraim. To effect, bring to pafs.

Roc. A plain, a field.

Rofhial. Very hofpitable.

Rofhoghtharach. Very gracious

Rofhonn. An earneft longing.

Rofhonnmhor. Very well pleafed, willing.

Rofhuachd. Great cold.

Rogh. An order, cuftom.

Rogh. A wreath.

Rogh. Choice.

Roghaim. To choofe.

Roghainach. Optative.

Rogha. }
Roghain. } Choice.

Roghainiocadh. Chofen, elected.

Roghanigham. To choofe.

Roghear. Very fharp, fevere.

Roghlach. An election of foldiers.

Roghlach. Very angry, enraged.

Roghmhal. Election of a prince.

Roghmhar. Digging

Roghmhai. Very dangerous, valiant.

Roibin. A fmall rope, or cord, a whifker.

Robhreadha. Excellent

Roibne. A lance, dart

Roicam. To tear.

Roichidh. Infomuch that, fo that.

Roicham. To come to, arrive at; to appertain.

Roictadh. A great cry.

Roid. Gale.

Roid. Momentum, force, race.

Roidam. To run faft.

Roidheas. Very handfome, pretty.

Roidin, mearbhull. Wild fire.

Roigham. To attain to, arrive at.

Roighlic. Very prudent, wife.

Roighne. Chief, choice.

Roighneadhadh. Election.

Roighnam. To elect, choofe.

Roilbhe. Mountains.

Roilbheoir. A mountaineer.

Roilig. A church.

Roille. Together.

Roille. Darnel.

Roimh. The city of Rome.

Roimh. Earth, foil, the burning place of any family.

Roimh, roimhe. Before, before that.

Roimhchubhidh. Fitted, adapted.

Roimheolas. Precognition.

Roimhbheachd. Preconception.

Roimhordaghadh. Predeſtination.

Roimhe cheile. Higgledy piggledy.

Roimhfheuchin. Forecaſt.

Roimhthoghta. Forechoſen.

Roimhſe. Sin, iniquity.

Roimhradh. A preface, preamble.

Roimhbhriathir. Adverb.

Roimſe A pole, ſtake.

Roine A hair, ſtreak.

Roineach. ⎫
Roineagach. ⎬ Hairy
Roinigh. ⎭

Roineadach. ⎫
Roinfaith. ⎬ Haircloth.
Roinchailt. ⎭

Roin. Gen. of Ron.

Roinn. A ſhare, diviſion, claſs.

Roinn. A point, edge.

Roinnam. To divide, ſhare.

Roinne. Horſe-hair.

Roinneadh. Diviſion.

Roinnphartach. Sharing, partaking.

Roipeir. A tuck, rapier.

Roiſceal. A ſentence, decree, verdict.

Roiſeal. The loweſt, moſt baſe.

Roiſeir. Angry.

Roiſg. Vide Ruiſg.

Roiſgmhearleach. A Tory.

Roiſin. ⎫
Roiſaid. ⎬ Roſin.

Roiſire. Anger, choler.

Roiſteach. A roach.

Roiſtim. To arrive, attain to.

Roiſtin. A gridiron.

Roith. A wheel.

Roithleoir. A wheelwright.

Roithidh. Until.

Roithleagan. A circle, wheel.

Roithlinge. A breach.

Roithnam. To pleaſe.

Roithre. A babbler, prating fellow.

Roithreachd. Loquacity, rhetorick.

Roithreabhar. Moſt prudent.

Roithreim. A ruſhing.

Roithrich. Rhetorick.

Roladh. ⎫
Rollan. ⎬ A roll, volume.

Rollagfheoir. A ſwathe.

Rolaim. To roll.

Rollair. A cylinder.

Romach. Hairy.

Romhad. Forward, before thee, through thee

Romhair. A rower.

Romhaiſeach. Very handſome.

Romhaith. Excellent.

Romham. Before me, through me.

Romhar. Digging

Romharam. To dig.

Romhan. French wheat, brank.

Romhianghas. Earneſt deſire.

Romhoide. Greatneſs, exceſs.

Romhradh. The ſight.

Romhuibh. Before you.

Romhuinn. Before us.

Romnacois. Yellow and grey.

Rompa. Before them, through them.

Ron. A ſea calf.

Ron The hair of the mane or tail of a horſe, cow, &c.

Ronadh. A club, ſtake.

Roncam. To ſnore.

Ronga. ⎫
Rongais. ⎬ A joining ſpar.

Rongalar. A rheumatiſm.

Ronn Saliva.

Ronnaigham. To ſpit, ſlaver.

Ronn. A chain, tie, bond.

Ronnach. Full of ſaliva, dirty with ſpittle.

Ronnadh. A club, ſtaff.

Ronnſaghadh. Search, inquiry.

Ronnaireachd. Saliva dropping from the mouth.

Ront. Fierce, cruel.

Ropadh. A rope.

Ropan. A little rope.

Ropaire. A rapier, treacherous, violent perſon.

Ropadoir. A ropemaker.

Roppam. To entangle, ravel.

Rordaim. To run, to race.

Rortaim. To pour out.

Ros. A roſe, a diſeaſe ſo called.

Ros. Science, knowledge.

Ros. Pleaſant.

Roſal. Judgment.

Roſam. }
Roſdam. } To roaſt.

Roſd. Grillade.

Roſdadh. }
Roſann. } Roaſting.

Roſarnach. A place where roſes grow.

Roſbhan. The apple of the eye.

Roſg An eye; Roſg aluin, a beautiful eye.

Roſg. The underſtanding.

Roſg. Proſe.

Roſgchlochd. }
Roſgmudh. } Idea.

Roſg catha. A ſpeech to an army.

Roſgdhalladh. Error, miſtake.

Roſs A promontory.

Roſſachd. Enchantment, charm or witch-craft.

Roſta. Roaſted.

Roth A wheel.

Roth. A hoary white froſt.

Rotheredha. A bodkin.

Rothlein. A whirl.

Ru, run. A ſecret.

Ru, run. Yellow lady's bedſtraw.

Ruadh. Red, reddiſh, ſtrong.

Ruadhag. A young hind.

Ruadhan. Any thing that dyeth red, red-diſhneſs.

Ruadhbhuidhe. Of reddiſh yellow.

Ruadhbhoc. A ſtag.

Ruadhbhoine. Flood water.

Ruadhchriot. Red, ruddle.

Ruadhlaith. }
Ruadhlaithineas. } Choler, cholera mor-bus.

Ruadhr. Declivity.

Ruagadh. Chaſing and hunting away, ba-niſhing.

Ruagam. To hunt, chaſe, put to flight.

Ruagaire. A hunter, any inſtrument to drive a thing from its place; ſwan ſhot.

Ruagaireachd. Hunting.

Ruaichillam. To buy, purchaſe.

Ruaichillte. Bought, purchaſed.

Ruaidh. Red.

Ruaidhneach. Hair.

Ruaidhe. A diſeaſe ſo called.

Ruaidham. To redden.

Ruaidhrin. A ſharp point.

Ruaig. Flight, chaſe.

Ruaim. A fiſhing-line.

Ruaimle. Standing water impregnated with clay.

Ruainne. A hair.

Ruainidh. Charitable.

Ruamh. A ſpade.

Ruamhar. Delving, digging.

Ruamharam. To dig, delve.

Ruamnadh. Reproof, reprehenſion.

Ruanidh. Red, reddiſh.

Ruanidh. Strong, able.

Ruanaigh. Anger.

Ruar. An expedition.

Ruaracan. Floundering.

Ruarach. A liar.

Ruathar. }
Ruatgar. } A ſkirmiſh, expedition.

Ruathradh. To higgle.

Rubam. To rub.

Rubha Patience, longanimity.

Rubha. A wound.

Rubin. A ruby.

Rucas. Friſking.

Ruihail. Tearing, cutting.

Ruchan. The throat.

Ruchd, riochd. Stead, room.

Ruchd.

Ruchd. Sudden, vehement.
Rucht. A fow.
Rucht. A great fhout, clamour.
Ruchdam. To cry out.
Rucis. Arrogance.
Rud, rod. A thing.
Rudan. A knuckle.
Rudhbluaithre. Sawduft.
Rudhrach. A fojourner.
Rudhrach. Very ftraight, long.
Rudhrach. Darkening.
Rudhrachas. Length.
Rug. Perfect tenfe of the verb Beiram.
Rug. A wrinkle.
Rugach. Wrinkled.
Rugadh. A paft tenfe of Beiram.
Rugadh. Was hurt or wounded.
Rugaire. A bar, latch.
Rugga. An old perfon.
Rugh. Rue.
Rugha. A fmall point of land jutting into the fea.
Rughadh. Hanging.
Rudmhodh. A bond-flave.
Ruibe. A pair.
Ruibh. Brimftone.
Ruibhne. A lance.
Ruibheachtain. A prop, fupport.
Ruibhneach. Armed with a lance, a fpear-man.
Ruibhneach. Strongly guarded.
Ruibhneadha. Great bands.
Ruibin. A riband.
Ruice. A rebuke, reproach.
Ruiceach Exaltation, lifting up.
Ruicead. A collection.
Ruiceat. Exalting, lifting up.
Ruidheadh. Reproof, cenfure.
Ruidheadh. A ray.
Ruidhleas, rodhilas. Very faithful.
Ruideis. Frifking.
Ruigam. To reach, arrive at.
Ruigh. An arm.

5

Ruigfin. } Arriving, reaching, attain-
Ruigeachd. } ing.
Ruigham. To reach.
Ruigheanas. Brightnefs.
Ruimneadh. Cafting, throwing.
Ruine, roine. Horfehair.
Ruine. A ftreak.
Ruinn. A divifion.
Ruinnecc. Grafs.
Ruinnfeam. To whip, fcourge.
Ruinnte. Divided.
Ruinreathoir. A fecretary.
Ruire A champion, a knight
Ruireaeh. Famous, renowned, celebrated.
Ruireach. Vide Ruire.
Ruireachas. Lordfhip, dominion.
Ruifg. } A veffel made of bark of
Rufgan. } trees.
Ruis. A way, road.
Ruis. An elder-tree, the name of the let-ter R.
Ruifeanta. Hafty.
Ruifg. A fkirmifh.
Ruifg. Naked.
Ruifg. Pl. of Rufg.
Ruifgam. To ftrip, peel, undrefs.
Ruifgam. To fmite, ftrike, pelt.
Ruifam. To tear in pieces.
Ruifgte. Stripped naked.
Ruifgfhuil. Hairs of the eyelids.
Ruith. An army, troop.
Ruith Running.
Ruitheach. Moving, on the march
Ruitham. To run.
Ruiteag. Rednefs.
Ruiteach. Ruddy.
Ruithean. Red-hot, blazing
Ruithean. Delight, pleafure
Ruitheanam. To fhine, glitter
Ruitheanas. Glittering, brightnefs.
Ruithneadh. A flame.
Ruitin. The ankle-bone, a fetlock, pof-tern.

Ruladh.

Ruladh. Maſſacreing, ſlaughtering.

Rum. A floor, a room, place or ſpace, room.

Rumaicham. To make room.

Rumhar. A mine.

Rumhram. To dig, mine.

Rumpal. A rump.

Run. A ſecret, ſecrecy, myſtery.

Runach. Confident, truſty, dark, myſterious. Inde, Runick.

Run. A purpoſe, deſign.

Run. Love, inclination.

Runbhocan. A pretence.

Runaigh. Dark, obſcure, myſtical.

Runaighe. A diſcreet perſon, a confident.

Runairm. A council-chamber.

Runchleirach. } A ſecretary.
Runghraibhthoir. }

Rundiamhair. A ſecret myſtery.

Rundiamhrach. Myſtical.

Runnadh. } A diviſion.
Runntail. }

Runphairtach. Partaker of a ſecret.

Runpartuighte. Communicable.

Runphairtam. To communicate, conſult, adviſe with.

Rurgoid. Rhubarb.

Rus. Knowledge, ſkill.

Rus. A wood.

Ruſg. The bark of a tree, huſk, ſhell, a fleece.

Ruſgadhal. Epiſpaſtic.

Ruſgam. To ſtrip, heal, undreſs, to gall, chafe, ſhave.

Ruſgan. A piece of ſkin peeled off; a ſhip made of bark.

Ruſgam. To ſtrike vehemently.

Ruſs. A check.

Ruſtaca. Rude, ruſtic.

Ruſtacachd. Rudeneſs, ruſticity.

Ruſtach. A boor, clown, churl.

Ruſtan. A lump, hillock.

Ruta. A herd, rout, a ram.

Ruta. A tribe of people.

Ruth. Wages.

Rutha. A thornback.

Ruthadh. A point of land in the ſea.

S.

S Is the fifteenth letter of the Iriſh alphabet. Before and after E and I, it ſounds like ſh, in other reſpects as in the Engliſh language. The Iriſh have called it Suil. Vide Analyſis.

Sa. In, in the.

Sa, & ſe. Self, ſelves; Thuſa, thyſelf; Miſe, myſelf.

Sa. Whoſe, whereof.

Sa, 'us a. And his.

Sab. Strong, able.

Sab. Death.

Sabad. A ſquabble.

Sabail. A granary, barn.

Sab, ſamh. A bolt, bar of a door.

Sabh. } Spittle.
Sabhlach. }

Sabha. Sorrel.

Sabhadh. To quarrel.

Sabhadh. A ſaw.

Sabham. To ſaw.

Sabhadoir. A ſawyer.

Sabhadoirachd. Sawing.

Sabhan.   } A cub, a young maſtiff
Sabhairle. } dog.

Sabhail.   } Saving, ſparing, protecting,
Sabhaladh. } preſervation.

Sabhailach. Careful, ſparing.

Sabhailam. To ſpare, ſave, preſerve.

Sabhas. Sauce.

Sabhaſair. A ſauſage.

Sabhul. A barn, granary.

Sabhadh-ſgriobe. } A whip ſaw.
Sabhadh-duirne.   }

Saboid. The ſabbath.

Sac. A ſack, bag.

Sacadh.   }
Sacaghadh. } Preſſing in a ſack.
Sacail.   }

Sacaigham. To preſs down a ſack, to
fill.

Sacan, ſaicin. A ſmall bag.

Sacan. An unmannerly trifling fellow.

Sacarbhuig. Confeſſion.

Sacham. To attack, ſet upon.

Saccraighe. Baggage.

Sacſrathair. A pack-ſaddle.

Sachir. Reſt.

Sadhall. A ſaddle.

Sadhaile. Neglect; delight, ſatisfaction.

Saddach. Mill-duſt.

Sadhail. Pleaſant, a good houſe, habitation.

Sadhbh. Salve, any thing good.

Sadhbh. Proper name of a woman, common in Ireland.

Saclan. A ſtandard.

Saeghulan. A king or prince, a judge, a
ſenior, elder; a pillar.

Sagart. A prieſt.

Sagartachd. Prieſthood.

Sagartamhuil. Prieſtly, holy, pious.

Sagh. A bitch.

Saghaidh. An attacking.

Saghal. Nice, tender.

Sagham. To drink, ſuck.

Sagharlachd. Delight, content.

Saghin. A little bitch.

Sagmhaire. A ſink, kennel.

Sagſun, Saſgun, Sacſun. England.

Sagſonach. Engliſh, an Engliſhman.

Sagsbheurla. The Engliſh tongue.

Sagsbheurlamhuil. According to the Engliſh tongue.

Saibhir. Plentiful, rich, opulent.

Saibhiram. To make rich, wealthy.

Saibhreas. Riches.

Saibhſeir. A ſaucer.

Saic. Pl. of Sac

Saich. Plenty, bellyfull, enough.

Saicdhiolaid. A pack-ſaddle.

Saiceadach. Sackcloth.

Saichſiot. They came.

Saide.   } A ſeat.
Saidhiſte. }

Saidheadh. A ſitting, ſeſſion, aſſize.

Saidh. A treaſury; prow of a ſhip.

Saidolach. Baſhful.

Saidolachd. Baſhfulneſs.

Saifear. A ſaphire-ſtone.

Saigain. A little ſhort man.

Saighead. An arrow, a dart.

Saighaidoir. A ſoldier, archer.

Saighaidoireachd. Brave actions, the army.

Saighaidairamhuil. Like a ſoldier.

Saigheas. Oldneſs, antiquity.

Saighnen. Lightning, a hurricane.

Sail. A beam; pl. Sailteacha.

Sail. A heel; pl. Salltan.

Sail. A guard, cuſtody.

Sail.   } A willow-tree, a name of the
Saileog. } letter S.

Sail.   } The ſalt-water, the ſea.
Saileas. }

Sailbhreaghadh. A rejoicing, merry-mak-
ing.

Sailbhrughadh. A bruiſe in the heel

Sailbhrugham. To bruiſe the heel.

Sailchuach.

Sailchuach. A violet, a panfy.

Sailgha. Brinifh.

Sailghad. Brinifhnefs.

Sailghiolla. A footman, page.

Sailam. To falute, hail.

Sailin. An arm of the fea.

Sailleadh. Pickle, brine.

Saillair. A faltcellar.

Saillam. To falt, pickle, feafon.

Sailleann. A fort of pafte ufed by weavers to fmooth their thread.

Saill. Fat, fatnefs.

Sailleach. Being fat.

Saillte. Salt, falted, feafoned.

Sailm A pfalm.

Sailmadoir. A pfalmift.

Sailfpiorad. A guardian fpirit.

Sailtairt. Treading.

Sailtairam. To tread upon, trample.

Sailthein. Beams.

Saim. Rich.

Saimh. Sweet.

Saimh. Pleafure, delight.

Saimh. A pair, couple.

Saimhbhearthach. Bearing twins.

Saimhbhriathraigham. To flatter, fpeak fair.

Saimhbhriochdam. } To allure, entice.
Saimhgriofam. }

Saimhbhriochtadh. Allurement.

Saimhcheilg. Hypocrify.

Saimhchealgach. Hypocritical.

Saimhdile. A mallet, beetle.

Saimheachd. Pleafure, delighr.

Saimhghriofadh. Enticement.

Saimhnigheadh. A yoking, coupling.

Saimhnigham. To yoke, couple.

Saimhrighe. Lovers of pleafure.

Saimhrigheacht. Eafe, quiet, fatisfaction.

Saimhrigheach. Eafy, fatisfied.

Saimhfeler. A counfellor.

Sain. Unequal.

Sainchreach. Healed.

Saindrean. A feat, fociety.

Saine. } Variety.
Saineas. }

Saine. Sound.

Saine. Good, divers.

Saineadh. Variation.

Sainrhios. Etymology.

Sainam. To vary, alter.

Sainre. A reddifh-purple, fanguine colour.

Saintheafam. To differ.

Saint. Covetoufnefs.

Saintieabh. A houfe, family.

Sai, far A compofitive particle fignifying very, exceeding.

Sairbhrigh. An attribute.

Sairfhios. Certain knowledge.

Saifde. Sage.

Saitean. A foil.

Saith. A vertebrum.

Saith. Satiety, fufficiency.

Saith. } A fwarm.
Saitheamhuin. }

Saith. Vulgar, vile.

Saith. A thruft, piercing.

Saith. A treafure, ftore of money.

Saithe. A fpace, a multitude.

Saitheas. Vilenefs, cheapnefs.

Saithionmhais. A treafurer.

Saitge. A fpace.

Saithach. Glutted, fated.

Sal, failin. A heel.

Sal. Drofs, ruft.

Sal-cluaife. Ear-wax.

Salach. Unclean, dirty.

Salachadh. Defilement, defiling.

Salaigham. To defile, pollute.

Salaim. To wait on, follow.

Salann. Salt.

Salannan. A falt-pit.

Sallaraim. To procure, provide.

Sallartha. Provided, procured.

Salchar. Naftinefs, filth.

Salchadh. Dirt, pollution.

Salchaim. Vide Salaigham.

Salchuach. A violet.

Sall. Bitterneſs, ſatire.

Sallann. Singing, harmony.

Salmaire. Pſalmiſt, choriſter.

Salmaireachd. Singing pſalms.

Salmcheatlach. A pſalmiſt.

Salmcheatladh. Singing of pſalms.

Salmhor. Salty.

Salt. Colour.

Saltacha. Beams.

Saltair. A pſalter; the title of ſeveral Iriſh chronicles, as Saltair na Teamhrach, Saltair Chaiſſil.

Saltoir. A ſaltmonger.

Saltairam. To tread, trample.

Saltairt. Treading, trampling.

Sam.
Samh. } The ſun.

Sam. I am.

Samh. That part of ſorrel that beareth ſeed.

Samh.
Samhach. } Pleaſant.

Samhach. Still, calm, pleaſant.

Samhagh tuaighe. The edge of a hatchet.

Samhadh. A congregation.

Samhail. Like, alike, equal.

Samhain. All Saints tide, hallowday, gen. Samhna.

Samhan. Savin.

Samhas. Delight, pleaſure.

Samhaircain. A primroſe.

Samhaſach. Pleaſant, agreeable.

Samhaſaiche. A ſuttler.

Samhaſtdheanta. Factitious.

Samhghubha. Sea nymphs.

Samhlachas. A ſample, pattern.

Samhlachadh. A ſimilitude.

Samhlaim. To reſemble.

Samhla. Apparitions.

Samhlut. Briſk, active.

Samhlughadh. Comparing, a ſimilitude, image.

Samhluigham. To compare.

Samhna. Of All Saints-tide.

Samhradh, i. e. Samhthrath. Summer, pleaſant ſeaſon.

Samhrog. Clover.

Samhſheaſamh. A diſtance.

Samhthach. A helve, handle.

Samhuil.
Samhuilt. } Like.

Samhuilt. Comparing, likeneſs, image, apparition.

Samhuiltam. To compare.

Samhſa. Sorrel.

San 's An. In the.

San. Holy.

San. Put after pronouns, and particulariſes the word to which it is joined.

San cann. Thither and hither.

Sanadh. Releaſing.

Sanam. To releaſe, diſſolve.

Sanarc. Red orpiment.

Sanas. A ſecret, a whiſper, knowledge.

Sanas. Greeting, ſalutation.

Sanas. A gloſſary, etymology.

Sanaſanuidhe. An etymologiſt.

Sanct. Holy.

Sanctoir. A ſanctuary.

Sandrong. A ſect.

Sannadh. Looſeneſs.

Sannt.
Santachd. } Greed, covetouſneſs.

Santach. Covetous.

Santaigham. To covet, deſire, to luſt.

Santughadh. Coveting, luſting after.

Santbhiodh. Appetite.

Saobh. Silly, fooliſh, mad, aſide.

Saobhadh. To amuſe, delight, charm.

Saobhadh. Going aſide.

Saobham. To infatuate, lead aſtray.

Saobhchiall. Nonſenſe, folly.

Saobhchaint. Gibble-gabble.

Saobhchrabhadh. Hypocrify.

Saobhchreideamh. Heterodoxy.

Saobhdholbha. Enchantment.

Saobhmhiannach. Punctilious.

Saobhnos. Anger, indignation, bad manners.

Saobhnofach. Morofe, peevifh.

Saobhfhruth. An eddying tide.

Saobhfgriobhadh imchaine. A libel.

Saoa. A track, a journey.

Saod. Care, attention, ftate, condition.

Saoduigham. To take care of.

Saoghal. The world, life, an age, generation.

Saoghalach. Worldly, long-lived.

Saoghalta. Secular, worldly.

Saoghaltachd. Worldlinefs.

Saoghalan. An old man.

Saoi. Good, generous, godly.

Saoi, faoith. A worthy, generous man; a man of letters.

Saoithfgeal. Idle ftories; the gofpel.

Saoidh. Hay.

Saoidhaaair. A mower, hay-cutter.

Saoidhadairachd. Mowing, hay-cutting.

Saoilam. To think, fuppofe, imagine, feem.

Saoiltin. Thinking, fuppofing, imagining.

Saoir. Pl. of Saor.

Saoirad. Cheapnefs.

Saoirfe. } Freedom, liberty, releafe;
Saoirfeachd. } cheapnefs.

Saoirfe. Belonging to a carpenter.

Saoirfeach. }
Saoirfeamhuil. } Free.
Saor. }

Saoirfeachd. } The trade of a carpenter,
Saoirfineachd. } joiner, &c.

Saoirfi. Any art, freedom.

Saoithcheap. A pillory.

Saoithe. A tutor, guardian.

Saoitheamhuil. Expert, fkilful, generous.

Saoitheamhlachd. Generofity.

Saor. A carpenter, wright, joiner.

Saor-chloch. A mafon.

Saor. Woe.

Saoradh. Freedom, exemption, deliverance.

Saoram. To free, acquit, deliver, refcue, liberate.

Saoranach. A freeman.

Saorchriodhach. Candid.

Saorchriodhaiche. Candour.

Saorcuairt. Circulation.

Saorcuairt na fola. Circulation of the blood.

Saordhail. Acquittance.

Saordhalach. Cheap, free

Saorfanach. A helper at work.

Saorfa. Freedom.

Saorfin. Salvation, deliverance.

Saoth. Labour, tribulation, punifhment.

Saothair. Labour, pains, travel, work, drudgery.

Saoth. A diforder, difeafe.

Saothach. A veffel, difh.

Saothach ionnlaid. A bafon.

Saothach-fgeulachd. Angiography.

Saothadh. Exculpating.

Saotharcan. A fort of grey plover.

Saothdhamh. A labouring ox.

Saothmhor. Toilfome, laborious.

Saothoir. A torturer, wrecker.

Saothphurt. An impofthume.

Saothrach. Servile, hard-working, difficult, plodding.

Saothraiche. A working man, labourer, plodder.

Saothraighthoir. A hufbandman.

Saothraghadh. Tillage.

Saothruigham. To labour, work, till.

Sar. Very, exceffive.

Sar. } A loufe.
Sarog. }

Saraigham. To conquer, overcome, to wrong, injure.

Saraghadh. Conqueft, victory.

Saraighte. Forced, taken by force, conquered.

Saraightheoir. A violent refcuer, a conqueror, infringer.

Saraghadh. Refcuing illegally, conquering, diftrefs, fatigue.

Saraigham. To refcue violently, overcome, exceed, injure, opprefs, to tire, fatigue.

Saruighte. Tired, fatigued, conquered, injured.

Saruightheach. An oppreffor, extortioner.

Sardil. A fprat.

Sarmhaith. Excellent.

Sarnigh. An endeavour.

Sarog. A glofs.

Sarralam. To prefent.

Sartulidh. Strong.

Saruich. Trefpafs.

Sas. An inftrument, means, arms, engines.

Sas. Capable.

Sas, Ann fas. Faft, laid hold of.

Sas. Straitened.

Safa. Standing.

Safachd Sufficiency.

Safadh. Satisfaction, comfort.

Safaigham. To fatisfy, fatiate.

Safaighte. Satisfied, fated.

Safamh. An amends, pleafure, fatisfaction.

Safat. Sufficient, capable.

Safdach. Eafy.

Safdadh. Eafe.

Safmhort. A maffacre.

Sath. Food, plenty.

Sathadh. A pufh, thruft.

Satham. To pufh, thruft, fhove.

Sathch. Full.

Sathach. A veffel, difh.

Sathainn Saturday, the fabbath of the Jews.

Sathbhach. A helve, handle.

Sathrach. Vide Saothrach.

Sbairn. A wreftle, exertion, conteft.

Sbairnam. To wreftle, ftrive earneftly

Spairnamhuil. Given to wreftling.

Sprogal. The dewlap, a crop, craw.

Sc & Sg Are ufed indifcriminately.

Scabadh. Difperfion, difperfing, fcattering.

Scabal. A helmet, hood, a fcapular.

Scabam. To fcatter, difperfe.

Scabar. Thin.

Scabhal. A booth, hut, a fhop, fcaffold, a fcreen covering the entrance at a door.

Scabhal. A cauldron, kettle.

Scabhas Good.

Scabhaifte. Advantage.

Scafa. A fkiff or cock-boat.

Scafal. Scaffold.

Scafthroid. A naval engagement.

Scagadh. A ftraining, cleanfing, burfting, a chink.

Scagaim. To ftrain, cleanfe, to burft, fhrink.

Scagaite. Strained, cleanfed, burft, fhrunk.

Scaich. To finifh.

Scail. A fhadow.

Scailain. A fan, umbrella.

Scaileach. Shady.

Scaileachd. Darknefs.

Scailam. To caft a fhade.

Scailp. A cave, den.

Scainnea. A fudden eruption or attack.

Scainam. To burft.

Scainadh. Burfting, a rent.

Scair. Any place where a thing is laid to dry.

Scaireacht. Crying, fhrieking.

Scairap. Lavifhnefs.

Scairt. The caul of a beaft, pl. Scartacha, the midriff.

Scairt. A thick tuft of fhrubs or branches

Scaiteach. Cutting, ftormy, ruinous.

Scala. A great bowl.

Scaithte. Cut, difperfed, deftroyed.

2   Scal.

Scal. A man, a champion.

Scalbhain. A multitude.

Scallach. Bald.

Scallachan. An unfledged bird.

Scalan A shadow.

Scalog. A servant, an old man.

Scalois. A bowl.

Scaluighe. Balances.

Scamhghlonn. ⎫
Scamhibhain. ⎬ A prank, villainous deed.

Scanbughadh. A reproaching, scandaliz-ing.

Scann. A swarm, multitude.

Scannal. Scandal, slander.

Scannalach. Scandalous, slandering.

Scanncried. A herd, drove.

Scannan. A thin membrane, skin.

Scannan faille. The cawl.

Scanradh. Dispersing, a surprise, fright.

Scanram. ⎫ To disperse, scatter, to con-
Scanraigham. ⎬ found, affright.

Scanraidhte. Dispersed by fright.

Scaoile. A loosenefs.

Scaoileadh. A loosing, untying.

Scaoilam. To loose, untie, scatter, dis-perse, dismifs, to unfold.

Scaoilte. Dismissed, untied, unfolded.

Scaoilteachd. A loosenefs, lax, a dispersed state.

Scaoin. Peace.

Scaoth. A swarm, multitude.

Scarachdin. Separating, separation.

Scaradh. A separation.

Scaram. To separate, to part, quit, to un-fold for drying.

Scaramhain. Parting.

Scarbh. A cormorant.

Scaramhuil. Separable.

Scarloid. Scarlet.

Scaroid. A table-cloth.

Scartha. Separated, parted.

Scartail. Vigorous, bold.

Scaffa. A skiff or boat.

Scaithanaigh. Dawn, parting of light and darkness

Scat. A skate.

Scath. A shadow, shade, a veil, covering, pretence, sake of protection, bashfulnefs or fear.

Scathach. Shady, bashful, timid.

Scathadh. To shun.

Scathan. A mirrour.

Scathmhor. Fearful, timorous, bashful.

Sce. The white thorn, hawthorn.

Sce. Vide Sceith.

Sceach. A bush, bramble, brier.

Sceachog. A hawthorn-berry, a haw.

Sceachradh. A prickle.

Sceal. Gen. Sceil, a relation, story, tale.

Scallan. A kernel.

Scealp. A cliff, a splinter.

Scealuidhe. A tale-bearer, romancer, his-torian.

Sceath. Vomiting.

Sceathach. Bushy, full of brambles.

Sceathrach. A vomit.

Sceatham. ⎫
Sceathraigham. ⎬ To vomit, spue.

Scecer. A gander.

Sceile. Misery, pity.

Sceilm. Boasting, vain-glory.

Sceimh. A scheme, draught.

Sceimhard. High bloom, good plight, good habit of body.

Sceimhach. Handsome, bloomy.

Sceinmneach. Swift, quick, nimble.

Sceinnead. An eruption, gushing forth, bouncing, sliding.

Sceip sheillan. A bee-hive.

Sceir. A sharp sea rock.

Sceite. Scattered, dispersed.

Sceitham. To vomit, spew, to spawn.

Sceith. Vomiting, spewing, spawning.

Sceng. A bed, a small bed-room.

Sceo. Much, over and above.

Sceot. A target.

Sceul.

Sceul. A ftory, tale, news.

Sceimh.
Sci, fciamh. } Beauty, bloom.

Sciach, fciathach, fciog. A hawthorn.

Sciamh. Beauty.

Sciamhach. Beautiful, fair.

Sciamham. To beautify, adorn.

Scian. A knife.

Scianbheartha. A razor.

Sciath. A wing, a fhield, buckler, fin.

Sciathan A little wing or fhield.

Sciath. A twig bafket.

Sciathach. Winged, having a fhield or buckler, ftreaked with white.

Sciathch. A cow that has white ftreaks on her fide.

Sciathanach. Winged.

Scib. A hand, fift.

Scib. A fhip, fkiff.

Sciberneog. A hare.

Scibhordan. A fyringe.

Scibeadh. The courfe or order of a thing.

Scibbadh. A crew.

Scile. Affright, confternation.

Scildaimhne. A minnow.

Scinnam. To fpring, gufh out.

Sciobal. A barn, granary.

Sciog. A hawthorn.

Sciorram. To flip.

Sciordam. To purge, fquirt.

Sciordain. A fquirt.

Sciorbhe. Gall.

Sciot. A dart, arrow.

Sciothach. White thorn.

Sciothag. A haw.

Scioth. A partition of rods wattled, a partition.

Scioth. Tired, fatigued.

Sciothaigham. To fatigue, tire.

Sciothaghadh. Tiring.

Sciothas. Fatigue.

Scitena. Scythia.

Sciulong. A deferter, fugitive.

Sciuram. To purge, fcour.

Sciurin. A fcouring.

Sciurlang. A fugitive.

Sciurs. A whip, woe, affliction.

Sciurfadh. Whipping, afflicting.

Sciurfam. To whip, fcourge.

Sclabhuidhachd. Slavery, fervitude.

Sclabhadh.
Sclabhaidhe. } A flave, bondfman.

Sclamhadh. Seizing and fnatching by force.

Sclamham. To feize or fnatch away by force.

Sclamhaire. An ufurper, one that feizeth violently.

Sclamhachd. A violently feizing on

Sclat. A flate.

Scleo. Shade, mifery, compaffion.

Scleo. Great pomp of words, high puffing

Scleoid. A filly fellow.

Sclongaide. Copious fnot.

Scloid. Filth.

Scod.
Scodan. } A corner of a cloth, fheet of a fail

Scoid. A neck.

Scoidais. Coquetry, flirting.

Scoidaifach.
Scoidamhuil. } Coquetifh, flirting, formal.

Scoil, fcol. A fchool.

Scoilair. A fcholar.

Scoilardha. Scholaftic.

Scoilairdhachd. Scholarfhip.

Scoiltain. A flit, flice, fplinter.

Scoiltam. To flit, rend, tear, burft.

Scoilteadh. A cleft.

Scoinnadh deifgadh. Cutting off.

Scoincam. To withdraw.

Scoitiche. A quack, mountebank.

Scoitichachd. Quackery.

Scolb. A prick, prickle, a fkirmifh or battle with knives and dirks.

Scolb.
Scolbach. } A fpray or wattle ufed in thatching with ftraw.

Scolb. A fplinter.

Scoltadh

Scoltadh. A slit, cleft, slitting, cleaving.

Scornan. } The throat.
Scornach. }

Scor. Much, many, plenty.

Scor. A champion.

Scor. A notch or mark made by the stroke of a knife or sword.

Scor. A concealed rock jutting into the sea, the tail of a bank.

Scoraid. A table-cloth.

Scoradh. Scarification

Scoram. To scarify.

Scot. Much.

Scot-bheurla. The Scotch tongue.

Scoth. A disease.

Scoth. The choice or best part of any thing.

Scoth. A flower.

Scotten. A small flock.

Scrabach. Rough.

Scraidain. A diminutive little fellow.

Scraidag. A diminutive little female.

Scraiste. A sluggard, slothful person.

Scraisteachd. Laziness, slothfulness.

Scraisteamhuil. Slothful, lazy.

Scraisteamhlachd. Laziness, sloth.

Scrantha. Divided.

Scrath. A turf, sod.

Scrathal. Tearing, destructive.

Screab. A scab, eschar.

Screabach. Scabbed

Screach. A screech, shriek.

Screachadh. Screeching, shrieking.

Screachag. A jay.

Screacham. To shriek, screech.

Scread. A cry, shout, bawling.

Screadadh. Crying, shouting, bawling.

Screadag. A sharp, sour drink.

Screadam. To cry out, bawl, shout.

Screadan. The noise of any thing rending.

Screadal. Shrieking, crying.

Screadalach. Crying, bawling.

Screitidh. Abhorrent.

Screapal. A scruple in weight

Scretidhachd. } Abhorrence.
Screamh. }

Scribhinn. A rugged rocky side of a hill.

Scrid. A breath, least breath of life or air.

Scrin. A shrine.

Scriob. A scratch, scrape, a furrow.

Scriobach. The itch.

Scriobam. To scratch, scrape, to curry a horse.

Scrioban. A curry-comb.

Scriobhadh. Writing.

Scriobhadoir. } A writer, notary, clerk, scri-
Scriobhneoir. } vener, scribe.

Scriobham. To write.

Scriobhte. Written.

Scriobhadoirachd. The profession of writing.

Scriobhuin. A bill, evidence.

Scrios. Ruin, destruction.

Scriosam. To sweep the skin, the surface, &c. off from a thing, to destroy, ruin.

Scriosadair. A destroyer.

Scriosadairachd. Flaying or sweeping every thing away, destroying.

Scriosta. Destroyed.

Scriotachan. A little squawler, an infant.

Scrobadh. Scratching.

Scrobam. To scratch.

Scroban. The crop or craw of a bird.

Scrobha. A screw.

Scrubaire. A scrub.

Scrudadh. An examination, searching,

Scrudam. To search, examine

Scruduighte. Examined, tried, searched.

Scruinge. An ensign.

Scuab. A sheaf, a besom.

Scuabadh. Sweeping, sweepings.

Scuabachan. A little brush or besom.

Scuabag. A little sheaf.

Scuabam. To sweep, brush.

Scuaptha. Swept.

Scuablion. A drag, or sweep-nest.

Scuchsam. To pass, proceed, go.

Scud. A ſhip.

Scud. A cluſter.

Scuird. The lap.

Scuiram. To ceaſe, deſiſt.

Scuiſeadh. To go, proceed.

Scuite. A wanderer.

Sculog, ſcalog. An old man, a ſervant.

Scur. Ceaſing, deſiſting.

Sda. Uſe.

Sdad. } A ſtopping, ſtaying, a let.
Sdadadh. }

Sdadam To ſtop, ſtay, remain.

Sdaid. State, condition, a furlong.

Sdaipal A ſtopper, cork.

Sdair. Hiſtory.

Sdairgha. Hiſtorical.

Sdeall. A caſt of water as from a ſyringe.

Sdealladh. Squirting.

Sdealladoir. A ſquirt, ſyringe.

Sdeallam. To ſquirt.

Sdeig. A ſlice of meat, a ſteak.

Sdeig-bhraghad. The gullet.

Sdeigh. Protection.

Sdeud. A ſteed.

Sdiallach. A ſtripe, ſtreak, ſplit of a plank, chop taken from any thing.

Sdiallach. Striped, ſtreaked.

Sdiobhart. A ſteward.

Sdiorap. A ſtirrup.

Sdiuir. A rudder, rule, guide.

Sdiuram. To ſteer, guide, direct.

Sdiuradh. Steering, guiding, directing.

Sdoc. A trumpet, a ſtock.

Sdodach. That kicketh.

Sdoid. Sulkineſs.

Sdoil. Beads.

Sdoirm. A ſtorm.

Sdoirmamhuil. Stormy.

Sdol. A ſtool, a ſeat.

Sdol-coiſe. A foot-ſtool.

Sdopadh. A meaſure of capacity, a ſtoup.

Sdor, ſdoras. Proviſion, ſtores.

Sduic. Pl. of Sdoc.

Sduipeal. Wandering, roving.

Sduir. Vide Sdiuir.

Se. He, it, him.

Se. For Is e, 'tis he, it.

Se. Six.

Seabhac. A hawk, falcon.

Seabhacoir. A falconer.

Seabhag. The ſpleen.

Seabhacamhuil. Hawk-like, fierce.

Seabhaidach. A wandering, ſtraying

Seabhais. A wandering, ſtrolling, ſtraying.

Seabhaiſach. Diſcurſive.

Seabhrach. Certain, ſure, true.

Seaca. Gen. of Sioc. Froſt.

Seacadh. } Parched, dried.
Seacanta. }

Seacaghadh. Parching, drying.

Seacaigham. } To parch, dry, freeze.
Seacaim. }

Seach. A turn, rather, elſe, aſide

Seach a cheile. One by or from another.

Seachad. By, aſide, out of the way, paſt.

Seachadadh. Tradition.

Seachadam. To deliver, ſurrender.

Seachadtha. Delivered, ſurrendered.

Seachaduighe. Further.

Seachuimſe. Beyond, before me.

Seachain. Idle tales.

Seachainam. To avoid, ſhun, ſeparate.

Seachantach. Straying, wandering.

Seachantachd. A ſhunning or avoiding.

Seachaintach. Diſmal, ominous, to be avoided, ſhunning.

Seacham. Beyond me.

Seacham. To paſs by, to paſs over.

Seachamhal. Further.

Seachbho A heifer.

Seachcang. Space of ſeven years.

Seachd. } Seven.
Seacht. }

Seachduan. } A fold.
Seachdhrud. }

Seachdhubla. Sevenfold.

Seachdmhadh. } Seventh.
Seachdo. }

Seachdmhain. A week.

Seachdmhain an luathreimhain. Ember-week.

Seachdmhad. Seventy.

Seachdmhado. Seventieth.

Seachdmhios. September.

Seachdrinn. The seven stars.

Seachdshliosnach. A heptagon, heptagonal.

Seachgairam. To call aside or apart.

Seachlabhradh. An allegory.

Seachlabhram. To allegorize.

Seachlabhrach. Allegorical.

Seachluigham. To lay apart.

Seachloc. A park, a field.

Seachmaillam. To forget.

Seachmal. Forgetfulness, oblivion.

Seachmall. Digression, partiality.

Seachmhallach. Oblivious.

Seachmalta. Forgetful.

Seachnadh. Avoiding, shunning, an avoiding.

Seachnam. To separate, avoid, escape.

Seachnain. By or through.

Seachoileabhar. For another cause, thereabouts.

Seachraith. Filth, dirt.

Seachran An error, straying

Seachrannach. Erroneous, straying.

Seachranam. To go astray.

Seachrod. A bye-way.

Seachtair. Without, on the outside, before, beyond.

Seachtar. The number seven.

Seachtdeug. Seventeen.

Seachto-deug. Seventeenth.

Sead, seod, seud. A jewel, precious stone, a present, favour, substance.

Seachtmhain. A week.

Sead. A way, road, a feat.

Sead. The likeness of a thing.

Seadaire. A dolt.

Seadal. A short time, space.

Sedar. The cedar-tree

Seadchoimhadaighe. Keeper of a museum. Vide Cimeliarcha.

Seadchomhthara. An attribute.

Seadh. Yes, be it so.

Seadh. Sense, meaning.

Seadh. A discourse, a dialogue.

Seadh, seach. By turns, alternately.

Seadh. Strong, able, stout.

Seadh. The crop or craw of a bird.

Seadha. A saw.

Seadham. To esteem, to value.

Seadham. To saw, smooth, plane.

Seadhbhail. Sawing.

Seadh-suirigh. A love-token.

Seafaid. A heifer.

Seafnadh. A blowing, breathing.

Seafnaim. To blow, breathe.

Seagal. Rye.

Seagh. Esteem, respect, worth, value.

Seagha. } Curious, ingenious.
Seaghar. }

Seaghach. Courteous, gentle.

Seaghach. A he-goat.

Seaghlan. An old man.

Seal. } A-while, space, distance, course,
Sealad. } or time.

Seala. A seal, signet.

Sealadh. Yet, one's course or stead.

Sealadach. Alternate, by turns.

Sealadh. Sealing.

Sealaidh. A cutting, hewing.

Sealaidheachd. A vicissitude, change.

Sealanta. Rigid.

Sealbh. A herd, drove.

Sealbh. Possession, inheritance.

Sealbh. A field.

Sealbh. A pretence, colour.

2

Sealbhaghadh.

Sealbhaghadh. Poffeffing.

Sealbhaigham. To poffefs, enjoy.

Sealbhuighe. ⎫ A proprietor, ownei, occu-
Sealbhadoir. ⎭ pant.

Sealbhag. Sorrel.

Sealbhag nam fiadh. Round-leaved mountain forrel.

Sealbhan. A great number, drove, heid,
multitude.

Sealg. Hunting, a chafe.

Sealg. The milt of fwine, the fpleen of
man or beaft, belly-ach.

Sealgaire. A fportfman, fowler, falconer.

Sealgaireachd. Hunting, hawking.

Sealgam. To hunt, fowl, hawk.

Sealgbhata. A hunting-pole.

Seall. Behold thou, fee.

Sealladh. A fight, profpect, view.

Seallam. To look at, behold, to fee.

Sealladh-nafach. A raree-fhow.

Sealta. Sealed.

Sealtuir. A fword.

Seaman. A fmall nail rivetted.

Seamar. ⎫ Trefoil, clover.
Seamrog. ⎭

Seamh, feimh. Mild, modeft, keen, fmall,
tender.

Seamhas. Good-luck.

Seamhafal. Fortunate, lucky.

Seamhfganach. Quick, foon.

Seamfa. A nail, a peg.

Sean. Old, antient.

Sean. Profperity, happinefs.

Sean. A charm.

Seanach. Crafty, cunning, wily.

Seanachidh. An antiquary.

Seanachas. Antiquities, hiftory, narration.

Seanadh. A denial, refufal ; a fynod, council of elders.

Seannadh. A bleffing, benediction.

Seanaid. A fenate.

Seanaidh. To fow corn, to drop, pour.

Seanaidhe. A fenator, member of pa-lia-
ment, antiquary.

Seanaidham. To fend.

Seanailtiras. A decree.

Seanam. To blefs, to defend from the
power of enchantments.

Seanan. To refufe, deny, decline.

Seanafan. Etymology.

Seanmhor. ⎫ Happy, profperous.
Seanamhuil. ⎭

Sean-aois. Old-age.

Seanarafg. A proverb, old faying.

Seanas. Shortnefs of fight.

Seanathair. A grandfather.

Seanbhean. An old woman.

Seanbheanachd. Anility.

Seadbholadh. An old fmell.

Seanchas. Antiquity.

Seancha. ⎫ An antiquary, genealo-
Seanchuidhe. ⎭ gift.

Seanchomhartha. An old token, a monument.

Seanchuimhne. Tradition.

Seanchus. Antiquity, a chronicle, regifter, a genealogy, pedigree.

Seanda. ⎫ Antient, antique, aged.
Seandidh. ⎭

Seandachd. Age, a being antient.

Seanduine. An old man.

Seanfhocal. An old faying, proverb.

Seanfhoirne. The old inhabitants.

Seang. Small, flender, flender-waifted.

Seangaim. To make flender or thin, to di-
minifh, grow flender.

Seangal. Wife, prudent.

Seangan. An ant, pifmire.

Seangarmhathair. The great-grandfather's
or great-grandmother's mother.

Seanghaid. ⎫ A grandmother.
Seanmhathair. ⎭

Seanghain. A child about to be born.

Seanghein. A child begot in old age.

Seanghille,

Seanghille. An old bachelor.

Seanlith. Happiness.

Seanma. Musical.

Seanmhuire. }
Seanmhuireachd. } Happiness, prosperity.

Seanmhur. Happy, prosperous, great, huge.

Seanmoir, searmoin. A sermon.

Seanmoirighe. A preacher, sermonist.

Seanmoiram. To preach, exhort, proclaim.

Seanmor. Very great, huge.

Seannach. A fox.

Seannachaigham. To play the fox.

Seannachal. Cunning, crafty, fox-like.

Seannfair A chanter.

Seanoir. An elder, senator, an old bard or Druid.

Seanoireachd. Old-age.

Seanradh. An old saying, a proverb, pl. Seanraite.

Seanfgeulachd. Archaiology.

Seanta. Blessed, having a charm of protection, refused, denied.

Seantiomna. The Old Testament.

Seanuaire. Good luck.

Seapam. To flinch back, sneak off, to pursue close.

Searb. Theft, felony.

Searbaid. The rowers feat in a boat.

Searbh. Bitter, four.

Searbhadas. }
Searbhas. } Bitterness, fourness.

Searbhadair. A towel, napkin.

Searbham. To embitter.

Searbhan. Oats.

Searbhghal. Blue, azure.

Searbhos. A deer, stag.

Searbhraite }
Searbhghloir. } Cacophony.

Searbhubhal. Coloquintida.

Searc. Love, affection.

Searcam. To love, be in love.

Searcairminnam. To reverence.

Searcamhuil. Affectionate, loving.

Searcog. A sweetheart, a mistress.

Searcall. Flesh, delicate meat, the best flesh.

Searcthoir. A gallant, a lover.

Searg. Dry, withered.

Seargam. To wither, dry, pine away, confume.

Seargadh. Withering, consuming.

Searganach. Dried up, withered.

Seargfamh. A consumption, wasting.

Seargtha. Dried up, withered, consumed.

Searmoin. A sermon.

Searmonaigham. To preach.

Searmonaighe. A preacher.

Searn. A youth, stripling.

Searnadh. Extension, yawning, stretching.

Searnam. To loose, untye.

Searpan. A swan.

Searpan. An order, custom.

Searb. Theft.

Searr. }
Searrach. } A colt, a foal.

Searrachal. Like a foal, small, flim.

Searr. A scythe, sickle.

Searrag. A bottle.

Searraigh. The herb pilewort.

Searraim. To yawn, stretch the limbs.

Searraim. To reap, mow, slaughter, kill, make havock.

Searrdha. An edge or point, edged.

Searfhuil. Squint-eyed.

Searthonn. A chief poet or prince.

Searthonna. Art, skill, knowledge.

Seas. Stand thou. Vide Seafam.

Seas. A board from land to the fide of a boat for passengers to go out and in by.

Seafachas. Sitting, a truce.

Seafadh. Standing.

Seafal. A fan.

Seafam. To stand, rise up.

Seafamh. Standing up.

Seafda. A defence.

Seafdubh. A ftandifh.

Seafg. Dry, barren, unprolific.

Seafgad, feafga. Sixty.

Seafgado. Sixtieth.

Seafgach. Seven battles.

Seafgachd. A herd of barren cattle.

Seafgaidhe. A barren cow.

Seafgaire. At eafe, quiet, well fixed or fettled.

Seafgaire. } Cozinefs, reft, quietnefs,
Seafgaireachd. } being in an eafy way.

Seafgaireach. Delightful, calm.

Seafgan. A fhock or handful of gleaned corn.

Seafgan. Land that hath been gleaned.

Seafganach. A bachelor.

Seafgar. Soft, effeminate, ftill.

Seafgbho. A heifer, barren cow.

Seafgchorpach. Barren.

Seafmhach. Stiff, ftedfaft, firm, perfevering.

Seafmhachd. Firmnefs, fteadinefs, conftancy.

Seafrach. A lad, youth.

Seafuir. Seafon.

Seafunta. Profperous.

Seata. A quean.

Seathadh. A hide, fkin.

Seathadair. A fkinner.

Seathbhog. Marjoram.

Seathnar. Number fix.

Seathar. A ftudy, library.

Seathar. Strong, able, good.

Seathar. God.

Seathardha. Divine.

Secnach. A body.

Sed. A cow with calf.

Sed. A way.

Sed gabnala. Augmentation.

Sedde. } Full made.
Seddidh. }

Segh. Milk.

Segh. An ox, buffalo, a hind of the moofe kind.

Seic. A bone.

Seich. A combat.

Seich. An adventurer.

Seicham. To follow, purfue.

Seichdmhi. September.

Seicibtan. Whenfoever.

Seicle. } A hatchel.
Seical. }

Seicladh. Hatcheling.

Seiclam. To hatchel.

Seicilte. Hatcheled.

Seicin. } The fkull, pellicle of the brain
Seicne. } meninx.

Seic. } The peritoneum.
Seicne. }

Seid. Blow thou.

Seidadh. Blowing, a blowing, a blaft.

Seidain. A panting, anhelation.

Seidam. To blow, breathe upon.

Seidean. Quickfand.

Seidigh. Afpiration.

Seidthe. Blown upon.

Seidd. A full belly, tympany.

Seigh. A hawk.

Seighion. A champion, warrior.

Seigheoir. A falconer.

Seighnean. A hurricane, tempeft; lightning.

Seighar. Vide Seaghar.

Seilbh. Poffeffion, a herd, drove.

Seilchide. } A fnail.
Seilichag. }

Seiladan. A fpitting-box.

Seile. Spittle.

Seileach. Mucous.

Seileach. A willow.

Seiladan. } A handkerchief.
Seileadach. }

Seilair. A cellar.

Seilg. Hunting, fowling; venifon

Seilighide. A fnail.

Seiligham. To spit.

Seilasdair. Yellow flower de luce.

Seilloin. A bee, humble bee.

Seilioda. }
Seilunn. } A sheep ked.

Seilt. Dropping, drivelling.

Seimh. Mild, little, single.

Seimhachd. Mildness.

Seimhdrean. A duel.

Seimilair. A chimney.

Seimhidh. Vide Seimh.

Seimhide. A snail.

Seimne. Elder.

Seineachd. Old-age.

Seinister. A window.

Seinn Sing thou.

Seinn. Singing.

Seinnam. To sing, play.

Seinsirachd. Eldership, seniority.

Seinsiras Antiquity in a place.

Seipeal. A chapel.

Seipinn. A quart, chopin.

Seirbh. Vide Searbh.

Seirbhe, seirbhachd. Bitterness.

Seire. A meal of victuals.

Seir. A heel.

Seirbhais. Service.

Seirbhaisach. A servant.

Seirbhaisaigham. To serve.

Seirc. Charity, affection.

Seircal Charitable, affectionate.

Seirceoir. A wooer.

Seircin. A darling, a beloved.

Seircin. A jerkin, coat.

Seirdin. A pilchard.

Seirg. Clover, trefoil.

Seirg. A consumption, decay.

Seirgidhe. Withered.

Seirgne. Sickly.

Seiric. Silk, superfine silk.

Seiric. Strong, able.

Seiricean. A silk-worm.

Seirseanach. An auxiliary.

Seirsin. A girdle, a band.

Seirt. Strength, power.

Seis. Pleasure, delight.

Seis. Skill, knowledge.

Seis. A troop, band, company; one's match or equal.

Seis. He sat.

Seisde. A siege.

Seisdadh. Besieging.

Seisdam. To besiege.

Seise. A tumult, noise, bustle.

Seiseach. Chearful, pleasant, agreeable.

Seiseachd. Pleasure, sensuality.

Seiseadh. The sixth.

Seisean. He, he himself.

Seiseilbh. Talk, discourse.

Seisain Session, fiting of a court; assizes.

Seisg. Sedge, bog-reed.

Seisg. Vide Scafg.

Seisgeann. A fenny boggy country.

Seisir. }
Seisim. } Six.

Seisim. To sit.

Seisreach. A plough of six horses, a plough.

Seisreach fearainn. A plowland.

Seitche. }
Seiteach. } A wife.

Seithe, seith. A skin, hide.

Seilreach. Neighing, braying, sneezing.

Seilide. }
Seilmide. } A snail.

Selian. A rill.

Semeann. A small snail.

Sen. A birding net.

Sene. A supper.

Sengilbhroth. Venison of wild boar.

Seo. Substance.

Seod, feud. A jewel.

Seodcha. A treasury, museum.

Seodchomhartha. A tomb, or grand monument; a triumphal arch.

Seoid. A hero.

Seoid. Jewels.

Seoid aonaich. A fairing.

Seoid. Strong.

Seol. A bed.

Seol. A fail.

Seol. A weaver's loom; mode or way of doing a thing, method.

Seolmara. The tide.

Seoladh. Sailing, directing, teaching.

Seoladair. A failor.

Seoladaireachd. Sea life.

Seolam. To fail, direct, inftruct, guide, conduct.

Seolbhata. A goad, ftaff or club for guiding cattle.

Seolta. Digefted, fet in order, fkilful, methodical.

Seoltachd. Skilfulnefs, neatnefs.

Seomar. A room, chamber.

Seomar-leape. A bed-chamber.

Seomar na culidh. A veftry.

Seomar na droitte. A dining-room.

Seomar-araich. A nurfery.

Seomrach. Full of chambers, cellular, vafcular.

Seomradoir. A chamberlain.

Seona faobha. Augury, forcery, druidifm.

Seorfa. A fort, fpecies.

Seothach. Meaning.

Seothag, feabhag. A hawk.

Sepeal. A chapel.

Serbos. A hart, ftag.

Ses. A befom.

Seuch. Vide Seach.

Seth, Go feth. Severally.

Seud. A jewel. Vide Sead.

Seud. A way, path.

Seudcha. ⎫
Seudachan. ⎬ A jewel-houfe, mufeum.
Seudlann. ⎭

Seudoir. A jeweller.

Seula. A feal.

Seuladh. Sealing.

Seulam. To feal.

Scunta. Denied, facred, enchanted.

Seunmhor. Enchanted.

Seun. A charm for protection.

Seuntas. ⎫
Seunbholadh. ⎬ Stench.

Sforrach. A perch.

Sg, fc, Indifcriminately written.

Sga, fgath. Sake of.

Sgabadh. Scattering.

Sgabam. To fcatter, difperfe.

Sgabte. ⎫
Sgabthe. ⎬ Difperfed.

Sgabaifte. Robbery, rapine.

Sgabard. A fheath, fcabbard.

Sgabhrach. ⎫
Sgabhrag. ⎬ Club-footed.

Sgabul. A garment.

Sgadan. A herring.

Sgadan garbh. The fifh called Alewife

Sgaire. A bold hearty man.

Sgafanta. Spirited, hearty.

Sgaffa. Vide Scaffa.

Sgaffadh. Codded.

Sgaga. To cleanfe, winnow, filter, to fplit, fhrink.

Sgagadh. A fplit, chink.

Sgagham. To fort, digeft.

Sgaifirr. The ftern of a fhip.

Sgaighnean. A winnowing fan.

Sgail. A flame, brightnefs.

Sgail. A fhade.

Sgailbhain. A multitude, fwarm.

Sgailc. A bumper of whifky in a morning.

Sgailcara. That giveth hard blows.

Sgailin. ⎫ An umbrella, veil; a little difh,
Sgaileog. ⎬ plate.

Sgailleas. Difdain.

Sgailleafach. Difdainful.

Sgailleog A fmall difh.

Sgailtam. Vide Sgoiltam.

Sgailtean. A billet, or cleft wood.

Sgaineadh. Splitting, cleaving.

Sgaineam. To split, cleave, burst.

Sgaipeadh. Difperfing.

Sgaipam. To difperfe.

Sgaipitheach. Profufe, lavifh.

Sgaird. A fmock.

Sgairneil. Shrieking, crying out.

Sgairnich. Separation, broken pieces.

Sgairioch. Prodigal.

Sgairp. A fcorpion.

Sgairt. }
Sgairteachd. } A loud cry, fhout, crying, roaring.

Sgairteoir. A cryer, bawler.

Sgairteach. That bawleth loud.

Sgairtaim. To cry, bawl.

Sgairtal. Vigorous.

Sgaiteach. Sharp, deftructive, ftormy.

Sgaith. A flower.

Sgaithin A fmall fhadow

Sgal. A fhriek, a loud fhrill cry.

Sgal. A man, a calf.

Sgala. A bowl.

Sgalam. To ring, tinkle, to give a fhrill cry.

Sgalain. A hut, cottage.

Sgalan. A fcaffold.

Sgalanta. Loud and fhrill founding.

Sgaldach Stubble.

Sgaldruth. A fornicator.

Sgallach. Troublefome, bald.

Sgallam To trouble, difturb, to fcald.

Sgalladh. A burning, fcalding.

Sgallagach. Bird-feed.

Sgallta. Burnt, fcalded.

Sgallta. Bare, bald.

Sgallog. A ruftic, fervant. Vide Scalog.

Sgamail. Scales.

Sgamal. Exhalation.

Sgamh. }
Sgamhan } The lungs.
Sgamhog }

Sgamhangha. Pulmonary.

Sgamhar. Saw-duft.

Sgannal. Abufe, fcandal, offence.

Sgamhchnaoigh. }
Sgamhghalar. } Phthific, or confumption of the lungs.
Sgamhfaoth. }

Sgannalach. Scandalous, abufive.

Sgannan. The caul, a film, an awn.

Sgann. A membrane.

Sgann. A multitude.

Sgannairbhuartha. Confufed, confounded.

Sganram. To difperfe through fear.

Sganruigh. Defamation, aftonifhment.

Sgaoigh. A rout, herd, drove.

Sgaog. A foolifh giddy fickle woman.

Sgaol. Spread, fcatter thou.

Sgaoladh. Difmiffing, feparating, ripping up, untying.

Sgaolam. To difmifs, feparate, untie.

Sgaolteach. Profufe.

Sgaolte Loofe, fpread.

Sgaolteachd. Profufenefs.

Sgaoll. Fright, fhynefs.

Sgaollaire. A fhy, timid creature.

Sgaollmhor. Timid, fhy.

Sgaollmhorachd. Shynefs, coynefs.

Sgaoim. Fear.

Sgaoth. A fwarm.

Sgapam. Vide Sgabam.

Sgarachdin. Separation, parting.

Sgaradh, fgarachdin. Separating.

Sgaram. To feparate.

Sgartha. Separated.

Sgarbh. A cormorant.

Sgarbh. A ford, fhallow water.

Sgarbham. To wade.

Sgardadh. Pouring, fprinkling, feparation.

Sgardaire. A water-gun, fquirt.

Sgardam. To fprinkle.

Sgarnal. A fcreaming, fcreeching.

Sgat. A fkate.

Sgath. A fhadow, fear.

Sgath. For the fake of.

Sgath. A large bundle of rods tied together, ufed in the Highlands inftead of a door.

Air fgath. For the fake of, behind.

Sgath. Deftruction, wafte.

Sgatham. To lop, cut off, deftroy.

Sgathach. Shady, fearful, timid.

Sgathachan A tail, the privities.

Sgathach. Loppings

Sgathadh A fegment, fhred, fkirmifhing, bickering

Sgathaire A fpruce fellow.

Sgathamh. A while, fhort fpace.

Sgathan. A mirrour.

Sgathanam. To behold.

Sgathara. Hewing, lopping.

Sgathbharra. A parafol.

Sgathbhard. A fatirift.

Sgathbhardachd. Satire, Bilingfgate-talk.

Sgathlann A booth, fhop, cover.

Sgathag Trefoil in flower.

Sgathmhor. Sharp.

Sgeach. } A haw
Sgeachog. }

Sgeachchaor A white thorn berry.

Sgeach. A buft.

Sgeachfpionnan. A goofeberry-bufh.

Sgeadach. Speckled, fky-coloured.

Sgeadachadh. Drefs, clothes, ornament.

Sgeaduigham. To drefs, adorn.

Sgeadaighoir. A decker.

Sgeadas. Ornament, various colours.

Sgealb, fgealb A fplinter.

Sgeallagach. Wild muftard.

Sgeallan. A flice, a kernel.

Sgealpag. A pinch, fplinter, a rent.

Sgealpach. In pieces, in fplinters.

Sgealpam To tear, rend, fplit, to pluck, fnatch.

Sgealptha. Torn, fnatched away.

Sgeamh. } Polypody.
Sgeamhchrainn. }

Sgeamhaim. To reproach.

Sgeamhcrom. A pinch.

Sgeamhle. A fkirmifh.

Sgeamhlaigham. To bicker, fkirmifh.

Sgeanadh, fgean. A wild, mad look

Sgearach Happy.

Sgeathach. Vide Sgeach.

Sgeathach. Emetic.

Sgeathchofg. Anti-emetick.

Sgeatham. } To vomit, reject.
Sgeathraigham. }

Sgeigaire. A buffoon.

Sgeigairachd. Buffoonery, waggery.

Sgeil. Skill, knowledge.

Sgeilamhuil Skilful, knowing.

Sgeil, gen. of Sgeul, fgeal. A ftory

Sgeilbhearthach. A tale-bearer, tale-bearing

Sgeiltheachdaire. A tale-bearer

Sgeimh. Beauty, ornament.

Sgeimham. To beautify, adorn, to fkim, to fcum.

Sgeimhiolta. A fcout.

Sgein. Flight.

Sgeinam. To bounce, leap up.

Sgeinmeile. }
Sgeinmeach. } Quick, fmart, fwift, nimble.
Sgeinmneach. }

Sgeip. A bee-hive

Sgeir. A rock in the fea.

Sgeith. The better part of any thing, rather Scoth.

Sgeith. Vomit.

Sgeith. Gen. of Sgiath.

Sgeithin. A little bufh.

Sgeitinnfcis. The quinzey.

Sgeitram. To crafh.

Sgeo. Underftanding.

Sgeog. Vide Sgeachog.

Sgeolach. One of Fingal's cups fo called.

Sgethe The handle of a target.

Sgeul. A ftory, news.

Sgeulaiche. A newfmonger.

Sgeulachd. Hiftorical narration.

Sgeun. Aftonifhment.

Sgeunal. Pruned, neat, in good order.

Sgiamhach. Beautiful, adorned, lovely.

2   Sgiam-

Sgiamhaiche. More beautiful.

Sgiamhaichad. Beautifulness.

Sgiamhalach. Squalling.

Sgiamhbhreacam. To gild, adorn.

Sgian. A knife.

Sgianadhaircach. Name of a sheep having sharp horns.

Sgianadhaircach Having sharp horns.

Sgian-bhuird. A table-knife.

Sgian-chollag. A chopping-knife

Sgian-bhearthaidh. A razor.

Sgiath. A wing, pinion, target, buckler.

Sgiathach. Winged, shielded, having a buckler.

Sgiathanach. Winged.

Sgibheal. Eaves of a roof

Sgiberneag. A hare.

Sgige. A jeering, derision.

Sgigeamhuil. Scornful.

Sgigam To jeer, deride.

Sgigthe Ridiculous.

Sgilghre. Gravel.

Sgille Quick, soon.

Sgilleog. A small pebble.

Sgillin. A shilling.

Sgillin Albanach. A penny.

Sgillin Shasgunach. A shilling.

Sgimheal. A pent-house.

Sgiomhiolach. A scout.

Sgimhleaghadh. An excursion.

Sgineadh. ⎫
Sgineal ⎬ A leap, skip.

Sgineadhach. Apt to start, skittish.

Sgineog. A flight.

Sgiobair. A skipper, master of a ship, helmsman.

Sgiobadh. The crew, men at work.

Sgiobal. A barn, granary.

Sgiobtha. Snatched away.

Sgiopidh. ⎫
Sgioptidh. ⎬ Tight, tidy, neat, spruce.
Sgiobalta. ⎭

Sgiolladh. Decidence. Vide Sgiollam.

Sgiollam. To shell or prepare grain, by grinding the husks of it.

Sgiollta. So prepared, neat, tight.

Sgiorram. To slip, stumble.

Sgiorradh Mischance.

Sgirthan A stumbler, a slipper.

Sgiothal. Ridiculous.

Sgioth A partition of wattled rods.

Sgiothlaich. A haunch

Sgire. ⎫
Sgireachd. ⎬ A parish.

Sgisthire. A prater, talkative.

Sgite. The fish called Maiden-ray.

Sgith. Wearied, tired, fatigued.

Sgiths. ⎫
Sgiothas. ⎬ Weariness, fatigue.

Sgitham. ⎫
Sgithaigham. ⎬ To tire, fatigue

Sgithaghadh. Tiring, fatiguing.

Sgiucham. To startle, leap.

Sgiurs. A scourge.

Sgiursadh. A whipping, whipping.

Sgiursam. To whip.

Sglaigin. A draught tree, beam of a wain.

Sglamham. To scold, wrangle, snatch.

Sglamhoide. A glutton.

Sglamhidhe. One that snatcheth away.

Sglamhach. That snatcheth.

Sglata. A slate, tile.

Sgleip. Ostentation.

Sgligeanach. Speckled.

Sgliurach. A slut, bad woman, slattern.

Sgliurachd. Idle gossiping.

Sgoballach. A piece, morsel.

Sgoid. A lappet.

Sgobam. T pluck from.

Sgobadh. A pluck, or pull.

Sgoidaisach Shewy, flirting, foppish.

Sgoidais. Pageantry, shew, flirting.

Sgoignean. A fan.

Sgoilt. Split thou.

Sgoiltain. A splinter.

Sgoilte. Cleft, split.

Sgoiltam.

Sgoiltam. To split, cleave.

Sgoithin. The prime, best.

Sgol.
Sgolghaire. } Loud laughter.

Sgol. A scull, or great quantity of fish; a school.

Sgolb. A splinter, a wattle, doubt.

Sgolbanach. A stripling, a youth.

Sgolbanta. Thin, slender.

Sgolog. An olive tree, a rustic, a servant.

Sgoloide. A schoolmaster.

Sgoltadh. A split, crack, chink.

Sgomhalsgartha. Astride.

Sgonaire. A trifler, whiffler.

Sgonasach. Trifling.

Sgonbabhraim. To blab out foolishly.

Sgonog. A hasty word, a fart.

Sgor. A stud of horses or mares. Vide Scor.

Sgoradh. Lancing, scarifying.

Sgoram. To lance, scarify, cut in pieces.

Sgorn.
Sgornach. } The throat.
Sgornan.

Sgorn frathrach. The pin or peg of a straddle.

Sgorchailbhe. The epiglottis.

Sgorthanach. A stripling.

Sgot. A shot, or reckoning.

Sgoth. A flower, son, a skiff.

Sgothadh. A pull.

Sgotham. To pull.

Sgothag. A cut.

Sgothlong. A yacht.

Sgrabach.
Sgrabanach. } Rough, rugged, scarce, rare.

Sgrabachan. Roughness.

Sgram. To wipe off.

Sgragall. Gold foil, a thin leaf, ray of gold or silver; a spangle.

Sgraibhsaidh. A hand-saw.

Sgraideog. A small puny person.

Sgraitach. Ragged, shabby.

Sgruit. A rag.

Sgraith.
Sgrathog. } A turf, green sod, green-sward.

Sgrathal. Destructive.

Sgramneirachd. Extortion.

Sgreabh bhathais. Baptismal fees.

Sgreabhal. An annual tribute of three-pence, paid at the command of the monarch by the provincial kings of Ireland, to St. Patrick, a favour given by new married people.

Sgreabhog. Crust.

Sgreach. A moan, a screeching.

Sgreachal. Crunkling.

Sgreacham. To make a noise, to whoop, shriek, crunkle.

Sgreachag, sgreachag reilge. An owl.

Sgreachan criosach. A vulture.

Screachtadh. A jocose bantering.

Sgread A screech.

Sgreadadh. Screeching, shrieking.

Sgreadam. To shriek, screech, squawl.

Sgreadaire. A cryer.

Sgreagan. Rocky ground.

Sgreagmhar. Rocky.

Sgreasta. Destruction.

Sgreataidham. To hate, abhor.

Sgreatachd. Hate, abhorrence.

Sgreatidh. To be abhorred, fearful.

Sgreathail. Fearful, frightful.

Sgreigam. To frig.

Sgribhin. A writing.

Sgribhisg. Notes, comments.

Sgrid. A breath.

Sgrideil. Lively.

Sgrin. A shrine.

Sgriob. A notch, a furrow, rut of a wheel, an itching of the lip superstitiously believed to precede an approaching kiss from a favourite, or a feast.

Sgriobach.
Sgrutach. } The itch.

Sgriobadh.

Sgriobadh. Scratching, rubbing, graving, picking.

Sgriobam. To fcrape, fcratch, write, engrave.

Sgriobaire. A graving tool.

Sgriobadoir. A grater.

Sgrioban. A wool-card, a rake.

Sgriobhadh. A writing, writing.

Sgriobhadoir A writer, clerk, notary.

Sgriobham. To write.

Sgriobhan A grammar.

Sgriobhantoir. A grammarian.

Sgrios. Ruin, deftruction.

Sgriofam. To deftroy, cut off. Vide Scriofam

Sgriobtuir. The fcripture.

Sgrobam. To fcratch, fcrape.

Sgroban. Crop of a bird.

Sgrioth. A long rhime.

Sgrubal. A fcruple.

Sgruibleach. Rubbifh.

Sgrudadh. Searching, fcrutinizing.

Sgrudam. To fearch, examine, fcrutinize.

Sgruigain. Neck, neck of a bottle.

Sgruta An old man.

Sgrutach. Lean, meagre.

Sguab. A fheaf, befom.

Sguabag A little fheaf.

Sguabadh. Sweeping, fweepings, refufe.

Sguabam. To fweep.

Sguab-aodaich. A clothes-brufh.

Sguab-lair. A befom.

Sguab-lion. A fweep-net.

Sguain A train, tail.

Sguaine. A fwarm, croud.

Sguibhir. An Efquire.

Sguileach. Rubbifh.

Sguille. A fcullion.

Sguird. A fhirt, fmock, a lap.

Sguir. Ceafe, defift thou.

Sguiram. To ceafe, defift.

Sguitfeadh. Threfhing.

Sguitfeam. To threfh, beat, to drefs flax.

Sgula. ⎫
Sgulag. ⎬ An old man, a little old man.
Sgulin. ⎭

Sgum. Scum.

Sgumadoir. A fcummer.

Sguman. The train when tucked up.

Sgumhara. Fat, good plight.

Sgumrag. A fort of fire-fhovel, a cinderwench, a dowdy.

Sgur. Ceafing, defifting.

Sguradh. Scouring.

Sguram. To fcour.

Sgurtha. Scoured.

Sguthaigh. A ftepping.

Shiar. Eaft

Si. She, her.

Sia. Far off, the utmoft, remoteft fiom you.

Sia. Six.

Siabhra. A fairy, hobgoblin.

Siabham. To rub, wipe.

Siabhaidhe. Fairies.

Siabunn. Soap.

Siachadh. A fprain.

Siacham. To fprain.

Siachcarnach. Hexangular.

Siacht. He came.

Siachtar. They came.

Siad. They.

Siadhail. Sloth, fluggifhnefs.

Siadhan. Confufed, topfy-turvy.

Siair. Afide.

Sian. A voice, found.

Sian. Storm, rain.

Sianal. Screaming, roaring.

Sianaidhe. One that cries out, a bawler.

Sianaidheacht. A yelling.

Sianmhedh. An accent.

Sianfa. Harmony, melody, pleafure.

Sia. Backwards, behind, the weft, awry,

Siarthonna. Art.

         Siafair.

Siasair. He sat.

Siasar. A session, assizes.

Siashliosnach. A hexagon, hexagonal.

Siat. A tumour, swelling.

Siataim. To puff, swell up.

Siathnail. Vide Sianal.

Sibal. Garlick, a leek.

Sibh. Ye, you.

Sibht. A shift, industry, contrivance.

Sibht. Providing, shifting, making a shift.

Sibhteamhuil. Provident.

Sibhtamhlachd. Foresight, a providing for.

Sibhealta. Civil.

Sic. Dry.

Sic. Vide Sioc.

Sichd. The inside of the skull.

Sice. Sycamore.

Sid. A lair, that there.

Side.
Sidheadh, sighe. } A blast.

Sidhean gaoithe. A whirlwind.

Sidheang. Infamy.

Sidhigham. To prove.

Sidhiuccan. A reed, cane.

Sigh. Spiritual, of the other world, belonging to spirits.

Sighe.
Sigidh. } A fairy, goblin.

Sighaire. A mountaineer.

Sighbhrog. A fairy, fairy-house.

Sighdhraoithachd. Enchantment with spirits, interference with spirits.

Sighin. A sign, token.

Sighinigham. To mark, sign.

Sigir. Silk.

Sigireun. A silk-worm.

Sigle. A seal.

Sileadh. A dropping, spittle.

Silim. Vide Saoilam.

Silam. To drop, distil, to sow.

Sileadh nan suil. Twinkling of the eye.

Silain A dropping, dropping.

Silin. A cherry.

Silsigham. To shine.

Silt. Spittle, an issue, a drop.

Siltain. A drooping creature.

Silt.
Silteach. } Fading, drooping, thin

Siltear. For Saoltar, it seemeth.

Simide. A mallet, beetle.

Similear, simne. A chimney.

Simontachd. Simony.

Simplidh Simple, mean, plain.

Simplidhachd. Simplicity, plainness.

Sin. The pronoun That.

Sin. Vide Sion, Sian.

Sin. Round.

Sine. Weather, bad weather.

Sineadh. Singing, from Seinnam.

Sinne. A dug or teat, nipple of the breast.

Sinne. Elder, eldest.

Sinneach. A wen.

Sineadh. A stretching, extending.

Sineam. To stretch.

Sineamhfeadha. A yew tree.

Singil.
Singilte. } Single, alone, unmixed.

Singlicham. To mix, adulterate.

Sinm. A song or tune.

Siniolach. A nightingale.

Sinin. A nipple, little teat.

Sinn, sinne. We, us

Sinseanoir.
Sinseanathair. } Great grandfather

Sinseanmhathair. A great grandmother.

Sinsior. An elder.

Sinsior. A yew tree.

Sinsir. The presbytery.

Sinsireachd. Eldership, seniority, chieftainship.

Sinsireachd. A right by succession.

Sinisean. Uvula.

Sinsirra. Ancestors.

Sinte. Stretched.

Sinteach

...teach. Straight, long.	Siolain. Dropping.
...tag. A ftraight line.	Siolarnach. Snoring, fnorting.
...bal } A fcallion, onion.	Siolaftair. A flag, fedge, wild flower de
...baid. }	luce.
...dadh. Blowing.	Siolbhruifneach. A nurfery.
...bag A blaft of the mouth.	Siolidh. A ftallion.
...bam. To blow.	Sionlchonlach. Fodder.
...ban Drift, the blaft.	Siolchur. Sowing.
...bhag A ftraw.	Siolchurtha Sown.
...bhal. A thorn, a pin.	Siolflafga. Running of the reins.
...bhalta. Civil, courteous.	Siolgam. To pick and choofe.
...bhaltachd. Civility.	Siollo. A jill, a fyllable.
...bhas. Rage, madnefs.	Siollairamh. Scanning of a verfe.
...bhafach Frantic, furious.	Siollam. To ftrike, fmite.
...bhiag. A fairy.	Siolliuin. A diærefis.
...c. } Froft.	Siolmhor. Bearing feed, full of feed, fer-
...can. }	tile.
...c liath. Hoar froft.	Siolmhorachd. Fertility
...c. Regio umbilicus, or groin.	Siolradh A ftock or breed, offspring.
...cnighte Dried up, frozen, obdurate.	Siolta. A teal.
...crim To freeze, dry up, grow hard.	Sioltaiche. A goofeander.
...chaire. A very little creature	Sioltagham. To filter.
...cair. A motive, reafon, a natural caufe,	Sioltaghan. A ftrainer.
opportunity.	Sioltreabh. A family.
...da Silk.	Sioltfhuileas. The running of the eyes.
...damhuil Like filk.	Siom. Them, the fame as Iadfan.
...dgha. Silken.	Sioman. A rope, cord.
...dhchan. Atonement.	Siomaide. A mallet
...dlamnaim To leap, bound.	Sion. A chain, bond, tie.
...flachan. Vide Siothlag.	Sion. Any thing.
...og A ftreak, a rick.	Sion. Weather; a ftorm, fnow.
...ogach. } Streaked.	Siona. Delay.
...ogamhuil. }	Sionan. The river Shannon.
...oghfurnadh. A hiffing, whifpering.	Sionbuailte. Weather-beaten.
...oghann. Vide Sithann.	Sionnach. A fox.
...ogidh. A fairy, pigmy.	Sionnachla. A weathergaw.
...ol. Seed, iffue, a tribe or clan.	Sionnadh. A reproof, fcoffing.
...olam Race, offspring of beafts.	Sionradhach Single.
...oladh A fyllable, dropping, the prow of	Sionfa A cenfer.
a fhip.	Sior. Continual, long.
...olaim, To fow, to drop, fpell, drivel.	Siorathearrach. Variable, inconftant.
...olchuiram. To fow.	Siorblofgadh. } A continual ruftling, or
...olanam. To ftrain, filter.	Siorbhraoileadh. } rattling noife.

Siorbhai.

Siorbhai. Thievery, theft.

Siorchainteach. A babbler, eternal talker.

Siorchafaim. To turn to and again.

Siorda. A great favour or prefent.

Siordanam. To rattle.

Siordha. ⎱ Everlasting, for ever, perpe-
Siorruidh. ⎰ tual.

Siorruidheachd. Perpetuity, eternity

Siordhaigham. To eternize.

Siorfhuigham. To condole, lament.

Siorghanam. To giggle.

Siorghlacam. To gripe, rough-handle.

Siorgnathuigham. To ufe often or much.

Siorghnath. Continual ufe.

Sioriomairc. Tranfmigration

Siorarridh. Importunity.

Siorarridhach. Importunate.

Siormharthanach. Everduring.

Siorlamhach. Long-handed.

Siorlofgadh. Everburning.

Siorob. Sparing, frugal.

Siorol. Hard drinking.

Siorofdam. To gape, yawn often.

Siorr. ⎱ Broomrape.
Siorralach. ⎰

Siorfan. Good news or tidings.

Siorfanach. Slow, tedious.

Siorfuidham. To linger, loiter.

Siortaire. An executioner.

Siortam. To fmite.

Siortha. Sought, begged.

Siortham. To afk, beg.

Siorthoir. A beggar, petitioner; a flut.

Siorthoireas A requeft.

Sioruifge. Continual rain.

Sios. Down.

Shios. Below.

Sios-fuas. Topfy-turvy.

Siofa. A court, parliament.

Siofurnaich. Hiffing.

Siofur. A pair of fheers, fciffars.

Siofma. A fchifm, private conference, whifpering.

Siofmaire. A fchifmatic, whifperer.

Siota. A pet, ill-bred child.

Siotridhe. A trifle, a jot.

Sioth, fith Peace, quietnefs.

Sioth. Spiritual, belonging to fpirits and
the other world.

Siothadh. A gnafh, rufhing at.

Siothal. Peaceable.

Siothaichan. Fairies.

Siothaigeantachd. Placability.

Siothbhaliaidh. Having long limbs.

Siothbhalta. Civil.

Siothbholfaire. A herald to proclaim peace.

Siothbhuan. Perpetual.

Siothchaint. Peace.

Siothchainteach. ⎱ Peaceable, pacific.
Siothchanta. ⎰

Siothchaintaiche. A peace-maker.

Siothchoimhadaiche. A conftable.

Siothlaetha. Days of peace.

Siothlag. A ftrainer or filter.

Siothlaigham. To filter, ftrain.

Siothlan. A ftrainer, filter, a cullender, a
fack

Siothlodh. Peace, making of peace.

Siothmhaor. A herald.

Siothmhalta. Civil

Sir, fior. In compound words fignifies perpetual.

Sireadh. Seeking, afking, looking for.

Sireamh. A difeafe.

Siram. To feek, afk, enquire after.

Sirchleachdam. To exercife, ufe often.

Sirdiolam. To fell much or frequently

Sirbiodaire. A vain tattler.

Siredam. To handle much.

Siriomcharam. To bear often.

Sirfheuchin. A fteady look.

Sirfheucham. To look ftedfaftly.

Sirreach. Lean, poor.

Sirreachdam. To foak.

Sirriam. A fheriff.

Sirfilt. Continual dropping.

Sirt.

Sirt. A little.

Silt. A time, a-while.

Sisteal. A flaxcomb, a cistern.

Sit-sit! Whist!

Sithbheach. Civil, of the city.

Siteirtnin A small cittern.

Siteog. Nice, effeminate.

Siterne. A harp.

Sith. Peace, rest, reconciliation.

Sithbhe. A rod.

Sithbhe. Continual, perpetual.

Sithbhe. A general.

Sithbhe. A city.

Sithbhein A fort or turret.

Sithbheo. }
Sithbhuan. } Lasting, perennial.

Sithbhrog. A fairy or fairy-house.

Sitheadh. Bending, declining.

Sitheal. A drinking-cup, a trowel, a body.

Sitheann. Venison.

Sitham. }
Sithaigham. } To pacify, reconcile.
Sithghnidham. }

Sithfhear. A strong man.

Sithne. Of venison.

Sithghliocas. Policy, cunning.

Sithbhristeach. A rebel, rebellious.

Sithcheanglam. To confederate.

Sithdruim An old name of Cashel.

Sithfhearc. Constant affection.

Sithim. A sequel, consequence.

Sitreach. The neighing of a horse.

Sitrigham. To neigh, bray.

Sitroighthoir. A husbandman.

Sittig otrach. A dunghill.

Siu. Before that, before.

Siu Here.

Siu & tall. Here and there.

Siubhal. A going, moving, walking.

Siubhalbhach A stroller, wayfaring-man.

Siubhal. A measure in music between fast and flow.

Siubhlach. Fleet, swift.

Siubhlaim. To walk, go, travel, depart, die.

Siuc. Dry, parched up.

Siucar. }
Siucra } Sugar.

Siudam. To swing, rock to sleep, to dandle, to nod.

Siulbhre. Chearfulness.

Siulmhaire. Delight.

Siulmhor. Bright, chearful, delightful.

Siunas. Lovage.

Siunsa. Sense.

Siur. A sister.

Siurdanadh. A rattling or making a noise.

Siurdanam. To rattle, make a noise.

Siurram. A sheriff.

Siurtach. A strumpet.

Siurtachd. Whoring.

Siurtag. A sudden sally or skipping.

Siurtagach. Frisky.

Siusan. A humming noise.

Siusarnadh. A whispering.

Siutharras. A wandering or strolling.

Slabhagan. A sort of edible sea-weed gathered from rocks, but different from dilse or duilliasg.

Slabhridh. A chain, a pot-hanger, a crook.

Slacairt. Beating as with a mallet.

Slacairam. To beat with a mallet.

Slacan. A beetle or bat.

Slacan-draoitheachd. A magical wand.

Slad. Theft.

Sladadh. Thievery, robbery.

Sladaighe. A thief, a robber.

Sladam, slaidam. To rob, steal.

Sladmharbham. To rob and murder on the highway.

Sladmhoir. }
Sladthoir. } A thief, a robber.

Sladmhoireachd. }
Sladuigeachd. } Robbery.

Sladthe. Robbed, ftripped.

Sladuire. } A thief.
Slaiteoir. }

Slaib. Mire on the ftrand or river's bank.

Slaibhre. A purchafe.

Slaibhreas. Chains.

Slaid. Theft, robbery.

Slaighe. Slaughter.

Slaighdean. A cough or cold.

Slaigham. To flay or kill.

Slaighre. A fword or fcymitar.

Slaim. Great booty.

Slainte. Health, falvation, a toaft or health.

Slainteamhuil. Healthy, falutary.

Slaiteoirachd. Thievery.

Slait, flatra. Strong, robuft.

Slam. A lock or flock of hair or wool.

Slamam. To draw and caid wool.

Slammam. } Curdled milk.
Slagan. }

Slamhan. An elm-tree.

Slamhagan. Locks.

Slamhach. A frothftick.

Slan. Healthy, found, entire.

Slan. A defiance, challenge. Vide Dubh-fhlan.

Slanaidheachd. A paffport.

Slanaigham. To heal, cure.

Slanaighthoir. A healer, faviour, faid of Jefus as the healer of the world.

Slanaghadh. Healing, faving.

Slanlus. Ribwort.

Slaod. A raft, float, a fledge.

Slaodam. To drag after, to flide.

Slaodan. A cough or cold, the rut of a wheel.

Sladrach. A hinge.

Slapach. Lukewarm.

Slapar A fkirt, the trail or train of a nobleman or king's robe.

Slaparach. Having long fkirts.

Slapaire. A floven.

Slapog. A flut or dirty woman.

Slas. Killing, flaughtering.

Slafaidheachd. } A private grudge.
Slafdachd. }

Slat. A rod, a yard.

Slatag. A twig.

Slataira. Straight, tall, ftately.

Slat-riogha. A fceptre, baton.

Slatbhroid. A goad.

Slat-mhara. Tangle.

Slat-mharcachd. A whip.

Slat-fhuaichiontas. A mace.

Slat-reul. An aftrolabe.

Slat-fhiul. A fail-yard.

Slat-iafgaich. A fifhing-rod.

Sleachd Vide Sliochd.

Sleachd-cuimhne. A monument.

Sleachdadh. A lancing, cutting, fcarifying.

Sleachdadh. } Kneeling, ftooping, bowing
Sleachdin. } reverently, adoration.

Sleachdam. To kneel, ftoop, bow reverently.

Sleachtam. To cut, diffect.

Sleagadh. Sneaking off, drawling.

Sleagach. Drawling.

Sleagaire. A drawler.

Sleagam. To fneak, drawl.

Sleagh. A fpear or lance.

Sleaghan. A fort of turf-fpade.

Sleaghach. Armed with a fpear.

Sleamhain. Smooth, flippery, plain.

Sleamhan, The elm tree.

Sleamhnan. Smoothnefs,, flipperinefs.

Sleamhnachd. Mucoufnefs.

Sleamhnaghadh. Slipping, fliding.

Sleamhnaigham. To flip, flide.

Sleamhnad, Slipperinefs.

Sleantach. A flake, a flice.

Sleas A mark, a fign; a fide, a ridge.

Sleafgadh. A crack.

Sleafgam. To crack.

Sleibh. Gen. of Sliabh.

Sleibthe. } Pl. of Sliabh.
Sleibhte. }

Sleibhteach. Mountainous.

Sleimhne. } Slipperiness, polish.
Sleimhneachd. }

Sleimhneach. Slipping.

Sleifs. The thigh.

Sleifde. Gen. of Sliafid.

Sleithe. A section, division.

Slethe. Cutting, striking.

Sleogam. To make sick or nauseate.

Sliabh. A mountain of the first magnitude, a heath land whether mountain or plain.

Sliabhaire. A mountaineer.

Sliachadairachd. Craft.

Sliachtadh. To pierce through.

Slias. } The thigh, the coarse part of a
Sliafaid. } thread.

Sliafparam. To daggle.

Sliafpairt. Daggling.

Slidach. Sly.

Slige, sligean. A shell.

Sligeanach. Sky-coloured, spotted.

Slighe. A way, a road.

Slighbhreac. Indifferency.

Slightheach. Sly, artful.

Sligheadoireachd. The practice of stratagems.

Slighthoireachd. Craftiness.

Slinn. A flat stone or tile.

Slinn. A weaver's sleay.

Slinnain. A shoulder, shoulder-blade.

Slinnteach. House-tiles.

Slintcrann. An ensign-staff.

Sliobham. To polish.

Sliobhram. To drag.

Sliobhtha. Sharp-pointed.

Sliobhtha. Polished, smoothed.

Sliobradh. A draught.

Sliochd. Seed, offspring, a tribe, descendants, posterity.

Sliocht. A troop, company, a rout, multitude.

Sliocht. A track, impression, print.

Slioge. A shell, a bomb.

Sliogeach. Full of shells.

Slioge creachuin. A scollopped shell which in antient times was used generally over the Highlands and Ireland as a drinking-cup, it is not yet out of fashion.

Slioge-neamhuin. Mother-of-pearl.

Slioge tomhais. The scales of a ballance.

Sliogam. To smooth, stroke.

Sliogard. A pumice.

Sliogarnach. Made of shells.

Sliom. Slim, sleek.

Sliommam. To flatter.

Sliomair, sliomfhear. A thief.

Slioncam. To beat.

Sliop. A lip.

Slios. A side, side of a county.

Sliofda. Fair, courteous, flattering.

Slis. } A chip, a lath, thin board.
Slifeog. }

Slifam. To slice.

Slifcheimnughadh. A digression.

Slifagaicham. To chip, slice.

Slifagan. Shavings.

Slifneach. Chips; scales.

Sliudhacach. } Horned.
Sliudhacanach. }

Sliughtheadh. A stratagem.

Sloch fine. A flake of snow.

Sloc. A pit, hollow.

Slocan. A little pit, hollow.

Sloc-guail. A coal-pit.

Slod. } A little standing water.
Slodan. }

Sloidhe. A section, division.

Sloighthe. Beaten, obbair sloighthe, beaten work.

Sloighreadh. A sword.

Sloinne. A firname, patronymic.

Sloinnam. To give a firname.

Slointe sios ann. Pointedly explained.

Sloitire. A thief, villain.

Sloitireachd. Villainy.

Sloitireach. Villainous.

Slomsliobh. Sharp.

Sluagh. An army, multitude, host.

Sluagh-coise. Infantry.

Sluagh-imirc. A marching army.

Sluaigheachd. An expedition.

Sluasaid.
Sluasghad. } A shovel.

Slucham. To stifle, overwhelm.

Sludhach
Sludhacan. } A horn.

Sludraighe.
Slaodrach. } A foundation.

Slugaire. A glutton, spendthrift.

Slugadh. The swallowing.

Slugaid. A slough, deep miry place.

Slugam. To swallow, devour.

Slugach. That swalloweth.

Slugthan.
Slugpholl. } A whirlpool.

Sluigain. The neck of a bottle.

Sluinn. A telling, declaring.

Slusam. To dissemble, counterfeit.

Smachd. Reproof, correction, awe, subjection, authority.

Smachda.
Smachdaighte. } Reproved, corrected.

Smachdaigham. To reprove, chastise, afflict.

Smachdaghadh.
Smachtadh. } Reproof, chastisement.

Smachdal. Authoritative, commanding.

Smachtbhann. A penal law, penalty.

Smachtlann. A house of correction.

Smadan. Soot, smut.

Smadanach. Smutted.

Smag A paw.

Smaig. Authority.

Smal
Smalan. } Dust, sorrowfulness, decay, obscurity, dimness.

Smalan. A hillock.

Small. Snuff of a candle.

Smallam. To snuff a candle, to blow up.

Smalladoir. Snuffers.

Smallog. A fillip.

Smaogal. A husk.

Smaolach. A thrush, an ouzle.

Smaosrach.
Smaostrach. } A cartilage, gristle.

Smarag. An emerald.

Smeacadh. A palpitation, panting.

Smeach. A neck, a fillip.

Smeach.
Smeachan. } The chin.

Smeanrachd. Groping.

Smear. Grease, tallow.

Smearadh. A greasing, unction.

Smearaim. To grease, anoint.

Smearthachd. Greasing.

Smeartha. Besmeared with grease, &c.

Smearthachan. A kitchen-brat, lickplate.

Smeathroid. A coal.

Smederneach. Slumber.

Smeid
Smeidag. } A nod, a wink.

Smeidadh. Nodding, winking, hissing.

Smeidach. One that winks.

Smeidam. To nod, beckon, wink, hiss.

Smeig
Smeigad. } The chin.
Smeigin.

Smeil. A pale, chill, ghastly look.

Smeilain. A poor, puny, pale creature.

Smeirne. A spit, broach.

Smeilag. A pale puny female.

Smeorach. A mavis, a linnet, name of a lap-dog.

Smeoradh. Anointing.

Smeorne. The point of a dart.

Smeorthoigh-theine. Firebrands.

Smeur. A blackberry, brambleberry.

Smeurach. Full of brambleberries.

Smid. Mum, not a syllable.

Smigeadach. A chincloth.

Smig.   } The chin, mirth.
Smigein. }

Smiol. Philomela.

Smior. Marrow, strength.

Smior caillaich. A poor puny fellow.

Smiot. An ear.

Smiot. A small portion of any thing.

Smiota. Of, belonging to the ear.

Smistam. To smite.

Smistin. A short thick stick.

Smodan   } Dirt, smut.
Smoiglcadh. }

Smogairneach. Large-boned.

Smoit. Sulkiness.

Smoitach. Sulky, techy.

Smol Snuff of a candle, coal, ember.

Smoladan.   }
Smoladair.   } Snuffers.
Smolghlantoir. }

Smot.   } A mouthful, a pluck.
Smotan. }

Smotan. A block, log, stock.

Smuaineadh. A thought, reflection.

Smuainam. To think, imagine, devise.

Smuaintughadh. Meditation.

Smuaintid. A thought, sentiment.

Smuaintigham. To think, consider.

Smuairain. Grief.

Smuais. In pieces, broken in shivers.

Smucil. Snoring.

Smudan. A ringdove, quest.

Smug Snot, spittle.

Smug na cumhag. Woodseare, cuckow spittle.

Smugadh. Spitting.

Smugam. To spit.

Smugaighil. Nose phlegm.

Smuid. Vapour, smoke.

Smuideamhuil. Smoky.

Smuidam. To smoke, exhale.

Smuigeadh. Filth, dirt.

Smuigeadach. A handkerchief.

Smuintigham. To imagine, think, design.

Smuintighe. Thought, imagination.

Smuir. A beak or snout.

Smuirnein. A mote.

Smuis. Sweat.

Smuit. A beak, snout.

Smur, smurach. Dust.

Smutach. Short-snouted.

Smutan. A block, log.

Snadhadh. Protection, defence.

Snadh. A sup.

Snadhghairm. An appellation, naming, appeal.

Snag. The hickup.

Snag.   } A woodpecker.
Snagardarach. }

Snagaighil. A stammering.

Snaglabhram. To stammer, hesitate in speech.

Snaidhadh. A cutting down, lopping, whetting.

Snaidham. To cut down, defalcate, lop, whet, to protect, defend, patronize.

Snaidhm. A knot, band.

Snaidhmcheanglam. To confederate.

Snaidhmam To knot, splice.

Snaighte. Cut, lopped.

Snaigheoireachd. Cutting chips.

Snaigheach.   }
Snagach.   } Creeping, crawling.
Snamhaighil. }

Snaigheam. } To creep, crawl.
Snagam.   }

Snagan. A slow creeping motion.

Snaggan. A short drink or draught.

Snaimias. A rout, multitude.

Snamh. Swimming.

Snamhaiche. A swimmer.

Snamhaim. To swim, float.

Snamhluath. Swift in swimming.

Snamhuighill. Floating.

Snamhan. Slow swimming or sailing.

Snaoi. A bier.

Snaoir. A slice.

                          Snaoisin.

Snaoifin. Snuff, powder.

Snaoifinadh. Calcination.

Snaoifinam. To reduce to powder.

Snapam. To pull the trigger of a gun.

Snapach. That fireth, ftriketh faft.

Snas. Decency, elegancy, colour.

Snafadh. Analyfis, analizing.

Snafam. To analize.

Snafmhor. Neat, elegant.

Snafta. Brave, gallant.

Snaftu. Colour.

Snath. Thread, line.

Snatha. An eafing, riddance of pain, grief, trouble.

Snathad. A needle.

Snathadachan. A needle-cafe.

Snathaim. To fup.

Snathfuaidhail. Pack-thread.

Sneachd. Snow.

Sneachda. Snowy.

Sneagh. A nit.

Sneaghach. Full of nits.

Sneigh. Straight, direct.

Sneigh. Little, fmall.

Sneigh. Sadnefs, forrow, vexation.

Snig. Vide Sneagh.

Snidhe. A drop, drops of rain through the roof of a houfe; a tear.

Snidham. To drop, diftil, let in water.

Snidhach. That droppeth.

Snightheach. Creeping.

Sniomh. Spinning, twifting, winding.

Sniomham. To fpin, twift, wind.

Sniomhain. Curling, that curleth, helical.

Sniomha. A fpindle.

Sniomhare. A wimble.

Sniofiot. They encountered.

Snifin. Snuff.

Sno. Vifage, appearance.

Snodhach Sap, juice.

Snoidheadoir. A hewer.

Snoighte. Hewn, chipped, pleafant, decent.

Snoigham. To hew, chip.

Snuadh. A river, brook.

Snuadh. Hair of the head, hue, colour, appearance

Snuadhmhor. Well-looked.

Snuadham. To flow, ftream.

Snuadhchlais. The channel of a river.

Snuot. An ear.

So. This, this here.

So. In compound words, fignifies goodnefs, or aptnefs, or eafy, equal to the Englifh termination Ble.

So Young.

Soaclach. Eafy.

Soadh. A bed.

Soadh, fodh. An eclipfe.

Soadhbharaigheachd. Towardnefs.

Soailce. A good fafhion.

Soainmhne. Vegetable.

So-airamh. Countable.

Soalt. A good leap.

So-aomidh. Flexible, exorable.

Soas. Experience.

Sobha. Sorrel.

Sobha-craobh. Rafberries.

So-bhintighte. Coagulable.

Sobha-talmhuin. Strawberries.

Sobholadh. A fweet fmell, fragrance.

Sobholtanachd. Fragrancy.

Sobhlafda. Savoury.

Sobhogtha. Moveable, pliable.

Sobhrach Primrofe.

Sobhrifde. Frangible.

Sobhuailtach. Eafy to ftrike.

Soc. A plough-fhare, a beak, fnout, chin.

Socach. Having a fnout, beak.

Socair. Eafe, reft, mildnefs.

Socarach. Eafy, quiet, mild, fmooth, plain, equal.

Socamhuil. Reft, eafe.

Socamhlach. Eafy, mild.

Socan, focin. Dim. of Soc.

5

Sochaidh.

Sochaidh. } An army, hoft, multitude.
Sochuidh.

Sochairde. Good friends.

Sochairdeas. Friendfhip.

Sochar. Profit, emolument, an obliging deed, a favour.

Socharach. Yielding profit, obliging.

Sochafta. Handy, manageable.

Sochd. Silence.

Sochdar, focarach. Stayed, fedate.

So-chiuinuicham. Eafy to appeafe.

So-chiuinuighte. Placable.

Sochla. Fame, reputation, renown.

Sochlairthe. Parted, divided.

Sochlaochloidh. } Changeable, convertible.
Sochloidh.

Sochlaonadh. Towardnefs.

Sochluintin. Audible, eafy to be heard.

Sochinhoi. Abftemious.

Sochobhaifte. Conformable.

Sochoduighte. Addible.

Sochomhraidhe. } Affable.
Sochomhraidhte.

Sochomhthodha. Convertible.

Sochonradh. Cheapnefs.

Socra, focras. Eafe, tranquillity.

Socrughadh, Quieting, affuaging, comfort.

Sochraid. A multitude of people.

Sochraide, fochairde. Friends.

Sochramhte. Digeftible.

Sochroidheach. Kind, good-natured.

Socraigham. To mitigate, affuage, quiet, calm, appeafe.

Sochuidhe. A number, multitude of people, an affembly.

Sochumte. Mouldable.

Socul Eafe, tranquillity.

Sodal. Vide Sotal.

Sodan Joy

Sodanach. Joyful, glad.

Sodarnach. Able to trot, ftrong and found for marching.

Sodar. A trotting.

Sodaram. } To trot.
Sodram.

Sodarthoir. A trotter.

Sodh. A burning, winding, changing.

Sodhaing. Still, quiet.

Sodhan. Profperous.

Sodham. To turn.

Sodhoirte. Apt to pour out, free in talking.

Sodhochanta. Damageable.

Sodhraife. Eafy to fhut.

Sodheanta. Eafy to be done, poffible.

Sodhearbhtha. Evincible.

Sodhionta. Defenfible.

Sofais. Vegetative, apt to grow.

Sofhaigfeach. } Vifible, apparent.
Sofhaicfinach.

Sofhaotin. Acquirable, impetrable.

Sofar. } Strong, ftout.
Soforaith.

Sofhirinachadh. Juftifiable.

Sofholach. Concealable.

Sogh. Profperity, delicacy, eafe, pleafure, fumptuoufnefs.

Soghamhuil. } Pleafant, cheaiful.
Soghan.

Soghmhor. } Sumptuous, profperous.
Soghach.

Soghchu. A greyhound.

Soghda. Provocation.

Soghiulan. Portable.

Soghlacaighte. Acceptable, agreeable.

Soghluaifte. Moveable, tractable, wavering.

Saghnaidh. Fair, comely.

Soghnuifeas. Comelinefs, beauty.

Soghointe. Vulnerable.

Soghradhach. Acceptable, a primrofe.

Soghraidham. To love exceedingly.

Soghfur. Fatnefs.

Soib. The hand.

Soibheufach. Well bred.

Soibh.

Soibh. For So, in compounds beginning with vowels.

Soibhfgeul. The gofpel.

Soibhfgeulaiche. An evangelift.

Soibhfgeulam. To preach the gofpel.

Soicead. A focket.

Soiche. Until.

Soicheadfaghach. Senfible.

Soichearnfa. Liberality, generofity.

Soicheal. Joy, mirth.

Soicham. To reach, arrive.

Soi-chinealta. Noble, high-born.

Soi-chinealtas. Nobility, noblenefs.

Soichle. Pleafure, mirth, gladnefs.

Soichreidche. } Credible.
Sochreidfin. }

Sochreidmheach. A credulous perfon.

Soidheach. A veffel.

Soidealach. Rude, ignorant.

Soighdeoir. A foldier, archer

Soighdiurtha. Exercifed in military difci-pline, brave.

Soighead. A dart, arrow, fhaft.

Soigheam. A precious ftone or gem.

Soighne. } Pleafure, delight.
Soighneas. }

Signhne. } A thunder-bolt, flafh of light-
Soighnein. } ning.

Soighnidh. To do good.

Soighnean gaoithe. A blaft, puff.

Soighniomhach. A benefactor.

Soighnifam. To do good.

Soilbheim. A flafh or bolt of light, a thunder-bolt.

Soilbhir. Happy, chearful

Soilbhire. } Chearfulnefs, good hu-
Soilbhireachd. } mour.

Soilbheachd. A jeft.

Soileaghta. Fufible.

Soileas. Officioufnefs.

Soileafach. Officious.

Soilfeachd. A charm.

Soilleir. Clear, manifeft.

Soilleirachd. Clearnefs, perfpicuity.

Soilleiruigham. To manifeft, clear, ex-plain, dilucidate.

Soilleirfe. An axiom.

Soilioftair. Vide Seilifdair.

Soillear. A cellar.

Soilleog. A willow, fallow.

Soillfe. Brightnefs, clearnefs.

Soillfeach. Bright, clear.

Soillfaghadh. Brightening.

Solllfigham. To fhine, brighten.

So-iomchar. Tolerable, portable.

Soimhianngha. Defireable.

So-impoighte. Convertible.

Soin. A found.

Soin For Sin, that, o fhin, from thence.

Soinas Sulkinefs.

Soinchearb. Synalaepha.

Soinean. } Fair weather, i. e. So-fhion,
Soinneann. } chearfulnefs, gaiety.

Soineannta. Meek, well tempered, plea-fant.

Soinam. To found, make a noife.

Soinine. Gen. of Soinean.

Soinmheach. Happy, fortunate.

Soinneach. A race-horfe.

Soinnion. A blaft.

Soinnfidh. Effable.

Soipin. A handful, wifp.

Soir, fhoir. The eaft.

Soirbh. Affable, eafy, pliable, profperous.

Soirbhigham. To profper, fucceed.

Soirbhaghadh. Profpering.

Soirbhas. Profperity, fuccefs, a fair wind.

Soirbheachd. Affability.

Soirbhrifte. Ductile.

Soirche. Clear, manifeft, bright.

Soircheacht. Brightnefs.

Soireidh. Convenient, agreeable.

Soircubthachd. Brittlenefs.

Soireann. Serenity, mildnefs, pleafantnefs, chearfulnefs.

Soireannta, Serene, mild, pleafant.

Soirin. Eaftern.
Soirnliach A baker's peel.
Soirthe Readinefs.
So rthe na cloine The womb
Soifgeul. The gofpel.
Soifgculadh Good news, tidings.
Soifgeulaidhe. An evangclift.
Soifciod Even unto.
Soifil. Proud, haughty.
Soifhinte. Ductile, pliable.
Soifhion Freedom, privilege.
Soifior Younger
Soifle. Brightnefs.
Soiflen. A fhining.
Soiftean. A good habitation, refidence.
So-ithte Edible.
Soithe Till, until.
Soitham Vide Soicham.
Soitheach A veffel, pitcher.
Soithleag. A circle.
Soitheamh. } Comely, gentle, pliable.
Soithidh
Soithearthe. The youngeft.
Soithinneach. Defirous
Soithnuigham. To allure.
Sol Ere, before.
Solabhra. Affable, exorable.
Solaitheach. Venial.
Solamh Quick, ready.
Solamhrachdich. Tangible.
Solar. A provifion, providing.
Solaraim To provide, prepare.
Solas, folus A round ball thrown into the air in honour of the fun, but it now means a coit.
Solas. Comfort, confolation, vaft pleafure; applied to the intellects.
Solafach. Comfortable, full of pleafure.
Solafaim. To comfort, confole
Solafda Bright, luminous.
Solafdach.
Solafmhaire. } Brightnefs.
Solafmhor. Luminous.

Solathar. A provifion, earning.
Solathraim. To provide, prepare.
So-leabhtha Legible.
So-leaghta. Colliquable
So-leighas Curable, medicable.
So-leonta. Vulnerable
Soll. Bait to catch fifh with.
Sollain. A welcome
Sollus. Light
Sollufta. Lighted.
Sollamuin Solemnity.
Sollamunta. Solemn, folemnized.
Sollamuntachd. Solemnization.
So loghtha. Venial, pardonable.
So-loghthachd. Pardonablenefs, flightnefs of a fault.
So-lubidh. Flexible.
So-lubteachd Flexibility.
Soma. A flock of fwans.
Somalta. Bulky, eafy, gentle.
Somaltachd. Negligence.
So-mharbhtha. Mortal.
So-mharbhthachd. Mortality.
Somharcin. A primrofe.
Somhlan. Safe and found.
So-mhuinte. Tractable.
Sompla. A pattern.
Son. Sake, caufe, account of
Son. A voice, found.
Son. A word.
Son. Tall.
Son. Good, profit, advantage.
Son. A ftake, beam
Son, fonn. Here.
Sonadh. Happy, bleffed, profperous.
Sonairte. Strength, courage.
Sonas. Happinefs, blifs, profperity.
Sonann. Fertile land, profperous foil.
Sonn. A club, ftaff.
Sonn. A hero.
Sonnach A wall, a caftle.
Sonnadh Contention, ftrife.
Sonnmharcach. A courier on horfeback.

[4 O]   Sonnaim.

Sonnaim. To pierce through, to thruft, to opprefs.

Sonnta. Bold, couragious.

Sonntach. Vide Sundach.

Sonntachd. Boldnefs, confidence.

Sonrach. } Special, particular
Sonradhach. }

Sonradhachd. Efpecalty, feveralty.

Sonraic. Righteous

Sonraichte. Particular.

Sonraigham To particularize, fignalize.

Sontach. Bold, merry.

So-oibruighte. Figurable.

Sop. A wifp, handful, bundle, the top or creft of a hen or other bird.

Sopan A little wifp.

Soplach. A wifp of ftraw

Sopar. A well.

Sop-reic. A tavern-fign.

Sor. To hefitate.

Sora. Soap.

Soraideadh. Salutation.

Soridh. Bleffing, farewel, compliments.

So-riaghlighte. Governable.

So raonuighte. Eligible.

So-reamhraighte. Coagulable.

So-rainnte. Divifible.

Soridh. Happy, fuccefsful.

Sorb A fault, blemifh, foul, dirty.

Sorbam. To pollute, defile.

Sorb-aorachas. A lampoon, fatire.

Sorbcharn. A dunghill.

Sorca, forcha. Light.

Sorcha. A woman's name. Lat. Clara.

Sorchaghadh. A manifeftation, clear declaration.

Sorchaigham. To manifeft, make clear.

Sorchaineadh A fatire, lampoon.

Sorchan. A little ftool or eminence.

Sorchan-leighidh A gawntree.

Sorcoir. A cylinder.

Soird. Order, thriftinefs.

Sordal Thrifty.

2

Sorn. A flue of a kiln or oven; a fnout

Sornach. Long-chinned.

Sornaireachd. The baker's trade, baking.

Sornam To forn.

Sornan. A tump, hillock.

Sornan. A fkate-fifh.

Sorn-raca. An oven-rake or fwoop.

Sort. A fpecies, fort.

Sortan. Praife.

Sorthan. Reproof.

Sorthan Profperity.

Soruaifleaghadh. Contempt.

Soruite. Parted, divided.

Sos. Knowledge.

Sos. A ceffation, giving over.

Sofi. Civil behaviour.

Sofir. The younger, youngeft.

Sofciodh Even to.

So-fgoilte. Fiffible.

So-fharuighte. Conquerable.

So-fdiuridh. Governable.

So-fheachanta. Avoidable.

So-fgaolte. Diffoluble.

So-fhamhlaghadh. Application.

So-fhamhluighte. Applicable.

So-threobhach. Arable.

So-thollidh. Borable.

So-theitheach. Ceffible.

So-fheolta. Navigable.

Softa. An abode, habitation.

Softan. A noife, cry.

Softanach. Clamorous.

Sotal. Pride, flattery.

Sotalach. Proud, arrogant, fawning, flattery.

Sotalaigham. To boaft, brag, flatter.

Sotla. Pride, arrogance.

Soth. Offspring.

Soth. Luxury.

Sothamhuil. Luxurious.

Sothamlachd. Epicurifm.

Sothaire. A fpruce fellow.

So-thaofgi. Exhauftible, eafily drained.

So-tharrangtha

So-tharrangtha. Eafily drawn.

So-theagafgte. Docile.

Sotlaige. Harm, damage.

Sotlaigh. Bad, naughty.

Sotinge. A judge.

So-thuigfiona. Intelligible.

So thuigthe. Senfible.

So-uinfughidh. That may be wielded.

So-uifgeamhuil. Moift, waterifh.

Spad. A clod, flat, dead.

Spadach. Full of clods.

Spad, fpadhad. A fpade.

Spadag. A fillip.

Spadal. A paddle, a plough-ftaff.

Spalim. To knock in the head, knock down, to fell.

Spadlanta. Mean, niggardly.

Spadantachd. Sluggifhnefs, niggardlinefs.

Spadchofach. Flat-nofed.

Spadchlufach. Flat-eared.

Spadphluicach. Blub-cheeked.

Spag. A claw, a club-foot.

Spagach. Having claws, club-footed.

Spagaire. An aukward club-footed fellow.

Spagaire-tuinn. The bird called a little grebe.

Spaid. A clod.

Spaid. Heavy, dull, unfruitful, infipid.

Spaidhair. The pocket-hole of a petticoat.

Spaidthalamh. Unfertile ground.

Spaideamhuil. Sluggifh.

Spaideamhlachd. Sluggifhnefs.

Spaidthion. Dead or flat wine.

Spaidam. To benumb.

Spaidthinnas. Lethargy.

Spaig. A lame leg.

Spailleadh. A check, abufe.

Spailp. Notable.

Spailpin. A rafcal.

Spain. A fpoon.

An Spain. Spain.

Spairn. A log of wood.

Spairn. An effort, wreftling.

Spairnachd. Wreftling.

Spairnam. To wreftle.

Spairt. A turf, clod, a fplafh of water.

Spairtam. To fplafh.

Spaifdeoirachd. Walking.

Spaiftram. } To walk about.
Spaiftrigham. }

Spal. A weaver's fhuttle.

Spalag. The cod or hufk of peafe or beans.

Spalla. A wedge, a pinning in building; the fragment of a ftone or wall.

Spallam. To beat, ftrike.

Spalpaire. A fpruce fellow.

Spalpam. To obtrude.

Sparaig. The bit of a bridle.

Sparan, fporan. A purfe, pouch, he fcrotum.

Sparan. A crifping-pin.

Sparn. A quarrel, wreftle.

Sparnam. To difpute, quarrel, wreftle.

Sparnaidheachd. Wreftling, quarreling.

Sparnpupa. A champion, chief-wreftler.

Sparr. A joift.

Sparra. A fpar, nail.

Sparram. To faften, drive a nail, to rivet, to enforce an argument.

Sparran-doruis. The bolt of a door, a doornail.

Sparfan. A dew-lap.

Spart. A clod.

Sparthhlucach. Blub-cheeked.

Spe. Froth.

Speal. A fcythe, mowing-hook.

Speal. A little while.

Spealadoir. A mower.

Spealaire. One that cutteth faft.

Spealadoireachd. Mowing.

Spealam. To cut, mow.

Spealanta. Acute, cutting, ready fpoken.

Spealantachd. Acutenefs.

Spealg. A fplinter.

Spealgach.

Spealgach.   Splinters.

Spealgadh   Cutting, splitting, shiving.

Spealgim. } To split, shive.
Spealtam. }

Spealtain.   Shavings.

Spearthach   A sort of fetter for cattle.

Speic. } A bar, spar, prop, stroke.
Speice. }

Speicam.   To put bars, to strike.

Specialta   Especial, peculiar

Spcicleir   Spectacles, glasses.

Speid.   A great river-flood; a being busy.

Speidal.   Busy, industrious.

Speidalachd.   Notableness.

Speil.   Cattle.

Speilagraicham.   To climb.

Speilp   A belt, armour.

Speir.   The ham, hough, pl. Speirthacha.

Speir, speur.   The sky, firmament.

Speir. } A sparrow-hawk.
Speirge. }

Speirag.   A slender-limbed female creature.

Speireach.   Slender-limbed

Speis.   A liking, fondness, attachment.

Speisal.   Fond, cleanly.

Speisalachd   Fondness, cleanliness.

Speur   The sky, firmament.

Speurgha.   Belonging to the sky.

Speurghlan.   Fair weather.

Spice.   A spike, long nail.

Spialam.   To pull asunder.

Spialadair.   Pincers.

Spid.   Spite, malice.

Spiddeal.   A spital or hospital.

Spideamhuil.   Spiteful.

Spideamhlachd.   Contempt, reproachfulness.

Spideog.   A nightingale, Philomela.

Spidshuileach.   Purblind

Spigeam.   To mock, scoff.

Spile.   A wedge.

Spinan, sprionan   A gooseberry-bush

Spiochog.   A purse or bag.

Spiochan.   A wheezing in the throat

Spiod.   An affront, reproach.

Spiodam.   To reproach.

Spionadh.   Motion, action.

Spionadach.   A little stirring.

Spionadh.   Pulling, plucking.

Spionam   To pluck, pull, spoil.

Spionnadh.   Strength, force

Spiontag.   Currants.

Spiorad.   A spirit.

Spioradalta.   Spiritual.

Spiorthacha.   Pl. of Speir, a ham, hough

Spios.   Pl. of Spiosra, spice.

Spiothog.   A small stone, such as one cast at an object.

Spiothoire.   A spy, scout.

Spiothoireachd.   Spying.

Spiris.   A sort of hammock.

Spirlin.   Chance.

Spirsog.   A sparrow-hawk.

Spiulgan.   Picking.

Spiullam.   To pick or shell, to decorticate

Spiunadh.   Strength.

Spiunam.   To stir up, examine.

Splanc. } A sparkle, blaze, flash of fire.
Splancradh. }

Splancam.   To sparkle, blaze, flash

Splancadan   Snot.

Spleadh. } Flattery, dependance, boasting, vain-glory, exploits.
Spleadhachas. }

Spleadhach.   Flattering, fabulous, verbose.

Spliuchan.   A bladder, purse, tobacco pouch.

Spocham.   To rob.

Spochaim.   To provoke, affront

Spogach   Vide Spagach

Spodhla. } A joint of meat, a fragment.
Spolla. }

Spol.   A weaver's shuttle.

Spoldaich,

Spoldaich. Slain bodies.

Spolla laoigh. A loin of veal.

Sponc. Tinder, spunge.

Sponog. A spoon.

Spor A spur, a gun-flint, a talon.

Sporach. Having spurs or claws.

Sporam. To spur, stir on.

Spors. Sport, derision.

Sporsal. Sportful.

Sporsalachd. Sportfulness.

Spotham. To geld, castrate.

Spothadair. A gelder.

Spracadh. ⎫ Strength, vigour, exertion,
Spraic.   ⎭ sprightliness.

Spraical. Strong, active.

Spraicalachd Activity, exertion.

Spraid. A blast, puff.

Spre. A sparkle, flash of fire.

Spre.   ⎫ Cattle, herd, the portion of a
Spreidh. ⎭ new married wife.

Spreaghadh. Stirring up, provocation, reproof.

Spreagaim. To blame, chide, reprove, prompt, to press, enforce any thing.

Spreaghadh. A sudden burst or blow.

Spreigham. To scatter, dismiss, to lunge, to burst suddenly.

Spreidhte. Dispersed, scattered.

Spreilleach. Blubber-lipped.

Spreote. A useless thing, a fragment, a drone, idler.

Sprineog. A pebble.

Sprios. A twig or wicker.

Spriosan. A small twig.

Spriuchar. A sting.

Spriumhacan A budget, satchel.

Spriunan. Currant or corinth.

Spro nd. Sadness.

Sprogaille Dewlap, a craw.

Sproth. A sprat.

Spruille   ⎫
Spruileach. ⎬ Crumbs, fragments.
Sprunnan.   ⎭

Spruan. Brushwood.

Spruisal. Neat, spruce.

Spruisalachd. Neatness, spruceness.

Spuaic. Callosity, pinnacle of a tower, pettishness.

Spuilin.   ⎫ Plunder.
Spuincadh. ⎭

Spuinam. To plunder.

Spuinadair. A plunderer.

Spuinc. A claw.

Spuise. A pocket.

Spuirse. Spurge, milkweed.

Spursan. A gizzard, giblets.

Sput. An eunuch; hog wash, a word of contempt for bad drink, a spout.

Sputam. To spout.

Srabh. Much, plenty, diffusion.

Srabhan. Superfluity.

Srabhach. Plentiful, squandering.

Sracadh. A young twig, shoot, sucker; a rent, a thrust.

Sracaire. An extortioner.

Sracaireachd. Extortion, tearing away.

Sracaireach. Given to extortion or tearing.

Sracanta. Oppressive, tearing.

Sracam. To tear, pull, rob, spoil.

Srad.   ⎫ A spark of fire.
Sradag. ⎭

Sradaidhe. Idle.

Sradaidheachd. Idleness.

Sradam. To sparkle.

Sraid, sraidin. A street; a lane.

Sraideog. A mat.

Sraiden. A lane.

Sraidin. The herb Shepherd's pouch.

Sraidmachd. Walking abroad.

Srait. A tax or fine.

Sraith. A layer, course, line or swath of hay cut down by the mower.

Sraith. The quartering of soldiers.

Sraith, srath. A bottom or valley, the side of a valley on the banks of a river, marshy grounds.

Sramh. A jet of milk gushing from a cow's udder.

Srann A snoring.

Srannam. To snore, make a snoring noise.

Srannartich. Snorting.

Srannan A great hoarseness, or rattling in the throat.

Srannan seididh. A sort of whirlgig.

Sraodr, sraoth A sneezing

Sraodham. To sneeze.

Sraoileag. A dirty huffey, flovenly woman, quean.

Sraoilleam. To tear.

Sraoilleanach. A scullion.

Sraoin. A huff.

Sraoinais. Huffingly.

Sraonadh. The impetus of one walking fast.

Sraonam. To turn, scatter.

Srath. A tax, general fine.

Srath. The bottom of a valley, fields on the banks of a river, a Srath, vide Sraith.

Srathac. Abounding in Sraths.

Srathair. A pack-saddle, straddle.

Srathaire. A stroller.

Sratham.
Srathaigham. } To tax, assess.

Sread. A herd, troop, flock.

Sreadaidhe. A herdsman.

Sreadaigheacha. Herding.

Sreamh. A stream, a spring.

Streamham. To flow.

Srean. A wheezing.

Sreang. A string, cord.

Sreangach. Stringed

Sreangam. To draw, extend, to tear.

Sreangtart. A load-stone.

Sreangthartach· An opprobrious word for a thin raw-boned fellow.

Sreath. A row, swath, rank, order, class.

Sreathaigham. To put in rows.

Sreathal. That is in rows.

Sreathnaighte. Spread, scattered.

Sreathnaigham. To wet, moisten, to extend.

Sreinglion. A casting net.

Srian. A bridle, restraint.

Srianam. To bridle, check, pull down an enemy.

Sruitan. A long and quick repetition of news or poetry.

Sro. Vide Stro.

Srobadh. A push, thrust.

Sroghall. A whip, rod.

Sromeadach. A handkerchief.

Sroineifeach. Snorting.

Sroiniall-freine. Mufrol.

Srol. Sattin, silk, gauze, or cyprus.

Srolgha, sroil. Of or belonging to Srol.

Sron. The nose, a promontory.

Sronagraigham. To smell.

Sronagrich. Smelling.

Sronamhuil. Nasal.

Sronfaith. Grunting.

Sroth. A stream.

Srothan. A brook. rivulet.

Srothfurtach Sneezing.

Srotham. To flow. Vide Srutham

Srothfhaobha. A gulph, whirlpool.

Sruamach. A meeting of streams.

Sruban. A drawing or sucking in.

Scrubadh. Inhaustus.

Srubam. Inhaurio, to snuff.

Siudhar. In small pieces.

Sruich. A speech.

Sriuth. Knowing, discerning.

Sruth. A stream.

Sruthan. A streamlet, brook, rivulet.

Sruthach. Full of streams.

Sruth. A man in religious orders, a clerk, a man of letters.

Srutham. To stream, flow, pour, derive.

Sruthanach. Full of streamlets.

Sruthchlais. A brook, channel.

Sruthladh. Rinsing, cleansing.

Sruthlam. To rinfe, cleanfe.

Sruthfhleach. Channel of a river.

Sta. Stand.

Sta. Ufe.

Stabha. A veffel.

Stabhaigham. To ftraddle.

Stabham. To ftave.

Stabhach. Afunder, wide-forked.

Stabul. A ftable.

Stac. A ftake.

Stacan. A thorn.

Staccadh. A ftack.

Staccan. A little ftack.

Stacach. Deaf.

Stad. A ftop, delay, hindrance, period.

Stadaighil. A ftanding ftill.

Stadam. To ftand, ftop, ftay.

Stadh. The ftays of a fhip.

Stadthach. Apt to ftop.

Staduid. A ftatute.

Staid. A craft, wile.

Staid. A furlong.

Staid. State, condition.

Staidhg, fteig. } The gullet or wind-
Staidhg bhraghad. } pipe.

Staidal. } Stately, portly.
Staidmhor. }

Staidamhlachd. } Statelinefs, portlinefs.
Staidmhorachd. }

Staidhair. } A ftair, ftep.
Staighre. }

Stail. A throw.

Stailadh. Stile, title.

Stailc. A ftop, impediment, ftubborn-
nefs.

Stain, ftainadh. Latten, tin.

Staipal. A ftopper.

Stair, fdair. Hiftory.

Stairiceach. Light.

Stairfeach. Threfhold.

Stairtheoir. An hiftorian.

Stal. A ftallion.

Stalacach. That ftareth.

Stalacaire. A fowler, gazer.

Stalacam. To ftare, gaze.

Stalcadh. Growing ftiff.

Stalcadair. Stiffening, ftarch.

Stalcam. To ftiffen.

Stalda. Stale, warm drink.

Stallam. To make drink lukewarm.

Stalic. A thump.

Stalicam. To thump.

Stalin. Steel.

Stam. To ftand.

Stamh. Tangle; the ifle of Staffa.

Stamha. A vafe.

Stamnidh. Manageable, pliable

Stang. A ditch.

Stanna. A tub, vat.

Stannart. Stint, a yard wand, a yard.

Staoig. A collop, ftake, a piece.

Staon. Awry, oblique.

Staonadh. Bias, bending, inclination

Staonaim. To decline, abftain.

Staonard. A creek in the neck.

Stapal. A link, torch.

Staplan. Noife of the fea.

Starbhanach. Firm, fteady.

Stargha. A fhield.

Stat. Pride, haughtinefs.

Statamhuil. Proud, ftately.

Statamhlachd. Statelinefs.

Steach, afteach. Within.

Steacham. To enter.

Steaffag. A ftaff, ftick, club.

Steall· A fhot of water from a fquirt, or
otherwife.

Steallach. That fquirteth.

Steallam. To fquirt, fprinkle.

Steallair. A fyringe, fquirt.

Stearnal. A bittern.

Snearnal tigh ofd. An innkeeper's fign.

Steic. Vide Staidhg.

Steic-bhraghad. The wind-pipe.

Steighe. A foundation.

Steilin. A gawntree.

Steileach.

Steileach. Laxative, loose.

Steille. A lax, loosenefs.

Steinle. The itch, mange.

Steinligham. To exulcerate.

Stiall. A ftreak, ftripe.

Stiallach. Striped, in ftripes.

Stiallam. To make in ftripes, to rend in pieces or fhreds.

Sticin. A little ftaff or club.

Stillam. To divide.

Stim. A hair-lace, fnood.

Stinleog. Hinge of a trunk.

Stiobhard. A fteward.

Stioram. To benumb.

Stirrin. A fturgeon.

Stiuram. Vide Sdiuram.

Stobam. To ftab.

Stobham. To ftew.

Stoc. A founding horn, a trumpet.

Stoc. A ftock, root, poft, or pillar.

Stoc leapa. The bed-fide.

Stoc, ftoc luinge. A gunwale.

Stocaire. A trumpeter.

Stoca. A wallet-boy, one that runs at a horfeman's foot.

Stoca. A ftocking.

Stocaigham. To grow ftiff or numb.

Stocach. An idler about the kitchen of great folks, and will not work for fub-fiftence.

Stoich. Funk, ftink.

Stoid. Sulks, pet.

Stoir. Stepping ftones.

Stoirm Storm.

Stoirmal.
Stoirmach. } Stormy.

Stoite. Prominent.

Stol. A ftool, feat.

Stolda. Steady, at leifure.

Stonta. A tub, vat.

Stor.
Storas. } Store, ammunition.

Storafach. Full of ftores.

3

Stothfhronach. Having a camois nofe, crook-nofed.

Strabaid. A proftitute.

Strac. A ruler to meafure grain in a difh, a ftripe, ftreak.

Stracam. To rule, meafure a difh by drawing the rule along the brim.

Strach. An arch, vault.

Straic. Pride.

Straical. Proud.

Straicain. A truncheon.

Straif. A floe-bufh.

Straighlich. The rattling of arms or other implements.

Straill.
Straille. } Delay, neglect.

Straille. A carpet, a mat.

Straillam. To pluck, tear in pieces.

Strangadh. Plucking, twitching.

Strangam. To pull, draw.

Stranglaim. To pull, twitch.

Strangtha. Pulled, plucked.

Strangadh.
Strangaireachd } Strife, contention, lazinefs.

Strangaire. A lazy fellow.

Strantrich. Snorting.

Straoidhach. Prodigal, wafteful.

Straoileadh. A flut, floven.

Straoileog. A drag-tail.

Straoidham. To wafte, fquander.

Straoidhair. A wafter, or prodigal one.

Straoilam. To pull, draw after.

Straoithal.
Straithlidh. } Noife.

Strath. The ftay betwixt the top-maft and fore-maft, by which it is fupported.

Strathnaigham. To fpread.

Streachla. A trifle.

Streachtan.
Streachlan. } A band, a garter.

Streachla. Torn, rent, ripped.

Streachlaghadh. Sport.

Strillin. A garter.

Streap. } Strife, insurrection, skir-
Streapag. } mish.

Stribrid } A whore, a harlot.
Strioboid }

Strioc. A streak.

Striocach. Streaked.

Striocam. To fall, submit, strike, to be humbled.

Striolla. A girth.

Striopach A whore, prostitute.

Striopachas. Fornication.

Striopachamhuil. Whorish.

Stro Prodigality.

Stroda. A strand, a shore.

Stroic A shive, piece.

Stroicam. To tear, cut off.

Stroidham To squander, waste.

Stroidhair. A squanderer, waster.

Strothamhuil. Prodigal.

Strothamhlachd. Prodigality.

Stroighin. Cement, mortar.

Stroill, straill. Delay.

Struth. } An ostrich.
Struthchamhull. }

Stuacach. Gruff, boorish.

Stuadh. A sheet, a scroll.

Stuadh } A gable, a pinnacle, a ridge.
Stuaidh. }

Stuadhbhraghdeach. Stiff-necked.

Stuaic A little hill or round promontory.

Stuaim. Device, air, mien.

Stumach. } Modest, temperate.
Stumadh. }

Stuamachd. Moderation.

Stucach. Stiff, rigid, horned.

Stucaire Shot-free.

Stucan. A little hill jutting out from another.

Stuidear. A student.

Stuideartha. } Studious.
Stuidearthach. }

Stuidaradh. Study.

Stuircin. A crest.

Stuirt. Huffiness, pride.

Stuirtal. Stately, proud.

Stuirtalachd. Stateliness, pride.

Stumpe. A post, stump.

Stur. Dust.

Sturach. Uneven.

Sturric. Summit of a hill, pinnacle.

Stuth. Stuff, matter or substance, corn.

Suabh. Mannerly, well-bred, mild.

Suabhais. Mildness, gentleness.

Suachgan. } An earthen pot.
Suacan. }

Suadh. Prudent, discreet.

Suadh. Counsel, advice.

Suadh A learned man.

Suadidh. Moving.

Suaichiontas. Vide Suaithchiontas.

Suaigh. Prosperous, successful.

Suaill. Small, little, mean.

Suaillmheasta. Homely, ordinary.

Suaim. A tone, accent.

Suaimhnas. Rest, quietness, pleasure.

Suaimhneach. Quiet, calm, safe, pleasant.

Suaimhnaicham. To please, charm.

Suaimhneasach. Full of pleasure.

Suain. Sleep, deep sleep; Sweden.

Suainartarch. That sleepeth heavy or fast, soundly.

Suairc. Civil, facetious, kind, affable.

Suanam. To sleep.

Suarcas. Facetiousness, affability, kindness, mirth, urbanity.

Suaissinam. To lay with the face up, to lay supine.

Suaite. Kneaded, mixed.

Suaiteachd. A tempering or mixing together, fatigue.

Suaithchiontas. A flag, colour, ensign, standard, an escutcheon.

Suaitheantais. A prodigy, portent.

Suaithreach. A soldier.

Sual. A wonder.

Suall. Famous, renowned.

Suan. Sleep, deep sleep.

Suanach. A Highland plaid, a fleece.

Suanairm. A bed-chamber, dormitory.

Suanghalar. A lethargy

Suanmhar. Inclined to sleep.

Suanmharachd. A being inclined to sleep.

Suantach. Drowfy, fleepy.

Suarach. Infignificant, trifling

Suaraighe. Cheapnefs, meannefs.

Suaraichas. Neglect, indifference.

Suarcas. Mirth, drollery.

Suarcrodh. Endowed.

Suas. Up, upward.

Suafmhollam. To flatter, puff, footh, to magnify, extol.

Suathain. Lafting, perennial.

Suathadh. Kneading.

Suatham. To knead, rub, mix.

Suathameafg. Chaos.

Suathleus. Dazzling.

Suathran. A vertigo.

Subh, fugh. Juice

Subh. A berry.

Subh-craobh. Rafpberry.

Subh-lair.
Subhtalmhin } A ftrawberry.

Subha. Pleafure, delight.

Subhach. Merry, cheaiful.

Subhachas. Mirth, chearfulnefs, gladnefs.

Subhailce. A virtue.

Subhailceach. Virtuous.

Subham.
Sucham. } To fuck in, inhaurio.

Subhan. Juice, fap.

Subhled. Exprefled juice, liquor.

Subhrifteach. Brittle.

Subhrifteachd. Brittlenefs, weaknefs.

Subftaint. Vide Sufbuin.

Suchadh. Suction, a wave, evaporation.

Sucridh. Eafy.

Sud. That there, yonder.

Sudh. Secure.

Sudog. A cake.

Sudrall. Light, brightnefs.

Sudire. A tanner.

Sugach. Merry, chearful, pleafant.

Sugaidham. To be merry or droll

Sugaighal. Joy.

Sugai dhe
Sugaire. } A droll.

Sugan. A ftraw rope.

Sugancha. A ropery.

Sugh. Juice, liquor.

Sughainte.
Sughmhaire. } A whirlpool, gulf.

Sugham. To fuck in, attract.

Sugradh. Mirth, playing, fporting.

Suibhealtan. A parafite.

Suibhealtas. Spunging, fharking.

Suibh. A ftrawberry tree.

Suibhe. A feffion, affize.

Suidh. A hero.

Suidhe.
Suidheachan. } A feat.
Suidheog.

Suidhuicham. To fet, plant.

Suidhughadh. Setting, planting.

Suidhuighte. Set, planted, fedate.

Suidham. To fit, to prove, enforce an argument.

Suidheann. The cable of a veffel.

Suidhiomh. A proof.

Suidhal. Quiet, calm, fedate, noble.

Suidhte. In order, well-proportioned.

Suidhte. Proved, maintained.

Suidhteachd. Steadinefs, equanimity.

Suigeort. A frifking, gladnefs.

Suigeortach. Frifking of joy.

Suigleadh. Snot.

Suil. The eye, hope, expectation.

Suil. Tackle.

Suilach. Having eyes, fharp, quick-fighted.

Suilag. A little eye, orifice.

Suilagach.

Suilagach. Full of little holes.

Suilaire. A Soland goose.

Suilbhire. Delight, chearfulnefs

Suilbhir. Chearful, pleafant.

Suilbhireachd Chearfulnefs.

Suilchrith. A quagmire.

Suilgha Ocular.

Suilmhalari. A cockatrice.

Suilmhangaire. A foreftaller of the market.

Suilmhear. A wave.

Suilradharcam. To fafcinate.

Suim. A fum, refpect, regard, confideration.

Suimal Refpectful, regardful of.

Suinean. Fair weather.

Suineann. Stammering.

Suipeir. Supper.

Suinich. Late.

Suire. Sea nymphs, mermaids.

Suiridh. Nimble, active.

Suiridh. Courting, wooing.

Suirigh. A fool.

Suiridheach. A fweetheart, fuitor.

Suifte. A flail.

Suiftaram. To threfh.

Suitchearnach. A prefent, donation.

Suithean. The mob, multitude.

Suithche. Soot.

Suithinge Merry, joyful.

Sul. The fun, an eye.

Sulairam. Vide Sollaram.

Sulbhaire. Oratory, eloquence.

Sulbeim Bewitching with the eye.

Sulchor. Quick-fighted.

Sulradharc. Forefight, fate.

Sulradharcam. To look before, provide, forefee.

Sult. Mirth, joy, jeft, delight.

Sult, f. Fat.

Sultmhar. Fat, fertile.

Sultmhor. Pleafant, jocofe.

Sultmhuire. Mirth, facetioufnefs.

Sumhar. A fpring.

Sumhl. Clofe packed.

Sumhlachadh. Packing clofe.

Sumhlaigham. To pack clofe.

Sumhlichte. Packed.

Summag. A pack-faddle.

Summaineadh. A wave.

Sunach. Vide Suanach.

Sunais. Lovage.

Sunn caiflean. A fortified caftle.

Sunnd. Joy, chearfulnefs, good-humour.

Sunndach. Good-humoured, merry.

Sunghaoth. Boafting.

Sunrach. Particular, fpecial.

Suntaidh. Quick, active.

Suntraigh. Strong, ftout.

Sur. A fearch, enquiry.

Suraim. To inveftigate, enquire.

Suram. To follow.

Surd Induftry.

Surdal. Induftrious.

Surdalachd. Induftry.

Susbuin. Subftance, ftrength, virtue.

Suth. The weather.

Suth. Juice.

Suthbrith. Decoction.

Suthor. Juicy.

Sutche. } Soot.

Suthaighe. }

Suthaigheach. Sooty.

Suthain. Profperous, eternal, everlafting,

Suthuineacht. Eternity.

T.

T, Is the fixteenth letter in the Galic alphabet, and is foft as in the Italian. It bears an afpirate, and then is mute; as Tog, lift up; Thog e, he lifted up, is Hog e. The Irifh writers have called it Teine, and no one of them has given the reafon of that appellative. This letter hath often, in the Irifh manufcripts, been commuted for D, as G hath for C, which is prejudicial to the affinity roots in one language beareth to thofe of another. Vide Analyfis.

T Is euphonic before nouns beginning with S.

Ta. I am, is.

Taachd. Dull of hearing.

Taag. A blow on the cheek.

Taainm A nick-name.

Tabar. A tabor, timbrel.

Tabh. A fort of fifhing-net, the ocean.

Tabhachd. Effect, good ufe.

Tabhachdach. Beneficial, efficient, valid.

Tabhachta. State, condition.

Tabhagh. To pull.

Tabhuan. Perfeverance.

Tabhair. Give thou.

Tabhairn. The fea.

Tabhairn. A tavern, inn.

Tabhairneoir. An innkeeper.

Tabhairt. Giving.

Tabhairtach. Dative, generous.

Tabhairam. To give, beftow, confer.

Tabhal. A fling, out of which darts and ftones were caft, as from the Roman catapulta, a chief.

Tabhartana. A leader, a general.

Tabhartas. A prefent, tribute.

Tabhartha. Given, delivered.

Tabhuigham. To profit, exact.

Tabhul. A horfe-fly, a breeze.

Tabhun Baying of dogs.

Taboid. A broil.

Tac. Time. A leafe.

Taca. Neat, valuable.

Taca. A prop, a tacket, peg.

Taca. A furety.

Tacaid. A tacket.

Tacaidheachd. Giving fecurity

Tacamhuil. Firm, folid, able.

Tacamhlachd. Firmnefs, folidity.

Tacan. A fhort time, a minute.

Tacar. Provifion, gleaning, plenty.

Tacar. Good, agreeable.

Tacha. Scarcity.

Tachalofgadh. } The itch.
Tachas.

Tachan. A fort of martin.

Tachair. He came, arrived.

Tachar. A fight, battle, fkirmifh.

Tachairam. To meet.

Tacharan. An orphan, a fprite.

Tachaifam. To fcratch.

Tachdadh. Strangling, choaking.

Tachdam. To ftrangle, choak.

Tachdaighte. Strangled.

Tachdar. Many, provifion.

Tacheoll. Subftantial.

Tacmang. A compafs, circuit.

Tacmangam. To encompafs, furround.

Tacmangtha. Surrounded.

Tacoid. A peg, fmall nail.

Tad. Lownefs of fpirits.

Tadh. }
Tadhad. } A thief.

Tadhal. The fenfe of feeling.

Tadhal A flefh-hook.

Tadhallam. To vifit often, frequent, to haunt

Tadhafg. An account, news.

Tadhbadh. }
Tadhbhaifteadh. } A fpectre.

Tadhbhachd. Subftance, confequence, e-fteem.

Tadhbbachdach Effectual, important.

Tadhbhas. Solidity, firmnefs.

Tadhbhas. A fhewing, appearance.

Tadhbhafach. Solid, weighty.

Tadhg. A poet.

Tadhg. A man's name.

Tadhlach. Hard, difficult.

Tadhorduigham. To predeftinate.

Taecht. Unfavourinefs.

Taem. Heed.

Taen. The root of bent.

Tafach An exhortation.

Tafach. Craving.

Tafaigham. To prefs, urge.

Tafan. A yelping, barking

Tafanaim. To yelp, bay, bark ; to expel, drive away, rout.

Taga Teazle.

Tagaidh. Come ye on, advance.

Tagair. Plead thou.

Tagairam. To plead.

Tagairt. Pleading.

Tagam. To deliver, furrender.

Tagar. An order, courfe.

Tagaradh. A pleading.

Tagarthoir. A pleader.

Tagartha. Pleaded.

Tagbhais. }
Tagbhail. } A hap, chance.

Taghairm. A fort of divination.

Taghal. A feeling, fenfe of feeling.

Tagham. To choofe, kick out.

Taghar. A fight, diftant noife.

Tagmhodh. A poem.

Taghte Chofen. Vide Tagham.

Tagraim. To plead a caufe, to debate, fpeak.

Tagradn. Proceeding, feries.

Tagrach. Argumentative.

Tagradoir. An advocate, pleader.

Tai, taoi. Silent, mute.

Taibh. The ocean.

Taibheirt. Difparagement.

Taibhle. Tables.

Taibhle fileadh. Planed tables, whereon the Irifh wrote before they had parchment.

Taibhleoir. An ambaffador.

Taibhleoirachd. Sporting, playing.

Taibhreadh. A dream, vifion, appearance, revelation, difcovery.

Taibhreal. Laurel.

Taibhream. To dream, to appear intellectually, fpiritually, or in dream.

Taibhfe. A vifion, apparition, phantom.

Taibhfigham. To feem, appear.

Taibhfion. A fhewing or appearing.

Taibhe. Vide Taibhle.

Taibid. A fquib in fpeech.

Taic. A quantity, dependence, prop, near, in conjunction.

Taiceachd. A man's utmoft exertions

Taiceam. To recommend.

Taiceamhuil. Firm, ftrong, folid.

Taicamhlachd. Strength.

Taichre. A combat, battle.

Taicial. A provider.

Taide. A beginning, commencing.

Taidhe. Theft.

Taidhean. A troop, multitude.

Taidhin. A mill-pond.

Taidheoir. A pleader, difputant.

Taidhim. To apply, join. Vide Tatham.

Taidhleach. Pleafant, delightful, fplendid.

Taidhleachd.

Taidhleachd. Delight, fplendour.

Taidhleoir. An ambaffador, meffenger.

Taidhun. Objecting.

Taifnighte. Driven, forced away.

Taifnam. To banifh, expel.

Taifeid. A bow-ftring.

Taig. Habit, cuftom.

Taigh Vide Tigh.

Taigais. A haggefs , the fcrotum.

Taighleachd. Delight.

Taigiar. Pleafant.

Taill. Subftance, product, a lump.

Tailcanach. Stately.

Tailcas. Defpite, reproach, contempt.

Taileafg. Sport, chefs.

Taileol, Solid.

Tailgean. A holy name fuppofed to have been given by the Druids to St. Patrick.

Tailmh. A fling.

Taille. Wages.

Tailm. A tool, inftrument.

Tailp. A bundle, bunch.

Taim. I am.

Taimh. Death, mortality, fainting.

Taimhfhion. Dead wine.

Taimhleachd. A burying carn, or heap of loofe ftones raifed by thofe who accompany corpfes on the highway to the burying-place, each perfon carrying a fingle ftone to be thrown into the heap or carn. The cuftom ftill continues in the Highlands, to which I have been an eye witnefs, and have added a ftone to the heap.

Taimhliofg. Chefs.

Taimhneam. To banifh.

Taimhneul. Slumber, trance, extacy.

Taimhneulam. To flumber.

Taimhthin. A natural death.

Tain. Water

Tain, tan. A land, country, region.

Tainad. Rarity, thinnefs.

Tainc.
Taincalachd. } Thanks, gratitude.

Taincal. Thankful.

Tainic. Came

Tainfiomh. A reflection, cenfure, reproach.

Taip A mafs, lump.

Taipeiftreach. Tapeftry.

Tair Contempt, reproach.

Tair. Vile, bafe.

Tair, thairis. Over.

Tairal. Contemptuous.

Tairbeit. A peninfula.

Taire. Bafer.

Tairad. Bafenefs.

Taireachd. Contempt, low life, bafenefs

Tairbh Pl. of Tarbh.

Tairbhe. Profit, advantage

Tairbhealach. A ferry, paffage.

Tairbheartach. Profitable, beneficial

Tairbhfheach. A thigh.

Tairc. A clod

Taircheadalt. Prophecy.

Taircheimnughadh. A paffage over.

Tairchreich. Defert, merit.

Taircfionach. Mean, vile.

Tairdhingam. To force, thruft through.

Taireadh. Praife, commendation

Taireag Provifion, preparation.

Tairealbh. Shewing, reprefenting.

Tairean. A defcent.

Taireim. Difpraife, difrepute.

Taireimadh. Difparagement.

Taireofg. A faw.

Taireis. After, afterwards.

Tairgeal An offering, oblation.

Tairgeag. An imp, graft.

Tairghrim. To prophecy.

Tairgam. To try, endeavour, offer

Tairgam. To efcape, get away.

Tairgire. Prophecy, divination.

Tairgne. A nail.

Tairgnine. A little nail.

Tairgnachd. Prophecy.

Tairic. He came.

Tairigam, tairgam. To render, offer.

Tairgfc. }
Tairgfin } An offer, proffer.

Tairal. Contemptuous.

Tairam To live, exift.

Tairiofgluathre Sawduft.

Tairiotalaim. To fly over.

Tairis. Trufty, loving, kind.

Tairife. }
Tairifeachd. } Lovingnefs, affection, friend-ſhip.

Tairis, thairis. Over, beyond, by.

Tairifam. To love, ſtay, remain, conti-nue.

Tairifce. A file.

Tairifcam. To ſhave off, file.

Tairifin. A band, tye.

Tairifiomh. Dear, intimate, friendly, trufty.

Tairifiomh. Tarrying, continuance, dwelling.

Tairifionach. Good.

Tairleach Moifture.

Tairlearach. Tranfmarine.

Tairleofaim. To appear through.

Tairm. Necromancy.

Tairmcheal. A circuit.

Tairnge. A nail, pin, peg.

Tairngam. To pull, draw, to brew, diftil.

Tairngthe, Drawn.

Tairngthoir. A drawer.

Tairnig. Was finiſhed.

Tairpeach Strong, grand, pompous.

Tairreimniughadh. Tranfition.

Tairrianach From beyond fea.

Tairrngam. To pull, draw.

Tairrngire. A promife.

Tairfeach. Hinge of a door, threfhold.

Tairfgam. To offer.

Tairfgiona. An offer.

Tairfhliabhach. Beyond the mountains.

Tairfiubhlam. To pafs over.

Tairtbhe. A circuit, compafs.

Tairthigham. To fave.

Tairthiudh. News, tales.

Tairthreoiram. To convey, carry over.

Tairthreortha. Conveyed.

Tais Wet, moift, dank.

Taifaigham. To moiften.

Taifaodach. Winding-fheet.

Taife. }
Taifad. } Moifture.

Taifalachd Wet, rain, moifture.

Taifal. Soft.

Taife. Dead bodies, ghofts, relicks, extacy.

Taifbeun. A vifion, appearance.

Taifbeunaid. A fhew, revelation.

Taifbeunam. To fhew, prefent, produce, appear, reveal.

Taifbeunta. Revealed, fhewn, prefented.

Taifceallach. Efpying, viewing.

Taifcealladh. A betraying.

Taifceallam. To view, obferve, reconnoi-tre.

Taifdeal. A journey, voyage.

Taifeachd. Moifture.

Taifeag. Reftitution.

Taifealbhadh. A reprefentation, likenefs.

Taifealbham. To perfonate, reprefent.

Taifg. }
Taifge. } A pledge, ftake, treafure.

Taifg. Keeping, laid up.

Taifgairm. An armoury.

Taifgam. To lay up, to keep fafe.

Taifgealach. A pilgrim, paffenger.

Taifgealachd. Pilgrimage.

Taifgidh. A hoarding, laying up.

Taifgiodan. A ftorehoufe.

Taifginntin. Equivocation.

Taifligham. To be wet or moift.

Taiflighte. Wetted.

Taifmangadh. Birth.

Taifte. Taches.

Taifteal. A journey, voyage, ftraying, wandering.

Taiftealach. A vagabond, traveller.

Taiftealam. To ftray, travel.

Taiftigham.

Taiſtigham. To water.

Taiſteamhuil. Momentary.

Taiſteog. Moment.

Tait. Pleaſure.

Taithcheannach. Exchange, traffic.

Taitheaſg. A repartee.

Taithleach. Peace, quietneſs.

Taithleach. Peaceable, quiet, depending on.

Taithliagh. A chirurgeon

Taithligham. To appeaſe, mitigate.

Taithlioch. An excuſe.

Taithmhead. Remembrance, memorial, monument.

Taithneamh. Splendour, brightneſs, a thaw.

Taithneamhach. Bright, ſhining, fair, beautiful.

Taithneamhas. Pleaſantneſs.

Taithnam. To thaw.

Taitneach. Agreeable, acceptable.

Tal. A cooper's ax or adze.

Taldeis. }
Talcuil. } A ſort of planes.

Talach. Diſpraiſe, reproach.

Talach. Diſſatisfied, murmuring.

Tala. An elegy.

Taladh. To huſh, rock to reſt.

Talaidh. Vide Aile.

Talamh. The earth, ground, ſoil.

Talamh-chumſgughadh. An earthquake.

Talamhchrithach. Earthſhaking.

Talamhanta. Mineral.

Talamhuidh. Earthy, earthly, terreſtrial.

Talan. Feats of arms, chivalry.

Talban. A partition.

Talca. Force, vigour, courage.

Talcanta. Strong, luſty.

Talchara. A generous lover.

Talcarra. Sturdy, corpulent.

Talcuil. A cooper's plane.

Talcumha. A tub.

Taleog. Deliver thou.

Taliſg. Some Iriſh inſtrument of war.

Talfuin. A hoe.

Talgadh. A quieting, pacifying.

Tall. Theft.

Tall, thall. Over, beyond.

Talla. A hall.

Tall. Eaſy.

Tallaim. To cut.

Tallaithe. Robbed, ſpoiled.

Tallan. A talent.

Talbhe. He that bereaves a man of a thing.

Tallthoir. A robber.

Talmhan. Gen. of Talamh.

Talmhuidhe. Terreſtrial.

Talpa. The tranſlator of the Iriſh bible uſes this Latin word for a mole, although the language, at leaſt the Scotch dialect, affords one. There are no moles in Ireland.

Talradharc. Warineſs, caution.

Tam. Truly, certainly.

Tamach. Dull, ſluggiſh.

Tamailte. Slothful, weak, faint, humiliating, diſparaging.

Tamailtin. Abuſive ſtories.

Tamal, tamul. Space, a little while.

Tamh. Reſt, quiet.

Tamh. The ocean.

Tamh. Plague, peſtilence, extacy.

Tamhach. A dolt.

Tamhaich. Inhabitants.

Tamhaighe. Dulneſs.

Tamhaigham. To ſettle, reſide, inhabit.

Tamhaim. To be ſilent.

Tamhait. Habitation.

Tamhan. A trunk, body, block, ſtock.

Tamhanach. A dolt, blockhead.

Tamhanta. Doltiſh, ſluggiſh, ſplenetic.

Tamhantas. Slowneſs.

Tamhaſg. A fool.

Tamhaſg. A fool.

Tamhnaim. To behead, lop off.

Tamhſhuan. A trance, extaſy.

Tan, An tan, An tam. When.

Tan. A herd of cows.

Tan. A country, region, territory.

Tanadh. }
Tanaidhe. } Thin, rare, slender.

Tanaidheachd. Thinness.

Tanaigham. To make thin, slender, diminish, rarify.

Tanaiste. A lord, dynast, governor of a country, heir apparent in Ireland to a prince.

Taraiste. The middle finger.

Thanaisteachd. Thanistry, law of regal succession.

Tanaisteach. Swaying, acting like a Thane.

Tanalich. Shallow water.

Tanas Dominion, lordship, government.

Tanas. }
Tanasg } A ghost, spirit of the deceased.

Tancard. A tankard.

Tangadar. They arrived, came.

Tangmangadh. An environing, guarding.

Tangnachd. Fraud, malice, grudge.

Tanic, thanic. Came.

Tannaladh. Often bellowing, agony.

Tannaidh aodaich. Woof.

Tansin. Then, at that time.

Taobh. A side.

Taobh amuidh. Outside.

Taobh astigh. Inside.

Taobhach. Partial.

Taobhachd. Presumption.

Taobgha. Lateral.

Taobhadh. Trusting, relying, a commission

Taobham. To join, take part with, incline, come nigh to, trust, depend.

Taobhan. A rafter.

Taobhcheimne. Digression.

Taobhghabhail. A hankering, kindness.

Taobhgheal. Having a white side.

Taobhghreim. A stitch in the side.

Taobhshlighe. A bye-way.

Taobhtha. Trusted, joined.

Taobhthoir. A creditor, commissary.

Taobhthrom. Pregnant.

Taod. Going, coming.

Taod. A halter.

Taodbhalc. Very strong, puissant.

Taodhaire. An apostate.

Taoghach. Elective.

Taoghal. A frequenting, visiting.

Taogham. To choose, elect.

Taoghte. Elected.

Taoidham. To turn, revolt.

Taoi. A trope, turning, winding.

Taoi. Deaf, silent.

Taoibhreim. }
Taoibhreimnughadh. } Digression.

Taoibhmheise. }
Taoibhmheithamh. } A commissary.

Taoicreidhm. }
Taoieasadh. } A giddiness, dizziness.

Taoig. A fit of passion.

Taoim. Bilge water in a ship.

Taois, taoise. Of dough.

Taoiseach. A chieftain, general.

Taoisg. Nearly full.

Taoisnaigham. }
Taoisnam. } To knead.

Taoisnighte. Kneaded.

Taoitheannach. Silent.

Taoitheannachd Silence.

Taolomach. A parricide.

Taom. A fit of sickness, madness, or passion.

Taom. Lave, empty thou. Vide Taoim.

Taomach. Subject to fits, emptying.

Taomam. To lave, pour out, to pump.

Taoman. A vessel to lave with.

Taomaire. A drawer, a pump.

Taombaoile. A mad fit.

Taos. Dough.

Taothchoir. Blame, dispraise.

Taoschua. A flesh pie.

Taofga. Rather, firft, fooner than.

Taofgach. Brim-full.

Taofgadh. Pumping, draining.

Taofgam. To drain, pour out, pump.

Taofgoir. One employed at the pump.

Taofgtha. Drained.

Taothalam. To come, vifit.

Taothal. Subfidy.

Tap. } Quick, active.
Tapidh. }

Tap. Tow or wool on the diftaff.

Tapadh. } Succefs, activity, good chance.
Tapachd. }

Tapaidham. To haften.

Tapag. Accident, chance words, a flip.

Taphuinam. To bark.

Taphun. Barking.

Taplich. A repofitory of fmall things, a wallet.

Taponta. At your peril, doing quickly.

Tar. Beyond, out of.

Tar. Come thou.

Tar, tair. Contempt.

Tar. Rather than, before.

Tara. Active, a multitude.

Tarachd. Activity.

Tarachair. An augre, gimlet.

Tharad. Over thee.

Taradharc. Squinting.

Tarail. To go round.

Taraifeach. From beyond the mountains.

Taralpach. Tranfalpine.

Tharam. Over me.

Taran. The ghoft of an unbaptized child.

Tarbert. A neck of land.

Tarbh. A bull.

Tarbh uifge. A fea bull or cow.

Tarbhan. A little bull.

Tarbhach. Profitable, fubftantial.

Tarbhachd. Gain, profit.

Tarbhach-iuil. A good guide, fkilful man.

Tarbhanta. Grim, ftern, bull-faced.

Tarbhaidh. A hindrance, impediment, misfortune.

Tarbheiram. To carry over, transfer.

Tarbhochnach. Tranfmarine.

Tarbhaillam. To pierce, thruft through.

Tarbh-tana. A parifh or public bull.

Tarcabal. Sins, tranfgreffions.

Tarceann. Moreover.

Tarcheann. Although, though.

Tarcim fuain. A deep fleep.

Tarchomhladh. A going, marching.

Tarcchonnair. A ferry, paffage.

Tarchuiram. To pafs over.

Tarcodhach. Naught, bad.

Tarcuis. } Contempt.
Tarcuifne. }

Tarcuifneach. Contemptuous, defpicable.

Tarcuifnigham. To defpife, revile.

Tard. He gave.

Taidharc. Squinting, looking afkew.

Tareis. After, afterwards.

Tarfhairmheadh. A paffing over.

Tarfas. An apparition.

Tarfuinneog. A cafement.

Targadh. A governing, ruling.

Targadh. } An affembly.
Targlomadh. }

Targaid. A target.

Targaidach. Armed with a target.

Targhan. A noife.

Targhraidh. An expedition.

Targhno. Ill-countenanced.

Tharibh. Over you.

Tharis. Over, over him, it.

Tharinn. Over us.

Tarla. He, it came to pafs, happened.

Tarlaic. He threw, caft.

Tarlaid. A drudge, flave.

Tarlaidham. To collect, bring together, feize, lay hold on.

Tarlodh. A draught, leading in of corn or hay.

3

Tar-

Tarlaidham. To meet, visit.

Tarlodham. Vide Tarlaidham.

Tarmadh. To dwell, to settle.

Tarman. A sanctuary, protection.

Tarman, torman. Noise.

Tarmchruthughadh. Transfiguration.

Tarmochan.}
Tarmonach.} The bird termagant.

Tarna. Cross, bye.

Tarnac It was finished.

Tarnach }
Tarnainach. } Thunder.

Tarnachd. Forwardness, perverseness.

Tarp A clod, lump.

Tarpan A cluster.

Tarr. The lowest part of the belly.

Tarrachtin. Revenge.

Tarrachtair. It happened.

Tarradh. Protection.

Tarradh. A drawing, draught.

Tarraghalaidhe. A prophet.

Tarraighil. Prophecy.

Tarraghlaim. To prophecy, foretel.

Tarrang }
Tarrann. } A nail.

Tarrangart. A load-stone.

Tarrangoir. A nailer.

Tarrangtha. Drawn, pulled.

Tarrastair. It happened.

Tarrfhionn Having white buttocks.

Tarrghraidh A journey.

Tarrningireacht. A prophecy.

Tarrnochd. Stark-naked.

Tarrsa. Come thou.

Tarrthaigham. To save, deliver.

Tarrthail. Preservation, safety.

Tarrthaim. To seize, lay hold of, to assert, affirm.

Tarthaim. To grow.

Tarrudh. A drawing.

Tarruing. A haul-yard, draught.

Tarruingam. To draw, pull, teaze, launch, distil.

Tarruingham suas. To take up with a person, cultivate acquaintance.

Tarruing air ais. Revulsion.

Tarsa. Over, past, over them.

Tarsnan. A transom, cross beam, or stick.

Tarsin. Across, awry, athwart.

Tarsnamham. To swim over.

Tarsoillseach. Transparent.

Tarsoillsigham. To be transparent.

Tart. Thirst, drought.

Tartan. A party-coloured stuff worn by Highlanders.

Tartar. Noise.

Tartarach. Noisy.

Tharte. Over her.

Tharta. Over them.

Tarthadoir. }
Tarthalaidhe. } A saviour.

Tarthach. A girth.

Tarthaigham. To assist, depend.

Tarthail. Help, assistance

Tarthailam. To assist, protect.

Tartmhor. Thirsty, dry.

Tas. A dwelling, habitation.

Tas. A whip, scourge.

Tasaim. To dwell, remain.

Tasan. A flow, tedious, plaintive discourse.

Tasanach. Slow, tedious.

Tasbeunam. To reveal, shew, present.

Tasc. Fame.

Tascor. A navy.

Tascor. An assembly, cavalcade, mark.

Tascoram. To march, migrate.

Tasdail. To examine.

Tasg. A report, rumour.

Tasga. A task.

Tasgaire. A slave, servant.

Tasgamhuil. Renowned.

Tasgidh. Laying up, keeping.

Tass. Half done.

Tatag. A clash.

Tath. Slaughter.

Tath. Solder, glue.

Tath. Withered.

Tath. A fide.

Tatha. Bail, fecurity.

Tathad. They have.

Tathaigheach. Converfant, acquainted.

Tathaigheachd Ufe, familiarity.

Tathaigham To frequent, haunt, ufe. Vide Tatham

Tataim. To kill, deftroy; to dye.

Tathaire A fluggifh trifling fellow.

Tathalam. To call, vifit.

Tatham. To apply, join by articulation.

Tathamh A nap of fleep.

Tathaoir. Heavy, dull.

Tathaoir. A reproach, contempt, difregard.

Tathoiram. To reproach, defpife.

Tathas. He gathered, affembled.

Tathbheim. A mortal blow, antiently the exercife of cafting darts and other miffiles from the Cranntabhuil.

Tathfan. Barking, baying.

Tathfanam. To bark.

Tathlaigham. To tame, fubdue, pacify.

Tathlan. A reproach, calumny.

Tathughadh. A foldering, joining, future.

Tathuighe. Acquaintance, haunting, frequenting, refort.

Tathuighbam. To be accuftomed. Vide Tathaigham.

Tathuighte. Frequented, accuftomed, publick.

Tathunn. Bay of a deer.

Te, An te. She, fhe that, whofoever.

Te, teth. Hot.

Teacclaim. A collection.

Teaccmais. A hindrance, impediment.

Teach. A houfe.

Teachadh. A ftrangling.

Teache re teachd. Coming, to come.

Teachd ann tir. Livelihood, fubfiftence.

Teachd afteach. Income.

Teachd amach. Encreafe.

Teachd. Innavigable. Vide Muir.

Teachda ⎫
Teachdach. ⎬ A meffenger, poft, ambaffador.
Teachdaire ⎭

Teachdaireachd. Meffage, embaffy, errand, legation.

Teachdaighte. Strangled.

Teachdmhor. Fruitful.

Teachtadh. Poffeffion

Teacmaic It came to pafs, happened.

Teacmhuail. Affliction, at death's door.

Teacmoc. Riches, wealth

Tead. A rope, cord, chord.

Teadidh. Quick, active.

Teadaidhe. A harper.

Teadarrachdoir. An avenger

Teadham. To go.

Teaga. Perhaps.

Teagamh. Doubt, perhaps.

Teagar. Provifion.

Teagafg. Teaching, doctrine, text, inftruction.

Teagafga. Sorcery, druidifm.

Teagafgam. To teach, inftruct.

Teagafgte. Taught, inftructed.

Teagafgthoir. A teacher.

Teagbhall. Afflicted even to death.

Teagh. A houfe, a room.

Teagh. Vapour, exhalation.

Teaghais. A fmall room, clofet, a cafe.

Teaghalach. A family, houfehold, habitation.

Teaghalach. Belonging to a family or houfe.

Teagham. To heat, warm, to grow hot.

Teaglachas. Soothing, flattery, playing the parafite.

Teaghlach. A family or houfehold, court, palace.

Teaghladhach Fair-fpoken.

Teaghlaigham. To footh, flatter

Teagmhail. Meddling, interfering, ftrife.

Teagm-

Teagmhailach. Contentious, contending, striving.

Teagmhaim. To meet, to strive, contend.

Teagmhach. Doubtful.

Teagmhuis. An accident.

Teagmhuiseach. Accidental, peradventure.

Tealach. A loosing.

Tealgadh. Casting, throwing.

Tealgam. To cast, throw.

Teilla }
Teailach. } The hearth.

Teallachag A domestic concubine.

Teallaid A bunchy woman.

Teallam. To steal

Teallur The earth.

Tealsanach. A philosopher.

Tealsanachd. Philosophy.

Tealsanta. Philosophical.

Tealtic. Silly, cowardly.

Tealtachd. Simplicity.

Teamhair } Pleasant ; Tara or Temora,
Teamhra. } the seat of the kings of Meath.

Teampull A church or temple.

Tean. Vide Teann.

Teanal, tional. Collecting, gathering.

Teanalam. To lay up, gather, glean.

Teanalaiche A gleaner.

Teanalta Gleaned.

Teanam. To writhe, twist.

Teanbhuaidhreadh. Fervency.

Teanchair. Pincers, tongs ; a vice.

Teanga. A tongue, dialect, language, pl. Teangtha.

Teanga mortair. Pestle.

Teanga mhion. Dead nettle.

Teangach. Tongued.

Teangair. A linguist.

Teangas. A pair of pincers.

Teann. Stiff, rigid, bold, powerful, tense.

Teannadh. Stiffness, rigidness, violence, beginning to.

Teanngug. Stiff and strong.

Teannaire. The roar of the sea in a cave.

Teannam. To strain, press, bind straight, embrace, to hold or get away, to begin.

Teannfaisgam. To press, wring, squeeze close.

Teannlamh. A tinder-box.

Teannradh. Shewing, manifestation, discovery.

Teannshaith. Abundance, full meal.

Teanntan. A press, bruising.

Teannta. Joined.

Teanntraidhe. Grief, sorrow.

Teannorcanus. The counter-tenor in musick. Cantus medius.

Tearbadh. A separation.

Tearbaidham. To separate.

Tearc. Few, rare.

Tearcadh, teirce. Fewness, scarcity, rareness.

Tearinam To descend, go down hill.

Tearischuidachd. Pastime.

Tearmann. } A limit, glebe land, protecTearmunn. } tion, sanctuary.

Tearmannoir. } A patron, protector.
Tearmannuidhe. }

Tearnadh. Descending, going down hill.

Tearnam. } To descend, escape.
Tearnodham. }

Tearnam. } To escape, fly from, evade,
Tearnodham. } recover ; to fall into a pit.

Tearnodh. A fall, hap, chance.

Tearnadh. An escape, recovery from sickness.

Tearr. Pitch, tar.

Tearrgha. Of pitch.

Tearram. To tar, pitch, daub.

Tearran. Anger, vexation.

Tearuinam. To save, deliver.

Tearuinte. Safe, delivered.

Tearuinteachd. Security.

Teas. Heat, warmth, a meſſage.

Teaſach. A fever.

Teaſaire. A meſſenger.

Teaſairgte. Saved, delivered.

Teaſargin. } Reſcuing, ſaving, delivering
Teaſargadh. } from danger.

Teaſargaim. To ſave, deliver, reſcue.

Teasbhach. Sultrineſs, hot weather.

Teasbuala. Hot-baths.

Teaſdaigham. To prove, try, fail.

Teaſdughadh. A trial.

Teaſgaigham. To preſerve.

Teaſgal. A ſcorching wind, a ſtorm, a wave.

Teaſgam. To cut, lop off.

Teaſghradh. Fervent love.

Teaſmhach. Vide Teaſbhach.

Teaſruigham. To deliver, reſcue.

Teaſruiguin. Deliverance.

Teaſtaghadh. Experience, trial, diſcuſſing, ſifting of a matter, abſence.

Teaſtaigham. To teſtify, bear witneſs, to lack, need, want.

Teaſtail. Want, defect.

Teaſtun. A groat, fourpence.

Teaſuidhe. Hot, burning.

Teaſuidheachd. A heat, warmth.

Teath ! Hold off ! a page.

Teathadh. A flight, running away.

Teathaigham. To celebrate, ſolemnize.

Teathadh. Flight.

Teatham. To flee, run away.

Teathmhach. Fleeting.

Teathra. The ſea.

Teathra. A Royſton crow.

Teb. Unreſolved.

Tebidich. Irreſolution.

Tebim. To fruſtrate.

Tec. A bone.

Tedaidh. Wild, fierce.

Tedarrachd. Revenge, vengeance.

Tedarnach. Revengeful.

Tedhmneach. Furious, headlong.

I

Tedhbhais. A phantom.

Tednos. Fierceneſs, ſeverity.

Tegearrach. A purchaſer.

Tegh, teth. Hot, ſcalding.

Teghbhal. Ground-rent.

Tegus. A purchaſe.

Teibiadh. A drawing, taking away.

Teibhearſam. To drop, diſtil.

Teibidh. Smart, pedantic.

Teibidh. Phyſicians.

Teich. Flee thou.

Teichd-reult. The north.

Teiclidh. Quiet, peaceable.

Teid, theid. Shall go.

Teide. A ſmooth plain hill.

Teidealtach. Valetudinary.

Teidin. A ſmall cord or rope.

Teidhm. Death.

Teidhmneach. Perverſe.

Teigeamhus. Shall happen, befal.

Teighiollas. A ſalimander.

Teile. } A lime or linden-tree.
Teileag. }

Teilgin. Caſting, throwing, vomiting

Teilgam. To vomit, caſt, throw, over-turn.

Teilglion. A caſting-net.

Teiligham. To refuſe, reject.

Teiligham To build.

Teilightheach. Fertile.

Teilis. A houſe, habitation.

Teimeal. Droſs.

Teimheal. Dark, obſcure.

Teimheal. A ſhadow, ſhade, covert.

Teimhliughadh. A darkening, obſcuring.

Tein. Coming.

Teinn. Great haſte, hurry, or diſtreſs, power, force.

Teinnbhealach. Perverſe, obſtinate.

Teinne. Fire, link of a chain.

Teinne, teinngha. Of fire.

Teinnas. Vide Tinnas.

Teinnmheach.

Teinnmheadh. A cutting, dividing, opening.

Teinne. ⎰ Tension, severity, rigidness.
Teinnad. ⎱

Teinne-athair. Lightning.

Teinne-chrios. An iron to strike fire from a flint

Teinnteach. Lightning; pl. of Teinne.

Teinntidh Fiery.

Teinntein. The hearth.

Teinntreach. Flashes of lightning; pl. of Teinne, a link.

Teinntrigham. To cast lightning.

Teirbeirt. Fatigue.

Terbheirt. Distributing, bestowing.

Teir. Shall say.

Teirachdin Decaying, weary, wasting.

Teirce. Scarcity, fewness.

Teircfheolach. Lean, meagre.

Teireadh. A commendation.

Teiricam. To be spent, to fail, wear.

Teirin A descent.

Teirinam. To descend.

Teiris Said to quell cattle when they quarrel.

Teirmasg. A mishap, misfortune.

Teirmasgach. That meeteth with many accidents.

Teirme. Season, while.

Teirmasgam. To meet with, to find.

Teirphonta. Three pounds weight.

Teisbeirt. Increase, growth.

Teisidh. They halted.

Teisite. A dropping, distilling.

Teisruigham. Vide Teasargam.

Teisruig. Rescue thou.

Teisteadh To be wanting.

Teith. Hot.

Teith. Flee thou.

Teithcheamh. ⎰ Flight.
Teitheadh ⎱

Teitham. To flee.

Teithmheach. A fugitive, rennagade.

Teithneas. Haste.

Teithneasach. Hasty, in haste.

Teitne. A player on the tabor or timbrel.

Tel. Fertile ground.

Telightheach. Fertile.

Tellur. The earth.

Temhe. Death, sickness.

Tenam. I pray thee.

Teochriodhach. Warm-hearted.

Teoghradhach. Kind, affectionate, zealous.

Teoilt. ⎰ Weak in temper.
Teoiltie. ⎱

Teoir Thrice, three.

Teoirfheac. A trident.

Teoiriolach. ⎰ Triumph.
Teorghairde. ⎱

Teoirinneach. Three-footed, three-forked.

Teoitachan-mhias. A chaffing-dish

Teol. Plenty, abundance.

Teol. A thief.

Teora, teoran. A border, limit, boundary.

Teora. Three, thrice.

Teorchan. The space of three hours.

Teorghar-athair. The great-grandfather's great grandfather.

Teorchosach. Three-footed.

Teorghabhlach. Three-pronged.

Teorlaethan. Three days space.

Teoruilleann. ⎰ A triangle.
Teoruile. ⎱

Teoruileannach. Triangular.

Teotham, teothaicham. To warm.

Teothaighte. Warmed.

Teothair. A halter, tether.

Teothram. To tether.

Teothchriodhach. Open and warm-hearted.

Teothughadh. Excandescence.

Ternodh. Falling.

Ternodh. Escaping. Vide Tearnadh.

                    Tesdughadh.

Tefdughadh. Trial.

Teftiall. Spouting up water.

Teftar. A fhilling.

Tet. A tabor, drum.

Tet, tethe. The north.

Teth. Hot, fcalding.

Teth. Fine, fmooth.

Tethin. The fun.

Teuchd. Deeds.

Teud. A ftring, cord, rope, fiddle-ftring.

Teudach. Stringed.

Teudchleafaidhe
Teudfhiubhlaiche. } A rope-dancer.

Teudaoire. A tack-rope.

Teullodham. To fteal away. Vide Ealaigham.

Teum. Expert.

Teumadh. To bite.

Teumam. To teach, break to any thing.

Teurnadh. Defcending, paffing away. Vide Tearnadh.

Ti. He, he who, him that ; An ti is oige, the youngeft.

Ti. Unto, to ; Go ti fo, hitherto.

Ti. Defign, intention.

Ti mhor. The Supreme Being, God.

Tiachair. Perverfe, ill-difpofed.

Tiachra. Prudence.

Tiachdidh. A common haunter, reforter, gueft, cuftomer.

Tiachtam. To accompany, attend, go to, arrive at.

Tiacht air. Talking, treating of.

Tiadhan. A little hill, ftone, tefticle.

Tiag, tiachog, tiagh. A bag, wallet.

Tiaghais. A manfion, dwelling-houfe.

'Tiaghuim. To come to, to vanifh, to appeal.

Tiamhdha. Dark, obfcure.

Tiamhdha. Slow, tedious.

Tiamhidh. Solitary, gloomy.

Tiamhidhachd. A folitary gloom or fadnefs.

Tiarna. A lord, prince, ruler.

Tiarnas. Dominion, lordfhip.

Tiarpan. A tefticle.

Tiarrthoch. A tripe.

Tias. A tide.

Tiafgadal. Induftry, contrivance.

Tibheadh. Laughter.

Tibham. To laugh.

Tibhfhiacal. The fore-teeth.

Tibharfan. Springing, fprouting, overflowing.

Tibhad. Thicknefs.

Tibhghra. Affeveration.

Tibhre. A fool.

Tibhreach. Given to laughing.

Tibhram. To fpring.

Tig. Come.

Tigam. To come.

Tigh. A houfe ; Gen. Tighe.

Tighe, tigheachd. Thicknefs, fatnefs.

Tigh-leanna. An alehoufe.

Tigh-ofd. An inn.

Tigh-moid. A court-houfe.

Tigh-cainach. A cuftomhoufe.

Tigh-cuinaidh. A mint.

Tigh-aifdighachd.
Tigh-cluith. } A playhoufe.

Tigh-fcoil. A fchool-houfe.

Tigh-eiridin. An infirmary.

Tigh-togalach. A brewhoufe.

Tigh-bainne. The dairy.

Tigh-beg. The jakes.

Tigh-nighadairachd. A wafhing-houfe.

Tigh-cearc. The hen-houfe.

Tigh-malairt A houfe of exchange.

Tigh-nuadh-nofda. A night-wake.

Tigheamhuil. Domeftic, belonging to a houfe.

Tigheadas. Houfekeeping, hufbandry.

Tigheadafach. Diligent, careful, bufied about houfekeeping.

Tighean. A bag or fatchel.

Tighearna. Vide Tiarna.

Tigh-

Tighearnamhuil. Lordly.

Tighearnalachd. Lordlinefs.

Tighearnas. Vide Tiarnas.

Tigheafach. A houfekeeper.

Tigheas. } Houfekeeping, hufban-
Tigheafachd. } dry.

Tigheafaim. To manage a farm, follow hufbandry.

Tighim, tigam. To come, go.

Tighin, tein. Coming

Tigh mail. A hired houfe.

Til. A welt, mark of a wound.

Tile. Much, plenty, a great deal.

Tileadh. A fhip's poop.

Tilig Caft thou ; a fhot, throw.

Tiligam. To caft, throw, vomit.

Tiligadh. } Cafting, vomiting.
Tiligin. }

Tillam. To turn, to return.

Tilladh. A returning.

Tim. Fear, dread.

Tim. Time.

Timchioll About, circuit, compafs.

Timchiollach. Circuitous.

Tiomchiollam. To furround, environ, encompafs.

Timchiollghearradh. } Circumcifion.
Timchiolltheafgadh. }

Timchiollghearram. } To circumcife.
Timchiolltheafgam. }

Timchiollghearrtha. Circumcifed.

Timchiollfgriobham. To circumfcribe, define.

Timchiolltha. Surrounded, environed.

Timtheanamh Form, fafhion.

Timdhibhe. A leffening, abatement, ruin, deftruction.

Time. Pride, dignity, eftimation ; thence the Latin Eftimo.

Time Heat, warmth.

Time. Fear, dread.

Timcach. Hot, warm.

Timheal. Darknefs, glimmering light.

Timhealach. Dark, obfcure.

Timearnam. To celebrate, folemnize.

Timich. Enticing.

Timtire. A minifter, fervant, agent.

Timtireachd. Service, miniftration.

Tinam. To fmelt, foften.

Tin. A beginning.

Tin. Fat, tender.

Tinchreachadh. A prey.

Tinciofdal. A march.

Tineach. Kindred.

Tineas. Thicknefs, clofenefs.

Ting. A tongue.

Tinn. Sick.

Tinn. Vide Teann.

Tinge, tinne. Strange, wonderful.

Tinge, tinne. Almoft.

Tinnas Sicknefs.

Tinnas cloinne. Travail, childbirth.

Tinneafach. Evil.

Tinim. To thaw, diffolve.

Tinm. Underftanding.

Tinne. The letter T according to O Flaherty.

Tinne. A chain. Vide Teinne.

Tinneafach. Stout, ftrong, literally ftrong-ribbed.

Tinnriomh. A conclufion.

Tinnfcra. A portion, dowry.

Tinnteach. Lightning.

Tinnteagal. Corruption.

Tinntean. The hearth.

Tinntighe. Fiery.

Tinntuirfeach. Miferable.

Tinfceadal. Inftruction, judicioufnefs.

Tint. A ton weight.

Tinteannas. Great hafte, expedition.

Tiobar. } A well; O thiobraidh, from the
Tiobrad. } mountains.

Tiocfaid. They fhall come. Vide Tigam.

Tioch. } A bag, budget, fatchel.
Tiochog. }

Tiodal. A title, epitaph, monument.
Tiodhlacadh. A gift, present.
Tiodhlacaim. To present, bestow.
Tiodhlaictheach. Bountiful.
Tiodhnacadh. } A present, offering, fa-
Tiodhnacal. } vour.
Tiogar. A tiger.
Tiolpadh. Snatching, cutting away.
Tiolpam. To snatch, cut away.
Tiolpadair. A cutpurse.
Tiom. Soft, tender, fearful.
Tiomachd. Softness, tenderness.
Tiomaltas. Victuals, eatables.
Tiomallaim. To eat.
Tiomam. To soften the passions.
Tiomanaim. To drive, turn away, push, thrust off.
Tiomargadh. A collection.
Tiomargaim. To collect, gather together.
Tiomarnadh. A command.
Tiomarnaim. To command, order.
Tiomchaire. Pity, mercy.
Tiomchriodheach Tender-hearted.
Tiomchuairt. A friendly visit; a period.
Tiomchuairteach. Periodical.
Tiomghaire. A request.
Tiomghairam. To ask, require.
Tiomna. A will, testament.
Tiomna nuadh. The New Testament.
Tiomnaim. To make a will, to swear.
Tiompan. A timbrel, tabor, drum, cymbal.
Tiompanuiche. A harper, minstrel.
Tiomsaigham. To collect, bring together.
Tiomsughadh. Collection.
Tiomuinam. To deliver, commit, commend, entrust.
Tionadh. Melting, dissolving. Vide Tinam.
Tionad. Whereas.

Tionail. Collecting, gathering.
Tionailam. To assemble, congregate.
Tioncam. To attend.
Tionlacadh. A funeral.
Tioncar. } Attendance.
Tionramh. }
Tionchaisin. The sight.
Tionchosg. Instruction.
Tionndadh. A turning about or back
Tionndaigham. To turn.
Tionsgnadh. } A beginning, device, pro-
Tionsgnamh. } ject, plot.
Tionsgnam. To begin, devise, plot
Tionnsgra. A reward, portion, dowry.
Tionnur. A slumber, nap.
Tional A congregation.
Tionolaim. Vide Tionalam.
Tionsaigham. To assemble, gather together.
Tionsanadh. A dropping, flowing down
Tionsanam. To drop, distil.
Tionscantach. Adventurous, diligent, industrious.
Tionscra. A buying, purchasing, a reward, stipend.
Tionsgain. A beginning, element.
Tionsgiodal. A managing, projecting, industry.
Tiontanas. Haste, speed, expedition.
Tionuigh. Frequenting, sojourning in a place.
Tionur. A tenon.
Tionus. A tan-yard.
Tiopal. A water-spider.
Tior. Vide Tir.
Tioradh. Drying, scorching.
Tioram. To dry, to kiln-dry.
Tiortha. Dried on a kiln.
Tioramh. Threshing.
Tioranach. A tyrant.
Tioranachd. Tyranny.
Tiorcomhrac. An assembly.
Tior-shochraic. A reward.

Tiormachd.
Tiormalachd. } Drought, thirst.

Tiormaigham. To dry up, make dry, desiccate.

Tiormachal. Desiccative.

Tiorthach. Born of a country, a patriot

Tiortha. Pl. of Tior or Tir.

Tiotal A title.

Tiotan. The sun.

Tiotadh.
Tiotan. } A moment.

Tipeadh. A regulating, disposing things in order.

Tir. A land, country, region.

Tir-mor. A continent.

Tirachas. Colonization, planting.

Tiraigham. To colonize.

Tiral. Snug, comfortable.

Tire, tirgha Of, belonging to a country.

Tirbheartha. Proper, peculiar to one's country.

Tlachdgrabhaiche.
Tirebheartaidhe. } A geographer.

Tirim. Dry.

Tirimaigham. Vide Tiormaigham.

Tir re thol. A church-yard.

Tirteach. Demesnes, a mansion-house.

Tisean. A grudge.

Tith. Neat.

Tithin The sun.

Tiubhram. To give, deliver. Vide Tabhairam.

Tiubiuid. A well, cistern.

Tiucfam To come. Vide Tigam.

Tiuchag
Tiuchan. } A pore.

Tiugh. Thick, close.

Tiughe.
Tiughad } Thickness.

Tiughmhuilleann A tucking-mill.

Tiughaigham To condense, thicken.

Tiughalach.
Tiughalachd } The thickest of liquids, dregs.

Tla. Soft.

Tlachd. Pleasure, delight, will, inclination

Tlachd. The earth.

Tlachd. A fair, market.

Tlachd. A garment, vesture, colour.

Tlachdairm. A market-place.

Tlachdadh A burying.

Tlachdaigham. To inter, bury.

Tlachdam. To colour.

Tlachdbhaile. A market-town.

Tlachdbhogadh. A quick-sand, quagmire.

Tlachdbhothi A booth in a fair.

Tlachdchomhthroman. A roller, cylinder.

Tlachdchorughadh.
Tlachdchumargadh. } An earthquake.

Tlachdgha. A fire kindled for summoning all the Druids to meet on the first of November to sacrifice to their gods. They burnt the sacrifice in that fire, nor was there any other fire to be kindled in Ireland that night. Vide Keat, in Tuathal teachtmhor.

Tlachgraibhachd. Geography.

Tlachdmhor. Pleasant, handsome, smooth.

Tlachdmhach. Fumitory.

Tlachdshubh
Tlaichdsheist. } A strawberry.

Tlachdthomhas. Geometry

Tlaith. Weak-spirited, timorous, slack.

Tlaim A handful of wool or flax.

Tlamadh. Teazing.

Tlamam. To teaze.

Tlas.
Tlasach. } A fair.

Tlas, tlus. Cattle.

Tlath, tla. Soft, tender.

Tlathas. Softness, weakness.

Tlathaigham. To reduce, weaken.

Tli, Colour.

Tlu, tlugh. A pair of fire-tongs.

Tlus. A lie, untruth.

Tlusaigheachd. Dissimulation.

Tnu, truth. Gen. Tnutha. Fire.

Tnu, tnuth, tnudh. Envy, indignation, expectation.

Tnuthach. Envious, jealous, a rival.

Tnuthaim. To envy.

Tnuthmhor. Envious.

Tnuthoir. A jealous lover.

To. Dumb, mute.

To. Silence.

To. A tongue.

Toamhlachd. } Silence.
Toanche. }

Tobach. Sudden, surprifing.

Tobar. A well.

Toban. A cowl.

Tobar-fiorghlan. A fpring-well.

Tobar-tarruinge. A draw-well.

Tobhach. To wreft.

Tobhtha, taoghtha. Chofen, elect.

Tocadh. Profperity.

Tocha. Love, loving.

Tocha. Choice.

Tochailt. Digging, a mine, quarry.

Tochailaiche. A miner, pioneer.

Tochailam. To dig, mine.

Tochailta. Dug, digged.

Tochailteach. Foffile.

Tochamlaidh. Marched.

Tochar. A caufeway, pavement.

Tochar. A croud, multitude, great quantity.

Tochar, tocharadh. A portion, dowry.

Tocharais. Winding, reeling thread or yarn.

Tocharaifam. To wind or reel yarn or thread.

Tocharaifta. Wound up.

Tochd. A fit or trance, filence.

Tochd. A bed-tick.

Tochas. Vide Tachas.

Tochdach. Still, filent.

Tochdaim. To be filent.

Tocheim. A flow ftep, pace.

Tochlaim. Vide Tochailam.

Tochradh. A gift, prefent, dowry.

Tocht. A piece, fragment.

Tochtam. To filence.

Tochtha. Chofen.

Tochus. Vide Tachas.

Tocomhladh. A ftepping, ftriding.

Tocfaid. A hogfhead.

Tod. A clod, fod.

Todan. A fmall clod.

Todam. To caft clods.

Todhas. Silence.

Todhernamh. Punifhment.

Todhochaide. The future, time to come.

Tofas. Topaz.

Togaidhe. Chofen, choice.

Togal. } A lifting up, raifing, taking,
Togbhal. } fhewing, demonftrating

Togbhalach. A builder, one that raifeth.

Togam. } To raife up, lift, to take, to
Togbham. } build, brew.

Togar. Defire, will, pleafure.

Togarach. Defirous, keen.

Togha. A choice.

Toghaidh. Attention, refpect.

Toghairm. A fummons, citation

Toghairm. A prayer, interceffion, petition, requeft.

Togham. To choofe.

Togh-ghuth. Confent, voice, choice.

Toghtha. Chofen, elect.

Toghuil. A deftruction.

Togra. A defire, choice.

Tograim. To defire, to pleafe, choofe.

Togtha. Heaved, lifted up, built, brewed or diftilled.

Toi, taoi. A bearing, birth.

Toibheim. Reproach, ftain, blemifh.

Toibheimach. Reproachful.

Toibhram. To appear.

Toic, toice. Wealth, riches, a fwelling

Toice. An opprobrious name for an ill-behaved young woman.

Toiceach.

Toiceach.   } Rich, wealthy.
Toiceamhuil. }

Toicam.   To fwell.

Toich.   Land, ground, territory.

Toich.   A natural right or property.

Toiche   Wall-eyed.

Toicheal.   A journey.

Toicheamach.   Gradually, ftep by ftep.

Toiched.   An arreft, confifcation.

Toichedte.   Confifcated.

Toichiol   Victory.

Toichim.   A going, departing.

Toichiofdal.   Arrogancy, prefumption.

Toichiofdalach.   Prefuming, felf-opinion-ated.

Toichneadh.   A faft.

Toid.   Whole.

Toidhearnamh. } Punifhment.
Toigearnamh. }

Toidhligh.   A flame, blazing fire.

Toidhrighte.   Seafoned to a thing.

Treifiun.   Heat, warmth.

Toifiunach.   Hot, fcalding.

Toigh.   A houfe. Vide Tigh.

Toigh.   Agreeable.

Toighe.   Notice, attention.

Toil.   The will, defire.

Toileach.   Willing, voluntary.

Toileachaf-inntin.   Contentment.

Toileamhuil   Wilful, obftinate.

Toileas.   The will.

Toilamhlachd.   Wilfulnefs, willingnefs, obftinacy.

Toilfheidhmnigham.   To enjoy.

Toiligham.   To be willing, to pleafe, in-dulge.

Toilighte.   Pleafed, fatisfied.

Toilirel.   Obftinate.

Toill.   Deferve thou.

Toillam.   To deferve, merit.

Toille.   A hollow, cavity.

Toillin   A little hollow.

Toilltin.   Deferving.

Toilltanach.   Deferving, meritorious.

Toilltanas.   Defert.

Toilfeimhnighe.   Enjoyment.

Toilteach.   Voluntary.

Toilteamhlachd.   Willingnefs.

Toimhdigh.   A tincture.

Toimhela.   Difmounting, hindrance.

Toimhfhreagraim.   To anfwer.

Toimhlam.   To eat.

Toimhfeach.   A farm.

Toimhfeachan.   A meafure, balance.

Toin.   Gen. of Ton.

Toin.   Tone, accent.

Toineal.   A trance, aftonifhment.

Toineamh.   A falmon.

Toineamh.   A monument.

Toinifg.   Senfe, underftanding.

Toiniudh.   A coming, going.

Toinnam.   To twift, wreathe, fpin.

Toinnadh.   Twifting, fpinning.

Toinneamh.   Death.

Toinneolas.   Profody.

Toinngrith.   Idem.

Toinnleaffaichoir.   A tanner, currier.

Tointe lin.   A fpindle of yarn.

Tointain.   A long thread in fpinning.

Toir.   A church-yard.

Toir.   Belonging to a church.

Toir.   For Tabhair, give thou.

Toir, thoir.   Give thou. Vide Tabhairam.

Toir.   A purfuit, diligent fearch.

Toirais.   A keen enquiry, anxiety.

Toiraifach.   Anxious.

Toireacht.   A purfuing, fearching for.

Toirdhealbhach, Turlogh.   Name of a man.

Toirbheartas.   Delivering, tradition, a dofe, bounty, difpenfation or gift.

Toirbheartha. } Delivered, given up.
Toirbhirt. }

Toirbheirt. } Giving up, delivering, dif-
Toirbhreadh. } penfing.

Toirbheirtach.   Bountiful.

Toirbhram. To give, deliver, yield, surrender; to affign.

Toirbhleafgadh. To rumble.

Toirchimeach. Benumbed.

Toirchimeachd. Stupidity.

Toirchimam. To burden, benumb.

Toirchios. A conception, fœtus, encreafe, plenty.

Toirdas Dotage.

Toireamh. A plowman.

Toireimnuigham. To walk ftately.

Toirigham. To purfue, follow clofely.

Toirighthe. Purfued, chafed.

Toiriofg. A faw.

Toirleimam. To alight.

Toirm. Noife, found.

Toirmeafg. A hindrance, impediment.

Toirmeafgam. To forbid, hinder, impede.

Toirmeafgte. Prohibited, reftrained.

Toirn. A great noife.

Toirnam. } To thunder, make a loud
Toirnigham. } noife.

Toirneach. } Thunder.
Toirneis. }

Toirrcheaghadh. Impregnating, begetting.

Toirrchigham. To impregnate, get with child, conceive.

Toirrchios. Fruit, conception.

Toirriomchram. To carry over.

Toirrfe. A lamp, torch.

Toirfe. Vide Tuirfe.

Toirfeach. Vide Tuirfeach.

Toirt. Quantity, bulk, value, refpect.

Toirtal. Tight, ftout; refpectful.

Toirtean. Ufeful, ferviceable.

Toirtheamhuil. Fruitful, plentiful.

Toirtheamhlachd. Fruitfulnefs, plenty.

Toirtin. A thin cake.

Toirtis. A tortoife.

Toifcidhe. Will, defire.

Toifeach. The beginning, van, a leader, chief.

Toifaigham. To begin.

Toifaghadh. Beginning.

Toifg. A wholefome admonition.

Toifg. A thing, circumftance.

Toifgal. Left, finifter.

Toifgbheodha. Expeditious in travelling.

Toit. Smoke, vapour.

Toit. A fragment, piece.

Toit. Whole, entire.

Toit. A fmall rick of corn.

Toitam. To perfume, to fmoke or roaft expeditioufly.

Toiteamhuil. Smoky.

Toitean. Burning, a fat collop, fteak.

Toitear. Lumpy.

Toith. Stink.

Toithghiobhair. A whore, proftitute.

Toithleannan. A concubine.

Toithfhearach. A filly or colt.

Toithealach. Vainglorious.

Toitheaftal. Arrogancy.

Toitrigham. To burn, fcorch.

Tol. A church-yard.

Tola. A church officer.

Tola. Superfluity.

Toladh. Deftruction.

Tolaibh. A multitude.

Tolanta. Holland.

Tolch. A hole, crevice.

Tolc. A wave.

Tolg. A bed.

Tolgdha. Proud, haughty, warlike.

Toll, Poll. A hole.

Toll. Hollow.

Toll. A head.

Tollachd. A hollow, cavity.

Tollam. To bore, pierce, penetrate, perforate.

Tollthach. Piercing, penetrating.

Tolteanas. Vide Toilteanas.

Tollta. Bored, perforated.

Toll-cluaife. A touch-hole.

Tolman. } A hillock.
Tolmag. }

Tolmanach. }
Tolmagach. } Full of small hills.

Tom. A bush, a thicket.

Tomach. Full of bushes.

Toman. }
Tomag } A small bush, tuft.

Tomadh A dip

Tomag-mhaddaidh.

Tomam To dip, drench.

Tombaca. Tobacco.

Tomhaidhm. A rupture of water.

Tomhailt. To eat. Vide Toimhlam.

Tomheisam. To unriddle, guess, resolve, to weigh, measure.

Tomhaisughadh. }
Tomhas. } Measuring, mensuration.

Tomhashlat. A measuring wand.

Tomhsean. Weights

Tomhseacham. A riddle, rebus.

Tomhaitheamh. Threatening, threats.

Tomhia. Protection.

Tomhraidhe. A patron, protector.

Tomhurus. Silence.

Tomhus, tomhseachan. A riddle, paradox.

Tomlachd. Thick milk, curds.

Tomonta. Rude

Tomthach. One that threatens, a swaggering fellow.

Ton. The breech, arse.

Tona. A tune.

Tonach. A shirt, covering, garment.

Tonalais. Cringing.

Tonnag. A wrapper round the shoulders of women in the Highlands like a shaul, a shaul, veil.

Tonchlodhach. A turncoat.

Tonlagan. Going or sliding on the breech.

Tonn. A wave, billow.

Tonn Strengthening.

Tonn. A hide, skin, pelt.

Tonn Quick.

Tonna. A tub, tun.

Tonnach. Waved, undulated.

Tonnach. Glittering.

Tonnach. A mound, rampier.

Tonnadh. Poisoned water, undulating.

Tonn a chladaich. The herb thrift.

Tonnach. Undulous.

Tonnam. To undulate, dip in water.

Tonnadair. A tunning dish.

Tonnadairachd. Tunning liquor.

Tonnchastach. A turn-coat.

Tonnag. A duck or drake, any aquatic palmiped.

Tonnghail. Wavy.

Tonnluasgadh. Wave-tost.

Tonnta. Waved.

Topnasca. A ball, bottom of yarn.

Tor, torr. A tower.

Tor. A bush, shrub, fear.

Tor, toras. Weariness, fatigue.

Tor. A sovereign, lord.

Torachd. Pursuit of, enquiry, search, retaliation.

Toradh. Regard, fruit, profit.

Toraidheach. Fertile, fruitful.

Toraidhtheach. Flexible, pliant.

Torain. A sort of vermin that destroys seed corn.

Toram. To reign.

Toramh. An augre.

Toran. A sounding or great noise.

Toras. Weariness, a journey.

Torathair. A monster.

Torc. A hog, swine.

Torc. The heart, face.

Torcar. Killing.

Torcbhaill. The præcordia.

Torchar. A fall.

Torchair. He fell, died, was killed; it happened.

Torchathair. A throne.

Torchios breige. A mooncalf.

Torchios anabaidh. Embryo, fœtus.

Torchraim. To fall down, die, perish, happen.

Torchuirt.

Torchuirt. Over-turning.

Torchur. A ferrying, paffing over.

Torcmhuin. The neck of a hog.

Tordhan. An elegy.

Torg. A killing, deftroying.

Torgan. A noife.

Torin. Thunder.

Torla. A furety.

Tormach. Increafe, feeding of cows or their being near calving.

Tormachaim. To magnify.

Tormaghadh. Encreafing.

Tormaigham. To encreafe, augment.

Tormaightheoir. An augmenter, improver.

Torman. A noife, found, the drone of a bagpipe.

Tormanach. Noify, having drones.

Tormanaim, To make a noife, murmur, tingle.

Tormuilt. Eating.

Tornalaim. To turn with a lath.

Torpan. A crab fifh.

Torr. A tower, heap, pile, body of men.

Torrach. Pregnant, with child

Torrachd. Round.

Torrachtaim. To make round.

Torrachtain. Going to vifit.

Torradh. Heaping, piling.

Torradh. A burial, watch, guarding.

Torram. To heap, pile.

Torramhuim. To watch, guard, to wake the dead, to vifit holy places as a pilgrim.

Torrthach. }
Torrthamhuil. } Fruitful, fertile.

Toirthamhlachd. Fertility.

Torrunn. Thunder.

Tort. A cake, little loaf.

Tort. By you, afide.

Tort. Giving. Vide Tabhairam.

Tort-fanear. Attention, obfervation.

Tort fanearach. Regardful, obferving.

Tortaobh. Confidence.

Tortaobtha. Confiding, depending on.

Tortaobhthach. A commiffary.

Torthach. }
Torthamhuil. } Fierce.

Torthuin. Exuberance, great fruitful nefs.

Torughan. Bafe in mufic.

Toruibh. Over you.

Toruig Event.

Toruigheachd. Purfuit, purfuing.

Toruigham. To purfue.

Toruinnfe, tarinnfe. Over us.

Torufcadh. To fall, be ruined, killed.

Tofach, toifach. A beginning, front, foundation.

Tofaiche. Former.

Tofaigham. To begin.

Tofanaibh. Thorns.

Tofd. Weighty, deadly.

Tofd. Silence.

Tofdach. Silent.

Tofdaigham. To confute.

Tofgaire. Ambaffador.

Tofgughadh. Motion.

Tofguigham To move.

Toftal. Arrogance.

Toftalach. Prefumptuous, arrogant

Tot. A wave, fod, turf.

Tota. The rower's feat in a boat.

Totchornhua. A fhe coufin.

Toth. Feminence, female

Totham. To tow, lead aftern.

Tothbhachain. A lafs.

Tothbhall. The female parts of generation.

Tothmhaol. A fhe flave.

Totta. A fhaft.

Tra. Vide Trath. Seafon, time.

Trachant. Ebbing of the tide.

Trachd. A treatife, tract, draught.

Trachdaire. An hiftorian.

Trachdam. To treat of, handle, negotiate

Trachdalaighe. A negotiator.

Trachladh. To loofen.

Tracht. Strength, bank or fhore of a river

Trachat

Trachta. A treatife, difcourfe.

Trachtaladh. Trade, negotiation.

Tradh. A lance.

Tradanach. Quarrelfome, contentious.

Traghrod. A way by the fea-fhore.

Traid. Quick, active.

Traide. Firft.

Traideach, troideach. A war-horfe.

Traigh The fea-fhore, ebb

Traigh-gheadh. A fhore-goofe.

Traigham. To ebb.

Traighadh-mara. Ebb-tide.

Traighighe A tragedian.

Traighigheachd. Tragedy.

Traighlaightheoir. A fcout.

Traill. A flave, fervant.

Traill. A kneading-tub, trough, tray.

Traillidheachd. } Slavery.
Traillamhlachd. }

Traillidh. } Slavifh.
Traillamhuil. }

Trainigham. To cull, choofe.

Traifgam. To be hungry.

Trait. A cataplafm.

Traitham. Vide Traigham.

Traocham To drain.

Traochluithe. Tilts, tournaments.

Traogh. Empty, ebbed.

Traogham. To empty, ebb.

Traoigh. A foot in length.

Traoileadh To drag.

Traona. A rail.

Traonoir. Idle, vacant.

Traonoirachd. Leifure, eafe.

Traotham. To leffen, abate.

Trapan. A bunch, clufter.

Trafda. Hitherto; crofs.

Trafgaram. To abrogate, deftroy.

Trafgradh. } Deftruction, oppreffion.
Trafgar. }

Trafgraim. To opprefs, overwhelm.

Trafnan. A ledge.

Trath. Time, feafon; foon, fpeedy.

Trath. Prayer-time, canonical hours.

Trath-nona. Noon, noontide, noontide-prayers; and noon of the antients, or ninth hour, being three in the afternoon, Trath-nona fignifies alfo the afternoon and evening.

Trathal. } In good or due time.
Trathamhuil. }

Trathrach. } A little ftalk of grafs.
Trathnin. }

Trathfoin. Then.

Tre, trid, tres. Through, by.

Treabh. A tribe, family, clan, pl. Treabhtha.

Treabhach. Pertaining to a family or tribe, powerful, valiant.

Treabhachas. Great feats.

Treabhadh. A ploughing, cultivating.

Treabham. To plough, till, cultivate.

Treabhaire. A plowman, a furety.

Treabhan. A tribune.

Treabhar. Skilful, difcreet.

Treabhlacht. A family, houfhold, tribulation.

Treabhlaim. } To trouble, diftruft.
Treabhlaigham. }

Treabhtha. Ploughed, earing.

Treabhtha. A village, homeftal.

Treabhthach. A farmer, hufbandman, one of the fame tribe.

Treabhthaire. A plowman.

Treabhur. A ftock or kindred.

Trecheann. Three tops, heads, or ends.

Treachladh. A loofing.

Treacail. Digging.

Tread. A herd or flock.

Treadach. Having flocks.

Treadhan. A faft.

Treadhmo. Wounds.

Treaduighe. A fhepherd, herdfman.

Treagh. A fpear, trident.

Treaghaim. } To pierce through, penetrate.
Treaghdaim. }

Trealamh. Apparel.

Treall. A fhort fpace, time.

Treallich. Lumber, trafh.

Treamaghadh. Binding, obligation.

Treamaigham. To bind, tie, faften unto.

Treamham. Through him.

Treampa. Through them.

Treanadh. Lamentation, wailing.

Treanadh. The week from Thurfday before to Thurfday after Whitfuntide.

Trean ri trean. The bird called a corncrake.

Treanam. To lament.

Treanas. Abftinence.

Trean, treun. Strong, brave, ftout.

Trean lamhchomhairt. Clapping of hands.

Treananta. Triangular.

Treartha. Art, fcience.

Trearthach. Artificial.

Treas. }
Treafo. } The third.

Treas. }
Treimhid. } By, through.

Treas. A fkirmifh, a battle.

Treas. Adverfity.

Treafumha. Drofs.

Treaftarruing. Thrice diftilled.

Treata. A plaifter.

Treath. Vide Treagh.

Treathaid. A pain, ftitch.

Treathan. A wave.

Treathan. The fea, high water.

Treathan. A foot.

Treathlich. Luggage, lumber.

Treatuir. A traitor.

Treatuirachd. Treafon, rebellion, treachery.

Treacheann. Three heads.

Trebi. Strong.

Tred. Tread. Vide Treud.

Tredeinas. For three days.

Tredheanas. Abftinence from flefh.

Trefid. Blowing, a blaft.

Treibhain. Steps.

Treibfe, treibhfe. Room, place, ftead.

Treibhdhiras. Set apart.

Treibhfeachd. Viciffitude, change.

Treibhfeach. Apt to change.

Treid. Vide Troid.

Treidhim To pierce through.

Treigeal A departure.

Treigean }
Treigfin. } Leaving, forfaking

Treigam. To leave, forfake, quit, abandon.

Treighanas. Abftinence from flefh.

Treigthe. Forfaken.

Treighthe. Virtuous qualification

Treightheach. Virtuous.

Treighion. A lofs.

Treimhdhirach. Upright, fincere.

Treimhdhireas. Sincerity.

Treine }
Treinas. } Might, power.

Treine. More powerful.

Treinfhear. A brave man, champion.

Treinfe. A trench.

Treis A-while, fhort fpace of time.

Treife. Force, ftrength.

Treifmhor. Strong, powerful.

Treifiner. A treafurer, as of a church

Treite. Embrocation.

Treith. Weak, ignorant.

Treitiol. A champion, warrior.

Treodas. Food

Treodfa, tridfa. Through, by thee.

Treoghdham. To pierce, bore.

Treoir. Strength, force, direction.

Treoradh. }
Treoraghadh. } A leading, direction.

Treoraghtheoir A guide, leader.

Treoraigham. To guide, direct, lead.

Treoraighte. Directed, guided.

Treoran. Three parts or pieces.

Treot. Trotting.

Treotam. To trot, come.

Tres.

Tres. For, becaufe.

Trefc. Brewers grains.

Treuille. A triangle.

Treuilleach.
Treuillineach. } Triangular.

Treubha. A rail.

Treubhachas.
Treubhantas. } Bravery, virtue, chivalry.

Treud. A flock or herd.

Treudach. Gregarious.

Treudaighe. A fhepherd, herdfman.

Treun.
Treunmhor. } Strong, brave.

Treunas.
Treunachas. } Strength, bravery.

Treun ri treun. The bird corn-crake or rail

Tri. Three.

Trid. Through, by means.

Trich. Vide Triath.

Trochan. A fock or fhoe.

Triad. Through thy means.

Triaghairdham. To triumph.

Trial A journey, going, gait.

Trial A purpofe, defign, plot, device.

Trialaire. A traveller.

Triallam. To go, march, walk, move.

Triallam. To imagine, devife, plot, defign

Triallan. A wayfaring-man.

Triamhin. Weary, fatigued.

Triamhna. Weaknefs, lownefs of fpirits

Triamhuin. A wailing, lamentation.

Trian A third part.

Trianach. Three by three, of the third part.

Triantan. A triangle, three-cornered bread.

Triath. A lord, king.

Triath. A hog, fow.

Triath. A wave.

Triath. A hill, hillock.

Tric. Often.

Tricad. Frequency.

Trichofach. Tripedal.

Trifiolaidh. A trifyllable.

Triramhach. A trireme.

Trichad.
Triochad. } Thirty.

Trichado.
Triochado. } Thirtieth.

Trid. Through.

Trid amach. Utterly, wholly.

Trid a cheile. Helter-fkelter, promifcuoufly.

Tri-deug. Thirteen.

Tridne. By us, through us.

Tridfa. By thee.

Tridfan. By, through him.

Tridfhoillfe. Tranfparency.

Tridfhoilfeach. Tranfparent.

Trifillte Threefold, triple.

Trilis. Bufhy hair

Trilifeach. Bufhy hair, crefted.

Trilfin. A fmall torch, lanthorn.

Trileonta. A quivering found.

Trillachan traighe. Collared oyfter-catcher.

Trimfa. By, through me.

Trimheas. Three pounds weight.

Trinfe. A trench.

Trinnfair. A trencher.

Triobloid. Trouble, affliction.

Trifhoghar. A triphthong.

Trioll. A plot, ftratagem.

Triollachan. A grey plover.

Triolonta. Trifling.

Trionoid. The trinity, godhead.

Triopol. A bunch, clufter.

Trifhrumhan. A triangle.

Trift. A curfe; tired, fad.

Triubhas. Trowfers.

Triucha. A canthred, fmall tripe.

Triugh. The hooping-cough.

Triun. Poor.

Triune. Poverty.

Triur.

Triur. Three, number three.

Triufan. Trowfers, or breeches and stock-ings in one piece.

Trocair. Mercy.

Trocairach. Merciful.

Trochladh. A loofening.

Trochlughadh. Profaning.

Trod. Scolding, ftrife, an elephant.

Trodach.
Trodanach. } Quarrelfome, riotous.

Trodamhuil. Serious, fcolding.

Trodhain.
Troghan. } A raven, bird of prey.

Trogh. Children.

Trogbhail. A difpute, wrangle.

Trogha. Miferable, unhappy.

Troghain. Sun-rifing.

Troghtheach. A footman, foot-foldier.

Troiath. An helmet.

Troich. A dwarf, evil body, bad perfon, coward.

Troid. A fighting, quarrelling.

Troidam. To ftrive, fcold, contend, wran-gle, quarrel.

Tioidh, troigh. A foot.

Troighe. Sorrow, grief.

Troighin. A brogue, flipper.

Troighleathann. A broad flipper.

Troightheach. A footman, foot-foldier.

Troighthin. A fock, dizzinefs.

Troimchill. A fanctuary.

Troimdhe. Tutelary gods.

Troime.
Troimad. } Heavinefs, more heavy.

Troimeachd. Heavinefs, weight.

Troifgeadh. Fafting, a faft.

Troifgeach. Severe, rigid, given to faft-ing.

Troifgam. To faft.

Troifte. A three-foot ftool, tripod.

Troirthligham. To confume, pine away.

Troitarachd. Treafon.

Trom. Weighty, heavy.

Trom. Protection.

Trom. Blame, rebuke.

Trom-tric. Pell-mell.

Tromam.
Tromaigham. } To aggravate, make heavy, to load, burden.

Tromaghadh. Making heavy.

Troman A great weight, bore-tree.

Tromara. A client.

Trombhanoglach. A woman client.

Trombhod Vervain, mallow.

Trombhuidhann. A tribe, clan of vaf-fals.

Tromchafair. A great fhower.

Tromchumhal. A woman flave.

Tromchuifeach. Important.

Tromdha. Weighty, heavy, grave.

Trominntin. Dejection.

Trominntinach. Dejected, melancholy.

Tromluidhe.
Tromlighe. } The night-mare.

Tromluidham To overlay.

Tromm. The elder-tree, bore-tree.

Trom mhathair. A matron.

Tomoglach. A client, a fervant.

Trompa, trompaid. A trumpet, trump.

Trompairachd. Playing on a trump or trumpet.

Trompoir.
Tromroir. } A trumpeter.

Tromthura. A tribe of vaffals.

Troraid. A fpire.

Trofdamhuil. Serious, faithful.

Trofdan. A pace, foot.

Trofg. A cod-fifh.

Trofgair. One that catcheth cod-fifh.

Trofgadh. A faft, fafting.

Trofnan. A crutch.

Trofta. A crack.

Troftal. Dwarfifh.

Troftamhlachd. Serioufnefs.

Trothailte.
Trothlaighthe. } Wafted, confumed.

Trotlughadh. Candying.

Truacanta.

Truacanta. Compaffionate, pitiful.

Truacantachd. Compaffionatenefs, pity.

Truadh. Lean, piteous.

Truadhas. Leannefs.

Truaghan. A poor, wretched creature.

Truagh. Pity.

Truaghanta. Lamentable.

Truaighe. Mifery, woe; favour, pity.

Truaighmheil. Compaffion, pity, mifery.

Truaill, A fheath, fcabbard.

Truaill. A body, carcafe.

Truailleaghadh. Profanation, polluting, adulterating.

Truaillidheachd. Corruption.

Truaillidh. Miferable, wretched.

Truailligham. ⎫ To pollute, unhallow, pro-
Truaillam. ⎬ fane, adulterate.

Truaillanach. A niggard, mifer, wretch.

Truas. Pity, compaffion.

Trucha. A fhort life.

Trudaire. A ftammerer.

Truid. ⎫ A ftarling, ftare.
Truideog. ⎭

Truill. A kind of veffel.

Truime. ⎫ Heavier, heavinefs.
Truimad. ⎭

Truinfigham. To inclofe, intrench.

Trull. A head.

Trumpa A jewifh harp. Vide Trompa.

Truis. To tear; a fuit of cloaths.

Trumpadoir. Vide Trompair.

Truifbhraghad. A neck-lace.

Truifaladh. The clothes when tucked up from the ground.

Trufam. To gird, trufs up, gather, warp.

Trufadh. Gathering, girding up.

Trufach. A fheaf; that gathereth.

Trufc. Vide Trofg.

Trufaros. A ward-robe.

Trufcan. A fuit of clothes.

Trufcan A fmelt or fparling.

Trufgan. Goods, chattels, furniture.

Trufgar. Oarweed.

Trufdar. Duft, filth.

Trufdalaim. To trufs up, gird up the loins.

Trutham. To feparate, funder.

Trutrach. Chattering.

Tu. Thou, you.

Tua. Silence.

Tuachail. Prudent, cunning.

Tuachioll. Winding, eddying, moving round againft the fun, left about.

Tuachiollach. Vortical, vermicular.

Tuadh. A hatchet, axe.

Tuadhmaoile. Fair, bufhy hair.

Tuadh. Fame, renown.

Tuadhana. Fleams.

Tuadh. Vide Tuath.

Tuagh. Dominion.

Tuagha. Hooks, hinges, crooks.

Tuaghrod. A way, road.

Tuai. Bad, naughty.

Tuaichle. Wit, cunning, prudence, augury.

Tuaileach. The twilight.

Tuaileas. Reproach, calumny.

Tuaileafach. Reproachful, calumnious.

Tuaileafam. To reproach, accufe.

Tuaileafog. A fcold.

Tuailam. To be able.

Tualang. Able, capable.

Tuailt. A towel.

Tuaim. A village, farm, a dyke fide, moat, hillock, rifing ground, a grave, tomb.

Tuainalach. Giddinefs.

Tuaiphair. A boor, clown, aukward fellow.

Tuairim. A guefs, opinion, conjecture, drift.

Tuair. Chief.

Tuairimam. To conjecture, guefs.

Tuairifg. An account, detail, a fymbol.

Tuairnin. A mallet, hammer.

Tuairnair. A turner.

Tuaifaid. A quarrel, wrangle.

Tuaifceart. The north quarter.

Tuaith. }
Tuaithean. } Northern.

Tuaith. A tract, territory.

Tuaitheach. A country-man, ruftic.

Tuaithe. Rural.

Tuaithleas. A ruftic trick, cunning.

Tualaing. Patience.

Tualaingam. To endure, bear patiently.

Tualthachd. Poffibility.

Tuama. A tomb or grave.

Tuamain. Fierce, morofe.

Tuapholl. A whirlpool.

Tuar. An omen, prefage, fore-runner.

Tuai. Foreboding.

Tuara. Satisfaction.

Tuara. Growth, life.

Tuaraim. To bode, portend.

Tuarcaim. To knock, fmite.

Tuargabh. Was taken.

Tuargnadh. Sedition.

Tuargnach-cath. Chief commander, generaliffimo.

Tuarufgbhail. A report, character.

Tuarafdal. Hire, wages, a fee.

Tuarafdalaigham. To hire.

Tuareip. Confufion, a foul houfe.

Tuas. Above, before.

Tuafaid. Tumult, buftle, quarrel.

Tuafaideach Tumultuous.

Tuafgeart. Northern, the north.

Tuaflagadh. A releafing, diffolving.

Tuata. }
Tuath. } Lay, of the country, northern.

Tuath. The north, a lordfhip.

Tuath. The country, the laity or people.

Tuathanach. A countryman, farmer, ruftic.

Tuathach. A north country perfon, a lord,
fovereign.

Tuatha de Danann. The fourth colony of
Ireland.

Tuathchaint. Gibberifh.

Tuatha fiodhgha. The name of fome Britons who ufed poifoned darts in Ireland,
K. ad A. M. 2737.

Tuathachd. A lordfhip, feigniory.

Tuathal. Left, aukward, ungainly.

Tuathallach. Aukward.

Tuathallan. An aukward, ungainly perfon.

Tuathamhuil. Rude, ruftic.

Tuathamhlachd Rufticity.

Tuathchund. Sorcery.

Tuathlios Calumny. Vide Tuaileas.

Tubag. A tub, vat.

Tubag-fhiolaidh. A dropping-tub.

Tubaift. Misfortune, mifchief.

Tubaifteach. Unlucky, unfortunate.

Tubaifteachd. Accidentalnefs.

Tubha. A fhew, appearance.

Tubhe. Thatch.

Tubhailt. A towel.

Tuc, teec. A bone.

Tuca. A tuck, rapier.

Tuccaid. A caufe, reafon.

Tucalam. To full.

Tucaluidhe. A fuller.

Tuchairaim. To rub.

Tuchan Hoarfenefs, a hoarfe-fong.

Tuchanach. Hoarfe.

Tucra. Meat.

Tuchr. A pore.

Tucht. A form, fhape

Tucht. Time. Vide Trath.

Tuchlach. Powerful.

Tuchtaigham. To choofe.

Tudan. A fmall heap, as a cock of hay.

Tudanachd. Making fmall heaps

Tudhamlach. Carriage, behaviour.

Tudhchadar. They came.

Tudhcham. }
Tudhchaidham. } To come, arrive.

Tufog. Crepitum.

Tug. Gave, brought.

Tughe, tuighe. Thatch, ſtraw.

Tugham. To thatch.

Tughte. Thatched.

Tughnaim. To apply, adjoin.

Tuidhle. Pleaſant, delightful.

Tuidhme. A confederacy, conjunction.

Tuidhmeach. A yoke-fellow.

Tuidhmim. To join, yoke.

Tuighe. Straw, thatch.

Tuigham To thatch.

Tuigam. To underſtand, diſcern, perceive.

Tuigſe, tuiſgin. Underſtanding, knowledge, ſkill.

Tuigſeach. ⎱Knowing, ſkilled, intelli-
Tuigſineach ⎰ gent.

Tuile. A flood, deluge, rain, pl. Tuilteach.

Tuile ruadh. Noah's flood.

Tuil Sleep, reſt.

Tuilbhein A torrent.

Tuilcheimnughadh. Progreſs, proceſſion.

Tuilg. A hillock.

Tuiligham. To overflow, encreaſe.

Tuill. Holes.

Tuillim To ſleep.

Tuille. More, a remnant, addition.

Tuille fos. Moreover.

Tuilleamh. Wages, hire.

Tuillam. To augment, encreaſe, enlarge; to deſerve, earn.

Tuillin. Deſert, merit.

Tuilſam. To ſleep.

Tuillte. Floods.

Tuillthe. Earned, deſerved.

Tuilm Elm, oak tree.

Tuimpe. A pump.

Tuinge. An oath.

Tuinidhe. Immoveable.

Tuinaiſg Senſe, underſtanding.

Tuinneamh Death.

Tuinnam. ⎱
Tuinnicham. ⎰ To dwell, ſojourn.

Tuinnachas. Sojourning.

Tuinnidhe. A den

Tuinnidhe. Poſſeſſion.

Tuir. Pl. of Tor.

Tuir. A lord, ſovereign, general.

Tuirbheach. ⎱
Tuirmheach. ⎰ Shame-faced, baſhful.

Tuirchimigham. To make ſorry, grieve, trouble.

Tuirchreich. A reward.

Tuirean. A troop, multitude.

Tuireann. Wheat.

Tuireadh. A requeſt, crying, weeping, a dirge.

Tuireann. A ſparkle of fire from an anvil.

Tuiriofg. A ſaw.

Tuiridh. A pillar, ſupporter of an edifice.

Tuirigham. To reign.

Tuirighin. A tongue, a prince, a judge.

Tuirifc-taidhe. Conviction of theft.

Tuirlin. A deſcent.

Tuirlingam. To deſcend.

Tuirliſteoir. A manger.

Tuirmheach. Modeſt, baſhful.

Tuirmheachd. Modeſty, ſhamefacedneſs.

Tuirſe. Wearineſs, ſadneſs.

Tuirſeach. Weary.

Tuirſigham. To weary, tire, fatigue.

Tuirtheachda. A rehearſal, relation.

Tuirt. Time, quantity, conſideration.

Tuis. Incenſe, frankincenſe.

Tuis. A gentleman, jewel.

Tuis, tus. A beginning, origin.

Tuiſbeanadh. A front.

Tuiſdeach. ⎱
Tuiſdigh. ⎰ A parent.

Tuiſdin. Creation.

Tuiſeach, taoiſeach. A commander, officer.

Tuiſear. A cenſer.

Tuiſill. A treſpaſs.

Tuiſleadh. ⎱
Tuiſlighe. ⎰ A ſtumbling, delivering.

Tuiſle.

Tuifle. The hinge of a door.

Tuifligham. To ſtumble, to bring forth, deliver.

Tuiſlighte. Fallen, ſtumbled, delivered.

Tuiſmeadh. } Delivery, travel, or bring-
Tuiſmeaghadh. } ing forth young.

Tuiſmigham. To ſtumble, bring forth young.

Tuiſmighthoir. A parent.

Tuiſtiun. A groat.

Tuiſteamhach. Frail, ruinous, ready to fall.

Tuith. A ſide.

Tuitam. } To fall.
Tuitim. }

Tuitam. A fall, chance, reſult.

Tuitamach. That falleth, accidental.

Tuitamachd. Contingence.

Tuitamas. The falling ſickneſs.

Tul. The front, countenance, face.

Tul. A beginning, entrance.

Tul. More.

Tul. Quick, ſoon.

Tul. A manner, faſhion.

Tul. Naked.

Tula. }
Tulach. } A hill, hillock.
Tuloch. }

Tulaga. A change of labourers.

Tulagam. To rock, move.

Tulagan. Rocking.

Tulaidhe. Treaſure.

Tulaigne. Intention.

Tulgach. Jolting much.

Tulla. A green or common.

Tulbhreicneach. Spotted, freckled.

Tulca. Bands.

Tulcach. } Full of hillocks.
Tulcanach. }

Tulchan. Dim. of Tulach.

Tulchomhraic. An aſſembly, congregation.

Tulchromachd. } A declivity.
Tulchlaonachd. }

Tulchoir. Obſtinate.

Tulchlaon. Declivous.

Tulchuiſeach. Confident, bold.

Tulghaiream. To provoke.

Tulglan. A handſome hillock.

Tulghluaſachd. Promotion.

Tulbhallſgadha. Spots, freckles.

Tullog. The fiſh called Pollock.

Tulradharcachd. Providence, foreſight.

Tulradharcach. Provident, foreſeeing.

Tulradharcam. To foreſee.

Tulſcan. A ſpreading, looſening.

Tulſtaonachd. A declivity.

Tultaradh. By mere chance, accidentally.

Tum. A buſh.

Tuma. Vide Tuama.

Tumadh. A dipping.

Tumaim, tomam. To dip.

Tumtha. Dipped.

Tumthaire. A dipper, diver.

Tunicam. To know.

Tunna. A ton.

Tunnog. A duck or drake.

Tur. Dry, bare, alone.

Tur. A requeſt, petition.

Tur, go tur. Totally, altogether.

Tur. A reſearch.

Tur. A tower.

Tur. Heavineſs, wearineſs.

Tur. A journey, tour.

Tura. Much, plenty, abundance.

Turadan. Nodding.

Turas, turus. A journey, expedition, voyage.

Turaſgar. Sea ore, ſea weed, ſhell-fiſh.

Turuſan. A pilgrim.

Turbit. A turbot, rhomboid.

Turbhaidh. Miſchance, miſfortune.

Turcach. A Turk, Turkiſh.

Turchar. Riches.

Turchomhroc. An aſſembly, congregation.

Turgaibh. He took up.

Turgabhail greine. Courſe of the ſun.

Turgbhala

Turgbhala. Guilt, iniquity.

'Turgabhalach. Guilty.

Turgnaim. To collect, gather.

Turlach. Ground covered with water in winter.

Turna. A furnace, a spinning-wheel.

Turna. A job of work.

Turnaidhe. A minister, servant.

Turnaim. To humble, descend.

Turnamh. A descent.

Turnamh. Rest, quiet.

Turnoir. A turner.

Tuiric. A push, thrust.

Turricam. To push over.

Tuisach. Sad, weary, exhausted in spirits.

Tuiscolbadh. Frequent skirmishes, a splinter.

Turse. Weariness, dejection. Vide Tuirse.

Turigan. Implements.

Turtuir. A turtle.

Turus. A journey, voyage, expedition.

Turusan. A traveller.

Turusgur. Giblets.

Tus. A beginning, commencement.

Tusa. Thou, thou thyself.

Tuscarnadh. Fiction.

Tusdin. The beginning.

Tusga, toisaiche. Rather, the former.

Tusga. Incense.

Tusimtheachd. Anti-ambulation.

Tuslogach. Desultory, skipping.

Tuslog. A leap, or little jump.

Tuslogam. To leap, skip.

Tusmhodh. A bond-slave.

Tusornach. A parricide.

Tut. Stink, filth.

Tutach. Stinking, filthy, ungainly, aukward.

Tutaighil. Dirt, filth, aukwardness.

Tuthan. Reproach, slander.

Tutaire. A dunghill.

U.

U

U Is the seventeenth and last letter of the Galic alphabet. Grammarians have called it U, which according to Flaharty signifies Heath, i. e. in Galic Fraoich It hath also, and with greater propriety, been called Ur, i. e. Ubhar, Iubar, or the Yew-tree. Its power and sound is the same as in the Latin and Italian languages. U seems once commuted for V in the name Ualtair, Walter, which the Gael pronounce Valtair. Bh and mh having the force, with little difference from each other, of V, sometimes supply the place of V in other languages, and

UAC

as the grammatical reader must be no stranger to the frequent commutations mh, bh, v, u, and w, little here need be said on that head.

Ua. From, of, a descendent, grandchild, commonly in English written O, as O'Connor, O'Neil, O'Brian.

Uabhan. Fear, dread, horror.

Uabhar. Pride, pomp, vainglory.

Uabhrach. Proud, haughty, arrogant.

Uacha. From them.

Uachd. A will, testament.

Uachdar. The top, surface, cream, summit, upper part.

Uachdarach. Uppermoſt, higheſt.

Uachdaraiche. Topmoſt, uppermoſt.

Uachdaran. A governor, ruler.

Uachdaranachd. Government, ſovereignty, ſupremacy.

Uadha. } From him, it.
Uaidhe. }

Uaahbhachd. Terror, horror.

Uadarſan. Eating.

Uadhbhaſach. Terrible.

Uagh. A grave.

Uaghbha.. A choice, election, option.

Uaibh. From you.

Uaibhreach. Proud, vainglorious.

Uaibhreas. Pride.

Uaiche. From her, it.

Uaidh. }
Uaidhe. } From him.
Uaidheſan. }

Uaigh. A den, grave, cave.

Uaighreir. Full of arbitrary ſway.

Uaignas. Secrecy, privacy, ſolitarineſs.

Uaigneach. Loneſome, ſolitary, ſecret.

Uaill. Wailing, lamentation, howling, cry.

Uaill. Vanity, pride, vainglory.

Uailleot. Vain, boaſting, proud.

Uaill. Famous, illuſtrious, renowned.

Uailleadh. A roaring, howling.

Uaillfeartach. Howling, yelling.

Uailligham. To roar, howl.

Uaillmhiannach. Ambitious.

Uailtheart. The howling of a wolf or dog.

Uaim, fuaim. A ſound, report.

Uaim. Notes on the harp.

Uaimb. A den or cave.

Uaimhneach. Dreadful, terrible, horrid.

Uaimhinn. An oven.

Uaimhnigham. To terrify.

Uaiminiche. A club.

Uain, uine. Time, opportunity, reſpite.

Uain. Loan.

Uaineachd. Vacation.

Uaine. Green.

Uainad. Greenneſs.

Uainn. }
Uainne. } From us.

Uainnarach. Secret, retired.

Uainnaras. Retirement.

Uair. Vide Oir.

Uair. An hour.

Uairachan. An horary.

Uairadair. A clock, time-keeper.

Uairadairaiche. A watch or clock maker.

Uairiodhach. Chilly.

Uairlan. A ſun-dial.

Uais. Noble, well deſcended.

Uaiſle. Nobility, gentry; generoſity.

Uaiſlad. }
Uaiſleachd. } Gentility.

Uaiſligham. To ennoble.

Uaiſlughadh. Making noble.

Uait From thee.

Uaithcligham. To diſmay.

Uaithdhligheadh. Privilege

Uaithchrith. Horror.

Uaithi, uaithe. From her, or it.

Uaithle. Horrible.

Uaithne. Menſtrua muliebria.

Uaithne. Green, greeniſhneſs.

Uaithne. A pillar, poſt.

Uaithne. Union, i. e. Comhardughadh, which ſee.

Uaithnigham. To prop, ſupport.

Uallach. A burden, charge, taſk.

Uallaigham. To load, burthen, encumber.

Uallach. Vide Eolach.

Uallach. Vain, vain-glorious, oſtentatious, freakiſh.

Uallaire. A coquet.

Uallaigh. Lewd.

Uallachus. Sillineſs, vanity, conceit.

Uallachan. A coxcomb.

Uallfult. Treaſon.

Ualmhaigham. To howl, roar.

Ualmhurnach. An outcry.

Uam. From me.

Uamchafaim. To encompafs, furround.

Uamh A cave, den, oven.

Uamhann. Dread, terror.

Uamhainach. }
Uamhafach. } Dreadful, terrible.

Uamhortha. Dreadful, abominable.

Uathmhorthachd. Abomination.

Uan. A lamb.

Uan caifg. The pafchal lamb.

Uan. Froth, foam. Vide Oghan.

Uanid. A chief or great perfon.

Uarcin Side of the head.

Uarach-mhullaich. The herb Devil's Bit.

Uarach. Temporary.

Uas Upon, more than, upwards, above.

Uafal. Noble, gentle, well-born, Sir, a gentleman.

Uath. Fear, dread.

Uath. The earth, mould.

Uath. A hawthorn, white thorn.

Uath. A fmall number.

Uathmhar. Dreadful, terrible.

Uathmhorachd. Dreadfulnefs.

Uath. Lonefome, folitary, alone, N'a uath 's n'a aonar, all alone.

Uatha. Single.

Uathadh A little, fmall quantity, a few.

Uathamhuil. Single, folitary.

Uathartan. A pocket.

Uathbhas. Aftonifhment, furprife, wonder

Uathbhafach. Shocking, dreadful, terrible.

Uathchomhradh. }
Uathlabhradh. } Soliloquy.

Ubh. The point of a weapon.

Ubhal. An apple.

Ucaire A cottoner or napper of frize, a fuller.

Ucfaim. To abolifh, extinguifh.

Uch Oh! alas!

Uchd. The breaft, bofom.

Uchbhadach. Groaning.

Uchdach. An afcent, fteepnefs, ftomacher, breaft-plate, extenfion of voice, delivery in fpeech.

Uchdal. That carrieth the head high, erect.

Uchdan. A hillock.

Uchdmhac. An adopted fon.

Uchdmhacachd. Adoption.

Uchdaodach. Clothes, or armour for the breaft.

Ud, od. That there, yon.

Uddacag. A woodcock.

Udal. Diftrefs.

Udail. Inhofpitable.

Udalach. Wavering.

Udalan. A fwivel.

Udhbhrann. A joint.

Udhmadh. An inclofure.

Udhmadh. A withe ufed to bolt the door of a cow-houfe.

Udhthair. A bile.

Udmall. Quick, active, ftirring, wavering.

Uga. Choice, election.

Ugadh. Birth.

Ugh. An egg.

Ughaim. Horfe-harnefs, traces.

Ughachd. A will, teftament.

Ughaimam. To accoutre, to harnefs.

Ughagan. A cuftard.

Ughamtha. Harneffed, equipped, accoutred.

Ughamhuil. Oval.

Ughbreithach. Oviparous.

Ughbhuidheacan. Yolk of an egg.

Ughchrath. Spawn, ovaria.

Ughdar. An author.

Ughdargha. }
Ughdarafach. } Authentic.

Ughdarach. Authoritative.

Ughdaras. Authority.

Ughdarafaim. To authorize, empower, authenticate.

Ughia.

Ughra. A conflict, fkirmifh, fight.

Ugin. Fore-part of the neck.

Uiateach. A farmei's houfe.

Uibhir. A number.

Uibne. A fmall pitcher, or cann.

Uibne. Drinking.

Uidh. Care, heed.

Uidh. A degree, ftep, fpace ; Uidh air uidh, gradually, ftep by ftep.

Uidhe. A journey.

Uidhghiolla. A running-footman.

Uidheach. Mufical, harmonious.

Uidhidheachd. Harmony, melody.

Uige. A jewel, precious ftone.

Uige. A web, carded wool for fpinning.

Uige Knowledge, fkill, ingenuity, under-ftanding.

Uigh. Pleafure.

Uighdeall. Trembling.

Uiginge. A fleet or navy.

Uil, for Uidhil. The Jews.

Uilc, Pl. of Olc. Evils.

Uile. All.

Uile.   } An elbow, nook, corner, an-
Uileann. } gle.

Uileannach. Angled, cornered.

Uileachd. Univerfality, generality.

Uilechumhachd. Omnipotence.

Uilechumhachdach. Omnipotent.

Uilelathairachd. Ubiquity.

Uilelathairach. Omniprefent.

Uileleirfin Attribute of feeing all things.

Uileinntinach. Without refervation.

Uilechruthach. Omniform.

Uilechinntach. All-fufficient.

Uilefhiofrach. Omnifcient.

Uilefhiofrachd. Omnifcience.

Uileleirfineach.   } All-feeing.
Uilefhaicfinach. }

Uilebheothaighach. All-chearing.

Uilebheannuighte. Truly bleffed.

Uilethorach. All-bearing.

Uilefhlugach. All-devouring.

2

Uileghlic. All-wife.

Uile-iomlan. All-perfect, all-fufficient.

Uile-iomlanachd. All-fufficiency.

Uile go leir. Altogether.

Uilidh. All, Go h uilidh, univerfally.

Uille, oille. Greater.

Uilleann. Honeyfuckle, name of the diph-thong ui.

Uillean. Vide Uileann.

Uille. Oil.

Uillgha. Oily, of oil.

Uim. The earth.

Uim. Brafs, copper.

Uimcheallach.   } Any clofe private place.
Uimcheallog. }

Uimchrith. An earthquake.

Uime. About, about him or it.

Uime-fin. Therefore.

Uimedim. To encompafs, embrace.

Uimfhalraftaim. To amble, pace.

Uimitalaigham, To circumvolate.

Uimitalaich. Circumvolution.

Uimtabhradh. Circumlocution.

Uimfhcolam. To circumnavigate.

Uimchladhadh. Circumvallation.

Uimfhilladh. Circumplication.

Uimfhuidhachadh. Circumpofition.

Uimfhiuth.   } Circumfluence
Uimfhruthadh. }

Uimfhruthach. Circumfluent, circunfluous.

Uimdhortam. To circumfufe.

Uimdhortadh. Circumfufion.

Uimrothladh. Circumgyration, revolution.

Uimrothlam. To circumgyrate, revolv

Uimpe. About her, it.

Uimhir. Number, arithmetic.

Uimhirach. Numerous.

Uimhrachal. Arithmetical.

Uimhrachan. Arithmetician.

Uimleac, uimleacan. The navel.

Uimleachta. Umbilical.

Uimmheirg.

Uimmheirg. Ruft.

Uimphliochdam. To embrace.

Uimreamhar. Very fat.

Uinamaid Ointment.

Uinche. A battle.

Uinge. An ounce.

Uine. Time.

Uinne. Blind.

Uinneamh. Strength.

Uinneog. A window.

Uinrun. An onion.

Uinfiunn. An afh-tree.

Uinfi. Is, it is.

Uinfuigham. To manage, fway.

Uir. Mould, earth, duft.

Uir. Fire.

Uirchur A cricket, chur-worm, fen-cricket.

Uircin. A pig, grice.

Uirdhuighadh. An eclipfe of the fun, or confonants.

Uirdhreachadh. A delineation.

Uire. More frefh, fiefhnefs.

Uireafbhach. Indigent, needy, a needy perfon.

Uireafbhuidh. Want, indigence.

Uirfhiacla. The fore-teeth.

Uirghairdachas. Rejoicing.

Uirghairdaigham. To rejoice.

Uirghiol Eloquence, utterance, a command.

Uirghiollach. Eloquent

Uirghreannachd. Puberty, iipcnefs of age.

Uraghadh. Renewing, refrefhing, refrefhment.

Uirad. A fhare, portion, as much as.

Uirid. Whilft, as long as.

Uirigh A couch.

Uiriofal. Bafe, mean, flavifh, cringing.

Uiriofle.
Uiriofleachd. } Lowlinefs, meannefs.

Uirioflaigham. To debafe, difparage.

Uirliofteoir. A manger.

Uirlis. Tools, inftruments.

Uirliocan. A vomiting.

Uirlios. A walled garden.

Uirneis A furnace.

Uirre. Upon, unto her.

Uir-reathadh. A mole.

Uirreachaire. Readier, more watchful.

Uirtreana. Pits of water in the fand left by the ebb.

Uis. Humble, obedient.

Uis. Ufe.

Uifal. Snug, comfortable.

Uifedeolachd. Supplication.

Uifeog. A lark.

Uifg.
Uifge. } Pl. Uifgidhe. Water, a river.

Uifge beatha. i. e. Aqua vitæ, whifgy.

Uifge neartmhor. Aqua fortis.

Uifgeul. A fable, ftory.

Uifgeulgha. Fabulous.

Uifgeulaiche. A fabulift.

Uifgamhuil. Watery.

Uifgamhlachd. Waterinefs.

Uifgeacha. Waters.

Uifgaigham. To water, irrigate.

Uifire. An oyfter, ufurer.

Uifiarram. To befeech, humbly entreat.

Uifiarrthach. Importunate.

Uifneach. An old name of the county of Longford.

Ulachd. Colour.

Ulladh.
Ullin. } Ulfter.

Ulog. A pulley.

Ullaigh. Ultonians.

Ulaidh. A pack-faddle, a hoard or hidden treafure.

Ulbhuadhach. All-victorious, triumphant.

Ullcach. The quinfey.

Ulcha. A beard.

Ulla. A place of devotion, a burying-place, the crofs or calvary of a cathedral church.

     Uldach,

Uldach. A burden.

Ullabheift. A lamprey.

Ullamh. Vide Ollamh.

Ullamh Ready, prepared.

Ullamhaim. } To prepare, procure, pro-
Ullamhaigham. } vide.

Ullamhaghadh. Preparation, preliminary.

Ullamhaighte. Prepared, provided, made ready.

Ullmhoid. A preparation, provision.

Ullchabhacan. An owl.

Ulmudh. Tongs.

Ullthach, ualach. A burden, load, armful.

Ultach. Ultonian.

Um. For Uime, about, near.

Um With, together with.

Umad. About thee, upon thee.

Umainn. About us.

Umaibh. About you.

Umaidhe. Vulgar, ignorant.

Umpa. About them.

Uman. Human.

Umaire, iomaire. A ridge.

Umar. A trough, a veffel.

Umar-baifdaidh. A font.

Umbracam. To embrace.

Umchafadh. A vertigo, dizzinefs.

Umchriodheal. The pericordium.

Umchadh. Ready.

Umdhruidam. To fhut up clofe, to befiege.

Umdhruidte. Clofed up, fhut up, befieged.

Umfaifgam. To embrace.

Umghaoth. A whirlwind.

Umghlacam. To gripe or grafp.

Umha. Copper, brafs.

Umha, uamha. A cave, den.

Umhail. Heed, attention, confideration, doubt.

Umhaire. A tinker, brazier.

Umhal. Obedient.

Umhaloid. Agony.

Umhalachd. } Humility, obedience.
Umhlaigheachd. }

Umchlodh. A vertigo.

Umhladh. Obedience, fubmiffion, a fine.

Umhlaigham. To obey, fubmit, humble.

Umhlughadh. Humbling, humiliation, making obeifance, faluting.

Umlabhradh. Circumlocution.

Umorro But, even, moreover.

Umpa About them.

Umpidh. An ideot.

Umfhuidnam. To befiege.

Una. Hunger, famine.

Una. Proper name of women common in Ireland.

Unfairt. } Wallowing.
Unfairtich. }

Unfairtam. To tumble, tofs, wallow, neftle.

Unga. Brafs, an ingot.

Ung. } Ionga. The nail, claw, hoof.
Unga. }

Ungadh. Unction, ointment.

Unga dheirionach. Extreme unction.

Ungam. To anoint.

Ungtha. Anointed.

Unich. Buftle, hurry.

Unicham. To tumble and tofs.

Unfa. An ounce.

Umfhuidham. To befiege.

Untas. A windlafs.

Uptha. Sorcery, witchcraft.

Ur. Frefh, new.

Ur, uir. Mould, earth.

Ur. Evil, mifchief, hurt.

Ur, ar. Slaughter.

Ur. Generous, noble-hearted.

Ur-fhliochd Noble race.

Ur. A brink, border.

Ur. Heath; hence the letter U takes its name.

Ur.

3

Ur. A beginning.

Ur. Fire, hence.

Urchuil. A cricket, falamander, or fire-fly

Ur. A moift place, a valley.

Ur. Very.

Ural. Frefh, flourifhing.

Urghranna. Very ugly, monftrous.

Uriofal. Very humble.

Urach. Earth, a beginning.

Urach bhallach. Orchis.

Urach. A bottle, pail, fmall tub.

Urachair. A fhot.

Urchairam. To fhoot, caft.

Uracht. A fupport.

Urad As much, many.

Uraiceachd. An accidence, primer, rudiments of education.

Uraige. The former.

Uran. Courtefy, affability, a fong.

Uranach. An upftart.

Uras. A fprout, bud.

Urbhaidh. A ward, cuftody.

Urbhaidhe. Bane, ruin, deftruction.

Urbhidh. Ruftling, noife, tumbling and tofling.

Urbhlaith. Fruitful, full of bloffom.

Urbhath. A hut, cottage.

Urcain A pig, grice.

Urchail. Fetters, fhackles.

Urchaillte. Fettered, fhackled, forbidden.

Urchailach. A heifer of a year and a half old.

Urchoid. Hurt, harm, detriment, malice, mifchief

Urchoideach. Mifchievous, malicious, factious

Urchoidam. To hurt, damage, bear malice.

Urchofg. A prefervative againft evil, antidote, a fpell.

Urchradhachd. Wretched, miferable.

Urchur. A throw, caft, fhot.

Urchuiram. To fhoot, caft, throw.

Urchuidmheadh. A denial, put off, excufe.

Urchuidmhigham. To excufe.

Urdhaithe. Defect.

Urdhubha. A darkening, eclipfe.

Urfomhar. Autumn.

Urgbhail A lifting, or taking up.

Urghairdeach. Joyful.

Urghairdeachas. Rejoicing, congratulation.

Urghairdam. To rejoice.

Urghais. An exchange, alteration.

Urgnamh. A feaft.

Urnamhog A goffip.

Urgnamhoir. A fmell-feaft.

Uila. } A lock of hair, hair, front.
Urlamh. }

Urlabhair. } Utterance, fpeech.
Urlabhradh. }

Urlaidhe. A fkirmifh, conflict.

Urlaimh. Poffeffion.

Urlaithe. Quick, active, ready.

Urlaimh. Quick, ready.

Urlamhuidh. A poffeffor.

Urlamhus. Poffeffion, fupreme power and authority.

Urlann. A ftaff.

Urlar. A floor.

Urlar-buailte. A threfhing floor.

Urlataidh. Active of body, tumbling.

Urluachair. Green rufhes.

Urmhor. Frefh, cooling, flourifhing, budding.

Urmhorachd. Frefhnefs, coolnefs, newnefs.

Urmam. To erafe.

Urmais. He refolved, intended.

Urmumhin. Ormond.

Urfhnaidhm. A knot, tie; a pin or jack to faften the chords of a harp.

Urnaigh. A prayer.

Urradh. A furety, good author, defendant in a procefs.

Urradh.

Urradh. A chieftain.

Urradh tighe. Houfehold furniture or goods.

Uirae. Obedience, fubmiffion.

Uirad. High.

Urraid. A principal perfon.

Urram. Refpect, honour, obedience, deference.

Uraigham. To renew, refrefh.

Urrain. A ftay, fupport.

Urramach. Refpectful, fubmiffive.

Urramachd. Homage, fubmiffion.

Urran na leife. The hip or huckle bone.

Urranta. Bold, daring, dauntlefs.

Urrflugaim. To vomit.

Urflugidh. Emetic.

Urrflugan. Vomiting.

Urras. Awe, bond, check, infurance.

Urrudhas. ⎫ Security, furetyfhip, courage,
Urras.   ⎬ undauntednefs.

Urrudhufach. Bold, confident, fecure.

Urrtha Upon her, it.

Urrthaigh. An oath.

Urfa.   ⎫ The fide poft of a door.
Urfin. ⎬

Urfa. A bear.

Urfcar.   ⎫ A cleanfing.
Urfcartadh. ⎬

Urfgeul. A fable, novel, ftory.

Urfgar-bhraghad. A necklace.

Urfag. A little bear.

Urful. A pair of tongs.

Urthaidhe. An oath.

Uruladh. An altar.

Urufa.   ⎫ Eafy, feafible, practicable.
Urufda. ⎬

Us. News, tidings, a narrative, ftory.

Us, for Agus. And.

Ufa. Juft, righteous, true.

Ufachd. Power, faculty.

Ufa.   ⎫ Eafier.
Ufaidhe. ⎬

Ufarb. Death.

Ufga, tufga. Incenfe.

Ufgaraim. To clear or rid.

Uflain. Play, fport, joftling, wreftling.

Uflainneach. Chearful, brifk, merry, nimble, active.

Uflainneachd. Chearfulnefs, brifknefs, activity.

Ufpairneachd. Wreftling, ftruggling, ftrife, contention.

Ufpag. A pang, thou.

Ufpairnam. To ftruggle, ftrive, contend.

Ufuir. An ufurer.

Ufuireachd. Ufury.

Uulp. A fox.

Utan. A knuckle.

Utraid. A way for cattle.

Ut ! Out !

Uth. Udder, dug.

Lightning Source UK Ltd.
Milton Keynes UK
UKHW030626240521
384271UK00007B/521

9 781140 836551